Japan and the World, 1853–1952

A Study of the East Asian Institute

Japan and the World 1853–1952

A Bibliographic Guide to
Japanese Scholarship in
Foreign Relations

EDITED BY
Sadao Asada

*A project of the Japan Association
of International Relations*

Columbia University Press
NEW YORK

Library of Congress Cataloging-in-Publication Data
Japan and the world, 1853-1952: a bibliographic guide to Japanese scholarship
in foreign relations.

   (A Study of the East Asian Institute)
   Based on: Sengo Nihon no kokusai seijigaku.
   "A project of the Japan Association of International
Relations."
1. Japan — Foreign relations — 1868-   — Bibliography.
2. Reference books — Japan — Foreign relations. 3. Refer-
ence books, Japanese — Bibliography. I. Asada, Sadao,
1936-   . II. Nihon Kokusai Seiji Gakkai. III. Sengo
Nihon no kokusai seijigaku. IV. Series: Study of the
East Asian Institute, Columbia University.
Z3308.R4J36   1989   [DS881.96]   016.32752   89-944
ISBN 0-231-06690-2

Columbia University Press
New York   Oxford
Copyright © 1989 Columbia University Press
All rights reserved
Printed in the United States of America

Casebound editions of Columbia University Press books are Smyth-sewn
and printed on permanent and durable acid-free paper

Book design by Ken Venezio

The East Asian Institute
of Columbia University

The East Asian Institute is Columbia University's center for research, education, and publication on modern East Asia. The Studies of the East Asian Institute were inaugurated in 1962 to bring to a wider public the results of significant new research on modern and contemporary East Asia.

Contents

Preface

This English-language edition of bibliographical essays is a collaborative undertaking of the Japan Association of International Relations (JAIR), representing the fruit of close cooperation among JAIR members. The original Japanese edition was published in 1979 as *Sengo Nihon no kokusai seijigaku* (Post–World War II Japanese research in international studies) to commemorate the association's twentieth anniversary. It is a comprehensive compilation of post–World War II Japanese scholarly works in the field of international studies, both historical and theoretical.

From the beginning, a strong interest was expressed by some of our overseas colleagues in having at least portions of this book translated and made widely available in English. Naturally, the most appealing part of the book for overseas scholars is the chapter on Japanese diplomatic history. We have, therefore, decided to build on and expand this chapter into a solid volume providing the most recent information on significant Japanese works as well as archival sources.

In recent years Japanese scholarship in this field has made rapid progress, but this state of affairs is not widely known abroad. Few Japanese diplomatic historians have published their studies in the Western languages, and only non-Japanese scholars who have a command of the language have been able to exploit new works. To be sure, English translations of some Japanese historical writings have appeared, but they are very few in number, and many of them tend to be popular, if not journalistic, in nature. In an age when trans-Pacific scholarly exchanges and communication have become increasingly important, this unfortunate situation must be rectified. One of the first steps, we believe, is to compile a basic bibliographical guide that will acquaint non-Japanese scholars with what their Japanese colleagues have been writing during the past forty years.

To make this English-language edition as useful and relevant as possible for overseas scholars, we have thoroughly reedited, greatly expanded, and updated the Japanese original. Major portions have been rewritten by both the original and newly recruited contributors. The result, without exaggeration, is an entirely new book.

For this English edition we have added three new chapters. One of them (chapter 1) provides a comprehensive guide to Japanese diplomatic documents and archives, the army and navy records, important personal papers, and other relevant manuscript collections. This chapter also introduces the reader to essential reference works and basic research tools. Finally, we comment on representative survey works on Japanese diplomatic history—both multivolume series and one-volume works.

Chapter 4 presents a broad historiographical survey of writings on the crucial period 1931–1945. The heated historical controversies over the causes and nature of the so-called "fifteen years war" (1931–1945) have become such an important part of contemporary Japanese intellectual history that it deserves a separate treatment on its own—even at the risk of some overlapping with the three chronological chapters that follow. Unlike in other chapters, we have not refrained from taking an ideological position and, at times, even polemical stands on basic controversies in Japanese scholarship. We have tried, however, to be fair in our presentation of the Marxist and other positions to which we do not subscribe.

The second half of chapter 4 is devoted to an extensive bibliographical essay on rich materials relating to the turbulent period, 1931–1945. More documents, personal papers, diaries, and memoirs have been published for this era than for any other. Since a large body of source materials has been published as a series covering these fifteen years, we deal with them in chapter 4.

Our English version carries the story up to the Allied occupation of Japan (1945–52), a period that has become a "boom field" in recent years. As chapter 8 shows, this is a research field where Japanese and foreign scholars (mostly American) have increasingly turned to joint symposia and research projects, and the results have been quite impressive. It also is a field where Japanese scholars can make, and have made, genuine international contributions to the study of intercultural relations between the Japanese people and the occupying forces.

We were tempted to trace Japan's foreign relations up to the 1980s, and indeed chapters were drafted to cover the current period. For the post-1952 years, however, the Japanese archives are only now beginning to be opened, and that quite selectively. Few documented studies have yet appeared. For this reason, we decided not to include these chapters but to incorporate them in a companion volume, *International Studies in Japan* (tentative title), that is shortly scheduled to be published in Japan.

Aside from chapter 4, statements preceding bibliographical lists are not meant to be tightly argued historiographical essays; rather, they consist of running commentaries on the works listed. In our coverage we have tried to be as comprehensive as possible, often winnowing out relevant articles from the countless number of small-scale, specialized journals published by each university or even each department.

This does not mean, of course, that we have refrained from selective judgment: we have taken the responsibility of excluding outdated works as well as writings of ephemeral or insignificant nature. Our emphasis throughout has been on original studies that either utilize new sources or present fresh interpretations.

From time to time we have been tempted to refer to contributions made by overseas scholars in the field of Japanese diplomatic history, to evaluate and compare them with works by Japanese scholars. However, we decided to adhere to our editorial policy and make only occasional references to exceptionally significant works by foreign scholars that have had an important impact on Japanese scholarship. (For the same reason, works by foreign scholars are not listed in the bibliographies.) This, of course, does not mean that we are unaware of an increasing number of studies by foreign scholars that are important especially for their interpretations and—most notably—for their non-Japanese perspectives.

Most of the works treated in this volume belong to "diplomatic history" in the conventional sense of the term. However, as Hosoya

Chihiro emphasizes in the Introduction, increasing efforts are being made by Japanese scholars to go beyond the traditional confines to study broader topics and to apply theoretical approaches derived from political science methodologies in the West. In the bibliographical essays, we have taken note of these less orthodox works.

More to the point, Hosoya notes the recent trend toward collaborative research with overseas scholars in various projects and conferences. It is in this context that the present volume becomes particularly relevant. Our hope is that this English version will serve as a standard reference work and provide a needed stimulus to promote mutual scholarly exchanges between Japanese specialists and their overseas colleagues.

The bibliographical volume, prepared during 1980–86, covers books and articles that appeared up to 1986; for the archives and personal papers as well as works of exceptional importance that came to our attention thereafter, last-minute efforts were made to incorporate information as of Novermber 1987.

A brief explanatory note is in order here. Our bibliographical entries generally follow the format established in *Japan's Foreign Policy, 1868–1941: A Research Guide,* edited by James W. Morley (Columbia University Press, 1974). As to names, we have followed Japanese practice: giving family names first (with the exception of scholars resident abroad and publishing extensively in English, such as Akira Iriye). Concerning Korean scholars resident in Japan, we often give both their romanized Korean names and the Japanese names by which they are known. When looking for governmental publications in the bibliography, the reader should first look for the heading "Japan" and then for the name of relevant ministry to find wanted entries. "Gaimushō" stands for the Foreign Ministry; other ministries should be self-evident.

Since most books are published in Tokyo, we have noted the places of publication only when published elsewhere. Occasionally the bibliographical lists include articles not mentioned in the preceding essays, partly because these articles, though regarded as worthy of mention, do not quite fit into our bibliographical narratives. We have tried, in these translations, to be as faithful as possible to the Japanese originals while respecting the English translations provided by the authors. In some cases, this practice has resulted in minor discrepancies between the original versions and the English translations.

The organization of the book makes it necessary to mention the same title more than once in different chapters at the risk of unnecessary duplications. Articles by the same author are differentiated in the text by the use of serial numbers printed within brackets. To identify the particular article, the reader should check the numbers, also in brackets, that appear at the end of that particular author's bibliographical entries.

A collaborative work of this kind must depend on the assistance of numerous scholars and colleagues. From the inception of the project, Professor Hosoya Chihiro, former president of the JAIR, provided leadership; he obtained financial aid for translation from the Japanese Ministry of Education, as well as additional assistance from the Suntory Foundation. His successors as JAIR president—Professors Tanigawa Yoshihiko, Kawata Tadashi, and Nagai Yōnosuke—continued to support the project. Professor Saitō Makoto helped us receive a grant for editorial/administrative expenses from the Japan-United States Friendship Commission.

Professor Ōhata Hideki, then head of JAIR's Administrative Office, and Professor Uno Shigeaki, its treasurer and later president of JAIR, have patiently sustained the project. Professor Hatano Sumio spent countless hours with me carefully going over several drafts of chapters 1 and 3 to 7.

As for technical problems involved in translation, I am indebted to the professional advice of Kano Tsutomu, editor of *The Japan Interpreter.* Professor Roger Buckley of the International Christian University read the entire manuscript and offered stylistic suggestions. Professor Bernard Susser of Doshisha Women's College provided me with emergency assistance. And across the Pacific, Professor Akira Iriye of the University of Chicago has been most supportive throughout.

I have exercised my editorial prerogative in heavily editing (and sometimes rewriting) the manuscript for the sake of clarity and stylistic consistency. Those who prepared the initial English drafts are: Glenn D. Hook and Hosoya Masahiro (Introduction); William Tyler (the first half of chapter 2); Hosoya Masahiro (chapter 3); Ishii

Osamu (chapters 5 and 6); Satō Kyōzō (chapters 7 and 8); and William Tyler (portions of chapter 8). The rest of the book was translated (or written in English) by this editor.

Last but not least, I must commend my student assistants, Kawasaki Tsuyoshi and Takeuchi Manabu, on their valiant efforts to check bibliographical information.

We tried to cover the field as thoroughly as possible, but also kept in mind John Foster Dulles' remark on the Japanese peace treaty drafts: "The perfect is the enemy of the good." It goes without saying that, as the editor-*cum*-translator, I alone am responsible for any errors of omission or commission, as well as infelicity of expression.

KYOTO, JAPAN   *Sadao Asada*

Japan and the World, 1853–1952

Introduction:
An Overview

Hosoya Chihiro

This collection of bibliographical essays provides a basic guide to post–World War II Japanese scholarship in the field of Japanese diplomatic history. As such the volume attempts to offer, in chronological chapters, surveys of significant works to acquaint overseas scholars with the range and content of what Japanese historians have been writing during the past forty years.

Yet these chapters do not claim to totally analyze shifting interpretations and dominant trends in the field. In this introduction I shall present an overview, sketching some of the major developments in diplomatic history in contemporary Japan. Since the postwar studies in diplomatic history depended on the groundwork already laid by our predecessors in the prewar and wartime periods, however, brief remarks on their works will be in order.

Prewar Legacy

The standard of research in Japanese diplomatic history, given the handicaps with which the historian had to cope, was relatively high even in the prewar period. Solid monographs on Japanese diplomatic history of the Meiji period (1868–1912) were written in the 1930s, extensively employing primary sources. For example, Shinobu Seizaburō's work (1934) on the Sino-Japanese War of 1894–95 analyzed the "dual diplomacy" of the Japanese army and government during this war,[1] while Tabohashi Kiyoshi's study (1930) of modern Sino-Korean-Japanese relations utilized documents of the office of the Korean governor-general.[2]

Also noteworthy are the substantial surveys of Japanese diplomatic history by Kajima Morinosuke (1938), Kiyosawa Kiyoshi (1941), and Shinobu Seizaburō (1942). Kajima, a former diplomat turned historian, had access to the Foreign Ministry archives when he wrote his solid account of the period from the Triple Intervention of 1895 to Japan's treaty with the Soviet Union in 1925.[3] Essentially, he based his narrative on confidential Japanese records, while disguising this practice by liberally providing footnotes from published Western sources.

Kiyosawa Kiyoshi's highly readable survey from Perry to the Tripartite Pact of 1940 is broader in scope and more critical in its treatment.[4] A liberal and internationally minded journalist, who had spent many years in the United States, Kiyosawa had the courage to write with "objectivity," "detachment," and "honesty" (his words in the Preface) at a time when freedom of expression was very much in jeopardy. Published in June 1941, his work remains useful to this day.

Shinobu Seizaburō's brief analytical survey came out the following year.[5] Covering the period from the "opening" of Japan in 1854 to the Washington Conference of 1921–22, this work was unique in its methodology. In his own words, he attempted to systematize Japanese diplomatic history in terms of "the characteristics of Japanese capitalism." Given this approach, it was natural that the author emphasized the role of domestic economic factors in shaping Japanese foreign policy during the seventy years that he reviewed.

Postwar Growth

Three factors, in particular, contributed to the transformation of research facilities in postwar Japan and to the remarkable growth of study in diplomatic history. First, following Japan's defeat, historians in Japan came to enjoy the freedom to conduct their research without fear of government censorship. Released from the fetters of militarism, they embarked on investigation into topics and issues previously held to be taboo, and began to publish their research freely. The new Japanese Constitution, guaranteeing freedom of inquiry, worked to the special advantage of diplomatic historians, particularly those intent on clarifying the inner workings of the government.

The second major change is access to and availability of Japanese government documents on diplomatic and military affairs. Before the war most of these documents were strictly confidential, and only a limited perusal was permitted to a small number of in-house historians. This changed dramatically under the Allied occupation of Japan (1945–1952). First, highly confidential diplomatic and military records of the prewar and wartime periods were released in order to provide evidence for the International Military Tribunal for the Far East. Also, during the American occupation, a substantial portion of the archives of the Japanese Foreign Ministry were microfilmed by a team of American scholars for the Library of Congress. The "opening" of these documents proved of epoch-making significance in the progress of research in Japanese diplomatic history.

The third factor that has contributed to raising the standard of scholarship in Japan has been the impact of political science approach, particularly of decision making and the behavioral sciences developed mostly in the United States. Thus, Japanese diplomatic historians began to use conceptual and analytical frameworks of a theoretical nature in their attempt to reconstruct the past. Let us next examine these three factors.

In regard to the first point—release from government suppression —it was Marxist historians who most actively put to use their newly gained freedom of speech. They opened a controversy in which they totally repudiated the Pacific War as an aggressive and imperialistic war, strongly called prewar and wartime leaders to account for their role in starting and waging the war, and fundamentally attacked the social and political systems which they claimed had made the war inevitable. Ironically enough, their stand was in a sense similar to the verdict passed by the International Military Tribunal for the Far East. It also accorded with the dominant mood during the Allied occupation of Japan. One of the studies reflecting the intellectual trend of this period is *Taiheiyō sensōshi* (A history of the Pacific War), edited by the left-wing Rekishigaku Kenkyūkai (Historical Science Society) and published in 1953–1954.[6]

Newly Available Documents

With regard to the second point—new access to historical documents —the records of the International Military Tribunal for the Far East served as a great impetus for diplomatic historians in the early 1950s. In due time, research groups were organized to utilize these records. An example of such work is *Taiheiyō sensō gen'inron* (The origins of the Pacific War), edited by Nihon Gaikō Gakkai (Association for the Study of Japanese Diplomacy) in 1953.[7] The most penetrating work based on the records of the Tokyo war crimes trials remains Maruyama Masao's essay on the thought and behavior of Japanese wartime leaders, which is a brilliant comparative analysis of the mentalities and leadership of the warlords of imperial Japan and Nazi Germany.[8]

From the first half of the 1950s on, Japanese historians began to utilize the Foreign Ministry archives, and this enabled them to make great strides in their research. At the same time the Foreign Ministry took the initiative in 1952 by compiling and publishing *Shūsen shiroku* (The historical record of the termination of the Pacific War).[9] This basic work brought together all the materials then available that relate to the efforts to end the war. Another essential publication was *Nihon gaikō nenpyō narabini shuyō bunsho, 1840–1945* (A chronology and major documents on Japanese foreign policy, 1840–1945),[10] compiled and edited by the Foreign Ministry in 1955. This work attracted considerable attention from both scholars and the general public, for it made available for the first time the minutes of Imperial conferences, cabinet decisions and instructions on major foreign policy problems, and secret treaties and agreements from the Meiji period to the end of the Pacific War.

In this connection, it would be in order to mention the great contribution by Kurihara Ken, an archivist par excellence, who not only compiled both of the above-mentioned works but also unstintingly gave of his unmatched knowledge of Foreign Ministry records to many researchers, including those from overseas. In this way, Kurihara played a major but little-publicized role in promoting research in Japanese diplomatic history. (I might parenthetically add that I greatly benefited from the "opening" of the Foreign Ministry archives when I conducted my research, which resulted in *Shiberia shuppei no shiteki kenkyū* [An historical study of the Siberian expedition]).[11]

In addition to diplomatic records, it became also possible, from the latter half of the 1950s onwards, to use the official documents and manuscripts (diaries and other personal papers) of the Japanese army and navy which were unearthed by and kept under the custody of the War History Department of the Defense Agency.

The Road to the Pacific War Series

Among empirical studies based on these newly opened documents as well as numerous interviews with the surviving participants, one notable landmark is the eight-volume series edited by Nihon Kokusai Seiji Gakkai (Japan Association of International Relations, abbreviated as JAIR), *Taiheiyō sensō e no michi: Kaisen gaikōshi* (The road to the Pacific War: a diplomatic history of the origins of the war),[12] published in 1962–63. The fruit of an ambitious collaborative research project, these volumes consist of detailed monographic essays that are filled with new factual information and analyses of the complex processes of Japan's policymaking and implementation. The project had originally been organized by Tanaka Naokichi, with Tsunoda Jun playing a coordinating role in its completion. An English version of major parts of the series is being published by Columbia University Press under the general editorship of James W. Morley.[13] In Japan this series has just been republished with a slightly different format: in a postscript each author briefly describes new works that have appeared since the original version was published. These facts would indicate that the majority of studies in the series retain their scholarly value to this day.

The publication of the *Taiheiyō sensō e no michi* series, however, evoked sharp criticism from the Marxist school of historians. The main charges were that the contributors to this series, by sticking so closely to the newly discovered "facts" as they found them, slighted the larger problem of the "war responsibility" of Japan's leaders and thus tended to be "reactionary" in general orientation.

In the early 1960s this controversy came to have wider ramifications when it was linked with a "great debate" over historical inter-

pretation of the Shōwa period (1926–   ). Provoked by Takeyama
Michio's *Shōwashi no seishinshi* (An intellectual history of the Shōwa
period), published in 1956, this debate unfolded itself around 1960,
and it became further heated when Hayashi Fusao began publishing
serialized articles in justification of the "Greater East Asian War" in
the influential opinion magazine *Chūō kōron* in September 1963.
Hayashi's contention was that the war had been fought for the
"liberation" of the Asian peoples from Western domination. (For
details on this debate, the reader is referred to historiographical discussions in chapter 4.)

It was in this period, too, that the historical controversy on the
meanings of the Russo-Japanese War was enlivened by the publication of an excellent joint study of the subject by a research group led
by Shinobu Seizaburō and Nakayama Jiichi.[14]

International Cooperation

While joint research projects became increasingly prevalent in Japan,
some of them developed on an international scale. The first international attempt of this sort was a conference between Japanese and
American specialists held in the summer of 1969 at Kawaguchiko. The
papers and summary proceedings of the conference were published in
1971–72 as *Nichi-Bei kankeishi: Kaisen ni itaru 10-nen, 1931–1941* (A
history of Japanese-American relations: The decade preceding the
war, 1931–1941).[15] The English version is Dorothy Borg and Shumpei
Okamoto, eds., *Pearl Harbor as History: Japanese-American Relations,
1931–1941* (Columbia University Press, 1973).

This work addressed itself not only to narrowly diplomatic relations but also to their institutional, domestic, economic, and intellectual backgrounds. There are chapters on senior leaders in both
governments and their foreign policy machineries, army and navy
establishments and strategies, economic and financial bureaucracies,
the Congress and the Diet, business circles, nongovernmental and
private organizations, the press and mass media, and academic and
intellectual figures. Papers by Japanese and American scholars were
paired for comparative purposes. The focus on parallel governmental
organizations was effective in bringing out the characteristics of the
decision-making process in the two countries.

The companion volume, examining the decade preceding the Manchurian Incident, is *Washinton taisei to Nichi-Bei kankei* (The Washington system and Japanese-American relations).[16] It contains papers by Japanese and American scholars who gathered in Kauai Island, Hawaii, in 1976 for a binational conference. Though not as tight in its conceptual framework as its Kawaguchiko predecessor, this volume is in one sense broader in coverage: it contains several chapters that examine the quadruple relationship between Japan, China, the United States, and Britain. (Unfortunately, the English version was never published.)

A somewhat similar joint project, on a more modest scale, resulted in Satō Seizaburō and Roger Dingman, eds., *Kindai Nihon no taigai taido* (Attitudes toward international affairs in modern Japan), published in 1974.[17] It consists of eight analytical essays that examine how the Japanese have perceived the external environment and reacted to it in various periods from the late Shogunate period to the post–World War II era. Although the authors vary in their methodologies, all of them attempt to go beyond the narrow confines of traditional diplomatic history to show new lines of investigation.

The most recent binational conference was held in London in the summer of 1979, and its theme was Anglo-Japanese relations during the period 1917–1949. Similar in conception and format to the Kawaguchiko meeting, this conference attempted to add a new dimension of our understanding of the origins of the Pacific War by re-examining them from the perspective of Anglo-Japanese relations. The Japanese and British historians, who gathered at the Imperial War Museum, reappraised, among other subjects, the role of Britain in East Asia especially during the 1930s and the wartime period. The papers presented at this conference were simultaneously published in Japan as Hosoya Chihiro, ed., *Nichi-Ei kankeishi, 1917–1949* (Essays on the history of Anglo-Japanese relations, 1917–1949),[18] and in Britain as Ian H. Nish, ed., *Anglo-Japanese Alienation, 1919–1952: Papers of the Anglo-Japanese Conference on the History of the Second World War* (Cambridge University Press, 1982). The importance of such joint research projects with foreign scholars will further increase in the future with new openings of the archives of the countries concerned.

It is to be regretted, however, that these joint undertakings have been limited to collaboration with American and British colleagues.

Ideally, there should be opportunities for joint research and discussions with historians from other countries in multinational projects. A promising start in this direction was made when Hōsei University held in November–December 1983 an international symposium on the theme of "The Allied Occupation of Japan in World History."[19] It aimed at comparing the Allied occupation of Japan with the Japanese occupation of Southeast Asia during the Pacific War and the American occupation of Micronesia, Okinawa, and South Korea. In addition to hosting Japanese, American, and British experts, the symposium was enlivened by the papers and comments by participants from the Philippines, Malaya, Korea, and the Soviet Union.

New Methodologies

Finally, I shall discuss the third factor that stimulated research in Japanese diplomatic history—interest in political science theories and attempts to apply their analytical frameworks to historical studies.

To cite one early example, Seki Hiroharu applied Richard C. Snyder's model of decision-making process (*Decision-Making as an Approach to the Study of International Relations* [Princeton University Press, 1954]) and Karl Deutsch's communication theory (*Nationalism and Social Communication* [New York: Wiley, 1953]) to analyze concrete political processes in his work on the Harbin revolution of 1917.[20] The theoretical interest in the foreign policy decision-making process can also be found in such works as Hosoya Chihiro's works on the Siberian intervention and its aftermath,[21] Kobayashi Yukio's study on Japanese policy toward the nascent Soviet Union,[22] and Ogata Sadako's monograph on Japan's policymaking at the time of the Manchurian Incident.[23]

In the early 1970s, Graham Allison's three models for analyzing foreign policy decision-making process, particularly the "bureaucratic politics model" (*Essence of Decision: Explaining the Cuban Missile Crisis,* [Boston: Little, Brown, 1971]), had a strong impact on Japanese diplomatic historians. Asada Sadao's study comparing Japanese and American decision-making process at the time of the Washington Conference may be cited as a representative case study that applies the "bureaucratic politics model."[24]

Interest in the theory of political leadership and the attempt to apply it to Japanese political processes were already apparent in Oka Yoshitake's early work on modern Japanese statesmen and his succinct biography of Yamagata Aritomo.[25] But it was not until the mid-1960s that studies of this kind became prevalent in Japan. For example, Mitani Taichirō in his study on Japanese foreign policy during the "transition period" of 1918–1921[26] made a penetrating analysis of Prime Minister Hara Kei's leadership. In 1967 and 1977 JAIR devoted two issues of its organ *Kokusai seiji* (International Relations) to "foreign policy leadership."[27]

An attempt to understand foreign policy leadership by delving into depth psychology is found in Kurihara Akira's analysis of Konoe Fumimaro's personality and his concept of the "New Order."[28] Kurihara's approach to psychohistory is based partly on the postulates of Erik H. Erikson's *Insight and Responsibility* (New York: Norton, 1964). In addition, there are studies on other Japanese leaders, in which the authors' interest in the psychological approach is partially evident: for example, Bamba Nobuya's analysis of Tanaka Giichi and Shidehara Kijūrō,[29] and Miwa Kimitada's biography of Matsuoka Yōsuke.[30]

Another major characteristics of studies in Japanese diplomatic history is the tendency, conspicuous since the mid-1960s, to emphasize the role of the images, perceptions, and attitudes held toward foreign nations by political, military, and opinion leaders, and from this angle to analyze the historical development of bilateral relations. Representative of this kind of work are the essays published in the special issue of *Kokusai seiji* (1966) featuring "Images in Japanese-American relations" and Akira Iriye's survey of shifting images in Sino-American relations.[31] The abstraction of images, however, has tended to be arbitrary, often lacking in objectivity. The analysis of cognitive structures has not always been conducted with sufficient exactitude, and new findings on a theoretical level were not always brought to bear on actual historical analyses.[32]

In regard to research on Japanese attitudes toward foreign affairs, there has emerged a strong tendency to view attitude formation as a reflection of the intellectual tradition in Japan or of domestic factors such as Japan's political culture, or to see it as a reaction of Japan to international environment. Works along these lines have yielded some important results. One example is the above-mentioned joint work edited by Satō Seizaburō and Roger Dingman.

An important case study on the linkage between domestic politics and foreign policy is Itō Takashi's monograph on domestic political alignments at the time of the London Naval Conference.[33] In this study, Itō attempts to analyze Japanese responses to the London Naval Treaty as the output of a political process in which various domestic political groups cooperated with or confronted each other over the issues.

Among studies in diplomatic history that focus on political forces in Japan, the following works deal with the role of the Japanese navy: essays by Asada Sadao on the Japanese navy and the United States from the Washington Conference to Pearl Harbor;[34] Kobayashi Tatsuo's monographic essay on the naval conferences of 1921–1936;[35] and Ikeda Kiyoshi's study on the London Naval Treaty.[36] The role of the army is examined in Fujiwara Akira's survey of Japanese military history;[37] Hata Ikuhiko's monograph on fascist movements in the military;[38] Imai Seiichi's essay on the political role of the Japanese military during the Taishō period;[39] and Banno Junji's analysis of the Japanese army's view on the West and its continental policy.[40] Kitaoka Shin'ichi's solid and richly documented monograph on the Japanese army and its continental policy (1906–1918) is a major recent contribution.[41] It traces how the army acquired increasing political autonomy by examining its policy toward China and Manchuria during this period.

Finally, the monumental *Senshi sōsho* (war history) series, published by Bōeichō Senshishitsu (War History Office, the Defense Agency), contains volumes that are indispensable to all who wish to understand the political role of the army and the navy in prewar Japanese foreign policy (see chapter 4).

As for studies on the influence of public opinion on foreign policy, *Kokusai seiji* has devoted one issue to the examination of this subject.[42] Ogata Sadako has written on the role of liberal nongovernmental organizations in Japan during the interwar period.[43] There is also Kakegawa Tomiko's essay on the governmental control of mass media and Japanese public opinion toward the United States during the 1930s.[44] While scholarly works on the role of public opinion in foreign policy are not rich in Japan, one noteworthy piece of research is Etō Shinkichi's case study on Tanaka diplomacy—particularly the diplomatic negotiations concerning the suspension of traffic on the Peking-Mukden Railway in 1927. In this work Etō attempts to abstract nationalistic feelings in Japan by means of content analysis of two local Japanese newspapers, and he tries to incorporate this theoretical technique into a more traditional historical analysis.[45]

As illustrations of more explicit applications of the content analysis method, I must mention the works by Mushakōji Kinhide,[46] Watanabe Akio,[47] and Usui Hisakazu.[48] These three political scientists attempt to analyze the values held by Japanese political leaders and their attitudes toward foreign affairs as expressed in their parliamentary speeches. Although their studies do not properly belong to the category of diplomatic history as such, there is no doubt that their findings have enriched the field by injecting new methodological insights.

Intellectual stimulation to Japanese diplomatic historians did not come solely from their colleagues in political science. From abroad, Akira Iriye of the University of Chicago has played an important role in provoking Japanese historians. Proposing a new conceptual framework and using a multiarchival approach in his first monograph, *After Imperialism: The Search for a New Order in the Far East, 1921–1931*,[49] Iriye challenged the conventional interpretation of Japanese foreign policy under the Washington system during the 1920s. In his most recent and prize-winning work, *Nichi-Bei senso* (The Japanese-American war),[50] he took a "revisionist" stand in his analysis of debates in both countries concerning war aims and postwar plans, emphasizing similarities rather than differences.

In contrast to the somewhat "unconventional" approaches discussed above, there have been a number of Japanese diplomatic historians who adhere to traditional methods, using primary sources and orthodox research tools. Foremost among such historians is Usui Katsumi, who has produced voluminous works on the history of Sino-Japanese relations extensively based on primary sources. I should add in passing that, so far as research on bilateral relations is concerned, studies on Sino-Japanese relations are the most advanced, perhaps followed by those on Japanese-American relations.

In this brief introductory essay I have selectively mentioned only those works that would serve to illustrate the development of the field. There are, of course, numerous other studies of importance, and they will be treated in detail in the chapters to follow.

New Trends

As has been suggested, a shift has occurred from "traditional" studies of diplomatic history to more innovative studies. A good index of the changing trends of research is the choice of themes featured in the JAIR's organ, *Kokusai seiji*. (For a list of issues devoted to Japanese diplomatic history, see chapter 1.)

Earlier issues featured chronological periods, viz., the Bakumatsu, Meiji, Taishō, and Shōwa periods. Second, there were also issues devoted to the major events in Japanese diplomatic history: the first Sino-Japanese War and Russo-Japanese War, the period of World War I, the Manchurian Incident, and the Sino-Japanese War. Third, several issues have appeared that examine bilateral relations, such as Japan's relations with China, the United States, Korea, Russia and the Soviet Union, Britain, and (more recently) Australia and Canada.

In contrast, there has been an increasing tendency for the editorial board of *Kokusai seiji* to give overall themes to each issue such as: Japanese perceptions of international relations; diplomatic thought and ideas in modern Japan; Japanese diplomacy and public opinion; leadership in modern Japanese diplomacy; informal channels in Japanese diplomacy; and East Asia and Japan during periods of transition. Organized in this fashion, *Kokusai seiji* in recent years has published more analytical and theory-oriented articles utilizing what one might call theoretical or "less orthodox" approaches.

The State of the Art

During the past decade the history of the Allied occupation of Japan (1945–52) has become a flourishing field, attracting an increasing number of contemporary Japanese historians, specialists in Japanese history, American history, or—more broadly—international history. In the past few years books and articles treating the period 1945–1952 have proliferated with such a speed that it is impossible even to summarize them in this introductory chapter. (The reader is referred to chapter 8 for an extensive bibliographical treatment of this period.)

The declassification of U.S. documents under the "twenty-five-year rule" and British records under the "thirty-year rule" has stimulated Japanese scholars to undertake multiarchival research. The bitter irony, is that Japanese scholars need to rely mainly on these foreign sources; recently opened Japanese documents are heavily "sanitized," with some of the crucial documents strangely missing.

Most recently, the research interest of Japanese scholars has been shifting to the diplomacy of peacemaking. One example is my own monograph on the subject, *San Furanshisuko kōwa e no michi* (The road to the San Francisco Peace Treaty),[51] based on American, British, and Japanese sources.

The Internationalization of Japanese Scholarship

Another important new trend is a more multilateral approach, which goes beyond the confines of Japanese diplomatic history as narrowly defined. One outstanding example is Yōnosuke Nagai and Akira Iriye, eds., *The Origins of the Cold War in Asia* (University of Tokyo Press and Columbia University Press, 1977). Most of the essays in this volume were originally presented at an international symposium on "The International Environment in Postwar Asia," chiefly organized by Nagai and held in Kyoto in November 1975. Availing themselves of the newly opened archives, the participants—American and Japanese scholars as well as a British expert, Donald C. Watt—examined the period 1941–1950 to find the roots of the cold war in Asia. The resulting book made it clear to overseas scholars that they can no longer afford to ignore Japanese scholarship in this field. See, for example, a shrewd review article by Warren Cohen that appeared in *Reviews in American History* (June 1978), 6(2):146–54. As Cohen states, the question had been: "Could Japanese scholars make significant contributions in a field where Western scholars had done so much?" The answer, he declares, is "an unequivocal yes."

The thirtieth anniversary of the Japan Association of International Relations provided the most recent occasion for an ambitious multinational conference. Held in Yokohama during September 5–8, 1986, this conference reexamined "International Affairs in Asia and the Pacific: Their Past, Present, and the Future." Among the speakers and commentators who gathered from abroad were some of the most distinguished diplomatic historians and political scientists from the United States, Britain, China, Korea, Thailand, and Malaysia.

Conclusions

It appears that Japanese scholars in the field of *Japanese* diplomatic history are beginning to move in the direction of *international* history. There is a sense of excitement over new research opportunities as the constant opening of fresh American and British archives presents new challenges and encourages equal competition with our Western colleagues on equal terms. This research trend is particularly noticeable in studies on the post–Pacific War period, especially the way in which the Allied occupation policy toward Japan was affected by the emergence of the cold war in Asia.

Reviewing the entire field of Japanese diplomatic history, one is struck with the fact that the proliferation of monographic works has not yet been matched by a similar growth in synthetic works. This is reflected in the dearth of substantial surveys of Japanese diplomatic history based on recent specialized studies.

Tasks for the future will necessarily involve reinterpretations on the macro level, incorporating the large and ever-expanding body of specialized works. At a time when Japan remains less than certain about how to contribute to global peace, stability, and progress, any such assignment will not be an easy one.

Notes

1. Shinobu Seizaburō 信夫清三郎, *Nisshin sensō* 日清戦争 (The Sino-Japanese War) (Fukuda Shobō, 1934). An enlarged edition was published in 1970 by Nansōsha.
2. Tabohashi Kiyoshi 田保橋潔, *Kindai Nissen kankei no kenkyū* 近代日鮮関係の研究 (A study of modern Japanese-Korean relations), 2 vols. (Munetaka Shobō, 1940). Reprinted by Bunka Shiryō Chōsakai, 1963. Its original edition, *Kindai Nisshi-Sen kankei no kenkyū* 近代日支鮮関係の研究 2 vols. Munetaka Shobō (A study of modern Sino-Japanese-Korean relations), was published in 1930.
3. Kajima Morinosuke 鹿島守之助, *Teikoku gaikō no kihon seisaku* 帝国外交

の基本政策 (Basic foreign policies of the Japanese empire) (Ganshōdō Shoten, 1938). Reprinted as *Nihon gaikō seisaku no shiteki kōsatsu* 日本外交政策の史的考察 (A historical study of Japan's foreign policy) (Kajima Kenkyūjo Shuppankai, 1964).

4. Kiyosawa Kiyoshi 清沢洌, *Nihon gaikōshi* 日本外交史 (A diplomatic history of Japan), 2 vols. (Tōyō Keizai Shinpōsha, 1941).

5. Shinobu Seizaburō 信夫清三郎, *Kindai Nihon gaikōshi* 近代日本外交史 (A diplomatic history of modern Japan) (Chūō Kōronsha, 1942). Reprinted in 1948 by Kenshinsha.

6. Rekishigaku Kenkyūkai 歴史学研究会 (Historical Science Society), ed., *Taiheiyō sensōshi* 太平洋戦争史 (A history of the Pacific War), 5 vols. (Tōyō Keizai Shinpōsha, 1953–54).

7. Nihon Gaikō Gakkai 日本外交学会 (Association for the Study of Japanese Diplomacy), ed., *Taiheiyō sensō gen'inron* 太平洋戦争原因論 (Origins of the Pacific War) (Shinbun Gekkansha, 1953).

8. Maruyama Masao 丸山真男, "Gunkoku shihaisha no seishin keitai" 軍国支配者の精神形態 (Thought patterns of wartime leaders), *Chōryū* (May 1949), 4(5): 15–37. This essay is reprinted in Maruyama Masao, *Gendai seiji no shisō to kōdō* 現代政治の思想と行動 (Thought and behavior in modern politics) (Miraisha, 1956), 1:83–124. For its English translation, see Ivan Morris, ed., *Thought and Behaviour in Modern Japanese Politics* (London: Oxford University Press, 1963), pp. 84–134.

9. Gaimushō 外務省 (Foreign Ministry), ed., *Shūsen shiroku* 終戦史録 (The historical record of the termination of the Pacific War), 2 vols. (Shinbun Gekkansha, 1951).

10. —— ed., *Nihon gaikō nenpyō narabini shuyō bunsho* 日本外交年表並主要文書 (A chronology and major documents on Japanese foreign policy), 2 vols. (Nihon Kokusai Rengō Kyōkai, 1955). Reprinted by Hara Shobō, 1966.

11. Hosoya Chihiro 細谷千博, *Shiberia shuppei no shiteki kenkyū* シベリア出兵の史的研究 (A historical study of the Siberian expedition) (Yūhikaku, 1955).

12. Nihon Kokusai Seiji Gakkai, Taiheiyō Sensō Gen'in Kenkyūbu 日本国際政治学会, 太平洋戦争原因研究部, ed., *Taiheiyō sensō e no michi* 太平洋戦争への道 (The road to the Pacific War), 7 vols., 1 supp. (Asahi Shimbunsha, 1962–63). Reprinted in 1987–88.

13. *Japan Erupts: The London Naval Conference and the Manchurian Incident, 1928–1932* (1984); *China Quagmire: Japan's Expansion on the Asian Continent, 1939–1941* (1983); *Deterrent Diplomacy: Japan, Germany, and the USSR, 1935–1940* (1976); *The Fateful Choice: Japan's Advance Into Southeast Asia, 1939–1941* (1980).

14. Shinobu Seizaburō and Nakayama Jiichi 信夫清三郎, 中山治一, eds., *Nichi-Ro sensōshi no kenkyū* 日露戦争史の研究 (Studies on the history of the Russo-Japanese War) (Kawade Shobō Shinsha, 1959).

15. Hosoya Chihiro, Saitō Makoto, Imai Seiichi, and Rōyama Michio 細谷千博, 斎藤真, 今井清一, 蠟山道雄, eds., *Nichi-Bei kankeishi: Kaisen ni itaru 10-nen, 1931–1941* (日米関係史—開戦に至る十年, 1931–1941) (A history of Japanese-American relations: The decade preceding the war, 1931–1941), 4 vols. (Tokyo Daigaku Shuppankai, 1971–72). Its English edition is Dorothy Borg and Shumpei Okamoto, eds., *Pearl Harbor as History: Japanese-American Relations, 1931–1941* (New York: Columbia University Press, 1973).

16. Hosoya Chihiro and Saitō Makoto 細谷千博, 斎藤真, eds., *Washinton taisei to Nichi-Bei kankei* ワシントン体制と日米関係 (The Washington system and Japanese-American relations) (Tokyo Daigaku Shuppankai, 1978).

17. Satō Seizaburō 佐藤誠三郎 and Roger Dingman, eds., *Kindai Nihon no taigai taido* 近代日本の対外態度 (Attitudes toward foreign affairs in modern Japan) (Tokyo Daigaku Shuppankai, 1974).

18. Hosoya Chihiro, ed., *Nichi-Ei kankeishi, 1917–1949* 日英関係史 (Essays on the history of Anglo-Japanese relations, 1917–1949) (Tokyo Daigaku Shuppankai, 1982).

19. Sodei Rinjirō 袖井林二郎, ed., *Sekaishi no naka no Nihon senryō* 世界史のなかの日本占領 (The Allied occupation of Japan in world history) (Nihon Hyōronsha, 1985).

20. Seki Hiroharu 関寛治, "1917-nen Harubin kakumei: Shiberia shuppeishi josetsu" 1917年ハルビン革命—シベリア出兵史序説 (The revolution in Harbin in 1917: Prelude to the history of the Siberian expedition) (Fukumura Shuppan, 1966).

21. Hosoya Chihiro 細谷千博, *Roshia kakumei to Nihon* ロシア革命と日本 (The Russian Revolution and Japan) (Hara Shobō, 1971). Most of the articles contained in this work originally appeared around 1960.

22. Kobayashi Yukio 小林幸男, "Nihon tai-So gaikō seisaku kettei kateiron josetsu" 日本対ソ外交政策決定過程論序説 (An introduction to a discussion of the policymaking process in Japan's relations with the Soviet Union), *Kindai hōgaku* (March 1960), 3(3–4):1–30.

23. Ogata Sadako 緒方貞子, *Manshū jihen to seisaku no keisei katei* 満州事変と政策の形成過程 (The Manchurian Incident and the policy-making process in Japan) (Hara Shobō, 1966). Its original English edition is *Defiance in Manchuria: The Making of Japanese Foreign Policy, 1931–1932* (Berkeley: University of California Press, 1964).

24. Asada Sadao 麻田貞雄, "Washinton kaigi o meguru Nichi-Bei no

seisaku kettei katei no hikaku" ワシントン会議をめぐる日米政策決定過程の比較 (A comparative study of the American and Japanese decision-making process at the time of the Washington Conference), in Hosoya Chihiro and Watanuki Jōji 細谷千博, 綿貫譲治, eds., *Taigai seisaku kettei katei no Nichi-Bei hikaku* 対外政策決定過程の日米比較 (A comparative study of the foreign policy decision-making process in Japan and the United States), pp. 419–64 (Tokyo Daigaku Shuppankai, 1977).

25. Oka Yoshitake 岡義武, "Kindai seijika no sutorateji" 近代政治家のストラテジー (The strategy of modern statesmen), in Oka Yoshitake, Nagahama Masatoshi, and Tsuji Kiyoaki 岡義武, 長浜政寿, 辻清明, eds., *Kindai kokkaron* 近代国家論 (On modern states), vol. 2. (Kōbundō, 1950); Oka Yoshitake, *Yamagata Aritomo: Meiji Nihon no shōchō* 山県有朋―明治日本の象徴 (Yamagata Aritomo: Symbol of Meiji Japan) (Iwanami Shoten, 1958).

26. Mitani Taichirō 三谷太一郎, "'Tenkanki' (1918–1921) no gaikō shidō" 「転換期」(1918―1921)の外交指導 (Foreign policy leadership at a "transition period," 1918–1921), in Shinohara Hajime and Mitani Taichirō 篠原一, 三谷太一郎, eds., *Kindai Nihon no seiji shidō* 近代日本の政治指導 (Political leadership in modern Japan), pp. 293–374 (Tokyo Daigaku Shuppankai, 1965).

27. *Kokusai seiji* (1967), no. 33; (1977), no. 56.

28. Kurihara Akira 栗原彬, "Konoe Fumimaro no pāsonaritī to shin taisei" 近衛文麿のパーソナリティと新体制 (Konoe Fumimaro: Identity and the New Order), in *Nenpō seijigaku, 1972: "Konoe shintaisei" no kenkyū* 年報政治学・1972,「近衛新体制」の研究 (The annuals of the Japanese Political Science Association, 1972: Studies on Konoe's "New Order"), pp. 181–230.

29. Bamba Nobuya 馬場伸也, *Manshū jihen e no michi* 満州事変への道 (Japan's road to the Manchurian Incident) (Chūō Kōronsha, 1972).

30. Miwa Kimitada 三輪公忠, *Matsuoka Yōsuke: Sono hito to gaikō* 松岡洋右―その人と外交 (Matsuoka Yōsuke: His personality and diplomacy) (Chūō Kōronsha, 1971).

31. See, for example, Akira Iriye 入江昭, *Bei-Chū kankei no imēji* 米中関係のイメージ (Images in Sino-American relations) (Nihon Kokusai Mondai Kenkyūjo, 1965); and *Kokusai seiji* (1976), no. 34.

32. See, for example, Kenneth E. Boulding, *The Image: Knowledge in Life and Society* (Ann Arbor: University of Michigan Press, 1956); Leon Festinger, *A Theory of Cognitive Dissonance* (New York: Row, Peterson, 1957); Harold and Margaret Sprout, "Environmental Factors in the Study of International Politics," *Journal of Conflict Resolution* (December 1957),

1(4):309–28; and Robert Jervis, *Perception and Misperception in International Politics* (Princeton University Press, 1976).

33. Itō Takashi 伊藤隆, *Shōwa shoki seijishi kenkyū: Rondon kaigun gunshuku mondai o meguru sho seiji shūdan no taikō to teikei* 昭和初期政治史研究 ―ロンドン海軍軍縮問題をめぐる諸政治集団の対抗と提携 (A study of the political history of the early Shōwa period: Conflict and collaboraion among political groups over the London Naval Treaty controversy) (Tokyo Daigaku Shuppankai, 1969).

34. Asada Sadao 麻田貞雄, "Nihon kaigun to tai-Bei seisaku oyobi senryaku" 日本海軍と対米政策および戦略 (The Japanese navy: Its policy and strategy toward the United States), in Hosoya et al., eds., *Nichi-Bei kankeishi* (1971), 2:87–149.

35. Kobayashi Tatsuo 小林龍夫, "Kaigun gunshuku jōyaku (1921–1936-nen)" 海軍軍縮条約(1921—1936年) (Naval treaties, 1921–1936), in *Taiheiyō sensō e no michi*, 1:3–160 (Asahi Shimbunsha, 1963).

36. Ikeda Kiyoshi 池田清, "Rondon kaigun jōyaku to tōsuiken mondai" ロンドン海軍条約と統帥権問題 (The London Naval Treaty and the question of the "right of supreme command"), *Hōgaku zasshi* (Osaka Ichiritsu Daigaku) (October 1968), 15(2):1–35.

37. Fujiwara Akira 藤原彰, *Gunjishi* 軍事史 (A military history of Japan) (Tōyō Keizai Shinpōsha, 1961).

38. Hata Ikuhiko 秦郁彦, *Gun fashizumu undōshi* 軍ファシズム運動史 (A history of fascist movements in the military) (Kawade Shobō Shinsha, 1962).

39. Imai Seiichi 今井清一, "Taishōki ni okeru gunbu no seijiteki chii" 大正期における軍部の政治的地位 (The political status of the military during the Taisho period), *Shisō* (September 1957), no. 399, pp. 3–21.

40. Banno Junji 坂野潤治, "Nihon rikugun no Ō-Beikan to Chūgoku seisaku" 日本陸軍の欧米観と中国政策 (The Japanese army's views of the West and its policy toward China), in Hosoya Chihiro and Saitō Makoto, eds., *Washinton taisei to Nichi-Bei kankei*, pp. 441–64.

41. Kitaoka Shin'ichi 北岡伸一, *Nihon rikugun to tairiku seisaku, 1906–1918* 日本陸軍と大陸政策, 1906–1918. (The Japanese army and its continental policy, 1906–1918) (Tokyo Daigaku Shuppankai, 1978).

42. *Kokusai seiji* (1970), no. 41.

43. Ogata Sadako 緒方貞子, "Kokusaishugi dantai no yakuwari" 国際主義団体の役割 (The role of liberal nongovernmental organizations), in Hosoya et al., eds., *Nichi-Bei kankeishi* (1972), 3:307–53.

44. Kakegawa Tomiko 掛川トミ子, "Masu media no tōsei to tai-Bei ronchō" マス・メディアの統制と対米論調 (The governmental control of the Japanese press and public opinion on the United States), in Hosoya Chihiro et al., eds., *Nichi-Bei kankeishi* (1972), 4:3–80.

45. Etō Shinkichi 衛藤瀋吉, "Keihōsen shadan mondai no gaikō katei" 京奉線遮断問題の外交過程 (Diplomatic negotiations concerning the suspension of traffic on the Peking-Mukden railway), in Shinohara Hajime and Mitani Taichirō, eds., *Kindai Nihon no seiji shidō*, pp. 375–429.

46. Mushakōji Kinhide 武者小路公秀, "Seiji no kotoba to kinchō kanwa: Teikoku gikai ni okeru shushō enzetsu no kachi naiyō bunseki" 政治の言葉と緊張緩和―帝国議会に於ける首相演説の価値内容分析 (The language of politics and tension reduction: Value content analysis of prime ministers' addresses before the Imperial Diet), in *Nenpō seijigaku, 1969: Kokusai kinchō kanwa no seiji katei* 年報政治学, 1969 : 国際緊張緩和の政治過程 (The annuals of the Japanese Political Science Association, 1969: Political process of international tension reduction), pp. 145–80.

47. Watanabe Akio 渡辺昭夫, "Taigai ishiki ni okeru 'senzen' to 'sengo': Shushō gaishō no gikai enzetsu no bunseki ni motozuku jakkan no kōsatsu" 対外意識における「戦前」と「戦後」―首相・外相の議会演説の分析に基づく若干の考察 ("Prewar" and "postwar" periods in Japanese perceptions of foreign affairs: Some observations on the basis of an analysis of premiers' and foreign ministers' addresses before the Diet), in Satō Seizaburō and Roger Dingman, eds., *Kindai Nihon no taigai taido*, pp. 225–74.

48. Usui Hisakazu 臼井久和, "Settoku komyunikēshon no Nichi-Bei hikaku: Gikai enzetsu no ichi kōsatsu" 説得コミュニケィションの日米比較―議会演説の一考察 (Comparison of persuasive communications in Japan and the United States: A study of parliamentary speeches), in Hosoya Chihiro and Watanuki Jōji eds., *Taigai seisaku kettei katei no Nichi-Bei hikaku*, pp. 347–72.

49. Akira Iriye, *After Imperialism: The Search for a New Order in the Far East, 1921–1931* (Cambridge: Harvard University Press, 1965). A somewhat condensed Japanese version was published as *Kyokutō shin chitsujo no mosaku, 1921–1931* 極東新秩序の模索, 1921―1931 (The search for a new order in the Far East, 1921–1931) (Hara Shobō, 1969).

50. Akira Iriye 入江昭, *Nichi-Bei sensō* 日米戦争 (The Japanese-American war) (Chūō Kōronsha, 1978). Its English version is *Power and Culture: The Japanese-American War, 1941–1945* (Cambridge: Harvard University Press, 1981).

51. Hosoya Chihiro, *San Furanshisuko kōwa e no michi* サンフランシスコ講和への道 (The road to the San Francisco Peace Treaty) (Chūō Kōronsha, 1984).

1

Guide to Documents, Archives, Encyclopedias, and Reference Works

Ōhata Tokushirō
Asada Sadao
Hatano Sumio

Unlike the following chapters, this chapter is not a bibliographical essay but a research guide. As such it attempts, first, to show the researcher the way to the rich archival materials of the Japanese Foreign Ministry (Gaimushō) and its serial publication of diplomatic documents. In addition, it provides practical information on other manuscript collections of major importance and relevance to the history of Japanese foreign policy, such as the army and navy records, personal papers, and other manuscript materials.

Second, this chapter presents reference materials. It introduces the reader to essential research tools—encyclopedias and chronologies of

Japanese diplomatic and military history, bibliographies, and other research aids.

Finally, for the convenience of students, we shall list published works of a general nature: multivolume series, survcy histories, and basic textbooks of Japanese diplomatic history.

FOREIGN MINISTRY DOCUMENTS AND ARCHIVES

Diplomatic Documents: The Bakumatsu Period

The records of the Foreign Ministry naturally constitute the basic primary source of any serious study of Japanese diplomatic history. However, we must start with collections of documents that antedated the establishment of the Foreign Ministry.

The beginning of the compilation of diplomatic documents in Japan may be said to be "Tsūkō ichiran" (Survey of foreign relations), 350 vols, which was completed in 1953. These volumes contain documents relating to the Shogunate's relations with foreign powers from 1566 to 1825. This compilation was followed by "Tsūkō ichiran: Zokushū" (Sequel to survey of foreign relations), in 152 volumes covering the years 1826–1854.[1] The documents of the Tokugawa (late Shogunate) period before Japan's opening to the Western powers were classified according to countries and subjects. This basic pattern was carried over into "Tsūshin zenran" (A complete record of foreign relations) and its sequel, as well as the subsequent records of the Foreign Ministry.[2]

"Tsūshin zenran," as preserved at the Diplomatic Record Office (Gaikō Shiryōkan) today,[3] consists of 320 volumes of diplomatic documents edited by the Tokugawa Shogunate, covering 1859–1860.

"Zoku tsūshin zenran" (Sequel to "Tsūshin zenran")[4] was compiled by the newly established Gaimushō (Foreign Ministry) to continue this series up to the first year of the Meiji period (1868). This collection consists of 505 chronological volumes, and 1,366 volumes arranged by subject. The chronological volumes contain diplomatic correspondence with twelve countries: the United States, Russia, the Netherlands, Britain, France, Portugal, Prussia, Switzerland, Belgium,

Italy, Denmark, and Hawaii. The subject volumes are classified into twenty-seven parts according to events they deal with; and depending on the issues involved, the collection includes documents as old as the early 1800s. "Tsūshin zenran" and its sequential volumes have been edited by Tsūshō Zenran Henshūkai and were published in facsimile form. Without including the index, they amount to 60 volumes.[5]

Foreign Ministry Documents

The task of systematically arranging, editing, and publishing the documents held by the Japanese Foreign Ministry was undertaken in 1936, when *Dai Nippon gaikō bunsho* (Diplomatic documents of imperial Japan) began to be published.[6] After the ninth volume appeared in 1940, the publication of the series was suspended because of the outbreak of the Pacific War.

After the end of the war, publication was resumed under the new overall title, *Nihon gaikō bunsho* (Documents on Japanese foreign policy). Those volumes published prior to the war were republished in 1949 under this new title. *Nippon gaikō bunsho* for the Meiji period (1868–1912) devotes one volume to each year. For example, the third volume contains documents pertaining to 1870, and the fourth volume (divided into two parts) prints documents relating to 1871.

When relevant documents grew too numerous to be contained in a single annual volume, they came to be printed in several installments or parts. Accordingly, the traditional format was changed, and starting with the Taishō period (1912–1926) each volume was designated not by serial number but by year. Thus, diplomatic documents for 1913, for example, were printed as *Nihon gaikō bunsho: Taishō 2-nen* (Documents on Japanese foreign policy: 1913), 3 vols. This basic format has been retained to date. As of March 1988, *Nihon gaikō bunsho* covers up to the end of 1926.

The rising interest in contemporary history has prompted publication of special volumes devoted to more recent events—parallel to the chronological volumes. Since 1977 carefully edited documents relating to the Manchurian Incident have been published in seven volumes. Similarly "the series on naval conferences" (covering the

Geneva and London conferences) has been published since 1979; to date, seven volumes have appeared.

The *Nihon gaikō bunsho* series also contains various collections of documents pertaining to special subjects. Some of them were published as "supplements" to annual volumes, such as the collections on the Boxer Rebellion (three-volume supplement to vol. 33), on the Russo-Japanese War (five-volume supplement to vols. 37 and 38), and on the Chinese Revolution of 1911 (supplement to vols. 44 and 45).[7]

Others were published as "special volumes." They include: collections on the Paris Peace Conference; the Washington Conference of 1921–22 (4 vols.); and the above-mentioned series on the Geneva and London naval conferences; and the Manchurian Incident.[8]

Also, there are "extra volumes" of *Nihon gaikō bunsho* relating to subjects that span several years: treaty revision (the negotiations to revise the unequal treaties with the Western powers during the Meiji period);[9] commercial treaties; and the Hague peace conferences of 1899 and 1907.[10]

Still another category of Foreign Ministry publications is not collected documents but is more in the nature of monographic studies originally compiled for desk use at the Foreign Ministry. These volumes include (with some overlapping with the previously cited series): *Jōyaku kaisei keika gaiyō fu nenpyō* (A summary of the progress of negotiations for treaty revision, with a chronology); *Tsūshō jōyaku to tsūshō seisaku no hensen* (Changes in commercial treaties and trade policy);[11] *Komura gaikōshi* (The diplomatic biography of Komura Jutarō);[12] *Pari kōwa kaigi keika gaiyō* (A summary of the developments at the Paris Peace Conference of 1919;[13] and *Tai-Bei imin mondai keika gaiyō* (The summary of the development of the Japanese immigration question in the United States).[14] The most recent addition to the series is *Nihon gaikō tsuikairoku, 1900–1935* (The diplomatic memoirs of Nagaoka Harukazu, 1900–1935).[15] The more important of these supplementary volume will be discussed in the chapters that follow.

A cumulative index of the *Nihon gaikō bunsho* series has not been printed, but the Document Section of the Foreign Ministry has prepared for its own desk use comprehensive tables of contents arranged by countries and covering the period 1868–1906.[16] It can be consulted at the Diplomatic Record Office.

As the above description shows, the pace of compilation and publication of the *Nihon gaikō bunsho* series has been painfully slow. In order to fill the gap, the Foreign Ministry edited and published in 1955 *Nihon gaikō nenpyō narabini shuyō bunsho* (A chronology and major documents of Japanese foreign policy),[17] which in a compact form encompasses the entire century from the Bakumatsu period to 1945. The first volume covers the years 1840–1921, the second volume 1922–1945. They provide a careful selection of major diplomatic documents and crucial papers relating to the Japanese government's decision making, together with a detailed chronology of Japanese foreign policy originally prepared by Kiyosawa Kiyoshi. The adenda provides a roster of major Foreign Ministry figures, ambassadors to and from Japan, and cabinet members during the period covered by this work. These volumes are an essential reference for any student of Japanese diplomatic history.

Among specialized reference works, students of Bakumatsu and Meiji diplomacy will find useful *Kindai in'yōreki taishōhyō* (A conversion table of the lunar and solar calendars), compiled by the Foreign Ministry, because the Japanese government prior to 1873 used the lunar calendar.[18]

Foreign Ministry Archives up to 1945

As to the archives of the Foreign Ministry, all the extant manuscript documents prior to 1945 can be examined at the Diplomatic Record Office of the Foreign Ministry. These original documents, contained in 48,000 files, are roughly arranged by periods and subjects. The documents of the Meiji and Taishō periods, in 22,000 files, are grouped as follows: (a) political affairs; (b) treaties; (c) commercial affairs; (d) judiciary and police matters; (e) military matters; and protocol and routine affairs. Those of the pre–World War II Shōwa period (1926–45), contained in 26,000 files, are arranged as follows: (a) political-diplomatic affairs; (b) treaties, agreements, and international conferences; (c) military affairs; (d) judiciary and police matters; (e) financial, economic, industrial, and commercial affairs; and others.

Each of these groups is divided and subdivided, and the reseacher must identify each set of documents by consulting the catalogue and cards at the search/reading room of the Diplomatic Record Office. Researchers are warned that Cecil H. Uyehara, ed., *Checklist of Archives in the Japanese Ministry of Foreign Affairs, Tokyo, Japan, 1868–1945* (Washington, D.C., 1954) is useful only for those documents (some two million pages) that were microfilmed by the team of American scholars who worked in Tokyo during 1949–51 on a cooperative project sponsored by the U.S. Library of Congress and the State Department. It should be emphasized that there is a vast quantity of Foreign Ministry documents, especially outside category (a), which were never microfilmed by the visiting team and can be examined only at the Diplomatic Record Office.

An explanation is called for documents that are marked with the sign "Matsu" in the card catalogue at the Diplomatic Record Office— documents that correspond to the items prefaced with "PVM" in Cecil H. Uyehara's *Checklist.* "Matsu" and "PVM" stand for the papers of Matsumoto Tadao, a scholarly parliamentary vice-minister during 1937–39.[19] During his term in this and other offices in the Foreign Ministry, he had transcribed a large body of important documents. After his death these copies were donated to the Foreign Minstry by his widow and were integrated into the ministry's archives. The core of the Matsumoto papers are documents—dispatches, position papers, and memoranda—relating to Sino-Japanese relations roughly from 1927 to 1939. The Matsumoto collection is an essential supplement to the archival materials relating to the Shōwa period, because many of the original documents were destroyed by fire.

Numerous Foreign Ministry materials were lost—some by accidental fires, others by American bombings, and still others were deliberately destroyed by Japanese officials who feared an imminent American invasion. They include records relating to such important subjects as the first Anglo-Japanese Alliance, the annexation of Korea, and the Nine-Power Treaty of the Washington Conference. On the Shōwa period, where the loss was greatest, missing documents include records relating to the assassination of Chang Tso-lin, the Tripartite Pact, and the Japanese-Soviet Neutrality Pact.

In November 1942, the Greater East Asia Ministry was established to deal with diplomatic and political affairs in the area defined as Greater East Asia—Manchuria, China, and Southeast Asia. Thus, the new ministry took over much of the substantial functions of the Foreign Ministry. The records of the Greater East Asia Ministry were, however, destroyed by air raids during the war.

Foreign Ministry Archives Since 1945

The Foreign Ministry documents for the post-1945 period have only recently been opened to researchers, both Japanese and foreign, and a "thirty-year rule" has been adopted as the rough guideline for archival opening. According to this principle, documents on the Allied occupation of Japan have been opened in stages. By the eighth release (March 1985), documents declassified were, among others, those relating to the ratification of the San Francisco Peace Treaty of 1952, the conclusion of commercial treaties, and the problem of Japan's participation in the United Nations. The most recent release—the ninth—of December 1987, makes available documents relating to the Japanese-Republic of China Peace Treaty, the U.S.-Japan Security Pact, and the executive agreement accompanying it. The Diplomatic Record Office has published a list of each group of documents with the opening of each new installment.[20] However, these lists are too general to be of much use for the historian searching for particular items.

Although the Foreign Ministry materials made available for 1945–1952 are huge in quantity, much of them are of low quality. The "declassification" process has been a highly selective, if not arbitrary, process; some key documents are strangely missing or withheld. Strongly worded appeals for a more liberal archival policy, sent to the prime minister's office by a group of Japanese and American scholars, went unanswered. Unfortunately, there exists no legislation in Japan that prohibits former bureaucrats from withholding documents that may prove embarrassing, either personally or collectively. Nor does a Japanese counterpart of America's Freedom of Information Act seem likely to be enacted in the near future.

Foreign Ministry Registers and Almanacs

In the Diplomatic Record Office, there are convenient handbooks on the organization of the Foreign Ministry and legations overseas, statutes and regulations governing Japanese diplomatic service, and a list of foreign service personnel with brief career records. They are *Gaimushō shokuinroku* (Register of the members of the Foreign Ministry),[21] which was prepared annually for the periods 1884–1912 and 1940–44, and *Gaimushō nenkan* (The Foreign Ministry almanac),[22] which is available for the years 1907–1942 and since 1952. *Gaimushō nenkan* has been divided since 1957 into two volumes, the first covering organization and statutes, and the second containing personnel lists.

One neglected source is *Kakankai kaihō* (1944–   ),[23] a monthly newsletter circulated among the former members of the Foreign Ministry; it often contains interesting "reminiscences" by retired diplomats about episodes in which they played a part.

OTHER MANUSCRIPT SOURCES

Aside from the Foreign Ministry archives, there are several major depositories of manuscript sources on Japanese diplomatic-military history that are open to the historian: Kokuritsu Kokkai Toshokan (National Diet Library); Kokuritsu Kōbunshokan (National Archives of Japan); and Bōeichō Bōei Kenkyūjo, Senshibu (War History Department, National Institute for Defense Studids, Defense Agency); and others.

Kensei Shiryō Shitsu

The National Diet Library's Kensei Shiryō Shitsu (The Depository for Documents on Political and Constitutional History)[24] holds the unpublished personal papers of nearly two hundred political and military leaders of modern and contemporary Japan. Each collection is divided broadly into letters and correspondence arranged alphabetically by names; and manuscript documents subdivided into private papers (diaries and personal memoranda) and original drafts of official papers arranged by subjects. For some of the better-organized collections (fourteen at the time of this writing), catalogues have been published to help the researcher identify the relevant documents quickly. For the bulk of the collections, however, scholars must rely on tentative catalogues (in the nature of card catalogues) that can be consulted at Kensei Shiryō Shitsu. Perhaps the quickest and most comprehensive guide is *Kensei Shiryō Shitsu yōran* (A handbook of collections at the Depository for Documents on Political and Costitutional Materials),[25] which was printed in 1981. It lists all the personal papers held at Kensei Shiryō Shitsu with brief comments on each item. Since this handbook was not printed for general sale, its availability is restricted.

The most up-to-date inventory was published in 1984 by the Diet Library in its bulletin (in nine installments). It gives a full list of its manuscript holdings with brief explanations.[26] Since this bulletin has only limited circulation abroad, we shall list here, in alphabetical order, relevant papers of individuals who played a role in Japanese foreign policy.

Akashi Motojirō (1864–1919)
Enomoto Takeaki (1836–1908)
Fukai Eigo (1871–1945)
Hirata Tōsuke (1849–1925)
Hoshi Tōru (1850–1901)
Ijūin Hikokichi (1864–1924)
Inoue Kaoru (1836–1915)
Inukai Tsuyoshi (1855–1932)
Ishiwara Kanji (1889–1949)
Itō Hirobumi (1841–1909)
Itō Miyoji (1857–1934)
Iwakura Tomomi (1825–83)
Kabayama Sukenori (1837–1922)
Kaneko Kentarō (1853–1942)
Katō Takaaki (1860–1926)
Katsu Kaishū (1823–99)
Katsura Tarō (1848–1913)
Kawakami Sōroku (1848–99)
Makino Nobuaki (1861–1949)
Matsukata Masayoshi (1835–1924)
Miura Gorō (1847–1926)
Mori Arinori (1847–89)

Munakata Kotarō (1864–1923)
Mutsu Munemitsu (1844–97)
Nishi Tokujirō (1847–1912)
Ogawa Heikichi (1870–1942)
Oka Ichinosuke (1860–1916)
Ōtori Keisuke (1832–1911)
Ōyama Iwao (1842–1916)
Sakatani Yoshiro (1863–1941)
Saitō Makoto (1858–1936)
Samejima Hisanobu (1846–80)
Shinagawa Yajirō (1843–1900)
Shishidō Tamaki (1829–1901)
Soejima Taneomi (1828–1905)
Takarabe Takeshi (1867–1949)
Terauchi Masatake (1852–1919)
Tsuzuki Keiroku (1861–1923)
Ueno Kagenori (1845–88)
Ugaki Kazushige (1868–1956)
Yamagata Aritomo (1838–1922)
Yanagihara Sakimitsu (1850–94)
Yamamoto Gonnohyōe (1852–1933)

Also available at Kensei Shiryō Shitsu are the microfilmed papers of the following figures:

Den Kenjirō (1855–1930)
Gotō Shinpei (1857–1929)
Hanabusa Yoshitomo (1842–1917)
Inoue Kowashi (1843–95)
Ishiwara Kanji (1889–1949)
Kido Takayoshi (1833–77)
Kido Kōichi (1889–1977)
Konoe Atsumaro (1863–1904)
Konoe Fumimaro (1891–1945)

Megata Tanetarō (1853–1926)
Nagaoka Gaishi (1858–1933)
Nishihara Kamezō (1873–1954)
Sanjō Sanetomi (1837–91)
Sone Arasuke (1849–1910)
Tanaka Giichi (1864–1929)
Terauchi Masatake (1852–1919)
Terajima Munenori (1832–93)

Gendai Seijishi Shiryō Shitsu

More recently, Gendai Seijishi Shiryō Shitsu (the Office of Contemporary Political History) of the National Diet Library has been collecting documents broadly relating to contemporary political and diplomatic history. For example, it holds the documents that had been seized by the American military during the Allied occupation and have since been returned to Japan. (The bulk of such returned documents—mostly the army and navy records—is, however, available at the War History Department, the National Institute for Defense Studies, as explained below.)

More importantly, Gendai Seijishi Shiryō Shitsu has been microfilming a vast store of original records in the United States relating to the Allied occupation of Japan.[27] These materials from Suitland, Maryland, and Washington, D.C. have been carefully organized and indexed by that office, so that many of the American documents on the occupation of Japan are, ironically, easier to use in Tokyo than in Suitland or Washington. (However, the sheer volume of card catalogue is such that it has proved impracticable to publish a guide to these documents.)

In May 1986, Gendai Seiji Shiryō Shitsu was incorporated into Kensei Shiryō Shitsu.

Finance Ministry

Zaiseishi Shitsu (the Office of Financial History, the Ministry of Finance)[28] has gathered a large and well-selected collection of Japanese and American documents on the Allied occupation of Japan (relating not only to economic and financial but also political-diplomatic matters). These documents were energetically collected by Hata Ikuhiko (then head of the Office of Financial History) and his colleagues in preparation for *Shōwa zaiseishi* (Economic and financial history of the Shōwa period).[29] Unfortunately, these materials are not open to the general public, but "in principle" qualified scholars with "letters of introduction" may examine them.

Kōbunshokan

In 1971 Kokuritsu Kōbunshokan (the National Archives of Japan)[30] was opened as a subsidiary agency of the Prime Minister's office. It has brought together to preserve documents (approximately 230,000 volumes) transferred from various administrative organs of the state. Among them, the most bulky and well-arranged collections are the following four: (a) "Kōbunroku" (Official documents of the cabinet, 1868–1886); (b) "Dajō ruiten" (Manuscript and statute books, 1867–1883); (c) "Kōbun ruishū" (Official documents of the cabinet concerning laws and ordinances, 1886–1950); and (d) "Kōbun zassan" (Official documents of the cabinet concerning miscellaneous matters, 1887–1945). "Kōbunroku" consists of documents received from various ministries. "Dajō ruiten" contains copies of records compiled chronologically. "Kōbun ruishū," which took over the above two collections and continued up to 1950, contains important documents on the cabinet's decision making. "Kōbun zassan" collects materials of lesser importance which were not contained in the above three categories. All four collections include materials on foreign policy.[31]

Whereas *Nihon gaikō bunsho* consists mainly of exchanges between the home office and its overseas legations, the above-described collections are useful for tracing the process through which the cabinet made decisions on important foreign policy issues. However, the materials of interest to the diplomatic historian are concentrated in the early Meiji period. The indices of these collections are at present being published.[32]

Privy Council

The most important single body of materials at Kōbunshokan is "Sūmitsuin bunsho" (records of the Privy Council). Established in 1888 as the supreme advisory council for the Emperor under the Meiji

Constitution, this council deliberated on important foreign policy questions and approved all treaties before their ratification. Especially important are the records of discussions in this council and its committee meetings on major foreign policy problems. Most of these materials became available to researchers only in 1973.

From these Privy Council materials, the proceedings of its plenary sessions are currently being published. To date, the proceedings for the Meiji period and the Taishō period have been published.[33] For the later period, only a small but important segment (1939–45) has been printed in Fukai Eigo's *Sūmitsuin jūyō giji oboegaki* (Notes on important sessions of the Privy Council).[34]

ARMY AND NAVY RECORDS

The records of the army and navy are under the custody of the War History Department of the National Institute for Defense Studies.[35] Needless to say, the role played by the Japanese military in foreign policy was of crucial importance, but the diplomatic historian will not find it easy to use these materials. Since the army and navy ministries and their general staffs hastily destroyed confidential documents at the time of Japan's surrender, the materials that have survived are patchy and full of gaps.

Seized Documents

During the occupation of Japan, the American military authorities seized and in 1947 shipped to the Washington Document Center a vast quantity of the surviving army and navy records, which were deposited at a warehouse in Franconia in the suburbs of Washington, D.C. under the custody of the U.S. National Archives. The first scholar to note the importance of these records and survey them was James W. Morley, who wrote a basic article, "Checklist of Seized Japanese Records in the National Archives," *Far Eastern Quarterly* (May 1950), 9(3): 306–33.

Shortly before these documents were returned to Japan in 1958, a group of American scholars headed by John Young selected and microfilmed a small portion of the army and navy documents that were considered historically valuable. The microfilm reproduction, sponsored by the U.S. Library of Congress and the U.S. Navy, consists of some 400,000 pages in 163 reels. They focused on various activities of the Japanese military mainly in China between 1900 and 1945. Because the time and funds available for the project were limited, a mere 5 percent of the seized documents could be microfilmed.

In 1959 John Young compiled the *Checklist of Microfilm Reproduction of Selected Archives of the Japanese Army, Navy, and Other Government Agencies, 1868–1945* (Washington, D.C.: Georgetown University Press, 1959). The usefulness of this checklist to Japanese scholars, in the absence of a similar guidebook, is clear from the fact that Gunjishi Kenkyūkai (Study group on military history) of Hitotsubashi University translated it into Japanese in 1970. Subsequently, the War History Department of the Defense Agency has prepared a more accurate translation of Young's checklist by carefully collating its entries with the returned documents.[36]

Despite Young's checklist and its Japanese translations, the historian cannot expect to locate easily the items he needs, given the accidental nature of the surviving documents. He will not find many systematic collections ready at hand. With a large body of still unorganized materials, he will have to find his own way, as if through a maze, to identify the particular documents he needs—that is, if they exist at all.

War History Office

In addition to the army and navy records returned from the United States, the War History Office of the Defence Agency (Bōeichō Senshishi Shitsu), inaugurated in 1955 and incorporated into the National Defense College a year later, collected a large body of primary sources. These materials contained roughly 13,800 items of official documents transferred from the Demobilization Agency. (This agency, though initially charged with the duty of demobilizing Japanese troops, had also assumed as early as June 1946 the task of collecting materials bearing on the history of the Pacific War in accordance with a directive from the General Military Intelligence Section, G-2, under General Douglas MacArthur, for compilation of the "MacArthur Report.")[37]

During its first ten-year period beginning in 1956, the War History Office concentrated on collecting both official documents and private manuscripts as basic sources for writing its massive series on the military history of the Pacific War, commonly known as the *Senshi sōsho* (War History series). In several instances, it turned out that collections of crucial documents, presumed to have been destroyed on the eve of Japan's surrender, were secretly (and against the order of the Imperial Headquarters) preserved by officers who were sensitive to their historical significance. It is estimated that the War History Office has gathered some 78,900 items from scattered sources. To fill the gap in documentary sources, the staff of the War History Office also conducted extensive interviews with former army and navy officers.

In 1976 the War History Office was reorganized as the War History Department (Senshibu) of the National Defense College, and the emphasis has shifted from collection of documents to research activities. In recent years, thanks to the dedicated work of the staff, card catalogues have become available for an increasing number of documents; they can be consulted in the new library of the National Defense College. In principle, "official" documents are entirely open to researchers, who must, however, request specific items.

Since an additional chapter or two would be needed to give a working guide to the manifold holdings at this library, suffice it here to make some explanatory remarks on the major collections, "Dai nikki" (Army general files) and "Kōbun bikō" (Navy general files). These two collections are the official records of the Army and Navy Ministries and contain few documents of their general staffs. (Most of the important documents of the general staffs relating to national policy, together with significant dispatches and reports, were destroyed at the time of Japan's surrender.)

Army Record

The "Dai nikki" (literally meaning "General diary") series amounts to roughly 7,700 volumes of official records for the period 1867–1942, consisting of chronologically arranged documents that emanated from or were received by the Army Ministry. The records for each year are broken down horizontally according to the degree of confidentiality. Thus they are grouped into "Gunji kimitsu dai nikki" (Confidential military files), "Riku kimitsu dai nikki" (The army's confidential files), "Mitsu dai nikki" (Confidential general files), and "Dai nikki" (General files).[38]

Since the bulk of these annual files pertains to purely military matters, it is not easy to locate documents relating to diplomatic and political affairs. "Mitsudai nikki," containing a section on diplomacy, includes a relatively large number of items relating to politico-diplomatic subjects.

In addition to such a system of classification, "Dai nikki" utilizes another method that groups confidential records according to subjects, including records relating to World War I, the Siberian expedition, the Manchurian Incident, the Sino-Japanese War, and the Pacific War. "Dai nikki" also contains a series of army records relating to the League of Nations and the Versailles treaties, the Washington Naval Conference, and other conferences of arms limitation during the 1920s. These records are especially valuable for the light they throw on the Japanese army's attitude toward interwar naval conferences.[39]

Next, we shall list, by way of illustration, some of the important files, not contained in the "Dai nikki", that should interest both military and diplomatic historians:

"Manshū jihen sakusen shidō kankei tsuzuri" (Files relating to strategy during the Manchurian Incident), 4 vols.; and "Bessatsu" (supplementary volumes), 3 vols.[40] These files record in great detail the activities of the Operations Section of the Army General Staff, from the Mukden Incident to the end of July 1932.

"Shina jihen sensō shidō kankei tsuzuri" (Documents relating to the conduct of the China Incident), 5 vols.[41]

"Kokubō taikō kankei jūyō shorui tsuzuri" (Files of important documents relating to the fundamentals of national defense), 5 vols.[42] These documents were collected by Lieutenant Colonel Shimanuki Shigeyoshi during his service at the Military Affairs Section of the Army Ministry. They contain important materials pertaining to defense and foreign policy during the latter part of the Pacific War.

"Dai tōa sensō sensō shidō kankei tsuzuri" (Files relating to the war guidance of the Greater East Asia War), 6 vols.[43] A collection of policy papers prepared by the War Guidance Office of the Army General Staff during 1943–45.

"Miyazaki Shūichi shiryō" (Miyazaki Shūichi's collection), 139 vols.[44] Head of the Operations Division of the Army General Staff at the time of Japan's surrender, Miyazaki served in the Demobilization Agency and collected crucial army documents. This huge and valuable collection consists of a large body of important papers drafted by the Army General Staff and the Imperial Headquarters from 1900 to 1945, and is especially rich in documents relating to Japan's surrender. Also, the Miyazaki collection contains personnel files for the period 1872–1933.

"Shōwa nikki" [1940–45] (Diary of the Shōwa period [obviously an innocuous pseudonym]), 80 vols.[45] Preserved by the War Guidance Office of the Army General Staff, this important collection contains the records of the Imperial Conferences, the Imperial Headquarters–Cabinet Liaison Conferences, and the Supreme War Council. Of special interests is "Kimitsu sensō nisshi" (Confidential war diary), 18 vols., from June 1, 1940 to August 1, 1945.[46] The last-mentioned diary, "Kimitsu sensō nisshi," is a detailed daily record kept by the War Guidance Office on such important matters as deliberations at the Imperial Headquarters–Cabinet Liaison Conferences, activities within the Army General Staff, contacts with the navy counterparts, and information from the Foreign Ministry.

Navy Record

The "Kōbun bikō" (Navy general files)[47] consists of official documents (1871–1937) emanating from the Navy Ministry. Unlike their army counterparts, these naval files are, on the whole, arranged consistently in chronological order. However, because these files do not include confidential documents but deal mainly with routine matters, the researcher must look elsewhere to find important documents bearing on foreign policy.

By way of examples, we shall list below some of the special collections germane to diplomatic history. Few, if any, of these naval documents are printed in the Foreign Ministry's *Nihon gaikō bunsho* (Documents on Japanese foreign policy), and to date they remain largely untapped by the diplomatic historian.

"Meiji 33-nen Shinkoku jihen shorui" (Documents relating to the Boxer Rebellion, 1900), 132 vols.[48]

"Meiji 44—Taishō 3-nen Shinkoku jihen shorui" (Documents relating to the Chinese Republican Revolution, 1911–1913), 85 vols.[49]

"Senji shorui" (Documents relating to the World War I period, 1914–1920), 716 vols.[50] Rich materials relating to the Japanese administration of the former German islands (Micronesia)—Pacific islands north of the equator and south of the Tropic of Cancer.

"Futsu-In mondai keii" (Particulars regarding the French Indochina question, September 1940), 2 vols.[51] The Navy General Staff's record relating to Japan's advance to northern French Indochina in September 1940.

Special mention must be made of the most recent acquisitions by the War History Department: the Enomoto collection and the Takagi collection. These materials are as important for naval as for political-diplomatic history:

"Gunbi gunshuku kankei shiryō" (Documents relating to naval armaments and [conferences of] naval limitation), 259 vols.[52] This huge and well-organized collection was preserved by the late Enomoto Jūji, a specialist in international law and naval limitation who served as a professor at the Naval Staff College. In his official capacity as an advisor to the Japanese delegation, he participated in all the naval conferences from the Washington Conference of 1921 to the second London Naval Conference of 1936, and he kept under his careful custody all the basic materials relating to naval limitation. A catalogue has been prepared by the War History Department on the Enomoto Collection, which is now open to the researcher.

Another important collection is:

"Takagi Sōkichi shiryō" (Records of Rear Admiral Takagi Sōkichi).[53] A "naval intellectual," Takagi intermittently headed the Research Section of the Navy Ministry during 1936–1940 and served in the Navy General Staff from 1943 in order to collect and analyze information that was necessary for naval policymaking. Takagi's activities as the navy's "political antenna" during this period were wide-ranging, and his efforts for an early termination of the Pacific War are well known. As is to be expected, his collection is an unusually rich one, containing many papers recording extremely delicate information gathered from the top leadership of the two services, cabinet members, senior statesmen, and court circles. There is a plan to publish in the near future the entire Takagi collection, including his valuable diary (1936–45).

Personal Papers

In addition to official records, the library of the War History Department holds several thousand items of personal papers: diaries and memoirs, memoranda and notes on particular problems, and the records of interviews with surviving former officers. Access to many of these personal manuscripts, especially diaries, is restricted in accordance with the conditions specified by their donors or surviving relatives. No list of these papers has been published. We shall mention here a few well-organized personal manuscripts available to the researcher:

The papers of Lieutenant General Saitō Hitoshi.[54] Useful for Japan's China policy during 1911–1931.

The papers of Lieutenant General Sasaki Tōichi[55] and Major General Katakura Tadashi.[56] Important for any study of the Manchurian Incident and the creation of Manchukuo.

The papers of Lieutenant General Watanabe Wataru.[57] They relate to the army's policy toward North China at the time of the Sino-Japanese War and Japan's military administration of Malaya during the Pacific War.

The quickest way to find out whose diaries or personal papers are deposited at the library of the War History Department is to check the footnotes of the *Senshi sōsho* (War History series). Most of the important manuscript sources of interest to the diplomatic historian are heavily utilized in the following volumes:

Daihon'ei rikugunbu (The Imperial Headquarters, army), 10 vols.[58]
Daihon'ei kaigunbu (The Imperial Headquarters, navy), 7 vols.[59]
Daihon'ei rikugunbu: Dai Tōa sensō kaisen keii (The Imperial Headquarters, army: Circumstances leading to the outbreak of the Greater East Asia War), 5 vols.[60]
Daihon'ei kaigunbu: Dai Tōa sensō kaisen keii (The Imperial Headquarters, navy: Circumstances leading to the outbreak of the Greater East Asia War), 2 vols.[61]

As has been noted, navy materials are not as extensive as army records. To supplement this deficiency, the researcher can utilize Shiryō Chōsaki, Kaigun Bunko (Naval Library, Historical Materials Research Society).[62] Most of their collection consists of printed (but rare) materials, but there are some manuscript sources mostly relating to the naval command immediately prior to and during the Pacific War.

Guides to Archives

Additional information and useful guides to the archives of various government offices and agencies—the state of their preservation, organization, etc.—can be found in Akamatsu Toshihide et al., eds., *Nihon komonjogaku kōza,* vol. 9: *Kindaihen 1* (Series on Japanese diplomatics, vol. 9: The modern period).[63] Briefer and more up-to-date guides for beginners are contained in Nakamura Takafusa and Itō Takashi, eds., *Kindai Nihon kenkyū nyūmon* (An introduction to the study of modern Japan).[64]

For materials held in the archives outside the Tokyo area, a convenient guide is Chihōshi Kenkyū Kyōgikai, ed., *Rekishi shiryō hozon kikan sōran* (A comprehensive survey of institutions for the preservation of local historial materials).[65]

MATERIALS ON JAPAN'S COLONIAL ADMINISTRATIONS

There exists no single organ in Japan that systematically collects source materials on Japan's colonial rule. These materials are scattered in some forty universities and research institutions.

The integrated agencies for Japan's colonial administration were Takushokumushō (the Ministry of Colonial Administration, 1896—97), Takushokushō (the Ministry of Colonial Affairs, 1929—42), and Dai Tōashō (the Greater East Asia Ministry, 1942—45).[66] The last-mentioned ministry, created in 1942 at the peak of Japan's military expansion, took over all the other colonial institutions, and became the central body for Japan's colonial administration. However, most of its records were destroyed by bombings during the war. The small remnants of the materials of these ministries, preserved at the Diplomatic Record Office and Kokuritsu Kōbunshokan, are hardly sufficient to trace their colonial activities.

Bibliographies

The local records of governmental agencies that administered colonial rule in various areas are widely dispersed both in Japan and many parts of Asia. Since the late 1960s Ajia Keizai Kenkyūjo (the Institute of Developing Economies) undertook broad surveys to locate the materials printed by colonial administrative agencies in Taiwan, Korea, Manchukuo, and the Kwantung Territory, as well as materials pertaining to the South Manchuria Railway Company. From 1973 to

1981 this institute published comprehensive catalogues in five volumes, mentioning the locations of these materials.[67]

Useful in this connection are broad historiographical essays published by Asada Kyōji, which treat Japan's colonialism as a whole.[68]

Korea

Korea was Japan's most important colony in terms of size, geographical propinquity, and long historical ties. Relating to the period 1905–1910, when Korea was Japan's protectorate controlled by the Japanese resident-general, Ichikawa Masaaki has energetically collected basic source materials and published them in three noteworthy volumes.[69]

For the postannexation period, 1910–1945, when Korea was ruled by the Japanese governor-general, extant documentary sources are meager. The personal papers of Terauchi Masatake and Saitō Makoto, which are available at Kensei Shiryō Shitsu of the National Diet Library, contain rich materials pertaining to their administration of Korea. The former served as governor-general during 1910–1916 and the latter during 1919–1927 and 1929–1931.

The important documents of the office of the governor-general of Korea are said to have been destroyed immediately after the end of the Pacific War. A portion of them, however, came into possession of the government of the Republic of Korea. Preserved at its Government Archives and Records Service, the Ministry of Government Administration, these surviving documents are being microfilmed.[70]

Concerning independence movements in Korea, basic documents are collected in vols. 25–30 (Chōsen) of Gendaishi shiryō series (Documents on contemporary history).[71]

A useful historiographical study on Japan's rule of Korea is a brief essay by Kajimura Hideki.[72]

Taiwan

Taiwan was Japan's first colony, acquired in 1895 following the Sino-Japanese War. Documents relating to the government-general of Taiwan are scattered among Kokuritsu Kōbunshokan, the War History Department of the Defense Agency, the Diplomatic Record Office, and other places. Most of the important documents emanating from the government-general of Taiwan are preserved at Taiwansheng Wen-xian Weiyuanhui (Commission on Documents Relating to the Taiwan Province)[73] in Taizhong. This commission possesses 14,000 volumes of the official records of the governor-general, covering the fifty years of Japanese rule. Since 1978 these records have been published in Taiwan in Chinese.

Regarding independence and anti-Japanese movements in Taiwan, important documents have been collected from scattered sources and published as vols. 21–22 *(Taiwan)* of the *Gendaishi shiryō* series.[74] A historiographical article on the Japanese administration of Taiwan has been published by Sasamoto Takeji.[75]

SMRC Materials

A semiofficial Japanese company, the South Manchuria Railway Company (SMRC) not only managed railroads but also served as an agent for Japanese expansion in Manchuria. At the same time, SMRC's huge Research Division (today, we might call it a "think tank") was engaged in extensive investigations of economic and political affairs not only in Manchuria but also in China and Siberia. Until recently the only bibliographical guide was John Young, *Research Activities of the South Manchurian Railway Company, 1907–1945: A History and Bibliography* (East Asian Institute, Columbia University, 1966).

New information was added with the publication in 1979 of the previously mentioned catalogue by Ajia Keizai Kenkyūjo: *Kyū shoku-minchi kankei kikan kankōbutsu sōgō mokuroku: Minami Manshū Tetsudō Kabushiki Kaishahen* (A comprehensive bibliography of the former Japanese colonies: South Manchuria Railway Company.)[76] According to this catalogue, materials relating to the South Manchuria Railway Company are scattered among forty-four Japanese and six American institutions. The bulk of the SMRC materials in the United States are deposited at the Library of Congress, whose Japanese section holds roughly 70 percent of all SMRC materials. These materials, originally preserved at the SMRC agencies in Tokyo, were seized during the Allied occupation by General Douglas MacArthur's General Headquarters.

Since 1979 the National Diet Library has been photocopying the SMRC materials at the Library of Congress. It is expected that in the very near future, these materials can be examined at the Diet Library on microfilm.

Little is known about the fate of those portions of SMRC materials that were seized by the Soviet Union in 1945. Much the same can be said about the records of the government of Manchukuo and its administrative branches. A large portion of these records was either seized by the Soviet authorities or had been destroyed when the Soviets entered the war against Japan. The surviving documents are collected in *Gendaishi shiryō* series.[77]

In the absence of basic source materials, the researcher must of necessity rely on such official histories as Manchukuo government, ed., *Manshū kenkoku jūnenshi* (A ten-year history of the founding of Manchukuo)[78] or postwar publications like *Manshūkokushi*, ed, (A history of Manchukuo)[79] and *Manshū kaihastsu shijūnenshi* (A forty-year history of the development of Manchuria).[80] These works provide only outline surveys of the history of Manchuria.

For this reason, Kaneko Fumio's historiographical essays on the state of "Manchurian studies" in the 1970s are all the more helpful. Together, these essays survey recent studies on developments in Manchuria from 1905 to 1932.[81]

Micronesia and Sakhalin

A short note will be in order because the bibliographies published by Ajia Keizai Kenkyūjo do not cover these areas.

In 1922 the South Seas Agency ('Nan'yōchō) was established in the Palau Islands to administer the Pacific Islands (most of Micronesia and other scattered islands), which had been awarded Japan as Class-C mandate territory according to the Versailles peace treaty. At first under the direct command of the prime minister, this agency was placed under the colonial minister in 1929, and finally came under the jurisdiction of the Greater East Asia Ministry in 1942.

Unfortunately, the records of the South Seas Agency have presumably been destroyed during the Pacific War. Those interested in the background of establishing this agency will be found useful the record of the Japanese navy's administration of these islands prior to 1922. It is titled "Senji shorui" (Wartime documents, 1914–20), 260 vols.[82]

In southern Sakhalin, obtained by the Treaty of Portsmouth of

1905, the Japanese government established the Colonial Agency of Sakhalin (Karafutochō). The record of this agency is totally missing, because it was seized by the Soviets in 1945 when they occupied Sakhalin. The only remaining documents are those of the Tokyo office of the Agency of Sakhalin—a mere 320 volumes, covering the years 1923–1945. First transferred to the Foreign Ministry, they are now preseved under the custody of the General Affairs Division, Hokkaido Government Office. In 1970 this office compiled a catalogue of these documents as well as those of the Bakumatsu and early Meiji periods relating to Sakhalin.[83]

ORAL HISTORY MATERIALS

The oral history approach has not been sufficiently developed in Japan as a research method in the field of Japanese diplomatic history.

In 1965 the Foreign Ministry attempted to establish Kokumin Gaikō Kenkyū Kyōkai (The Research Association for Japanese Diplomacy)[84] and began interviewing former diplomats. The attempt failed, however, because the project did not receive enough support from the parties concerned.

The Finance Ministry was more successful. Its Zaiseishi Shitsu (Office of Financial History) conducted 150 interviews with former financial bureaucrats in the process of preparing *Shōwa zaiseishi* (The economic and financial history of the Shōwa period). These records are preserved as "Shōwa zaiseishi shidankai kiroku" (The records of historical discussion meetings on the financial history of the Shōwa period).[85] A portion of them has been published as *Ōkura daijin kaikoroku* (Memoirs of finance ministers).[86]

From the 1960s to the early 1970s the staff of the War History Office of the Defense Agency conducted interviews with a large number of former army and navy officers as well as diplomats to fill gaps in surviving documents. Most of these interviews were recorded on tapes.

More informally, a group of scholars, who during the early 1960s, conducted joint research for the multivolume *Taiheiyō sensō e no michi* (The road to the Pacific War),[87] also used the oral history approach. Among the important interviewees are: on the army side, Lieutenant General Tanaka Shin'ichi, Lieutenant General Satō Kenryō, Lieutenant General Doi Akio, Major General Imai Takeo, Major General Katakura

Tadashi, and Colonel Imoto Kumao; and on the navy side, Admiral Inoue Shigeyoshi, Rear Admiral Yokoi Tadao, and Commander Shiba Katsuo; and diplomats Arita Hachirō, Nishi Haruhiko, and Yoshizawa Kenkichi. Their taped interviews (in 83 reels) are preserved by the War History Department of the Defense Agency.

The first full-scale oral history project was launched in the 1960s by Naiseishi Kenkyūkai (Study group on the history of domestic [Japanese] politics)[88] headed by Tsuji Kiyoaki. It has published recorded interviews with about one hundred former bureaucrats and politicians. However, this project included only a few diplomats: Yoshizawa Seijirō, Suzuki Tadakatsu, and John K. Emmerson (an American diplomat with considerable experience of Japan).

In the 1970s Nihon Kindai Shiryō Kenkyūkai (Study group on source materials on modern Japan), in cooperation with Kido Nikki Kenkyūkai (Study group on the Kido diary),[89] began publishing an oral history series. Of interest for our purposes are transcribed interviews with military officers who became deeply involved in the politics and diplomacy of the period 1928–1945, such as Suzuki Teiichi, Katakura Tadashi, Maki Tatsuo, Inada Masazumi, and Nishiura Susumu.

Less systematic are the interviews (more in the nature of dialogue) that Nakamura Kikuo conducted in the late 1960s with twenty-seven former army and navy officers. On the basis of these interviews, he published two popular books that purport to give a "confidential history" of the army and navy in the Shōwa period up to 1945.[90]

Another approach to oral history was shown when several historians, in cooperation with the major newspaper *Mainichi*, interviewed seventy-two "witnesses" to major events from the Great Depression to Japan's recovery of independence in 1952. These "witnesses" constitute important materials; they were edited by Andō Yoshio to reconstruct the history of the Shōwa period in three volumes.[91]

Another newspaper company *Yomiuri* fully mobilized its resources to organize a huge project in which interviews were conducted with some 10,000 individuals involved in political and diplomatic events from 1935 to 1945. The result is an impressive series, *Shōwashi no tennō* (The Emperor in the history of the Shōwa period).[92] Although journalistic in origin and style, these volumes are a mine of detailed information of great value to the historian (see chapter 4, pp. 239–41).

ENCYCLOPEDIAS AND REFERENCE WORKS

Encyclopedias

A veritable treasure house for information on Japanese diplomatic history, for beginners and specialists alike, is: Gaimushō Gaikō Shiryōkan Nihon Gaikōshi Jiten Hensan Iinkai, ed., *Nihon gaikōshi jiten* (The encyclopedia of Japanese diplomatic history).[93] This is a unique encyclopedia specifically devoted to the nation's diplomatic history and its international environment. Broad in conception and comprehensive in coverage, *Nihon gaikōshi jiten* contains not only the usual items on diplomatic history but also the names of persons, both Japanese and foreign, who have played significant roles in Japan's foreign relations; explanations of basic technical terms and concepts; administrative institutions and diplomatic practices; and numerous items on Chinese and Western matters germane to Japan's diplomatic history.

In the field of military history there are two general encyclopedias: Jinbutsu Ōraisha, ed., *Kindai no sensō*, vol. 8: *Gunji jiten* (Modern warfare, vol. 8: Encyclopedia of military affairs);[94] and Ōhama Tetsuya and Ozawa Ikurō, eds., *Teikoku riku-kaigun jiten* (Dictionary of the imperial Japanese army and navy).[95] Both works are useful for the beginner, but their entries are too brief and not comprehensive enough for the researcher.

Institutional References

The official history of the Foreign Ministry is Gaimushō Hyakunenshi Hensan Iinkai, eds., *Gaimushō no hyakunen* (A century of the Japanese Foreign Ministry).[96] The first volume covers 1869 to 1931, and the second volume 1931 to 1969. A product of collaboration between Foreign Ministry members (mainly archivists) and academic historians, this work is not a mere institutional history; it may also be regarded as an historical account of a century of Japanese foreign relations since the Meiji period, centering on the Foreign Ministry. Never meant to be a general survey of Japanese diplomatic history, the work is somewhat uneven and occasionally episodic in treatment, but it contains valuable chapters on such subjects as the changing

structures and reorganizations of the Foreign Ministry, shifts in budgetary appropriations for the ministry over the years, and personnel
policy. The final chapter includes directories of Foreign Ministry staff
for certain given years and lists of chief posts, both in the home office
and legations abroad.

For further details on the changing structure, organization, and
personnel administration of the pre–World War II Foreign Ministry
(as well as other civilian ministries), the essential reference tool is
Hata Ikuhiko (Senzenki Kanryōsei Kenkyūkai, ed.), *Senzenki Nihon
kanryōsei no seido, soshiki, jinji* (System, organization, and personnel
administration of the prewar Japanese bureaucracy).[97] It conveniently
shows the holders of upper and middle-ranking offices in chronological charts. One of the most valuable portions of this authoritative and
thorough volume is succinct and accurate biographical entries of civil
bureaucrats, some of them now quite obscure, who were in one way
or another involved in making or implementing Japanese foreign
policy.

The most comprehensive and indispensable reference work on
the army and navy establishments is Nihon Kindai Shiryō Kenkyūkai, ed., *Nihon riku-kaigun no seido, soshiki, jinji* (System, organization and personnel administration of the Japanese army and navy).[98]
It is similar in conception and format to its companion volume on
civilian bureaucrats. It is specially useful for indicating this line of
command and the positions held by army and navy officers—both
in the home offices in Tokyo and those stationed abroad or on sea
duty.

A more compact book is Jōhō Yoshio and Toyama Misao, eds., *Riku-
kaigun shōkan jinji sōran* (A comprehensive personnel record of the
generals and admirals of the Japanese army and navy).[99]

As for atlases and maps of Japanese diplomatic history, the only
modern collection is Kajima Heiwa Kenkyūjo, ed., *Nihon gaikōshi,
Bekkan 4: Chizu* (Japanese diplomatic history, supplementary vol. 4,
Atlas).[100] In the field of military history, Maehara Tōru and Kuwata
Etsu have coedited a convenient volume, *Nihon no sensō: Zukai to dēta*
(Japan's wars: Maps and data).[101] It contains all the operational maps
of the wars in which Japan participated, from the Sino-Japanese War
of 1894–1895 to the Pacific War.

Chronology

The basic chronology of Japanese diplomacy from 1849 to 1945 is contained in the previously cited *Nihon gaikō nenpyō narabini shuyō bunsho*. (A chronology and major documents on Japanese foreign policy (2 vols), edited by the Foreign Ministry. The main body of this detailed chronology had been originally prepared by Kiyosawa Kiyoshi, a liberal commentator on foreign affairs, during the war years, and it was revised by the archivists of the Foreign Ministry for this publication. Its usefulness is enhanced by parallel columns listing major events abroad.

A comparable chronology for post–World War II years is found in Kajima Heiwa Kenkyūjo, ed., *Nihon gaikō shuyō bunsho, nenpyō* (Major documents and chronology of Japanese foreign policy, 1941–1980).[102] For our purposes, the first volume, covering the years 1941–1960, is relevant. The global context of Japanese foreign policy can be grasped at one glance, because the chronology of Japanese diplomacy is set against four columns of chronologies relating to the Asia-Pacific region, the Soviet–Eastern European areas, North America and Western Europe, and the Middle East–African–Latin American areas. These volumes also contain the more important published documents.

A one-volume diplomatic chronology that spans the period from 1842 to 1972 is Kajima Heiwa Kenkyūjo, ed., *Nihon gaikōshi, Bekkan 3: Nenpyō* (Japanese diplomatic history, Supplementary, vol. 3: A comprehensive chronology).[103]

An authoritative and massively detailed chronology of Japanese military and naval history from the outbreak of the Sino-Japanese War in 1937 to the surrender of Japan in 1945 is Suekuni Masao, ed., *Riku-kaigun nenpyō fu heigo, yōgo no kaisetsu* (A chronology of the Japanese army and navy, and a dictionary of military terminology).[104] This chronology, which is useful not only to the military historian but also to the diplomatic historian, can be used most conveniently in conjuction with the massive *Senshi sōsho* (War History series) of which this chronology is one volume. Cross-references are provided so that each entry directs the reader to the appropriate volumes and pages of *Senshi sōsho*. The volume contains a dictionary of military terminology that provides useful information on the background of diplomatic history for the years 1937–1945.

An authoritative one-volume chronology that covers in detail the politico-diplomatic together with other fields of Japanese history is Iwanami's *Kindai Nihon sōgō nenpyō* (A comprehensive chronology of modern Japan).[105] The usefulness of this chronology for the historian is enhanced by the careful documentation of each chronological entry by end notes as well as by an index.

Bibliographies

The only bibliographical guide (in Japanese) to Japanese diplomatic history is Hanabusa Nagamichi, ed., *Nihon gaikōshi kankei bunken mokuroku* (A bibliography of Japanese diplomatic history) and its addendum, published in 1961 and 1968 respectively.[106] This volume contains books published in Japanese, Chinese, and Western languages and articles in Japanese published from the early Meiji years to 1967. Its usefulness is marred by awkward organization, i.e., alphabetical arrangement by titles without any cross-index. The book is convenient, however, for locating articles that appeared in such influential journals as *Gaikō jihō* (Revue diplomatique), *Kokusaihō gaikō zasshi*, (The journal of international law and diplomacy), and *Chūō kōron* (The central forum).[107]

The basic English-language bibliographical work is contained in James W. Morley's *Japan's Foreign Policy, 1868–1941: A Research Guide* (Columbia University Press, 1974). Its "Bibliography of Foreign Policy: Standard Works" and "Bibliography of Recent Works" have become outdated. But they retain their usefulness precisely because these bibliographies comprehensively list older works and studies in the West (which our volume advisedly eschews).

Turning to specific fields of Japanese diplomatic history, Sino-Japanese relations are relatively well served by bibliographers: Yamane Yukio, ed., *Kindai Nitchū kankeishi bunken mokuroku* (A bibliography of works on the history of modern Sino-Japanese relations);[108] and Ichiko Chūzō, ed., *Kindai Chūgoku kankei bunken mokuroku, 1945–1978* (A bibliography of works relating to modern China, 1945–1978).[109] The former is devoted to works on the history of Sino-

Japanese relations from the early Meiji year to 1941. It lists about 3,500 books, essays, and magazine articles according to major topics. The latter—a comprehensive catalogue of roughly 20,000 books and articles arranged by author—is an extremely useful reference work, because it contains works on the history of Sino-Japanese relations, Japanese policy toward China, and the Japanese figures who were deeply involved in Chinese affairs. In addition, Ichiko Chūzō, ed., *Kindai Chūgoku: Nitchū kankeishi bunken mokuroku* (A bibliography of modern China and Sino-Japanese relations) contains works on Sino-Japanese realtions published since 1945.[110]

Although not a bibliography as such, it would be appropriate to mention here a useful handbook on the history of Sino-Japanese relations: Kawahara Hiroshi and Fujii Shōzō, eds., *Nitchū kankei no kiso chishiki* (Basic information on Sino-Japanese relations).[111]

For the history of Japanese-Korean relations up to the 1890s, Moriyama Shigenori has published a highly useful work in two installments; he discusses research trends in this field, comments on documents available, and presents a bibliography.[112]

On Japan's relations with the United States and the USSR, no comprehensive bibliography has yet appeared. The JAIR organ, *Kokusai seiji,* has published two issues devoted to the development of Japanese-American relations (1961, no. 17) and Japanese-USSR relations (1966, no. 31), but the bibliographies contained in them are too brief and outdated.

For the history of relations with Southeast Asia, there is a recent bibliography in English: Iwasaki Ikuo, ed., *Japan and Southeast Asia: A Bibliography of Historical, Economic and Political Relations.*[113] This volume lists roughly 2,200 books and articles written from the nineteenth century to 1983.

JAIR Journal

Passing references have been made to *Kokusai seiji* (International relations), the organ of Nihon Kokusai Seiji Gakkai (the Japan Association of International Relations). Since its inauguration in 1957, this journal has printed more than two hundred articles on aspects of Japanese diplomatic history. This emphasis is explained by the special efforts made by the late Professor Kamikawa Hikomatsu, the founder of JAIR, and his associates to promote research in Japanese diplomatic history. A list of special issues devoted to Japanese diplomatic history follows:

No. 3 (1957): *Nihon gaikōshi kenkyū—Meiji jidai* (Studies in Japanese diplomatic history—The Meiji period).[114]

No. 6. (1958): *Nihon gaikōshi kenkyū—Taishō jidai* (Studies in Japanese diplomatic history—The Taishō period).[115]

No. 11 (1960): *Nihon gaikōshi kenkyū—Shōwa jidai* (Studies in Japanese diplomatic history—The Shōwa period.)[116]

No. 14 (1960): *Nihon gaikōshi kenkyū—Bakumatsu-ishin jidai* (Studies in Japanese diplomatic history—The late Shōgunate and Meiji Restoration period).[117]

No. 15 (1961): *Nihon gaikōshi kenkyū—Nitchū kankei no tenkai* (Studies in Japanese diplomatic history—The development of Sino-Japanese relations).[118]

No. 17 (1961): *Nichi-Bei kankei no tenkai* (The development of Japanese-American relations).[119]

No. 19 (1962): *Nihon gaikōshi kenkyū—Nisshin Nichi-Ro sensō* (Studies in Japanese diplomatic history: The Sino-Japanese War and Russo-Japanese War).[120]

No. 22 (1963): *Nikkan kankei no tenkai* (The development of Japanese-Korean relations).[121]

No. 23 (1963): *Nihon gaikōshi kenkyū—Daiichiji sekai taisen* (Studies in Japanese diplomatic history—World War I).[122]

No. 26 (1964): *Nihon gaikō no shomondai, 1* (Problems in Japanese diplomatic history, 1).[123]

No. 28 (1965): *Nihon gaikō no shomondai, 2* (Problems in Japanese diplomatic history, 2).[124]

No. 31 (1966): *Nichi-Ro Nisso kankei no tenkai* (The development of Russo-Japanese and Soviet-Japanese relations).[125]

No. 33 (1967): *Nihon gaikōshi kenkyū—Gaikō shidōsharon* (Studies in Japanese diplomatic history—the leaders of Japanese diplomacy).[126]

No. 34 (1967): *Nichi-Bei kankei no imēji* (Images in Japanese-American relations).[127]

No. 37 (1968): *Nihon gaikōshi no shomondai, 3* (Problems in Japanese diplomatic history, 3).[128]

No. 41 (1970): *Nihon gaikōshi kenkyū—Gaikō to yoron* (Studies in Japanese diplomatic history—Foreign policy and public opinion).[129]

No. 43 (1970): *Manshū jihen* (The Manchurian Incident).[130]

No. 47 (1972): *Nitchū sensō to kokusaiteki taiō* (The Sino-Japanese War and international response).[131]

No. 51 (1974): *Nihon gaikō no kokusai ninshiki—Sono shiteki tenkai* (Japanese perception of international relations—Its historical development).[132]

No. 56 (1977): *1930-nendai no Nihon gaikō—Yonin no gaishō o chūshin to shite* (Japanese diplomacy in the 1930s—Uchida, Hirota, Arita, and Matsuoka).[133]

No. 58 (1978): *Nichi-Ei kankei no shiteki tenkai* (The historical development of Anglo-Japanese relations).[134]

No. 66 (1980): *Hendōki ni okeru higashi Ajia to Nihon—Sono shiteki kōsatsu* (East Asia and Japan during a period of transition—Historical studies).[135]

No. 68 (1981): *Nichi-Gō kankei no shiteki tenkai* (The historical evolution of Australia-Japan relations).[136]

No. 71 (1982): *Nihon gaikō no shisō* (Thought and ideas in modern Japanese foreign policy).[137]

No. 75 (1983): *Nihon gaikō no hikōshiki channeru* (Informal channels in Japanese diplomacy).[138]

No. 79 (1985): *Nihon-Kanada kankei no shiteki tenkai* (The historical evolution of Canadian-Japanese relations).[139]

Periodical Index

In Japan the number of small-scale periodicals and organs of universities and research institutions is so staggeringly large that even the specialist has difficulties keeping abreast of all of them.

For this purpose, bibliographical guides to current periodical literature are essential. Since 1948 the National Diet Library (NDL) has published *Zasshi kiji sakuin (Jinbun, shakaihen)* (Periodical index: Humanities and social sciences).[140] Its value has been enhanced by the compilation of a cumulative index based on the NDL volumes. First published in 1976, each cumulative edition, covering the time span of five to ten years, is printed in ten to eleven volumes.[141] The most recent edition covers up to 1984.

For articles that have appeared since the last index, one needs to consult bibliographies that appear in such monthly journals as *Shigaku zasshi*[142] and *Kokusai mondai*.[143] Historiographical essays reviewing the previous year's publications, printed annually in *Shigaku zasshi*, are one guide to the most recent trends of research and writing.

More convenient for non-Japanese scholars who wish to keep up with current publications is *An Introductory Bibliography for Japanese*

Studies, annually published in English by the Japan Foundation. The social sciences and the humanities are dealt with in alternate years. This series contains chapters on international politics, political science, and history—all written by recognized specialists in their fields. Its format is somewhat similar to the present volume: bibliographical essays are followed by a list of books and articles published during the previous year.

For biographical works on historical figures, there are two convenient bibliographies: Kokkai Toshokan Sankō Shoshibu (NDL, Bibliographical Division), ed., *Kindai Nihon seiji kankei jinbutsu bunken mokuroku* (Bibliography of works on political figures in modern Japan)[144] and Hōsei Daigaku Bungakubu Shigaku Kenkyūshitsu (History Department, Hōsei University), eds., *Nihon jinbutsu bunken mokuroku* (Bibliography of Japanese biographical works).[145]

SURVEY HISTORIES AND TEXTBOOKS

Prewar Works

Until the end of the Pacific War, Japanese diplomatic history was called "a sterile field of research," because essential documents remained closed to the researcher and censorship placed severe restrictions on historical writings. For these reasons, there are few surveys of Japanese diplomacy published before the conclusion of the Pacific War that can still be read profitably. One notable exception is *Nihon gaikōshi* (A diplomatic history of Japan), 2 vols., by Kiyosawa Kiyoshi, a liberal commentator on international affairs, which was first published in June 1941.[146] In lucid prose he critically examines the entire course of Japanese diplomacy from Perry to the eve of Pearl Harbor in terms of the principle of the balance of power. One important thesis of the book is that for most of this period the Japanese government tended to take a realistic and cautious stand, whereas popular opinion demanded a more ideological and chauvinistic policy.

In terms of intellectual depth, readability, and fullness of treatment, none of the postwar surveys matches Kiyosawa's prewar book. One reason may be that so many monographic works and articles have recently appeared that no single historian has been able to fully absorb and synthesize them into a full-length survey.

The Kajima Series on Japanese Diplomatic History

It would be convenient to mention here the multivolume series *Nihon gaikōshi* (Japanese diplomatic history), edited by Kajima Heiwa Kenkyūjo, because many of the individual volumes of this series will be referred to in later chapters. These volumes are very uneven in quality. The first part of the Kajima series (vols. 1–13), bearing the authorship of Kajima Morinosuke, seem like "in-house" histories and they contain a modicum of analysis and interpretation. The second part of the series, covering later years, were authored or co-authored by former diplomats who had access to materials not generally available, or who personally participated in the events they describe. These volumes have no footnotes and lack the usual scholarly apparatus:

Vol. 1: *Bakumatsu gaikō: Kaikoku to ishin* (Bakumatsu diplomacy: The opening of Japan and the Meiji Restoration).[147]

Vol. 2: *Jōyaku kaisei mondai* (Treaty revision).[148]

Vol. 3: *Kinrin shokoku oyobi ryōdo mondai* (Neighboring countries and territorial issues).[149]

Vol. 4: *Nisshin sensō to sangoku kanshō* (The first Sino-Japanese War and the Triple Intervention).[150]

Vol. 5: *Shina ni okeru rekkyō no kakuchiku* (Rivalry among powers over rights and interests in China).[151]

Vol. 6: *Daiikkai Nichi-Ei dōmei to sono zengo* (The first Anglo-Japanese Alliance).[152]

Vol. 7: *Nichi-Ro sensō* (The Russo-Japanese War).[153]

Vol. 8: *Dainikai Nichi-Ei dōmei to sono jidai* (The second Anglo-Japanese Alliance).[154]

Vol. 9: *Daisankai Nichi-Ei dōmei to sono jidai* (The third Anglo-Japanese Alliance).[155]

Vol. 10: *Daiichiji sekai taisen sanka oyobi kyōryoku mondai* (Japan's entry into World War I and its cooperation with the Allies).[156]

Vol. 11: *Shina mondai* (The China question).[157]

Vol. 12: *Pari kōwa kaigi* (The Paris Peace Conference and Japan).[158]

Vol. 13: *Washinton kaigi oyobi imin mondai* (The Washington Conference and the immigration question).[159]

Vol. 14: *Kokusai Renmei ni okeru Nihon* (Japan's activities in the League of Nations).[160] Drafted by seven middle-ranking diplomats under the supervision of Satō Naotake, it does not contain scholarly analysis but provides a record of administrative work. One feature of the book is its emphasis on Japan's activities in the cultural, financial, and economic areas.

Vol. 15: *Nisso kokkō mondai, 1917–1945* (The problem of diplomatic relations between Japan and the Soviet Union, 1917–1956).[161] Drafted, under the supervision of Nishi Haruhiko, by three middle-ranking diplomats who took part in negotiations with the Russians before the Pacific War, it contains useful information on fisheries and economic problems between Japan and the Soviet Union. For the most part, however, the book is based on "Nisso kōshō koshōshi" (A history of Japanese-Soviet relations), compiled by the Foreign Ministry for desk use.

Vol. 16: *Kaigun gunshuku kōsho, Fusen jōyaku* (Negotiations for naval limitation and the Kellogg-Briand Pact), drafted by Unno Yoshirō under the editorship of Horinouchi Kensuke.[162] Based only on the Foreign Ministry record, the book is weak in its treatment of the naval aspects of the Geneva (1927) and London naval conferences (1930–36).

Vol. 17: *Chūgoku nashonarizumu to Nikka kankei no tenkai* (The development of Chinese nationalism and Sino-Japanese relations), by Kamimura Shin'ichi.[163] Written by Kamimura, who had long experience in negotiating with the Chinese, this volume purports to study the impact of Chinese nationalism on Sino-Japanese relations after World War I. Instead, the book consists of mere narratives of Sino-Japanese diplomatic relations.

Vol. 18: *Manshū jihen* (The Manchurian Incident), drafted by Baba Akira under the editorship of Morishima Gorō and Yanai Tsuneo.[164] A solid and important monograph focusing especially on the Foreign Ministry's response to the Manchurian Incident.

Vols. 19 and 20: *Nikka jihen* (The China Incident), by Kamimura Shin'ichi.[165] Capitalizing on the author's own experiences, this volume provides useful information on the developments leading to the establishment of the Wang Ching-wei regime in 1940.

Vol. 21: *Nichi-Doku-I dōmei, Nisso Chūritsu jōyaku* (The Tripartite Pact and the Japanese-Soviet Neutrality Pact).[165] Drafted, under the supervision of Horinouchi Kensuke,[166] by Andō Yoshirō and Narita Katsushirō (who held middle-ranking positions in the Europe-America Bureau of the Foreign Ministry at the time), the volume is a mixture of personal recollections and postwar historical studies.

Vol. 22: *Nanshin mondai* (The problem of the southward advance), by Nagaoka Shinjirō under the editorship of Matsumoto Shun'ichi and Andō Yoshirō.[167] The contents are almost the same as Nagaoka's monographic work that appeared in Nihon Kokusai Seiji Gakkai, ed., *Taiheiyō sensō e no michi*, vol. 6.

Vol. 23: *Nichi-Bei kōshō* (The Japanese-American negotiations), by Kase

Toshikazu.[168] The author was secretary to the Foreign Minister at the time of the Japanese-American negotiations (1940–41), but in this volume he bases his account strictly on the Foreign Ministry record, instead of weaving his personal recollections.

Vol. 24: *Dai Tōa sensō, senji gaikō* (The Greater East Asia War and wartime diplomacy).[169] This volume was written on the basis of official government records, under the supervision of Ōta Ichirō, by Ikeda Chikata, who served for many years in the East Asia Bureau of the Foreign Ministry. The volume contains detailed information on Japan's diplomacy with the neutral nations and relations with Southeast Asian countries under Japanese occupation.

Vol. 25: *Dai Tōa sensō, shūsen gaikō* (The Greater East Asia War and the termination of war), drafted by Kurihara Ken and Matsuzawa Tetsunari under the supervision of Matsumoto Shun'ichi and Andō Yoshirō.[170] The volume quotes liberally from official documents but provides little new information.

Vol. 26: *Shūsen kara kōwa made* (From the end of the war to the peacemaking), supervised by Suzuki Tadakatsu.[171] Jointly authored by three diplomats (including Suzuki) and three legal specialists, the volume is mainly devoted to legal aspects on the Allied occupation policy, but the portions written by the former diplomats contain interesting information.

vol. 27: *San Furanshisuko heiwa jōyaku* (The San Francisco Peace Treaty), by Nishimura Kumao.[172] Nishimura, as the head of the Foreign Ministry's Treaty Bureau, assisted Prime Minister Yoshida Shigeru in negotiations over the Japanese peace treaty. This volume, containing a considerable amount of information not available elsewhere, is one of the most valuable works in the Kajima series on Japanese diplomatic history.

Short Surveys

We shall mention here some of the more useful textbooks and short surveys. Gaimushō, ed., *Nihon gaikō hyakunen shōshi* (A short history of the past century of Japanese diplomacy)[173] is a plain account from the Bakumatsu period to Japan's admission to the United Nations. Because the emphasis is placed on the Shōwa period, the treatment of earlier periods is too brief.

Akira Iriye's *Nihon no gaikō: Meiji ishin kara gendai made* (Japanese diplomacy: From the Meiji Restoration to the present, 1966)[174] is compact in format yet rich in content. Eschewing a factual account, Iriye concentrates on the ideas and images in Japanese diplomacy,

56 ŌHATA, ASADA, HATANO

setting them against the international environment at each important stage. In drawing contrasts between realism in the government's policy and idealism prominent in public opinion, he employs an analytical framework quite similar to Kiyosawa's previously cited survey. An interpretive history written in bold strokes, this book makes for interesting reading, but it needs updating.

Ōhata Tokushirō's *Kokusai kankyō to Nihon gaikō* (Japanese diplomacy and its international environment, 1966)[175] is a rather unusual work: it is meant to serve both as a general survey for beginners and as a bibliographical guide to advanced students. The same author's more recent text, *Nihon gaikōshi* (A Japanese diplomatic history, 1978),[176] attempts to place Japanese foreign policy in the context of world history from the Bakumatsu period to the normalization of Sino-Japanese relations in 1972.

Ikei Masaru's *Nihon gaikōshi gaisetsu* (A history of Japanese diplomacy, 1973; enlarged ed., 1982)[177] is a well-balanced textbook that is prefaced by an introductory chapter on "the basic conditions of Japanese diplomacy" and follows its course from the Bakumatsu period to the conclusion of the Sino-Japanese treaty of 1972. In his treatment of historical events, the author looks back to the past in order to examine which foreign policy alternatives Japan chose, for what reasons, and with what results.

Shinobu Seizaburō, ed., *Nihon gaikōshi, 1853–1972* (A history of Japanese diplomacy, 1853–1972)[178], published in 1979, is a more detailed survey which is a product of joint study among eight historians headed by Shinobu. It attempts to go beyond a mere "survey history" and to analyze basic policies of Japanese diplomacy from a leftist viewpoint. The theme of the book, in the author's words, is to "clarify the history of the growth and development of the modern Japanese nation, its imperialistic expansion, its collapse and [postwar] revival."

Notes

1. "Tsūkō ichiran" 通航一覧 (Survey of foreign relations), This series as well as its sequel, *Tsūkō ichiran zokushū*, were published by Tosho Kankōkai in 1938 and were reprinted in five volumes by Seibundō (Osaka) in 1967. For more detailed descriptions of these earlier documents, see Mikami Terumi 三上昭美, ed., *Nihon komonjogaku kōza*, vol.

11: *Kindaihen, 3* 日本古文書学講座11：近代篇, 3 (Series on Japanese paleography, vol. 11: The modern period, 3), pp. 99–103 (Yūzankaku, 1979).

2. "Tsūshin zenran" 通信全覧 (A complete record of foreign relations).

3. The address of Gaikō Shiryōkan 外交史料館: Azabudai 1-5-3, Minatoku, Tokyo 108.

4. "Zoku tsūshin zenran" 続通信全覧 (Sequel to a complete record of foreign relations, 1983–88).

5. Yūshōdō, 1983.

6. Gaimushō 外務省 (Foreign Ministry), *Dai Nippon gaikō bunsho* 大日本外交文書 (Nihon Kokusai Renmei Kyōkai, 1936–1940).

7. *Nihon gaikō bunsho*, vol. 33: *Bessatsu: Hokushin jihen* 別冊北清事変 (Documents on Japanese foreign policy: Supplementary volumes: The Boxer Rebellion), 3 vols. (1956–57); vols. 37–38: *Bessatsu: Nichi-Ro sensō* 別冊日露戦争 (Supplementary volumes: The Russo-Japanese War), 5 vols. (1958–60); vol. 45: *Bessatsu: Shinkoku jihen* 別冊清国事変 (Supplementary volume: The 1911 Revolution in China) (1961); *Meiji nenkan tsuiho* 明治年間追補 (Addendum to the documents on the Meiji period), 2 vols. (1963).

8. *Pari kōwa kaigi keika gaiyō* 巴里講和会議経過概要 (A summary of developments at the Paris Peace Conference) (1971); *Washinton kaigi* ワシントン会議 (The Washington Conference), 2 vols. (1977–78); *Washinton kaigi: Gunbi seigen mondai* ワシントン会議—軍備制限問題 (1974) (The Washington Conference: The problem of naval limitation (1974); *Washinton kaigi: Kyokutō mondai* ワシントン会議—極東問題 (The Washington Conference: The Far Eastern questions) (1976); *Junēbu kaigun gunbi seigen kaigi* ジュネーブ海軍軍備制限会議 (The Geneva Conference for the limitation of naval armaments) (1982); *Rondon kaigun kaigi: Yobi kōshō, jōyaku setsumeisho* (1972) ロンドン海軍会議—予備交渉, 条約説明書 (Preliminary negotiations for the London Naval Conference and written explanations of the London Naval Treaty) (1982); *1930-nen Rondon kaigun kaigi* 1930年ロンドン海軍会議 (The London Naval Conference of 1930), 2 vols. (1983–84); *Rondon kaigun kaigi keika gaiyō* ロンドン海軍会議経過概要 (A summary of the developments at the London Naval Conference) (1979); *Kaigun gunbi seigen jōyaku Sūmitsuin shinsa kiroku* 海軍軍備制限条約枢密院審査記録 (Records of the Privy Council's examination of the London Naval Treaty) (1978); *1935-nen Rondon kaigun kaigi* 1935年ロンドン海軍会議 (The London Naval Conference of 1935) (1986); 1935-nen Rondon kaigun kaigi keika hōkokusho 1935年ロンドン海軍会議経過報告書 (Report on the development of the 1935 naval conference) (1986); *Manshū jihen* 満州事変 (The Manchurian Incident), 7 vols. (1977–81).

9. *Jōyaku kaisei kankei Nihon gaikō bunsho* 条約改正関係日本外交文書 (Documents on Japanese foreign policy relating to treaty revision), 4 vols. (1941–50); *Jōyaku kaisei kankei Nihon gaikō bunsho: Tsuiho* 条約改正関係日本外交文書追補 (Documents of Japanese foreign policy relating to treaty revision: Addenda) (1953). *Jōyaku kaisei kankei Nihon gaikō bunsho: Kaigihen* 条約改正関係日本外交文書—会議編 (Documents on Japanese foreign policy relating to treaty revision: Conferences), 2 vols. (1956); *Jōyaku kaisei keika gaiyō fu nenpyō* 条約改正経過概要付年表 (A summary of the development of negotiations for treaty revision, with a chronology) (1950).

10. *Tsūshō jōyaku kankei Nihon gaikō bunsho* 通商条約関係日本外交文書 (Documents on Japanese foreign policy relating to commercial treaties), 4 vols. (1954); *Hāgu bankoku heiwa kaigi Nihon gaikō bunsho* 海牙万国平和会議日本外交文書 (Documents on Japanese foreign policy relating to the Hague Peace Conferences of 1899 and 1907), 2 vols. (1955).

11. *Tsūshō jōyaku to tsūshō seisaku no hensen* 通商条約と通商政策の変遷 (Changes in commercial treaties and trade policy), edited by Kawashima Nobutarō 川島信太郎, 1951. This volume was originally drafted by Kawashima after World War I as "Honpō jōyaku kaiseishi: zenpen" 本邦条約改正史—前編 (A history of the revision of Japanese treaties), vol. 1, which treated the subject up to the conclusion of Mutsu Munemitsu's treaty of 1889. The second volume was published as "Tsūshō jōyaku to tsūshō seisaku no hensen" 通商条約と通商政策の変遷 (Changes in commercial treaties and trade policy).

12. *Komura gaikōshi* 小村外交史 (The diplomatic biography of Komura Jutarō), 2 vols. Originally written by Shinobu Junpei 信夫淳平 in 1921, and extensively revised by Usui Katsumi 臼井勝美, *Komura gaikōshi* was reprinted by Shinbun Gekkansha in 1953 and later by Hara Shobō in 1966.

13. This volume prints "1919-nen Pari kōwa kaigi no keika ni kansuru chōsho" 1919年巴里講和会議の経過に関する調書 (A record of developments at the Paris Peace Conference of 1919) (1970) in 10 volumes prepared by the Political Affairs Bureau for its desk use.

14. *Tai-Bei imin mondai keika gaiyō* 対米移民問題経過概要 (A summary of the development of the Japanese immigration question in the United States) (1971); *Tai-Bei imin mondai keika gaiyō fuzokusho* 対米移民問題経過概要付属書 (1972) ([English-language] documents accompanying the summary of immigration question in the United States). The former volume prints the staff study of the negotiations on the immigration question in the United States drafted by Tsūshō Kyoku (the Commerce Bureau) of the Foreign Ministry.

15. *Nihon gaikō tsuikairoku, 1900–1935* 日本外交追懐録, 1900–1935 (The diplomatic memoirs [of Nagaoka Harukazu], 1900–1935). These are the "official" memoirs of Ambassador Nagaoka Harukazu 長岡春一 who made notable contributions to Japan's conference diplomacy during the years 1920–1930, especially at the League of Nations.

16. Gaimu Daijin Kanbō Bunshoka 外務大臣官房課文書課 "Nihon gaikō bunsho: Meiji gannen—Meiji 39-nen, Sōmokuji" 日本外交文書—明治元年—明治39年総目次 (Comprehensive index to *Nihon gaikō bunsho*, 1868–1906) (1960).

17. Gaimushō (Foreign Ministry), ed., *Nihon gaikō nenpyō narabini shuyō bunsho* 日本外交年表並主要文書 (A chronology and major documents on Japanese foreign policy), 2 vols. (Nihon Kokusai Rengō Kyōkai, 1955. Reprinted by Hara Shobō in 1966).

18. Gaimushō, ed., *Kindai in'yōreki taishōhyō* 近代陰陽暦対照表 (A conversion table of the lunar and solar calendars).

19. On the basis of documents he copied (which are never cited explicitly), Matsumoto Tadao 松本忠雄 has written an objective study which was unusual in war years: *Kinsei Nihon gaikōshi kenkyū* 近世日本外交史研究 (Studies in modern Japanese diplomatic history) (Hakuhōdō, 1942).

20. Gaikō Shiryōkan, comp., *Gaimushō kiroku maikurofirumu kensakubo* 外務省記録マイクロフィルム検索薄 (Indices to the [postwar] record of the Japanese Foreign Ministry) (Gaikō Shiryōkan, 1971–87), in 9 vols. in mimeograph (available on request from Gaikō Shiryōkan). The system of classifying postwar documents basically follows the prewar pattern.

21. *Gaimushō shokuinroku* 外務省職員録. For the period from 1866 to 1883, see *Shokuinroku* 職員録, which lists not only Foreign Ministry but also all government ministry officials.

22. *Gaimushō nenkan* 外務省年鑑.

23. *Kakankai kaihō* 霞関会会報. For details, *cf.* Gaimushō no Hyakunen Hensan Iinkai, ed., *Gaimushō no hyakunen*, vol. 1 (Hara Shobō, 1969), pp. 1486–88 (see n. 96).

24. Kokuritsu Kokkai Toshokan, Kensei Shiryō Shitsu 国立国会図書館憲政資料室. Address: 1-10-1 Nagatachō Chiyoda-ku, Tokyo 100.

25. *Kensei Shiryō Shitsu yōran* 憲政資料室要覧 (National Diet Library, 1981) is a one-volume guide to all the manuscript sources deposited there, containing a brief explanation of each collection.

26. "Kensei Shiryō Shitsu shozō bunsho no gaiyō" 憲政資料室所蔵文書の概要 (A summary of manuscripts in the possession of the Depository for Documents on Political and Constitutional Materials), *Kokuritsu kokkai*

toshikan geppō 国立国会図書館月報 (National Diet Library monthly bulletin) (January 1984), no. 274; (September 1984), no. 282.

27. Kumata Atsumi 熊田淳. "Kokuritsu Kokkai Toshokan: Senryō kankei bunsho ni tsuite" 国立国会図書館占領関係文書について (On records relating to the occupation of Japan available at the National Diet Library), *Rekishigaku kenkyū* (July 1979), no. 470, pp. 54–56; "Gendai Seijishi Shiryō Shitsu shozō Nihon senryō kankei shiryō no genjō" 現代政治史資料室所蔵日本占領関係資料の現状 (The present status of materials relating to the occupation of Japan collected by the Office of Contemporary Political History, the National Diet Library), *Kokuritsu kokkai toshokan geppō* (September 1981), no. 244, pp. 1–6.

28. Ōkurashō Zaiseishi Shitsu 大蔵省財政史室 (Office of Financial History, Ministry of Finance). Address: Kasumigaseki 3-1, Chiyoda-ku, Tokyo 100.

29. *Shōwa zaiseishi: Shūsen kara kōwa made* 昭和財政史—終戦から講和 まで. 20 vols. Tōyō Keizai Shinpōsha.

30. Kokuritsu Kōbunshokan 国立公文書館. Address: 3-2 Kitanomaru Kōen, Chiyoda-ku, Tokyo, 102.

31. "Kōbunroku" 公文録; "Dajō ruiten" 太政類典; "Kōbun ruishū" 公文 類聚; "Kōbun zassan" 公文雑纂.

32. Kokuritsu Kōbunshokan, ed., *Dajō ruiten mokuroku* 太政類典目録, 7 vols. (1973–83); *Kōbun ruishū mokuroku* 公文類聚目録, 4 vols. (covering up to 1906) (1985–   ).

33. *Sūmitsuin kaigi gijiroku: Meijihen* 枢密院会議議事録明治篇 (The proceedings of the sessions of the Privy Council: The Meiji period), 15 vols. (Tokyo Daigaku Shuppankai, 1984–85). *Sūmitsuin kaigi gijiroku: Taishōhen* (The proceedings of the sessions of the Privy Council: The Taishō period) (1985–88).

34. Fukai Eigo 深井英五, *Sūmitsuin jūyō giji oboegaki* 枢密院重要議事覚書 (Iwanami Shoten, 1953).

35. Bōei Kenshūjo, Senshibu 防衛研究所戦史部. Address: Nakameguro 2-chōme 2-1, Meguro-ku, Tokyo 153.

36. Gunjishi Kenkyūkai, Hitotsubashi Daigaku, tr., *"Kyū riku-kaigun kankei bunsho mokuroku"* 旧陸海軍関係文書目録; Bōei Kenshūjo, Senshi Shitsu, *Riku-kaigun kiroku bunsho mokuroku: Bei-gawa satsuei maikurofirumuhen* 陸海軍記録文書目録—米側撮影マイクロフィルム編 (not published, 1974).

37. For concise authoritative descriptions of these documents, see Kondō Shinji 近藤新治, "Gunreibu kikan bunsho" 軍令部機関文書 (Manuscript documents relating to the Navy General Staff); and "Rikugunshō, Kaigunshō" 陸軍省, 海軍省 (The Army and Navy Ministries), in *Nihon*

komonjogaku kōza, vol. 9, *Kindaihen*, 1, pp. 97–107, 160–68. Morimatsu Toshio, "Official Research Agencies," in La commission japon d'histoire militaire, *Revue Internationale d'Histoire Militaire*, no. 38, pp. 80–92 (Hara Shobō, 1978).

38. "Dai nikki" 大日記; "Gunji Kimitsu dai nikki" 軍事機密大日記; "Riku kimitsu dai nikki" 陸機密大日記; "Mitsu dai nikki" 密大日記.

39. They include the following documents of the Army Ministry: "Kokusai renmei, heiwa jōyaku kankei shorui" 国際連盟, 平和条約関係書類 (Files relating to the League of Nations and the Versailles Peace Treaty, 1918–20), 22 vols.; "Washinton kaigi kankei shorui" ワシントン会議関係書類 (Files relating to the Washington Conference, 1921–22), 17 vols.; "Gunshuku kaigi kankei shorui" 軍縮会議関係書類 (Papers relating to arms limitation conferences, 1928–31), 51 vols.

40. "Manshū jihen sakusen shidō kankei tsuzuri" 満州事変作戦指導関係綴; "Bessatsu" 別冊.

41. "Shina jihen sensō shidō kankei tsuzuri" 支那事変戦争指導関係綴.

42. "Kokubō taikō kankei jūyō shorui tsuzuri" 国防大綱関係重要書類綴.

43. "Dai Tōa sensō shidō kankei tsuzuri" 大東亜戦争指導関係綴.

44. "Miyazaki Shūichi shiryō" 宮崎周一史料.

45. "Shōwa nikki" 昭和日記. Aside from "Kimitsu sensō nisshi," the bulk of these documents has been printed in Sanbō Honbu, ed., *Sugiyama memo* 杉山メモ (The memoranda of General Sugiyama Hajime), (2 vols. Hara Shobō, 1967) and Sanbō Honbu, ed., *Haisen no kiroku* 敗戦の記録 (The record of defeat) (Hara Shobō, 1969).

46. "Kimitsu sensō nisshi" 機密戦争日誌.

47. "Kōbun bikō" 公文備考.

48. "Meiji 33-nen Shinkoku jihen shorui" 明治33年清国事変書類.

49. "Meiji 44—Taishō 3-nen Shinkoku jihen shorui" 明治44年—大正3年清国事変書類. The file contains numerous important materials on foreign policies advocated by the navy and the Foreign Ministry, reports from Japanese agencies in China, and telegraphic correspondence between Tokyo and its representatives in China. Especially useful are "Gaimu hōkoku" 外務報告 (Reports on foreign affairs), 57 vols., which consist of dispatches exchanged between the Foreign Ministry and its representatives and agencies in various parts of China (chronologically arranged). A convenient catalogue of this group of documents has been prepared by Fujii Shōzō 藤井昇三 as "Kyū kaigunshō hensan no Shingai kakumei kankei shiryō" 旧海軍省編纂の辛亥革命関係資料 (Materials relating to the Chinese revolution of 1911 compiled by the Japanese navy), *Shingai kakumei kenkyū* (Studies on the Chinese revolution of 1911) (May 1984), no. 4, pp. 109–14.

50. "Senji shorui" 戦時書類.
51. "Futsu-In mondai keii" 仏印問題経緯.
52. "Gunji gunshuku kankei shiryō" 軍備軍縮関係資料, collected by Enomoto Jūji 榎本重治.
53. "Takagi Sōkichi shiryō" 高木惣吉資料.
54. Saitō Hisashi 斉藤恒.
55. Sasaki Tōichi 佐々木到一.
56. Katakura Tadashi 片倉衷.
57. Watanabe Wataru 渡辺渡.
58. *Daihon'ei rikubungu* 大本営陸軍部 (Asagumo Shinbunsha, 1967–75).
59. *Daihon'ei kaigunbu* 大本営海軍部. (1970–75).
60. *Daihon'ei rikugunbu: Dai Tōa sensō kaisen keii* 大本営陸軍部・大東亜戦争開戦経緯 (1973–74).
61. *Daihon'ei kaigunbu: Dai Tōa sensō kaisen keii* 大本営海軍部・大東亜戦争開戦経緯 (1979).
62. Shiryō Chōsakai 史料調査会. Address: 10-45 Kami Ōzaki, Shinagawa-ku, Tokyo 141.
63. Akamatsu Toshihide 赤松俊秀 et al., eds., *Nihon komonjogaku kōza*, vol. 9: *Kindaihen 1* 日本古文書学講座, 9：近代編1 (Kyōko Shoin, 1981), vol. 2.
64. Nakamura Takafusa and Itō Takashi 中村隆英, 伊藤隆, eds., *Kindai Nihon kenkyū nyūmon* 近代日本研究入門, rev. and enlarged ed. (Tokyo Daigaku Shuppankai, 1983).
65. Chihōshi Kenkyū Kyōgikai 地方史研究協議会, ed., *Rekishi shiryō hozon kikan sōran* 歴史資料保存機関総覧 2 vols. (Yamakawa Shuppansha, 1979).
66. Takushokumushō 拓殖務省; Takushokushō 拓殖省; Dai Tōashō 大東亜省.
67. Ajia Keizai Kenkyūjo アジア経済研究所, ed., *Kyū shokuminchi kankei kikō kankōbutsu sōgō mokuroku: Taiwanhen* 旧植民地関係機関刊行物総合目録ー台湾編 (Comprehensive bibliography of materials published by Japan's former colonial agencies: Taiwan (Ajia Keizai Shuppankai, 1973.)
—— *Chōsenhen* 朝鮮編 (Comprehensive bibliography: Korea) (1978).
—— *Manshūkoku, Kantōshūhen* 満州国, 関東州編 (Comprehensive bibliography: Manchukuo and the Kwantung Territory) (1975).
—— *Minami Manshū Tetsudō Kabushiki Kaishahen* 南満州鉄道株式会社編 (Comprehensive bibliography: The South Manchuria Railway Company) (1979).
—— *Manshūkoku, Kantōshū, Minami Manshū Tetsudō Kabushiki Kaisha:*

Sakuinhen 満州国, 関東州, 南満州鉄道株式会社—索引編 (Manchu-kuo, the Kwantung Territory, and the South Manchuria Railway Company: An index (1982).

68. Asada Kyōji 浅田喬二 "Nihon shokuminchi kenkyū no genjō to mondaiten" 日本植民史研究の現状と問題点 (The current state and problems in studies on the history of Japanese colonialism), *Rekishi hyōron,* (April 1975), no. 300, pp. 178–98; "Nihon shokuminshi kenkyū no kadai to hōhō" 日本植民史研究の課題と方法 (Tasks and methodologies for studies of the history of Japanese colonialism), *Rekishi hyōron* (December 1975), no. 308, pp. 63–86; "Saikin ni okeru shokuminchi kenkyū no dōkō" 最近における植民地研究の動向 (Recent trends in studies on [Japanese] colonies), *Tochi seido shigaku* (April 1984), 26(3): 58–65.

69. Ichikawa Masaaki 市川正明, ed., *Kankoku heigō shiryō* 韓国併合史料 (Materials on the annexation of Korea), 3 vols. (Hara Shobō, 1978).

70. The Korean Archives: 大韓民国総務処政府記録保存所·

71. Kan Dok-san 姜徳相, ed. and intro., *Chōsen* 朝鮮 (Korea) (Misuzu Shobō, 1966–76).

72. Kajimura Hideki 梶村秀樹, "Chōsen—Kindaishi" 朝鮮—近代史 (Korea —its modern history), *Ajia keizai* (February 1978), 19(1–2): 18–26.

73. Taiwansheng Wenxian Weiyuanhui 台湾省文献委員会·

74. Yamabe Kentarō 山辺健太郎, ed., *Taiwan* 台湾, 2 vols. (Misuzu Shobō, 1971).

75. Sasamoto Takeji 笹本武治, "Chūgoku—Taiwan" 中国—台湾 (China-Taiwan), *Ajia keizai* (February 1978), 19 (1–2): 79–88.

76. See also note 68, Asada Kyōji's articles.

77. Itō Takeo 伊藤武雄 et al., eds., *Mantetsu* 満鉄, 3 vols. (*Gendaishi shiryō vols.* 31–33) (Misuzu Shobō, 1966–67).

78. Manshūteikoku seifu 満州帝国政府, ed., *Manshū kenkoku jūnenshi* 満州建国十年史 (Minami Manshū Tetsudō Kabushiki Kaisha, 1943, reprinted by Hara Shobō, 1969).

79. Manshūkokushi Hensan Iinkai 満州国史編纂委員会, ed., *Manshūkokushi* 満州国史, 2 vols. (Manshū Dōhō Engokai, 1970–71).

80. Manshikai 満史会, ed., *Manshū kaihatsu shijūnenshi* 満州開発四十年史, 2 vols. (Manshū Kaihatsu Shijūnenshi Kankōkai, 1964).

81. Kaneko Fumio 金子文夫, "1970-nendai ni okeru 'Manshū' kenkyū no jōkyō, part 1: Nichi-Ro sengo kara Manshū jihen made" 1970年代における「満州」研究の状況(1)—日露戦後から満州事変まで (A survey of the "Manchurian" studies in the 1970s: From the end of the Russo-Japanese War to the Manchurian Incident), *Ajia keizai* (March 1979),

20(3):28–55; part 2: "1970-nendai ni okeru 'Manshū' kenkyū no jōkyō:Manshū jihen kara Manshūkoku seiritsu made" 1970年代におけ る「満州」研究の状況—満州事変から満州国崩壊まで (A survey of the "Manchurian" studies in the 1970s: From the Manchurian Incident to the demise of Manchukuo), *Ajia keizai* (November 1979), 20(11):24–43.

82. "Senji shorui" 戦時書類.

83. Hokkaidō Sōmubu Gyōsei Shiryō Shitsu 北海道総務部行政資料室, ed., *Karafuto kankei bunken sōmokuroku* 樺太関係文献総目録 (1970).

84. Kokumin Gaikō Kenkyū Kyōkai 国民外交研究協会·

85. "Shōwa zaiseishi shidankai kiroku" 昭和財政史史談会記録·

86. Ōkura Daijin Kanbō Chōsa Kikakuka 大蔵大臣官房調査企画課, ed., *Ōkura daijin kaikoroku* 大蔵大臣回顧録 (Ōkura Zaimu Kyōkai, 1977).

87. Nihon Kokusai Seiji Gakkai 日本国際政治学会, ed., *Taiheiyō sensō e no michi* 太平洋戦争への道 (The road to the Pacific War), 7 vols. (Asahi Shimbunsha, 1962–63).

88. Naiseishi Kenkyūkai 内政史研究会, *Naiseishi kenkyū shiryō* 内政史研 究資料 (Materials for the study of the history of [Japanese] domestic politics) (Tokyo Toritsu Daigaku Hōgakubu, 1963–); 250 vols. printed so far, but not for general sale.

89. Nihon Kindai Shiryō Kenkyūkai 日本近代史料研究会 and Kido Nikki Kenkyūkai 木戸日記研究会, eds., *Nihon kindai shiryō sōsho B*. 日本近 代史料叢書B (Tokyo Daigaku Kyōyō Gakubu, 1975–), 19 vols. printed so far, but not for general sale.

90. Nakamura Kikuo 中村菊男 *Shōwa rikugun hishi* 昭和陸軍秘史 (A con- fidential history of the army in the Shōwa period) (Banchō Shobō, 1968); *Shōwa kaikugun hishi* 昭和海軍秘史 (A confidential history of the navy in the Shōwa period) (Banchō Shobō, 1969).

91. Andō Yoshio 安藤良雄, ed., *Shōwa seiji keizaishi e no shōgen* 昭和 政治経済史への証言 (Witnesses to the political and economic history of the Shōwa period), 3 vols. (Mainichi Shinbunsha, 1965–66).

92. Yomiuri Shinbunsha, *Shōwashi no tennō* 昭和史の天皇, 30 vols. (Yomi- uri Shinbunsha, 1969–76).

93. Gaimushō Gaikō Shiryōkan Nihon Gaikōshi Jiten Hensan Iinkai 外務省外交史料館日本外交史辞典編纂委員会, ed., *Nihon gaikōshi jiten* 日本外交史辞典 (The encyclopedia of Japanese diplomatic his- tory) (Ōkurashō Insatsukyoku, 1979).

94. Jinbutsu Ōraisha 人物往来社, *Kindai no sensō*, Vol. 8: *Gunji jiten* 近代 の戦争, 8, 軍事辞典 (Jinbutsu Ōraisha, 1966).

95. Ōhama Tetsuya and Ozawa Ikurō 大濱徹也, 小沢郁郎, eds., *Teikoku riku-kaigun jiten* 帝国陸海軍事典 (Dōseisha, 1979).

96. Gaimushō Hyakunenshi Hensan Iinkai 外務省百年史編纂委員会, ed., *Gaimushō no hyakunen* 外務省の百年 (A century of the Japanese Foreign Ministry), 2 vols. (Hara Shobō, 1969).

97. Hata Ikuhiko (Senzenki Kanryōsei Kenkyūkai, ed.) 秦郁彦（戦前期官僚制研究会）, ed., *Senzenki Nihon Kanryōsei no seido, soshiki, jinji* 戦前期日本官僚制の制度, 組織, 人事 (The system, organization, and personnel of the prewar Japanese bureaucracy) (Tokyo Daigaku Shuppankai, 1981).

98. Nihon Kindai Shiryō Kenkyūkai 日本近代史料研究会, comp., *Nihon riku kaigun no seido, soshiki, jinji* 日本陸海軍の制度, 組織, 人事 (The system, organization, and personnel of the Japanese army and navy) (Tokyo Daigaku Shuppankai), 1971.

99. Jōhō Yoshio, editorial supervisor; Toyama Misao, ed. 上法快男監修, 外山操編, *Riku-kaigun shōkan jinji sōran* 陸海軍将官人事総覧 (Fuyō Shobō, 1981).

100. Kajima Heiwa Kenkyūjo 鹿島平和研究所, ed., *Nihon gaikōshi, Bekkan 4: Chizu* 日本外交史, 別巻 4 —地図 (Japanese diplomatic history, supplementary vol. 4: Atlas) (Kajima Kenkyūjo Shuppankai, 1974).

101. Maehara Tōru and Kuwata Etsu 前原透, 桑田悦, eds., *Nihon no sensō: Zukai to dēta* 日本の戦争 —図解とデータ (Hara Shobō, 1982).

102. Kajima Heiwa Kenkyūjo 鹿島平和研究所, ed., *Nihon gaikō shuyō bunsho, nenpyō* 日本外交主要文書. 年表 (Major documents and a chronology of Japanese foreign policy, 1941–1980), 3 vols. (Hara Shobō, 1983–85).

103. Kajima Heiwa Kenkyūjo 鹿島平和研究所, ed., *Nihon gaikōshi, Bekkan 3: Nenpyō* 日本外交史, 別巻 —年表 (Japanese diplomatic history, supplementary vol. 3: A chronology) (Kajima Kenkyūjo Shuppankai, 1974).

104. Suekuni Masao 末国正雄, ed., *Riku-kaigun nenpyō fu heigo, yōgo no kaisetsu* 陸海軍年表付兵語用語の解説 (Asaguno Shinbunsha, 1980) (Published as a volume in the War History series).

105. Iwanami Shoten 岩波書店, ed., *Kindai Nihon sōgō nenpyō* (A comprehensive chronology of modern Japan), rev. ed. (Iwanami, rev. ed., 1984).

106. Hanabusa Hidemichi 英修道, ed., *Nihon gaikōshi kankei bunken mokuroku* 日本外交史関係文献目録 (A bibliography of Japanese diplomatic history) (Keiō Gijuku Daigaku Hōgaku Kenkyūkai, 1961); enlarged edition, 1968.

107. *Gaikō jihō* 外交時報 (monthly journal, founded in February 1898, suspended during 1953–57); *Kokusaihō gaikō zasshi* 国際法外交雑誌

(monthly journal, founded in 1902); *Chūō kōron* 中央公論 (monthly journal, founded in January 1899).

108. Yamane Yukio 山根幸夫, eds., *Kindai Nitchū kankeishi bunken moku-roku* 近代日中関係史文献目録 (A bibliography of the history of modern Sino-Japanese relations) (Tokyo Joshi Daigaku Tōyōshi Kenkyū-shitsu, 1977).

109. Ichiko Chūzō 市古宙造, ed., *Kindai Chūgoku kankei bunken mokuroku, 1945-1978* 近代中国関係文献目録, 1945—1978 (A bibliography of works relating to modern China, 1945-1978) (Chūō Kōron Bijutsu Shuppan, 1980).

110. Ichiko Chūzō, ed., *Kindai Chūgoku, Nitchū kankeishi bunken mokuroku* 近代中国. 中日関係文献目録 (A bibliography of modern China and Sino-Japanese relations) (Kyūko Shoin, 1979).

111. Kawahara Hiroshi and Fujii Shōzo 河原宏, 藤井昇三, eds., *Nitchū kankei no kiso chishiki* 日中関係の基礎知識 (Basic information on Sino-Japanese relations) (Yūhikaku, 1974).

112. Moriyama Shigenori 森山茂徳, "Kindai Nikkan kankeishi kenkyū no dōkō to shiryō oyobi bunken" 近代日韓関係史研究の動向と史料及び文献 (Research trend in the history of modern Japanese-Korean relations, documents, and bibliography), *Kokka gakkai zasshi* (November 1975) 88(11–12):66–98.

113. Published by Ajia Keizai Kenkyūjo アジア経済研究所, 1983.

114. *Nihon gaikōshi kenkyū—Meiji jidai* 日本外交史研究—明治時代 (1957).

115. *Nihon gaikōshi kenkyū—Taishō jidai* 日本外交史研究—大正時代 (1958).

116. *Nihon gaikōshi kenkyū—Shōwa jidai* 日本外交史研究—昭和時代 (1959).

117. *Nihon gaikōshi kenkyū—Bakumatsu-ishin jidai* 日本外交史研究—幕末・維新時代 (1960).

118. *Nihon gaikōshi kenkyū—Nitchū kankei no tenkai* 日本外交史研究—日中関係の展開 (1961).

119. *Nichi-Bei kankei no tenkai* 日米関係の展開 (1961).

120. *Nihon gaikōshi kenkyū—Nisshin Nichi-Ro sensō* 日本外交史研究—日清・日露戦争 (1961).

121. *Nikkan kankei no tenkai* 日韓関係の展開 (1962).

122. *Nihon gaikōshi kenkyū: Daiichiji sekai taisen* 日本外交史研究—第一次世界大戦 (1962).

123. *Nihon gaikōshi no shomondai, 1* 日本外交史の諸問題, 1 (1963).

124. *Nihon gaikōshi no shomondai, 2* 日本外交史の諸問題, 2 (1964).

125. *Nichi-Ro Nisso kankei no tenkai* 日露・日ソ関係の展開 (1965).

126. *Nihon gaikōshi kenkyū—Gaikō shidōsharon* 日本外交史研究—外交指導者論 (1966).
127. *Nichi-Bei kankei no imēji* 日米関係のイメージ (1966).
128. *Nihon gaikōshi no shomondai, 3* 日本外交史の諸問題, 3 (1967).
129. *Nihon gaikōshi kenkyū—Gaikō to yoron* 日本外交史研究—外交と世論 (1969).
130. *Manshū jihen* 満州事変 (1970).
131. *Nitchū sensō to kokusaiteki taiō* 日中戦争と国際的対応 (1972).
132. *Nihon gaikō no kokusai ninshiki—Sono shiteki tenkai* 日本外交の国際認識—その史的展開 (1974).
133. *1930-nendai no Nihon gaikō: Yonin no gaishō o chūshin to shite* 1930年代の日本外交—四人の外相を中心として (1976).
134. *Nichi-Ei kankei no shiteki tenkai* 日英関係の史的展開 (1977).
135. *Hendōki ni okeru higashi Ajia to Nihon: Sono shiteki kōsatsu* 変動期における東アジアと日本—その史的考察 (1980).
136. *Nichi-Gō kankei no shiteki tenkai* 日豪関係の史的展開 (1981).
137. *Nihon gaikō no shisō* 日本外交の思想 (1982).
138. *Nihon gaikō no hiseishiki channeru* 日本外交の非正式チャンネル (1983).
139. *Nihon-Kanada kankei no shiteki tenkai* 日本・カナダ関係の史的展開 (1985).
140. Kokuritsu Kokkai Toshokan 国立国会図書館, comp., *Zasshi kiji sakuin (Jinbun, shakaihen)* 雑誌記事索引（人文・社会編）, published since 1948 by the compiler.
141. Nichigai Asoshiētsu, Inc. 日外アソシェーツ, comp., *Zasshi kiji sakuin (Jinbun, shakaihen): Ruiseki sakuinban* 雑誌記事索引（人文・社会編）累積索引版 (Japanese periodicals index, humanities and social science: Cumulative edition) (Kinokuniya Shoten, 1976–86). Each cumulative edition is accompanied by two supplements, one devoted to an author index and the other to a subject index.
142. *Shigaku zasshi* 史学雑誌. This journal publishes historiographical essays each year in issue no. 5. For our particular purposes, see the section on Japan (modern and contemporary).
143. *Kokusai mondai* 国際問題.
144. Kokkai Toshokan Sankō Shoshibu 国会図書館参考書誌部, ed., *Kindai Nihon seiji kankei jinbutsu bunken mokuroku* 近代日本政治関係人物文献目録 (Kokkai Toshokan, 1986).
145. Hōsei Daigaku Bungakubu Shigaku Kenkyūshitsu 法政大学文学部史学研究室, ed., *Nihon jinbutsu bunken mokuroku* 日本人物文献目録 (Bibliography of Japanese biographical works) (Heibonsha, 1974). This

volume contains scholarly articles and essays that have appeared in magazines.

146. This book originally appeared as Kiyosawa Kiyoshi 清沢洌, *Gendai Nihon bunmeishi: Gaikōshi* 現代日本文明史, vol. 3, 外交史 (History of contemporary Japanese civilization, 3: Diplomatic history) (Tōyō Keizai Shinpōsha, 1941). For an excellent biography of Kiyosawa, see Kitaoka Shin'ichi 北岡伸一, *Kiyosawa Kiyoshi: Nichi-Bei kankei e no tōsatsu* 清沢洌―日米関係への洞察 (Kiyosawa Kiyoshi: Insights into Japanese-American relations) (Chūō Kōronsha, 1987).

147. Kajima Morinosuke 鹿島守之助, *Bakumatsu gaikō: Kaikoku to ishin* 幕末外交―開国と維新 (1970).

148. Kajima Morinosuke, *Jōyaku kaisei mondai* 条約改正問題 (1970).

149. Kajima Morinosuke, *Kinrin shokoku oyobi ryōdo mondai* 近隣諸国及び領土問題 (1970).

150. Kajima Morinosuke, *Nisshin sensō to sangoku kanshō* 日清戦争と三国干渉 (1970).

151. Kajima Morinosuke, *Shina ni okeru rekkyō no kakuchiku* 支那における列強の角逐 (1970).

152. Kajima Morinosuke, *Daiikkai Nichi-Ei dōmei to sono zengo* 第一回日英同盟とその前後 (1970).

153. Kajima Morinosuke, *Nichi-Ro sensō* 日露戦争 (1970).

154. Kajima Morinosuke, *Dainikai Nichi-Ei dōmei to sono jidai* 第二回日英同盟とその時代 (1970).

155. Kajima Morinosuke, *Daisankai Nichi-Ei dōmei to sono jidai* 第三回日英同盟とその時代 (1970).

156. Kajima Morinosuke, *Daiichiji sekai taisen sanka oyobi kyōryoku mondai* 第一次世界大戦参加及び協力問題 (1971).

157. Kajima Morinosuke, *Shina mondai* 支那問題 (1971).

158. Kajima Morinosuke, *Pari kōwa kaigi* パリ講和会議 (1971).

159. Kajima Morinosuke, *Washinton kaigi oyobi imin mondai* ワシントン会議及び移民問題 (1971).

160. [Most of vols. 14–27 were drafted by middle-ranking diplomats (sometimes in collaboration with young scholars) under the supervision or editorship of senior diplomats. In accordance with the format of the Kajima series, we shall cite supervisors here, but notations in the text indicate who actually authored or co-authored these volumes.] Satō Naotake 佐藤尚武 *Kokusai Renmei ni okeru Nihon* 国際連盟における日本 (1972).

161. Nishi Haruhiko 西春彦, *Nisso kokkō mondai, 1917–1945* 日ソ国交問題, 1917—1945 (1970).

162. Horinouchi Kensuke 堀内謙介, *Kaigun gunshuku kōshō, Fusen jōyaku* 海軍軍縮交渉・不戦条約 (1973).
163. Kamimura Shin'ichi 上村伸一, *Chūgoku nashonarizumu to Nikka kankei no tenkai* 中国ナショナリズムと日華関係の展開 (1971).
164. Morishima Gorō 守島伍郎 and Yanai Hisao 柳井恒夫 *Manshū jihen* 満州事変 (1973).
165. Kamimura Shin'ichi 上村伸一, *Nikka jihen* 日華事変, 2 vols. (1971).
166. Horinouchi Kensuke 堀内謙介 *Nichi-Doku-I dōmei, Nisso chūritsu jōyaku* 日独伊同盟・日ソ中立条約 (1971).
167. Matsumoto Shun'ichi and Andō Yoshirō 松本俊一安東義良, eds., *Nanshin mondai* 南進問題 (1973).
168. Kase Toshikazu 加瀬俊一, *Nichi-Beo kōshō* 日米交渉 (1970).
169. Ōta Ichirō 太田一郎, *Dai Tōa sensō, senji gaikō* 大東亜戦争, 戦時外交 (1971).
170. Matsumoto Shun'ichi and Andō Yoshirō 松本俊一安東義良, *Dai Tōa sensō, shūsen gaikō* 大東亜戦争・終戦外交 (1972).
171. Suzuki Tadakatsu 鈴木九萬, *Shūsen kara kōwa made* 終戦から講和まで (1973).
172. Nishimura Kumao 西村熊雄, *San Furanshisuko heiwa jōyaku* サンフランシスコ平和条約 (1971).
173. Gaimushō (Foreign Ministry), ed., *Nihon gaikō hyakunen shōshi* 日本外交百年小史 (Yamada Shoin, 1954); revised ed. 1958.
174. Akira Iriye 入江昭, *Nihon no gaikō: Meiji ishin kara gendai made* 日本の外交—明治維新から現代まで (Chūō Kōronsha, 1966).
175. Ōhata Tokushirō 大畑篤四郎, *Kokusai kankyō to Nihon gaikō* 国際環境と日本外交 (Azuma Shuppan, 1966).
176. Ōhata Tokushirō, *Nihon gaikōshi* 日本外交史 (Azuma Shuppan, 1978).
177. Ikei Masaru 池井優, *Nihon gaikōshi gaisetsu* 日本外交史. (History of Japanese diplomacy) (Keiō Tsūshin, 1973; revised ed., 1986).
178. Shinobu Seizaburō 信夫清三郎, ed., *Nohon gaikōshi, 1853–1972* 日本外交史 1853-1972 (A history of Japanese diplomacy) (Mainichi Shimbunsha, 1974). 2 vol.

2

From the Opening of Japan to the West to the Conclusion of the Russo-Japanese War

Yasuoka Akio

SOURCE MATERIALS ON THE BAKUMATSU THROUGH MEIJI PERIOD

Before World War II, the University of Tokyo Historiographical Institute (Tōkyō Daigaku Shiryō Hensanjo) initiated an ongoing project of publication of documents relating to diplomacy in the Bakumatsu period. The series, *Dai Nippon komonjo: Bakumatsu gaikoku kankei monjo* (Old Japanese documents: Documents relating to foreign affairs in the Bakumatsu period), commenced with 1853 and proceeded in chronological order. After World War II, this work was resumed with the publication of an additional nineteen more volumes (vols. 23 through 41), the last of these covering materials through October 1860. Unfortunately, the documents from the Meiji government's newly formed diplomatic arm, that are to be found in the Foreign Ministry's *Dai Nippon gaikō monjo* (Documents on Imperial Japan's foreign policy), date only from November 1867. Because this leaves a gap of nearly seven years, a sequel to *Bakumatsu gaikoku kankei monjo* would be most welcome.

Moreover, the compilation of materials on the Shogunate's overseas negotiations, originally edited by the Shogunate and made available in printed form as *Tsūkō ichiran: Zokushū* (Survey of foreign relations: A sequel) under the editorship of Yanai Kenji, extends only through 1856. The Foreign Ministry publication, *Zoku tsūshin zenran ruishū* (Sequel to the complete record of foreign relations), is divided into various sections, one of which is *Bakumatsu ishin gaikō shiryō shūsei* (Collected historical records on foreign relations: 1853–1868), 6 vols. Its publication by Ishinshi Gakkai began in 1943 but was suspended the following year and has never been resumed. It should also be added that the publication in facsimile of the Foreign Ministry's manuscripts of *Tsūshin zenran* (the complete record of foreign relations) was finally brought to a conclusion in March 1988; a total of sixty volumes.

Finally, it should be noted that the celebration of the centennial of the Treaty of Amity and Friendship between Japan and the United States saw the publication in seven volumes of *Man'en gannen kenbei shisetsu shiryō shūsei* (Materials from the Japanese delegation to America of 1860) compiled by Nichi-Bei Shūkō Tsūshō Hyakunen Kinen Jigyō Un'ei Kai. This work, however, is made up primarily of the travel diaries of the members of the delegation.

Nihon gaikō bunsho (Documents on Japanese foreign policy), compiled by Gaimushō (the Foreign Ministry), constitutes a resumption of the prewar series and, commencing with 1877, now extends to the end of 1926. In addition, the Foreign Ministry compiled *Nihon gaikō nempyō narabini shuyō bunsho* (Chronology and major documents of Japanese foreign policy, 1840 to 1945; 2 vols.). Published in 1955, it is very handy, for it provides a detailed chronology and the key official documents relating to Japan's state policy. (See chapter 1.)

In the area of Japanese-Korean relations, Kim Chong-myong, ed., *Nikkan gaikō shiryō shūsei* (Collection of materials on Japanese-Korean diplomatic relations), presents relevant records in chronological order and contains "Nikkan kōshō jikenroku" (A record of crises in

Japanese-Korean negotiations). This work is now being expanded and reprinted as Ichikawa Masaaki, ed., *Nikkan gaikō shiryō* (Materials on Japanese-Korean diplomatic relations).

There are several publications that are useful as source materials, though they are not diplomatic records as such. These include: *Itō Hirobumi kankei monjo* (Documents relating to Itō Hirobumi); the papers of Ōkuma Shigenobu (Waseda University); and *Inoue Kowashi den: Shiryōhen* (Biography of Inoue Kowashi: Historical materials). Also important is Kunaishō (Ministry of the Imperial Household), ed., *Meiji Tennōki* (Annals of Emperor Meiji).

FOREIGN RELATIONS DURING THE BAKUMATSU PERIOD

Before World War II, research into Japan's overseas negotiations during the Bakumatsu period and the years of the Meiji Restoration was undertaken by such pioneering scholars as Tabohashi Kiyoshi in his *Zōtei: Kindai Nihon gaikoku kankeishi* (A history of modern Japan's foreign relations, revised and enlarged edition; 1943). This work, reprinted in 1976, remains a useful general book.

Opening of Treaty Ports

The most comprehensive study on the conclusion of treaties and opening of treaty ports is Haga Shōji's article examining Shogunate foreign policy at the time of the treaties of amity and friendship.

On the conclusion of the Japanese-American Treaty of Amity and Friendship in 1854, Akimoto Masutoshi's article [1] and Nakamura Takeshi's essay are recommended. On the treaty and the first American consul general, Townsend Harris, Ōyama Azusa has written a good article [9]. Motohashi Tadashi's recent work, *Nichi-Bei kankeishi kenkyū* (Studies in the history of [early] Japanese-American relations), contains a detailed account of Japanese reaction to the arrival of Commodore Perry and the images of the United States held by the Japanese from the opening of Japan to the 1880s. On the opening of relations with Britain, see Fujii Sadafumi's study [3] on Japan's first treaty with Britain.

The most recent important work that treats the subject against the broad international background is: Ishii Kanji and Sekiguchi Hisashi, eds., *Sekai shijō to bakumatsu kaikō* (The world market and Japan's opening in the Bakumatsu period). This is a product of an ambitious conference held in December 1981, which widely mobilized Japanese specialists in such diverse fields as British, American, French, and Chinese studies. The work attempts to reexamine the opening of Japan, with all its significance for both Asia and the world at large, and to place this historical event in the development of a world market. The initial chapter by Sekiguchi, which raises important questions on Japan's opening of treaty ports in the context of world economic history, is followed by chapters which relate Japan's opening to British, American, and French capitalism. One chapter is devoted to a comparison of Japanese and Chinese opening of treaty ports. Each paper is accompanied by an informative series of discussions. Altogether, the volume, representing new comparative approaches and outside perspectives, is a unique contribution.

Katō Yūzō, one of the contributors to this volume, has also published an essay on the opening of Japan with particular reference to the article of 1858 treaties banning the opium trade. In addition, Katō has published a serial study (in eight parts) on the international setting at the time of the visitation of the "Black Ships" to Japan. These essays were collected in Katō's new book, *Kurobune zengo no sekai* (The outside world at the time of the visitation of the "Black Ships" to Japan).

The Foreign Powers' Policy Toward Japan

Ishii Takashi has actively engaged himself in the study of the policies that foreign countries adopted toward Japan. In 1957 he presented his magnum opus, *Meiji ishin no kokusaiteki kankyō* (The Meiji restoration and its international environment), revising and expanding it in 1966. Subsequently he published a survey history of the opening of Japan in the Bakumatsu period, *Nihon kaikokushi* (A history of the opening of Japan). Ishii is especially interested in a detailed examination of British policy toward Japan, and he illuminates the underlying policy of neutrality that Great Britain adopted in its diplomatic relations with Japan from 1860 through the early 1870s, or during its "Little Eng-

land" phase. Ishii supports his thesis by referring to his discovery
in the pages of the *Japan Times* of the dates of publication of the
"English Policy" articles by Ernest Satow, then language attaché to
British Ambassador Harry S. Parkes. These dates were subsequently
revised by Hirose Shizuko [2], and the subject was further commented
on by Ishii [1]. Concerning Ernest Satow as diplomatist, Hagiwara
Nobutoshi has published his *Tōi gake* (The distant precipice), which is
based on the Satow papers in the British Public Record Office. Concerning Ambassador Parkes' predecessor, Sir Rutherford Alcock, the
reader is referred to Masuda Tsuyoshi's recent work, *Bakumatsuki no
Eikokujin* (The British in the Bakumatsu period).

Foreign Settlements. When treaty ports were opened to trade,
quarters were established for foreign residents. In his contribution to
Yokohamashi-shi (A history of Yokohama city), vols. 2 and 3, Akimoto
Masutoshi compares the case of Yokohama with that of Shanghai.
Ōyama Azusa, *Kyū-jōyakuka ni okeru kaishi kaikō no kenkyū* (A study
of open cities and ports under the old treaty system) makes a clear-cut
distinction between "open cities" and "open ports" as they were
established under the terms of the treaties concluded in 1854–1860,
and then proceeds to discuss the nature of foreign settlements in
general as well as the specific characteristics of Hakodate, Kobe, and
other ports. Finally, he discusses the steps that led to their abolition
through treaty revision.

Stationing of Foreign Troops. Because of pressure from the foreign
powers, foreign troops continued to be stationed in Japan until 1875.
On the foreign troops in Yokohama, see Hirose Shizuko's article [1] on
the origins of stationing foreign troops and Hora Tomio's essay on the
stationing of British and French troops. For negotiations concerning
the withdrawal of these troops, see Kishi Motokazu's study on the
withdrawal of British troops from Yokohama.

Consular Jurisdiction. There is considerable room for research into
actual case studies of consular courts. Besides Hora Tomio's *Bakumatsu
ishinki no gaiatsu to teikō* (Foreign pressures and resistance to them
during the Bakumatsu and Restoration periods), the only other study

to date is Imai Shōji's article [2] on British consular justice at the time of the opening of Japan. It is a case study on the consular trial (1860) of a British subject for firing a gun.

The Tsushima Incident. On the subject of the temporary occupation of Tsushima Island by the Russian navy in 1861, no work has yet appeared in the postwar period that goes beyond Nezu Masashi's 1934 study. The only new study that deserves our attention is the work by a historian from Tsushima Island, Hino Kaizaburō, *Bakumatsu ni okeru Tsushima to Ei-Ro* (Tsushima island, England, and Russia in the Bakumatsu period), which draws upon local historical materials.

The Bonin and the Ryūkyū Island. Concerning the jurisdictional questions that arose as a result of the foreign ships making frequent calls at the Bonin Islands, two principal studies were published before World War II. One is Tabohashi Kiyoshi's detailed study that appeared in 1921–22, and the other is Okudaira Takehiko's work (1940) which was based on British documents.

In the postwar years, as Japanese began to return to the islands and progress was made over their reversion to Japan, Ōkuma Ryōichi published *Rekishi no kataru Ogasawaratō* (The Bonin Islands speak of their past), a work that, drawing on sources both at home and abroad, covers the history of the islands through their possession by Japan in the early Meiji period. Tanaka Hiroyuki's articles on diplomatic relations concerning the recovery of the Bonins during the early 1860s draw almost exclusively on domestic materials and limits its focus to the Bakumatsu period. The period from 1771 to 1882 is covered by Ōkuma Ryōichi, *Ikokusen Ryūkyū raikōshi no kenkyū* (A historical study of foreign ships calling at the Ryūkyū Islands). The plans proposed by the Satsuma leadership to deal with the problem of foreign ships calling at Ryūkyūan ports are examined by Iwasaki Masao's study on the foreign policies of Shimazu Nariakira, which draws upon Shimazu's records (*Shimazu Nariakira monjo;* 3 vols. to date).

Russo-Japanese Relations/Northern Territories. Abe Kōzō's article [1] on Russo-Japanese relations during the Bakumatsu period provides a general introduction to the subject. For a more extensive historical survey of Russo-Japanese relations, the reader is directed to Manabe

Shigetada's *Nichi-Ro kankeishi* (A history of Russo-Japanese relations) which, drawing upon both Japanese and Russian sources, covers the period 1697–1875. Takano Akira's *Nihon to Roshia* (Japan and Russia) provides a bibliographical treatment of materials ranging from the period of initial contacts between the two countries through the period of Efim V. Putyatin's negotiations with Japan. Kōriyama Yoshimitsu's posthumously published *Bakumatsu Nichi-Ro kankeishi kenkyū* (Studies in the history of Russo-Japanese relations in the Bakumatsu period) is not a historical survey but rather a collection of individual papers dealing with periods up to the time of Ambassador N. P. Rezanov's arrival in Japan in 1804.

Hora Tomio's *Hoppō ryōdo mondai no rekishi to shōrai* (The problem of the northern territories: their history and their future) reviews the manner in which both Japan and Russia came to lay claim to the Kurile Islands. The book contains an essay arguing that the southern Kuriles be treated as Japan's "indigenous territory." There is also Ōkuma Ryōichi's monograph, *Hoppō ryōdo mondai no rekishiteki haikei* (The historical background of the northern territories problem). Other works on this subject are: Abe Seiji's essay on the Russian occupation of Kushunkotan on Sakhalin; Akizuki Toshiyuki's study [2] on its occupation during 1853–54; and the same author's essay [1] that traces the Japanese-Russian mixed residence in Sakhalin during the Bakumatsu period.

Dutch-Japanese Relations. By virtue of the fact that Holland was the only Western nation to have enjoyed trading relations with Japan during Japan's years of national seclusion, a wealth of materials had been produced on Dutch-Japanese relations in the prewar period, but there was a tendency to emphasize what was called "histories of Dutch studies," or more broadly, "histories of Western studies." In the postwar era, the pioneer in this field, Itazawa Takeo, published such works as *Nichi-Ran bōekishi* (A history of Japanese-Dutch trade), *Nihon to Oranda* (Japan and Holland), and *Shiiboruto* (An account of the life of Philipp Franz von Seibold). In addition, Itazawa published *Nichi-Ran bunka kōshōshi no kenkyū* (A study of the history of cultural exchange between Japan and Holland), which is a compilation of his prewar research. A work in a similar vein is Iwao Seiichi, ed., *Oranda fūsetsugaki shūsei* (Transcriptions of Dutch comments on Japan), which is a compilation of materials available in the Netherlands. Yamawaki Teijirō, *Nagasaki no Oranda shōkan* (The Dutch trading house in Nagasaki) treats the realities of Deshima island trade by drawing on the records of the Dutch East India Company preserved in the Het Algemeen Rijksarchief (The General National Archives in the Hague, Netherlands). He also treats the question of Deshima in its final years.

For scholarship concerning Japanese-Dutch diplomatic relations, the reader is directed to Morioka Yoshiko's article on William II's call for the opening of Japan and Shōji Mitsuo's essay on the history of Dutch-Japanese relations during the Bakumatsu period. Kanai Madoka's article on the contribution of Donker Curtius is informative for its explanation of the preservation of the Dutch Company's Nagasaki records.

Franco-Japanese Relations. In the area of Japan's relations with France, there are the prewar writings of Ōtsuka Takematsu, which were followed by Nezu Masashi's postwar works, such as his articles on negotiations between the Shogunate and French governments at the time of the Paris Agreement of 1864 [2] and on French policy toward Japan as seen from French diplomatic records of the Bakumatsu period [1].

For a case study on foreign capital moving into the Japanese market at this time, the reader is directed to an article by Shibata Michio and Shibata Asako, which examines on the basis of French sources the plans for the formation of the Compagnie française d'exportation et d'importation.

On Frenchmen who played important roles in Franco-Japanese relations, there are several noteworthy works. Tomita Hitoshi's study traces the career of Mermet Cachon, who acted as language officer for French Ambassador Leon Roches. Takahashi Kunitarō's book, *Oyatoi gaikokujin, vol. 6: Gunji* (Foreign advisors in the employment of the Japanese government, vol. 6: Military affairs) deals with figures such as F. L. Verny, who established the Yokosuka Iron Works (a naval dockyard), and C. S. Chanoine, an instructor of military science. In addition, Nishibori Akira has published his study on the French-language school opened in Yokohama and the French citizens employed by the Meiji government. Tomita, Takahashi, and Nishibori have traveled in France to investigate and collect materials, and have contributed to empirical research in Franco-Japanese relations including the history of cultural exchange. For example, Tomita speculates on the role of Murakami Hidetoshi, the pioneer of French studies in Japan, in the conclusion of the Franco-Japanese Treaty of Amity of 1858.

German-Japanese Diplomatic Relations. There is a series of prewar works by Maruyama Kunio, including *Shoki Nichi-Doku tsūkō shōshi* (A short history of early German-Japanese relations), but in the postwar period there has been a dearth of materials. The only work that can be cited is Imamiya Shin, *Shoki Nichi-Doku tsūkōshi no ken-kyū* (Researches into the early history of German-Japanese relations). Using materials obtained from the Preussische Geheimes Staatsarchiv prior to World War II, Imamiya examines the role of the mission of Friedrich A. B. Eulenburg which resulted in the Prussian-Japanese treaty of 1861. This work also describes the activities of the Japanese delegation that visited Prussia in the early 1860s; the role of Henry C. J. Heusken, the Dutchman attached to the American consulate Townsend Harris, who acted as interpreter for Count Eulenburg in his treaty negotiations with Japan; and the contributions of Alexander G. G. von Siebold, the German attached to the British legation.

As a result of the translation and publication in Japanese of his great work *Nippon: Archiv zur Beschreibung von Japan* (twenty parts, 1832–54), there has been mounting interest in Siebold's father, Philipp B. F. von Siebold, but considerable room remains for study of the activities of Philipp's twin sons, Alexander and Heinrich. Regarding Max A. S. von Brandt, the Prussian government's first consul general in Japan, there are very few works except Tanaka Masahiro's article [1], and much remains to be done in this field to investigate historical materials on the German side.

THE FIRST YEARS OF THE MEIJI PERIOD

The Beginnings of Meiji Diplomacy

On the subject of the transference of diplomatic functions from the Tokugawa Shogunate regime to the newly established Meiji government, Irie Keishirō's essay on the Meiji restoration and the switch from a system of dual sovereignty is an especially useful study, as is Nakamura Hidetaka's article on an earlier period that examines the "view of world order in Tycoon diplomacy."

For an authoritative official account of the establishment of the institutional and organizational structure for the conduct of foreign affairs, the reader is referred to Gaimushō Hyakunenshi Hensan Iinkai, ed., *Gaimushō no hyakunen* (A century of the Japanese Foreign Ministry), 1:22–163. Other works include Mikami Terumi's articles on the establishment of the Foreign Ministry: [1], [2]. Uchiyama Masakuma has written a succinct essay [1] tracing the origins of pro–Anglo-American policy traditional in the Japanese Foreign Ministry.

Foreign Involvements in the Japanese Civil War. Concerning the period of civil war, i.e., the Boshin war, that led to the Meiji restoration, the reader is referred to Ishii Takashi's survey treatment, *Ishin no nairan* (Civil disturbances during the restoration), and his basic article [4] on the international relations in the last stage of the Boshin war. Shimomura Fujio's general study, *Meiji ishin no gaikō* (The diplomacy of the Meiji restoration) contains a wide-ranging discussion of diplomatic issues related to the war. It covers such topics as the statement of neutrality issued by the foreign powers. Among the problems treated in this book are: the issue with the United States over the latter's detention of the ironclad S. S. *Stonewall Jackson;* French military officers' participation in the war; foreigners' sales of military supplies, and the problem of currencies. Shimomura has also published an article [1] examining the diplomacy of Boshin war.

Concerning foreigners' involvement in the Boshin war, Tanaka Masahiro's essays on the following topics deserve attention: French military instructors and the Toba-Fushimi war [2]; the Schnell brothers (German weapons salesmen) and their involvement in the Tōhoku war [3], and Hiramatsu Buhei and the Yonezawa domain [4]. On this subject, see also Ayuzawa Shintarō's article on the secret role Schnell played in the history of the Bakumatsu/early restoration years. Tanaka also touches upon the activities of the Schnell brothers, Henry and Edward, in his previously cited article [3], but the aforementioned works by no means exhaust the topic.

The "Expel-the-Barbarians" Movement.   Among the very first diplomatic problems to be faced by the newly formed Meiji government were the "expel-the-barbarians" incidents (i.e., the Kobe incident on February 4, 1868; the Sakai incident on March 8, 1868; and the interruption of British Ambassador Parkes' visit to the Emperor on March 23, 1868). A survey on the subject is found in Wagatsuma Sakae et al., eds., *Nihon seiji saiban shiroku* (Historical records of Japanese political trials). This problem is also treated in Ishii Takashi's previously cited work, *Meiji ishin no kokusaiteki kankyō*. Oka Yoshitake's distinguished essay on the aftermath of the antibarbarian movement is contained in his collection of essays, *Reimeiki no Meiji Nihon* (Meiji Japan at dawn). The most recent work in this vein, based on both Japanese and foreign documents, is Uchiyama Masakuma's *Kōbe jiken* (The Kōbe incident). Uchiyama regards this incident, involving the clash between foreign troops with the forces of Bizen Province, as "a starting point of Meiji diplomacy" in the sense that the incident led the new government to pronounce a complete opening of Japan. Noda Hideo's article on the Nawate incident, which takes its name from the locale in Kyoto where the incident occurred, examines the attack on Parkes' retinue.

Concerning the various diplomatic problems that resulted from the new Meiji government's prohibition of Christianity, Hirose Shizuko has published a useful article [4]. Suzuki Yūko's essay on the Meiji government's policies on Christianity covers the evolution of the government's policy that led to the lifting of the official prohibition of Christianity in 1873.

The Iwakura Embassy.   One record dating from the mission itself is Kume Kunitake, ed., *Tokumei zenken taishi Bei-Ō kairan jikki* (The authentic record of the embassy to the United States and Europe). It has been reissued by Iwanami Shoten in its pocket paperback series with annotations by Tanaka Akira (5 vols., 1977–82). This record has attracted attention from specialists in comparative culture, but it cannot be regarded as a record of actual diplomatic negotiations. The political maneuvering that lay behind the dispatching of the embassy is discussed in Ōkubo Toshiaki, ed., *Iwakura shisetsu no kenkyū* (Researches on the Iwakura embassy), which examines the role played by Ōkuma Shigenobu in initiating the idea. Shimomura Fujio had also touched upon this subject in his *Meiji shonen jōyaku kaiseishi no ken-kyū* (Researches on the history of treaty revisions in the early Meiji period). The most recent work is Mōri Toshihiko's article [1] on the composition of the Iwakura embassy, which focuses on the problems attendant on the appointment of Kido Takayoshi as vice-envoy.

The Iwakura embassy was confronted at various points in the course of his mission by questions related not only to the matter of the persecution of Christians in Japan but also the restrictions imposed upon the internal travel of foreigners in Japan. For a full discussion of this topic, see Hirose Shizuko's essay [7] on the question of internal travel by foreigners. Ishii Takashi's *Meiji shoki no kokusai kankei* (International relations in the early Meiji period) also devotes a chapter to this subject.

The Maria Luz Affair.   Concerning the *Maria Luz* affair of 1872, which arose from the release of Chinese coolies aboard the Peruvian ship, the prewar studies of Tabohashi Kiyoshi provide the greatest details. For postwar scholarship, see Kaizuma Haruhiko's essay on Etō Shinpei and the *Maria Luz* affair. The episode is examined as a case study on the legal autonomy of nationals from nonsignatory countries in the previously cited *Nihon Seiji saiban shiroku* (Historical records of Japanese political trials) by Wagatsuma Sakae. Ōyama Azusa's recent study [7] on the trial procedures in the *Maria Luz* affair points out, however, that Tabohashi erred in his interpretation that the foreign consuls stationed in Yokohama attempted to strip Japan of its right to try foreigners from nontreaty nations. As Shimomura Fujio observes in his *Meiji ishin no gaikō* (The diplomacy of the Meiji restoration), one cannot overlook the fact that the issue of the "Sakhalin problem" was an important factor underlying the arbitration decision rendered by the czar in 1875.

The Northern Territories.   On diplomatic policy adopted in the early years of the Meiji government with respect to the "Ezo lands" (which meant both Hokkaidō and Sakhalin), Ōyama Azusa has published a basic article [8]. Drawing upon Japanese materials, he examines shifts in the government's policies. Ōkuma Ryōichi's monograph on the historical background of the northern territories problem gives a general account of this problem in the Bakumatsu and early Meiji years on the basis of both Japanese and foreign sources. Shinobu Seizaburō's succinct essay on the Sakhalin-Kurile islands exchange treaty was written as a rebuttal to arguments advanced by Soviet historians.

Other important works include Oka Yoshitake's essay [4] on Britain and the Ezo lands in the early Meiji years, which makes use of British diplomatic documents; and Ishii Takashi's articles on Russo-Japanese relations in the restoration period [6] and on American Envoy Charles E. De Long's arbitration over the Russo-Japanese boundaries dispute [3]. Ueda Toshio's essays [2], discussing the history of negotiations on territorial possessions [3], deal with not only Sakhalin and the Kuriles but also the Ryūkyūs and the Bonin Islands. The most recent work on the subject is Yasuoka Akio's *Meiji ishin to ryōdo mondai* (The Meiji restoration and territorial questions). Based mainly on Japanese documents, the book surveys the history of negotiations on the northern and southern territories during the Bakumatsu and early Meiji years. Though a compact volume, it contains a comprehensive bibliographical guide to Japanese works on the subject, which will provide a useful guide to research in this field.

RELATIONS WITH KOREA

General Studies

On Japan's diplomatic relations with Korea, there is a considerable accumulation of scholarship from the prewar years, including Tabohashi Kiyoshi's detailed work, *Kindai Nissen kankei no kenkyū* (A study of modern Japanese-Korean relations, 2 vols., originally published in 1940 and reissued 1963); and Okudaira Takehiko, *Chōsen kaikoku kōshō shimatsu* (Diplomatic negotiations concerning the opening of Korea; originally published in 1934 and reissued in 1969).

In the postwar era, Yamabe Kentarō has published a series of studies that are based on exhaustive research into source materials in the National Diet Library (such as the papers of Inoue Kaoru, Tōyō Bunko, and Seikadō Bunko). He has also published a historical survey, *Nikkan heigō shōshi* (A short history of the Japanese annexaion of Korea), which commences with the events leading up to the opening of Korea to the outside world. Shin Kukju's *Kindai Chōsen gaikōshi kenkyū* (A study of the diplomatic history of modern Korea) deals primarily with Japanese-Korean relations from the time of the opening of Korea through the beginning of the Sino-Japanese War.

The Movement to "Invade Korea"

Since the publication of Kemuyama Sentarō's *Seikanron jissō* (The actual facts concerning the movement to "invade Korea") as early as 1907, a considerable number of works have appeared that examine the origins and nature of the so-called "seikanron." In the postwar era, Inoue Kiyoshi in his *Nihon no gunkokushugi* (Militarism in Japan), vol. 1, has argued that as a result of the political changes of 1873 a bureaucratic dictatorship was established in opposition to the samurai militarism of Saigō Takamori and others. Ōe Shinobu's essay [2] on the emergence and significance of the "Invade Korea" debate takes the argument one step further and points to the basic compatibility of Japan's modern imperial state with Saigō's orientation toward a warlike foreign policy. And Fujimura Michio [7] sees the differences as being merely between one of calling for total war (as advocated by Saigō), and one of calling for limited war. Fujimura regards the subjugation of Formosa in 1874 as the implementation of Ōkubo Toshimichi's concept of limited war.

On the other hand, Mōri Toshihiko [2] argues that, while Kido Takayoshi's call for a Korean expedition in the early Meiji years was conceived initially as a strategy for coping with domestic politics, it shortly became the basis of the debate on Japan's Asian policy. In his *Meiji rokunen seihen no kenkyū* (Researches into the political changes of 1873), Mōri historiographically reviews various interpretations of the "invade Korea" debate and breaks sharply with existing scholarship by calling Saigō the "advocate of peaceful negotiations." Subsequently Mōri partially revised this thesis in his *Meiji rokunen seihen* (The political changes of 1873), written for a general readership, but there was no retreat from his hypothesis on Saigō.

Banno Junji [2] agrees with Mōri that even if Saigō had prevailed in the controversy and had gone to Korea as an envoy himself, a Japanese-Korean war would not have ensued. Yet Banno insists that the historical framework of the "internal reforms party" versus "foreign expedition party" is a valid one for explaining Japanese

policy toward Korea and China up to 1876. Writing in response to
Mōri's new thesis, Ōyama Azusa [14] argues that the act of dispatching
a mission to open Korea was by its nature inseparably linked with the
call for invasion. Iechika Yoshiki takes issue with another important
point made by Mōri, i.e., that the political changes of 1873 were
mainly aimed at driving Etō Shinpei out of the government: [2], [3].
Rather, Iechika emphasizes, one of the major factors in the political
changes was a move to eliminate the influence of Foreign Minister
Soejima Taneomi as well as Kuroda Kiyotaka. Scholarly debate will
continue in the future.

The Kanghwa Incident and the Opening of Korea.   This incident of
1875, which brought about a Japanese-Korean crisis, is examined in
detail in Kobayashi Katsumi's article on the Kanghwa incident and
Kido Takayoshi's stand, and Peng Tse-chou (Hō Takushū)'s essay [3]
on the positions of Kido and Itagaki. Both of them discuss this incident
in terms of Kido's stand. An orthodox diplomatic history treatment
is found in Hanabusa Nagamichi's article [1], which deals with the
treaties concluded between Korea and Japan (1876) and between
Korea and the United States (1882). Hirose Shizuko draws on British
sources to elucidate the international environment at the time of the
opening of Korea: [5], [6]. In particular, her studies throw light on the
role played by Envoy Parkes and the British government.

A special edition of a journal for Korean studies, *Kan* (The Han),
issued to celebrate the centennial of the opening of the port at
Kanghwa, includes Ōhata Tokushirō's essay [1] on the Kanghwa treaty
from the viewpoint of the history of treaties. Shin Kukju's article [1]
on Korean-Japanese diplomacy immediately following the Kanghwa
Treaty of 1876 clarifies the contents and significance of the addendum
to the treaty and its provisions on trade, which had previously been
unknown to diplomatic historians.

The Seoul Incidents of 1882 and 1884

These incidents have been one of the focal points of postwar Japanese
scholarship, because of their importance in relations between the
Japanese, Korean, and Ch'ing governments. The first Seoul incident of

1882 is treated in Yamabe Kentarō's article [2] on the Imjin rebellion and Tanaka Naokichi's study [2]. In a separate article [1] Tanaka covers the second Seoul incident of 1884. Yamabe Kentarō's article on the Kabsin incident [3] is solidly based on relevant documents but raises controversial points. On the one hand he is highly critical of the descriptions given in the official history of the Liberal Party (*Jiyūtōshi*, 1910), but at the same time he criticizes the role played by the reformist statesman, Kim Ok-kiun. However, Kang Imon's *Chōsen no jōi to kaika* (Exclusionism and modernization in Korea), from the perspective of intellectual history, evaluates Kim as the founder of a Korean bourgeois political reform movement. Similarly, the collection of essays on *Kin Gyoku-kin no kenkyū* (Studies on Kim Ok-Kiun)— edited by the Center for Historical Studies, People's Democratic Republic of Korea (Chōsen Minshushugi Jinmin Kyōwakoku, Shakai Kagakuin Rekishi Kenkyūjo), and translated and published by the Japanese Institute for Korean Studies—is critical of Yamabe's, and by extension, Tabohashi's interpretations. It credits Kim with a considerably more significant role as a leader calling for the modernization of Korea.

Apart from this issue, there has been a controversy on the authenticity of the account in the official *Jiyūtōshi* on the meeting that purportedly took place between Itagaki and Gotō and the French ambassador to Japan. Peng Tse-chou (Hō Takushū)'s article [1] on the discussions between the Japanese Liberal Party and the French authorities concerning the Korean problem, based on materials from French sources, rebuts the Yamabe thesis which claims that the official account was a fabrication. Peng Tse-chou has also used French diplomatic documents to write several papers on Japan's policy toward Korea during the period of the Sino-French War: [2], [4], [7]. His book, *Meiji shoki Nichi-Kan-Shin kankei no kenkyū* (A study of relations between Japan, Korea, and China in the late nineteenth century), broadly examines the "invade Korea" controversy (Seikanron), Japanese-Korean trade competition, and the cultural policies of Japan and China toward Korea, but it does not discuss the Kabsin rebellion of 1884.

In addition, Nose Kazunori's articles on Takezoe Shin'ichirō and Shimamura Hisashi [2] and on the Sino-French War and Japanese diplomacy [1], both deal with the events surrounding the Kabsin rebellion. Moreover, one must not overlook such specialized studies as Sassa Hirō's article on the Sino-French War and the establishment of the School of Tung-yang hsueh-kuan at Shanghai. Although the study of the Sino-French War is handicapped by the loss of Foreign Ministry documents, which were destroyed by fire, the question of the effect of the war on Japan, apart from its relation to the Korean situation, remains an important task for future research.

One problem in Japanese-Korean relations in the period 1889–1893 was the grain export controversy, but the only noteworthy postwar study on this subject is Karasawa Takeko's article on incidents arising from the prohibition of grain exports.

Concerning the Korean internal reforms of 1894–95, in which Japan participated, Japanese and Korean historians differ in their interpretations, just as they did about Kim Ok-kiun. In addition to Pak Chong-kun's article [2] on the Sino-Japanese War and the Kabo reform (1894–95), there is a detailed introduction to this question in Moriyama Shigenori's essay [2] on research trends on the history of modern Japanese-Korean relations.

New developments in research on Japanese-Korean relations are now appearing from a number of organizations whose membership includes Korean scholars. Among such organizations are: Chōsenshi Kenkyūkai (Association for the Study of Korean History), whose monograph series *Chōsenshi Kenkyūkai ronbunshū* numbers twenty four volumes to date; Chōsen Gakkai (The Academic Association of Koreanology in Japan), which publishes its journal *Chōsen gakuhō*; and Kankoku Kenkyūin (Tokyo Institute for Korean Studies), which publishes *Kan* (The Han).

THE SINO-JAPANESE WAR: ITS PRELUDE AND AFTERMATH

The Sino-Japanese Treaty of 1871

The Treaty of Peace, Commerce and Navigation between China and Japan, signed in 1871, marks the beginning of modern diplomatic relations on an equal basis between Japan and China. This subject had been studied in detail by Tabohashi Kiyoshi as early as 1930. In the postwar period, the process of concluding this treaty was examined by Fujimura Michio in his articles on the new Meiji government's response to the old system of international relations [2], and on the change in Japanese policy toward China in the early Meiji [4].

The Question of the Ryūkyū Islands

In recent years there has been an increasing amount of research by scholars from Okinawa working on the subject of the Meiji government's disposition of the Ryūkyūs. Two of the earliest postwar works were Satō Saburō's article [3] on the disposition of the Ryūkyū domain and Ueda Toshio's article [3] on Sino-Japanese negotiations on jurisdiction over the Ryūkyūs, which clarifies the negotiating points on both sides. Hanabusa Nagamichi's article [3] on the history of sovereignty over Okinawa presents a general survey of the Ryūkyū problem on the basis of Japanese, Chinese, and Ryūkyūan sources. Ōyama Azusa [13] has also written on the Sino-Japanese dispute concerning jurisdiction over the Ryūkyūs, and Fujimura Michio [6] examines the diplomatic negotiations over the Ryūkyū Islands in the context of shifting Japanese policy toward Asia. Two Okinawan scholars have published collections of previously printed articles: Kinjō Seitoku, *Ryūkyū shobunron* (Essays on the disposition of the Ryūkyūs); and Gabe Masao, *Meiji kokka to Okinawa* (The Meiji state and Okinawa).

The Formosan Expedition

The question of the Ryūkyū Islands cannot be studied apart from the Formosan expedition, a comprehensive treatment of which may be found in Hanabusa Nagamichi's article [4] on the 1874 incident of Taiwanese aborigines and Watanabe Ikujirō's essay on the Formosan expedition. Koh Se-kai's article on the Taiwan incidents (1871–74) makes use of Chinese sources. The reader is also referred to Segawa Yoshinobu's article [2] on the Formosan expedition of 1874, and Kurihara Jun's article, which sees the Formosan expedition as a turning point in the policy toward the Ryūkyūs.

The Sino-Japanese War

Sino-Japanese relations, worsened by the problem of the Ryūkyū islands and Formosa, came to a head over Korea and led to the outbreak of hostilities in 1894.

The Tonghak rebellion of 1894 provided both China and Japan with the excuse to send troops to Korea. Shin Kukju's article [2] examines the Tonghak problem and the outbreak of the Sino-Japanese War. There is a tendency, among Korean scholars living in Japan, to regard and evaluate the Tonghak rebellion as the "peasants' uprising of 1884."

On the Sino-Japanese War itself there is the prewar pioneering work by Shinobu Seizaburō, *Mutsu gaikō: Nisshin sensō no gaikōshiteki kenkyū* (Mutsu diplomacy: A historical study of the diplomacy of the Sino-Japanese War), which examines the causes of the war, pointing to Japan's "dual diplomacy" pursued by diplomats and the military. As another cause of the war, Shinobu emphasizes the "imperatives of Japanese industrial capital." However, postwar research has shown, on the basis of analyses of the actual conditions of international trade at the time, that Japan's bourgeoisie was not particularly desirous of entering the Korean market. Furthermore, Nakatsuka Akira's *Nisshin sensō no kenkyū* (A study of the Sino-Japanese War) rejects the dual diplomacy thesis and sees the war as a logical outcome of a government under an "absolutist imperial system." On the other hand, Fujimura Michio's *Nisshin sensō* (The Sino-Japanese War) is based on the author's wide-ranging research and attempts a synthesis of the military, diplomatic, and political aspects.

The Triple Intervention and the Treaty of Shimonoseki

In his study [3] of diplomatic strategy and leadership with respect to the Sino-Japanese War, Hiyama Yukio concentrates on the problem of how the conditions for the peace were determined through several stages. Nakatsuka Akira, in his above-mentioned *Nisshin sensō no kenkyū*, devotes a chapter to an analysis of the "provisional draft of the Treaty of Shimonoseki." Tabohashi Kiyoshi's *Nisshin sen'eki gaikōshi no kenkyū* (A study of the diplomatic history of the Sino-Japanese War), published posthumously in 1951, is the final work of this scholar; it covers the war from its prelude through the peace negotiations. Its approach can be gleaned from the subtitle: "Research on the international political history of East Asia."

Among studies that examine the question of the Triple Intervention from the perspective of theories of international relations, the most informative is Abe Kōzō's article [3] on the treaty of Shimonoseki and the Triple Intervention, which follows the events through the return of the Liaotung Peninsula to China. After Japan felt compelled to accept the conditions of the tripartite intervention, the only remaining area for its expansion pointed to Formosa. Recent studies have brought open the previously neglected ("tabooed" in pre–World War II days) subject of the Taiwanese resistance movement to Japanese rule. Notable works on the subject are: Teh Ten-chiau's essay on the Triple Intervention and Formosa; Huang Chao-t'ang's articles on Japan's seizure of Taiwan [1] and on the Republic of Taiwan [2]; and Koh Sa-Kai's essay on Taiwan under Japanese rule.

On the murder of Queen Min of Korea (October 8, 1895)—"the incident of 1895"—both Yamabe Kentarō [1] and Pak Chon-kun [1] argue that it may have been the Japanese military rather than civilians who played the prinicipal role in the assassination.

THE REVISION OF THE UNEQUAL TREATIES

The basic source materials for the negotiations concerning treaty revision have been published as Gaimushō (Foreign Ministry) ed., *Jōyaku kaisei kankei Nihon gaikō bunsho* (Documents on Japanese foreign policy: Treaty revision), 4 vols. and a supplementary volume, *Jōyaku kaisei keika gaiyō* (A summary of the development of treaty revision). As for survey histories, no full-scale study has been published since Yamamoto Shigeru's *Jōyaku kaiseishi* (A history of treaty revision) appeared in 1943. The only study that is worthy of mention is Inoue Kiyoshi's *Jōyaku kaisei* (Treaty revision).

The early stages of treaty revision are covered in Shimomura Fujio's monograph, *Meiji shonen jōyaku kaiseishi no kenkyū* (Research on the history of treaty revision in the early Meiji period), which uses, among others, American sources and covers the period from the drafting of the proposal for treaty revision through the Iwakura embassy's negotiations in the United States. Hanabusa Nagamichi's article [2] surveys the course of the negotiations to revise the unequal treaties. Essays that discuss the principals responsible for the negotiations as they developed are numerous. Ōyama Azusa [3] studies the drafts for treaty revision by Iwakura and Terashima, and Inō Tentarō [3] discusses the so-called Ōkuma treaty draft. Hirose Shizuko [3] examines Inoue's treaty revision diplomacy, while Sakane Yoshihisa [1] addresses himself to Foreign Minister Aoki Shūzō's negotiations with England on treaty revision. One work that deals with a question closely related to treaty revision is Ōyama Azusa's article [5] on treaty revision and foreign judges.

Foreign Settlements

Ōyama Azusa [4] has also published an article on treaty revision and the foreign settlements, and another essay on this subject that is contained in his *Kyū jōyakuka ni okeru kaishi kaikō no kenkyū* (A study of open cities and ports under the old treaty system). Akimoto Masutoshi's article [2] on the Yokohama and Shanghai foreign settlements presents a comparative analysis of the Japanese and Chinese situations. In addition, Tōkairin Shizuo examines the attitudes of foreign missionaries resident in Yokohama, Tokyo, Osaka, and Kobe during the period when Foreign Minister Aoki was conducting negotiations on treaty revision. It concludes that the missionaries and others who hoped for early revision of the treaties did so out of a desire for the freedom to pursue their evangelical activities. This included a desire for the abolition of the foreign settlements, and permission for foreigners to live and travel in the interior.

The Debate Over Westernization

Inō Tentarō has made a bibliographical study [5] of books and magazines of the period to throw light on trends in domestic public opinion regarding treaty revision and the question of permitting foreigners to live in the interior. Together with his research on early official drafts for treaty revision, his works are collected in his book *Jōyaku kaiseiron no rekishiteki tenkai* (The historical development of the call for treaty revision).

On Meiji Japan's perceptions of the external world, Oka Yoshitake has written several distinguished essays. One of them [3] analyzes the perceptions of Japan's international situation as revealed in representative newspapers supporting the popular rights movement during the years 1879–1881. It clearly brings out the acute sense of external crisis felt in the age of imperialism. He has also written articles on the Sino-Japanese War and the Japanese attitude toward foreign countries [5] and on the controversy over treaty revision and Japanese perceptions of the powers [2]. The latter two articles examine the arguments of such leading intellectuals as Fukuzawa Yukichi and Taguchi Ukichi, as well as of the organs of political parties.

Among contemporary articles and editorials dealing with Japan's relations with the rest of the world, Fukuzawa Yukichi's 1885 editorial "Datsu-A ron" (Throwing off Asia) has often been cited as an example of his view of Asia; it has been quoted as indicating his transition from the "reconstruction" to the "conquest" of Asia. Taking issue with this conventional interpretation, Banno Junji, in his *Meiji: Shisō no jitsuzō* (Meiji concepts of Asia: Reality and ideology), closely analyzes Fukuzawa's views on international affairs during the period of the Seoul incidents (1882–84), and he concludes that Fukuzawa's views of Asia was actually more aggressive when he was advocating the "reconstruction of Korea" than after he came to call for "throwing off Asia." In a chapter dealing with Japanese perceptions at the time of the Chinese revolution of 1911, Banno points out that there was one thing in common between Fukuzawa from 1877 to 1886 and General Yamagata Aritomo from 1907 to 1912: in both cases, the call for "throwing off Asia" basically stemmed from the realization that China should never be underestimated. While so many scholars tend to take the rhetorics of intellectuals at face value, Banno's study is noteworthy for utilizing a new methodology in order to question the conventional wisdom and present new interpretations.

The views on foreign affairs of Kuga Katsunan, who was a critic of "throwing off Asia," are now receiving considerable scholarly attention. One example is Tōyama Shigeki's essay on Kuga's views on foreign policy, analyzing his editorials written during the Sino-Japanese War period. Recently, there has been a considerable amount of research on the so-called "hard-line" or chauvinistic view of foreign relations, as seen in studies such as Sakeda Masatoshi's *Kindai Nihon ni okeru taigaikō undō no kenkyū* (Research on the chauvinistic foreign policy movement in modern Japan), Sakai Yūkichi's article on Konoe Atsumaro and chauvinism around the turn of the century, and Miyaji Masato's essay on the nationalistic chauvinism of this period.

The Ōtsu Incident

The Ōtsu incident of 1891, in which the crown prince of Russia on a visit to Japan was attacked and wounded by a Japanese, occurred when Aoki Shūzō was foreign minister. Taoka Ryōichi's distinguished study, *Ōtsu jikin no saihyōka* (A reappraisal of the Ōtsu incident) examines this question from the viewpoint of international law. Kino Kazue has published an article on the Ōtsu incident and Inoue Kowashi, pointing out that Japan's terms for the settlement of this incident accorded with the memorandum submitted by Alessandro Paternostro, an influential Italian adviser to the Japanese Ministry of Justice. It is to be hoped that studies utilizing Russian sources will appear in the future.

The Boxer Rebellion

There are several excellent studies on specific aspects of the rebellion. Inō Tentarō has written an article [1] on the Boxer Rebellion and the diplomacy of Japan's expedition—the dispatching of a contingent of Japanese troops to China. Nakatsuka Akira's article discusses "Japanese imperialism" and the suppression of the Boxer Rebellion. For Japanese response to the rebellion, see Kawamura Kazuo [3] and Yamaguchi Kazuyuki. Yet there is no single work that comprehensively treats the Japanese response to the Boxer Rebellion. *Giwadan no kenkyū* (A study of the Boxers), the posthumous work of Muramatsu Yūji, a specialist in East Asian history, shows the strong influence of Tabohashi Kiyoshi's article on Russo-Japanese relations and the Boxer Rebellion, devoting a chapter to the military contingents sent by each foreign power.

For source materials there is *Hokushin jihen* (The Boxer Rebellion), a three-volume supplement to the Foreign Ministry's *Nihon gaikō bunsho* (Documents on Japanese foreign policy). On the Peking or

Boxer protocol of 1901, Sugano Tadashi's article traces the process of concluding the protocol, with special attention to Minister Komura's negotiations.

The Amoy Incident

In 1900, during the Boxer Rebellion, there was an abortive attempt on the part of a Japanese military group to occupy Amoy. Japanese documents relating to the deliberations on this maneuver have been lost, and it is unclear whether this resulted from the frustration of the Japanese government's southward advance policy or a local action executed by the military and consular officials with the collusion of the Formosan governor-general's office. Articles by Kotani Yoshiko and Satō Saburō [1] both see the plan to dispatch troops as an act of the government originating in Tokyo. To support their argument, they rely on the account found in the official biography of Gotō Shinpei by Tsurumi Yūsuke. Its second volume covers the period when Gōto was in the Formosan Governor-General's office. Quoted in this biography is an observation that sees Navy Minister Yamamoto Gonnohyōe as the driving force behind the Yamagata cabinet's plan to dispatch troops. On the other hand, Ōyama Azusa [1] argues that the above-mentioned scholars have ignored basic materials in the Navy Ministry. Using the official history of the navy to bolster his point, he contends that the Tokyo government attempted to put a stop to the local agencies which so willfully misinterpreted the cabinet deicision in order to launch the attack.

Other works on this question include articles by Kawamura Kazuo [1], Yamamoto Shirō, and Takahashi Shigeo, the last of which examines the position of Navy Minister Yamamoto. However, these works, too, offer differing opinions about the reason why the plan was aborted, so that there is no definitive interpretation. The problems of the Amoy incident, with its many mysteries, are well-organized and presented in Mukōyama Hiroo's essay on the Amoy incident and the Waichow revolt; Mukōyama also suggests a relationship between this incident and the failure of a military uprising led by Sun Yat-sen at Waichow in Canton Province, which occurred at the same time. Other works include: Nakamura Naomi's article [2] on Japan's Asian policy after the Sino-Japanese War, which examines the

Amoy incident from the perspective of the Korean problem; and Iwakabe Yoshimitsu's study [1] on administration in South China after the Sino-Japanese War. Iwakabe examines the call for construction of railroads in southern China at the time when the Japanese government adopted a state policy that called for "protection of the north while advancing to the south."

The Anglo-Japanese Alliance

Studies on the Anglo-Japanese Alliance include articles by Shigemitsu Osamu, Ueda Toshio [1], Murashima Shigeru, and Imai Shōji [3], [4].

On the relationship between the Anglo-Japanese Alliance and the question of railways in China, Inoue Yūichi has published an essay [3] on the construction of the Peking-Pusan railway, solidly based on both the Japanese and British archives. The nature of this article is indicated by its subtitle: the railway question as a factor in the formation of the Anglo-Japanese Alliance. Inoue has also written a series of related articles dealing with such subjects as the Seoul-Wiju railway as a factor in the coming of the Russo-Japanese War [4]; and Japan's construction of a railroad for military use during the Russo-Japanese War [5].

The broad historical background of the alliance is found in Uchiyama Masakuma's essay [3], tracing pro-British feelings in Japan. This essay is contained in his book *Gendai Nihon gaikō shiron* (Historical essays on modern Japan's diplomacy).

Factual details with a modicum of analytical interpretation are presented in Kajima's series on Japanese diplomatic history, vol. 6: *Daiikkai Nichi-Ei dōmei to sono zengo* (The first Anglo-Japanese Alliance); vol. 8: *Dainikai Nichi-Ei dōmei to sono jidai* (The second Anglo-Japanese alliance); and vol. 9: *Daisankai Nichi-Ei dōmei* (The third Anglo-Japanese Alliance). All of these volumes were authored by Kajima Morinosuke himself. A more compact treatment is Kajima's *Nichi-Ei gaikōshi* (A history of Anglo-Japanese diplomatic relations).

Kurobane Shigeru's *Nichi-Ei dōmei no kenkyū* (A study of the history of the Anglo-Japanese alliance) is the only monographic work available on the entire history of the alliance; the author traces its formation in 1902 to subsequent changes and to its termination in 1922. It would be fair to observe that Japanese scholarship on the

Anglo-Japanese Alliance has yet to produce a major monograph that is comparable to Ian Nish's superb two-volume study: *The Anglo-Japanese Alliance: The Diplomacy of Two Island Empires, 1894–1907* (London: Athlone Press, 1966); and *Alliance in Decline: A Study in Anglo-Japanese Relations, 1908–23* (1972).

THE RUSSO-JAPANESE WAR

As early as 1927 there was a controversy over the nature of the Russo-Japanese War within a broader framework of an academic debate on the nature of Japanese capitalism. One school defined the Russo-Japanese War as a war of defense against the threat posed by tsarist Russia. The other school, committed to the thesis of "Japanese imperialism," argued that the imperatives inherent in a backward capitalist nation like Japan compelled it to a monopolistic control of Manchuria, which in turn led to an inevitable war with Russia. This latter interpretation was advanced, for example, by Shinobu Seizaburō in his survey work, *Kindai Nihon gaikōshi* (The diplomatic history of modern Japan), which appeared in 1942.

In the years since World War II, the nature of the Russo-Japanese War has become a key issue in the academic debate over the periodization of Japan's modern history, particularly with reference to the rise of imperialism. In his *Nihon no gunkokushugi* (Militarism in Japan), left-wing historian Inoue Kiyoshi asserted that the Russo-Japanese War was in and of itself an imperialistic war, whereas Moriya Fumio argues in his *Shinpan Nihon shihonshugi hattatsushi* (A history of capitalistic developments in Japan) that it was Japan's victory in the war that marked the emergence of Japanese imperialism.

The joint research project on the Russo-Japanese War by historians at Nagoya University (the so-called "Nagoya group") resulted in the publication in 1959 of an important volume, *Nichi-Ro sensōshi no kenkyū* (Studies on the history of the Russo-Japanese War), jointly edited by Shinobu Seizaburō and Nakayama Jiichi. Two members of the team that contributed to this work, Shimomura Fujio and Fujimura Michio, caused something of a historical controversy by expressing their dissenting view; they argued that the Russo-Japanese War can hardly be said to have resulted from the bourgeoisie's demands for a Manchurian market when one examines the stage of development of domestic industrial capital and the then prevailing mood in Japan's economic circles. Their contentions against Marxist interpretations are also found in Shimomura's articles on the nature of the Russo-Japanese War [3] and on the Russo-Japanese War and the Manchurian market [4], and Fujimura's interpretive essay [5] on the nature of the Russo-Japanese War. In 1962 *Kokusai seiji,* the organ of Nihon Kokusai Seiji Gakkai (Japan Association of International Relations), featured the Sino-Japanese and Russo-Japanese wars. This special issue contains, in addition to research articles, a useful historiographical essay on the two wars, written by four members of the Nagoya group.

Japan's diplomatic relations with Korea in the period from the Sino-Japanese War through the Russo-Japanese War are discussed in Maejima Shōzō's article. On the so-called Masan incident (caused by Russian leasing of land in Masan, Korea in 1900), Yamawaki Shigeo has written a detailed study based on Japanese Foreign Ministry records. This study was followed by Ōyama Azusa's article [10]. A new view on the matter of Russian leasing of territory at Yongam, Korea in 1903 is also presented in his article [12] on the Yongam incident.

Russo-Japanese diplomatic relations and diplomacy prior to the commencement of hostilities are examined in articles by Ōhata Tokushirō [2] and Ōyama Azusa [11] respectively.

On the conduct of diplomacy during the war, Matsumura Masayoshi has written an interesting article [1] on the Russo-Japanese War and Japan's public relations diplomacy. This article is the summary of a portion of the same author's detailed monograph, *Nichi-Ro sensō to Kaneko Kentarō: Kōhō gaikō no kenkyū* (The Russo-Japanese War and Kaneko Kentarō: A study in public relations diplomacy). The author's new approach, particularly his emphasis on "public relations diplomacy"—a concept that had not been used before in the study of diplomatic history—is refreshing and noteworthy.

Among the works devoted to Russo-Japanese peace negotiations, Yoshimura Michio's article concentrates on the Japanese position with respect to China. Likewise, Satō Saburō's study [2] on the military administration of occupied territory in Manchuria during the Russo-Japanese War takes up the subject in the context of the history of Sino-Japanese relations. Ōyama Azusa's monograph, *Nichi-Ro sensō no gunsei shiroku* (Historical records of military administration during the Russo-Japanese War) is a comprehensive treatment of the subject, including the military administration of Sakhalin and the enemy territory occupied outside of Manchuria. This work is also useful because it prints many relevant source materials.

General histories of the war include: Furuya Tetsuo's compact volume on the Russo-Japanese War and Kurobane Shigeru's *Sekaishijō yori mitaru Nichi-Ro sensō* (The Russo-Japanese War as seen from the standpoint of world history). A revised version of Shinobu Seizaburō and Nakayama Jiichi, eds., *Nichi-Ro sensōshi no kenkyū* (Studies on the history of the Russo-Japanese War) appeared in 1972; it is especially valuable for its comprehensive bibliography. The Russo-Japanese War has many aspects, including not only domestic and foreign policy and military matters, but also industrial and economic problems, so that multilateral studies elucidating these complex features are needed in the future.

The Japanese-Soviet Historical Symposium; held every other year since 1973, alternately in Tokyo and Moscow, took up as one of its themes at the fourth conference (Moscow, 1979) "The Russo-Japanese War in World History," but the papers presented by both Japanese and Soviet scholars tended to concentrate on topics related to military history and strategy. Ōe Shinobu, who presented a paper at the symposium, has published *Nichi-Ro sensō no gunjishiteki kenkyū* (A study on the military history of the Russo-Japanese War). It presents well-documented research on the wartime military arrangements. For Ōe, this war, as the world's first full-scale war fought between imperialist powers, was an epoch-making event. Among military histories, Tani Hisao's *Kimitsu Nichi-Ro senshi* (Confidential history of the Russo-Japanese War) is most valuable for its presentation of hitherto confidential archival materials of the army. First prepared as a text for a special advanced course at the Army Staff College, it was finally published in 1966. Other works in this area include Sanbō Honbu (Army General Staff), ed., *Himitsu Nichi-Ro senshi* (Secret history of the Russo-Japanese War).

For diplomatic documents on this crucial period, see Foreign Ministry, ed., *Nichi-Ro sensō* (The Russo-Japanese War), a five-volume supplement to *Nihon gaikō bunsho* (Documents on Japanese foreign policy).

PERSONALITIES IN MEIJI DIPLOMACY

Foreign Employees

Foreigners in the employ of the Japanese government made a definite contribution to building a modern state. The role of these foreigners who worked behind the scenes in Meiji diplomatic affairs is not to be overlooked. For example, the Iwakura embassy was sent overseas in part on the "suggestion" of Guido H. F. Verbeck, Dutch advisor to the Japanese government.

The best introduction to the subject is Umetani Noboru's *Oyatoi gaikokujin: Meiji Nihon no wakiyaku tach:* (Foreign employees: Hidden contributors to Meiji Japan). In this compact yet readable volume, the author expertly sketches the accomplishments of fourteen foreigners who were hired to work in a variety of fields.

The subject receives a closer examination in seventeen volumes— *Oyatoi gaikokujin* (Foreigners in the employ of the Japanese government)—in wide-ranging fields (including medicine, fine arts, architecture, music, and many other areas). Quite readable and informative, these volumes provide fascinating accounts of intercultural relations. Umetani wrote the first volume, *Gaisetsu* (Introductory survey), in which he systematically discusses the historic roles of these foreign employees and their contributions to Japan's modernization. It will be sufficent here to list other volumes in this series with particular relevance to our purposes—vol. 2: *Sangyō* (industry and business), by Yoshida Mitsukuni; vol. 5: *Kyōiku, Shūkyō* (Education and Religion), by Shigehisa Tokutarō; vol. 6: *Gunji* (Military affairs), by Takahashi Kunitarō; and vol. 11: *Seiji hōsei* (Political and legal institutions), by Umetani. This volume by Umetani prints in addendum the above-mentioned draft (in Japanese translation) of Guido Herman Fridolin Verbeck's advice ("Brief Sketch") to Ōkuma Shigenobu on the Iwakura embassy. Vol. 12: *Gaikō* (Dilomacy), by Imai Shōji describes foreigners who served as advisors to the Japanese Foreign Ministry.

The last-mentioned volume examines contributions made by foreign employees to Japanese diplomacy. The author traces the careers and activities of such individuals as E. Pershine Smith, the first foreign adviser to the Foreign Ministry; Alexander G. G. von Siebold; Durham W. Stevens; and Henry Willard Denison. The most important among them, Denison was employed by the Foreign Ministry from 1880 to 1914. His story has also been warmly told in Shidehara

Kijūrō's diplomatic memoirs, *Gaikō gojūnen* (Fifty years as a diplomat). Also, former ambassador Ōno Katsumi's essay on Denison's "singular devotion" is printed in *Gaimushō no hyakunen* (A century of the Japanese Foreign Ministry) edited by Gaimushō Hyakunenshi Hensan Iinkai, vol. 2.

Another American, far more colorful than Denison, who was deeply involved in Japanese diplomacy is Charles W. Le Gendre. A portion of written diplomatic opinions presented by Le Gendre, preserved in the Ōkuma Papers at Waseda University, was printed in Nakamura Naomi's article [3]. The first volume of Ōkuma monjo (The Okuma papers), published in 1958, contains three items by Le Gendre and two by Gustave E. Boissonade on the Formosan expedition. On the Frenchman Boissonade, who played an important role as a legal adviser to the Meiji government, we have Ōkubo Yasuo's *Nihon kindai hō no chichi: Boasonado* (Boissonāde: The father of modern law in Japan).

Interest in foreign employees has grown in recent years. In 1975 a basic list of foreigners who were hired in the years between 1868 and 1889 was compiled as *Shiryō: Oyatoi gaikokujin* (Source materials on foreign employees). This volume contains very useful introductory essays, commentaries on each field or area and a bibliography and locations of manuscript sources. A product of cooperation between Japanese and American scholars is Ardath W. Burks, ed., *The Modernizers: Overseas Students, Foreign Employees, and Meiji Japan* (Boulder: Westview Press, 1985).

Leaders of Meiji Diplomacy

A special 1967 issue of *Kokusai seiji* (no. 33) was devoted to Japan's foreign policy leadership. For the Meiji period, the following essays are relevant: Yasuoka Akio on Foreign Minister Inoue Kaoru [2] and Sakane Yoshihisa [1] on Foreign Minister Aoki Shūzō, with special emphasis on his diplomatic strategy and negotiations with Britain for treaty revision. (Aoki's autobiography, edited by Sakane, was published in 1970.) On Soejima Taneomi, who presided over the Foreign Ministry in the years 1871–73, there are the following works: Kobayashi Rokurō's article on the Meiji government and Le Gendre; and Itō Kazuhiko's essay on Soejima's position on the debate over the Formosan expedition in 1872–73. Research on Terashima Munenori, foreign minister during 1873–79, has been scanty. It is to be expected, however, that more studies will appear with the publication of Terashima Munenori Kenkyūkai, ed., *Terashima Munenori kankei shiryo* (Papers relating to Terashima Munenori).

Regarding Foreign Minister Mutsu, Tamura Kōsaku has written an article evaluating Mutsu's diplomacy on the basis of the following standards: Japan's international position at the time; the degree of difficulty of the problems at hand; the appropriateness of the national policy formulated by the foreign minister; the domestic situation; skill in implementing foreign policy; and the results of policy execution. Mutsu's own account of his diplomatic strategy at the time of the Sino-Japanese War is *Kenkenroku* (Memoirs of a devoted subject). The English version of these important memoirs has been prepared by Gordon M. Berger as *Kenkenroku: A Diplomatic Record of the Sino-Japanese War, 1894–95* (Princeton University Press, 1982). A new edition of this valuable record has recently been published with careful annotations by Nakatsuka Akira. The introductory essay by Nakatsuka throws new light on the circumstances under which this memoirs was published. In addition, Hiyama Yukio [2] has published a bibliographical study on Mutsu's manuscript.

The accomplishments of Foreign Minister Komura Jutarō rank clearly with those of Mutsu Munemitsu. On Komura, we have Shinobu Junpei's superb diplomatic biography, *Komura gaikōshi* (A history of Komura diplomacy), originally published in 1933 as a supplementary volume to Foreign Ministry, ed., *Nihon gaikō bunsho* (Documents on Japanese foreign policy). Subsequently it was extensively revised by Usui Katsumi, who utilized collateral documents, and was republished in 1953 and reprinted in 1966.

Okamoto Shumpei has written a stimulating reappraisal of Komura diplomacy. It reexamines the earlier role of Komura as minister to China and also touches on the view of China held by his Sinologist advisor, Naitō Konan. Okamoto points out that Komura's inflexibly hard-line attitude toward China at the time of the Peking negotiations in 1904 was one of "utter disregard for China."

In a similar vein, Sugano Tadashi, in his article on the process of the conclusion of the Boxer protocol, attributes Japan's inability to obtain nothing but a relatively small indemnity to the nation's international position at the time and to the immaturity of its diplomatic skills. Komura's two greatest diplomatic achievements are said to be the conclusion of the Anglo-Japanese Alliance and the fruits of the Russo-Japanese War, but Uchiyama Masakuma [2] has published a severe indictment of Komura on these scores as well.

Whatever the case may be, a reexamination and reappraisal of historical figures from fresh viewpoints seem to be in order. Much more research is needed not only on the leaders who played a key role in diplomatic history but also on their subordinates and supporters. For example, one can cite highly readable works by Shimada Kinji, a specialist in comparative literature, who has published pioneering works on legendary naval heroes. *Roshia ni okeru Hirose Takeo* (Lieutenant Commander Hirose Takeo in Russia) is Shimada's first venture into a study of nationalism in the Meiji period. It was followed by *Amerika ni okeru Akiyama Saneyuki* (Lieutenant Akiyama Saneyuki in the United States), which describes in detail, on the basis of extensive research in American and Japanese materials, the full portrait of the young lieutenant studying in the United States and preparing himself to become the "mastermind of the Battle of the Japan Sea" during the Russo-Japanese War. It discusses not only naval-strategic aspects but also the diplomatic and political background of the period under study, 1897–99.

Bibliography

Note: The author would like to acknowledge the assistance of Iwakabe Yoshimitsu, a doctoral candidate at the graduate school of Hōsei University, in compiling the original bibliography.

Abe Kōzō 阿部光蔵. "Bakumatsuki Nichi-Ro kankei" 幕末日露関係 (Russo-Japanese relations during the Bakumatsu period). *Kokusaihō gaikō zasshi* (March 1962), 60(4–6):5–38. [1]
—— "Bakumatsuki Nichi-Ro kankei: Karafuto kokkyō kakutei kōshō o chū-shin to shite" 幕末期日露関係：樺太国境劃定交渉を中心として (Russo-Japanese relations during the Bakumatsu period: Focusing on the negotiations over the border settlement of Sakhalin). *Kokusai seiji* (1960), no. 14: *Nihon gaikōshi kenkyū: Bakumatsu ishin jidai,* pp. 44–58. [2]
—— "Nisshin kōwa to sangoku kanshō" 日清講和と三国干渉 (The treaty of Shimonoseki and the Triple Intervention) *Kokusai seiji* (1961), no. 19: *Nisshin Nichi-Ro sensō,* pp. 52–70. [3]
Abe Seiji 阿部誠士. "Roshia no Kyokutō seisaku to Karafuto Kushunkotan

senkyo" ロシアの極東政策と樺太久春古丹占拠 (Russia's Far Eastern policy and its occupation of Kushunkotan on Sakhalin). *Shakai keizai shigaku* (December 1979), 45(4):64–80.

Aihara Ryōichi 相原良一. *Tenpō 8-nen Bei-sen Morisongō torai no kenkyū* 天保8年米船モリソン号渡来の研究 (A study on the arrival of the U.S.S. *Morrison* in 1838). Yajinsha, 1945.

Akimoto Masutoshi 秋本益利. "Beikoku no tai-Nichi seisaku to Nichi-Bei washin jōyaku no teiketsu" 米国の対日政策と日米和親条約の締結 (America's policy toward Japan and the conclusion of the Treaty of Amity and Friendship in 1854). *Kokusai seiji* (1960), no. 14: *Nihon gaikōshi kenkyū: Bakumatsu ishin jidai*, pp. 14–29. [1]

—— "Yokohama kyoryūchi to Shanhai sokai" 横浜居留地と上海租界 (The Yokohama and Shanghai foreign settlements). In Kyoto Daigaku Bunga-kubu Dokushikai, ed., *Kokushi ronshū*, 2:1475–1492. Dokushikai, 1959. [2]

Akizuki Toshiyuki 秋月俊幸. "Bakumatsu Karafuto ni okeru Nichi-Ro zakkyo no seiritsu katei" 幕末樺太における日露雑居の成立過程 (A history of Japanese-Russian mixed residence in Sakhalin during the Bakumatsu period). *Hoppō bunka kenkyū* (1977), no. 11, pp. 63–81; (1979), no. 12, pp. 171–206. [1]

—— "Kaei-nenkan Roshia no Kushunkotan senkyo" 嘉永年間ロシアの久春古丹占拠 (Russian occupation of Kushunkotan during the Kaei era [1853–54]). *Surabu kenkyū* (August 1974), no. 19, 59–95. [2]

Aoki Shūzō 青木周蔵 (revised and annotated by Sakane Yoshihisa 坂根義久). *Aoki Shūzō jiden* 青木周蔵自伝 (The autobiography of Aoki Shūzō). Heibonsha, 1979.

Ayuzawa Shintarō 鮎沢信太郎. "Bakumatsu ishin shijō ni an'yaku shita kaigaijin Suneru" 幕末維新史上に暗躍した怪外人スネル (The mysterious foreigner Schnell and the secret role he played in the history of the Bakumatsu/early restoration years). *Nihon rekishi* (April 1962), no. 166, pp. 27–35.

Banno Junji 坂野潤治. *Meiji: Shisō no jitsuzō* 明治・思想の実像 (Meiji concepts of Asia: Reality and ideology). Sōbunsha, 1977.

—— "Meiji shoki [1873–85] no 'taigaikan'" 明治初期(1873—85)の「対外観」 (Japanese views of China in the early Meiji [1873–85]). *Kokusai seiji* (1982), no. 71, *Nihon gaikō no shisō*, pp. 10–20. [1]

—— "Seikan ronsō go no 'naichiha' to 'gaiseiha'" 征韓論争後の「内治派」と「外征派」 (The "internal reforms" party and the "foreign expedition" party after the "invade Korea" controversy). *Nenpō Kindai Nihon kenkyū*, no. 3: *Bakumatsu-ishin no Nihon* 年報近代日本研究, No. 3—幕末・維新の日本 (Studies in modern Japan, no. 3: Japan in the Bakumatsu restoration period), pp. 245–62.

Chōsen Gakkai 朝鮮学会 (The Academic Association of Koreanology in Japan), ed., *Chōsen gakuhō* 朝鮮学報 (Journal of the Academic Association of Koreanology in Japan).

Chōsen Minshushugi Jinmin Kyōwakoku, Shakai Kagakuin Rekishi Kenkyūjo 朝鮮民主主義人民共和国社会科学院歴史研究所 (The Center for Historical Studies, People's Democratic Republic of Korea), ed.; Nihon Chōsen Kenkyūjo 日本朝鮮研究所 (The Japanese Institute for Korean Studies), tr., *Kin Gyoku Kin no kenkyū* 金玉均の研究 (Studies on Kim Ok-kyiun). Nihon Chōsen Kenkyūjo, 1968.

Fujii Sadafumi 藤井貞文. "Bakumatsu gaikō ni okeru shinkyō jiyū no mondai" 幕末外交に於ける信教自由の問題 (The problem of religious freedom in the Bakumatsu period). *Kokugakuin zasshi* (June 1965), 66(6): 1–15. [1]

—— "Gokakoku jōyaku no teiketsu to shinkyō no jiyū" 五箇国条約の締結と信教の自由 (On the commercial treaties between Japan and five countries in the Bakumatsu period and the problem of the freedom of religion). *Kokugakuin zasshi* (February 1975), 76(2): 1–15. [2]

—— "Nichi-Ei jōyaku no kenkyū" 日英条約の研究 (A study on Japan's first treaty with Great Britain). *Kokugakuin daigaku kiyō* (March 1978), no. 16, pp. 1–34. [3]

—— "Uragami kyōto mondai o meguru Nichi-Futsu kankei: Bakumatsuhen" 浦上教徒問題を廻る日仏関係—幕末篇 (Franco-Japanese relations concerning Christians in Uragami: the Bakumatsu period). In Kaikoku 100-nen Kinen Bunka Jigyōkai, ed., *Kaikoku hyakunen kinen Meiji bunkashi ronshū* 開国百年記念明治文化史論集 (Essays on Meiji cultural history in commemoration of the centennial of Japan's opening to the West), pp. 73–121. Kengensha, 1952. [4]

Fujimura Michio 藤村道生. "Chōsen ni okeru Nihon tokubetsu kyoryūchi no kigen" 朝鮮における日本特別居留地の起源 (The origins of special Japanese settlements in Korea). *Nagoya daigaku bungakubu kenkyū ronshū: Shigaku* (March 1964), no. 12, pp. 21–56. [1]

—— "Meiji ishin gaikō no kyū kokusai kankei e no taiō: Nisshin shūkō jōki no seiritsu o megutte" 明治維新外交の旧国際関係への対応—日清修好条規の成立をめぐって (The new Meiji government's response to the old system of international relations: With special reference to the conclusion of a treaty of friendly relations between Japan and China, 1871). *Nagoya daigaku bungakubu ronshū: Shigaku* (March 1966), no. 41, pp. 29–46. [2]

—— "Meiji shoki ni okeru Nisshin kōshō no ichi danmen: Ryūkyū buntō jōyaku o megutte" 明治初期における日清交渉の一断面—琉球分島条約をめぐって (One episode in Sino-Japanese negotiations in the early

Meiji period: With particular reference to the question of dividing the Ryūkyū territory) 1, *Nagoya daigaku bungakubu kenkyū ronshū: Shigaku* (March 1968), no. 16, pp. 1–8. [3]

—— "Meiji shonen ni okeru Ajiya seisaku no shūsei to Chūgoku: Nisshin shūkō jōki sōan no kentō" 明治初年におけるアジア政策の修正と中国—日清修好条規草案の検討 (China and changes in Japanese policy toward Asia in the early Meiji period: A reexamination of the draft treaty of 1871 between Japan and China). *Nagoya daigaku bungakubu kenkyū ronshū: Shigaku* (March 1967), no. 15, pp. 3–26. [4]

—— "Nichi-Ro sensō no seikaku ni yosete" 日露戦争の性格によせて (On the nature of the Russo-Japanese War). *Rekishigaku kenkyū* (May 1956), no. 195, pp. 1–13. [5]

—— *Nisshin sensō: Higashi Ajia kindaishi no tenkanten* 日清戦争—東アジア近代史の転換点 (The Sino-Japanese War: A turning point in the history of East Asia). Iwanami Shoten, 1973.

—— "Ryūkyū buntō kōshō to tai-Ajia seisaku no tenkan" 琉球分島交渉と対アジア政策の転換 (Diplomatic negotiations over the Ryūkyū Islands and the shift in Japan's policy towards Asia). *Rekishigaku kenkyū* (June 1971), no. 373, pp. 1–13, and 56. [6]

—— "Seikan ronsō ni okeru gaiin to naiin" 征韓論争における外因と内因 (External and internal causes behind the "invade Korea" debate). *Kokusai seiji* (1968), no. 37: *Nihon gaikōshi no shomondai, 3*, pp. 1–22. [7]

—— *Yamagata Aritomo.* 山県有朋. Yoshikawa Kōbunkan, 1986.

—— "Yūshi sensei no gaikō seisaku: 1875-nen o chūshin ni" 有司専制の外交政策 (The despotism of clan government in Japan and foreign policy: With special focus on the year 1875). *Nihon rekishi* (March 1975), no. 322, pp. 2–21. [8]

Furuya Tetsuo 古屋哲夫. *Nichi-Ro sensō* 日露戦争 (The Russo-Japanese War). Chūō Kōronsha, 1966.

Gabe Masao 我部政男. "Meiji 10-nendai no tai-Shin gaikō: 'Ryūkyū jōyaku' no tenmatsu o megutte" 明治10年代の対清外交—「琉球条約」の顛末をめぐって (Japanese policy toward China in the 1880s: With particular reference to the "Ryūkyū treaty"). *Nihonshi kenkyū* (May 1971), no. 119, pp. 22–49.

—— *Meiji kokka to Okinawa* 明治国家と沖縄 (The Meiji state and Okinawa). San'ichi Shobō, 1979.

—— "Meiji shonen no hoppō mondai (Oboegaki): Karafuto Chishima kōkan jōyaku kōshō" 明治初年の北方問題〈覚え書〉—樺太千島交換条約交渉 (A note on the question of the northern territories in the early Meiji years: Negotiations over a treaty to exchange the northern Kuriles and Sakhalin). *Ryūdai hōgaku* (February 1972), no. 13, pp. 1–25.

Gaimushō Hyakunenshi Hensan Iinkai 外務省百年史編纂委員会, ed. *Gaimushō no hyakunen* 外務省の百年 (A century of the Japanese Foreign Ministry). 2 vols. Hara Shobō, 1969.

Haga Shōji 羽賀祥二. "Washin jōyakuki no bakufu gaikō ni tsuite" 和親条約期の幕府外交について (Bakumatsu foreign policy at the time of the conclusion of the treaties of amity and friendship). *Rekishigaku kenkyū* (July 1980), no. 482, pp. 1–13, 52.

Hagiwara Nobutoshi 萩原延寿. *Tōi gake: Ānesuto Satō nikkishō* 遠い崖（アーネスト・サトウ日記抄）(The distant precipice: Selections from the diary of Ernest Satow), vol. 1. Asahi Shinbunsha, 1980.

Hanabusa Nagamichi 英修道. "Chōsenkoku no kindaiteki kaikoku: Nissen kōkafu jōyaku (1876), Bei-Sen Shūferuto jōyaku (1882) no kenkyū" 朝鮮国の近代的開国―日鮮江華府条約(1876), 米鮮シューフ ルト条約(1882年)の研究 (Korea's modern "opening": A study on the Japanese-Korean treaty of Kangwa, 1876, and the American-Korean treaty of Shufeldt, 1882). *Hōgaku kenkyū*, (February 1967), 40(2): 1–44. [1]

—— "Jōyaku kaisei kōshō" 条約条正交渉 (Diplomatic negotiations for treaty revision). In Ueda Toshio 植田捷雄, ed., *Kamikawa sensei kanreki kinen: Kindai Nihon gaikōshi no kenkyū* 神川先生還暦記念―近代日本外交史の研究 (Festschrift for Professor Kamikawa Hikomatsu: Studies in modern Japanese diplomatic history), pp. 1–61. Yūhikaku, 1956. [2]

—— "Okinawa kizoku no enkaku" 沖縄帰属の沿革 (A history of sovereignty over Okinawa). *Kokusaihō gaikō zasshi* (April 1955), 54(1–3): 3–40. [3]

—— "1874-nen Taiwan bansha jiken" 1874年台湾蕃社事件 (The 1874 incident the Taiwanese aborigines clashing with the expeditionary Japanese forces). *Hōgaku kenkyū* (September–October 1951), 24(9–10): 51–79. [4]

Hayashi Tadasu 林董. "Tai-Shin seiryaku kanken" 対清政略管見 (My views on diplomatic strategy toward China), printed in *Kokusai seiji* (1957), no. 3: *Nihon gaikōshi kenkyū—Meiji jidai*, pp. 195–203.

Hayashi Yoshikatsu 林義勝 "Was the Russo-Japanese war really a turning point in Japanese-American relations?: An historiographical essay". *Kyōyō gakka kiyō* (Tokyo Daigaku) (March 1981), no. 13, pp. 11–36.

Hino Seizaburō 日野清三郎. *Bakumatsu ni okeru Tsushima to Ei-Ro* 幕末における対馬と英露 (Tsushima island, England, and Russia in the Bakumatsu period). Tokyo Daigaku Shuppankai, 1968.

Hirose Shizuko 広瀬靖子. "Bakumatsu ni okeru gaikoku guntai Nihon chūryū no tansho" 幕末における外国軍隊日本駐留の端緒 (The origins of stationing foreign troops in Japan during the Bakumatsu period). *Ochanomizu shigaku* (1973), no. 15, pp. 8–42. [1]

—— "'Eikokusakuron' no genbun keisai mondai ni tsuite"「英国策論」

の原文掲載問題について (On the problem of printing the original of "English Policy"). *Nihon rekishi* (November 1961), no. 161, pp. 48–66. [2]

—— "Inoue jōyaku kaisei kōshō ni kansuru ichi kōsatsu" 井上条約改正交渉に関する一考察 (An observation on Inoue's treaty revision diplomacy). In Kindai Chūgoku Kenkyū Iinkai 近代中国研究委員会, ed., *Kindai Chūgoku kenkyū* 近代中国研究 (Studies in modern China), vol. 7. Tokyo Daigaku Shuppankai, 1966, pp. 303–483. [3]

—— "Kirisutokyō mondai o meguru gaikō jōkyō" キリスト教問題をめぐる外交状況 (The diplomatic situation pertaining to the banning of Christianity), in three parts: *Nihon rekishi* (July 1972), no. 290, pp. 68–91; (August 1972), no. 291, pp. 14–39; (August 1973), no. 303, pp. 79–103. [4]

—— "Kōka jōyaku no seiritsu o megutte" 江華条約の成立をめぐって (On the conclusion of the Kanghwa Treaty). *Kokusai seiji* (1970), no. 41: *Gaikō to yoron*, pp. 98–121. [5]

—— "Kōkatō jiken no shūhen" 江華島事件の周辺 (Events surrounding the Kanghwa incident). *Kokusai seiji* (1968), no. 37: *Nihon gaikōshi no shomondai, 3*, pp. 23–40. [6]

—— "Meiji shonen no tai-Ō-Bei kankei to gaikokujin naichi ryokō mondai" 明治初年の対欧米関係と外国人内地旅行問題 (Japan-Europe/U.S. relations in the early years of the Meiji period and the question of internal travel by foreigners). *Shigaku zasshi* (November 1974), 83(11):1–29; (December 1974), 83(12):40–61. [7]

Hiyane Teruo 比屋根照夫. "Jiyū minkenha no Ryūkyūron" 自由民権派の琉球論 (The Ryūkyū problem as seen by advocates of the popular-rights movement). *Ryūdai hōgaku* (March 1974), no. 15, pp. 79–108.

Hiyama Yukio 桧山幸夫. "Itō naikaku no Chōsen shuppei kettei ni taisuru seiryakuronteki kentō: Nisshin sensō zenshi to shite" 伊藤内閣の朝鮮出兵決定に対する政略論的検討—日清戦争前史として (A study for the politicos-strategic discussions that led to the decision for the Korean expedition by Itō cabinet: A study of the prehistory of the Sino-Japanese war), 1, 2. *Chūkyō hōgaku* vol. 18, no. 1 & 2 (Feb. 1984) pp. 25–99; vol. 18, no. 3 (March 1984) pp. 36–134. [1]

—— "Mutsu Munemitsu cho 'Kenken yoroku sōkō'" 陸奥宗光著「塞々餘録草稿」 (Mutsu Munemitsu's draft of his 'Kenken yoroku'). *Chūkyō hōgaku* (July 1982), 17(1):113–136; (January 1983), 17(2):44–101. [2]

—— "Nisshin sensō ni okeru gaikō seiryaku to sensō shidō" 日清戦争における外交政略と戦争指導 (Diplomatic strategy and the conduct of the war during the Sino-Japanese War). In Fukuchi Shigetaka Sensei Kanreki Kinen Ronbunshū Kankō Iinkai 福地重孝先生還暦記念論文集刊行委員会 (ed.), *Kindai Nihon keisei katei no kenkyū* 近代日本形成過程の研究 (Researches into the process of modern Japan's formation). Yūzankaku, 1978, pp. 453–93. [3]

Hora Tomio 洞富雄. "Bakumatsu ishin ni okeru Ei-Futsu guntai no Yokohama chūton" 幕末維新における英仏軍隊の横浜駐屯 (The stationing of British and French troops in Yokohama during the Bakumatsu and restoration periods). *Ōkuma kenkyū* (October 1952), no. 2, pp. 40–101.

—— *Bakumatsu ishinki no gaiatsu to teikō* 幕末維新期の外圧と抵抗 (Foreign pressures and resistance to them during the Bakumatsu and restoration periods). Azekura Shobō, 1977.

—— *Hoppō ryōdo mondai no rekishi to shōrai* 北方領土問題の歴史と将来 (The problem of the northern territories: Its history and its future). Shinjusha, 1973.

Horiguchi Osamu 堀口修. "Nisshin tsūshō kōkai jōyaku teiketsu kōshō ni tsuite" 日清通商航海条約締結について (On the conclusion of the Sino-Japanese treaty of commerce and navigation). *Chūō shigaku* (March 1984), no. 7, pp. 21–72.

Huang Chao-t'ang 黄昭堂 (alias Yuzin Chiautong 黄有仁). "Nihon no Taiwan sesshū to taigai sochi" 日本の台湾接収と対外措置 (Japan's seizure of Taiwan, and external actions). *Kokusaihō gaikō zasshi* (May 1970), 69(1):63–93; (July 1970), 69(2):76–99. [1]

—— *Taiwan minshukoku no kenkyū* 台湾民主国の研究 (Research on the Republic of Taiwan). Tokyo Daigaku Shuppankai, 1972. [2]

Ichikawa Masaaki 市川正明, ed. *Nikkan gaikō shiryō* 日韓外交史料 (Materials on Japanese-Korean diplomatic relations). 10 vols. Hara Shobō, 1979–81.

Iechika Yoshiki 家近良樹. "Soejima gaimukyō haiseki undō to "Meiji 6-nen seihen" 副島外務卿排斥運動と「明治六年改変」(The movement to drive out Foreign Minister Soejima Taneomi and the political change of 1873). *Bunka shigaku* (November 1982), no. 38, pp. 55–71.

Imai Hiroshi 今井宏. *Meiji Nihon to Igirisu kakumei* 明治日本とイギリス革命 (Meiji Japan and the English revolution). Kenkyūsha Shuppan, 1974.

Imai Shōji 今井庄次. "Hesuperia-gō jiken ni tsuite: Ken'eki kisoku jisshi shimatsu" ヘスペリア号事件について―検疫規則実施始末 (On the incident of the German S. S. *Hesperia:* The implementation of quarantine regulations). *Rekishi kyōiku* (January 1964), 12(1):35–40. [1]

—— "Kaikoku tōsho no Eikoku ryōji saiban no ichirei: Kanagawa ni okeru Mosu happō jiken" 開国当初の英国領事裁判の一例―神奈川における モス発砲事件 (A case study of British consular justice at the time of the opening of Japan: The Moss incident of firing a gun at Kanagawa). *Kokusai seiji* (1960), no. 14: *Nihon gaikōshi kenkyū—Bakumatsu ishin jidai,* pp. 30–43. [2]

—— "Nichi-Ei dōmei kōshō ni okeru Nihon no shuchō" 日英同盟交渉における日本の主張 (Japan's case during the negotiations for the Anglo-Japanese Alliance). *Kokusai seiji* (1957), no. 3: *Nihon gaikōshi kenkyū—Meiji jidai,* pp. 119–36. [3]

—— "Nichi-Ei dōmei to Kurino Shin'ichirō" 日英同盟と栗野慎一郎 (The Anglo-Japanese Alliance and Kurino Shin'ichirō). *Rekishi kyōiku* (February 1962), 10(2):39–44. [4]

—— *Oyatoi gaikokujin,* vol. 12: *Gaikō* お雇い外国人，12—外交 Foreignes in the employ of the Japanese government (Foreign employees, vol. 12: Diplomacy). Kajima Kenkyūjo Shuppankai, 1975. [5]

Imai Teruko 今井輝子. "'Gannen mono' imin mumenkyo Hawai tokō mondai ni tsuite no ichi kōsatsu" 「元年者」移民無免許ハワイ渡航問題についての一考察 ("First year" emmigrants to Hawaii and the Japan-Hawaii Treaty of Commerce and Friendship). *Tsudajuku daigaku kiyō* (March 1979), no. 11, pp. 37–66.

Imamiya Shin 今宮新. *Shoki Nichi-Doku tsūkōshi no kenkyū* 初期日独通交史の研究 (Researches into the early history of German-Japanese relations). Kajima Kenkyūjo Shuppankai, 1971.

Inō Tentarō 稲生典太郎. "Giwadan jihen to Nihon no shuppei gaikō: Daigo shidan shutsudō ni itaru made no keii" 義和団事変と日本の出兵外交—第5師団出動に至るまでの経緯 (The Boxer Rebellion and diplomacy of Japan's expedition: To the dispatch of the Fifth Division). In Kaikoku 100-nen Kinen Bunka Jigyōkai 開国百年記念文化事業会, ed., *Kaikoku 100-nen kinen Meiji bunkashi ronshū* 開国百年記念明治文化史論集 (Collected papers on Meiji cultural history in commemoration of the centennial of the opening of the country), pp. 497–562. Kengensha, 1952. [1]

—— "Giwadan jihen to rengōgun sōshikikan sennin mondai" 義和団事変と連合軍総指揮官選任問題 (The Boxer Rebellion and the problem of selecting the commander in chief of the Allied expeditionary forces). *Kokushigaku* (July 1951), no. 55, pp. 29–40. [2]

—— "Higashi Ajia ni okeru fubyōdō jōyaku no kaisei to kaishō" 東アジアにおける不平等条約の改正と解消 (Revisions and abolition of the unequal treaties in East Asia). *Chūō daigaku bungakubu kiyō (Shigakuka)* (March 1985), no. 30, pp. 1–16. [6]

—— "Iwayuru Ōkuma jōyakuan ni kansuru ni, san no kōsatsu" 所謂大隈条約案に関する二，三の考察 (Some observations on the so-called Ōkuma treaty draft). In Mori Katsumi Hakase Koki Kinenkai 森克巳博士古稀記念会, ed., *Taigai kankei to seiji bunka* 対外関係と政治文化 (Foreign relations and political culture), 1 : 387–413. Yoshikawa Kōbunkan, 1974. [3]

—— *Jōyaku kaiseiron no rekishiteki tenkai* 条約改正論の歴史的展開 (The historical development of the call for treaty revision). Komine Shoten, 1976.

—— "'Jōyaku kaisei' to 'naichi zakkyo' ni kansuru shiryō ni tsuite" 「条約改正」と「内地雑居」に関する資料について (On materials regarding 'treaty revision' and 'mixed residence' [of foreigners outside concessions]. *Kiyō Nihon kindaishigaku* (August 1958), no. 1, pp. 83–96; (March 1960), no. 2, pp. 54–78. [5]

—— "Meiji 4-nen no gishintei jōyaku sōhon ni tsuite" 明治 4 年の擬新定条約草本について (On the false revised treaty draft of 1871). *Chūo daigaku bungakubu kiyō: Shigakuka* (November 1960), no. 6, pp. 40–64. [4]

—— "Meiji ikō ni okeru 'sensō miraiki' no shōchō 明治以降における「戦争末来記」,流行とその消長 (The rise and fall of the "war scare" literature since the Meiji period), printed in *Jōyaku kaiseiron no rekishi teki tenkai*, pp. 715–64.

—— *Zoku jōyaku kaisei-ron no tenkai* 続条約改正論の展開 (The historical development of treaty revision: A sequel). In *Nihon gaikō shisōshi ronkō* 日本外交思想史論考 (On the intellectual history of Japanese diplomacy), vol. 2. Komine Shoten, 1965.

Inō Tentarō and Ōyama Azusa 大山梓. "Kindai Higashi Ajia ni okeru fubyōdō jōyaku taisei no seiritsu" 近代東アジアにおける不平等条約体制の成立 (The establishment of the unequal treaty system in modern East Asia). *Chūo daigaku bungakubu kiyō (Shigakuka)* (March 1983), no. 28, pp. 61–81. [5]

Inoue Kiyoshi 井上清. *Jōyaku kaisei: Meiji Nihon no minzoku mondai* 条約改正—明治日本の民族問題 (Treaty revision: The national task of Meiji Japan). Iwanami Shoten, 1955.

—— *Nihon no gunkokushugi* 日本の軍国主義 (Militarism in Japan). 2 vols. Tokyo Daigaku Shuppanka, 1953 (reprinted in 4 vols., 1975).

—— *Senkaku rettō: Uotsuri shotō no shiteki kaimei* 尖閣列島—魚釣諸島の史的解明 (Senkaku Islands: An historical examination of *Uotsuri* islands). Gendai Hyōronsha, 1972.

—— "*Uotsuri* rettō (Senkaku rettō nado) no rekishi to kizoku mondai" 釣魚列島(尖閣列島等)の歴史と帰属問題 (A history of the Senkaku Islands and the question of the title to them). *Rekishigaku kenkyū* (February 1972), no. 381, pp. 1–8.

Inoue Kowashi Denki Hensan Iinkai 井上毅伝記編纂委員会 ed., *Inoue Kowashiden: Shiryōhen* 井上毅伝：史料篇 (The biography of Inoue Kowashi: Historical materials). 6 vols. Tokyo Daigaku Shuppankai, 1978.

Inoue Yūichi 井上勇一. "Ei-Ro tetsudō kyōtei to Kei-Hō tetsudō shakkan mondai: Nichi-Ei dōmei seiritsu e no ichi kōsatsu" 英露鉄道協定と京奉鉄道借款問題―日英同盟成立への一考察 (The Anglo-Russian railway convention and the problem of the Peking-Mukden railway loan contract: A study on the formation of the Anglo-Japanese Alliance). *Hōgaku kenkyū* Keiō Gijuka Daigaku (March 1980), 53(3):55–80. [1]

―― "Hōkomon tetsudō o meguru Nichi-Ei kankei: Mantetsu heikō sen mondai to Nichi-Ei dōmei no henshitsu" 法庫門鉄道をめぐる日英関係―満鉄平行線問題と日英同盟の変質 (The Fakumen railway dispute and the Anglo-Japanese relations: Changes Anglo-Japanese Alliance). *Hōgaku Kenkyū* (August 1984), 57(8):28–55. [2]

―― "Kei-Fu tetsudō no kensetsu o meguru kokusai Nichi-Ro kankei: Nichi-Ei dōmei seiritsu yōin to shite no tetsudō mondai" 京釜鉄道の建設をめぐる日露関係―日英同盟成立要因としての鉄道問題 (Russo-Japanese relations and the Seoul-Pusan railway as factors in the formation of the Anglo-Japanese alliance). *Kokusaihō gaikō zasshi* (November 1981), 80(5):38–67. [3]

―― "Kei-Gi tetsudō no kensetsu o meguru kokusai kankei: Nichi-Ro sensō kaisen gen'in to shite no tetsudō mondai" 京義鉄道の建設をめぐる国際関係―日露戦争開戦原因としての鉄道問題 (International relations and the Seoul-Wiju railway as factors in the coming of the Russo-Japanese War). *Kokusai seiji* (1982), no. 71; *Nihon gaikō no shisō,* pp. 173–88. [4]

―― "Nichi-Ro sensōki no Nihon no gun'yō tetsudō kensetsu mondai: Dai nikai Nichi-Ei dōmei e no ichi kōsatsu" 日露戦争期の日本の軍用鉄道建設問題―第2回日英同盟への1考察 (The problem of Japan's construction of a railroad for military use during the Russo-Japanese War: An observation on the second Anglo-Japanese Alliance). *Gunji shigaku* (December 1980), 16(3):9–20. [5]

Irie Keishirō 入江啓四郎. "Nigenteki genshusei to Meiji ishin" 二元的元首制と明治維新 (The Meiji Restoration and the switch from a system of dual sovereignty). *Kokusai seiji* (1957), no. 3: *Nihon gaikōshi kenkyū—Meiji jidai,* pp. 22–39.

Iriye Akira 入江昭. "Nichi-Bei tekitai ishiki no gensen" 日米敵対意識の源泉 (The roots of antagonism between Japan and the United States). *Kokusai seiji* (1967), no. 34: *Nichi-Bei kankei no imēji,* pp. 1–19.

Ishii Kanji and Sekiguchi Hisashi 石井寛治, 関口尚志, eds., *Sekai shijō to bakumatsu kaikō* 世界市場と幕末国際開港 (The world market and Japan's opening in the Bakumatsu period). Tokyo Daigaku Shuppankai, 1982.

Ishii Takashi 石井孝. "Bakumatsu kokusai seikyoku ni okeru 'shō-Eikokushugi' no tenkai" 幕末政局における「小英国主義」の展開 ("Little

Britain" and Japan's foreign relations in the late Shogunate). *Rekishigaku kenkyū* (August 1963), no. 279, pp. 44–51. [1]

Ishii Takashi. "Bakumatsu no ryōkō ryōto kaikō kaishi teigi o meguru gaikō kankei" 幕末の両港両都開港開市延期提議をめぐる外交関係 (Diplomatic problems concerning the proposal to open two ports and cities in the Bakumatsu period). *Rekishigaku kenkyū* (1952), no. 155, pp. 13–27. [2]

——— "Beikoku kōshi Derongu no Nichi-Ro kokkyō mondai chōtei kōsaku" 米国公使デロングの日露国境問題調停工作 (American envoy Charles E. De Long's arbitration over the Russo-Japanese boundaries dispute). *Nihon rekishi* (July 1974), no. 314, pp. 65–79. [3]

——— "Boshin nairan saishū dankai ni okeru kokusai kankei: Hakodate hanran o meguru rekkyō no dōkō" 戊辰内乱最終段階における国際関係 —箱館反乱をめぐる列強の動向 (International relations in the last stage of the Boshin war: With particular reference to the attitudes of the powers regarding Hakodate rebellions). *Tōhoku daigaku bungakubu kenkyū nenpō* (1964), no. 14, pp. 190–239. [4]

——— *Boshin sensōron* 戊辰戦争論 (Yoshikawa Kōbunkan, 1984).

——— "'Eikokusakuron' to Pākusu no tai-Nichi seisaku" 「英国策論」とパークスの対日政策 (The "English Policy" and Parkes' policy toward Japan). *Nihon rekishi* (January 1962), no. 163, pp. 13–29. [5]

——— "Ishinki ni okeru Nichi-Ro kankei no tenkai" 維新期における日露関係の展開 (The development of Russo-Japanese relations in the restoration period). *Rekishigaku kenkyū* (April 1974), no. 407, pp. 1–14, 29. [6]

——— *Ishin no nairan* 維新の内乱 (Civil disturbances during the restoration). Shiseidō, 1968.

——— "Iwakura shisetsudan no tai-Ei kōshō" 岩倉使節団の対英交渉 (The Iwakura embassy and negotiations with Great Britain, 1). *Bunka* (August 1972), 36(1–2):63–92. [7]

——— *Meiji ishin no kokusaiteki kankyō* 明治維新の国際的環境 (The Meiji restoration and its international environment). Yoshikawa Kōbunkan, 1957; 2d rev. ed., 1966.

——— *Meiji shoki no kokusai kankei* 明治初期の国際関係 (International relations in the early Meiji period). Yoshikawa Kōbunkan, 1977.

——— *Meiji shoki no Nihon to higashi Ajia* 明治初期の日本と東アジア (Japan and East Asia in the early Meiji period). Yūrindō, 1982.

——— *Nihon kaikokushi* 日本開国史 (A history of the opening of Japan). Yoshikawa Kōbunkan, 1972.

——— "Rekkyō no tai-Nichi seisaku" 列強の対日政策 (The policy of the powers toward Japan). In *Iwanami kōza: Nihon rekishi*, vol. 14: *Kindai 1*

岩波講座—日本歴史14, 近代1 (Iwanami series: Japanese history, vol. 14: The modern period), pp. 213–58. Iwanami Shoten, 1962. [8]

Ishinshi Gakkai 維新史学会, ed., *Bakumatsu ishin gaikō shiryō shūsei* 幕末維新外交史料集成 (Collected historical records on foreign relations: 1853–1868). 6 vols. The editor, 1942–44. Reprinted by Daiichi Shobō, 1968–69.

Itazawa Takeo 板沢武雄. *Nichi-Ran bōekishi* 日蘭貿易史 (A history of Japanese-Dutch trade). Heibonsha, 1949.

—— *Nichi-Ran bunka kōshōshi no kenkyū* 日蘭文化交渉史の研究 (A study of the history of cultural exchange between Japan and Holland). Yoshikawa Kōbunkan, 1978.

—— *Nihon to Oranda* 日本とオランダ (Japan and Holland). Shibundō, 1955.

—— *Shiiboruto* シーボルト (The life of Philipp Franz von Siebold). Yoshikawa Kōbunkan, 1960.

Itō Hirobumi 伊藤博文, ed., *Hisho ruisan: Chōsen kōshō shiryō* 秘書類纂—朝鮮交渉資料 (A collection of secret documents: Materials relating to the negotiations over Korea). 27 vols. Hisho Ruisan Kankōkai, 1933–36; Reprinted in 3 vols. Hara Shobō, 1970.

Itō Hirobumi Kankei Bunsho Kenkyūkai 伊藤博文関係文書研究会, ed. *Itō Hirobumi kankei monjo* 伊藤博文関係文書 (Documents relating to Itō Hirobumi). 9 vols. Hanawa Shobō, 1973–1981.

Itō Kazuhiko 伊藤一彦. "Meiji goroku nen 'sei-Tai' ronsō ni okeru Soejima Taneomi no ichi" 明治5—6年「征台」論争における副島種臣の位置 (Soejima Taneomi's position on the debate over the Formosan expedition in 1872–73). *Shakai undōshi* (1975), no. 5, pp. 26–42.

Iwakabe Yoshimitsu 岩壁義光. "Nisshin sengo no nan-Shin keiei ni kansuru ichi kōsatsu: Nan-Shin tetsudō fusetsu yōkyū o chūshin ni" 日清戦後の南清経営に関する一考察—南清鉄道敷設要求を中心に (A study on Japanese policy in South China after the Sino-Japanese War: With particular reference to the demands for construction of a southern China railway). *Hōsei daigaku daigakuin kiyō* (October 1978), no. 1, pp. 59–72. [1]

—— "Nisshin sensō to kyoryū Shinkokujin mondai: Meiji 27-nen 'Chokurei 137-gō' to Yokohama kyoryūchi" 日清戦争と居留清国人問題—明治27年「勅令第137号」と横浜居留地 (The Sino-Japanese War and the question of Chinese residents: Article 137 of the Imperial Ordinance and foreign settlements in Yokohama). *Hōsei shigaku* (March 1984), no. 36, pp. 61–79. [2]

Iwao Seiichi 岩生成一. supervisory ed.; Nichi-Ran Gakkai, Hōsei Rangaku Kenkyūkai, 日蘭学会, 法政蘭学研究会 ed., *Oranda fūsetsugaki shūsei* 和蘭風説書集成 (Transcriptions of Dutch comments on Japan). 2 vols. Yoshikawa Kōbunkan, 1977, 1979.

Iwasaki Masao 岩崎正雄. "Shimazu Nariakira no gaikō seisaku ni kansuru ichi kōsatsu: Kōka-nenkan no Ryūkyū gaikan jiken o chūshin to shite" 島津斉彬の外交政策に関する一考察 ： 弘化年間の琉球外艦事件を中心として (An inquiry into the foreign policies of Shimazu Nariakira: With particular reference to incidents involving foreign warships in Ryūkyū, 1844–47). *Komazawa shigaku* (March 1980), no. 27, pp. 77–85.

Japan, Gaimushō 外務省 (Foreign Ministry), ed. *Bakumatsu ishin gaikō shiryō shūsei* 幕末維新外交資料集成 (Collected historical records on foreign relations: 1853–1868). 6 vols.

—— *Jōyaku kaisei kankei Nihon gaikō bunsho* 条約改正関係日本外交文書 (Documents on Japanese foreign policy relating to treaty revision). 4 vols. Nihon Gakujutsu Shinkōkai, 1941–1950.

—— *Jōyaku kaisei kankei Nihon gaikō bunsho* 条約改正関係日本外交文書 (Documents on Japanese foreign policy: Treaty revision—Conferences). 4 vols. (1956).

—— *Jōyaku kaisei keika gaiyō fu nenpyō* 条約改正経過概要付年表 (A summary of the development of negotiations for treaty revision, with chronology). Nihon Kokusai Rengō Kyōkai, 4 vols., 1950. Supplement to *Jōyaku kaisei kankei Nihon gaikō bunsho*.

—— *Nihon gaikō bunsho*, vol. 33: *Bessatsu: Hokushin jihen* 別冊北清事変 (Documents on Japanese foreign policy: Supplementary volumes: The Boxer Rebellion), 3 vols (1956–57); vol. 38: *Bessatsu: Nichi-Ro sensō* 別冊, 日露戦争 (Supplementary volumes: The Russo-Japanese War), 5 vols. (1958–60); vol. 45: *Bessatsu: Shinkoku jihen* 別冊清国事変 (Supplementary volume: The 1911 Revolution in China) (1961).

—— *Meiji nenkan tsuiho* 明治年間追補 (Addendum to the documents on the Meiji period), 2 vols., 1963.

—— *Nihon gaikō nenpyō narabini shuyō bunsho, 1840–1945* 日本外交年表並主要文書, 1840—1945 (A chronology and major documents on Japanese foreign policy, 1840–1945). 2 vols. 1955; reprinted by Hara Shobō, 1966. *shiryōkan kiyō* (March 1983), no. 1, pp. 5–56. [1]

—— *Tsūshin zenran* 通信全覧 (The complete record of foreign relations) (Yūshodō, 1983–88). See chapter 1.

—— *Tsūshō jōyaku to tsūshō seisaku no hensen* 通商条約と通商政策の変遷 (Changes in commercial treaties and trade policy), edited by Kawashima Nobutaro 川島信太郎, 1951.

—— *Zoku Tsūshin zenran* 通信全覧 (Sequel to the complete record of foreign relations). 60 vols. Ed. Tsūshin Zenran Henshū Iinkai 通信全覧編纂委員会. Yūshodō, 1983–88.

Japan, Kunaichō 宮内省 (Ministry of the Imperial Household), ed. *Meiji Tennōki* 明治天皇紀 (The annals of Emperor Meiji). 13 vols. Yoshikawa Kōbunkan, 1968–1977.

—— Sanbō Honbu 参謀本部 (Army General Staff), ed. *Himitsu Nichi-Ro senshi* 秘密日露戦争史 (Secret history of the Russo-Japanese War). Gannandō, 1977.

Kaizuma Haruhiko 海妻玄彦. "Etō Shimpei to Maria-Rūzugō jiken" 江藤新平とマリアルーズ号事件 (Etō Shimpei and the *Maria Luz* Affair). *Ajia daigaku shogaku kiyō* (November 1965), no. 14, pp. 129–38.

Kajima Morinosuke 鹿島守之助. *Nichi-Ei gaikōshi* 日英外交史 (A history of Anglo-Japanese diplomatic relations). Kajima Kenkyūjo Shuppanka, 1957.

—— *Nihon gaikōshi*, vol. 6: *Daiikkai Nichi-Ei dōmei to sono zengo* 日本外交史, 6 — 第一回日英同盟とその前後 (Japanese diplomatic history, vol. 6: The first Anglo-Japanese Alliance). Kajima Kenkyūjo Shuppankai, 1970.

—— *Nihon gaikōshi*, vol. 7: *Nichi-Ro sensō* 日本外交史, 7 ：日露戦争 (Japanese diplomatic history, vol. 7: The Russo-Japanese War). Kajima Kenkyūjo Shuppankai, 1970.

—— *Nihon gaikōhsi*, vol. 8: *Dainikai Nichi-Ei dōmei to sono jidai* 日本外交史, 8 ：第二回日英同盟とその時代 (Japanese diplomatic history, vol. 8: The second Anglo-Japanese Alliance). Kajima Kenkyūjo Shuppankai, 1970.

—— *Nihon gaikōshi*, vol. 9: *Daisankai Nichi-Ei dōmei to sono jidai* 日本外交史, 9：第三回日英同盟とその時代 (Japanese diplomatic history, vol. 9: The third Anglo-Japanese Alliance). Kajima Kenkyūjo Shuppankai, 1970.

Kanai Madoka 金井圓. "Donkeru-Kurutiusu no mō hitotsu no kōken" ドンケル・クルティウスのもうひとつの貢献 (Donker Curtius' other contributions). *Nihon rekishi* (November 1963), no. 186, pp. 57–66.

Kang, Imon 姜在彦.*Chōsen no jōi to kaika* 朝鮮の攘夷と開化 (Exclusionism and modernization in Korea). Heibonsha, 1977.

Kankoku Kenkyūkai 韓国研究会, ed. *Kan* 韓 (The Han) (Journal of Korean studies).

Karasawa Takeko 唐沢たけ子. "Bōkokurei jiken" 防穀令事件 (Incidents arising from the prohibition of grain exports). *Chōsenshi kenkyūkai ronbunshū* (June 1969), no. 6, pp. 64–93.

Katō Yūzō 加藤祐三. "Bakumatsu kaikō kō: Tokuni Ansei jōyaku no Ahen kin'yū jōkō o chūshin ni shite" 幕末開国考—とくに安政条約のアヘン禁輸条項を中心して (A study on the opening of Japan in the Bakumatsu period: With particular reference to the article of 1858 treaties banning the opium trade). *Yokohama kaikō Shiryōkan kiyō*, no. 1 (March 1983), pp. 5–56.

—— *Kurofune ihen: Perī no chōsen* 黒船異変—ペリーの挑戦 (Shocks of the Black Ships: Perry's challenges). Iwanami Shoten, 1988.

—— *Kurofune zengo no sekai* 黒船前後の世界 (The outside world around the time of the visitation of the Black Ships to Japan). Iwanami Shoten, 1985.

Kawamura Kazuo 河村一夫. "Amoi jiken no shinsō ni tsuite" 厦門事件の真相について (The truth behind the Amoy incident). *Nihon rekishi* (February 1974), no. 309, pp. 46–53. [1]

—— "Gaikōkan to shite no Yano Ryūkei: Shinkoku ryūgakusei shōhei saku ni tsuite" 外交官としての矢野竜渓—清国学生招聘策について (The historical role of Yano Ryūhei as a diplomat in 1898: His views on the invitation of Chinese students). *Seiji keizai shigaku* (April 1980), no. 167, pp. 11–16. [2]

—— "Hokushin jihen to Nihon" 北清事変と日本 (The Boxer Rebellion and Japan). *Kokusai seiji* (1957), no. 3: *Nihon gaikōshi kenkyū—Meiji jidai*, pp. 93–118. [3]

—— *Kindai Nitchū kankeishi no shomondai* 近代日中関係史の諸問題 (Problems in modern Sino-Japanese relations). Nansōsha, 1983.

—— "Nichi-Ei dōmei no kiki no sai no Komura chū-Ei taishi" 日英同盟の危機の際の小村駐英大使 (The Role of Komura Jutarō as Japanese ambassador to England at the critical moment of the Anglo-Japanese Alliance). *Seiji keizai shigaku* (April 1981), no. 179, pp. 1–31. [4]

Kemuyama Sentarō 煙山専太郎. *Seikanron jissō* 征韓論実相 (The actual facts concerning the movement to "invade Korea"). Waseda Daigaku Shuppanbu, 1907.

Kim Chong-myong 金正明, ed. *Nikkan gaikō shiryō shūsei* 日韓外交資料集成 (A collection of materials on Japanese-Korean diplomatic relations). 10 vols. Gannandō, 1962–1966.

Kinjō Seitoku 金城正篤. *Ryūkyū shobunron* 琉球処分論 (Essays on the disposition of the Ryūkyūs). Naha; Okinawa Taimususha, 1978.

Kino Kazue 木野主計. "Ōtsu jiken to Inoue Kowashi" 大津事件と井上毅 (The Ōtsu incident and Inoue Kowashi). *Kokushigaku* (March 1968), no. 176, pp. 42–68.

Kishi Motokazu 岸甫一. "Ishinki no Yokohama chūton Igirisu guntai tettai mondai" 維新期の横浜駐屯イギリス軍隊撤退問題 (Problems related to the withdrawal of British troops stationed in Yokohama during the Restoration period). *Nihon rekishi* (October 1979), no. 377, pp. 69–87.

Kobayashi Katsumi 小林克巳. "Kōkatō jiken to Kido Takayoshi no tachiba" 江華島事件と木戸孝允の立場 (The Kanghwa incident [of 1875] and Kido Takayoshi's stand). *Nihon rekishi* (April 1955), no. 83, pp. 12–22.

Kobayashi Rokurō 小林六郎. "Meiji seifu to komon gaikō: Ru Jyandoru to sono shūhen" 明治政府と顧問外交—ルジャンドルとその周辺 (The Meiji government and the diplomatic advisor Le Gendre). In *Uchida Shigetaka sensei koki kinen: Seiji no shisō to rekishi* 内田繁隆先生古稀記念

—政治の思想と歴史 (A festschrift for Professor Uchida Shigetaka: Essays on the history of political thought), pp. 49–87. Kinen Ronbunshū Kankō-kai, 1963.

Koh Se-k'ai 許世楷. *Nihon tōchika no Taiwan: Teikō to dan'atsu* 日本統治下の台湾—抵抗と弾圧 (Taiwan under Japanese rule: Resistance and suppression). Tokyo Daigaku Shuppankai, 1972.

—— "Taiwan jiken, 1871–74" 台湾事件 (Japan's expedition to Formosa, 1871–74). *Kokusai seiji* (1965), no. 28: *Nihon gaikōshi no shomondai, 2,* pp. 38–52.

Kōriyama Yoshimitsu 郡山良光. *Bakumatsu Nichi-Ro kankeishi kenkyū* 幕末日露関係史研究 (Studies in the history of Russo-Japanese relations in the Bakumatsu period). Kokusho Kankōkai, 1980.

Kotani Yoshiko 故谷美子. "Amoi jiken no ichi kōsatsu: Nihon no nan-Shin sinshutsu keikaku to sono zasetsu" 厦門事件の一考察—日本の南清進出計画とその挫折 (A study on the Amoy incident: The Japanese plan to expand to south China and its failure). *Rekishi kyōiku* (March 1958), 6(3):41–50.

Koyama Hironari 小山博也. "Jōyaku kaisei mondai to bōeki seisaku: Meiji shonen no kaisei rongi o tōshite" 条約改正問題と貿易政策—明治初年の改正論議を通して (The problem of treaty revision and [Japan's] commercial policy: With particular reference to the call for treaty revision in the early Meiji period). *Saitama daigaku kiyō* (Shakai kagaku hen) (March 1958), no. 6, pp. 81–99.

Kume Kunitake 久米邦武, ed. *Tokumei zenken taishi Bei-Ō kairan jikki* 特命全権大使米欧回覧実記 (The authentic record of the embassy to the United States and Europe). 5 vols. Hakubunsha, 1878. Reissued in pocket paperback series with introduction by Tanaka Akira. 5 vols., Iwanami Shoten 1977–82.

Kurihara Jun 栗原純. "Taiwan jiken: Ryūkyū seisaku no tenki to shite no Taiwan shuppei" 台湾事件—琉球政策の転機としての台湾出兵 (The Formosan expedition of 1874: The expedition to Formosa as a turning point in Japan's policy toward the Ryūkyūs). *Shigaku zasshi* (September 1978), 87(9):60–85.

Kurobane Shigeru 黒羽茂. *Nichi-Ei dōmei shi no kenkyū* 日英同盟史の研究 (A study of the history of the Anglo-Japanese Alliance). Sendai, Tōhoku Kyōiku Shuppan, 1968.

—— *Nichi-Ro sensō shiron* 日露戦争史論 (A historical study of the Russo-Japanese War). Sugiyama Shoten, 1982.

—— *Sekai shijō yori mitaru Nichi-Ro sensō* 世界史上より見たる日露戦争 (The Russo-Japanese War as seen from the standpoint of world history). Shibundō, 1960.

Kuroha Shigeru. *Taiheiyō o meguru Nichi-Bei kōsōshi* 太平洋をめぐる日米抗争史 (A history of Japanese-American rivalry in the Pacific). Nansō-sha, 1968.

Maejima Shōzō 前島省三. "Nisshi Nichi-Ro sensō ni okeru tai-Kan seisaku" 日清・日露戦争における対韓政策 (Japanese policy toward Korea during the Sino-Japanese and Russo-Japanese Wars). *Kokusai seiji* (1962), no. 19: *Nihon gaikōshi kenkyū—Nisshin Nichi-Ro sensō*, pp. 71–86.

Manabe Shigetada 真鍋重忠. *Nichi-Ro kankeishi* 日露関係史 (A history of Russo-Japanese relations). Yoshikawa Kōbunkan, 1978.

Maruyama Kunio 丸山国雄. *Shoki Nichi-Doku tsūkō shōshi* 初期日独通交小史 (A short hisotry of early German-Japanese relations). Nichi-Doku Bunka Kyōkai, 1931.

Masuda Tsuyoshi 増田毅. *Bakumatsuki no Eikokujin* 幕末期の英国人 (The British in the Bakumatsu period). Yūhikaku, 1980.

Matsumura Masayoshi 松村正義. "Nichi-Ro sensō to Nihon no kōhō gaikō" 日露戦争と日本の広報外交 (The Russo-Japanese War and Japan's public relations diplomacy). *Gunji shigaku* (September 1980), 16(3):2–8. [1]

—— *Nichi-Ro sensō to Kaneko Kantarō: Kōhō gaikō no kenkyū* 日露戦争と金子堅太郎—広報外交の研究 (The Russo-Japanese War and Kaneko Kentarō: A study in public relations diplomacy). Shin'yūdō, 1980. [2]

—— "Kōkaron to Nichi-Ro sensō" 黄禍論と日露戦争 (The yellow peril and the Russo-Japanese War). *Kokusai seiji* (1982), no. 71; *Nihon gaikō no shisō*, pp. 38–53. [3]

Mikami Terumi 三上昭美. "Gaimushō setchi no keii: Wagakuni gaisei kikō no rekishiteki kenkyū, 1" 外務省設置の経緯—わが国外政機構の歴史的研究 (The establishment of the Ministry of Foreign Affairs in Japan: A historical study of Japan's foreign policy machinery, 1). *Kokusai seiji* (1963), no. 26: *Nihon gaikōshi no shomondai, 1*, pp. 1–26. [1]

—— "Gaisei kikō no kakuritsu ni kansuru ichi kōsatsu: Wagakuni gaisei kikō no rekishiteki kenkyū, 2" 外政機構の確立に関する一考察—わが国外政機構の歴史的研究, 2 (The process of establishing the Ministry of Foreign Affairs: A historical study of Japan's foreign policy machinery, 2). *Kokusai seiji* (1966), no. 28: *Nihon gaikōshi no shomondai, 2*, pp. 17–37. [2]

Miyaji Masato 宮地正人. "Kokuminshugiteki taigaikōha ron" 国民主義的対外硬派論 (On the hard-time nationalistic foreign policy, 1 and 2). *Shigaku zasshi* (November 1971), 80(11):1–36; (December 1971), 80(11):26–61.

Mōri Toshihiko 毛利敏彦. "Iwakura shisetsudan no hensei jijō: Sangi Kido Takayoshi no fukushi shūnin mondai o chūshin ni" 岩倉使節団の編成事情—参議木戸孝允の副使就任問題を中心に (Circumstances surrounding the composition of the Iwakura embassy: With particular reference to the appointment of Kido Takayoshi as the vice-envoy). *Kokusai seiji* (1980), no. 66: *Hendōki ni okeru Higashi Ajia to Nihon—Sono shiteki kōsatsu,* pp. 128–47. [1]

—— *Meiji rokuhen seihen* 明治六年政変 (The political changes of 1873). Chūō Kōronsha, 1979. [2]

—— *Meiji rokunen seihen no kenkyū* 明治六年政変の研究 (Researches into the political changes of 1873). Yūhikaku, 1978. [3]

—— "Meiji shoki gaikō no Chōsenkan" 明治初期外交の朝鮮観 (The view of Korea in early Meiji diplomacy). *Kokusai seiji* (1974), no. 51: *Nihon gaikō no kokusai ninshiki—sono shiteki tenkai,* pp. 25–42. [2]

Morioka Yoshiko 森岡美子. "Uiremu Nisei kaikoku kankoku ni kansuru Oranda gawa no jijō ni tsuite" ウイレム二世開国勧告に関するオランダ側について (Circumstances in Holland surrounding William II's call for the opening of Japan). *Shigaku zasshi* (January 1975), 84(1): 54–64.

Moriya Fumio 守屋典郎. *Shinpan Nihon shihonshugi hattatsushi* 新版・日本資本主義発達史 (A history of capitalistic developments in Japan). Aoki Shoten, 1969.

Moriyama Shigenori 森山茂徳. "Chōsen ni okeru Nihon to Berugī Shinjikēto: Sono keizaiteki kyōdō kōdō no zasetsu" 朝鮮における日本とベルギー・シンディケート―その経済的共同行動の挫折 (Japanese and Belgian syndicates: The failure of their joint economic activities). *Nenpō: Kindai Nihon kenkyū* (November 1980), no. 2, pp. 28–54. [1]

—— "Kindai Nikkan kankeishi kenkyū no dōkō to shiryō oyobi bunken" 近代日韓関係史研究の動向と資料及び文献 (Research trends in the history of modern Japanese-Korean relations: Sources and documents). *Kokka gakkai zasshi* (November 1975), 88(11–12): 66–98. [2]

—— "Nisshin, Nichi-Ro senkanki ni okeru Nikkan kankei no ichi sokumen: Zai-Nichi Kankokujin bōmeisha no shogū mondai" 日清，日露戦間期における日韓関係の一側面―在日韓国人亡命者の処遇問題 (One aspect of Japanese-Korean relations during the period between the Sino-Japanese and Russo-Japanese Wars: Treatment of Korean refugees in Japan). *Tōyō bunka kenkyūjo kiyō* (March 1982), no. 88, pp. 195–222. [3]

Motohashi Tadashi 本橋正. *Nichi-Bei kankeishi kenkyū* 日米関係史研究 (Studies in Japanese-American relations). Gakushūin Daigaku, 1986.

Mukōyama Hiroo 向山寛夫. "Amoi jiken to Keishū jiken" 厦門事件と恵州事件 (The Amoy Incident and the Waichow revolt). *Kokugakuin daigaku daigakuin kiyō* (1974), no. 6, pp. 35–54.

Muramatsu Yūji 村松祐次. *Giwadan no kenkyū* 義和団の研究 (A study of the Boxers). Gannandō, 1976.

Murashima Shigeru 村島滋. "Nichi-Ei dōmeishi no ichi sokumen: Ryōkoku gunji kyōshō no seiritsu o megutte" 日英同盟史の一側面―両国軍事

協商の成立をめぐって (An aspect of the history of the Anglo-Japanese Alliance: Problems of the military arrangements). *Kokusai seiji* (1978), no. 58: *Nichi-Ei kankei no shiteki tenkai,* pp. 15–31.

—— "Nichi-Ei dōmei to Nichi-Ro sensō" 日英同盟と日露戦争 (The Anglo-Japanese Alliance and the Russo-Japanese War). *Rekishi kenkyū* (February 1967), 15(2): 20–26.

Mutsu Munemitsu 陸奥宗光. *Kenkenroku* 蹇蹇録 (Memoirs of a devoted subject). Iwanami Shoten, 1939. For a new edition, see Nakatsuka Akira 中塚明 edited with introduction and annotations, *Shintei Kenkenroku* 新訂蹇蹇録 Iwanami Shoten, 1983.

Nakai Akio 中井晶夫. *Shoki Nihon Suisu kankeishi* 初期日本スイス関係史 (A history of the early years of Japanese-Swiss relations). Kawama Shobō, 1971.

Nakamura Hidetaka 中村栄孝. "Taikun gaikō no kokusai ninshiki" 大君外交の国際認識 (The view of world order in Tycoon diplomacy). *Kokusai seiji* (1974), no. 51: *Nihon gaikō no kokusai ninshiki—Sono shiteki tenkai,* pp. 1–24.

Nakamura Naomi 中村尚美. "Ajia shinryakuron to Nisshin sensō" アジア侵略論と日清戦争 (The call to invade Asia and the Sino-Japanese War). *Shakai kagaku tōkyū* (Waseda Daigaku) (December 1973), 19(1): 27–59. [1]

—— "Nisshin sensōgo no Ajia seisaku" 日清戦争後のアジア政策 (Japan's Asian policy after the Sino-Japanese War). *Shakai kagaku tōkyū* (March 1976), 21(3): 167–203. [2]

—— "Ru Jandoru gaikō iken: Ei-Ro no Kyokutō seisaku to Nihon gaikō" ル・ヂャンドル外交意見—英露の極東政策と日本外交 (Le Gendre's diplomatic opinions: Japanese diplomacy and the Far Eastern policies of Britain and Russia). *Ōkuma kenkyū* (October 1952), no. 2, pp. 164–83. [3]

Nakamura Takeshi 中村赳. "Kanagawa jōyaku mondaiten kenkyū" 神奈川条約問題点研究 (Problems relating to the U.S.-Japanese Treaty of 1854). In Iwao Seiichi 岩生成一, ed., *Kinsei no yōgaku to kaigai kōshō* 近世の洋学と海外交渉 (Western learning in modern Japan and negotiations with foreign powers), pp. 279–301. Gannandō, 1979.

Nakatsuka Akira 中塚明. "Giwadan chin'atsu sensō to Nihon teikokushugi" 義和団鎮圧戦争と日本帝国主義 (The armed suppression of the Boxer Rebellion, and Japanese imperialism). *Nihonshi kenkyū* (November 1964), no. 75, pp. 6–31.

—— *Nisshin sensō no kenkyū* 日清戦争の研究 (A study of Sino-Japanese War). Aoki Shoten, 1968.

Nakayama Jiichi 中山治一. "'Shin-Futsu kattō ikken' to Nihon no sentaku:

Iwayuru 'Datsu-A Nyū-Ō' no seiji katei'' 「清仏葛藤一件」と日本の選択 —いわゆる「脱亜入欧」の政治過程 (Japan's entrance into the family of Western nations: The Sino-Franco conflict and Japan's alternatives). *Kokusai seiji* (1982), no. 71; *Nihon gaikō no shisō*, pp. 21–37.

Nakayama Masaru 中山勝. ''Meiji shichinen, Hakodate ni okeru Doitsu ryōji satsugai jiken ni kansuru ichi kōsatsu'' 明治7年, 函館におけるドイツ 領事殺害事件に関する一考察 (A note on the murder of the German consul in Hakodate in 1874). In Tezuka Yutaka 手塚豊, ed., *Kindai Nihonshi no shin kenkyū* 近代日本史の新研究 (New studies in modern Japanese history), 2: 113–38. Hokuju Shuppan (Gakubunsha), 1983.

Nezu Masashi ねずまさし. ''Bakumatsu no Furansu qaikō bunsho kara mita Furansu no tai-Nichi hōshin'' 幕末のフランス外交文書からみたフラン スの対日方針 (French policy toward Japan as seen from French diplomatic records of the Bakumatsu period). *Shigaku zasshi* (March 1957), 69(3):94–112. [1]

—— ''1864-nen no Pari kyōyaku o meguru Furansu daini teisei to Tokugaka bakufu to no kōshō'' 1864年のパリ協約をめぐるフランス第二帝政と 徳川幕府との交渉 (Negotiations between the Shogunate government and France under the Second Empire over the Paris Agreement of 1864). *Rekishigaku kenkyū* (August 1957), no. 210, pp. 21–32. [2]

Nichi-Bei Shūkō Tsūshō Hyakunen Kinen Gyōji Un'ei Kai 日米修好通商百年 記念行事運営会, ed. *Man'en gannen ken-Bei shisetsu shiryō shūsei* 万延 元年遺米使節史料集成 (Materials from the Japanese delegation to America of 1860). 7 vols. Kazama Shobō, 1961.

Nihon Kokusai Seiji Gakkai 日本国際政治学会 (Japan Association of International Relations), ed. *Kokusai seiji* (1962), no. 19: *Nihon gaikōshi kenkyū— Nisshin Nichi-Ro sensō.*

—— *Kokusai seiji* (1967), no. 33: *Gaikō Shidōsharon.*

Nishibori Akira 西堀昭. ''Bakumatsu no Yokohama ni setsuritsu sareta Furansugogaku denshūjo no seiritsu to haikei'' 幕末の横浜に設立され た仏蘭西語学伝習所の成立と背景 (The background of founding the French-language school in Yokohama). *Chiba shōka daigaku ronshū* (1969– 72), 11(3–4):153–73.

Noda Hideo 野田秀雄. ''Nawate jiken ni kansuru jakkan no kōsatsu'' 縄手 事件に関する若干の考察 (A brief observation on the [1868] Nawate incident). *Nihon rekishi* (October 1978), no. 305, pp. 31–62.

Nose Kazunori 野瀬和紀. ''Kōshin seihen no kenkyū, 1: Shin-Futsu sensō to Nihon gaikō'' 甲申政変の研究, 1：清仏戦争と日本外交 (A study of the Kōshin incident, 1: The Sino-French War and Japanese diplomacy). *Chōsen gakuhō* (January 1977), no. 82, pp. 133–60. [1]

—— ''Takezoe Shin'ichirō to Shimamura Hisashi'' 竹添進一郎と島村久

(Takezoe Shin'ichirō and Shimamura Hisashi). *Kokusai hōsei kenkyū* (October 1971), no. 13, pp. 1–24. [2]

Ōe Shinobu 大江志乃夫. "Nichi-Ro sensō no gunjiteki bunseki: Rikugun o chūshin ni" 日露戦争の軍事的分析—陸軍を中心に (An analysis of the Japanese military in the Russo-Japanese War with particular reference to the army). *Shigaku kenkyū* (March 1974), no. 96, pp. 1–58. [1]

—— *Nichi-Ro sensō no gunjishiteki kenkyū* 日露戦争の軍事史的研究 (A study on the military history of the Russo-Japanese War). Iwanami Shoten, 1976.

—— "Seikanron no seiritsu to sono igi" 征韓論の成立とその意義 (The emergence of the "invade Korea" debate and its significance). In Ōtsuka Shigakkai 大塚史学会, ed., *Higashi Ajia kindaishi no kenkyū* 東アジア 近代史の研究 (Studies in modern East Asian history), pp. 59–91. Ochanomizu Shobō, 1967. [2]

Ōhata Tokushirō, 大畑篤四郎. "Kōkatō jōyaku no jōyakushiteki kōsatsu" 江華島条約の条約史的考察 (A study of the Kanghwa Treaty from the viewpoint of the history of treaties). *Kan* (September 1967), 5(9):60–79. [1]

—— "Nichi-Ro kaisen gaikō" 日露開戦外交 (Diplomacy before the outbreak of the Russo-Japanese War). *Kokusai seiji* (1962), no. 19: *Nihon gaikōshi kenkyū—Nisshin Nichi-Ro sensō*, pp. 102–18. [2]

—— *Nihon gaikō seisaku no shiteki tenkai* 日本外交政策の史的展開 (The historical development of Japanese foreign policy). Seibundō, 1983.

Oka Yoshitake 岡義武. "Ishin chokugo ni okeru jōi undō no yoen" 維新直後 における尊攘運動の余炎 (The aftermath of the Expel-the-barbarians movement in the immediate post-Restoration period). In Oka, *Reimeiki no Meiji Nihon*, pp. 5–50. [1]

—— "Jōyaku kaisei rongi ni arawareta tōji no taigai ishiki" 条約改正論議 に現われた当時の対外認識 (The controversy over treaty revision and Japanese perceptions of foreign powers, 1, 2). *Kokka gakkai zasshi* (August 1953), 67(1–2):1–24; (September 1953), 67(3–4):69–92. [2]

—— "Meiji shoki no jiyū minken ronja no me ni eijitaru tōji no kokusai jōsei" 明治初期の自由民権論者の眼に映じたる当時の国際情勢 (The international situation as seen by the advocates of the popular-rights movement in the early Meiji period). In Meiji Shiryō Kenkyū Renrakukai 明治史料研究連絡会, ed., *Minkenron kara Nashonarizumu e* 民権論から ナショナリズムへ (From the popular-rights movement to nationalism), pp. 33–83. Ochanomizu Shobō, 1957, [3]

—— "Meiji shonen no Ezochi to Igirisu" 明治初年の蝦夷地とイギリス (Ezo and Great Britain in the early Meiji era). *Kokka gakkai zasshi* (June 1943), 57(6):1–37. [4]

—— "Nisshin sensō to tōji ni okeru taigai ishiki" 日清戦争と当時における

対外意識 (The Sino-Japanese War and Japanese attitudes toward foreign countries, 1, 2). *Kokka gakkai zasshi* (December 1954), 69(3–4):1–29; (February 1955), 69(5–6):1–32. [5]

—— *Reimeiki no Meiji Nihon: Nichi-Ei kōshō no shikaku ni oite* 黎明期の明治日本—日英交渉の視角において (Meiji Japan at dawn: Seen from the perspective of Anglo-Japanese negotiations). Miraisha, 1964.

—— *Yamagata Aritomo: Meiji Nihon no shōchō* 山県有朋—明治日本, 象徴 (Yamagata Aritomo: Symbol of Meiji Japan). Iwanami Shoten, 1958.

Okamoto, Shumpei 岡本俊平. "Meiji Nihon no tai-Chūgoku taido no ichi danmen: Komura Jutarō no baai" 明治日本の対中国態度の一断面—小村寿太郎の場合 (One aspect of Japan's attitude toward China in the Meiji period: The case of Komura Jutarō). In Satō Seizaburō 佐藤誠三郎 and Roger Dingman, eds., *Kindai Nihon no taigai taido* 近代日本の対外態度 (Attitude toward foreign affairs in modern Japan), pp. 65–92. Tokyo Daigaku Shuppankai, 1974.

Ōkubo Toshiaki 大久保利謙, ed. *Iwakura shisetsu no kenkyū* 岩倉使節の研究 (Researches on the Iwakura embassy). Munetaka Shobō, 1977.

Ōkubo Yasuo 大久保泰甫. *Nihon kindaihō no chichi: Boasonādo* 日本近代法の父—ボワソナアド (Boissonade: The father of modern law in Japan). Iwanami Shoten, 1977.

Okudaira Takehiko 奥平武彦. *Chōsen kaikoku kōshō shimatsu* 朝鮮開国交渉始末 (Diplomatic negotiations concerning the opening of Korea). Tōkō Shoin 1934; republished by Tōkō Shoin, 1969.

Ōkuma Ryōichi 大熊良一. *Hoppō ryōdo mondai no rekishiteki haikei* 北方領土問題の歴史的背景 (The historical background of the northern territories problem). Nanpō Dōhō Engokai, 1964.

—— *Ikokusen Ryūkyū raikōshi no kenkyū* 異国船琉球来航史の研究 (A historical study of foreign ships calling at the Ryūkyū Islands). Kajima Kenkyūjo Shuppanka, 1971.

—— *Rekishi no kataru Ogasawaratō* 歴史の語る小笠原島 (The Bonin Islands speak of their past). Nanpō Dōhō Engokai, 1966.

Ōno Katsumi 大野勝巳. "Kasumigaseki no kageno hito: Denison" 霞が関の陰の人—デニソン (A hidden figure in Kasumigaseki: Henry Willard Denison). In Ōno Katsumi, *Kasumigaseki gaikō: Sono dentō to hitobito* 霞が関外交—その伝統と人々 (Kasumigaseki [Foreign Ministry] diplomacy: Its tradition and leaders), pp. 185–201. Nihon Keizai Shinbunsha, 1978.

Ōtsuka Takematsu 大塚武松. *Bakumatsu gaikōshi no kenkyū* 幕末外交史の研究 (Studies in the diplomatic history of the late Tokugawa Shogunate). Hōbunkan, 1952.

Ōyama Azusa 大山梓. "Amoi jiken" 厦門事件 (The Amoy incident). *Meiji bunka kenkyū* (1968), no. 1, pp. 139–53. [1]

Ōyama Azusa. "Edō yakusho" 江戸約書 (Edō convention). *Teikyō hōgaku* (January 1982), 13(1):39–54. [2]

—— "Iwakura kaisei sōan to Terashima kaisei sōan" 岩倉改正草案と寺島 改正草案 (Drafts for treaty revision by Iwakura and Terashima). *Kokusai seiji* (1957), no. 3: *Nihon gaikōshi kenkyū—Meiji jidai*, pp. 51–66. [3]

—— "Jōyaku kaisei to gaikokujin kyoryūchi" 条約改正と外国人居留地 (Treaty revision and foreign settlements). *Rekishi kyōiku*, (January 1961), 9(1):60–69. [4]

—— "Jōyaku kaisei to gaijin hōkan" 条約改正と外人法官 (Treaty revision and foreign judges). *Kokusaihō gaikō zasshi* (December 1960), 59(4):1–29. [5]

—— "Kyoryūchisei to chigai hōken" 居留地制と治外法権 (Foreign settlements and extraterritoriality). *Teikyō hōgaku* (December 1982), 13(2):15–26. [6]

—— *Kyū jōyakuka ni okeru kaishi kaikō no kenkyū* 旧条約下における開市・開港の研究 (A study of open cities and ports under the old treaty system). Otori Shobō, 1967.

—— "Maria-Rūsugō jiken to saiban tetsuzuki" マリア・ルース号事件と裁判手続 (Trial procedures in the case of the *Maria Luz* affair). *Seikei ronsō* (Hiroshima Daigaku) (January 1977), 26(5):11–33. [7]

—— "Meiji shoki no hoppō ryōdo mondai" 明治初期の北方領土問題 (The northern territories problem in early Meiji period). *Kokusaihō gaikō zasshi* (March 1962), 60(4–6):39–67. [8]

—— "Nichi-Bei jōyaku to Bei sōryōji" 日米条約と米総領事 (The U.S.-Japan treaty and the American consul general [Townsend Harris]). *Hiroshima hōgaku* (December 1978), 2(2–3):141–71. [9]

—— "Nichi-Ro sensō chokuzen ni okeru Nichi-Ro kankei no ichi mondai: Bazanpo jiken" 日露戦争直前における日露関係の一問題—馬山浦事件 (One issue in Russo-Japanese relations immediately before the outbreak of the Russo-Japanese War: The Masan incident). *Gunji shigaku* (November 1968), 4(3):71–80. [10]

—— *Nichi-Ro sensō no gunsei shiroku* 日露戦争の軍政史録 (Historical records of military administration during the Russo-Japanese War). Fuyō Shobō, 1973.

—— "Nichi-Ro sensō to kaisen gaikō" 日露戦争と開戦外交 (The Russo-Japanese War and prewar diplomacy). *Kokusaihō gaikō zasshi* (July 1969), 68(2):45–70. [11]

—— *Nihon gaikōshi kenkyū* 日本外交史研究 (Studies in Japanese diplomatic history). Ryōsho Fukyūkai, 1980.

—— "Ryūganpo jiken" 竜巌浦事件 (The Yongam incident). *Meiji bunka kenkyū* (1969), no. 3, pp. 41–55. [12]

—— "Ryūkyū kizoku to Nisshin fungi" 琉球帰属と日清紛議 (The Sino-Japanese dispute concerning jurisdiction over the Ryūkyūs). *Seikei ronsō* (Meiji Daigaku) (May 1970), 38(1–2):76–126. [13]

—— "Seikan ronsō to Karafuto mondai" 征韓論争と樺太問題 (The "invade Korea" controversy and the problem of Sakhalin). *Gunji shigaku* (June 1978), 14(1):2–17. [14]

Pak Chong-kun 朴宗根. "Bin hi gyakusatsu jiken no shorian o meguru shomondai" 閔妃虐殺事件の処理案をめぐる諸問題 (Problems concerning the handling of the murder of Queen Min). In Ōtsuka Shigakkai 大塚史学会, ed., *Higashi Ajia kindaishi no kenkyū* 東アジア近代史の研究 (Studies of modern East Asian history), pp. 156–220. Ochanomizu Shobō, 1967. [1]

—— *Nihon teikokushugi no Chōsen shihai* 日本帝国主義の朝鮮支配 (Korea under the rule of Japanese imperialism). 2 vols. Aoki Shoten, 1973.

—— *Nisshin sensō to Chōsen* 日清戦争と朝鮮 (Korea and the Sino-Japanese War). Aoki Shoten, 1982.

—— "Nisshin sensō to Chōsen no kōgo kaikaku: Tokuni gunkoku kimusho o chūshin ni" 日清戦争と朝鮮の甲午改革—とくに軍国機務処を中心として (The Sino-Japanese War and the Kabo reform of Korea: With particular reference to the Kungkuk Kimuch'o). *Kokusai seiji* (1963), no. 22: *Nikkan kankei no tenkai,* pp. 50–68. [2]

Peng Tse-chou (Hō Takushū) 彭沢周. "Chōsen mondai o meguru Jiyūtō to Furansu: Shutoshite Yamabeshi-setsu ni taisuru hihan" 朝鮮問題をめぐる自由党とフランス—主として山辺氏説に対する批判 (Discussions between the Japanese Liberal Party and the French authorities concerning the Korean problems: A criticism of Mr. Yamabe's thesis). *Rekishigaku kenkyū* (June 1962), no. 265, pp. 19–27. [1]

—— "Ferī naikaku to Nihon" フェリー内閣と日本 (Japan and the cabinet of Jules Ferry). *Shirin* (May 1962), 45(3):33–66. [2]

—— "Kōkatō jiken ni taisuru Kido/Itagaki no dōkō" 江華島事件に対する木戸，板垣の動向 (The behaviors of Kido and Itagaki during the Japanese-Korean crisis of 1875 over the Kanghwa incident). *Rekishigaku kenkyū* (July 1967), no. 326, pp. 36–46. [3]

—— "Kōshin jihen o meguru Inoue gaimukyō to Furansu kōshi tono kōshō" 甲申事変をめぐる井上外務卿とフランス公使との交渉 (The Kabsin rebellion and negotiations between Foreign Minister Inoue Kaoru and the French minister). *Rekishigaku kenkyū* (November 1963) no. 282, pp. 34–55. [4]

—— *Meiji shoki Nichi-Kan-Shin kankei no kenkyū* 明治初期日韓清関係の研究 (A study of relations between Japan, Korea, and China in the early Meiji period). Hanawa Shobō, 1969.

Peng Tse-chou. "Meiji zenki ken-Kan shisetsu ni kansuru kōsatsu" 明治前期遺韓使節に関する考察 (Japanese embassies to Korea in the early Meiji period). *Tōhōgaku* (1964), no. 27, pp. 91–102. [6]

—— "Shin-Futsu sensōki ni okeru Nihon no tai-Kan seisaku" 清仏戦争期における日本の対韓政策 (Japan's policy toward Korea during the Sino-French war of 1884). *Shirin* (May 1960), 43(3): 124–43. [7]

Sakai Yūkichi 坂井雄吉. "Konoe Atsumaro to Meiji 30-nendai no taigaikōha: 'Konoe Atsumaro nikki' ni yosete" 近衛篤麿と明治30年代の対外硬派—「近衛篤麿日記」によせて (Konoe Atsumaro and the foreign policy hard-liners around the turn of the century: Seen through his diary). *Kokka gakkai zasshi* (August 1970), 84(3–4): 50–119.

Sakane Yoshihisa 坂根義之. "Aoki Shūzō gaishō no tai-Ei jōyaku kaisei kōshō: Tokuni gaikō seisaku kettei katei ni tsuite" 青木周蔵外相の対英条約改正交渉—とくに外交政策決定過程について (Foreign Minister Aoki Shūzō's negotiations with England on treaty revision: With special reference to the foreign policy decision-making process). *Kokushigaku* (February 1979), no. 107, pp. 1–33. [1]

—— "Aoki Shūzōron: Tai-Ei jōyaku kaisei kōshō to gaikō seiryaku" 青木周蔵論—対英条約改正交渉と外交政略 (On Foreign Minister Aoki Shūzō: With particular reference to his diplomatic strategy and negotiations with Britain for treaty revision). *Kokusai seiji* (1966), no. 33: *Nihon gaikōshi kenkyū—gaikō shidōsha-ron*, pp. 10–26. [2]

Sakeda Masatoshi 酒田正敏. *Kindai Nihon ni okeru taigaikō undō no kenkyū* 近代日本における対外硬運動の研究 (Research on chauvinistic foreign policy movements in modern Japan). Tokyo Daigaku Shuppankai, 1978.

—— "Nisshin sengo gaikō seisaku no kōsoku yōin" 日清戦後外交政策の拘束要因 (Restraints on Japanese foreign policy after the Sino-Japanese War). *Nenpō, kindai Nihon kenkyū* (November 1980), no. 2, pp. 3–27.

Sassa Hiroo 佐々博雄. "Shin-Futsu sensō to Shanhai tōyōgakkan no setsuritsu" 清仏戦争と上海東洋学館の設立 (Sino-French war and the establishment of the School of Tung-yang hsueh-kuan at Shanghai). *Kokushikan daigaku bungakubu jinbungakkai kiyō* (January 1980), no. 12, pp. 55–76.

Satō Saburō 佐藤三郎. *Kindai Nitchū kōshōshi no kenkyū* 近代日中交渉史の研究 (A study on the history of modern Sino-Japanese negotiations). Yoshiwaka Kōbunkan, 1984.

—— "Meiji 33-nen no Amoi jiken ni kansuru kōsatsu" 明治33年の厦門事件に関する考察 (An observation on the Amoy incident of 1900). *Yamagata daigaku kiyō: Jinbun kagaku* (March 1963), 5(2): 1–49. [1]

—— "Nichi-Ro sensō ni okeru Manshū senryōchi ni taisuru Nihon no gunsei ni tsuite" 日露戦争における満州占領地に対する日本の軍政について

(On the military administration of occupied territory in Manchuria during the Russo-Japanese War). *Yamagata daigaku kiyō: Jinbun kagaku* (January 1967), 6(2):1–36. [2]

—— "Ryūkyūhan shobun mondai no kōsatsu" 琉球藩処分問題の考察 (An inquiry into the disposition of the Ryūkyū domain). *Yamagata daigaku kiyō: Jinbun kagaku* (March 1954), 3(1):47–68. [3]

Segawa Yoshinobu 瀬川善信. "Hokushin jihen ni okeru Nihon rikugun shuppei mondai: Kyoryūmin hogo to no kanren ni oite" 北清事変における日本陸軍出兵問題—居留民保護との関連において (The Japanese army's expedition during the Boxer Rebellion: In connection with the problem of protecting Japanese residents). *Saitama daigaku kyōyōbu kiyō* (March 1982), no. 29, pp. 1–32. [1]

—— "Taiwan shuppei (Meiji 7-nen) mondai: Sensen fukoku naki kaigai shuppei no kēsu to shite" 台湾出兵(明治7年)問題—宣戦布告なき海外出兵のケースとして (The Formosan expedition of 1874: A case of military expedition without a declaration of war). *Hōgaku shinpō* (June 1973), 80(6):1–42. [2]

Seki Shizuo 関静雄. "Tai-Ro kyōiron yori mitaru Karafuto seisaku: Meiji gannen yori Meiji 8-nen made" 対露脅威論より見たる樺太政策—明治元年より明治八年まで (Policy toward Sakhalin seen in the light of the perceived threat from Russia, 1868–75). *Hōgaku ronsō* (Kyoto Daigaku) (May 1982), 111(2):39–66; (October 1982), 112(1):44–69.

Shibata Michio and Shibata Asako 柴田三千雄, 柴田朝子. "Bakumatsu ni okeru Furansu no tai-Nichi seisaku" 幕末におけるフランスの対日政策 (French political policy toward Japan in the Bakumatsu period). *Shigaku zasshi* (August 1967), 76(8):46–71.

Shidehara Kijūrō 幣原喜重郎. *Gaikō gojūnen* 外交五十年 (Fifty years as a diplomat). Yomiuri Shinbunsha, 1951.

Shigehisa Tokutarō 重久篤太郎. *Oyatoi gaikokujin, 5: Kyōiku, shūkyō* お雇い外国人, 5 ：教育, 宗教 (Foreigners in the employ of the Japanese government, vol. 5: Education and religion). Kajima Kenkyūjo Shuppankai, 1968.

Shigemitsu Osamu 重光蔵. "Nichi-Ei dōmei" 日英同盟 (The Anglo-Japanese alliance). In Ueda Toshio 植田捷雄, ed., *Kamikawa sensei kanreki kinen: Kindai Nihon gaikōshi no kenkyū* 神川先生還暦記念—近代日本外交史の研究 (Festschrift for Professor Kamikawa Hikomatsu: Studies in modern Japanese diplomatic history), pp. 175–230. Yūhikaku, 1956.

—— "Nichi-Ei dōmei no shūmatsu ni tsuite" 日英同盟の終末について (On the termination of the Anglo-Japanese Alliance, 1–4). *Ōita daigaku keizai ronshū* (June 1955), 7(1):42–58; (October 1955), 7(2):47–74; (March 1956), 7(4):88–106; (September 1956), 8(2):99–126.

Shimada Kinji 島田謹二. *Amerika ni okeru Akiyama Saneyuki* アメリカにお

ける秋山真之 (Lieutenant Akiyama Saneyuki in the United States). Asahi Shimbunsha, 1969.

—— *Roshia ni okeru Hirose Takeo* ロシアにおける広瀬武夫 (Lieutenant Commander Hirose Takeo in Russia), revised and enlarged ed. Kōbundō, 1962.

Shimazu Nariakira Monjo Kankō Kai kai 島津斉彬文書刊行会, ed., *Shimazu Nariakira monjo* 島津斉彬文書 (The papers of Shimazu Nariakira). 3 (out of 4 projected) vols. published to date, Yoshikawa Kōbunkan, 1959–(69).

Shimomura Fujio 下村冨士男. "Boshin sensō to taigai kankei" 戊辰戦争と対外関係 (The Boshin war and Japan's external relations). *Nagoya daigaku bungakubu kenkyū ronshū:* Shigaku (1952), no. 2, pp. 77–125. [1]

—— "Iwakura kōshō izen ni okeru jōyaku mondai" 岩倉交渉以前における条約問題 (The unequal treaty problem prior to Iwakura Tomomi's negotiations). *Nagoya daigaku bungakubu kenkyū ronshū* (1953), vol. 5: *Shigaku, No. 2,* pp. 71–104. [2]

—— *Meiji ishin no gaikō* 明治維新の外交 (The diplomacy of the Meiji restoration). Oyashima Shuppan, 1948.

—— *Meiji shonen jōyaku kaiseishi no kenkyū* 明治初年条約改正史の研究 (Researches on the history of treaty revision in the early Meiji period). Yoshikawa Kōbunkan, 1962.

—— "Nichi-Ro sensō no seikaku" 日露戦争の性格 (The nature of the Russo-Japanese War). *Kokusai seiji* (1957), no. 3: *Nihon gaikōshi kenkyū—Meiji jidai,* pp. 137–52. [3]

—— "Nichi-Ro sensō to Manshū shijō" 日露戦争と満州市場 (The Russo-Japanese War and the Manchurian market). *Nagoya daigaku bungakubu kenkyū ronshū* (March 1956) no. 14, pp. 1–16. [4]

Shin Kukju 申国桂 *Kindai Chōsen gaikōshi kenkyū* 近代朝鮮外交史研究 (A study of the diplomatic history of modern Korea). Yūshindō, 1966.

—— "Kōka jōki chokugo no Kan-Nichi gaikō" 江華条規直後の韓日外交 (Diplomatic relations between Korea and Japan immediately after the conclusion of the Kanghwa Treaty). *Kokusai seiji* (1963), no. 22: *Nikkan kankei no tenkai,* pp. 13–34. [1]

—— "Tōgakutō mondai to Nisshin kaisen" 東学党問題と日清開戦 (The question of the Tonghak party and the outbreak of the Sino-Japanese War). *Kokusai seiji* (1962), no. 19: *Nisshin Nichi-Ro sensō,* pp. 31–51. [2]

Shinobu Junpei 信夫淳平. *Komura gaikōshi* 小村外交史 (A diplomatic biography of Komura Jutarō). Gaimushō, 1953; reprinted by Hara Schobō, 1966.

Shinobu Seizaburō 信夫清三郎. "Chishima Karafuto kōkan jōyaku" 千島樺太交換条約 (The Sakhalin-Kurile Islands exchange treaty). *Kokusai seiji* (1957), no. 3: *Nihon gaikōshi kenkyū—Meiji jidai,* pp. 40–50.

—— *Kindai Nihon gaikōshi* 近代日本外交史 (A diplomatic history of modern Japan). Chūō Kōronsha, 1942; reprinted in 1948 by Kenshinsha.

—— *Mutsu gaikō: Nisshin sensō no gaikōshiteki kenkyū* 陸奥外交—日清戦争の外交史的研究 (Mutsu diplomacy: A historical study of the diplomacy of the Sino-Japanese War). Sōbunkaku, 1935. First published as *Nisshin sensō*, Fukuda Shobō, 1934.

—— *Nisshin sensō* 日清戦争 (Fukuda Shobō, 1934). Revised and enlarged. Nansōsha, 1970.

Shinobu Seizaburō and Nakayama Jiichi 信夫清三郎, 中山治一, eds. *Nichi-Ro sensōshi no kenkyū* 日露戦争史の研究 (Studies on the history of the Russo-Japanese War). Kawade Shobō Shinsha, 1959 (rev. ed. 1972).

Shōji Mitsuo 庄司三男. "Bakumatsu Nichi-Ran gaikōshi no ichi kōsatsu: Shu to shite Oranda-gawa shiryō ni yoru" 幕末日蘭外交史の一考察—主としてオランダ側史料による (One observation on the history of Dutch-Japanese relations during the Bakumatsu period on the basis of Dutch documents). *Kokusai seiji* (1960), no. 14: *Nihon gaikōshi kenkyū—Bakumatsu ishin jidai*, pp. 59–71.

Sugano Tadashi 菅野正. "Pekin giteisho no teiketsu katei: Komura kōshi no baishō kōshō o chūshin ni" 北京議定書の締結過程—小村公使の賠償交渉を中心に (On the process of the conclusion of the Boxer protocol: With particular reference to Minister Komura's negotiations). *Hisutoria* (December 1967), no. 49, pp. 41–62.

Suzuki Yūko 鈴木裕子. "Meiji seifu no kirisutokyō seisaku" 明治政府のキリスト教政策 (The Meiji government's policies on Christianity). *Shigaku zasshi* (February 1977), 86(2):55–73.

Tabohashi Kiyoshi 田保橋潔. "Giwa kempi ran to Nichi-Ro" 義和拳匪乱と日露 (Japan, Russia and the Boxer Uprising). In Shigakukai, ed. *Tōzai kōshōshiron* 東西交渉史論 (A study of the history of East-West diplomatic relations). Fuzan Shobō, ed., 1939. [1]

—— *Kindai Nissen kankei no kenkyū* 近代日鮮関係の研究 (A study of modern Japanese-Korean relations). 2 vols. Chōsen Sōtokufu (Government-General of Korea), 1940 (reprinted by Munetaka Shobō, 1963).

—— "Kindai Nisshi-Sen kankei no kenkyū: Tenshin jōyaku yori Nisshi kaisen ni itaru" 近代日支鮮関係の研究—天津条約より日支開戦に至る (A study of Japan's diplomatic relations with China and Korea: From the Treaty of Tientsin to the outbreak of the Sino-Japanese War), *Keijō teikoku daigaku hōbungakubu kenkyū chōsa sasshi* (1930), no. 3.

—— *Nisshin sen'eki gaikōshi no kenkyū* 日清戦役外交史の研究 (A study of the diplomatic history of the Sino-Japanese War). Tōkō Shoin, 1951.

—— *Zōtei: Kindai Nihon gaikoku kankeishi* 増訂近代日本外国関係史 (A

history of modern Japan's foreign relations). Revised and enlarged edition, Tokō Shoin, 1943; reprinted by Hara Shobō, 1976.

Takahashi Kunitarō 高橋邦太郎. *Oyatoi gaikokujin,* vol. 6: *Gunji* お雇い 外国人, 6 ：軍事 (Foreign advisers in the employment of the Japanese government, vol. 6: Military affairs). Kajima Kenkyūjo Shuppankai, 1968.

Takahashi Shigeo 高橋茂夫. "Meiji 33-nen Amoi jiken no ichi kōsatsu: Yamamoto kaigun daijin no taido o chūshin to shite" 明治33年厦門事件 の一考察—山本海軍大臣の態度を中心として (A study of the Amoy Incident of 1900: With special reference to the position of Navy Minister Yamamoto). *Gunji shigaku* (March 1973), 8(4): 33–44.

Takano Akira 高野明. *Nihon to Roshia* 日本とロシア (Japan and Russia). Kinokuniya Shoten, 1971.

Tamura Kōsaku 田村幸策. "Nihon gaikō shijōni okeru Mutsu Munemitsu no chii" 日本外交史上における陸奥宗光の地位 (The place of Mutsu Munemitsu in Japanese diplomatic history). *Gaikō jihō* (January 1967), no. 1036, pp. 5–15.

Tanaka Hiroyuki 田中弘之. "Bakumatsu no ichi Ogasawara-tōmin o meguru ryōji saiban" 幕末の一小笠原島民をめぐる領事裁判 (The consular trial of a native of the Bonins during the late Shogunate). *Komazawa shigaku* (March 1976), no. 23, pp. 63–86.

—— "Bunkyūdo no Ogasawaratō kaishū o meguru gaikō" 文久度の小笠 原島回収をめぐる外交 (Diplomatic relations concerning the recovery of the Bonins during the early 1860s). *Komazawa shigaku* (March 1973), no. 20, pp. 35–45.

Tanaka Masahiro 田中正弘. "Ishin zengo ni okeru Fon Buranto" 維新前後 におけるフォンブラント (Von Brandt at the time of the Meiji Restoration). *Kokushigaku* (October 1980), no. 112, pp. 20–41. [1]

—— "Toba fushimi sensō to Futsukoku gunji kyōkan" 鳥羽伏見戦争 と仏国軍事教官 (French military instructors and the Toba-Fushimi war). *Kokushigaku* (September 1971), no. 85, pp. 40–49. [2]

—— "Tōhoku sensō ni katsuyaku seru Suneru no sujō" 東北戦争に活躍 せるスネルの素性 (The true story of the Schnells' involvement in the Tōhoku war). *Kokugakuin zasshi* (May 1973), 74(5): 14–27. [3]

—— "Yonezawahan to Hiramatsu Buhei" 米沢藩と平松武兵衛 (Hiramatsu Buhei and the Yonezawa domain). *Gunji shigaku* (September 1976), 12(2): 51–62. [4]

Tanaka Naokichi 田中直吉. "Chōsen o meguru kokusai kattō no hito maku: Keijō jingo no hen" 朝鮮をめぐる国際葛藤の一幕—京城甲申の変 (One act from the drama of international conflict over Korea: The incident of 1882 at Kyŏngsŏng, Imo pyon). *Hōgaku shirin* (November 1957), 55(2): 19–82. [1]

—— "Nissen kankei no ichi danmen: Keijō jingo no hen" 日鮮関係の一断面—京城壬午の変— (An episode in Japanese-Korean relations: The Imo Kunlan in Seoul). *Kokusai seiji* (1957), no. 3: *Nihon gaikōshi kenkyū—Meiji jidai*, pp. 67–92. [2]

Tani Hisao 谷寿夫. *Kimitsu Nichi-Ro senshi* 機密日露戦史 (The confidential history of the Russo-Japanese War). Hara Shobō, 1966.

Taoka Ryōichi 田岡良一. *Ōtsu jiken no saihyōka* 大津事件の再評価 (A reappraisal of the Ōtsu Incident). Yūhikaku, 1976 (rev. ed., 1983).

Teh Tehn-chiau 戴天昭. "Nisshin sengo sangoku kanshō to Taiwan" 日清戦後三国干渉と台湾 (The Triple Intervention after the Sino-Japanese War, and Formosa). *Hōgaku shirin* (February 1969), 66(3):1–53.

Teramoto Yasutoshi 寺本康俊. "Manshū no kokusai chūritsuka seisaku to Komura gaikō" 満州の国際中立化政策と小村外交 (The international neutralization of Manchuria, and Komura diplomacy). *Seiji keizai shigaku* (December 1983), no. 209, pp. 35–44.

Terashima Munenori Kenkyūkai 寺島宗則研究会, ed., *Terashima Munemori kankei shiryō* 寺島宗則関係資料 (Papers relating to Terashima Munenori). Shinjinsha, 1987. 2 vols.

Tōkairin Shizuo 東海林静男. "Jōyaku kaisei ni taisuru zai-Nichi kyoryū gaikokujin senkyōshi no dōkō" 条約改正にたいする在日居留外国人宣教師の動向 (Attitudes held by foreign missionaries resident in Japan on treaty revision). *Rekishi* (September 1966), no. 33, pp. 12–27.

Tokyo Daigaku Shiryō Hensanjo 東京大学史料編纂所 (University of Tokyo Historiographical Institute), ed., *Dai Nippon komonjo: Bakumatsu gaikoku kankei monjo* 大日本古文書—幕末外国関係文書 (Old documents of Japan: Official documents relating to foreign relations in the Bakumatsu period). Shiryō Hensan Gakkai, Tokyo Daigaku, 1910–1980.

Tomita Hiroshi 富田仁. "Nichi-Futsu shūkō tsūshō jōyaku o megutte" 日仏修好通商条約をめぐって (On the Franco-Japanese Treaty of Amity and Commerce). *Furansugaku kenkyū* (March 1982), no. 12, pp. 1–17.

—— *Merume Kashon* メルメ・カション (Mermet Cashon). Yūrindō, 1980.

Tōyama Shigeki 遠山茂樹. "Kuga Katsunan no gaikō ron: Tokuni Nisshin sensō zengo no jiki o chūshin to shite" 陸羯南の外交論—とくに日清戦争前後の時期を中心として (An essay on Kuga Katsunan's views on foreign policy: Especially around the period of the Sino-Japanese War). *Yokohama shiritsu daigaku ronsō: Jinbun kagaku keiretsu* (April 1973), 24(2–3):1–29.

Tsuda Takako 津田多賀子. "1880-nendai ni okeru Nihon seifu no higashi Ajia seisaku tenkai to rekkyō" 1880年代における日本政府の東アジア政策展開と列強 (The development of Japan's policy in East Asia during the 1880s, and the powers). *Shigaku zasshi* (December 1982), 91(12):1–33.

Tsurumi Yūsuke 鶴見祐輔. *Gotō Shimpei* 後藤新平 (Gotō Shimpei). 4 vols. Gotō Shinpei Haku Denki Hensankai, 1937–38 (reprinted in 1965 by Keisō Shobō).

Uchiyama Masakuma 内山正熊. *Gendai Nihon gaikō shiron* 現代日本外交史論 (Historical essays on modern Japan's diplomacy). Keiō Tsūshin, 1971, chs. 1–4.

—— "Kasumigaseki seitō gaikō no seiritsu" 霞ヶ関正統外交の成立 (The establishment of Kasumigaseki [Foreign Ministry] diplomacy). *Kokusai seiji* (1965), no. 28: *Nihon gaikōshi no shomondai, 2*, pp. 1–16. [1]

—— *Kōbe jiken: Meiji gaikō no shuppatsuten* 神戸事件—明治外交の出発点 (The Kōbe incident: The starting point of Meiji diplomacy). Chūō Kōronsha, 1983.

—— "Komura gaikō hihan" 小村外交批判 (A critique of Komura's diplomacy). *Hōgaku kenkyū* (Keiō Gijuku Daigaku) (May 1968), 41(5):123–50. [2]

—— "Nihon ni okeru shin-Ei-shugi no enkaku" 日本における親英主義の沿革 (The history of pro-British feeling in Japan). In Uchiyama, *Gendai Nihon gaikōshiron*, pp. 29–69. [3]

Ueda Toshio 植田捷雄. "Nichi-Ei dōmei: Sono seiritsu katei to igi" 日英同盟—その成立過程と意義 (The Anglo-Japanese Alliance: The history of its formation and its significance). *Hitotsubashi ronsō* (March 1967), 57(3): 23–47. [1]

—— "Ryōdo kizoku kankeishi" 領土帰属関係史 (A history of Japan's foreign relations pertaining to territorial jurisdiction). In Kokusaihō Gakkai 国際法学会 (The Japan Association of International Law), ed., *Heiwa jōyaku no sōgōteki kenkyū* 平和条約の総合的研究 (A comprehensive study of the Peace Treaty [of 1951], 1), pp. 119–96. Yūhikaku, 1952. [2]

—— "Ryūkyū kizoku o meguru Nisshin kōshō" 琉球帰属を繞る日清交渉 (Sino-Japanese negotiations concerning the disputed sovereignty of the Ryūkyūs). *Tōyō bunka kenkyūjo kiyō* (1951), no. 2, pp. 151–201. [3]

Umetani Noboru 梅渓昇. *Oyatoi gaikokujin* お雇い外国人 (Foreigners in the employ of the Japanese government). Nihon Keizai Shinbunsha, 1965, pp. 70–77.

—— *Oyatoi gaikokujin*, vol. 1: *Gaisetsu* お雇い外国人, 1 —概説 (Foreigners in the employ of the Japanese government, vol. 1: An overview). Kajima Kenkyūjo Shuppankai, 1968.

—— *Oyatoi gaikokujin*, vol. 8: *Seiji hōsei* お雇い外国人, 8 —政治, 法制 (Foreigners in the employ of the Japanese government, vol. 8: Political and legal systems). Kajima Kenkyūjo Shuppankai, 1968.

—— *Oyatoi gaikokujin: Meiji Nihon no wakiyakutachi* お雇い外国人—明治日本の脇役たち (Foreign employees: Hidden contributors to Meiji Japan). Nihon Keizai Shinbunsha, 1965.

UNESCO Higashi Ajia Bunka Kenkyū Sentā ユネスコ東アジア文化研究
センター. *Shiryō: Oyatoi gaikokujin* 資料—御雇外国人 (Source materials
on foreigners in the employ of the Japanese government). Shōgakkan,
1975.

Wagatsuma Sakae 我妻栄 et al., eds. *Nihon seiji saiban shiroku: Meiji, 1*
日本政治裁判史録, 明治 1 (Historical records of Japanese political trials:
The Meiji period, 1). Daiichi Hōki Shuppan, 1968.

Waseda Daigaku Shakai Kagaku Kenkyūjo 早稲田大学社会科学研究所
(Ōkuma Institute of Social Sciences, Waseda University), ed. *Ōkuma
bunsho* 大隈文書 (The papers of Ōkuma Shigenobu), vol. 1. Published
by the editor in 5 vols. 1958–1962.

Watanabe Ikujirō 渡辺幾治郎. "Seiban jiken to kindai Nihon no kensetsu"
征蕃事件と近代日本の建設 (The Formosan expedition and the building
of modern Japan). *Ōkuma kenkyū* (1954), no. 5, pp. 1–95.

Yamabe Kentarō 山辺健太郎. "Itsubi no hen ni tsuite" 乙未の変について
(On the murder of Queen Min). *Kokusai seiji* (1963), no. 22: *Nikkan kankei
no tenkai*, pp. 69–81. [1]

—— "Jingo gunran ni tsuite" 壬午軍乱について (On the Imjin rebellion).
Rekishigaku kenkyū (September 1961), no. 257, pp. 13–25. [2]

—— "Kōshin jihen ni tsuite: Tokuni 'Jiyūtōshi' no ayamari ni kanrenshite"
甲申事変について—とくに自由党史のあやまりに関連して　(On the
Kabsin incident: With particular reference to erroneous accounts in the
"History of the Liberal Party"). *Rekishigaku kenkyū* (August 1960), no.
244, pp. 23–34. [3]

—— *Nikkan heigō shōshi* 日韓併合小史 (A short history of the Japanese
annexation of Korea). Iwanami Shoten, 1966.

Yamaguchi Kazuyuki 山口一之. "Giwadan jihen to Nihon no hannō: Kachū
no kuri o hirou" 義和団事変と日本の反応—火中の栗を拾う (Japanese
reaction to the Boxer Uprising: To pull the chestnuts out of the fire).
Kokusai seiji (1969), no. 42: *Kokusai seiji no riron to hōhō*, pp. 106–26.

Yamamoto Shigeru 山本茂. *Jōyaku kaiseishi* 条約改正史 (A history of treaty
revision). Takayama Shoin, 1943.

Yamamoto Shirō 山本四郎. "Amoi jiken ni tsuite" 厦門事件について (On
the Amoy incident). In Akamatsu Toshihide Kyōju Taikan Kinen Jigyōkai,
ed., *Kokushi ronshū* (Essays in Japanese history), pp. 1135–48. 1972.

Yamashita Shigekazu 山下重一. "Tai-Shin kaiyaku buntō kōshō to Inoue
Kowashi" 対清改約分島交渉と井上毅 (Sino-Japanese negotiations in
1880, and Inoue Kowashi). *Kokugakuin hōgaku* (February 1982), 19(4):
115–164.

Yamawaki Shigeo 山脇重雄. "Bazanpo jiken" 馬山浦事件 (The Masan incident). *Tōhoku daigaku bungakubu kenkyū nenpō*, 1–3 (January 1959), no. 9,

pp. 1–45; (February 1960), no. 10, pp. 138–87; (February 1963), no. 13, pp. 47–125.

Yamawaki Teijirō 山脇悌二郎. *Nagasaki no Oranda shōkan* 長崎のオランダ 商館 (The Dutch company in Nagasaki). Chūō Kōronsha, 1980.

Yanai Kenji 箭内健次, ed., *Tsūkō ichiran: Zokushū* 通航一覧—続輯 (A survey of foreign relations: A sequel). 5 vols. Osaka; Seibundō, 1973.

Yasuoka Akio 安岡昭男. "Bankoku kōhō to Meiji gaikō" 万国公法と明治 外交 (International law and Meiji diplomacy). *Seiji keizai shigaku* (March 1983), no. 200, pp. 188–99. [1]

—— "Inoue Kaoruron" 井上馨論 (On Foreign Minister Inoue Kaoru). *Kokusai seiji* (1966), no. 33: *Nihon gaikōshi kenkyū—Gaikō shidōsharon*, pp. 10–26. [2]

—— "Iwakura Tomomi no gaikō seiryaku" 岩倉具視の外交政略 (Iwakura Tomomi's diplomatic strategy). *Hōsei shigaku* (March 1969) no. 21, pp. 1–23. [3]

—— *Meiji ishin to ryōdo mondai* 明治維新と領土問題 (The Meiji restoration and territorial questions). Kyōikusha, 1980.

Yokohamashi-shi Henshūshitsu 横浜市史編集室, ed., *Yokohamashi-shi* 横浜 市史 (A history of Yokohama City), vols. 2 and 3. Yokohama: Yūrindō, 1958–63.

Yoshida Mitsukuni 吉田光邦. *Oyatoi gaikokujin*, vol. 2: *Sangyō* お雇い外 国人, 2：産業 (Foreigners in the employ of the Japanese government, vol. 2: Industries). Kajima Kenkyūjo Shuppankai, 1968.

Yoshimura Michio 吉村道男. "Nichi-Ro kōwa mondai no ichi sokumen: Nichi-Bei no tai-Shin taido o chūshin ni" 日露講和問題の一側面—日米 の対清態度を中心 (One aspect of Russo-Japanese peace negotiations: With particular reference to Japanese and American attitudes toward China). *Kokusai seiji* (1961), no. 19: *Nihon gaikōshi kenkyū—Nisshin Nichi-Ro sensō*, pp. 119–33.

Yuzin Chiautong 黄有仁. See Huang Chao-t'ang 黄昭堂.

3

From the End of the Russo-Japanese War to the Manchurian Incident

Ikei Masaru
Hatano Sumio
Inoue Yūichi
Asada Sadao

Studies in Japanese diplomatic history for the period under consideration have made significant progress in recent years. The most obvious
reason is that the basic archival materials and manuscript sources are
available to researchers; unlike source materials for the 1930s, those
relating to this period were spared deliberate destruction on the eve of
Japan's surrender.

Second, a growing number of Japanese scholars are taking broader
perspectives in examining Japanese foreign policy within the context
of world politics. This approach entails the incorporation of recent

findings by scholars abroad as well as collaboration with them. Symposia with foreign scholars have also made a considerable contribution in this respect. One example is Hosoya Chihiro and Saitō Makoto, eds., *Washinton taisei to Nichi-Bei kankei* (The Washington system and Japanese-American relations), the outcome of a binational conference between Japanese and American scholars.

Third, the study of diplomatic history has expanded its scope to encompass an analysis of the decision-making process; the linkage between foreign and domestic policies; external images and perceptions held by policymakers and opinion leaders; and shifts in public opinion as reflected in mass media. Representative of such an approach is Itō Takashi's *Shōwa shoki seijishi kenkyū* (A study in the political history of the early Shōwa period), which analyzes the conflict between and collaboration among various political groups over the issue of the London Naval Treaty in 1930.

Fourth, there is a growing tendency among Japanese historians to apply behavioral science approaches. One early example is Seki Hiroharu's *Gendai Higashi Ajia kokusai kankyō no tanjō* (The emergence of the contemporary international system in East Asia).

AFTER THE RUSSO-JAPANESE WAR

Imperialistic or Defensive War?

Before we move on to post-1905 developments, it would be in order here to pose and summarize historiographical debates concerning imperialism and Japan's place in the international system in the early twentieth century. (The causes of the Russo-Japanese War as such are treated in chapter 1, with which our discussion overlaps to some extent.)

Was the Russo-Japanese War the first imperialistic war in Asia or was it a defensive war against tsarist Russia? This question is traced back to pre-World War II controversies. Phrased in simple Marxist-Leninist terms, the issue was boiled down essentially to when Japanese capitalism reached the stage of imperialism.

The first to open fire in the postwar controversy was Inoue Kiyoshi, who published *Nihon no gunkokushugi* (Militarism in Japan in 1953). According to him, Japanese imperialism emerged in 1899, and the

Russo-Japanese War was an imperialistic war caused by the ambitions of the military and bureaucrats that were linked with the demand of bourgeois forces for monopolistic control of the Manchurian market. Fujii Shōichi [1] further developed this thesis, particularly stressing the role of the Japanese bourgeoisie.

Refuting this thesis, Shimomura Fujio emphasized that the demands of the Japanese bourgeoisie for the Manchurian market had hardly grown strong enough to constitute the cause for war with Russia. Japanese policy was defensive in nature, he concluded, for Japan opposed Russian encroachment on Korea and posession of Manchuria. Fujimura Michio agreed that the war was not caused by Japan's desire for monopolistic control of the Manchurian market, but he admitted that, from the viewpoint of international politics, the Russo-Japanese War partook of the nature of an imperialistic war [3].

In 1959 an important joint study by historians at Nagoya University (the "Nagoya group") was published as Shinobu Seizaburō and Nakayama Jiichi, eds., *Nichi-Ro sensōshi no kenkyū* (Studies on the history of the Russo-Japanese War). Although this work diversified the controversy, its focus was the Manchurian market. Fujii Shōichi, one of the contributors, argued that the Russo-Japanese War was an imperialistic war fought in the worldwide context of struggles among imperialist powers in the early twentieth century. He also criticized Shimomura by emphasizing that the demands for the Manchurian market powerfully appealed to the Japanese military, bureaucrats, and bourgeoisie. The whole controversy began to wane in the 1970s.

International Setting After 1905

One of the early works on the transformation of Japan's international environment after 1905 is a compact volume, *Nichi-Ro sensō igo* (After the Russo-Japanese War) by Nakayama Jiichi and his colleagues in European history (the members of the "Nagoya group"). As the subtitle "International relations of imperialism in East Asia" suggests, the work is broad in scope: it attempts to examine the interaction between Far Eastern and European international politics in the age of imperialism. Japan, as a latecomer in the diplomacy of imperialism, attempted to overcome its economic vulnerability by cultivating military power and pursuing a politically monopolistic policy on the continent. When confronted with the "dollar diplomacy" of the United States in Manchuria, Japan was ready for rapproachement with Russia to counter the mutually perceived threat. Relations with Britian and Germany, as well as with the United States and Russia, are sketched up to the outbreak of the Chinese Revolution of 1911. This book, published in a somewhat popular format, has not been followed by more detailed monographs.

Recent years have seen several studies on the impact of the Russo-Japanese War on domestic political changes and foreign policy after the war. The growth of nationalistic chauvinism is examined in Miyaji Masando's *Nichi-Ro sensōgo seijishi no kenkyū* (A study in political history after the Russo-Japanese War). Another important study on the domestic political turmoil following the Russo-Japanese War is Banno Junji's *Taishō seihen* (The political change in the Taishō period), which is based extensively on unpublished sources.

Such political crises revolved largely around the issue of arms expansion at a time when Japan was close to financial bankruptcy as the result of the Russo-Japanese War. The army-navy conflict over the issue of arms expansion is examined in Masuda Tomoko's study on the political process of naval expansion, 1906–1914.

The Manchurian Question

The dynamics of international relations in Manchuria is treated by Hatano Yoshihiro. In his article [1], he focuses on U.S.-Japanese conflict over Manchuria, occasioned by E. H. Harriman's plan to introduce American capital into Manchuria and Secretary of State Philander Knox's scheme to neutralize the Manchurian railways.

A more recent study is found in Hata Ikuhiko, *Taiheiyō kokusai kankeishi: Nichi-Bei oyobi Nichi-Ro kiki no keifu, 1900–1935* (A history of international relations in the Pacific: Analysis of Japanese-American and Russo-Japanese war scares, 1900–1935), chs. 1–3. Hata analyzes these war scares within the context of conflicting interests among the three powers in Manchuria. For this purpose, Hata applies what he calls "equidistant analysis," a methodology that would place the historian's perspective at the midpoint (or "equidistant") from all the nations he treats.

Japanese policies toward the Manchurian problems that arose in the aftermath of the Russo-Japanese War are examined in a collection of essays edited by Kurihara Ken, ed., *Tai-Manmō seisakushi no ichimen* (Aspects of [Japan's] Manchurian-Mongolian policy). It contains Kurihara's study of the policy toward the Manchurian problems, focusing on the activities of Hagiwara Shūichi, the first Japanese consul-general in Mukden. His other article [5], on the Kwantung governor-generalship, examines, within the context of Japan's domestic politics, the activities of Japan's first governmental machinery established to manage Manchurian affairs. Baba Akira's contribution [2], an essay on the Manchurian policy of the first Saionji cabinet (1906–1908), examines Chinese attempts at enlisting the cooperation of Germany and the United States to oppose Japan's policy of expanding its railway and mining interests in Manchuria. These works agree in emphasizing the nature of Japan's "dual diplomacy"—policy conducted by the military independent of or in contradiction to the policy of the government (the Foreign Ministry).

Tago Keiichi [3] takes exception to this prevailing view of "dual diplomacy." In this article he argues that there was much in common between the policies of the military and the government on the administration of Manchuria immediately after the conclusion of the 1905 Sino-Japanese treaty.

The most detailed treatment of the development of Japanese foreign and defense policies from 1900 to 1912—with focus on the Manchurian question—is Tsunoda Jun's full-length study, *Manshū mondai to kokubō hōshin: Meiji kōki ni okeru kokubō kankyō no hendō* (The Manchurian question and Japan's defense policy: Changes in the defense setting [of Japan] after the late Meiji period). As the subtitle suggests, Tsunoda pays full attention to the international context of Japanese policies and strategies. His research on Japan's decision-making process is thorough, exhaustively utilizing the available Japanese archival and manuscript sources as well as printed documents of the powers involved. In the first half of the book Tsunoda traces in great detail the entire course of the "Manchurian question" from the Open Door notes, Japan's negotiations leading to the Anglo-Japanese Alliance, the decision for war with Russia, Japan's control of Manchuria after the war, and Secretary of State Philander Knox's neutralization scheme and the formation of the four-power China consortium. The second part of the book covers Japanese efforts to meet the Russian and American threat. There is a detailed discussion of the formulation of the Imperial National Defense Policy of 1907. On all these issues, Tsunoda's analyses are shrewd and judicious, although he eschews broader interpretations.

The South Manchuria Railway Company

Founded in 1906, this railway company (SMRC) formed the mainstay of Japanese expansion in Manchuria after the Russo-Japanese War. Andō Hikotarō, ed., *Mantetsu: Nihon teikokushugi to Chūgoku* (The South Manchuria Railway Company: Japanese imperialism and China) is the result of a joint project of a Waseda University research group. As the subtitle suggests, this work attempts to study the railway as an instrument for colonizing Manchuria. Miyasaka Hiroshi, a member of this research group, has published an article on the establishment of the SMRC with particular reference to Sino-Japanese relations over the three Eastern Provinces. Kaneko Fumio, in his article [4] on the early years (1907–16) of the SMRC, points out that since its establishment this railway had to compete with the Chinese Eastern Railway for the north Manchurian market and contend with the Korean Railway for Japanese-Manchurian trade routes. Harada Katsumasa's *Mantetsu* (The South Manchuria Railway Company) is a compact, readable volume that traces the company from its establishment in 1906 to its debacle in 1945. While the author discusses the role that the SMRC played in Japanese aggression in China, he also reminds the reader that the core of the railway was its operation of a railroad network.

The above-cited works are not based on the SMRC records. (The problem of access to them is discussed in chapter 1.) Instead, they rely heavily on its official histories: Minami Manshū Tetsudō Kabushiki Kaisha, ed., *Minami Manshū Tetsudō Kabushiki Kaisha jūnenshi* (A ten-year history of the South Manchuria Railway Company) and its sequel, *Minami Manshū Tetsudō Kabushiki Kaisha dainiji jūnenshi* (A history of the second decade of the South Manchuria Railway Company). Another useful work, *Minami Manshū Tetsudō Kabushiki Kaisha daisanji jūnenshi* (A history of the third decade of the

South Manchuria Railway Company), long out of print, has been reprinted. Manshikai, ed., *Manshū kaihatsu shijū nenshi* (A forty-year history of the development of Manchuria) is a broad survey of the administration of Manchuria, focusing on the South Manchuria Railway, that amply rests on primary sources.

A recent guide to the materials of the SMRC is: *Kyū-shokuminchi kankei kikan kankōbutsu sōgo mokuroku: Minami Manshū Tetsudō Kabushiki Kaishahen* (A comprehensive bibliography of materials published by Japan's former colonial agencies: The South Manchuria Railway Company), compiled and published by Ajia Keizai Kenkyūjo (Institute of Developing Economies). The *Gendaishi shiryō* (Documents on contemporary history) series prints source materials on the South Manchuria Railway Company that have survived; they relate to the period 1923–25 and have been published as *Mantetsu* (SMRC), 3 vols., edited and with an introduction by Itō Takeo, Ogiwara Kiwamu, and Fujii Masuo.

The Army's Continental Policy

Regarding the political activities of the Japanese army, which were enhanced following the Russo-Japanese War, Imai Seiichi has pointed out in his early essay [2] that the military sought political independence from the cabinet and a more powerful role in the formulation of Japan's continental policy. Kitaoka Shin'ichi's recent monograph, *Nihon rikugun to tairiku seisaku, 1906–1918* (The Japanese army and continental policy, 1906–1918), empirically examines the relationship between the military's political position and its active role in continental policy. Tracing the development of Japan's continental policy from the end of the Russo-Japanese War to World War I, Kitaoka studies the process through which the army attained growing political autonomy during this period. Drawing a line between Japan's policy toward China and its administration of Manchuria, Kitaoka examines Japan's Manchurian policy in three areas: railways, finance, and administrative agencies. Rejecting a monolithic view of the Japanese army, he analyzes the relationship among leading individuals of the major factions within the army. Kitaoka's well-documented study is one of the major contributions of recent years.

Continental Expansionists and Their Critics

Concerning the figures who played roles in Japan's continental policy, the following studies are useful. On the diplomat Yamaza Enjirō, who inherited the China policy of Komura Jutarō, Ichimata Masao has written *Yamaza Enjirō den: Meiji jidai ni okeru tairiku seisaku no jikkōsha* (The life of Yamaza Enjirō: An executor of Japan's continental policy during the Meiji period). The thought and behavior of Uchida Ryōhei, a representative right-wing "adventurer" *(rōnin)* in China, are closely examined by Hatsuse Ryūhei, *Dentōteki uyoku Uchida Ryōhei no kenkyū* (A study of Uchida Ryōhei, a traditional right-winger). Sugiyama Shigemaru, another political wire puller who maneuvered for continental expansion, is portrayed in a biography by Ichimata Masao, edited by Ōhata Tokushirō. A stimulating study of these "adventurers" is found in Masumi Junnosuke, *Nihon seitō shiron* (A history of Japanese party politics), vol. 3.

On the other hand, there was a small but vocal group, headed by journalist Ishibashi Tanzan, who urged relinquishing Japan's interests on the continent (even in Manchuria). Ishibashi's views are examined by, among others, Masuda Hiroshi. For a systematic study of *Tōyō Keizai Shinpō*, an important liberal journal, which Ishibashi presided over, see Inoue Kiyoshi and Watanabe Tōru, eds., *Taishōki no kyūshin-teki jiyūshugi* (Radical liberalism of the Taishō period). The specially relevant essays it contains of Japan's continental policy from the end of the Russo-Japanese War to the period of World War I are: Yamamoto Shirō's analysis [1] of the journal's treatment of the China question; Inoue Kiyoshi's essay on its critique of Japanese imperialism; and Iguchi Kazuki's discussion of the journal's treatment of Japan's colonial policy.

Transformation of the Anglo-Japanese Alliance

After the Russo-Japanese War, the Anglo-Japanese Alliance gradually lost its status as the main pillar of Japanese diplomacy, and historians have accordingly dealt with the problems relating to the revision of this alliance. Kajima Morinosuke's survey history, *Nichi-Ei gaikōshi* (A history of Anglo-Japanese diplomatic relations), reproduces major documents but lacks analysis. The same can be said about his detailed

studies, *Dainikai Nichi-Ei dōmei to sono jidai* (The second Anglo-
Japanese Alliance) and *Daisankai Nichi-Ei dōmei to sono jidai* (The
third Anglo-Japanese Alliance), vols. 8 and 9, respectively, of his
multivolume Kajima series on Japanese diplomatic history. Kurobane
Shigeru's *Nichi-Ei dōmeishi no kenyū* (A study on the history of the
Anglo-Japanese Alliance) covers the entire career of the alliance—not
only its origins and abrogation but also rather obscure periods in
between. It is the most thorough study of the alliance from the Japanese viewpoint. As noted in chapter 2, the most exhaustive work,
based on the archives of both nations, is Ian Nish's two-volume
masterly study: *The Anglo-Japanese Alliance, 1894–1907* (London:
Athlone Press, 1966) and *Alliance in Decline, 1908–1923* (1972).

The problems related to the termination of the alliance are treated
in Murashima Shigeru's article on the nature of the third Anglo-
Japanese Alliance and Ōhata Tokushirō's essay [2]. Murashima's
article examines from military-strategic viewpoints the changing
nature of the Anglo-Japanese Alliance from the Russo-Japanese War
to the Washington Naval Conference. The impact of anti-Japanese
movements in Canada is emphasized in Ōhara Yūko's study on Canada's
role in the abrogation of the Anglo-Japanese Alliance and Japan's
response.

China Policy During the 1911 Revolution

The foremost study on this subject is contained in Usui Katsumi's
Nihon to Chūgoku: Taishō jidai (Japan and China in the Taishō period),
which provides an overall perspective on Japan's China policy during
this period. Solidly based on primary sources, this book builds on his
earlier articles—among others, those on the Chinese Revolution of
1911 and Japan's response: [3], [5]. Usui carefully analyzes the conflict, competition, and cooperation between the Japanese Foreign
Ministry and the army in the decision-making process. Somura
Yasunobu has also examined Japan's response in two essays. In one of
them [2] he discusses the relation between the Manchurian question
and the Chinese Revolution, and in the other essay [3] he examines the
reaction of Japanese public opinion.

Ōhata Tokushirō's article [5] on Japan's response to the 1911 Revolution argues that Japan's basic policy to "protect" its Manchurian-

Mongolian interests, which would eventually result in the Twenty-One Demands of 1915, had already been formed during the period of the 1911 Revolution. A study that focuses on the moves of the Japanese military is Yui Masaomi's article [2]. A detailed examination of the Japanese navy's response to the outbreak of the 1911 Revolution is Hatano Masaru's study which is based on the diaries of Commander Takeshita Isamu (then serving in the Navy General Staff) and Vice-Navy Minister Takarabe Takeshi.

For more specific studies on Japan's dealings with Yuan Shih-k'ai, who attained power through a compromise with Sun Yat-sen, there are: Ikei Masaru, "Japan's Response to the Chinese Revolution of 1911" [3] and Somura Yasunobu's article [1] on Japan and the problem of Yuan Shih-k'ai's imperial regime. Somura has collected his essays on Sino-Japanese relations in his *Kindaishi kenkyū, 1: Nihon to Chūgoku* (A study of modern diplomatic history: Japan and China).

Important studies on the various responses of major powers to the 1911 Revolution include: Irie Keishirō's essay on the recognition of the new Chinese government; and Usui Katsumi's article [6] on the 1911 Revolution and Anglo-Japanese relations.

Among other works relating to the 1911 revolution and its aftermath, a series of essays by Kurihara Ken are noteworthy. In one [1] of them he examines the circumstances behind the 1913 assassination of Abe Moritarō, director of the Political Affairs Bureau of the Foreign Ministry, in the context of Japan's policy toward Manchuria and Mongolia. Abe was generally regarded as a spokesman of Japan's "weak-kneed" continental policy. Kurihara has also published an important article [2] on the first and second independence movements in Manchuria and Mongolia, in which he describes the Japanese military's abortive plans to establish a "Manchuria-Mongolia Kingdom" designed to restore the Ch'ing dynasty. These and other essays are collected in the above-mentioned book edited by Kurihara.

More recently, Yamaguchi Toshiaki published, with introductory comments, the newly discovered papers of Hamaomote Matasuke, chief of the China section of the Army General Staff. These papers are essential for our understanding of the extent to which the Japanese army interfered with domestic affairs in China at a time when it was racked with the rebellion against President Yuan Shih-k'ai's plan to end the republic and enthrone himself (the so-called third Chinese Revolution of 1915).

The Annexation of Korea

There have been almost no full-scale studies that analyze diplomatic developments from the Japanese-Korean treaty of 1905 to the annexation of Korea in 1910. The only works available are survey histories written for general readers: Yamabe Kentarō's *Nikkan heigō shōshi* (A short history of the annexation of Korea) and *Nihon no Kankoku heigō* (The Japanese annexation of Korea); and Nakatsuka Akira's *Kindai Nihon to Chōsen* (Modern Japan and Korea).

Until recently the main sources on Korean-Japanese relations were the Foreign Ministry's *Nihon gaikō bunsho* (Documents on Japanese foreign policy), vols. 38–43 (covering the years 1905–10), and Itō Hirobumi, ed., *Hisho ruisan: Chōsen kōshō shiryō* (A collection of secret documents: Materials relating to the negotiations over Korea). The gaps have been filled with the publication of *Nikkan gaikō shiryō shūsei* (A collection of diplomatic documents on Japanese-Korean relations), edited by Kim Chong-myong (Kin Sei-mei). The sixth volume of this collection contains diplomatic documents hitherto unpublished, and the eighth volume, *Chōsen no hogo oyobi heigō* (The protection and annexation of Korea), edited by Chōsen Sōtokufu (Office of the Korean Governor-General), reproduces some of the most important materials for our purposes. Another compilation of previously unpublished materials is Ichikawa Masaaki, ed., *Kankoku heigō shiryō* (Materials on the annexation of Korea). Ichikawa has also authored *Anjū-kon to Nikkan kankeishi* (An Chung-gŭn and the history of Japanese-Korean relations) mainly on the basis of new materials on An Chung-gŭn, who assassinated Itō Hirobumi in 1909.

As the above account shows, the output of writings on Japanese colonial policy toward Korea prior to 1910 has been meager. One reason is that Japanese historians have tended to regard the Office of the Resident General (opened in 1906) as, at least in form, an organ for merely indirect control of Korea, and to assume that the full-scale direct administration of Korea began with its annexation in 1910 when the Office of the Resident General was replaced by the Governor-General of Korea, who was bestowed with far-reaching authority.

Taking issue with this interpretation, Pak Kei-shik (Boku kei-shoku), in his *Nihon teikokushugi no Chōsen shihai* (The rule of Korea under Japanese imperialism), points out that many of the administra-

tive structures and institutions of the Office of the Resident General
were taken over by that of the Governor-General. His work would
suggest the need to take note of the continuities of the Japanese
control of Korea before and after its annexation.

Recently a few works have appeared that attempt to place Japan's
Korea policy within the broad context of the colonial policies of the
Western imperialist powers in the early twentieth century. Tanaka
Shin'ichi's essays attempt to show, from the perspectives of international law and land policy, that Japan's "protectorate" policy toward
Korea was based on careful examination of the powers' colonial policies. Moriyama Shigenori, in his most recent study, asserts that
Japan's policy toward Korea since the latter's "opening" in 1876 had
been strongly affected by the East Asian policies of the Western
powers, and that Japan's annexation of Korea was largely motivated
by its hope to forestall a crisis that would be precipitated by the
powers' intervention in the Korean and Manchurian issues.

Examining the political process leading to the annexation of Korea,
Tago Keiichi [2] [3] demonstrates how the Japanese military took the
initiative for controlling Korea as a necessary measure to counter
rising nationalist movements. Korea's "righteous army" movement
against the Japanese is discussed in detail by Kan Imon in his *Chōsen
kindaishi kenkyū* (A study of modern Korean history). To suppress this
anti-Japanese movement, Itō Hirobumi, the first Resident General in
Korea, found it increasingly necessary to develop a large-scale gen-
darme force *(kenpeitai)*. On this issue, a valuable collection of Korean
materials is: Dokuritsu Undōshi Hensan Iinkai, ed., *Dokuritsu undōshi
shiryōshū: Gihei kōsōshi shiryōshū* (Collection of materials on the history of Korea's independence movements: The history of resistance by
the righteous army).

For the period after Japan's annexation of Korea, there have been a
relatively large number of works, mostly written from the viewpoint of Japanese imperialism. Among them is Pak Kei-shik's above-
mentioned work. A more recent example is Takashima Masaaki's
Chōsen ni okeru shokuminchi kin'yūshi no kenkyū (A study of the
financial history of Korea as a colony), which empirically analyzes the
process of developing colonial finance at the time of the Japanese
annexation of Korea.

The mainstay of the administration of Korea was the Oriental

Development Company (Tōyō Takushoku Kaisha), a Japanese government-supported company to develop Korean agriculture and industries. The establishment of this company is the subject of Kimijima Kazuhiko's recent article. Kurose Ikuji has published an article on the Oriental Development Company and the "Korean administration" after the Russo-Japanese War. Megata Tanetarō's financial reform in Korea from 1904 to 1907 is treated in Hajima Takahiro's study.

There are numerous other studies on the various aspects of Japan's administrative policy toward postannexation Korea. One work that deserves special attention is Kan Don-chin, *Nihon no Chōsen shihai seisakushi kenkyū* (A study on the history of Japanese policy to rule Korea), which elucidates the realities of the "enlightened civil administration" (as opposed to the "militaristic administration") during the governor-generalship of Admiral Saitō Makoto (1919–27).

Russo-Japanese Relations

For basic sources on the period from the end of the Russo-Japanese War to the Russian Revolution, *Nichi-Ro kōshōshi* (A history of Russo-Japanese relations), compiled by the Europe-Asia Bureau of the Foreign Ministry in 1944, still remains useful. Extensively based on the Foreign Ministry archives, Yoshimura Michio's monograph, *Nihon to Roshia: Nichi-Ro sengo kara Roshia kakumei made* (Japan and Russia: From the end of the Russo-Japanese War to the Russian Revolution), provides a detailed account of Russo-Japanese relations with particular attention to the third and fourth agreements concluded in 1912–16. Refuting the widely accepted view that the fourth Russo-Japanese agreement (1916) was directed against the United States, Yoshimura persuasively argues that it was aimed against Germany as the common enemy. An early, but still useful, study on the subject is Tanaka Naokichi's essay on the Russo-Japanese agreement. Kobayashi Yukio has published a stimulating essay [4] on Japanese policy toward Russia during World War I.

From a strategic viewpoint, Russia was regarded as Japan's primary hypothetical enemy ever since the Imperial National Defense Policy was sanctioned in 1907. Tsunoda Jun presents a detailed discussion of this question in his previously cited book. Shimanuki Takeji has published a basic article [2] on the development of national defense policy since the Russo-Japanese War. The *Senshi sōsho* (War History) series, edited by the War History Office of the Defence Agency, includes *Daihon'ei rikugunbu, 1* (Imperial Headquarters, army, vol. 1) which traces in detail the history of the army's defense policy and strategy toward Russia (the Soviet Union). (See chapter 4 for the *Senshi sōsho* series.)

The Immigration Question

Akira Iriye has discussed the broader ramifications of the immigration question. According to him, this question became magnified out of all proportion and caused a Japanese-American crisis because it was linked with a broader image of a clash between Eastern and Western civilizations at the beginning of the twentieth century. Emphasizing the role of mutual perceptions, Iriye develops these themes in his seminal article [2] on the roots of antagonism between Japan and the United States and in "Japan as a Competitor, 1895–1917." [1] His full treatment of the subject appears in his *Pacific Estrangement: Japanese and American Expansion, 1897–1911* (Cambridge, Mass.: Harvard University Press, 1972).

On the other hand, Asada Sadao [5] places the immigration question and anti-Japanese racism in the context of power politics in the Pacific. On the basis of Japanese and American sources, he analyzes the process through which the ideology of "yellow peril" was formed. He also examines the impact of the immigration question on domestic political and intellectual developments in Japan.

Wakatsuki Yasuo's compact book, *Hai-Nichi no rekishi: Amerika ni okeru Nihonjin imin* (A history of anti-Japanese movements: Japanese immigrants in the United States), is a brief historical survey. His "Japanese Emigration to the United States, 1866–1924: A monograph" is a well-documented study.

Although somewhat outdated, the most comprehensive treatment of the saga of Japanese immigrants, including diplomatic aspects and fully based on primary Japanese sources, remains *Nichi-Bei bunka kōshōshi*, vol. 5: *Iminhen* (A history of Japanese-American cultural relations, vol. 5: Immigration), edited by Nagai Matsuzō, a Japanese diplomat stationed in the United States who was engaged in immigration affairs after the Russo-Japanese War. However, the volume lacks footnotes, a bibliography, and other scholarly apparatus, is weak in analysis, and does not entirely escape a filiopietistic tendency.

Indispensable for any study of Japanese-American relations over the immigration question is the basic collection of official Japanese documents on the immigration issue, *Tai-Bei imin mondai keika gaiyō* (A summary of the development of the Japanese immigration question in the United States), which was published as a supplementary volume of the Foreign Ministry's *Nihon gaikō bunsho* (Documents on Japanese foreign policy). It brings together, in one convenient volume, most of the important documents, which otherwise would have to be searched for in the annual volumes of *Nihon gaikō bunsho*. Its companion volume, *Tai-Bei imin mondai keika gaiyō fuzokusho* (Documents accompanying a summary of the development of the Japanese immigration question in the United States), is less useful, containing only English-language documents readily available elsewhere.

On the specific aspects of the immigration question, Kachi Teruko has published an article on the Treaty of 1911 and California land law. The subject is treated more fully in her *The Treaty of 1911 and the Immigration and Alien Land Law Issue Between the U.S. and Japan*.

The Immigration Act of 1924 has been studied in several articles. Segawa Yoshinobu [4] has written on the 1924 act and Japanese diplomacy, while Iino Masako dealt with anti-Japanese movements in the United States and the legislative process of the 1924 Immigration Act. Aruga Tadashi has published an interesting article, based mainly on the Japaness archives, on the anti-Japanese exclusion question, focusing on the origins of the famous "Hanihara letter." Miwa Kimitada's essay on the passing of the 1924 act and Japanese boycotts of American goods describes the process through which anti-American activities in Kobe City came to be colored by a tendency toward pan-Asianism.

The Japanese-American "crisis" over the immigration issue triggered off a war scare between the two nations. The recurrent pattern of U.S.-Japanese war scares is examined in Hata Ikuhiko's previously mentioned book. Focusing on the Japanese side, Inō Tentarō has published an article [1] on "books on future wars" with America, tracing the ebb and flow of their popularity since the Meiji era.

Turning to Canada, Uchiyama Masakuma has published an article

[1] on the history of Canadian policy to restrict Japanese immigration. Haraguchi Kunihiro's well-documented study discusses the revision of the Lemieux Agreement (1908) between Canada and Japan. Other recent works relating to Japanese immigration in Canada include the following articles: Iino Masako and Bamba Nobuya on Japanese-U.S.-Canadian relations centering on the immigration question; and Iino and Takamura Hiroko on developments from the Vancouver riots of 1907 to the Lemieux Agreement.

Concerning Latin America, the first systematic study is Kunimoto Iyo's article [3] on Japanese immigrants in Central and South America and anti-Japanese movements in the prewar period. An anti-Japanese incident of 1911 that flared up as an American response to the Japanese plan to buy a tract of land in Mexico's Bajay California is carefully studied in Kunimoto's article [1] on the Magdalena Bay incident, which is based on Mexican, Japanese, and other sources.

WORLD WAR I YEARS

Japan's Entry Into War

Japan took advantage of the outbreak of the European war to expand both on the China mainland and in the central Pacific. The standard studies of Japan's quick entry into World War I are articles by Ueda Toshio [1] and Nagaoka Shinjirō [3]. Nagaoka's work, fully based on Japanese documents, concentrates on Britain's efforts to restrict Japan's spheres of actions and Japan's refusal to be so bound.

In recent years, a growing number of Japanese historians are addressing themselves to the question of what impact the "total war" had on the Japanese political and economic system and how the military responded to this new mode of warfare by intervening in various aspects of political, social, and economic life at home. One example is an astute essay by Kisaka Jun'ichirō: he shows how quickly the Japanese army began preparations for autarky and national mobilization, and concludes that the opposition of the liberal intellectuals and political parties was in the end doomed. Kurosawa Fumitaka has also published an article elaborating on the Japanese army's plan for a total war, and Yamaguchi Toshiaki has written on national mobilization. Taking full account of these recent studies, Yoshii Hiroshi and his colleagues have published "Japanese Historiography on the First World War" [2].

A compact survey of Japanese policy during World War I, especially with regard to China, is presented in an essay by Imai Shōji. On the strained Sino-Japanese relations during the war, Usui Katsumi's previously cited work, *Nihon to Chūgoku: Taishō jidai,* contains a detailed and useful account.

Japan's diplomatic moves toward Germany during the war were ambivalent. Basing his analysis on German documents, Miyake Masaki [2] examines one of the secret Japanese diplomatic moves, Japanese-German peace talks in Stockholm. Hayashima Akira has also written detailed studies on the subject.

The Twenty-One Demands

World War I provided Japan with the opportunity to present to China the Twenty-One Demands (January 1915) with the hope of further strenthening its influence on the continent. The only full-length monograph on the subject is Horikawa Takeo, *Kyokutō kokusai seijishi josetsu: Nijūikkajō yōkyū no kenkyū* (Introduction to the history of Far Eastern international politics: A study of the Twenty-One Demands), published in 1958. This study is based only on printed materials; thus it lacks in-depth analysis of the policymaking process in Japan as well as the dynamics of interaction among the powers. In contrast, Nagaoka Shinjirō's article [4] is a well-documented study of the background and decision making with regard to the Twenty-One Demands.

The foreign policy of Ōkuma Shigenobu, the prime minister at the time of the incident, is defended by Ishida Hideo; why Prime Minister Ōkuma, a self-styled "liberal statesman," decided to impose such harsh conditions on China is the question to which Kimura Tokio addresses himself in his article.

The role of Foreign Minister Katō Takaaki is examined by Nomura Otojirō [2]. Challenging the generally accepted view that Katō unwillingly acquiesced in the inclusion of a motley of demands known as "group five" under pressures from various quarters, Nomura argues that Katō himself insisted on "group five" and that the Sino-Japanese negotiations "failed" because Katō held fast to his rigid position. The army's moves at that time are examined by Yamamoto Shirō [3] on the basis of Terauchi Masatake's papers.

Regarding the response of the powers to the Twenty-One Demands, Japanese works have concentrated on U.S.-Japanese relations. Hosoya Chihiro has written a solid study [6] based on both Japanese and American sources. It traces how President Wilson's attitude took on an increasingly anti-Japanese tone as he became more deeply involved in foreign policymaking until he issued the note of May 1915, a prototype of the later Stimson Doctrine. In addition, Shin Hee-suk focuses on U.S. opposition to Japanese claims to the Manchurian interests as spelled out in the Twenty-One Demands. The most recent work is Kitaoka Shin'ichi's incisive and well-documented article [2]. Tracing in details the misperceptions of Paul S. Reinsch (American minister to China), Kitaoka shows how President Wilson came to lean toward his minister's exaggerated views about Japan's ambitions. Thus the article illustrates the complicated process through which mutual "misunderstandings" escalated into mutual mistrust.

The Lansing-Ishii Agreement. Studies on the Lansing-Ishii Agreement of 1917, which gave rise to conflicting interpretations of "special interests" between Japan and the United States, include articles by Oka Toshitaka [2] and Nagaoka Shinjirō [1]. The latter article is fully based on the Japanese archives. Chapter 4 of Hata Ikuhiko's previously cited work, *Taiheiyō kokusai kankeishi,* throws light on this deliberately "ambiguous" agreement by analyzing the respective bargaining positions of Japan and the United States.

The Nishihara Loans

On the so-called "Nishihara loans" to China (1917–18), the essential sources are contained in Suzuki Takeo, ed., *Nishihara shakkan shiryō kenkyū* (Documents on the Nishihara loans). It is a rich collection of the family papers held by Finance Minister Shōda Kazue, a member of Premier Terauchi's brain trust for Japan's continental policy. Nishihara's own reminiscences, *Yume no shichijū yonen: Nishihara Kamezō jiden* (A dream of over seventy years: The autobiography of Nishihara Kamezō), still remains a revealing source.

Shōda Kazue's son, Shōda Tatsuo, has published *Chūgoku shakkan to Shōda Kazue* ([The Nishihara] loans to China and Shōda Kazue), which treats the loans in the broad context of Japan's diplomatic and financial policy during and after World War I. This book points out, among other things, the difference between Nishihara, who was obsessed with his idea of closer ties with China, and Shōda, who predicated his China policy on Japan's economic situation and relations with the United States.

More specialized studies based on the Nishihara papers (at the National Diet Library) include articles by Shimura Toshiko and Hatano Yoshihiro [2]. Shimura analyzes the formative process of the Nishihara loans and the underlying ideas and ideals. Hatano's work points out that the Nishihara loans were quite different in nature from the Twenty-One Demands because these loans were partially inspired by Nishihara's own idea of establishing a "sphere of autarky in the Orient."

The most recent works are fine studies by Yamamoto Shirō [4] and Saitō Seiji [2]. The former essay examines Sino-Japanese relations during the Terauchi cabinet (1916–18) with special reference to the role of Nishihara Kamezō and Colonel Banzai Rihachirō. The latter study discusses Nishihara's views of China and the China policy of the Terauchi cabinet. In addition, Yamamoto has edited *Terauchi Masatake nikki* (The diary of Terauchi Masatake) and *Nishihara kamezō nikki* (The diary of Nishihara Kamezō), which are vital to the understanding of this subject.

The specifically financial aspects of the Nishihara loans are studied with full documentation in articles by Takahashi Makoto, Kitamura Hironao, and Ōmori Tokuko.

The Advisory Council on Foreign Relations.   This extraconstitutional organ was created in 1917 ostensibly for the purpose of detaching foreign policy issues out of domestic strife for the duration of the World War I. From the outset, however, the Advisory Council on Foreign Relations (Gaikō Chōsakai) was beset by dissension. Political controversies and maneuvers that accompanied the establishment of this Council are detailed by Kobayashi Tatsuo [3]. The anomalous relationship between the Foreign Ministry and the Advisory Council (the latter often overshadowing the former) is fully described in Gaimushō Hyakunenshi Hensan Iinkai, ed., *Gaimushō no hyakunen* (A century of the Japanese Foreign Ministry), vol. 1. The functions of the Advisory Council are analyzed by Amamiya Shōichi in relation to the army's conduct of war: [1], [2].

Itō Miyoji, the vociferous speaker at its deliberations, kept a meticulous record of the proceedings of the Advisory Council on Foreign Relations. This record (in the form of a diary), together with other related documents, has been expertly edited with an introduction by Kobayashi Tatsuo as *Suiusō nikki: Rinji gaikō chōsa iinkai kaigi hikki nado* (Suiusō diary: The notes from meetings of the Advisory Council on Foreign Relations and other matters).

Until its demise in September 1922, the Advisory Council, taking over much of the Foreign Ministry, presided over such important agenda as the Siberian Expedition, the Paris Peace Conference, Japan's participation in the new four-power China consortium, and the Washington Conference. Unfortunately, *Suiusō nikki,* though rich in deliberations on the Siberian Expedition, covers only up to the end of the Paris Peace Conference; the sequel record is presumed to have been lost or destroyed. Despite these gaps, it remains a major source for this period, together with another magnificent mine of information—*Hara Kei nikki* (The diary of Hara Kei) edited by Hara Keiichirō.

The Siberian Expedition

The foremost work on the Siberian Expedition is Hosoya Chihiro's *Shiberia shuppei no shiteki kenkyū* (A historical study of the Siberian Expedition). Paying attention to the intertwining interests of the major powers concerned as well as rival forces within each country, particularly within Japan and the United States, Hosoya analyzes the dynamism of the process that set in motion the Siberian intervention. The first to use the records of the Japanese Foreign Ministry and *Suiusō nikki,* Hosoya clarifies the conflict and cooperation among Japanese leaders. In great detail he traces the decision-making process that involved forces favoring nonintervention, a "limited intervention," and a "total intervention."

In this sense, Hosoya's work is the antithesis of Inoue Kiyoshi's Marxist interpretation presented in *Nihon no gunkokushugi* (Militarism in Japan), vol. 2 (1953 edition). Inoue argues that the responsibility for the Siberian Expedition rested solely with "Japanese imperialism," which he paints as a monolithic force. Written from a similar viewpoint, Shinobu Seizaburō's *Taishō seijishi* (A political history of Taishō Japan) contains an account of the entire course of the Siberian Expedition.

Subsequently, Hosoya has published a series of studies on related subjects by utilizing such materials as the Army General Staff's *Taishō 7-nen naishi 11-nen Shiberia shuppeishi* (History of the Siberian Expedition, 1918–22), the American archives, and the best of scholarly works by foreign scholars such as James W. Morley's *The Japanese Thrust Into Siberia, 1918* (Columbia University Press, 1957). In his basic article [8] on the Siberian Expedition and Japanese-American relations, Hosoya examines splits as well as changes in the policy of the Wilson administration and relates them to Japan's Siberian policy. He has also published a substantial essay [5] on Japan and the issue of recognizing the Kolchak regime. These and other essays have been collected in Hosoya's *Roshia kakumei to Nihon* (The Russian Revolution and Japan).

Another scholar who has written extensively on Russo-Japanese relations during World War I is Kobayashi Yukio. Some of his essays, solidly based on Japanese and (some) Russian sources, were brought together in his recent book, *Nisso seiji gaikōshi: Roshia kakumei to chian iji hō* (A history of Japan-USSR political and diplomatic relations: The Russian Revolution and the Peace Preservation Law of 1925.) For this period, Kobayashi's book treats such topics as: World War I and Japanese policy toward Russia; Japan and the Russian Revolution; and the Manchurian- Mongolian question and shifting Japanese policies toward the Soviet Union [6].

Kobayashi [5] contends that Japan's reluctance to withdraw forces from Siberia was due to the establishment of the Bolshevik regime and the impact of the Nikolaevsk incident (March–May 1920), in which several hundred Japanese soldiers, sailors, and civilians were murdered by Russian partisans. This incident has been studied also by Hara Teruyuki [2] and Itō Shūichi. In addition, Hara has examined the military aspects of the Siberian Expedition, focusing on the battles at the Amur River. On the other hand, Amamiya Shōichi [3] discusses the role of the Eastern Conference (1921) in the decision leading to the withdrawal of forces from Siberia. The domestic political process revolving around the issue of withdrawal from Siberia is examined in Momose Takashi's article focusing on the period from December 1920 to May 1921.

Japan occupied north Sakhalin (1920–25) as retaliation against the Nikolaevsk incident, and this incident is studied in Ueda Toshio's article [2]. Yoshimura Michio [3] discusses the rivalry among Japan, the United States, and the Soviets over the oil interests in north Sakhalin in relation to the problem of the Japanese recognition of the Soviet Union. From a broader perspective Hosoya Chihiro [2] analyzes economic conflict between Japan, the United States, and Britain over oil resources in north Sakhalin.

Concerning a large question—the transformation of international politics in East Asia brought about by the Russian Revolution—Seki Hiroharu has written a series of articles. In 1958 he was one of the earliest to apply to historical writing behavioral science approaches such as the model of the decision-making process developed by Richard C. Snyder in his *Decision-Making as an Approach to the Study of International Relations* (Princeton University Press, 1954) and Karl Deutsche's communication theory, *Nationalism and Social Communication* (New York: Wiley, 1953). Seki's theoretical interest was explicit in his monographic essay [3] on the revolution in Harbin in 1917, which analyzed the dynamics of international politics centering on the establishment of the Harbin soviet. From a similar viewpoint, Seki has also examined in his detailed essay [2] the decision-making process that led to the Sino-Japanese Military Agreement of 1918. Subsequently, Seki collected both studies in his *Gendai higashi Ajia kokusai kankyō no tanjō* (The emergence of the contemporary international system in East Asia).

The Russian Revolution had a wide-ranging impact on Japanese politics, society, and thought. However, there have been few substantial studies of these subjects except for Kikuchi Masanori's *Roshia kakumei to Nihonjin* (The Russian Revolution and the Japanese). He describes Japanese reactions, using the memoirs and recorded observations of Japanese diplomats, journalists, and soliders who witnessed the Russian Revolution:

The Paris Peace Conference. Despite the importance of the subject, there are relatively few studies on the Paris Peace Conference. Kobayashi Tatsuo's substantial essay [2] on the Paris Peace Conference and Japanese diplomacy provides a comprehensive and balanced treatment of the Shantung controversy, the problem of the former German islands in the Pacific, and other issues. Another general account is Saitō Takashi's short article. The difficult role of Makino Nobuaki, the chief Japanese delegate at Paris and a believer in the "new diplomacy," is sympathetically described by Hosoya Chihiro [3]. Oka Yoshitake has critically analyzed Japanese public opinion with regard to the Paris Peace Conference and American diplomacy.

The Shantung question, which became one of the most disputed issues at Paris, is traced from its inception by Uchiyama Masakuma [2]. Shimizu Hideko has also examined this question, fully utilizing the Foreign Ministry archives. Ikei Masaru [7] deals with the final outcome of the Shantung question in relation to Japanese responses to the May Fourth Movement of 1919.

The Japanese efforts at Paris for the sake of the "abolition of racial discrimination" are carefully studied by Ikei [6]. He takes issue with the view of Ichimata Masao and some foreign scholars that Japan scrapped its demand for "racial equality" in exchange for acceptance of its claim to Shantung, arguing that there simply could not have been such a diplomatic "bargain," because the Japanese government regarded its Shantung claim as a sine qua non even to the extent of refusing to join the League of Nations, whereas it considered the "racial equality" issue ultimately as a matter of mere "face."

In addition to annual volumes the Foreign Ministry has published a "supplementary volume" on the Paris Peace Conference: *Pari kōwa kaigi keika gaiyō* (A summary of developments at the Paris Peace Conference).

The relationship between Japan and the League of Nations is discussed at length by Unno Yoshirō in his *Kokusai renmei to Nihon* (Japan and the League of Nations), a solid monograph fully based on the Foreign Ministry archives. Unno's work is the only book-length study that comprehensively covers Japanese activities at the League of Nations from 1920 to 1933. Unno has also published an article [1] on the able diplomat Satō Naotake, discussing his role at the League of Nations, disarmament conferences, and other interwar conferences.

On the other hand, Asada Sadao [4] analyzes Japanese perceptions of the United States in "the age of Woodrow Wilson." Particularly after its entry into W.W.I. Japan's leaders saw in the United States four "threats": economic, military, racial ("White Peril"), and ideological (Wilsonianism). Asada examines these perceived "threats" critically in the light of the realities—American policies and intentions. In a diplomatic offensive which the United States began to take after the Paris Peace Conference, Asada argues, the United States made use of these "threats" and that this in turn led to moderation of Japanese policy, thus setting the stage for the Washington Conference.

THE WASHINGTON SYSTEM

From Paris to Washington

Japanese diplomacy from the end of World War I to the Washington Conference of 1921–22 may be said to have undergone a "transitional period." Domestically, party leader Hara Kei took firm control of Japanese foreign policy as prime minister. Externally, the Anglo-Japanese Alliance—the traditional frame of reference for Japanese foreign policy—seemed virtually disintegrated, and as a result the United States came to assume more and more weight in Japanese diplomacy.

Focusing on Prime Minister Hara Kei and Army Minister Tanaka Giichi, Mitani Taichirō has brilliantly analyzed in his monographic essay [3] their foreign policy leadership during the years 1918–21. Mitani credits the Hara cabinet's China policy with having in essence preempted and prepared the way for the emergence of the Washington system. Thus, he concludes that Hara's policy constituted the prototype or precursor of "Shidehara diplomacy." The thesis that Shidehara inherited Hara's "liberal" foreign policy is argued by Kurihara Ken [4] in his aforementioned collection of essays, *Tai-Manmō seisakushi no ichimen*.

Japan's responses to the major changes in its international environment, triggered by World War I and further intensified by the invitation to the Washington Conference, are shrewdly analyzed by Satō Seizaburō. He emphasizes Japan's extremely passive stand at the Washington Conference and its tendency to pragmatic calculations and opportunistic accommodation with the "dominant trends of the time." Satō examines both the strengths and weaknesses of the Washington system by viewing it as a "system of tension reduction." It is of interest to note that his essay—together with Aruga Tadashi's work on the American side and Fujii Shōzō's study on China's reaction—appeared in the annual (1970) of the Nihon Seiji Gakkai (Japanese Political Science Association) that was devoted to "the political process of international tension reduction." In the intellectual climate reflecting detente during the late 1960s, the Washington Conference seemed to provide a good theme for a case study in "tension reduction."

The Washington Conference

The first scholar to exploit the Foreign Ministry archives for this period was Ōhata Tokushirō, who wrote on the following subjects: the problem of renewing the third Anglo-Japanese Alliance and the proposal for the Washington Conference [2]; Japan's participation in the Washington Conference [3]; and the calling of the Washington Conference and Japanese-American relations [6].

Among other subjects, Asada Sadao has continued to write on the Washington Conference ever since he published "Japan's 'Special Interests' and the Washington Conference, 1921–1922" in 1961 [2]. In that article he characterized the Washington treaties as a product of Japanese-American compromise and pointed out the ambiguous understanding on "special interests" as a potential weakness of the Washington system. Subsequently, he has written several essays, all based on archival and manuscript sources in Japan and the United States (and, to some extent, Britain), on both the naval and Far Eastern questions. His analytical essay [7] that compares the Japanese and American decision-making processes at the time of the Washington conference explicitly applies the "bureaucratic politics" model.

The naval question is treated in Asada's "Japanese Admirals and the Politics of Naval Limitation: Katō Tomosaburō vs. Katō Kanji" [3]. Pointing to fundamental differences in personality, attitudes toward the United States and Great Britain, and outlooks on national defense, Asada stresses the historical significance of the mutually opposing views held by Navy Minister Katō Tomosaburō, the chief Japanese delegate to the conference, and his chief naval aide Katō Kanji. The subject is also analyzed in his essay [6] on the Japanese navy and the politics of naval limitation, 1918–1930.

Japan's divided policy on the Far Eastern questions at the Washington Conference is examined in Asada's essay [8] on the Japanese response to and activities at the Washington Conference, which is subtitled "from the 'old diplomacy' to the 'new diplomacy.'" Applying, among others, the theories of perception and misperception developed in the United States, Asada untangles changing and often conflicting perceptions of the international situation held by Japan's decision makers. There are other studies that deal with more specific aspects of Japanese Policy. Unno Yoshirō has published a well-documented study [5] of the Foreign Ministry's preparations for the Washington Conference. Segawa Yoshinobu [5] has studied the subsidiary role of the army.

Most of the relevant Foreign Ministry documents on the conference were published in 1977–78 as *Nihon gaikō bunsho: Washinton kaigi* (Documents on Japanese foreign policy: The Washington Conference), 2 vols.; *Washinton kaigi: Gunbi seigen mondai* (The Washington Conference: The problem of naval limitation); and *Washinton kaigi: Kyokutō mondai* (The Washington Conference: The Far Eastern Questions).

The Nature of the Washington System

The most recent and comprehensive study of the "Washington system" (1918–31) is Hosoya Chihiro and Saitō Makoto, eds., *Washinton taisei to Nichi-Bei kankei* (The Washington system and Japanese-American relations). This volume is the result of the conference held between Japanese and American scholars on Kauai Island, Hawaii, in 1976. Conceived basically as a companion volume to Hosoya Chihiro, et al, ed., *Nichi-Bei kankeishi: Kaisen ni itaru 10-nen, 1931–1941*, this conference volume was different in that some of the papers examined Japanese-American relations in the trilateral framework of cooperation and conflict among Japan, the United States, and Britain in China.

As a general framework of the conference, most participants took for granted the existence of the Washington *system* as an interlocked structure of treaties and agreements. (On this point, the British authority Ian Nish has asserted elsewhere that such a phraseology is not found in British documents and that in the hasty preparation for and spontaneous give-and-take at the conference, there was simply not enough time to devise such a "master plan." *Japanese Foreign Policy, 1869–1942: Kasumigaseki to Miyakezaka* [London: Routledge and Kegan Paul, 1977], pp. 141–42).

The introductory essay [9] by Hosoya, the capstone of the entire volume, broadly analyzes East Asian international relations of the period in terms of a dominant-subordinate system. According to this systemic interpretation, China was allowed to participate as a subordinate actor in a system dominated by Japanese-American-British cooperation. He traces the multilayered interactions of cooperation and conflict among the East Asian policies of the respective countries. Specifically, Hosoya subdivides Japan's "policy of international cooperation" into "cooperation with the *United States*" and "cooperation with *Britain*." According to this framework, "Shidehara diplomacy" no doubt leaned heavily toward the United States. In contrast, "Tanaka diplomacy" sought cooperation with Great Britain by jointly confronting Chinese nationalism even by forcible means. In this sense, contends Hosoya, "Tanaka diplomacy" also sought a policy of "international cooperation," though it was "alliance oriented" and thus was tinged with the "old diplomacy." In short, Hosoya revises the traditional interpretation that "Tanaka diplomacy" rejected cooperative policy and followed Japan's own "independent" course.

One of the issues that attracted the attention of the conference participants was the theme of cooperation and conflict between Japan and the United States over investments in China. Hirano Ken'ichirō's contribution [2] examines the formation of the new four-power China consortium, which is said to have anticipated or preempted the economic underpinnings of the Washington system. Hirano focuses on Japan's demand to exclude Manchuria and Inner Mongolia from the scope of the new consortium against the background of domestic politics in Japan and China. On the other hand, Mitani Taichirō [4] deals with the role of international financiers in his essay on Wall Street and the "Manchurian-Mongolian question." Examining Japanese-American relations over the issuance of bonds proposed by the South Manchuria Railway Company and the Oriental Development Company, Mitani argues that Japan's request for American capital was the logical consequence of its effort to reconcile Japan's "special interests in Manchuria and Mongolia" with the "Washington system." (In this connection, Mitani's essay [1] on Japan's international bankers and international politics, published elsewhere, reexamines the significance of the Washington system in the context of the activities of Takahashi Korekiyo and Inoue Junnosuke, the two international financiers of Japan who shored up the economic props of the Washington system.)

Economic aspects of Japanese-American relations received due attention at the conference. Nakamura Takafusa [2] focuses on the Japanese policy of lifting the gold embargo and examines it from the broad perspective of the international economy in the 1920s. Satō Kazuo analyzes the structure of U.S.-Japanese trade, emphasizing the unbalanced growth of the Japanese economy which heavily depended on export of raw silk and silk products.

Asada Sadao's contribution is an essay [6] on the Japanese navy and naval limitation, focusing on Japan's policy and strategy toward the United States. He analyzes the decision-making process within the Japanese navy not only at the dramatic peaks of the naval conferences at Washington (1921–22), Geneva (1927), and London (1930), but also during the more obscure intervals between them. On the basis of newly discovered naval documents, he demonstrates how in the course of the 1920s a powerful faction, opposed to naval limitation and committed to destroying the Washington system, had come to gain supremacy.

Banno Junji's contribution is an essay on the Japanese army's continental policy and its perception of the United States and Europe. Although this study is devoted to the period before 1921, it shows how such army leaders as Tanaka Giichi and Ugaki Kazushige had quickly adjusted to the global changes in the diplomatic setting and switched their China policy to cooperation with the United States. However, theirs was a minority view. After the Washington Conference, there remained a strong undercurrent in the army that clamored for an "independent" China policy and withdrawal from the Washington system.

The last section of the book is devoted to "cultural contacts and assimilation." Saitō Makoto presents an essay on the role of Nitobe Inazō, a leading liberal intellectual and under-secretary-general of the League of Nations who devoted himself to cultural exchange between Japan and the United States. The focus of Saitō's study is on the basic premises that underlay Nitobe's pioneering work in "American studies." Homma Nagayo presents an essay on the "Americanization of Japanese culture" with particular reference to life-style and mass culture. However, the question remains of how to relate cultural history to diplomatic history of the period.

Whether conciously intended to do so or not, many of the conference papers amounted to challenges to Akira Iriye's *Kyokutō shin chitsujo no mosaku* (The search for a new order in the Far East). Lively discussions took place between Iriye and his critics. For example, Hosoya took issue with Iriye on the question of when the Washington system disintegrated as a cooperative international system to assure stability in East Asia. This controversy will be further examined later.

Since the English version of Iriye's monograph was published as *After Imperialism: The Search for a New Order in the Far East, 1921– 1931* (Cambridge: Harvard University Press, 1965), it will not be necessary to dwell on this important work. Suffice it here to note some of its characteristics that have provided considerable stimulus to Japanese scholars. On the basis of solid multiarchival research, Iriye examines the transformation of the "international system" in East Asia from the end of World War I to the Manchurian Incident from a broad perspective. He analyzes the disintegration of the "old diplomacy" ("imperialist cooperation") brought about by World War I and the search for a "new order" to replace the old. For this purpose Iriye unravels the intertwining relations between the subjective images of the international order held by the decision makers (mainly of Japan and the United States) and the objective realities of international politics in East Asia.

For this same period, Iriye has also written an analytical essay on "The Failure of Economic Expansionism, 1918–1931," in Bernard Silberman and H. D. Harootunian, eds., *Japan in Crisis* (Princeton University Press, 1974). Iriye introduces an alternative to the conventional concepts of "international cooperation" or "peaceful policy"; he suggests that the concepts of "economic expansionism" and "peaceful expansionism" are more relevant in explaining the characteristics of Japanese diplomacy under the Washington system.

From a different angle, Usui Katsumi has written a shrewd essay [9] on the Japanese ruling class and the "Versailles-Washington system." In it he examines the ambivalent attitude on the part of Japan's ruling elite: its acceptance of the status quo as one of the five great powers, and its "inferiority complex" as one of the "have-not nations" committed to the overthrow of the existing international order.

The above-mentioned studies by no means exhaust opportunities for research on the 1920s. For one thing, with the exception of Hosoya Chihiro [9], few Japanese scholars have utilized the British archives. The Chinese archives up to 1927, deposited at the Institute of Modern History, Academia Sinica, still remain to be tapped by Japanese diplomatic historians.

Recognition of the Soviet Union

The Soviet Union, not even invited to the Washington Conference, remained a bitter critic of the Washington system as an outsider and it attempted to create, under its own leadership, an international (and frankly anti-imperialistic) system in East Asia that would counter the edifice constructed at Washington.

The first detailed study of the subject is contained in Kobayashi Yukio's contribution [6] to the first volume of *Taiheiyō sensō e no michi*. Kobayashi examines the negotiations for normalizing Soviet-Japanese relations, which began with "private negotiations" between Gotō Shinpei (former foreign minister and at that time mayor of Tokyo) and Adolf Joffe. In two other articles Kobayashi emphasizes the pressures brought to bear by the Japanese fishing industry: [1], [3].

After the initiation of the Gotō-Joffe parley, the meeting held in 1924 between Leo Karakhan and Yoshizawa Kenkichi (minister to China) set the Japanese-Soviet negotiations on a more regular basis. Kobayashi [1] chronicles these negotiations and stresses the change of Japanese policy affected by the collapse of the Yamamoto cabinet and its replacement by the Katō Takaaki ministry. Kobayashi [2] also analyzes Japan's decision-making process that led to the Yoshizawa-Karakhan conference (1923–25). His other essays on related subjects are collected in Kobayashi's previously mentioned *Nisso seiji gaikōshi*.

One of the factors that entered into Japan's recognition of the Soviet Union was the oil interests in Sakhalin. Yoshimura Michio [3] describes the rivalries among Japan, the United States, and the Soviets over the oil interests that lay behind the Japanese occupation of north

Sakhalin (1920–25). His article [1] on the S.S. *Lenin* incident during the great Tokyo earthquake of 1923 takes up the episode of Japan ordering out a Russian relief ship on the charge of Communist propaganda. Yoshimura maintains that the negotiations to settle that incident provided one occasion for holding the Yoshizawa-Karakhan conference.

On Gotō Shinpei there are two able studies by Yoshimura Michio [1] and Kitaoka Shin'ichi [1]. Gotō sought an alignment with China and the Soviet Union in order to counter the Washington system. In addition, Sakai Tetsuya traces the advocacy of collaboration with the Soviets led by leaders like Gotō. As background, Sakai analyzes changing perceptions of the Soviet Union in Japanese diplomacy during and after this period.

Of course, the Foreign Ministry under Shidehara Kijūrō, strongly committed to the policy of cooperating with the United States, was opposed to the idea of joining hands with the Soviet Union to challenge the Washington system.

The First Period of Shidehara Diplomacy

There are conflicting interpretations of the so-called Shidehara diplomacy (1924–27, 1929–31). As a part of the historiographical controversy provoked by Tōyama Shigeki et al., *Shōwashi* (A history of the Shōwa period), Japanese scholars have argued about how to evaluate Shidehara diplomacy—whether it was a peace-oriented policy or simply a disguised form of imperialism.

New dimensions have been added to the study of Shidehara diplomacy by such works as Usui Katsumi's writings on Sino-Japanese relations in the 1920's; Hosoya's previously mentioned essay [9] on the changing characteristics of the Washington system; and Bamba Nobuya's *Manshū jihen e no michi: Shidehara gaikō to Tanaka gaikō*. The last-mentioned work is not an orthodox study of diplomatic history. Instead, the author applies the concepts of political sociology and social psychology to analyze the process through which the diplomatic principles of Shidehara and Tanaka were formed, and he contrasts personalities and the *Weltanschauung* between the two men.

Since the major characteristics of Shidehara diplomacy—nonintervention, international cooperation, and economic rationalism—

manifested themselves in that leader's China policy, Japanese historians have closely examined the subject. Usui Katsumi's *Nitchū gaikōshi: Hokubatsu no jidai* (A history of Sino-Japanese diplomatic relations: The northern expedition period) describes at length Sino-Japanese relations during the Kuomintung's northern expedition (1926–1928). This book, which is a sequel to the author's *Nihon to Chūgoku: Taishō jidai*, is one of the most reliable studies on this period.

There are various studies on specific incidents and topics. Fujii Shōzō analyzes one of the recurrent wars between Chinese warlords in his article [3] on Sino-Japanese relations during the Anhwei-Mukden war of 1920. Ikei Masaru has written two articles on the role of the Japanese army in subsequent battles between Chinese warlords: one [1] on the Japanese intervention in the first Mukden-Chihli war; and the other [2] on Japan's involvement in the second Chihli-Fengtien fight. In these articles Ikei demonstrates that the Japanese army, through clandestine interference in Chinese civil wars, betrayed Shidehara's policy of "noninterference." The Lingcheng incident of 1923 (involving the kidnapping of Japanese and other foreign residents in China) is examined by Baba Akira [4]. The Kuo Sung-ling incident of 1925 (in which Kuo Sung-ling, belonging to the Mukden military clique, attempted rebellion against Chang Tso-lin) is treated by Eguchi Keiichi [1]. Fujii Shōzō's article on Sino-Japanese relations centering on the Taku incident of 1926 [4] is a detailed analysis of the 1926 incident that resulted from a clash between the Chinese Nationalist forces and Japanese troops. All of these studies, based on the Foreign Ministry archives and unpublished army documents, discuss the so-called "dual diplomacy" or the Japanese military's intervention in the conduct of foreign affairs, forcing a reexamination of Shidehara's policy of "noninterference."

The representative works that critically treat Shidehara diplomacy in this respect are Eguchi Keiichi's essay [1] cited above and a joint study by Eguchi and Ono Shinji. According to them, Japan in the period of early Shidehara diplomacy regarded as vital the acquisition of the China market as an outlet for its products in order to overcome a recession following World War I. For this purpose, it would have been to Japan's disadvantage to interfere militarily with China's domestic affairs, which would only aggravate its political confusion. While admitting that Shidehara insisted on a noninterference policy,

Eguchi and his associate point out that Japan's economic expansion into China was dictated by the imperative of "the imperialist bourgeoisie" and was always pursued against the background of Japan's military power. They also argue that Shidehara diplomacy was no different from Tanaka diplomacy in not hesitating to interfere with Chinese domestic affairs when it came to the matter of protecting Japan's interests in Manchuria and Mongolia.

This thesis has been challenged, for example, by Usui Katsumi [7]. He points out that although both Shidehara and Tanaka talked about the defense of the Manchurian-Mongolian interests, there were great differences between what they meant. On the one hand, what Tanaka and the military had in mind was a "positive policy," which could lead to the separation of Manchuria and Mongolia from the rest of China. On the other hand, Shidehara accepted the unity of China. He subordinated the importance of Manchuria to that of China proper, a vast region for Japan's economic activities. Thus, his Manchurian policy was a "negative" one. Usui asserts that this difference between the two men pointed early on to the divergence of China policy during the ensuing years.

On the Japanese response to the upsurge of Chinese nationalism, there are a number of works. Usui expertly treats the 1925 anti-Japanese and anti-British movements in Shanghai in his article [2] on the May 30 incident and Japan. Nakamura Takafusa [1] traces the activities of the Japanese Cotton-Spinners' Association in China in relation to the May 30 incident.

The Peking Tariff Conference of 1925, designed to revise Chinese tariffs in accordance with the agreement at the Washington Conference, also has important bearing on the assessment of Shidehara diplomacy and the Washington system. Akira Iriye, in his *After Imperialism*, points out that "Shidehara diplomacy" as exemplified in Japan's tariff negotiations with China revealed the determined pursuit of Japan's economic interests, characterized by realism rather than idealism. Iriye also argues that the failure of this tariff conference spelled the "final collapse" of the Washington system. Taking issue with Iriye, Hosoya [9] emphasizes the resilience of the tripartite cooperative system, arguing that differences at the tariff conference did not necessarily herald the disintegration of the Washington system.

Hosoya argues that the demise of the Washington system came around 1929 when Japan's diplomatic isolation became complete.

Bamba Nobuya's *Japanese Diplomacy in a Dilemma: New Light on Japan's China Policy, 1924–1929* gives credit to Shidehara for a willingness to recognize China's tariff autonomy. In a well-documented article, specifically devoted to the Peking Tariff Conference, Bamba maintains, on the basis of a detailed analysis of Shidehara's decision making, that his rational personality and skillful leadership characterized the policymaking process throughout.

How did the Chinese view Shidehara diplomacy? Fujii Shōzō's article [1] that addresses itself to this question is an unusual study. According to his work, based on a careful analysis of the *Tung-fang tsa-chih* (a Shanghai bimonthly journal), the Chinese image of Shidehara diplomacy was quite different from that of "international cooperation"; rather, the Chinese found the policy of "international cooperation" in Tanaka diplomacy, because Tanaka sought accommodation with Great Britain. Interestingly, this interpretation roughly matches the British view of Shidehara diplomacy, as pointed out by Hosoya [9]. The most recent work on Shidehara diplomacy is Uno Shigeaki's article, which points out the limitations of Shidehara's "idealism" and "rationalism" by analyzing his policies toward China and the Soviet Union.

Tanaka Diplomacy

Banno Junji has published several important essays discussing the historical significance of the emergence of Tanaka diplomacy in the context of Japanese domestic politics. In his essay [2] on party politics and Japan's China policy, 1919–1926, Banno inquires into the reasons why the Seiyūkai party rejected Shidehara diplomacy and advocated Tanaka diplomacy with its emphasis on "independent policy," despite the Seiyūkai's public stand for a policy of international cooperation and nonintervention in China. In another article [1] examining the Japanese army's policy toward China during an earlier period, Banno emphasizes continuities in the interventionist orientation of the army since the World War I period, a tendency that would eventually result in Japan's departure from the Washington system. In yet

another article [3] on the Japanese army and the collapse of Shidehara
diplomacy, he suggests a more complex interpretation of "dual diplomacy," which goes beyond a simplistic view of Japan's continental
policy in terms of the dichotomy of the Foreign Ministry and the
army, by shedding light on the political party and the army as the
background of Tanaka diplomacy. These essays were collected by
Banno in his recent book, *Kindai Nihon no gaikō to seiji* (Diplomacy
and politics in modern Japan).

Further treatments of the various aspects of the subject include the
following studies: Usui Katsumi [8] on the nature of Tanaka diplomacy; Baba Akira [1] on the first Shantung expedition of 1927, which
aggravated relations with China; Etō Shinkichi [2] on Japan and the
United States during the Nanking incident of 1927; and Seki Hiroharu
[1] on the developments leading to the Manchurian Incident. These
works are all excellent and highlight various aspects of Tanaka's
"independent policy."

A most recent study of Tanaka diplomacy and the Japanese army is
a stimulating essay by Kurosawa Fumitaka. He argues that since World
War I the Japanese army, intent on establishing a system to cope with
coming total war, sought to stabilize both the domestic order and the
international order in East Asia. Tanaka prepared his foreign policy
along this line and seemingly succeeded in attaining domestic and
international stability in 1925. But it was not long before the activities
of the Soviet Union came to upset this stability, thus undermining
Tanaka diplomacy.

One notable case study of Tanaka diplomacy is Etō Shinkichi's
essay [1] on the question of suspending the traffic on the Peking-
Mukden railway in 1927. Etō analyzes the planned interception of this
railway as a coercive measure to force a solution to the pending
Manchurian-Mongolian questions immediately after the Eastern Conference of 1927. Examining various restraints (such as splits within
the government and the Seiyūkai party), Etō points to the limitations
of Tanaka's "positive diplomacy." In this study, Etō applies a new
methodology, a content analysis of two local Japanese newspapers,
and the result shows that most likely Japanese public opinion would
not have supported a hard-line policy. In his subsequent study [3] on
Sino-Japanese tension and Japanese attitudes from 1925–28 Etō utilizes

the technique of content analysis more extensively, using two major Japanese newspapers, the *Asahi* and *Nichi-Nichi*.

In June 1927 the Japanese government held the so-called Eastern Conference, recalling the key members of Japanese legations and military authorities from Manchuria and China, in order to exchange information and coordinate Japanese policy. This conference is said to have agreed on "positive" settlements of the Manchurian-Mongolian questions including the resort to military force. However, to this date, primary sources on the deliberations at the Eastern Conference have not been located; previous writings on this subject depend on secondary sources. Satō Motoei has searched with great care related documents scattered at the Diplomatic Record Office and the War History Department, and he has suceeded in discovering all the papers prepared for the conference and the conference agenda in detail. These materials with explanatory notes are published in Kindai Gaikōshi Kenkyūkai, ed., *Hendōki no Nihon gaikō to gunji* (Japanese diplomacy and the military during a turbulent period). The contents of the conference proceedings still remain unknown.

What attracted worldwide attention about this conference was the so-called "Tanaka memorial" that China published by seizing on the occasion. In this document, Prime Minister Tanaka allegedly recommended to the Throne a detailed plan for the conquest of Manchuria and Mongolia. However, Inō Tentarō's article [2], after carefully examining the "memorial" both in its format and contents, concludes that the document in question was forged.

On the assassination of Chang Tso-lin, killed by a bomb explosion in June 1928, Usui Katsumi has published a basic article [1]. Shimada Toshihiko's general book *Kantōgun* (The Kwantung Army) also contains a useful account of the incident. Baba Akira in his article [5] relates the incident to the fall of the Tanaka cabinet.

The Second Period of Shidehara Diplomacy

Following the fall of the Tanaka cabinet in July 1929, Shidehara was called back to lead Japan's foreign policy again. Among substantial studies that treat the collapse of Shidehara's diplomacy as a prelude to the Manchurian Incident, the following works are important: Imai

Seiichi's early article [1] on the decision-making process in Shidehara diplomacy; Eguchi Keiichi's *Nihon teikokushugi shiron: Manshū jihen zengo* (Historical studies on Japanese imperialism: The period of the Manchurian Incident); and Seki Hiroharu's monographic essay [1] on the prehistory of the Manchurian Incident (1927–31). The last-mentioned study by Seki is especially important; fully utilizing the military archives as well as the papers of Ishiwara Kanji, he clearly demonstrates the complicity of the Tokyo army authorities in the Mukden plot. The author reveals in detail how the key Kwantung Army staff officers Ishiwara Kanji and Itagaki Seishirō kept in close touch with the army leaders in Tokyo such as Nagata Tetsuzan, the chief of the important Military Affairs Section of the Army Ministry.

Seki's essay [4] on the March 1931 incident (an abortive coup d'état by middle-echelon army officers) and the crisis in Japan's China policy demonstrates, through a structural analysis of political leadership, that this incident was significant in having deprived Shidehara of any possibility of controlling the army's resort to military force in Manchuria.

Ōhata Tokushirō has published an article [1] on Sino-Japanese negotiations regarding the revision of the unequal treaties. Through an analysis of the negotiations, he examines the insurmountable gap between China's "revolutionary diplomacy" and Japan's "legalistic" stand.

The "Manchurian-Mongolian question," which was the direct occasion of the Manchurian Incident, consisted of many factors: an economic crisis that resulted from the spread of the world depression to Manchuria; the railway questions in Manchuria, which had remained unresolved since the end of the Russo-Japanese War; and the various movements among the Japanese residents in Manchuria. Nomura Kōichi [1] discusses the nature of the regimes in the Three Eastern Provinces in the context of interplay between the "peculiarities" of this region and Japan's claim for "special interests," carrying his account up to the eve of the Manchurian Incident.

The railway policy of the regimes in Manchuria is discussed in Ogata Yōichi's article [2] on the Tung-pei transportation committee and the so-called "plan to form a railway network to encircle the South Manchuria Railway." Ogata contends that the crisis of the South Manchuria Railway was caused by the decreased demand for soybeans during the depression, and not from the Chinese regime's plan to construct a railway competing with the South Manchuria Railway. In another article [1], Ogata focuses on Shidehara's role in the Manchurian railway negotiations. Kaneko Fumio's recent article [1] explains the process through which the management crisis of the South Manchuria Railway turned into a crisis in Japanese foreign policy.

In coping with these problems, the Japanese consulate general in Mukden played an extremely important role. Hayashi Kyūjirō, who served as consul general in Mukden during the years 1928–1932, has left a memoir, *Manshū jihen to Hōten sōryōji* (The Manchurian Incident and the consul general in Mukden), whose usefulness is enhanced by a careful introductory essay by Baba Akira.

Hirano Ken'ichirō [1] examines the Japanese residents' movements in Manchuria, 1921–1931. He also discusses their changing views of Manchuria and Mongolia (the idea of "interracial harmony") and asserts that Japanese residents influenced the development of the nature of the nascent "Manchukuo." From a different viewpoint, Matsuzawa Tetsunari discusses the activities of the Manchurian Youth League (Manshū Seinen Renmei).

In addition to the above works, there are studies on the economy, finance, emigration, and other issues in Manchuria and Inner Mongolia before the outbreak of the Manchurian Incident. For a general survey of these topics, the following historiographical essays are instructive: Kaneko Fumio's survey [2] of the Manchuria studies in the 1970s; Asada Kyōji's essay [2] on the history of Japanese colonialism; and Yanagisawa Asobu's survey of trends in the socioeconomic study of the Manchurian Incident.

The London Naval Conference

There already exist a number of studies on the London Naval Conference of 1930, a crucial event in the history of Shōwa Japan. Unno Yoshirō's early article [4] is a useful study, although it is based only on the Foreign Ministry archives. Kobayashi Tatsuo's excellent monographic essay [1] on the treaties of naval limitation, 1921–1936, extensively utilizes the primary materials of the navy, especially the records left by the "moderate" leaders of the Navy Ministry. For this reason, Kobayashi's account is fuller and more sympathetic in its treatment of the so-called "Treaty faction," which supported naval limitation. Its English version is contained in *Japan Erupts: The London Naval Conference and the Manchurian Incident, 1928–1932* (Columbia University Press, 1984), translated under the general editorship of James W. Morley.

From the naval perspective Nomura Minoru provides a concise account of the London Naval Conference and its background. Nomura is also the author of *Daihon'ei kaigunbu: Rengō kantai*, vol. 1: *Kaisen made* (Imperial Headquarters, navy: A history of the combined fleet, vol 1: Up to the opening of hostilities), a volume in the *Senshi sōsho* (War History) series. The most authoritative one-volume history of the Japanese navy, this book contains a concise account of the London Naval Conference. For the technical background of building plans and the effects of naval treaties on Japanese strategy, the most reliable work is Suekuni Masao, *Kaigun gunsenbi*, vol. 1: *Shōwa 16-nen jūichi-gatsu made* (Naval armaments and preparations for war, vol. 1: Up to November 1941), also a volume in the *Senshi sōsho* series. Much broader in scope than the title suggests, this massively documented volume, together with Nomura's work, represents the best of Japanese scholarship in naval history.

Ikeda Kiyoshi, one of the foremost civilian experts in naval history, published two important articles: one [2] discussing the London Naval Treaty and the question of the right of supreme command; and the other [1] printing the documents of the Navy General Staff concerning the London Naval Treaty, with commentaries. In these articles Ikeda points out that earlier studies have tended to give disproportionate weight to the "Treaty faction," and calls attention to the necessity of clarifying the position of the "Fleet faction," centering in the Navy General Staff, which opposed any naval limitation.

Regarding this point, Asada Sadao, in his essay [6] on the Japanese navy's policy regarding arms limitation, traces the increasing strength of the "Fleet faction" on the basis of new materials. Regarding the London Naval Conference, Asada points out the weakness of leadership in the navy and confusion resulting from poor communication between Tokyo and the Japanese delegates in London as well as within the Japanese delegation.

The domestic political effects of the London Naval Treaty and its aftermath are ably treated in essays contained in Nomura Minoru's recent book, *Rekishi no naka no Nihon kaigun* (The Japanese navy in historical perspective). The outline of the domestic upheaval following the London Naval Conference can be traced by reading the first volume of Harada Kumao, *Saionjikō to seikyoku* (Prince Saionji and politics). Portions of this book relating to the London Treaty problem are available in an English translation as Thomas F. Mayer-Oakes, tr., *Fragile Victory, Prince Saionji and the 1930 Treaty Issue* (Detroit: Wayne State University Press, 1968).

The most ambitious study on the development of domestic politics over the London Naval Treaty is Itō Takashi, *Shōwa shoki seijishi kenkyū: Rondon kaigun gunshuku mondai o meguru shoseiji shūdan no taikō to teikei* (A study of the political history of the early Shōwa period: Conflicts and alignments of political groups over the issue of the London naval limitation). Based on an enormous amount of research into new materials, Itō makes in-depth analyses of the Hamaguchi cabinet, senior statesmen *(genrō)*, and the House of Peers, the Lower House, the Seiyūkai party, and the ultra-right forces, depicting the structure of conflict and cooperation among these groups. What attracted the attention of scholars was the analytical framework Itō developed in this book. In order to diagram the dynamics of the changing alignment of various political groups over the issue of the London Naval Treaty, Itō presents two sets of contrasts: one axis showing "progressives" (favoring Westernization) versus "reactionaries," and another axis indicating "renovationists" (destruction) versus "gradualists" (representing the status quo). Applying this framework to the analysis of the political history of the 1920s and 1930s, he has made a significant contribution. One example, which focuses on an earlier period, is *Taishōki "Kakushinha" no kenkyū* (A study of the "renovation faction" during the Taishō period).

The Foreign Ministry has shown an unusual zeal in publishing a series of diplomatic records relating to the interwar conferences for naval limitation. It has been felt by the Foreign Ministry that at a time when arms control is much talked about, one can learn much from the "lessons" of the past naval conferences. Below we shall simply list these volumes: *Nihon gaikō bunsho: 1930-nen Rondon kaigun kaigi* (Documents on Japanese foreign policy: The London Naval Conference of 1930), 2 vols.; *Nihon gaikō bunsho: Rondon kaigun kaigi keika gaiyō* (A summary of the developments at the London Naval Conference); *Rondon kaigun kaigi, yobi kōshō, jōyaku setsumeisho* (Preliminary negotiations for the London Naval Conference, written explanations of the [London] treaty); and *Nihon gaikō bunsho: Kaigun gunbi seigen jōyaku Sūmitsuin shinsa kiroku* (Record of the Privy Council's examination of the London Naval Treaty).

The Geneva Naval Conference of 1927 has largely escaped scholarly attention in Japan. Recognizing the significance of Geneva as "a prelude to the London Naval Conference," the Foreign Ministry compiled *Nihon gaikō bunsho: Junēbu kaigun gunbi seigen kaigi* (The Geneva Conference for the limitation of naval armaments). Unno Yoshirō has examined the Geneva Conference in *Kaigun gunshuku kōshō, Fusen jōyaku* (Negotiations for naval limitation and the Kellogg-Britan Pact), which is vol. 16 of the Kajima series on Japanese diplomatic history. Unfortuntely, Unno's exclusive reliance on Foreign Ministry materials prevents him from untangling the politics of naval limitation within the navy as well as the government. Asada's essay [6] is the only work that studies the Geneva Conference from naval viewpoint and on the basis of the navy's record.

JAPAN AND THE NATIONALIST MOVEMENTS IN EAST ASIA

China

Usui Katsumi's previously cited books on Sino-Japanese relations in the Taishō period and during the northern expedition are useful on anti-Japanese movements and Chinese movements to recover their national rights; the author relates these movements to Japan's China policy. A more general study is Kikuchi Takeharu's *Chūgoku minzoku undō no kihon kōzō: Taigai boikotto no kenkyū* (The basic structure of Chinese nationalist movements: A study in antiforeign boycotts). Kikuchi describes at length major anti-Japanese boycotts: the *Daini Tatsu-maru* incident of 1908 (in which the seizure of a Japanese smuggling vessel by the Chinese authorities led to anti-Japanese boycotts); the Mukden-Antung railway question (1909); the Twenty-One Demands of 1915; the May Fourth Movement of 1919; the May 30th incident of 1925; and the Japanese military expeditions to Shantung (1927, 1928). More broadly, Banno Masataka has written a survey of the Chinese efforts to recover their national rights from World War I to the May 30 Incident.

It is well known that the results of the Paris Peace Conference, highly humiliating to the Chinese, provoked the outburst of the May Fourth Movement. On this movement, one should consult, in addition to Kikuchi Takaharu's previously cited work, Maruyama Matsuyuki's *Go-shi undō: Sono shisōshi* (The May Fourth Movement: Its intellectual history), which is valuable because it tells about the perspective of the Chinese Communist Party on this movement. Ikei Masaru's valuable article [7] on the Shantung question and the May Fourth Movement examines Japan's unsympathetic response to the outburst of Chinese nationalism in 1919 in comparison with friendly attitudes shown by the West. Also worthy of mention is Nohara Shirō's short essay on the Taishō intellectuals and the May Fourth Movement. The most recent study on the May Fourth Movement is: Kyōto Daigaku Jinbun Kagaku Kenkyūjo (The Institute of Humanistic Studies, Kyoto University), ed., *Go-shi undō no kenkyū* (Studies on the May Fourth Movement). As for relations with Japan, this work contains Fujimoto Hiroo's essay on Japanese imperialism and the May Fourth Movement.

A substantial work on Sun Yat-sen is Fujii Shōzō's *Son Bun no kenkyū: Tokuni minzokushugi riron o chūshin to shite* (A study of Sun Yat-sen: With particular reference to his theory of nationalism). *Son Bun to Nihon* (Sun Yat-sen and Japan), written by the Sinologist Kaizuka Shigeki, is an introductory book. The best study on the subject remains Marius B. Jansen, *The Japanese and Sun yat-sen* (Cambridge, Harvard University Press, 1954).

In addition to the works mentioned above, we have a large literature on various aspects of anti-Japanese movements in China. The following are only a few examples: Ajioka Tōru's article on Chinese nationalist movements during the early part of World War I; and Sugano Tadashi's essay on the Twenty-One Demands and anti-Japanese boycotts by Chinese overseas.

Korea

Japan's policy of governing Korea during the 1920s is expertly treated in Kan Don-chin (Kyō Tō-chin), *Nihon no Chōsen shihai seisaku-*

shi kenkyū: 1920-nendai o chūshin to shite (A study of the history of Japanese policy of governing Korea: with particular reference to the 1920s).

Regarding independence movements in Korea, essential sources are the six-volume collection *Chōsen*, expertly edited with an introduction by Kan Dok-san (Kyō Toku-sō), which are printed as volumes. 25–30 of the *Gendaishi shiryō* series (Documents on contemporary history). Volumes 25–26 contain documents on the March First Movement of 1919; volumes 27–30 print materials on the anti-Japanese movements led by the Korean Communist Party and on other topics covering the period from the March First Movement to the first half of the 1930s.

The March First Movement seems to dominate Japanese research on the history of Japanese-Korean relations. Important works include, to name only a few, articles by Yamabe Kentarō and Kan Dok-san. The Korean independence movement in Hsien-tao of Manchuria (1920), which was triggered by the March First Movement, is treated in Hayashi Masakazu's article [2] on the Hun-ch'un incident and Higashio Kazuko's essay on this incident and the Japanese military expedition to Hsien-tao.

Taiwan

Concerning independence movements in Taiwan, volumes 21 and 22 of the *Gendaishi shiryō* series, edited by Yamabe Kentarō, contain basic materials on the Taiwan Communist Party, the Taiwanese movement to establish its own parliament, agrarian movements, and the Musha incident of 1930 (in which the Taiwanese aborigines revolted against Japanese rule). For a comprehensive study on the anti-Japanese movements in Taiwan, To Shōgen's *Nihon teikokushugika no Taiwan* (Taiwan under Japanese imperialism) is recommended.

On Japan's administrative policy in Taiwan, *Nihon tōchika no Taiwan: Teikō to dan'atsu* (Taiwan under Japanese rule: Resistance and suppression) by Koh Se-kai is an excellent study. Wakabayashi Masahiro's *Taiwan kō-Nichi undōshi kenkyū* (A study on the history of Taiwanese resistance movement against Japanese rule) concentrates on the nature of Taiwan policy during the Taishō period, fully examining the relationship between "Taishō democracy" and the Taiwanese movement to establish their own parliament (1921–34). Ryū Mei-shū's recent work, *Taiwan tōchi to ahen mondai* (Japanese rule over Taiwan, and the opium question), is an unusual study that traces Japan's changing policies toward Taiwan with a special focus on opium consumption and cultivation there. Mukōyama Hiroo has published an article discussing law and politics in Taiwan under Japanese rule from the standpoint of ethnic law. On the Musha incident of 1930, the following works are useful: Tai Kok-fon, *Taiwan Musha hōki jiken: Kenkyū to shiryō* (The Musha incident: Research and documents); and Nakagawa Kōichi and Wakamori Tamio, *Musha jiken: Taiwan Takasagozoku no hōki* (The Musha incident: The uprising of the Taiwanese aborigines against Japanese rulers).

Bibliography

Ajia Keizai Kenkyūjo アジア 経済研究所 (Institute of Developing Economies), ed. *Kyū shokuminchi kankei kikan kankōbutsu sōgō mokuroku: Minami Manshū Tetsudō Kabushiki Kaishahen* 旧植民地関係機関刊行物総合目録―南満州鉄道株式会社 (A comprehensive bibliography of materials published by Japan's former colonial agencies: The South Manchuria Railway Company). Ajia Keizai Kenkyūjo, 1979.

Ajioka Tōru 味岡徹. "Daiichiji taisen shoki no Chūgoku minzoku undō" 第一次大戦初期の中国民族運動 (The Chinese nationalist movement in the early phase of World War I). *Rekishigaku kenkyū, Bessatsu tokushū* (October 1979), pp. 131–141.

Amamiya Shōichi 雨宮昭一. "Kindai Nihon no sensō shidō no kōzō to tenkai: Seiryaku to senryaku tono kankei o chūshin to shite", 1, 2 近代日本の戦争指導の構造と展開 (The conduct of war in modern Japan: Its structure and development, 1, 2). *Ibaragi daigaku kyōyōbu kiyō*, (April 1975), no. 7, pp. 21–71; (April 1976), no. 8, pp. 57–112. [1]

—— "Sensō shidō to seitō: Gaikō chōsakai no kinō to ichi" 戦争指導と政党―外交調査会の機能と位置 (The conduct of war and political parties: The functions and position of the Advisory Council on Foreign Relations). *Shisō* (April 1976), no. 622, pp. 103–25. [2]

—— "Shiberia teppei katei to tōhō kaigi" シベリア撤兵過程と東方会議 (The Eastern Conference [1920] and the process of Japan's withdrawal of troops from Siberia). *Rekishigaku kenkyū, Bessatsu tokushū* (October 1979), pp. 21–27. [3]

Andō Hikotarō 安藤彦太郎, ed. *Mantetsu: Nihon teikokushugi to Chūgoku*

178   IKEI, HATANO, INOUE, ASADA

満鉄—日本帝国主義と中国 (The South Manchuria Railway Company: Japanese imperialism and China). Ochanomizu Shobō, 1965.

Aruga Tadashi 有賀貞. "Hai-Nichi mondai to Nichi-Bei kankei: 'Hanihara shokan' o chūshin ni" 排日問題と日米関係—埴原書簡を中心に (The anti-Japanese exclusion question and Japanese-American relations: With particular reference to the "Hanihara letter"). In Iriye Akira and Aruga, eds., *Senkanki no Nihon gaikō,* pp. 65–96.

Asada Kyōji 浅田喬二. "Manshū ni okeru tochi shōsoken mondai" 満州における土地商租権問題 (The problem of commercial land leases in Manchuria). In Manshūshi Kenkyūkai 満州史研究会, ed., *Nihon teikoku-shugika no Manshū* 日本帝国主義下の満州 (Manchuria under Japanese imperialism), pp. 317–97. Ochanomizu Shobō, 1972. [1]

—— "Nihon shokuminshi kenkyū no genjō to mondaiten" 日本植民史研究の現状と問題点 (The current state and problems in studies on the history of Japanese colonization). *Rekishi hyōron* (April 1975), no. 300, pp. 178–98. [2]

Asada Sadao 麻田貞雄. "Amerika no tai-Nichi kan to 'Washinton taisei'" アメリカの対日観と「ワシントン体制」 (The "Washington system" and American images of Japan). *Kokusai seiji* (1966), no. 34: *Nichi-Bei kankei no imēji,* pp. 36–57. [1]

—— "Japan's 'Special Interests' and the Washington Conference, 1921–22." *American Historical Review* (October 1961), 67(1):62–70. [2]

—— "Japanese Admirals and the Politics of Naval Limitation: Katō Tomosaburō vs. Katō Kanji." In Gerald Jordan, ed., *Naval Warfare in the Twentieth Century,* pp. 141–66. London: Croom Helm, 1977, [3]

—— "Nichi-Bei kankei no imēji: Senzen" 日米関係のイメージ—戦前 (Japanese images of the United States: The prewar years). In Miwa, ed., *Sōgō kōza Nihon no shakai bunkashi,* vol. 7: *Sekai no naka no Nihon,* pp. 308–59. [4]

—— "Nichi-Bei kankei to imin mondai" 日米関係と移民問題 (Japanese-American relations and the immigration question). In Saitō Makoto 斎藤真 et al., eds., *Nihon to Amerika: Hikaku bunkaron,* vol. 2: *Demokurashī to Nichi-Bei kankei* 日本とアメリカ—比較文化論, 2：デモクラシーと日米関係 (Japan and America: Studies in comparative culture, vol. 2: Democracy and Japanese-American relations), pp. 161–210. Nan'undō, 1973. [5]

—— "Nihon kaigun to gunshuku: Tai-Bei seisaku o meguru seiji katei" 日本海軍と軍縮—対米政策をめぐる政治過程 (The Imperial Japanese Navy and naval limitation: The political process with regard to policy toward the United States). In Hosoya Chihiro and Saitō Makoto eds., *Washinton taisei to Nichi-Bei kankei,* pp. 353–414. [6]

—— "Washinton kaigi o meguru Nichi-Bei seisaku kettei katei no hikaku: Hito to kikō" ワシントン会議をめぐる日米政策決定過程の比較―人と機構 (A comparative study of the Japanese and American decision-making process at the time of the Washington Conference: Decision makers and mechanisms). In Hosoya and Watanuki, eds., *Taigai seisaku kettei katei no Nichi-Bei hikaku*, pp. 419–64. [7]

—— "Washinton kaigi to Nihon no taiō: 'Kyū gaikō' to 'shin gaikō' no hazama" ワシントン会議と日本の対応―「旧外交」と「新外交」のはざま (Japan's reaction to the Washington Conference: From the "old diplomacy" to the "new diplomacy"). In Iriye and Aruga, eds., *Senkanki no Nihon gaikō*, pp. 21–63. [8]

Asukai Masamichi 飛鳥井雅道. "Roshia kakumei to 'Nikō jiken'" ロシア革命と「尼港事件」 (The Russian Revolution and the "Nikolaevsk incident"). In Inoue and Watanabe, eds., *Taishōki no kyūshinteki jiyūshugi*, pp. 265–306.

Baba Akira 馬場明. "Daiichiji Santō shuppei to Tanaka gaikō" 第一次山東出兵と田中外交 (The first Shantung expedition: A case study of Tanaka diplomacy). *Ajia kenkyū* (October 1963), 10(3): 50–77. [1]

—— "Nichi-Ro sengo ni okeru daiichiji Saionji naikaku no tai-Man seisaku to Sinkoku" 日露戦後における第一次西園寺内閣の対満政策と清国 (China and the Manchurian policy of the first Saionji cabinet after the Russo-Japanese War). In Kurihara, ed., *Tai-Manmō seisakushi no ichimen*, pp. 61–86. [2]

—— "Nichi-Ro sengo no tairiku seisaku" 日露戦後の大陸政策 (Japan's continental policy after the Russo-Japanese War). *Kokusai seiji* (1962), no. 19: *Nihon gaikōshi kenkyū–Nisshin Nichi-Ro sensō*, pp. 134–50. [3]

—— *Nitchū kankei to gaisei kikō no kenkyū: Taishō, Shōwaki* 日中関係と外政機構の研究―大正・昭和期 (A study on Sino-Japanese relations and [Japanese] foreign policy machinery: Taishō and Shōwa periods). Hara Shobō, 1983.

—— "Rinjō jiken to Nihon no tai-Chūgoku seisaku" 臨城事件と日本の対中国政策 (The Lingcheng incident and Japan's policy toward China). *Kokugakuin daigaku kiyō* (March 1976), no. 14, pp. 35–66. [4]

—— "Tanaka gaikō to Chō Saku-rin bakushi jiken" 田中外交と張作霖爆死事件 (Tanaka diplomacy and the killing of Chang Tso-lin by a bomb). *Rekishi kyōiku* (February 1960), 8(2): 41–48. [5]

Bamba Nobuya 馬場伸也. *Japanese Diplomacy in a Dilemma: New Light on Japan's China Policy, 1924–1929*. Vancouver, Canada: University of British Columbia Press; Kyoto: Mineruva Shobō, 1973.

—— *Manshū jihen e no michi: Shidehara gaikō to Tanaka gaikō* 満州事変への道―幣原外交と田中外交 (The road to the Manchurian Incident: Shidehara diplomacy and Tanaka diplomacy). Chūō Kōronsha, 1972.

—— "Pekin kanzei tokubetsu kaigi ni nozomu Nihon no seisaku kettei katei'' 北京関税特別会議に臨む日本の政策決定過程 (Japan's decision-making process with regard to the Peking Tariff Conference, 1925–26). In Hosoya and Watanuki, eds., *Taigai seisaku kettei katei no Nichi-Bei hikaku,* pp. 375–417.

Banno Junji 坂野潤治. *Kindai Nihon no gaikō to seiji* 近代日本の外交と政治 (Diplomacy and politics in modern Japan). Kenbun Shuppan, 1985.

—— ''Nihon Rikugun no Ō-Beikan to Chūgoku seisaku'' 日本陸軍の欧米観と中国政策 (The Japanese army's views on Europe and the United States, and its policy toward China). In Hosoya and Saitō, eds., *Washinton taisei to Nichi-Bei kankei,* pp. 441–64. [1]

—— ''Seitō seiji to Chūgoku seisaku, 1919–1926'' 政党政治と中国政策, 1919–1926 (Political parties and their China policies, 1919–1926), *Nenpō kindai Nihon kenkyū,* no. 2: *Kindai Nihon to higashi Ajia* (Journal of Modern Japanese Studies, no. 2: Modern Japan and East Asia, pp. 96–113, 1980. [2]

—— ''Shidehara gaikō no hōkai to Nihon rikugun'' 幣原外交の崩壊と日本陸軍 (The collapse of Shidehara diplomacy and the Japanese army). In Tokyo Daigaku Shakai Kagaku Kenkyūjo 東京大学社会科学研究所 (Social Science Research Institute, University of Tokyo), ed., *Fashizumuki no kokka to shakai, 6* ファシズム期の国家と社会, (6) (The state and society during the fascist period, vol. 6), pp. 115–44. Tokyo Daigaku Shuppankai, 1979. [3]

—— *Taishō seihen* 大正政変 (The political change in the Taishō period). Kyoto: Mineruva Shobō, 1982.

Banno Masataka 坂野正高. ''Daiichiji taisen kara go-sanjū made: Kokken kaifuku undōshi oboegaki'' 第一次大戦から5.30まで―国権回復運動史覚書 (From World War I to the May 30th Incident: A note on the history of China's movement to recover national rights). In Ueda Toshio 植田捷雄, ed., *Gendai Chūgoku o meguru sekai no gaikō* 現代中国をめぐる世界の外交 (Modern China in world diplomacy), pp. 1–67. Nomura Shoten, 1951.

Eguchi Bokurō 江口朴郎 ''Nihon teikokushugi no kokusaiteki keiki'' 日本帝国主義の国際的契機 (The international setting of Japanese imperialism). In Eguchi Bokurō, *Teikokushugi to minzoku* 帝国主義と民族 (Imperialism and the peoples), pp. 70–140. Tokyo Daigaku Shuppankai, 1954.

Eguchi Keiichi 江口圭一. ''Kakushōrei jiken to Nihon teikokushugi'' 郭松齢事件と日本帝国主義 (The Kuo Sung-ling incident and Japanese imperialism). *Jinbun gakuhō* (Kyoto Daigaku) (November 1962), no. 17, pp. 71–88. [1]

—— *Nihon teikokushugi shiron: Manshū jihen zengo* 日本帝国主義史論―満州事変前後 (Historical studies on Japanese imperialism: The period of the Manchurian Incident). Aoki Shoten, 1975.

Eguchi Keiichi. "Santō shuppei, 'Manshū jihen' o megutte" 山東出兵・「満州事変」をめぐって (Editorial views on the Shantung expedition and the Manchurian Incident). In Inoue and Watanabe, eds., *Taishōki no kyū-shinteki jiyūshugi*, pp. 353–92. [2]

Eguchi Keiichi and Ono Shinji 小野信爾, "Nihon teikokushugi to Chūgoku kakumei" 日本帝国主義と中国革命 (Japanese imperialism and the Chinese Revolution). In *Iwanami kōza: Nihon rekishi, 20: gendai, 3*, 岩波講座日本歴史20, 現代, 3 (Iwanami series on Japanese history, vol. 20: The contemporary period, 3), pp. 1–50. Iwanami Shoten, 1963.

Etō Shinkichi 衞藤瀋吉. "Kei-Hō sen shadan mondai no gaikō katei" 京奉線遮断問題の外交過程 (The diplomatic negotiations concerning the suspension of traffic on the Peking-Mukden Railway). In Shinohara and Mitani, eds., *Kindai Nihon no seiji shidō*, pp. 375–429. [1]

—— "Nankin jiken to Nichi-Bei" 南京事件と日米 (Japan and the United States during the Nanking Incident). In Saitō, ed., *Gendai Amerika no naisei to gaikō*, pp. 299–324. [2]

—— "Nikka kinchō to Nihonjin: 1925-nen kara 28-nen made no *Asahi* to *Nichi-Nichi* no naiyō bunseki" 日華緊張と日本人—1925年から28年までの「朝日」と「日日」の内容分析 (Sino-Japanese tensions and the Japanese: Content analysis of the *Asahi* and *Nichi-Nichi* from 1925 to 1928). In Etō Shinkichi et al., eds., *Chūka Minkoku o meguru kokusai seiji* 中国をめぐる国際政治 (The Republic of China in international politics), pp. 183–235. Tokyo Daigaku Shuppankai, 1968. [3]

—— "Shidehara gaikō kara Tanaka gaikō e: Gaikō mondai o midarini seisō no gu ni suruto dōnaruka" 幣原外交から田中外交へ—外交問題をみだりに政争の具にするとどうなるか (From Shidehara diplomacy to Tanaka diplomacy: A lesson taken from party quarrels over diplomatic problems). *Sekai keizai* (June 1963), no. 82, pp. 2–12. [4]

—— "Tōten to Shinkoku kakumei wa dōshite musubitsuitaka" 滔天と清国革命はどうして結びついたか (How Miyazaki Tōten came to be involved in the Chinese Revolution of [1911]). *Shisō* (March 1968), no. 525, pp. 19–30. [5]

—— "Chūgokujin no Nihonkan: Daiichiji taisen chokugo kara Shidehara gaikō made" 中国人の日本観—第一次大戦直後から幣原外交まで (Japan as seen by the Chinese, 1919 to 1931). *Shakai kagaku tōkyū* (Waseda Daigaku) (March 1975) 20(2–3):5–42. [6]

Fujii Shōichi 藤井松一. "Nichi-Ro sensō" 日露戦争 (The Russo-Japanese War). In Iwanami Kōza: *Nihon rekishi 18, Gendai, 1* 岩波講座, 日本歴史18, 現代, 1 (Iwanami series on Japanese history: vol. 18, Contemporary period, 1), pp. 109–52. Iwanami Shoten, 1963.

—— "Teikokushugi no seiritsu to Nichi-Ro sensō" 帝国主義の成立と日露

戦争 (The emergence of [Japanese] imperialism and the Russo-Japanese War). In Rekishigaku Kenkyūkai 歴史学研究会, ed., *Jidai kubun jō no rironteki shomondai* 時代区分上の理論的諸問題 (Theoretical problems of historical periodization), pp. 44–59. Iwanami Shoten, 1956.

Fujii Shōzō 藤井昇三. "Chūgoku kara mita 'Shidehara gaikō'" 中国から見た「幣原外交」 ("Shidehara diplomacy" as seen from the Chinese side). In *Nitchū kankei no sōgo imēji: Showa shoki o chūshin to shite* 日中関係の相互イメージ, 昭和初期を中心として (Mutual images in Sino-Japanese relations, with special reference to the early Shōwa period), pp. 1–31. Ajia Seikei Gakkai, 1972. [1]

—— "Nijūikkajō jōyaku jiki no Son Bun to 'Chū-Nichi meiyaku'" 21ヶ条条約時期の孫文と「中日盟約」 (Sun Yat-sen and "the Sino-Japanese alliance" at the time of the negotiations of the Twenty-One Demands). In Ichiko Chūzō Kyōju Taikan Kinen Ronsō Henshū Iinkai 市古宙三教授退官記念論叢編集委員会, ed., *Ronshū kindai Chūgoku kenkyū* 論集近代中国研究 (Collected essays on modern China), pp. 335–59. Yamakawa Shuppansha, 1981. [2]

—— "1920-nen Anchoku sensō o meguru Nitchū kankei no ichi kōsatsu: Henbōgun mondai o chūshin to shite" 1920年安直戦争をめぐる日中関係の一考察—辺防軍問題を中心として (A consideration of Sino-Japanese relations during the Anhwei-Mukden war of 1920: With special reference to the problem of troops in defense of the borderline). *Kokusai seiji* (1961), no. 15: *Nihon gaikōshi kenkyū—Nitchū kankei no tenkai,* pp. 56–70 [3]

—— *Son Bun no kenkyū: Tokuni minzokushugi riron o chūshin to shite* 孫文の研究—特に民族主義理論を中心として (A study of Sun Yat-sen: With particular reference to his theory of nationalism). Keisō Shobō, 1966.

—— "Taku jiken o meguru Nitchū kankei: Chūgoku kokumin kakumei no ichi sokumen" 大沽事件をめぐる日中関係—中国国民革命の一側面 (Sino-Japanese relations over the Taku incident: An aspect of the Chinese nationalist revolution). In Hirano Ken'ichirō 平野健一郎, ed., *Kokusai kankeiron no furontia* 国際関係論のフロンティア (The frontier of studies in international relations), 2: 261–88. Tokyo Daigaku Shuppankai, 1984. [4]

—— "Washinton kaigi to Chūgoku no minzoku undō" ワシントン会議と中国の民族運動 (The Washington Conference and the nationalist movement in China). *Toyō bunka kenkyūjo kiyō* (March 1970), no. 50, pp. 203–53. [5]

—— "Washinton taisei to Chūgoku: Hokubatsu chokuzen made" ワシントン体制と中国—北伐直前まで (The Washington system and China: Up to the Northern Expedition). *Kokusai seiji* (1971), no. 46: *Kokusai seiji to kokunai seiji no renkei,* pp. 1–16. [6]

Fujii Shōzō. "Washinton taisei to Chūgoku Kyōsantō: 1921-nen kara 1924-nen made" ワシントン体制と中国共産党—1921年から1924年まで (The Washington system and the Chinese Communist Party: From 1921 to 1924). *Kokusai mondai kenkyū* (December 1968), no. 1, pp. 74–84. [7]

Fujimoto Hiroo 藤本博生. "Pari kōwa kaigi to Nihon, Chūgoku: 'Jinshu-an' Nisshi dōkatsu jiken" パリ講和会議と日本・中国—「人種案」日使恫喝事件 (Japan and China at the Paris Peace Conference: With particular reference to Japan's proposal for "racial equality"). *Shirin* (November, 1976), 59(6): 70–97. [1]

—— *Nihon teikokushugi to Go-shi undō* 日本帝国主義と五・四運動 (Japanese imperialism and the May Fourth Movement). In Kyōto Daigaku Jinbun Kagaku Kenkyūjo, ed., *Go-shi undō no kenkyū,* parts 1–3. Kyoto, Dōhō Shuppansha, 1982. [2]

Fujimura Michio 藤村道生. "Kankoku jijūbukan kara mita Nihon no Kankoku heigō" 韓国侍従武官から見た日本の併合 (The Japanese annexation of Korea as seen by an aide in Korea). *Kyūshū kōgyō daigaku kenkyū hōkoku: Jinbun shakai kagaku* (March 1973), no. 21, pp. 15–56. [1]

—— "Kindai Nihon gaikōshi no jiki kubun: Tsūshi jojutsu no tame no sagyō kasetsu" 近代日本外交史の時期区分—通史叙述のための作業仮説 (A tentative attempt at the periodization of Japanese diplomatic history). *Kyūshū kōgyō daigaku kenkyū hōkoku* (March 1971), no. 19, pp. 1–38. [2]

—— "Nichi-Ro sensō no seikaku ni yosete" 日露戦争の性格によせて (On the nature of the Russo-Japanese War). *Rekishigaku kenkyū* (May 1956), no. 195, pp. 1–13. [3]

Gabe Masaaki 我部政明. "Nihon no Mikuroneshia senryō to 'Nanshin': Gunseiki [1914–1922] o chūshin to shite, 1, 2." 日本のミクロネシア占領と「南進」—軍政期(1914—1922)を中心として (Japan's "southward advance" and occupation of Micronesia: With special reference to Japan's military administration, 1914–1922, 1, 2), *Hōgaku kenkyū* (Keiō Gijuku Daigaku) (July 1982), 55(7): 70–89; (August 1982), 55(8): 67–87.

Gaimushō Hyakunenshi Hensan Iinkai 外務省百年史編纂委員会, ed. *Gaimushō no hyakunen* 外務省の百年 (A century of the Japanese Foreign Ministry). 2 vols. Hara Shobō, 1969.

Hajima Takahiko 羽島敬彦. "Chōsen ni okeru shokuminchi kin'yū kaikaku: Megata o chūshin ni" 朝鮮における植民地金融改革—目賀田〔種太郎〕を中心に (Reforms of colonial finance in Korea: With particular reference to Baron Megata Tanetarō). In Ono Kazuichirō and Yoshinobu Susumu 小野一一郎, 吉信粛, eds., *Ryō taisenkanki no Ajia to Nihon* 両大戦間期のアジアと日本 (Asia and Japan in the interwar period), pp. 175–99. Ōtsuki Shoten, 1979.

Hara Keiichirō 原奎一郎, comp. *Hara Kei nikki* 原敬日記 (The diary of Hara

Kei). 9 vols. Kangensha, 1950–51. (Reprinted in 6 vols. by Fukumura Shuppan, 1965.)

Hara Teruyuki 原暉之. "Nihon no Kyokutō Roshia gunji kanshō no sho-mondai" 日本の極東ロシア軍事干渉の諸問題 (On Japan's military intervention in the Russian Far East). *Rekishigaku kenkyū* (March 1980), no. 478, pp. 1–14. [1]

—— "'Nikō jiken' no shomondai" 「尼港事件」の諸問題 (Problems of the "Nikolaevsk incident"). *Roshiashi kenkyū* (February 1975), no. 23, pp. 2–17. [2]

Harada Katsumasa 原田勝正. "Chōsen heigō to shoki no shokuminchi keiei" 朝鮮併合と初期の植民地経営 (The annexation of Korea and early colonial administration). In *Iwanami kōza: Nihon rekishi,* vol. 18: *Gendai, 1* 岩波講座日本歴史18, 現代 1 (Iwanami series on Japanese history, vol. 18: The contemporary period, 1), pp. 197–244. Iwanami Shoten, 1963.

—— *Mantetsu* 満鉄 (The South Manchuria Railway Company). Iwanami Shoten, 1983.

Harada Kumao 原田熊雄. *Saionjikō to seikyoku* 西園寺公と政局 (Prince Saionji and politics), vol. 1. Iwanami Shoten, 1950.

Haraguchi Kunihiro 原口邦紘. "Nihon-Kanada kankei no ichi kōsatsu: 'Rumyū kyōyaku' kaitei mondai" 日本・カナダ関係の一考察—「ルミュー協約」改訂問題 (The revision of the Lemieux Agreement and Japanese-Canadian relations). *Kokusai seiji* (1978), no. 58: *Nichi-Ei kankei no shiteki tenkai,* pp. 45–68.

Hata Ikuhiko 秦郁彦. "Meijiki ikō ni okeru Nichi-Bei Taiheiyō senryaku no hensen" 明治期以降における日米太平洋戦略の変遷 (Changes in Japanese and American strategies in the Pacific since the Meiji period). *Kokusai seiji* (1968), no. 37: *Nihon gaikōshi no shomondai,* no. 3, pp. 96–115.

—— *Taiheiyō kokusai kankeishi: Nichi-Bei oyobi Nichi-Ro kiki no keifu, 1900–1935* 太平洋国際関係史—日米および日露危機の系譜, 1900—1935 (A history of international relations in the Pacific: An analysis of Japanese-American and Russo-Japanese war scares, 1900–1935). Fukumura Shuppan, 1972.

Hatano Masaru 波多野勝. "Shingai kakumei to Nihon kaigun no taiō" 辛亥革命と日本海軍の対応 (The Chinese Revolution of 1911 and the response of the Japanese navy). *Gunji shigaku* (March 1986), 21(4):14–22 (part 1); (June 1986), 22(1):45–56 (part 2).

Hatano Yoshihiro 波多野善大. "Nichi-Ro sensōgo ni okeru kokusai kankei no dōin" 日露戦争後における国際関係の動因 (The dynamics of international relations after the Russo-Japanese War). *Kokusai seiji* (1957), no. 3: *Nihon gaikōshi kenkyū—Meiji jidai,* pp. 153–82. [1]

—— "Nishihara shakkan no kihonteki kōsō" 西原借款の基本的構想 (The

fundamental idea behind the Nishihara loans). In *Nagoya daigaku bunga-kubu 10-shūnen kinen ronshū*, pp. 393–416. 1959. [2]

Hatsuse Ryūhei 初瀬龍平. *Dentōteki uyoku Uchida Ryōhei no kenkyū* 伝統的右翼内田良平の研究 (A study of Uchida Ryōhei, a traditional right-winger). Fukuoka: Kyūshū Daigaku Shuppankai, 1980.

Hayashi Kyūjirō 林久治郎. (Introduction by Baba Akira 馬場明) *Manshū jihen to Hōten sōryōji* 満州事変と奉天総領事 (The Manchurian Incident and the Japanese consul general in Mukden). Hara Shobō, 1978.

Hayashi Masakazu 林正和. "Chō Saku-rin gunbatsu no keisei katei to Nihon no taiō" 張作霖軍閥の形成過程と日本の対応 (The process of the forma-tion of Chang Tso-lin's warlordism and Japan's reaction). *Kokusai seiji* (1970), no. 41: *Nihon gaikōshi kenkyū: Gaikō to yoron*, pp. 122–42. [1]

—— "Konshun jiken no keika" 琿春事件の経過 (The development of the Hun-ch'un incident of 1920). *Sundai shigaku* (September 1966), no. 19, pp. 107–26. [2]

Hayashima Akira 早島暎. "Doitsu no sensō mokuteki seisaku ni okeru iwayuru Sutokkuhorumu kōshō ni tsuite" ドイツの戦争目的政策における所謂ストックホルム交渉について (German war aims during World War I and the so-called "Stockholm negotiation"). *Seiyō shigaku* (June 1976), no. 101, pp. 1–21.

—— "Zur Japanischen Europolitik, 1914–1918." *Kansei Gakuin University Annual Studies* (1977), no. 26, pp. 89–105.

Higashio Kazuko 東尾和子. "Konshun jiken to Kantō shuppei" 琿春事件と間島出兵 (The Hun-ch'un incident and the [Japanese] expedition). *Chōsenshi kenkyūkai ronbunshū* (March 1977), no. 14, pp. 59–85.

Hirano Ken'ichirō 平野健一郎. "Manshū jihen zen ni okeru zai-Man Nihon-jin no dōkō: Manshūkoku seikaku keisei no ichi yōin" 満州事変前における在満日本人の動向—満州国性格形成の一要因 (The movements and attitudes of Japanese residents in Manchuria, 1921–1931: Their psychologic of "interracial harmony"). *Kokusai seiji* (1970), no. 43: *Manshū jihen*, pp. 51–76. [1]

—— "Nishihara shakkan kara shin shikoku shakkandan e" 西原借款から新四国借款団へ (From the Nishihara loans to the new four-power China consortium). In Hosoya and Saitō, eds., *Washinton taisei to Nichi-Bei kankei*, pp. 283–320. [2]

Hirata Ken'ichi 平田賢一. "'Chōsen heigō' to Nihon no yoron" 「朝鮮併合」と日本の世論 (The annexation of Korea and public opinion in Japan). *Shirin* (May 1974), 57(3): 103–23.

Homma Nagayo 本間長世. "Nihon bunka no Amerikaka: Raifu sutairu to taishū bunka" 日本文化のアメリカ化—ライフスタイルと大衆文化 (The Americanization of the Japanese culture: Changing life-style and mass culture). In Hosoya Chihiro and Saitō Makoto, eds., *Washinton taisei to Nichi-Bei kankei,* pp. 603–30.

Horikawa Takeo 堀川武夫. *Kyokutō kokusai seijishi josetsu: Nijūikkajō yōkyū no kenkyū* 極東国際政治史序説―二十一箇条要求の研究 (An introduction to the history of Far Eastern international politics: A study of the Twenty-One Demands). Yūhikaku, 1958.

―― "Nihon no Manshū ken'eki ni okeru tokushu rieki no hōteki seikaku" 日本の満州権益における特殊利益の法的性質 (The legal nature of Japan's "special interests" in Manchuria). *Ajia kenkyū* (April 1962), 9(1): 48–69.

Hosoya Chihiro 細谷千博. "Japanese Documents on the Siberian Intervention, 1917–1922: Part 1, November 1917–January 1919." *Hitotsubashi Journal of Law and Politics* (April 1960), 1(1): 30–53. [1]

―― "Kita Saharin no sekiyu shigen o meguru Nichi-Bei no keizai funsō" 北サハリンの石油資源をめぐる日米の経済紛争 (Economic conflict between Japan and the United States over oil resources in north Sakhalin). In Hosoya, ed., *Taiheiyō-Ajia ken no kokusai keizai funsōshi, 1922–1945,* pp. 183–205. [2]

―― "Makino Nobuaki to Verusaiyu kaigi" 牧野伸顕とヴェルサイユ会議 (Makino Nobuaki and the Versailles Conference). In Hosoya, *Nihon gaikō no zahyō,* pp. 4–17. [3]

―― *Nihon gaikō no zahyō* 日本外交の座標 (Thought and behavior in Japanese diplomacy [Collected essays]). Chūō Kōronsha, 1979. [4]

―― "Nihon to Koruchakku seiken shōnin mondai: Hara Kei naikaku ni okeru Shiberia shuppei seisaku no saikeisei" 日本とコルチャック政権承認問題―原敬内閣におけるシベリア出兵政策の再形成 (Janan and the issue of recognizing the Kolchak regime: Reformulation of the Siberian expedition policy under the Hara Kei cabinet). *Hitotsubashi daigaku kenkyū nenpō: Hōgaku kenkyū* (March 1964), no. 3, pp. 13–135. [5]

―― "Nijūikkajō yōkyū to Amerika no taiō" 「ニーケ条要求」とアメリカの対応 (The American reaction to the Twenty-One Demands). *Hitotsubashi ronsō* (January 1960), 43(1): 28–50. [6]

―― "The origins of the Siberian Intervention." *Annals of the Hitotsubashi Academy* (October 1958), 9(1): 91–108. [7]

―― *Roshia kakumei to Nihon* ロシア革命と日本 (The Russian Revolution and Japan). Hara Shobō, 1972.

―― *Shiberia shuppei no shiteki kenkyū* シベリア出兵の史的研究 (A historical study of the Siberian Expedition). Yūhikaku, 1955.

―― "Shiberia shuppei o meguru Nichi-Bei kankei" シベリア出兵をめぐる日米関係 (The Siberian Expedition and Japanese-American relations). *Kokusai seiji* (1961), no. 17: *Nichi-Bei kankei no tenkai,* pp. 73–90. [8]

Hosoya Chihiro, ed., *Taiheiyō-Ajia ken no kokusai keizai funsōshi, 1922–1945* 太平洋・アジア圏の国際経済紛争史, 1922—1945 (A history of international economic conflicts in the Asia-Pacific region, 1922–1945), Tōkyō Daigaku Shuppankai, 1983.

—— "Washinton taisei no tokushitsu to hen'yō" ワシントン体制の特質 と変容 (The characteristics and changes of the Washington system). In Hosoya and Saitō, eds., *Washinton taisei to Nichi-Bei kankei*, pp. 3–39. [9]

Hosoya Chihiro and Saitō Makoto 斎藤真, eds., *Washinton taisei to Nichi-Bei kankei* ワシントン体制と日米関係 (The Washington system and Japanese-American relations). Tokyo Daigaku Shuppankai, 1978.

Hosoya Chihiro and Watanuki Jōji 綿貫譲治, eds., *Taigai seisaku kettei katei no Nichi-Bei hikaku* 対外政策決定過程の日米比較 (Comparative studies of the foreign policy decision-making process in Japan and the United States). Tokyo Daigaku Shupankai, 1977.

Hosoya Chihiro et al., eds., *Nichi-Bei kankeishi: Kaisen ni itaru 10-nen, 1931–41-nen* 日米関係史—開戦に至る10年 (1931—41年) (A history of Japanese-American relations: The decade preceding the war, 1931–1941). 4 vols. Tokyo Daigaku Shuppankai, 1971–72.

Ichikawa Masaaki 市川正明. *An-jūkon to Nikkan kankeishi* 安重根と日韓関 係史 (An Chung-gǔn and the history of Japanese-Korean relations). Hara Shobō, 1979.

Ichikawa Masaaki, ed., *Kankoku heigō shiryō* 韓国併合史料 (Materials on the annexation of Korea). 3 vols. Hara Shobō, 1978.

Ichimata Masao 一又正雄. "Nichi-Bei imin mondai to 'kokunai mondai'" 日米移民問題と「国内問題」 (The Japanese immigration as a jurisdictional question in the United States). In Ueda Toshio, ed., *Kamikawa sensei kanreki kinen: Kindai Nihon gaikōshi no kenkyū*, pp. 423–39.

—— *Sugiyama Shigemaru: Meiji tairiku seisaku no genryū* 杉山茂丸—明治 大陸政策の源流 (Sugiyama Shigemaru: A genesis of Japan's continental policy during the Meiji period). Ed. by Ōhata Tokushirō. *Hara Shobō*, 1976.

—— *Yamaza Enjirō den: Meiji jidai ni okeru tairiku seisaku no jikkōsha* 山座 円次郎伝—明治時代における大陸政策の実行者 (The life of Yamaza Enjirō: An executor of Japan's continental policy during the Meiji period). Hara Shobō, 1974.

Iguchi Kazuki 井口和起. "Shokuminchi seisakuron: 1910-nendai no Chōsen seisakuron o chūshin to shite" 植民地政策論—1910年代の朝鮮政策論 を中心として (Discussions on colonial policy: With particular reference to Japan's policy toward Korea in the 1910s). In Inoue and Watanabe, eds., *Taishōki no kyūshinteki jiyūshugi*, pp. 187–217.

Iino Masako 飯野正子. "Beikoku ni okeru hai-Nichi undō to 1924-nen iminhō seitei katei" 米国における排日運動と1924年移民法制定過程

(Anti-Japanese movements in the United States and the legislative process of the 1924 Immigration act). *Tsuda juku daigaku kiyō* (1978), no. 10, pp. 1–41.

Iino Masako and Bamba Nobuya 馬場伸也. "Imin mondai o meguru Nichi-Bei-Ka kankei" 移民問題をめぐる日米加関係 (Japanese-U.S.-Canadian relations centering on the immigration question). In Hosoya, ed., *Taiheiyō-Ajia ken no kokusai keizai funsōshi, 1922–1945,* pp. 85–112.

Iino Masako and Takamura Hiroko 飯野正子, 高村宏子. "Vankūvā bōdō kara Rumyū kyōtei e" ヴァンクーヴァ暴動からルミュー協定へ (From the Vancouver riots to the Lemieux Agreement). *Tsuda juku daigaku kiyō,* (1982), no. 14, pp. 41–72.

Ikeda Kiyoshi 池田清 (ed., with commentaries). "Rondon kaigun jōyaku ni kansuru gunreibu gawa no shiryō 3-pen" ロンドン海軍条約に関する軍令部側の史料3編 (The London Naval Treaty and the Japanese navy: Materials relating to the Navy General Staff). *Hōgaku zasshi* (Osaka Ichiritsu Daigaku) (March 1969), 15(4):102–26. [1]

—— "Rondon kaigun jōyaku to tōsuiken mondai" ロンドン海軍条約と統帥権問題 (The London Naval Treaty and the right of the supreme command). *Hōgaku zasshi* (October 1968), 15(2):1–35. [2]

—— "Rondon kaigun jōyaku hiroku: Ko kaigun taishō Katō Kanji ikō, Shōwa 13-nen" 倫敦海軍条約秘録(故海軍大将加藤寛治遺稿) (Katō Kanji's "secret memoirs" about the London Naval Treaty). *Hōgaku zasshi* (August 1969), 16(1):123–42. [3]

Ikei Masaru 池井優. "Daiichiji Hōchoku sensō to Nihon" 第一次奉直戦争と日本 (The first Mukden-Chihli war and Japan). In Hanabusa Nagamichi Hakase Kanreki Kinen Ronbunshū Hensan Iinkai 英修道博士還暦記念論文集編集委員会, ed., *Hanabusa Nagamichi hakase kanreki kinen ronbunshū: Gaikōshi oyobi kokusai seiji no shomondai* 英修道博士還暦記念論集—外交史および国際政治の諸問題 (Festschrift for Professor Hanabusa Nagamichi: Studies in diplomatic history and international politics), pp. 351–78. Keiō Tsūshin, 1962. [1]

—— "Dainiji Hōchoku sensō to Nihon" 第二次奉直戦争と日本 (Japan's policy toward the second Mukden-Chili war, 1924). *Hōgaku kenkyū* (Keiō Gijuku Daigaku) (March 1963), 37(3):48–77. [2]

—— "Japan's Response to the Chinese Revolution of 1911." *The Journal of Asian studies* (February 1966), 25(2):213–27. [3]

—— "Nihon no tai-En gaikō (Shingai kakumeiki)" 日本の対袁外交(辛亥革命期) (Japan's policy toward Yuan Shik-K'ai during the Revolution of 1911, 1, 2). *Hōgaku kenkyū* (April 1962), 35(4):64–93; (May 1962), 35(5):49–83. [4]

—— "Nihon no tai-So shōnin, 1917–1925: Tai-So kōshō katei no gaikō-

shiteki kenkyū" 日本の対ソ承認, 1917—1925— 対ソ交渉過程の外交史
的研究 (Japanese recognition of the USSR: A historical study of the negotiation process with the Soviet Union). *Hōgaku kenkyū* (November 1973),
46(11): 1–46. [5]
—— "Pari heiwa kaigi to jinshu sabetsu teppai mondai" パリ平和会議と
人種差別撤廃問題 (The Paris Peace Conference and the problem of abol-
ishing racial discrimination). *Kokusai seiji* (1963), no. 23: *Nihon gaikōshi
kenkyū—daiichiji sekai taisen,* pp. 44–58. [6]
—— "Santō mondai, Go-shi undō o meguru Nitchū kankei" 山東問題・五四
運動をめぐる日中関係 (Sino-Japanese relations concerning the Shantung
question and the May Fourth Movement). *Hōgaku kenkyū* (January 1970),
43(1): 215–34. [7]
Imai Seiichi 今井清一 "Shidehara gaikō ni okeru seisaku kettei" 幣原外交
における政策決定 (Decision making in "Shidehara diplomacy"). In Nihon
Seiji Gakkai 日本政治学会 (Japanese Political Science Association), ed.,
Nenpō seijigaku, 1959: Taigai seisaku no kettei katei 年報政治学, 1959：
対外政策の決定過程 (The annuals of the Japanese Political Science Association, 1959: Aspects of foreign policymaking), pp. 92–112. Iwanami
Shoten, 1959. [1]
—— "Taishōki ni okeru gunbu no seijiteki chii" 大正期における軍部の
政治的地位 (The political position of the military during the Taishō
period). *Shisō* (September 1957), no. 339, pp. 3–21 (part 1); (December
1957), no. 402, pp. 106–27 (part 2). [2]
Imai Shōji 今井庄次. "Daiichiji sekai taisen to tai-Ka seisaku no tenkai"
第一次世界大戦と対華政策の展開 (World War I and the development
of [Japanese] policy toward China). In Mori Katsumi and Numata Jirō
森克己, 沼田次郎, eds., *Taigai kankeishi* 対外関係史 (Studies in the history
of Japanese foreign relations), pp. 297–365. Yamakawa Shuppansha, 1978.
Inō Tentarō 稲生典太郎. "Meiji ikō ni okeru 'sensō miraiki' no ryūkō to
sono shōchō" 明治以降における「戦争未来記」の流行とその消長 (The
rise and fall of war scare literature since the Meiji period). *Kokugakuin
daigaku kiyō* (February 1969), no. 7, pp. 129–65. [1]
—— "'Tanaka Jōsōbun' o meguru nisan no mondai" 「田中上奏文」をめぐ
る二三の問題 (Several problems concerning the "Tanaka Memorial").
Kokusai seiji (1963), no. 26: *Nihon gaikō no shomondai, 1,* pp. 72–87. [2]
Inoue Kiyoshi 井上清. *Nihon no gunkokushugi* 日本の軍国主義 (Militarism in
Japan). 2 vols. Tokyo Daigaku Shuppankai, 1953 (reprinted in 4 vols.,
1975).
—— "Nihon teikokushugi hihanron" 日本帝国主義批判論 (Criticism of
Japanese imperialism). In Inoue and Watanabe, eds., *Taishōki no kyūshin-
teki jiyūshugi,* pp. 115–86.

Inoue Kiyoshi *Nihon teikokushugi no keisei* 日本帝国主義の形成 (The formation of Japanese imperialism). Iwanami Shoten, 1968.

—— and Watanabe Tōru 渡辺徹, eds. *Taishōki no kyūshinteki jiyūshugi: "Tōyō Keizai Shinpō" o chūshin to shite* 大正期の急進的自由主義―「東洋経済新報」を中心として (Radical liberalism of the Taishō period: Studies on the *Tōyō Keizai Shinpō*). Tōyō Keizai Shinpōsha, 1972.

Inouye Yūichi 井上勇一. "Anpo tetsudō o meguru Nisshin kōshō: Man-Kan ittaika seisaku to Nichi-Ei dōmei no henshitsu 安奉鉄道をめぐる日清交渉―満韓一体化政策と日英同盟の変質 (Sino-Japanese negotiations over the Antung-Mukden railway: The changing nature of the Anglo-Japanese Alliance and Japan's policy to unify Manchuria and Korea). *Hōgaku kenkyū* (Keiō Gijuku Daigaku) (March 1983), 56(3):309–336. [1]

—— "Kin-Ai tetsudō o meguru kokusai kankei" 錦愛鉄道をめぐる国際関係 (Japan and the great powers over the Chinchow-Aigun railway). *Hōgaku kenkyū* (January 1985), 58(1):62–91. [2]

Irie Keishirō 入江啓四郎. "Shingai kakumei to shinseifu no shōnin" 辛亥革命と新政府の承認 (On the 1911 revolution in China and the recognition of the new government). In Ueda Toshio, ed., *Kamikawa sensei kanreki kinen: Kindai Nihon gaikōshi no kenkyū*, pp. 231–94.

Iriye, Akira 入江昭. *Kyokutō shin chitsujo no mosaku* 極東新秩序の模索 (The search for a new order in the Far East). Hara Shobō, 1970. The author's slightly abridged version of *After Imperialism: The Search for a New Order in the Far East, 1921–1931* (Cambridge: Harvard University Press, 1965).

—— "Kyōsō aitekoku Nihon, 1895-nen kara 1917-nen" 競争相手国日本，1895年から1917年 (Japan as a competitor, 1895–1917). In Katō Hidetoshi and Kamei Shunsuke, eds., *Nihon to Amerika*, pp. 145–80. [1]

—— "Nichi-Bei tekitai ishiki no gensen" 日米敵対意識の源泉 (The roots of antagonism between Japan and the United States). *Kokusai seiji* (1967), no. 34: *Nichi-bei kankei no imēji*, pp. 1–19. [2]

Iriye, Akira and Aruga Tadashi 有賀貞, eds., *Senkanki no Nihon gaikō* 戦間期の日本外交 (Japanese diplomacy in the interwar period). Tokyo Daigaku Shuppankai, 1984.

Ishida Hideo 石田栄雄. "Ōkuma rōkō to tai-Shi gaikō: Iwayuru Nijūikkajō yōkyū o megutte—Tokuni dai gokō kibōjōkō ni tsuite" 大隈老侯と対支外交―所謂二十一箇条要求を繞って―特に第五号希望条項について (Marquis Ōkuma and Japan's policy toward China: The problem of the Twenty-One Demands, in particular, group five). *Ōkuma kenkyū* (October 1954), no. 5, pp. 126–66; (May 1955), no. 6, pp. 86–142; (March 1956), no. 7, pp. 33–60.

Ishihara Naoki 石原直紀. "Taishō shoki no gaikō kikō: Nikyoku yonka sei no kakuritsu kara Rinji Gaikō Chōsakai setchi ni itaru keika" 大正初期の外交機構―二局四課制の確立から臨時外調査会設置にいたる経緯

(The foreign policy machinery in the early Taishō period: From the establishment of the two-bureau, four-section system to the instituting of the Advisory Council on Foreign Relations). *Shakai kagaku jānaru* (Kokusai Kirisutokyō Daigaku) (October 1981), 20(1): 113–32.

Itō Hirobumi 伊藤博文, ed. *Hisho ruisan: Chōsen kōshō shiryō* 秘書類纂—朝鮮交渉資料 (A collection of secret documents: Materials relating to the negotiations over Korea). 3 vols. Hisho Ruisan Kankōkai, 1933–36; reprinted by Hara Shobō, 1970.

Itō Shūichi 伊藤秀一. "Nikoraiefusuku jiken to Chūgoku hōkan" ニコライエフスク事件と中国砲艦 (The Nikolaevsk incident and the gunboats in China). *Roshiashi kenkyū* (February 1975), no. 23, pp. 18–36.

Itō Takashi 伊藤隆. *Shōwa shoki seijishi kenkyū: Rondon kaigun gunshuku mondai o meguru sho seiji shūdan no taikō to teikei* 昭和初期政治史研究—ロンドン海軍条約をめぐる諸政治集団の対抗と提携 (A Study of the political history of the early Shōwa period: Conflicts and alignments of political groups over the issue of the London naval limitation. Tokyo Daigaku Shuppankai, 1969.

—— *Taishōki "kakushinha" no kenkyū* 大正期「革新派」の研究 (A study of the "renovation faction" during the Taishō period). Hanawa Shobō, 1978.

Itō Takeo 伊藤武雄, Ogiwara Kiwamu 荻原極, Fujii Masuo 藤井満州雄 (ed., with an introduction). *Gendaishi shiryō*, vols. 31–33: *Mantetsu* 現代史資料 31—33, 満鉄 (Source materials on contemporary history, vols. 31–33: South Manchuria Railway Company). Misuzu Shobō, 1966–67.

Japan, Bōeichō 防衛庁 (Defense Agency), Bōei Kenshūjo Senshi Shitsu 防衛研修所戦史室 (The War History Office, National Defense College), ed. (Nomura Minoru, 野村実, author). *Senshi sōsho: Daihon'ei kaigunbu, Rengō kantai*, vol. 1: *Kaisen made* 戦史叢書：大本営海軍部連合艦隊(1)開戦まで (War history series: Imperial Headquarters, navy: A history of the Combined Fleet, vol. 1: Up to the opening of hostilities). Asagumo Shinbunsha, 1975.

—— (Shimanuki Takeji 島貫武治, author). *Senshi sōsho Daihon'ei rikugunbu*, vol. 1: *Shōwa 15-nen gogatsu made* 戦史叢書：大本営陸軍部(1)昭和15年5月まで (War history series: Imperial Headquarters, army, vol. 1: Up to May 1940). Asagumo Shinbunsha, 1967.

—— (Suekuni Masao 末国正雄, author). *Senshi sōsho: Kaigun gunsenbi*, vol. 1: *Shōwa 16-nen jūichigatsu made* 戦史叢書：海軍々戦備(1)昭和16年11月まで (War history series: Naval armaments and preparations for war, vol. 1: Up to November 1914). Asagumo Shinbunsha, 1969.

Japan, Chōsen Sōtokufu 朝鮮総督府 (Office of the Korean Governor General), ed., *Chōsen no hogo oyobi heigō* 朝鮮の保護及び併合 (The protection and annexation of Korea). Reprinted by Chūō Nikkan Kyōkai, Yūhō Kyōkai, 1956.

Japan, Gaimushō 外務省 (Foreign Ministry), *Nihon gaikō bunsho: Pari kōwa kaigi keika gaiyō* 日本外交文書—巴里講和会議経過概要 (Documents on Japanese foreign policy: A summary of the development at the Paris Peace Conference). 1971.

—— *Nihon gaikō bunsho: Tai-Bei imin mondai keika gaiyō* 日本外交文書—対米移民問題経過概要 (Documents on Japanese foreign policy: A summary of the development of the Japanese immigration question in the United States). 1972.

—— *Nihon gaikō bunsho: Tai-Bei imin mondai keika gaiyō fuzokusho* 日本外交文書—対米移民問題経過概要付属書 (Documents accompanying a summary of the development of the Japanese immigration question in the United States). 1973.

—— *Nihon gaikō bunsho: Washinton kaigi* 日本外交文書—ワシントン会議 (Documents on Japanese foreign policy: The Washington Conference), 2 vols., 1977–78.

—— *Nihon gaikō bunsho: Washinton kaigi, Gunbi seigen mondai* 日本外交文書—ワシントン会議：軍備制限問題 (Documents on Japanese foreign policy: The Washington Conference—The problem of naval limitation). 1974.

—— *Nihon gaikō bunsho: Washinton kaigi, Kyokutō mondai* 日本外交文書—ワシントン会議：極東問題 (Documents on Japanese foreign policy: The Washington Conference—The Far Eastern questions), 1976.

—— *Nihon gaikō bunsho: Junēvu kaigun gunbi seigen kaigi* 日本外交文書—ジュネーヴ海軍軍備制限会議 (Documents on Japanese foreign policy: The Geneva Conference for the limitation of naval armaments). 1982.

—— *Nihon gaikō bunsho: 1930-nen Rondon kaigun kaigi* 日本外交文書—1930年ロンドン海軍会議 (The London Naval Conference of 1930), 2 vols., 1983–84.

—— *Nihon gaikō bunsho: Rondon kaigun kaigi keika gaiyō* 日本外交文書—ロンドン海軍会議経過概要 (A summary of the developments at the London Naval Conference), 1979.

—— *Nihon gaikō bunshō: Rondon kaigun kaigi, yobi kōshō, jōyaku setsumeisho* 日本外交文書—ロンドン海軍会議予備交渉, 条約説明書 (Preliminary negotiations for the London Naval Conference, written explanations of the [London] treaty), 1982.

—— *Nihon gaikō bunsho: Kaigun gunbi seigen jōyaku Sūmitsuin shinsa kiroku* 海軍軍備制限条約枢密院審査記録 (Record of the Privy Council's examination of the London Naval Treaty), 1984.

Japan, Gaimushō, Ō-A-Kyoku 欧亜局 (Europe-Asia Bureau, Foreign Ministry). *Nichi-Ro kōshōshi* 日露交渉史 (A history of Russo-Japanese relations). 2 vols. 1944; reprinted by Hara Shobō, 1969.

Japan, Sanbō Honbu 参謀本部 (Army General Staff). *Shōwa 3-nen Shina jihen shuppeishi* 昭和三年支那事変出兵史 (A history of the military expedition during the 1928 incident in China). Sanbō Honbu, 1930.

—— *Taishō 7-nen naishi 11-nen Shiberia shuppeishi* 大正 7 年乃至11年西伯利出兵史 (History of the Siberian Expedition, 1918–22). 3 vols. Shin Jidaisha, 1972.

Kachi Teruko 佳知晃子. "Nichi-Bei tsūshō kōkai jōyaku to Kariforunia tochihō" 日米通商航海条約とカリフォルニア州土地法 (The Treaty of 1911 and California land law). *Kokusai seiji* (1961), no. 17: *Nichi-Bei kankei no tenkai,* pp. 21–45.

—— *The Treaty of 1911 and the Immigration and Alien Land Law Issue Betweeen the United States and Japan, 1911–1913.* Arno Press, 1979.

Kaizuka Shigeki 貝塚茂樹. *Son Bun to Nihon* 孫文と日本 (Sun Yat-sen and Japan). Kōdansha, 1967.

Kajima Morinosuke 鹿島守之助. *Nichi-Ei gaikōshi* 日英外交史 (A history of Anglo-Japanese diplomatic relations). Kajima Kenkyūjo Shuppankai, 1957.

—— *Nihon gaikōshi,* vol. 8: *Dainikai Nichi-Ei dōmei to sono jidai* 日本外交史，8 — 第二回日英同盟とその時代 (A history of Japanese diplomacy, vol. 8: The second Anglo-Japanese alliance). Kajima Kenkyūjo Shuppankai, 1970.

—— *Nihon gaikōshi,* vol. 9: *Daisankai Nichi-Ei dōmei to sono jidai* 日本外交史，9 — 第三回日英同盟とその時代 (A history of Japanese diplomacy, vol. 9: The third Anglo-Japanese alliance). Kajima Kenkyūjo Shuppankai, 1970.

Kan Dok-san 姜徳相 (Kyo Toku-sō), ed., with an introduction. *Chōsen* 朝鮮 (Korea), vols. 1–4. Vols. 25–30 of *Gendaishi shiryo* 現代史資料 (Documents on contemporary history). Misuzu Shobō, 1966–67.

—— "Nihon no Chōsen shihai to San-ichi dokuritsu undō" 日本の朝鮮支配と三・一独立運動 (Japanese colonial rule of Korea and the March 1 independence movement). In *Iwanami kōza: Sekai rekishi,* vol. 25: *Gendai, 2* 岩波講座—世界歴史25, 現代 2 (Iwanami series on world history, vol. 25: The contemporary period, 2), pp. 310–45. Iwanami Shoten, 1970.

—— "Nihon teikokushugi no Chōsen shihai to Roshia kakumei" 日本帝国主義の朝鮮支配とロシア革命 (Japan's imperialistic rule over Korea, and the Russian Revolution). *Rekishigaku kenkyū* (October 1967), no. 329, pp. 37–47.

Kan Don-chin 姜東鎮 (Kyō Tō-chin). *Nihon no Chōsen shihai seisakushi kenkyū: 1920-nendai o chūshin to shite* 日本の朝鮮支配政策史研究—1920年代を中心として (A study on the history of Japanese policy of governing Korea: With particular reference to the 1920s). Tokyo Daigaku Shuppankai, 1979.

Kan Zaigen 姜在彦. *Chōsen kindaishi kenkyū* 朝鮮近代史研究 (A study of modern Korean history). Nihon Hyōronsha, 1970.

Kaneko Fumio 金子文夫. "Nichi-Ro sengo no 'Manshū keiei' to Yokohama Shōkin Ginkō" 日露戦後の「満州経営」と横浜正金銀行 (The "administration of Manchuria" after the Russo-Japanese War, and the Yokohama Specie Bank." *Tochi seido shigaku* (January 1977), 19(2):28–52. [1]

—— "1920-nendai ni okeru Nihon teikokushugi to 'Manshū': Tetsudō kin'yū mondai o chūshin ni" 1920年代における日本帝国主義と「満州」—鉄道金融問題を中心に (Japanese imperialism and "Manchuria" in the 1920s: With emphasis on the railway and monetary problems, 1, 2). *Shakai kagaku kenkyū* (Tokyo Daigaku) (February 1981), 32(4):148–224; (March 1981), 32(6):195–286. [2]

—— "1970-nendai ni okeru 'Manshū' kenkyū no jōkyō" 1970年代における「満州」研究の状況 (A survey of "Manchuria" studies in the 1970s, 1, 2). *Ajia keizai* (March 1979), 20(3):38–55; (November 1979), 20(11):24–43. [3]

—— "Sōgyōki no Minami Manshū Tetsudō, 1907–1916" 創業期の南満州鉄道, 1907—1916 (The South Manchuria Railway Company in its first years of operation). *Shakai kagaku kenkyū* (January 1980), 31(4):171–201. [4]

Katagiri Nobuo 片桐庸夫. "Taiheiyō Mondai Chōsakai (IPR) to Manshū mondai: Daisankai Kyoto kaigi o chūsin to shite" 太平洋問題調査会(IPR)と満州問題—第3回京都会議を中心に (The Institute of Pacific Relations and the Manchurian question: With particular reference to the third Kyoto conference). *Hōgaku kenkyū* (September 1979), 52(9):48–81.

Katō Hidetoshi and Kamei Shunsuke 加藤秀俊, 亀井俊介, eds. *Nihon to Amerika: Aitekoku no imēji kenkyū* 日本とアメリカ—相手国のイメージ研究 (Japan and the United States: Studies in mutual images). Nihon Gakujutsu Shinkōkai, 1977.

Kawabata Masahisa 川端正久. *Kominterun to Nihon* コミンテルンと日本 (Communist International and Japan). Kyoto: Hōritsu Bunkasha, 1982.

Kikuchi Masanori 菊地昌典. "Roshia kakumei to Nihon" ロシア革命と日本人 (The Russian Revolution and Japan). In Miwa, ed., *Sōgo kōza Nihon no shakai bunkashi*, vol. 7: *Sekai no naka no Nihon*, pp. 267–305.

—— *Roshia kakumei to Nihonjin* ロシア革命と日本人 (The Russian Revolution and the Japanese). Chikuma Shobō, 1973.

Kikuchi Takaharu 菊地貴晴. *Chūgoku minzoku undō no kihon kōzō: Taigai boikotto no kenkyū* 中国民族運動の基本構造—対外ボイコットの研究 (The basic structure of Chinese nationalist movements: A study in antiforeign boycotts). Daian, 1966.

Kim Chong-myong 金正明 (Kin Sei-mei), ed. *Nikkan gaikō shiryō shūsei* 日韓外交資料集成 (A collection of diplomatic documents on Japanese-Korean relations). 8 vols. Gannandō Shoten, 1966–68.

Kimijima Kazuhiko 君島和彦. "Tōyō Takushoku Kabushiki Kaisha no set-suritsu katei" 東洋拓殖株式会社の設立過程 (The establishment of the Oriental Development Company). *Rekishi hyōron* (November 1973), no. 282, pp. 28–44; (January 1974), no. 285, pp. 47–57.

Kimura Tokio 木村時夫. "Tai-Ka nijūikkajō yōkyū to Ōkuma Shigenobu" 対華21ヶ条要求と大隈重信 (The Twenty-One Demands and Ōkuma Shigenobu). *Waseda jinbun shizen kagaku kenkyū* (March 1983), no. 23, pp. 1–24.

Kindai Nihon Kenkyūkai 近代日本研究会, ed. *Nenpō kindai Nihon kenkyū* 年報近代日本研究 (Journal of modern Japanese studies). (1979), no. 1: *Shōwaki no gunbu* 昭和の軍部 (The military in the Shōwa period); (1980), no. 2: *Kindai Nihon to Higashi Ajia* 近代日本と東アジア (Modern Japan and East Asia); (1982), no. 4: *Taiheiyō sensō* 太平洋戦争 (The Pacific War); (1985) no. 7: *Nihon gaikō no kiki ninshiki* 日本外交の危機認識 (Crises in Japan's diplomacy: Perceptions and Responses). Yamakawa Shuppansha.

Kisaka Jun'ichirō 木坂順一郎. "Taishōki minponshugisha no kokusai ninshiki" 大正期民本主義者の国際認識 (The understanding of international politics held by the Taishō democrats). *Kokusai seiji* (1974), no. 51: *Nihon gaikō no kokusai ninshiki—sono shiteki tenkai*, pp. 59–86.

Kitamura Hironao 北村敬直. "Kōtsū ginkō shakkan no seiritsu jijō" 交通銀行借款の成立事情 (Circumstances leading to the supply of credit to the Communication Bank). *Shakai keizai shigaku* (December 1961), 27(3):39–58.

Kitaoka Shin'ichi 北岡伸一. "Gaikō shidōsha to shite no Gotō Shimpei" 外交指導者としての後藤新平 (Gotō Shinpei as a foreign policy leader). *Kindai Nihon kenkyū* (1980), no. 2: *Kindai Nihon to Higashi Ajia*, pp. 55–95. [1]

—— *Nihon rikugun to tairiku seisaku, 1916–1918* 日本陸軍と大陸政策, 1906—1918 (The Japanese army and continental policy, 1906–1918). Tokyo Daigaku Shuppankai, 1978.

—— "Nijūikkajō saikō: Nichi-Bei gaikō no sōgo sayō" 21カ条再考—日米外交の相互作用 (A reconsideration of the Twenty-One Demands: The mutual interaction of Japanese and American foreign policies). *Kindai Nihon kenkyū, no. 7: Nihon gaikō no kiki ninshiki*, 1985, pp. 119–50. [2]

Kobayashi Tatsuo 小林龍夫. "Kaigun gunshuku jōyaku, 1921–1936" 海軍軍縮条約, 1921—1936 (Treaties of naval limitation, 1921–1936). In Nihon Kokusai Seiji Gakkai, ed., *Taiheiyō sensō e no michi*, 1:3–160. [1]

—— "Pari heiwa kaigi to Hihon no gaikō" パリ平和会議と日本の外交 (The Paris Peace Conference and Japanese diplomacy). In Ueda Toshio, ed., *Kamikawa sensei kanreki kinen: Kindai Nihon gaikōshi no kenkyū*, pp. 365–422. [2]

—— "Rinji Gaikō Chōsa Iinkai no setchi" 臨時外交調査委員会の設置 (Circumstances leading to the establishment of the Advisory Council on Foreign Relations). *Kokusai seiji* (1965), no. 28: *Nihon gaikōshi no shomondai, 2,* pp. 53–71. [3]

Kobayashi Tatsuo, ed. *Suiusō nikki: Rinji Gaikō Chōsa Iinkai kaigi hikki nado* 翠雨荘日記—臨時外交調査委員会会議筆記等 (Suiusō diary: Notes from meetings of the Advisory Council on Foreign Relations and other matters). Hara Shobō, 1965.

Kobayasi Yukio 小林幸男. "Nihon no tai-So shōnin to keizai mondai" 日本の対ソ承認と経済問題 (Japanese recognition of the Soviet Union and economic issues). *Kokusai seiji,* (1966), no. 31: *Nichi-Ro, Nisso kankei no tenkai,* pp. 86–98. [1]

—— "Nihon tai-So gaikō seisaku kettei kateiron josetsu: Yoshizawa-Karahan kaidan kaimaku no keika" 日本対ソ外交政策決定過程論序説一芳沢・カラハン会談開幕の経過 (An essay on the decision-making process in the Japanese policy toward the Soviet Union: Circumstances surrounding the start of the Yoshizawa-Karakhan parley). *Hōgaku* (Kinki Daigaku) (March 1960), 8(3–4):1–30. [2]

—— "Nisso kokkō chōsei no ichi danmen: Gotō-Yoffe kōshō kaishi no keika" 日ソ国交調整の一断面—後藤・ヨッフェ会談開始の経過 (A phase of adjustment of Soviet-Japanese diplomatic relations: The beginning of the Gotō-Joffe negotiations). *Kokusai seiji* (1958), no. 6: *Nihon gaikōshi kenkyū—Taishō jidai,* pp. 130–41. [3]

—— *Nisso seiji gaikōshi: Roshia kakumei to chian iji hō* 日ソ政治外交史—ロシア革命と治安維持法 (A history of Japan-USSR political and diplomatic relations: The Russian Revolution and the Peace Preservation Law of 1925). Yūhikaku, 1985.

—— "Ōshū taisen to Nihon no tai-Ro seisaku" 欧州大戦と日本の対露政策 (Japanese policy toward Russia during World War I). *Kokusai seiji* (1963), no. 23: *Nihon gaikōshi kenkyū—Daiichiji sekai taisen,* pp. 28–43. [4]

—— "Shiberia kanshō to Nikoraefusuku jiken" シベリア干渉とニコラエフスク事件 (The Siberian intervention and the Nikolaevsk incident.) *Kinki daigaku hōgaku* (January 1957), 5(3):181–223; (April 1957), 5(4):91–133; (July 1957), 6(1):93–134; (December 1957), 6(2–3):121–66; (April 1958), 6(4):105–34; (July 1958), 7(1):79–111. [5]

—— "Tai-So seisaku no suii to Manmō mondai, 1917–1927" 対ソ政策の推移と満蒙問題, 1917—1927 (Shifting policies toward the Soviet Union, and the Manchurian-Mongolian question). In Nihon Kokusai Seiji Gakkai, ed., *Taiheiyō sensō e no michi,* 1:163–284. [6]

Koh Se-kai 許世楷. *Nihon tōchika no Taiwan: Teikō to dan'atsu* 日本統治下

の台湾—抵抗と弾圧 (Taiwan under Japanese rule: Resistance and suppression). Tokyo Daigaku Shuppankai, 1972.

Kunimoto Iyo 国本伊代. "Magudarena-wan jiken: Monrō dokutorin to Nihon" マグダレナ湾事件—モンロー・ドクトリンと日本 (The Magdalena Bay episode, 1911–1912: The Monroe Doctrine and Japan). *Amerika kenkyū* (March 1977), no. 11, pp. 140–60. [1]

—— "Mekishiko kakumei to Nihon, 1913–1914" メキシコ革命と日本, 1913—1914 (The Mexican revolution and Japan, 1913–1914). *Rekishigaku kenkyū* (July 1976), no. 434, pp. 1–14. [2]

—— "Senzenki ni okeru Chūnan-Bei imin to hai-Nichi undō" 戦前期における中南米移民と排日運動 (The immigration and anti-Japanese questions in Central and South America in the pre-W. W. II period). In Kojima Reiitsu 小島麗逸, ed., *Nihon teikokushugi to higashi Ajia* 日本帝国主義と東アジア (Japanese imperialism and East Asia), pp. 331–81. Ajia Keizai Kenkyūjo, 1979. [3]

Kurihara Ken 栗原健. "Abe Gaimushō Seimukyokuchō ansatsu jiken to tai-Chūgoku (Manmō) mondai" 阿部外務省政務局長暗殺事件と対中国（満蒙）問題 (The assassination of Abe, director of the Political Affairs Bureau of the Foreign Ministry, and Japan's policy toward China, especially Manchuria and Mongolia). *Kokusaihō gaikō zasshi* (November 1956), 55(5):50–76. [1]

—— "Daiichiji, dainiji Manmō dokuritsu undō" 第一次, 第二次満蒙独立運動 (The first and second independence movements in Manchuria and Mongolia). *Kokusai seiji* (1958), no. 6: *Nihon gaikōshi kenkyū—Taishō jidai*, pp. 52–65. [2]

—— "Daiichiji dainiji Manmō dokuritsu undō to Koike seimukyokuchō no jishoku" 第一次, 第二次満蒙独立運動と小池政務局長の辞職 (The first and second independence movements in Manchuria and Mongolia and the resignation of Koike, director of the Political Affairs Bureau, Foreign Ministry). In Kurihara, ed., *Tai-Manmō seisakushi no ichimen*, pp. 139–61. [3]

—— "*Hara Kei nikki* saigo no memo" 『原敬日記』最後のメモ (The last memo in Hara Kei's diary). In Kurihara, ed., *Tai-Manmō seisakushi no ichimen*, pp. 225–35. [4]

—— "Kantō totokufu mondai teiyō" 関東都督府問題提要 (The problem of the governorship-general in Kwantung). In Kurihara, ed., *Tai-Manmō seisakushi no ichimen*, pp. 38–60. [5]

Kurihara Ken, ed. *Tai-Manmō seisakushi no ichimen: Nichi-Ro sengo yori Taishōki ni itaru* 対満蒙政策史の一面—日露戦後より大正期に至る (Aspects of [Japan's] Manchurian-Mongolian policy: From the end of the Russo-Japanese War through the Taishō period). Hara Shobō, 1966.

Kurobane Shigeru 黒羽茂. *Nichi-Ei dōmeishi no kenkyū* 日英同盟史の研究 (A study of the history of the Anglo-Japanese Alliance). Sendai: Kyōiku Tosho, 1968.

—— "Shiberia kanshō sensō to Nihon no tachiba" シベリア干渉戦争と日本の立場 (The war of intervention into Siberia, and Japan's position, 1, 2). *Nihon rekishi* (June 1963), no. 181, pp. 34–43; (July 1963), no. 182, 86–101.

—— *Taiheiyō o meguru Nichi-Bei kōsōshi* 太平洋をめぐる日米抗争史 (A history of Japanese-American rivalry in the Pacific). Nansōsha, 1968.

Kurosawa Fumitaka 黒沢文貴. "Tanaka gaikō to rikugun" 田中外交と陸軍 (Tanaka diplomacy and the army). *Gunji shigaku* (December 1985), 21(3): 17–34.

Kurose Ikuji 黒瀬郁二. "Nichi-Ro sensōgo no 'Chōsen keiei' to Tōyō Takushoku Kabushiki Kaisha" 日露戦後の「朝鮮経営」と東洋拓殖株式会社 (The "Korean administration" after the Russo-Japanese War, and the Oriental Development Company). *Chōsenshi kenkyūkai ronbunshū* (March 1975), no. 12, pp. 99–128.

Kyōto Daigaku Jinbun Kagaku Kenkyūjo 京都大学人文科学研究所 (Institute of Humanistic Studies, Kyoto University), ed. *Go-shi undō no kenkyū* 五・四運動の研究 (Studies on the May Fourth Movement). 3 parts. Kyoto: Dōhō Shuppansha, 1982.

Maeda Emiko 前田恵美子. "Dan Ki-zui seiken to Nihon no tai-Shi tōshi: Heikidai shakkan o chūshin ni" 段祺瑞政権と日本の対支投資—兵器代借款を中心に (The Tuan Chi-jui regime and Japanese investment in China: With particular reference to ammunition). *Kanazawa daigaku keizai ronshū* (March 1975), nos. 12–13, pp. 43–52.

Manshikai 満史会, ed. *Manshū kaihatsu shijūnenshi* 満州開発四十年史 (A forty-year history of the development of Manchuria). 2 vols. plus supplement. Manshū Kaihatsu Shijūnenshi Kankōkai, 1964.

Maruyama Matsuyuki 丸山松幸. *Go-shi undō: Sono shisōshi* 五・四運動—その思想史 (The May Fourth Movement: Its intellectual history). Kinokuniya Shoten, 1969.

Masuda Hiroshi 増田弘. "Ishibashi Tanzan no Manshū hōkiron: Shō-Nihonshugi ni kansuru ichi kōsatsu" 石橋湛山の満州放棄論—小日本主義に関する一考察 (Ishibashi Tanzan's proposal for relinquishing Manchuria: A note on "Little Japan"). *Kokusai seiji* (1982), no. 71: *Nihon gaikō no shisō* pp. 72–92.

Masuda Tomoko 増田知子. "Kaigun gunbi kakuchō o meguru seiji katei, 1906–1914" 海軍軍備拡張をめぐる政治過程, 1906—1914 (The political process of naval arms expansion, 1906–1914). *Kindai Nihon kenkyū* (1982), vol. 4: *Taiheiyō sensō*, pp. 411–33. Yanakawa Shuppansha, 1982.

Masuda Tsuyoshi 増田毅. "Hara Kei no Chūgokukan" 原敬の中国観 (Hara Kei's view of China). *Kobe hōgaku zasshi* (March 1969), 18(3–4), 413–60.

Masumi Junnosuke 升味準之輔. *Nihon seitōshi ron* 日本政党史論 (A history of Japanese political parties), vol. 3. Tokyo Daigaku Shuppankai, 1967.

Matsumoto Shigeharu 松本重治. *Shanhai jidai: Jānarisuto no kaisō* 上海時代—ジャーナリストの回想 (My days in Shanghai: Recollections of a journalist). Chūō Kōronsha, 1974, vol. 1.

Matsuo Takayoshi 松尾尊兊. "Yoshino Sakuzō to Chōsen: San-ichi undō o chūshin ni" 吉野作造と朝鮮—三・一運動を中心に (Yoshino Sakuzō and Korea: With particular reference to the March First Movement). *Jinbun gakuhō* (January 1968), no. 25, pp. 125–49.

Matsuzawa Tetsunari 松沢哲成. "Manshū jihen to 'Minzoku kyōwa undō'" 満州事変と「民族協和」運動 (The Manchurian Incident and the "interracial harmony" movement). *Kokusai seiji* (1970), no. 43: *Manshū jihen,* pp. 77–99.

Minami Manshū Tetsudō Kabushiki Kaisha 南満州鉄道株式会社, ed. *Minami Manshū Tetsudō Kabushiki Kaisha dainiji jūnenshi* 南満州鉄道株式会社第二次十年史 (A history of the second decade of the South Manchuria Railway Company). Dairen: Minami Manshū Tetsudō Kabushiki Kaisha, 1928; reprinted by Hara Shobō, 1974.

—— *Minami Manshū Tetsudō Kabushiki Kaisha daisanji jūnenshi* 南満州鉄道株式会社第三次十年史 (A history of the third decade of the South Manchuria Railway Company). 3 vols. Dairen: SMRC, 1938; reprinted by Ryūkeisha, 1976.

—— *Minami Manshū Tetsudō Kabushiki Kaisha jūnenshi* 南満州鉄道株式会社十年史 (A ten-year history of the South Manchuria Railway Company). Diaren: SMRC, 1919; reprinted by Hara Shobō, 1974.

Mitani Taichirō 三谷太一郎. "Nihon no Kokusai kin'yūka to kokusai seiji" 日本の国際金融家と国際政治 (Japan's international financiers and international politics). In Satō and Dingman, eds., *Kindai Nihon no taigai taido*, pp. 123–54. [1]

—— *Nihon seitō seiji no keisei: Hara Kei no seiji shidō no tenkai* 日本政党政治の形成—原敬の政治指導の展開 (The formation of party politics in Japan: The development of Hara Kei's political leadership). Tokyo Daigaku Shuppankai, 1967. [2]

—— "'Tenkanki' (1918–1921) no gaikō shidō: Hara Kei oyobi Tanaka Giichi o chūshin to shite" 「転換期」(1918—1921)の外交指導—原敬および田中義一を中心として (Foreign policy leadership at a turning point, 1918–1921; with particular reference to Hara Kei and Tanaka giichi). In Shinohara and Mitani, eds., *Kindai Nihon no seiji shidō*, pp. 293–374. [3]

—— "Wōru sutorīto to Manmō: Gaisai hakkō keikaku o meguru Nichi-

Bei kankei" ウォール・ストリートと満蒙—外債発行計画をめぐる日米関係 (Wall Street and the Manchurian-Mongolian question: Japanese-American relations over the flotation of American loans). In Hosoya and Saitō, eds., *Washinton taisei to Nichi-bei kankei,* pp. 321–50. [4]

Miwa Kimitada 三輪公忠. "1924-nen hai-Nichi iminhō no seiritsu to beika boikotto: Kōbe shi no baai o chūshin to shite" 1924年排日移民法の成立と米貨ボイコット—神戸市の場合を中心として (The passage of the 1924 anti-Japanese Exclusion Act and Japanese boycotts of American goods: The case of Kobe city). In Hosoya, ed., *Taiheiyō-Ajia ken no kokusai funsōshi, 1922–1945,* pp. 143–79.

Miwa Kimitada, ed., *Sōgō kōza Nihon no shakai bunkashi,* vol. 7: *Sekai no naka no Nihon* 総合講座日本の社会文化史，7 世界の中の日本 (Series on Japanese social and cultural history, vol. 7: Japan in the world). Kōdansha, 1974.

Miyaji Masando 宮地正人. *Nichi-Ro sensōgo seijishi no kenkyū* 日露戦争後政治史の研究 (A study in political history after the Russo-Japanese War). Tokyo Daigaku Shuppankai, 1973.

Miyake Masaki 三宅正樹. "Daiichiji sekai taisen ni okeru Doku-Ro tandoku kōwa to Nihon" 第一世界大戦における独露単独講和と日本 (Japan and the separate peace between Germany and Russia during World War I). *Rekishi kyōiku* (February 1967), 15(2):25–35. [1]

—— "Daiichiji taisen ni okeru Nichi-Doku kankei to Nichi-Ro kankei" 第一次大戦における日独関係と日露関係 (Japanese-German and Russo-Japanese relations during World War I). *Kokusai seiji* (1969), no. 38: *Heiwa to sensō no kenkyū, 2,* pp. 105–33. [2]

Miyasaka Hiroshi 宮坂宏. "'Mantetsu' sōritsu zengo: Tōsanshō o meguru Nitchū kankei" 「満鉄」創立前後—東三省をめぐる日中関係 (Sino-Japanese relations centering on the Three Eastern Provinces: At the time of the founding of the South Manchuria Railway Company). *Kokusai seiji* (1961), no. 15: *Nihon gaikōshi kenkyū—Nitchū kankei no tenkai,* pp. 29–42.

Momose Takashi 百瀬孝. "Shiberia teppei seisaku no keisei katei: Taishō kunen jūnigatsu—jūnen gogatsu" シベリア撤兵政策の形成過程—大正9 年12月—10年 5 月 (The policymaking process for the withdrawal of forces from Siberia). *Nihon rekishi* (January 1984), no. 428, pp. 86–101.

Moriyama Shigenori 森山茂徳. "Nikkan heigō no kokusai kankei: Chōsen mondai to Manshū mondai no renkan" 日韓併合の国際関係—朝鮮問題と満州問題の連関 (The Japanese annexation of Korea and international relations: Linkage between the Korean and Manchurian issues). *Kindai Nihon kenkyū,* no. 7: *Nihon gaikō no kiki ninshiki* pp. 69–94.

Mukōyama Hiroo 向山寛夫. "Nihon tōchi ka ni okeru Taiwan no hō to seiji: Minzoku hō no shiten ni tatte" 日本統治下における台湾の法と政治—

民族法の視点に立って (Law and politics in Taiwan under Japanese rule: From the standpoint of ethnic law). *Kokugakuin hōgaku* (September 1983), 21(2):61–106.

Murashima Shigeru 村島滋. "Daisanji Nichi-Ei dōmei no seikaku to igi" 第三次日英同盟の性格と意義 (The nature and significance of the third Anglo-Japanese Alliance). *Kokusai seiji* (1972), no. 45: *Sensō shūketsu no jōken*, pp. 75–92.

Nagai Matsuzō 永井松三, ed. *Nichi-Bei bunka kōshōshi*, vol. 5: *Iminhen* 日米文化交渉史 5 — 移民篇 (A history of Japanese-American cultural relations, vol. 5: Immigration). Yōyōsha, 1955; reprinted by Hara Shobō, 1979.

Nagaoka Shinjirō 長岡新次郎. "Ishii-Ranshingu kyōtei no seiritsu" 石井・ランシング協定の成立 (The conclusion of Lansing-Ishii Agreement). *Kokusai seiji* (1968), no. 37: *Nihon gaikōshi no shomondai, 3*, pp. 54–71. [1]

—— "Katō Takaakiron" 加藤高明論 (An essay on Katō Takaaki). *Kokusai seiji* (1967), no. 33: *Nihon gaikōshi kenkyū—Gaikō shidōsharon*, pp. 27–40. [2]

—— "Ōshū taisen sanka mondai" 欧州大戦参加問題 (The issue of the Japanese entry into World War I). *Kokusai seiji* (1958), no. 6: *Nihon gaikōshi kenkyū—Taishō jidai*, pp. 26–38. [3]

—— "Tai-Ka nijūikkajō yōkyū mondai no kettei to sono haikei" 対華二十一ケ条要求問題の決定とその背景 (The decision for the Twenty-One Demands to China and its background). *Nihon rekishi* (June 1960), no. 144, pp. 66–80. [4]

Nakagawa Kōichi and Wakamori Tamio 中川浩一, 和歌森民男, eds. *Musha jiken: Taiwan Takasagozoku no hōki* 霧社事件—台湾高砂族の峰起 (The Musha incident: The uprising of the Taiwanese aborigines against Japanese rulers). Sanseidō, 1980.

Nakamura Takafusa 中村隆英. "Go-sanjū jiken to zai-Kabō" 5・30事件と在華紡 (The May 30 incident and [Japanese] cotton industries in China). *Kindai Chūgoku kenkyū* (1964), no. 6, pp. 99–169. [1]

—— "Sekai keizai no nakano Nichi-Bei keizai kankei" 世界経済の中の日米経済関係 (Japanese-American economic relations in the context of the world economy). In Hosoya and Saitō, eds., *Washinton taisei to Nichi-Bei kankei*, pp. 467–87. [2]

Nakatsuka Akira 中塚明. *Kindai Nihon to Chōsen* 近代日本と朝鮮 (Modern Japan and Korea), rev. ed. Sanseidō, 1977.

Nakayama Jiichi 中山治一 *Nichi-Ro sensō igo: Higashi Ajia o meguru teikokushugi no kokusai kankei* 日露戦争以後—東アジアをめぐる帝国主義の国際関係 (After the Russo-Japanese War: International relations of imperialism in East Asia). Sōgensha, 1957.

Nihon Kokusai Seiji Gakkai 日本国際政治学会 (Japan Association of International Relations) ed. *Taiheiyō sensō e no michi* 太平洋戦争への道 (The road to the Pacific War). Vol. 1. Asahi Shimbunsha, 1963.

Nihon Seiji Gakkai 日本政治学会 (Japanese Political Science Association), ed. *Nenpō seijigaku, 1969: Kokusai kinchō kanwa no seiji katei* 年報政治学 1969—国際緊張緩和の政治過程 (The annuals of the Japanese Political Science Association, 1969: The political process of international tension reduction). Iwanami Shoten, 1970.

Nishihara Kamezō 西原亀三. *Yume no shichijū yonen: Nishihara Kamezō jiden* 夢の七十余年—西原亀三自伝 (A dream of over seventy years: The autobiography of Nishihara Kamezō). Ed. by Murashima Nagisa, Kyoto, 1949; reprinted by Heibonsha, 1965.

Nishikawa Jun 西川潤. "Nihon taigai bōchō shisō no seiritsu: Nishihara shakkan no keizai shisō" 日本対外膨張思想の成立—西原借款の経済思想 (The formation of Japanese thought on overseas expansion: The economic thought of the Nishihara loans). In Shōda Ken'ichirō 正田健一郎, ed., *Kindai Nihon no tōnan-Ajiakan* 近代日本の東南アジア観 (Modern Japanese views on Southeast Asia), pp. 29–67. Asia Keizai Kenkyūjo, 1978.

Nishio Yōtarō 西尾陽太郎. "Nikkan heigō to Uchida Ryōhei" 日韓併合と内田良平 (Japanese annexation of Korea and Uchida Ryōhei). *Shien* (March 1968), no. 100, pp. 105–17.

Nohara Shirō 野原四郎. "Go-shi undō to chishikijin" 五・四運動と知識人 (The May Fourth Movement and [Japanese] intellectuals). In *Sekaishikōza* 世界史講座 (Series on world history), 6:7–322. Tōyō Keizai Shimpōsha, 1956.

Nomura Kōichi 野村浩一. "Manshū jihen chokuzen no Tōsanshō mondai" 満州事変直前の東三省問題 (The problem of the Three Eastern Provinces just before the Manchurian Incident). *Kokusai seiji* (1961), no. 15: *Nihon gaikōshi kenkyū—Nitchū kankei no tenkai,* pp. 71–86. [1]

—— "Tairiku mondai no imēji to jittai" 大陸問題のイメージと実態 (The images and realities of the problem of the [China] continent). In Hashikawa Bunzō and Matsumoto Sannosuke 橋川文三, 松本三之介, eds., *Kindai Nihon seiji shisōshi* 近代日本政治思想史 (The history of political thought in modern Japan), 2:52–108. Yūhikaku, 1970. [2]

Nomura Minoru 野村実. *Rekishi no naka no Nihon kaigun* 歴史の中の日本海軍 (The Japanese navy in historical perspective). Hara Shobō, 1980.

Nomura Otojirō 野村乙二郎. "Ijūin Hikokichiron" 伊集院彦吉論 (A study of Ijūin Hikokichi). *Seiji keizai shigaku* (October 1974), no. 101, pp. 1–12. [1]

—— *Kindai Nihon seiji gaikōshi no kenkyū: Nichi-Ro sensō kara Daiichiji Tōhō kaigi made* 近代日本政治外交史の研究—日露戦争から第一次東方会議

まで (Studies in modern Japanese political and diplomatic history: From the Russo-Japanese War to the first Eastern Conference). Tōsui Shoin, 1982.

—— "Tai-Ka nijūikkajō mondai to Katō Takaaki: Tokuni dai gogō no rikai ni tsuite" 対華二十一ケ条問題と加藤高明—特に オ 5 号の理解について (The problem of the Twenty-One Demands and Katō Takkaaki: With particular reference to group five). *Seiji keizai shigaku* (April 1977), no. 131, pp. 1–10; (May 1977), no. 132, pp. 16–25; (July 1977), no. 134, pp. 8–19; (August 1977), no. 135, pp. 19–42. [2]

Ogata Sadako 緒方貞子. "Kokusaishugi dantai no yakuwari" 国際主義団体 の役割 (The role of liberal nongovernmental organizations in Japan.) In Hosoya et al., eds., *Nichi-Bei kankeishi: Kaisen ni itaru 10-nen*, 3: 307–53; also in Dorothy Borg, ed., *Pearl Harbor as History: Japanese-American Relations, 1931–1941*, Columbia University Press, pp. 459–86.

Ogata Yōichi 尾形洋一. "Dainiji 'Shidehara gaikō' to 'Manmō' tetsudō kōshō" 第二次「幣原外交」と「満蒙」鉄道交渉 (The second "Shidehara diplomacy" and negotiations over railways in South Manchuria and eastern Inner Mongolia). *Tōyō gakuhō* (March 1976), 57(3–4): 178–212. [1]

—— "Tōhoku Kōtsū Iinkai to iwayuru 'Mantetsu hōi tetsudōmō keikaku'" 東北交通委員会と所謂「満鉄包囲鉄道網計画」 (The Tung-pei transportation committee and the so-called "plan to form railway network to encircle the South Manchuria Railway"). *Shigaku zasshi* (August 1977), 86(8): 39–72. [2]

Ōhara Yūko 大原祐子. "Nichi-Ei dōmei haiki mondai ni hatashita Kanada no yakuwari to Nihon no hannō" 日英同盟廃棄問題に果したカナダの役 割と日本の反応 (The role of Canada in the abrogation of the Anglo-Japanese Alliance and Japan's response). *Kokugakuin daigaku kiyō* (March 1977), no. 15, pp. 197–220.

Ōhata Tokushirō 大畑篤四郎. "Chūgoku kokumin kakumei to Nihon no taiō: Fubyōdō jōyaku kaisei teigi o chūshin ni" 中国国民革命と日本の 対応—不平等条約改正提議を中心に (Chinese Nationalist Revolution and Japan's response: With particular reference to the Chinese proposal for abolition of the unequal treaties). In Iriye and Aruga, eds., *Senkanki no Nihon gaikō*, pp. 125–53. [1]

—— "Daisanji Nichi-Ei dōmei kōshin mondai: Washinton kaigi kaisai teigi ni kanren shite" 第三次日英同盟更新問題—ワシントン会議開催提議に 関連して (The problem of renewing the third Anglo-Japanese Alliance: In relation to the proposal for the Washington Conference). *Waseda hōgaku* (January–February 1959), 35(1–2): 275–302. [2]

—— *Nihon gaikō seisaku no shiteki tenkai: Nihon gaikōshi kenkyū* 日本外交

政策の史的展開―日本外交史研究 (The historical development of Japanese diplomacy: Studies in Japanese diplomatic history), vol. 1. Seibundō, 1983.

―― "Nihon no Washinton kaigi sanka" 日本のワシントン会議参加 (Japan's participation in the Washington Conference). *Waseda hōgakkaishi: Hōritsuhen* (July 1960), no. 10, pp. 21–48. [3]

―― "Nihon taigai keizai seisaku no tenkai: Teikokushugi kakuritsuki o chūshin to shite" 日本対外経済政策の展開―帝国主義確立期を中心として (The historical development of Japan's economic foreign policy: With focus on the period of establishment of Japanese imperialism). *Shakai kagaku tōkyū* (December 1973), 19(1):61–87. [4]

―― "Shingai kakumei to Nihon no taiō: Ken'eki yōgo o chūshin to shite" 辛亥革命と日本の対応―権益擁護を中心として (The Chinese Revolution of 1911 and Japan's response: With particular reference to protection of Japan's interests). *Nihon rekishi* (November 1982), no. 414, pp. 57–75. [5]

―― "Washinton kaigi kaisai to Nichi-bei kankei" ワシントン会議開催と日米関係 (The calling of the Washington Conference, and Japanese-American relations). *Kokusai seiji* (1961), no. 17: *Nichi-Bei kankei no tenkai*, pp. 91–106. [6]

―― "Washinton kaigi Nihon seifu kunrei ni tsuite no kōsatsu" ワシントン会議日本政府訓令についての考察 (A study of the Japanese government's instructions regarding the Washington Conference). In Hanabusa Nagamichi Hakushi Kanreki Kinen Ronbunshū Henshū Iinkai 英修道博士還暦記念論文集編纂委員会, ed., *Hanabusa Nagamichi hakushi kanreki kinen ronbunshū: Gaikōshi oyobi kokusai seiji no shomondai* 英修道博士還暦記念論文集―外交史及び国際政治の諸問題 (A Festschrift for Dr. Hanabusa Nagamichi: Studies in diplomatic history and international politics), pp. 257–74. Keiō Tsūshin, 1962. [7]

Oka Toshitaka 岡俊孝. "Manshū tokushu ken'eki to Beikoku no tai-Nichi gaikō" 満州特殊権益と米国の対日外交 (Japan's special interests in Manchuria and U.S. policy toward Japan). *Hō to seiji* (May 1965), 16(2): 29–71. [1]

―― "Robāto Ranshingu no tai-Nichi seisaku: Ishii-Ranshingu kyōtei o chūshin to shite" ロバート・ランシングの対日政策―石井・ランシング協定を中心として (Robert Lansing's policy toward Japan: With particular reference to the Lansing-Ishii Agreement). *Hō to seiji* (July 1961), 12(2): 63–102. [2]

Oka Yoshitake 岡義武. "Pari heiwa kaigi ni okeru Amerika gaikō to waga kuni yoron" パリ平和会議におけるアメリカ外交とわが国世論 (American diplomacy at the Paris Peace Conference, and public opinion in Japan). In Saitō, ed., *Gendai Amerika no naisei to gaikō,* pp. 275–97.

Okada Sadanori 岡田貞寛, ed. *Okada Keisuke kaikoroku: fu Rondon gunshuku mondai nikki* 岡田啓介回顧録—付ロンドン軍縮問題日記 (The memoirs of Okada Keisuke, with his diary on the London naval limitation issue). Mainichi Shinbunsha, 1977.

Okamoto Shumpei 岡本俊平. "Meiji Nihon no tai-Chūgoku taido no ichi danmen: Komura Jutarō no baai" 明治日本の対中国態度の一断面—小村寿太郎の場合 (An aspect of Meiji Japan's attitude toward China: The case of Komura Jutarō). In Satō and Dingman, eds., *Kindai Nihon no taigai taido,* pp. 65–92.

Ōmori Tokuko 大森とく子. "Nishihara shakan ni tsuite: Tetsu to kin'en o chūshin ni" 西原借款について—鉄と金円を中心に (Gold and iron: Some aspects of the Nishihara loans to China in the Taishō period). *Rekishigaku kenkyū* (April 1975), no. 419, pp. 36–51.

Ōura Toshihiro 大浦敏弘. "Kyokutō Roshia ni taisuru Bei-Nichi kanshō to sono hatan ni tsuite no ichi kōsatsu: 1918–1922 ni okeru" 極東ロシアに対する米日干渉とその破綻についての一考察—1918-1922年における (A study of the American-Japanese intervention in Far Eastern Russia and its failure, 1918–1922). *Handai hōgaku* (November 1954), no. 12, pp. 1–12; (August 1955), no. 15, pp. 23–59.

Ōyama Azusa 大山梓. "Nankin jiken to Shidehara gaikō" 南京事件と幣原外交 (The Nanking incident [of 1927] and Shidehara diplomacy). *Seikei ronsō* (Meiji Daigaku) (December 1971), 40(3–4):1–10. [1]

—— "Shingapōru bōdō (1915-nen nigatsu) to ryōji hōkoku" シンガポール暴動(1915年2月)と領事報告 (The mutiny of Zudian troops at Singapore in 1915, and the Japanese consul's report). *Seikei ronsō* (March 1971), 39(1–2):73–88. [2]

Pak Kei-shik 朴慶植. *Nihon teikokushugi no Chōsen shihai* 日本帝国主義の朝鮮支配 (The rule of Korea under Japanese imperialism). 2 vols. Aoki Shoten, 1973.

Ryū Mei-shū 劉明修 (Liu Ming-shou). *Taiwan tōchi to ahen mondai* 台湾統治と阿片問題 (Japanese rule over Taiwan, and the opium question). Yamakawa Shuppansha, 1983.

Saitō Makoto 斎藤真, ed. *Takagi Yasaka sensei koki kinen: Gendai Amerika no naisei to gaikō* 高木八尺先生古稀記念—現代アメリカの内政と外交 (Domestic politics and foreign policy of contemporary America). Tokyo Daigaku Shuppankai, 1959.

—— "Sōseiki Amerika kenkyū no mokuteki ishiki: Nitobe Inazō to 'Beikoku kenkyū'" 草創期アメリカ研究の目的意識—新渡戸稲造と「米国

研究」(The aims of American studies in Japan in early stages: Nitobe Inazō and "American studies"). In Hosoya and Saitō, eds., *Washinton taisei to Nichi-Bei kankei*, pp. 577–602.

Saitō Seiji 斉藤聖二. "Daiichiji taisen to Terauchi naikaku no seiritsu: Sengo 'kiki' naikaku no setchi" 第一次大戦と寺内内閣の成立—戦後「危機」内閣の設置 (World War I and the Terauchi cabinet: The establishment of the postwar "crisis" cabinet). *Jōchi shigaku* (November 1983), no. 28, pp. 98–118. [1]

—— "Nishihara Kamezō no tai-Chūgoku kōsō: Terauchi naikakuki tai-Chūgoku seisaku no zentei" 西原亀三の対中国構想—寺内内閣期対中国政策の前提 (Nishihara Kamezō and Japan's aggression on the continent: The major premises of the Terauchi cabinet's policy toward China). *Kokusai seiji* (1982), no. 71: *Nihon gaikō no shisō* pp. 54–71. [2]

Saitō Takashi 斎藤孝. "Pari kōwa kaigi to Nihon" パリ講和会議と日本 (The Paris Peace Conference and Japan). *Kokusai seiji* (1958), no. 6: *Nihon gaikōshi kenkyū—Taishō jidai*, pp. 105–17.

Sakai Tetsuya 酒井哲哉. "Nihon gaikō ni okeru Sorenkan no hensen, 1923–37" 日本外交におけるソ連観の変遷, 1923—37 (The changing perceptions of the Soviet Union in Japanese diplomacy, 1923–37). *Kokka gakkai zasshi* (April 1984), 97(3–4):106–36.

Satō Kazuo 佐藤和夫. "Nichi-Bei bōeki to Nihon keizai no fukinkō seichō" 日米貿易と日本経済の不均衡成長 (The unbalanced growth of the Japanese economy and Japanese-American trade), in Hosoya and Saitō, eds., *Washinton taisei to Nichi-Bei kankei*, pp. 488–510.

Satō Motoei 佐藤元英. "Tōhō kaigi to shoki 'Tanaka gaikō'" 東方会議と初期「田中外交」(The Eastern Conference and early "Tanaka diplomacy"). *Kokusai seiji* (1980), no. 66: *Hendōki ni okeru higashi Ajia to Nihon—Sono shiteki kōsatsu*, pp. 72–90.

Satō Motoei, ed. "Tōhō kaigi (1927-nen) ni kansuru Gaimushō kiroku" 東方会議(1927年)に関する外務省記録. In Kindai Gaikōshi Kenkyūkai 近代外交史研究会, ed., *Hendōki no Nihon gaikō to gunji* 変動期の日本外交と軍事 (Japanese diplomacy and the military during a turbulent period). pp. 181–231. Hara Shobō, 1987.

Satō Saburō 佐藤三郎. "Chūka Minkoku daini kakumeiji ni okkota Enshū, Kankō, Nankin no Nitchū funsō san jiken ni tsuite" 中華民国第二革命時に起った兗州・漢口・南京の日中紛争三事件について (On the Yenchow, Hankou, and Nanking incidents between Japan and China during the second Chinese Nationalist Revolution). *Yamagata daigaku kiyō: Jinbun kagaku* (January 1968), 6(3):1–42.

Satō Seizaburō 佐藤誠三郎. "Kyōchō to jiritsu no aida: Nihon" 協調と自立

の間—日本 (Between cooperation and autonomy: The case of Japan). *Nenpō seijigaku, 1969: Kokusai kinchō kanwa no seiji katei*, pp. 99–144.

Satō Seizaburō and Roger Dingman, eds. *Kindai Nihon no taigai taido* 近代日本の対外態度 (Attitudes toward foreign affairs in moden Japan). Tokyo Daigaku Shuppankai, 1974.

Segawa Yoshinobu 瀬川善信. "Nichi-Bei imin mondai to Gaimushō" 日米移民問題と外務省 (The Japanese-American immigration question and the Foreign Ministry). *Saitama daigaku kiyō: Shakai kagaku* (March 1968), no. 15, pp. 1–17. [1]

—— "Nichi-Fu imin mondai" 日布移民問題 (Japanese-Hawaiian immigration question, 1, 2). *Kokusaihō gaikō zasshi* (June 1967), 66(1):67–96; (October 1967), 66(3):28–56. [2]

—— "Obata kōshi agureman mondai" 小幡公使アグレマン問題 (The problem of Minister Obata Yūkichi's agrément [from the Chinese government]). *Kokusaihō gaikō zasshi* (November 1968), 67(3):72–101. [3]

—— "1924-nen Beikoku iminhō to Nihon gaikō" 1924年米国移民法と日本外交 (The U.S. Immigration Act of 1924 and Japanese diplomacy). *Kokusai seiji* (1964), no. 26: *Nihon gaikōshi no shomondai, 1*, pp. 55–71. [4]

—— "Washinton gunshuku kaigi (1921–1922) to Nihon rikugun" ワシントン軍縮会議(1921—1922)と日本陸軍 (The Washington Conference of 1921–22 and the Japanese army, 1–3). *Bōei ronshū* (April 1965), 4(1): 45–67; (July 1965), 4(2):163–88; (October 1965), 4(3):53–67. [5]

Seki Hiroharu 関寛治. *Gendai higashi Ajia kokusai kankyō no tanjō* 現代東アジア国際環境の誕生 (The emergence of the contemporary international system in East Asia). Fukumura Shuppan, 1966.

—— "Manshū jihen zenshi (1927–1931)" 満州事変前史 (A history of the developments leading to the Manchurian Incident [1927–1931]). In Nihon Kokusai Seiji Gakkai, ed., *Taiheiyō sensō e no michi*, 1:287–440. [1]

—— "1918-nen Nitchū gunji kyōtei no teiketsu" 1918年日中軍事協定の締結 (The conclusion of the Sino-Japanese military agreement of 1918). Reprinted in Seki Hiroharu, *Gendai higashi Ajia kokusai kankyō no tanjō*, pp. 197–395. [2]

—— "1917-nen Harubin kakumei: Harubin sobietto juritsu o meguru kokusai seijigakuteki ichi kōsatsu" 1917年ハルビン革命—ハルビン・ソビエット樹立をめぐる国際政治学的一考察 (The revolution in Harbin in 1917: A study in international politics centerning on the establishment of the Harbin soviet). *Kokusaihō gaikō zasshi* (August 1958), 57(3):36–83. [3]

—— "Tairiku gaikō no kiki to sangatsu jiken" 大陸外交の危機と三月事件 (The March incident and the crisis in Japan's continental policy). In Shinohara and Mitani, eds., *Kindai Nihon no seiji shidō*, pp. 433–90. [4]

Seki Shizuo 関静雄. "Hara naikaku gaikō no kōsoku yōin ni tsuite" 原内閣
外交の拘束要因について (The factors constraining the diplomacy of the
Hara cabinet, 1, 2). *Hōgaku ronsō* (June 1977), 101(3):36–63; (July 1978),
103(4):55–70.

Shidehara Heiwa Zaidan 幣原平和財団, ed. *Shidehara Kijūrō* 幣原喜重郎.
Published by the editor, 1955.

Shimada Toshihiko 島田俊彦. *Kantōgun* 関東軍 (The Kwantung Army).
Chūō Kōronsha, 1965.

—— "Tō-Shi tetsudō o meguru Chū-So funsō: Ryūjōkō jiken chokuzen no
Manshū jōsei" 東支鉄道をめぐる中ソ紛争―柳条溝事件直前の満州
情勢 (Sino-Soviet conflict over the Chinese Eastern Railway: The Manchurian situation just before the Liu-Tiao-Kou Incident). *Kokusai seiji*
(1970), no. 43: *Manshū jihen*, pp. 25–50.

Shimanuki Takeji 島貫武治. "Daiichiji sekai taisen igo no kokubō hōshin,
shoyō heiryoku, yōhei kōryō no hensen" 第一次世界大戦以後の国防
方針,所要兵力,用兵綱領の変遷 (The development of the national de-
fense policy, the estimate of requisite armament, and the outline of strategy
since World War I). *Gunji shigaku* (June 1973), 9(1):65–74. [1]

—— "Nichi-Ro sensō igo ni okeru kokubō hōshin, shoyō heiryoku, yōhei
kōryō no hensen" 日露戦争以後における国防方針,所要兵力,用兵綱領
の変遷 (The development of the national defense policy, the estimate of
requisite armament, and the outline of strategy since the Russo-Japanese
War). *Gunji shigaku* (March 1973), 8(4):2–16. [2]

Shimizu Hideko 清水秀子. "Santō mondai" 山東問題 (The Shantung question). *Kokusai seiji* (1977), no. 56: *1930-nendai no Nihon gaikō–Yonin no
gaishō o chūshin to shite*, pp. 117–36.

Shimomura Fujio 下村冨士男. "Nichi-Ro sensō no seikaku" 日露戦争の
性格 (The nature of the Russo-Japanese War). *Kokusai seiji* (1957), no. 3:
Nihon gaikōshi kenkyū—Meiji jidai, pp. 137–52. [1]

—— "Nichi-Ro sensō to Manshū shijō" 日露戦争と満州市場 (The Russo-
Japanese War and the Manchurian market). *Nagoya daigaku bungakubu
kenkyū ronshū* (March 1956), no. 14, pp. 1–16. [2]

—— *Nihon zenshi: Kindai, 2* 日本全史―近代, 2 (A complete history of
Japan: The modern period, 2). Tokyo Daigaku Shuppankai, 1968. [3]

Shimura Toshiko 志村寿子. "Terauchi naikaku to Nishihara shakkan" 寺内
内閣と西原借款 (The Terauchi cabinet and the Nishihara loans). *Tokyo
toritsu daigaku hōgakkai zasshi* (October 1969), 10(1):57–142.

Shin Hee-suk 申熙錫. "Manmō ken'eki o meguru Nichi-Bei kankei no
sōkoku: Tai-Chūgoku nijūikkajō yōkyū no shimatsu" 満蒙権益をめぐる
日米関係の相克―対中国21ケ条要求の始末 (Japanese-American rival-
ries over the interests in Manchuria and Mongolia: With special reference

to the problem of the Twenty-One Demands). *Kokusai seiji* (1980), no. 66: *Hendōki ni okeru higashi Ajia to Nihon,* pp. 91–108.

Shinobu Seizaburō 信夫清三郎. *Taishō seijishi* 大正政治史 (A political history of Taishō Japan). 4 vols. Kawade Shobō, 1951–52.

Shinobu Seizaburō and Nakayama Jiichi 信夫清三郎, 中山治一, eds. *Nichi-Ro sensōshi no kenkyū* 日露戦争史の研究 (Studies on the history of the Russo-Japanese War). Kawade Shobō Shinsha, 1965.

Shinohara Hajime and Mitani Taichirō 篠原一, 三谷太一郎, eds. *Kindai Nihon no seiji shidō* 近代日本の政治指導 (Political leadership in modern Japan). Tokyo Daigaku Shuppankai, 1965.

Shōda Tatsuo 勝田龍夫. *Chūgoku shakkan to Shōda Kazue* 中国借款と勝田主計 ([The Nishihara] loans to China and Shōda Kazue). Daiyamondosha, 1972.

Somura Yasunobu 曽村保信. "En Sei Gai teisei mondai to Nihon no gaikō" 袁世凱帝政問題と日本の外交 (The problem of Yuan Shik-k'ai's imperial regime and Japanese diplomacy). *Kokusaihō gaikō zasshi* (May 1957), 56(2): 1–34. [1]

—— *Kindaishi kenkyū: Nihon to Chūgoku* 近代史研究—日本と中国 (A study of modern diplomatic history: Japan and China). Komine Shuppan, 1961; enlarged ed., 1962.

—— "Shingai kakumei to Nihon" 辛亥革命と日本 (The 1911 revolution and Japan). *Kokusai seiji* (1961), no. 15: *Nihon gaikōshi kenkyū—Nitchū kankei no tenkai,* pp. 43–55. [2]

—— "Shingai kakumei to Nihon no yoron" 辛亥革命と日本の世論 (The 1911 revolution and Japanese public opinion). *Hōgaku shinpō* (September 1956), 63(9):26–50. [3]

—— "Tairiku seisaku ni okeru imēji no tenkan: Fukuzawa Yukichi no kōkeisha to tairikuha no hitobito" 大陸政策におけるイメージの転換—福沢諭吉の後継者と大陸派の人々 (Shifting images in Japan's policy toward the Asia continent: The successors of Fukuzawa Yukichi and the continentalists). In Shinohara and Mitani, eds., *Kindai Nihon no seiji shidō,* pp. 253–92. [4]

Sugano Tadashi 菅野正. "Nijūikkajō yōkyū to kakyō no tai-Nichi boikotto" 21条要求と華僑の対日ボィコット (The Twenty-One Demands and anti-Japanese boycotts by Chinese overseas). *Tōkai daigaku kiyō (Bungakubu)* (July 1979), no. 31, pp. 1–14. [1]

—— "1905-nen, Chūgoku ni okeru tai-Nichi boikotto" 1905年, 中国における対日ボィコット (On the anti-Japanese boycotts in China, 1905). *Tōkai daigaku kiyō (Bungakubu)* (July 1975), no. 24, pp. 19–27; (July 1976), no. 25, pp. 41–50. [2]

Suzuki Takeo 鈴木武雄, editorial supervisor. *Nishihara shakkan shiryō ken-*

kyū 西原借款資料研究 (Documents on the Nishihara loans). 2 vols. Tokyo Daigaku Shuppankai, 1972.

Tago Keiichi 多胡圭一. "Nichi-Ro sensō zengo ni okeru shokuminchi keiei no ippan ni tsuite" 日露戦争前後における植民地経営の一斑について (A study of Japanese colonial rule after the Russo-Japanese War). *Handai hōgaku* (March 1981), nos. 116–17, pp. 1107–24. [1]

―― "Nihon ni yoru Chōsen shokuminchika katei ni tsuite no ichi kōsatsu: 1904–1910 ni okeru" 日本による朝鮮植民地化過程についての一考察―1904―1910における (The process of Japan's colonization of Korea, 1904–1910). *Handai hōgaku* (March 1974), no. 90, pp. 39–68 (part 1); (March 1975), no. 94, pp. 1–23 (part 2); (January 1977), no. 101, pp. 175–205 (part 3). [2]

―― "1905-nen Nisshin jōyaku teiketsu chokugo no Manshū keiei ippan ni tsuite" 1905年日清条約締結直後の満州経営一斑について (On the administration of Manchuria immediately after the conclusion of the Sino-Japanese treaty of 1905). *Handai hōgaku* (March 1977), no. 102, pp. 1–21. [3]

Tai Kok-fon 戴国輝. *Taiwan musha hōki jiken: Kenkyū to shiryō* 台湾霧社蜂起事件―研究と資料 (The Musha incident: Research and documents). Shakai Shisōsha, 1981.

Takahashi Makoto 高橋誠. "Nishihara shakkan no tenkai katei" 西原借款の展開過程 (The development of the Nishihara loans). *Keizai shirin* (March 1971), 39(1–2):214–47. [1]

―― "Nishihara shakkan no zaisei mondai" 西原借款の財政問題 (The financial problems of the Nishihara loans). *Keizai shirin* (June 1968), 36(2): 27–56. [2]

Takashima Masaaki 高嶋雅明. *Chōsen ni okeru shokuminchi kin'yūshi no kenkyū* 朝鮮における植民地金融史の研究 (A study of the financial history of Korea as a colony). Ōhara Shinseisha, 1978.

Tanaka Giichi Denki Kankōkai 田中義一伝記刊行会, ed., *Tanaka Giichi denki* 田中義一伝記 (Biography of Tanaka Giichi). 3 vols. Published by the editor, 1958–1960.

Tanaka Naokichi 田中直吉. "Nichi-Ro kyōshōron" 日露協商論 (An essay on Russo-Japanese agreement). In Ueda Toshio, ed., *Kamikawa sensei kanreki kinen: Kindai Nihon gaikōshi no kenkyū*, pp. 295–364.

Tanaka Shin'ichi 田中慎一. "Chōsen ni okeru tochi chōsa jigyō no sekaishiteki ichi" 朝鮮における土地調査事業の世界史的位置 (Comprehensive land survey in Korea by Imperial Japan in the perspective of modern world history). *Shakai kagaku kenkyū* (October 1977), 29(3):1–84 (part 1); (August 1978), 30(2):1–99 (part 2).

—— "Hogokoku mondai: Ariga Nagao, Tachi Sakutarō no hogokoku ronsō" 保護国問題—有賀長雄, 立作太郎の保護国論争 (A controversy over the question of the protectorate between Ariga Nagao and Tachi Sakutarō). *Shakai kagaku kenkyū* (October 1976), 28(2):126–62.

Terunuma Yasutaka 照沼康孝. "Ugaki rikushō to gunsei kaikakuan: Hamaguchi naikaku to rikugun" 宇垣陸相の軍制改革案—浜口内閣と陸軍 (Army Minister Ugaki and the proposal for army reforms: The Hamaguchi cabinet and the army). *Shigaku zasshi* (December 1980), 89(12):38–61.

Tominaga Yukio 富永幸生. "Nishihara shakkan to hokushin seisaku: Daiichiji sekai taisen ni okeru Nihon no sensō mokuteki seisaku" 西原借款と北進政策—第一次世界大戦における日本の戦争目的政策 (The Nishihara loans and [Japanese] policy toward north China: Japan's war aims during World War I). *Rekishigaku kenkyū* (December 1977), no. 451, pp. 33–43.

To Shōgen 涂照彦. *Nihon teikokushugika no Taiwan* 日本帝国主義下の台湾 (Taiwan under Japanese imperialism). Tōkyō Daigaku Shuppankai, 1975.

Tōyama Shigeki, Imai Seiichi, and Fujiwara Akira 遠山茂樹, 今井清一, 藤原彰. *Shōwashi* 昭和史 (A history of the Shōwa period). Iwanami: Shoten, 1955; revised ed., 1959.

Tsunoda Jun 角田順. *Manshū mondai to kokubō hōshin: Meiji kōki ni okeru kokubō kankyō no hendō* 満州問題と国防方針—明治後期における国防環境の変動 (The Manchurian question and Japan's defense policy: Changes in the defense setting [of Japan] after the late Meiji period). Hara Shobō, 1967.

Uchiyama Masakuma 内山正熊. "Kanada honpō imin seigenshi no ichi danmen" カナダ本邦移民制限史の一断面 (One aspect of the history of Canadian policy to restrict Japanese immigration). *Hōgaku kenkyū* (Keiō Gijuku Daigaku) (January 1970), 43(1):37–70. [1]

—— "Nichi-Doku sensō to Santō mondai" 日独戦争と山東問題 (The German-Japanese war and the Shantung question). *Hōgaku kenkyū* (February 1960), 33(2):243–91. [2]

Ueda Toshio 植田捷雄. "Daiichiji taisen to Nihon no sansen gaikō" 第一次大戦と日本の参戦外交 (The negotiations concerning Japan's entry into World War I). In Gakujutsu Kenkyū Kaigi Gendai Chūgoku Kenkyū Tokubetsu Iinkai, ed., *Kindai Chūgoku kenkyū* 近代中国研究 (Studies on modern China), pp. 327–61. Kōgakusha, 1948. [1]

—— "Shiberia shuppei to kita Karafuto mondai" シベリア出兵と北樺太問題 (The Siberian expedition and the problem of north Sakhalin). *Kokusaihō gaikō zasshi* (March 1962), 60(4–6):99–126. [2]

Ueda Toshio, ed. *Kamikawa sensei kanreki kinen: Kindai Nihon gaikōshi no kenkyū* 神川先生還暦記念—近代日本外交史の研究 *Festschrift for Professor Kamikawa: Studies in modern Japanese diplomatic history* (神川先生還暦記念—近代日本外交史の研究). Yūhikaku: 1956.

Unno Yoshirō 海野芳郎. *Kokusai renmei to Nihon* 国際連盟と日本 (Japan and the League of Nations). Hara Shobō, 1972.

—— "Kokusai renmei oyobi gunshuku kaigi to Satō Naotake" 国際連盟および軍縮会議と佐藤尚武 (Satō Naotake and the League of Nations and disarmament conferences). In Kurihara Ken 栗原健, ed., *Satō Naotake no menboku* 佐藤尚武の面目 (The diplomatic highlights of Satō Naokate), pp. 25–84. Hara Shobō, 1981. [1]

—— "Nihon Indoshina keizai kōshōshi no ichimen: 1920-nendai nakaba no Meruran, Yamagata ryōshisetsudan o chūshin to shite" 日本・インドシナ経済交渉史の一面—1920年代半ばのメルラン，山県両使節団を中心として (An aspect of the history of economic relations between Japan and Indochina: With particular reference to the missions of M. Merlin and Yamagata Isaburō in the mid-1920s). *Nanpō bunka* (December 1980), no. 7, pp. 47–64. [2]

—— "Nihon to Indoshina no bōeki masatsu" 日本とインドシナの貿易摩擦 (Trade frictions between Japan and French Indochina). In Hosoya, ed., *Taiheiyō-Ajia ken no kokusai keizai funsōshi*, pp. 41–64. [3]

—— "Rondon kaigun gunshuku kaigi: Nihon no tachiba to shuchō" ロンドン海軍軍縮会議—日本の立場と主張 (The London Naval Conference of 1930: Japan's position and demands). *Kokusai seiji* (1960), no. 11: *Nihon gaikōshi kenkyū—Shōwa jidai*, pp. 36–49. [4]

—— "Washinton kaigi to Gaimushō" ワシントン会議と外務省 (The Washington Conference and the [Japanese] Foreign Ministry). *Gaimushō chōsa geppō* (September 1967), 8(9):33–71. [5]

Unno Yoshirō (Horinouchi Kensuke 堀内謙介, editorial supervisor). *Nihon gaikōshi, Vol. 16: Kaigun gunshuku kōshō, fusen jōyaku* 日本外交史，16—海軍軍縮交渉，不戦条約 (Japanese diplomatic history, Vol. 16: Naval limitation conferences and the Kellogg-Briand Pact). Kajima Kenkyūjo Shuppankai, 1973.

Uno Shigeaki 宇野重昭. "Shidehara gaikō hossoku zengo no Nihon gaikō to Chūgoku: 1924-nen no Nitchū, Nisso kankei" 幣原外交発足前後の日本外交と中国—1924年の日中，日ソ関係 (Japanese diplomacy and China in the early "Shidehara diplomacy": Sino-Japanese and Japanese-Soviet relations in 1924). In Iriye and Aruga, eds., *Senkanki no Nihon gaikō*, pp. 97–123.

Usui Katsumi 臼井勝美. "Chō Saku-rin bakushi no shinsō" 張作霖爆死の真相 (The real facts about Chang Tso-lin's death by explosion). *Bessatsu Chisei* (December 1956), no. 5: *Himerareta Shōwashi*, pp. 26–38. [1]

Usui Katsumi. *Chūgoku o meguru kindai Nihon no gaikō* 中国をめぐる近代日本の外交 (Modern Japan's foreign policy toward China). Chikuma Shobō, (1983).

—— "Go-sanjū jiken to Nihon" 5・30事件と日本 (The May 30th incident and Japan). *Ajia kenkyū* (October 1957), 4(2):43–64. [2]

—— *Nihon to Chūgoku: Taishō jidai* 日本と中国—大正時代 (Japan and China in the Taishō period). Hara Shobō, 1972.

—— "Nihon to Shingai kakumei: Sono ichi sokumen" 日本と辛亥革命—その一側面 (Japan and the Chinese Revolution of 1911: One aspect of the relationship). *Rekishigaku kenkyū* (May 1957), no. 207, pp. 49–52. [3]

—— *Nitchū gaikōshi: Hokubatsu no jidai* 日中外交史—北伐の時代 (A history of Sino-Japanese diplomatic relations: The northern expedition period). Hanawa Shobō, 1971.

—— "Ōshū taisen to Nihon no tai-Man seisaku: Nanman-Tōmō jōyaku no seiritsu zengo" 欧州大戦と日本の対満政策—南満・東蒙条約の成立前後 (World War I and Japan's policy toward Manchuria: The conclusion of the southern Manchuria—eastern Mongolia treaty). *Kokusai seiji* (1963), no. 21: *Nihon gaikōshi kenkyū—Daiichiji sekai taisen,* pp. 15–27. [4]

—— "Shingai kakumei: Nihon no taiō" 辛亥革命—日本の対応 (The Chinese Revolution of 1911 and Japan's response). *Kokusai seiji* (1958), no. 13: *Nihon gaikōshi kenkyū—Taishō jidai,* pp. 13–25. [5]

—— "Shingai kakumei to Nichi-Ei kankei" 辛亥革命と日英関係 (The 1911 Revolution and Anglo-Japanese relations). *Kokusai seiji* (1977), no. 58: *Nichi-Ei kankei no shiteki tenkai,* pp. 32–44. [6]

—— "Taishō-Shōwa shoki no gaikō" 大正・昭和初期の外交 ([Japanese] diplomacy during the Taishō and early Shōwa periods). In Nihon Rekishi Gakkai 日本歴史学会, ed., *Nihonshi no mondaiten* 日本史の問題点 (Issues in the study of Japanese history), pp. 367–74. Yoshikawa Kōbunkan, 1965. [7]

—— "Tanaka gaikō ni tsuite no oboegaki" 田中外交についての覚書 (A note on Tanaka diplomacy). *Kokusai seiji* (1960), no. 11: *Nihon gaikōshi kenkyū—Shōwa jidai,* pp. 26–35. [8]

—— "Verusaiyu-Washinton taisei to Nihon no shihaisō" ヴェルサイユ・ワシントン体制と日本の支配層 (The Versailles-Washington system and Japan's ruling class). In Hashikawa Bunzō and Matsumoto Sannosuke 橋川文三, 松本三之介, eds., *Kindai Nihon seiji shisōshi* 近代日本政治思想史 (Essays on the history of modern Japanese political thought), 2: 109–31. Yūhikaku, 1970. [9]

—— "Washinton kaigi kaisai no zentei ni tsuite no oboegaki" ワシントン会議開催の前提についての覚書 (A note on the precondition for holding the Washington Conference). *Shien* (March 1970), no. 102, pp. 77–97. [10]

Wakabayashi Masahiro 若林正丈. *Taiwan kō-Nichi undōshi kenkyū* 台湾抗日運動史研究 (Study on the history of the Taiwanese resistance movement against Japanese rule). Kenbun Shuppansha, 1983.

Wakatsuki Reijirō 若槻礼次郎. *Kofūan kaiko roku* 古風庵回顧録 (Memoirs), rev. ed. Yomiuri Shinbunsha, 1975.

Wakatsuki Yasuo 若槻泰雄. *Hai-Nichi no rekishi: Amerika ni okeru Nihonjin imin* 排日の歴史―アメリカにおける日本人移民 (A history of anti-Japanese movements: Japanese immigrants in the United States). Chūō Kōronsha, 1972.

──── "Japanese Emigration to the United States, 1866–1924: A monograph". *Perspectives on American History*, no. 12. Charles Warren Center for Studies in American History, Harvard University, 1979, pp. 387–516.

Yamabe Kentarō 山辺健太郎, ed., with an introduction. *Taiwan* 台湾, vols. 1–2. Vols. 21–22 of *Gendaishi shiryō*. Misuzu Shobō, 1971.

──── *Nihon no Kankoku heigō* 日本の韓国併合 (The Japanese annexation of Korea). Taihei Shuppansha, 1966.

──── *Nikkan heigō shōshi* 日韓併合小史 (A short history of the annexation of Korea). Iwanami Shoten, 1963.

──── "San-ichi jiken ni tsuite" 三・一事件について (On the March 1 movement). *Rekishigaku kenkyū* (June 1955), no. 184, pp. 1–12; (July 1955), no. 185, pp. 13–28.

Yamaguchi Toshiaki 山口利昭. "Hamaomote Matasuke bunsho: Chūgoku daisan kakumei to sanbō honbu" 浜面又助文書―中国第三革命と参謀本部 (The papers of Hamaomote Matasuke: The third Chinese revolution and Japan's Army General Staff). *Kindai Nihonshi kenkyū*, no. 2: *Kindai Nihon to higashi Ajia*, 1980, pp. 205–70.

Yamamoto Shirō 山本四郎. "Chūgoku mondairon" 中国問題論 (Treatment of the Chinese question [by the *Tōyō Keizai Shinpō*]). In Inoue Kiyoshi and Watanabe Tōru, eds., *Taishōki no kyūshinteki jiyūshugi*, pp. 85–113. [1]

──── "Daiichiji sekai taisen ni okeru Amerika no sansen to Nihon: Terauchi naikaku no keizai to seiji" 第一次世界大戦におけるアメリカの参戦と日本―寺内内閣の経済と政治 (The U.S. entry into World War I and Japan: The political and economic policies of the Terauchi cabinet). *Hisutoria* (March 1966), no. 43, pp. 24–41. [2]

──── "Sansen, Nijūikkajō yōkyū to rikugun" 参戦・二一ケ条要求と陸軍 (Japan's entry into war, the Twenty-One Demands, and the Japanese army). *Shirin* (May 1974), 57(3):1–33. [3]

──── "Terauchi naikaku jidai no Nitchū kankei no ichi men: Nishihara Kamezō to Banzai Rihachirō" 寺内内閣時代の日中関係の一面―西原亀三と坂西利八郎 (An aspect of Sino-Japanese relations during the Terauchi cabinet: Nishihara Kamezō and Banzai Rihachirō). *Shirin* (January 1981), 64(1):1–36. [4]

—— "Terauchi naikaku shoki no tai-Ka seisaku" 寺内内閣初期の対華政策 (China policy during the early years of the Terauchi cabinet). *Shisō* (Kyōto Joshi Daigaku) (March 1980), no. 37, pp. 51–114. [5]

Yamamoto Shirō, ed. *Nishihara Kamezō nikki* 西原亀三日記 (The diary of Nishihara Kamezō). Kyoto: Kyoto Joshi Daigaku, 1983.

—— ed. *Terauchi Masataka nikki 1900–1918* 寺内正毅日記, 1900—1918 (The diary of Terauchi Masataka). Kyoto: Kyoto Joshi Daigaku, 1980.

Yanagisawa Asobu 柳沢遊. "'Manshū jihen' o meguru shakai keizaishi kenkyū no shodōkō" 「満州事変」をめぐる社会経済史研究の諸動向 (Various trends in the socioeconomic study of the "Manchurian Incident"). *Rekishi hyōron* (September 1981), no. 377, pp. 50–59.

Yoda Yoshiie 依田憙家. "Musha hōki kenkyū no kon'nichiteki imi" 霧社蜂起研究の今日的意味 (The contemporary significance of studying the Musha uprising). *Shisō* (February 1973), no. 584, pp. 120–39.

Yoshida Yutaka 吉田裕. "Daiichiji sekai taisen to gunbu: Sōryokusen dankai e no gunbu no taiō" 第一次世界大戦と軍部—総力戦段階への軍部の対応 (World War I and the Japanese army: The military response in the age of total war). *Rekishigaku kenkyū* (September 1978), no. 460. pp. 36–41.

Yoshii Hiroshi 義井博. "Dai ichiji taisenchū no Santō oyobi Nan'yo guntō ni kansuru Nihon no himitsu kyōtei ni tsuite no ichi kōsatsu" 第一次大戦中の山東および南洋群島に関する日本の秘密協定についての一考察 (Japanese secret agreements of 1917 concerning Shantung and the South Seas islands during World War I). *Gunji Shigaku* (August 1966), no. 6, pp. 36–55. [1]

Yoshii Hiroshi et al. "Japanese Historiography on the First World War." In Jurgen Rohwer, ed., *Neue Forschungen zum Erstern Weltkrieg: Literaturberichite und Bibliographien* (Schriften der Bibliothek fur Zeitgeschichte), pp. 195–203. Bernard und Graefe Velag Koblenz, 1985. [2]

Yoshimura Michio 吉村道男. "Kantō daishinsai to Rēningō jiken" 関東大震災と「レーニン号」事件 (The great Tokyo earthquake and the S.S. *Lenin* incident). *Nihon rekishi* (November 1978), no. 366, pp. 68–86 [1]

—— "Nichi-Ro dōmei no ichi kōsatsu" 日露同盟の一考察 (A study on the Russo-Japanese treaty). *Kokusai seiji* (1963), no. 26: *Nihon gaikōshi no shomondai, 1*, pp. 36–54. [2]

—— "Nihongun no kita Karafuto senryō to Nisso kokkō mondai: Sekiyu riken o meguru shomondai" 日本軍の北樺太占領と日ソ国交問題—石油利権をめぐる諸問題 (Japan's military occupation of north Sakhalin and the problem of establishing diplomatic relations with the Soviet Union). *Seiji keizai shigaku* (May 1977), no. 132, pp. 1–15. [3]

—— *Nihon to Roshia: Nichi-Ro sengo kara Roshia kakumei made* 日本とロシア—日露戦後からロシア革命まて (Japan and Russia: From the end of the Russo-Japanese War to the Russian Revolution). Hara Shobō, 1969.

—— "1920-nendai kōhan ni okeru Nisso kyōchō no mosaku" 1920年代後半における日ソ協調の模索 (Search for Japanese-Soviet cooperation in the late 1920s). In Hosoya, ed., *Taiheiyō-Ajia ken no kokusai keizai funsōshi, 1922–1945*, pp. 113–41. [4]

—— "Shīmensu jiken no kokusaiteki haikei" シーメンス事件の国際的背景 (International background of the Siemens case). *Kokushigaku* (November 1975), no. 97, pp. 1–25. [5]

Yui Masaomi 由井正臣. "Niko shidan zōsetsu mondai to gunbu" 二個師団増設問題と軍部 (The problem of increasing two divisions, and the [Japanese] army). *Komazawa shigaku* (May 1971), no. 17, pp. 1–19. [1]

—— "Shingai kakumei to Nihon no taiō" 辛亥革命と日本の対応 (The 1911 Revolution and the Japanese response). *Rekishigaku kenkyū* (January 1969), no. 344, pp. 1–11. [2]

4

Japanese Foreign Policy: 1931–1945 Historiography and Notes on Basic Sources

A HISTORIOGRAPHICAL SURVEY FOR THE YEARS 1931–1945

Hatano Sumio

From the historiographical viewpoint, by far the richest and the most exciting field of Japanese diplomatic history is the period from the Manchurian Incident to the end of the Pacific War. There is a powerful school of historians in Japan who lump together and treat this period as a "fifteen years war" (not a precise term because this period adds up to only thirteen years and eleven months).

In this chapter I shall present a broad historiographical essay and notes on basic sources for this period in the hope that they will help to place the subsequent chapters in a proper perspective.

The Prevalence of Marxist Historiography

With Japan's defeat in 1945, historical writing on contemporary Japanese history made a fresh start. As has been noted in the introduction, early postwar Japanese historiography was predicated upon two factors: the resurgence of the Marxist school of historians and the impact of the International Military Tribunal for the Far East. The defeat of Japan reinstated, with fanfare, the Marxist historians, who considered it their most important task to locate where responsibility lay for having brought Japan into the war. Their efforts had something in common with the verdicts of the Tokyo war crimes trials in that both put the war guilt solely on the Japanese, whether individually or collectively.

These war crimes trials construed the East Asian war, lasting from the Manchurian Incident to the Pacific War, as a succession of aggressions by Japanese militarism, and their verdict pointed to a "conspiracy" plotted by a group of Japanese "militarists." However, the trials, by their very nature, concentrated on individuals who were presumed to be "guilty." In contrast, Japanese Marxists were more interested in examining the "structure" of Japan's socioeconomic and political leadership that caused the war. More specifically, they laid the blame on "Emperor-system fascism" as a uniquely Japanese form of fascism.

In the prewar years Marxist historians had of necessity refrained from openly discussing the question of political power (the "superstructure") and concentrated on its economic base (the "substructure"). As it became possible, with Japan's defeat, to talk freely about political power, a new perspective emerged. One powerful theoretical framework for explaining contemporary Japanese history, closely linked with the pursuit of war responsibility, was the concept of "Emperor-system fascism." Instead of locating the origins of the war in a "conspiracy" of "militarists," the holders of this concept denounced the whole power structure of prewar Japan and critically analyzed a fundamental "contradiction" between the military, monopoly capitalists, parasitic landlords, and the bourgeoisie on the one hand, and the "people" on the other.

An early (1952) survey history that represents this thesis of "Emperor-system fascism" was Inoue Kiyoshi, Suzuki Masashi, and Okonogi Shinzaburō, eds., *Gendai Nihon no rekishi* (A history of contemporary Japan).[1] Among recent surveys, I shall cite as a typical example Fujiwara Akira's *Nihon kindaishi* (A history of modern Japan).[2] Such a viewpoint naturally led to the conclusion that war responsibility was not confined to a group of "militarists," as the Tokyo trials decided, but must be assumed by Japan's entire ruling class.

A comprehensive study from such a perspective was the five-volume work, *Taiheiyō sensōshi* (History of the Pacific War), edited by the Rekishigaku Kenkyūkai (the Historical Science Society) and published in 1953–54.[3] The work was consistent in casting the blame on the Japanese ruling class that allegedly constituted the basis for the Emperor system—the military, bureaucrats, monopoly capitalists, landlords, and others.

Taiheiyō sensōshi also presented a framework for understanding World War II as the convergence of three different types of wars: war among imperialist powers; war between fascist and antifascist forces; and war for the liberation of oppressed peoples, especially in China. This perspective, along with the concept of "Emperor-system fascism," has long served as an analytical framework for Marxist historians.

The Shōwashi Controversy

Studies on Japanese fascism from non-Marxist viewpoints were initiated by the pioneering works of political scientists Maruyama Masao and Ishida Takeshi.[4] Especially important was Maruyama's *Gendai seiji no shisō to kōdō* (1953–54),[5] which is available in partial English translation under the title *Thought and Behavior in Modern Japanese Politics* edited by Ivan Morris Oxford University Press, 1963). It brilliantly presents an analytical framework for understanding the political structure of Japanese fascism, which remains useful to this day.

Comparing the processes of the emergence of fascism in Japan and Germany, Maruyama presented an analysis of "fascism from above" and "fascism from below." In the case of Germany, a new type of ultra-rightist movement was eventually integrated by the Nazi party into a mass movement led by Hitler—a process that Maruyama calls "fascism from below." By contrast, in the case of Japan, efforts to integrate "from below" the ultra-right groups that had mushroomed since the 1920s failed. Coups d'état by "radical" young army and navy officers affiliated with ultra-right groups saw their final collapse with the failure of the February 26 (1936) incident. Thereafter, the military elites and the "renovationist" bureaucrats attempted to use "fascism from below" by inciting volatile officers, but they found it impossible to overcome the pluralistic and diffused system of political power to bring about a dictatorship even remotely similar to the German type.

In 1953 an important historical work appeared that was aimed at refuting Marxist interpretations. Titled *Taiheiyō sensō gen'inron* (The origins of the Pacific War),[6] this solid volume was the result of joint research by empirically oriented scholars headed by Ueda Toshio. The book examined a wide scope of questions ranging from political institutions and the national economy, to anti-Japanese boycotts in China, and the problem of oil resources. The express purpose of this book, as spelled out in the preface, was to rectify Marxist interpretations that might "mislead people about Japan's real intention in regard to the war" and also to present a viewpoint "unfettered" by the verdicts of the Tokyo war crimes trials. To put it in another way, the very fact that such a scholarly rebuttal was felt to be necessary testifies to the strong influence wielded by the Marxist school and the judgment of the Military Tribunal during the early postwar period.

Gaimushō (Foreign Ministry), ed., *Shūsen shiroku* (The historical record of the termination of the Pacific War),[7] though important as a basic work, was not much more than a compilation of all the materials that could then be gathered about the circumstances leading to the end of the war. Even as such, the book, as soon as it was published in 1952, was criticized as a subterfuge to avoid responsibility for the war and a politically motivated justification of the Japanese government's policy since the Manchurian Incident. For example, the leftist historian Matsushima Eiichi denounced the book "as intended to 'resuscitate' [former Japanese leaders] and to exempt them from their war responsibility by emphasizing their peace efforts during the war" (*Mainichi Shinbun*, June 15, 1952). In the prevailing intellectual climate, such an accusation sounded plausible enough.

In 1955 three "leftist" historians—Tōyama Shigeki, Imai Seiichi, and Fujiwara Akira—published a collaborative book on contemporary Japanese history for general readers. Titled *Shōwashi* (A history of the Shōwa period),[8] the book instantly gained a wide audience. This time, however, the leftist interpretation was to meet a barrage of criticisms from non-Marxist historians.

The first to open fire was the literary critic Kamei Katsuichirō who

charged that the book treated contemporary Japanese history merely
as the struggle between two forces: the groups forming the core of the
Emperor system (the military, monopolistic capitalists, and bureaucrats) on the one hand, and the communists and liberals on the other.
In other words, Kamei was critical about the book's simplistic and
stereotyped division of the Japanese people, which fit them into an
abstract concept of "class struggle." Kamei's major objection to the
book was that it did not pay enough attention to the majority of the
Japanese people who had oscillated between these two groups.[9]

Just about the same time, Takeyama Michio also challenged *Shōwashi*
in his book, *Shōwa no seishinshi* (An intellectual history of the Shōwa
period).[10] According to Takeyama, Japan's elite groups in the 1930s—
court circles and elder statesmen, senior bureaucrats and political
parties—were not war-mongering "fascists," nor were they united in
their determination to commence and execute the war. The political
scientist Shinohara Hajime argued that the heart of the matter lay in
how to interpret the new "middle stratum" of the Japanese people,
whose behavior could hardly be explained by the crude concept of
class struggle.[11] Similarly, Maruyama Masao harshly criticized the
Marxist historians for their dogmatic tendency to reduce everything
to the basic structure of the state. He then advised Marxist historians
to liberate themselves from this sort of self-fulfilling thought process.[12]

To these criticisms Tōyama Shigeki, one of the co-authors of *Shōwashi,* responded that "an objective and critical understanding of
history" would become possible only when the historian takes the
viewpoint of the proletariat, the leading revolutionary force.[13] Such a
standpoint was to be the position of those who seek radical changes;
to put it more simply, it was by analyzing history from the viewpoint
of the Communist Party that the legitimacy of Marxism was to be
established.

In actuality, however, the Marxist historians were placed in a difficult situation by the turbulent developments within the socialist
camp: the major strategic shift of the Japanese Communist Party in
1955, the de-Stalinization of the following year, and the upheavals in
Poland and Hungary.

The so-called "great debate on *Shōwashi,*" which came to involve
not only historians and political scientists but also literary figures,

was never settled. The upshot was that the original edition underwent a wholesale rewriting in 1959 for a revised edition, which considerably toned down the initial thesis.

Marxists on the Defensive

In the early 1960s Marxist oriented interpretations met serious challenges from the advocates of "modernization theory," which was applied to reevaluate the rapid growth Japan and achieved since the Meiji restoration. This theory presented an alternative mode of explaining Japan's "modernization." The controversies erupted at the preparatory meeting, held in Hakone in the summer of 1960 under the auspices of Kindai Nihon Kenkyū Kaigi (the Conference on Modern Japan), which was connected with the Association for Asian Studies in the United States. John W. Hall, one of the leading scholars at the conference, spoke for the position taken by the majority at the conference who were intent on making a positive evaluation of the course of Japan's modernization. Although his attempt to establish a value-free approach appeared to have paved the way for comparative study, it came under heavy attack from Japanese Marxist scholars. The result of the Hakone conference was published as Marius B. Jansen, ed., *Changing Japanese Attitudes Toward Modernization* (Princeton University Press, 1965). Its Japanese version is Jansen and Hosoya Chihiro, eds., *Nihon ni okeru kindaika no mondai* (The problems of modernization in Japan).[14]

In 1961 Edwin O. Reischauer, one of the participants at the Hakone conference, was appointed ambassador to Japan. His writings—such as "A New Look at Modern Japan"[15]—aroused deep suspicions among leftist Japanese intellectuals, who felt that his "modernization" theory was politically motivated. They severely criticized it as a part of the "Kennedy-Reischauer line" or the "W. W. Rostow-Reischauer modernization line," constituting an ideological arm of "American imperialism." (Reischauer's role in historical controversies as well as his ambassadorship are examined in a sympathetic essay by Ikei Masaru.)[16]

The first half of the 1960s was a period when influential Japanese intellectuals became engaged in heated controversies on the meanings of the Pacific War. These debates constituted the background of the debates between advocates of the *Shōwashi* position and the modernization theorists.

The first to open fire was Hayashi Fusao, a literary personality, who published *Dai Tōa sensō kōteiron* (In defense of the Greater East Asian War) in 1964 and its sequel the following year.[17] In these provocative books he defined the course of Japanese history from Commodore Perry to the end of the Pacific War as Japan's "hundred years war" against the West for the realization of a Greater East Asia. Hayashi claimed that the war was for the "liberation" of the Asian peoples from subjugation by the West, and he went on to argue that it was a war of "self-defense" against America's "white Pacific" policy. It goes without saying that Hayashi's assertions caused intense controversy in Japanese intellectual circles.

On the other hand, Takeuchi Yoshimi, who rejected Marxism and developed his own philosophy of history, admitted that the Sino-Japanese War was definitely a war of Japanese aggression, but he contended that the "Greater East Asian War" was not necessarily a war of pure and simple aggression on Japan's part because it "gave certain opportunities" for independence to Asian peoples.[18]

The philosopher Ueyama Shunpei published his *Dai Tōa sensō no imi* (The significance of the Greater East Asian War) in 1964.[19] In it he broadly classified historical interpretations of World War II into three categories: the "imperialistic war" of the Marxists; the "war of national liberation" for Asian peoples; and the American view of the "Pacific War." Ueyama pointed out that these interpretations reflected respective national senses of values, and he criticized those Japanese historians who had uncritically swallowed the American interpretation, while eschewing as taboo the viewpoint of the Greater East Asian War, thus committing "double mistakes."

These bold questions raised in the first half of the 1960s were not followed by further controversies, but there is no doubt that they had a strong impact on Japanese specialists in contemporary diplomatic history.

The Road to the Pacific War Series

The seven-volume series *Taiheiyō sensō e no michi: Kaisen gaikōshi* (The road to the Pacific War: A diplomatic history of the origins of the war),[20] published in 1962–63, probably constitutes the most important scholarly contribution that had been made by Nihon Kokusai Seiji Gakkai (the Japan Association of International Relations). However, when placed within the above context, this richly documented work could be regarded as a response to Marxist historiography.

One of the contributors to this work, Hata Ikuhiko, had already expressed his criticism of Marxist interpretations in the preface of his own monograph, *Nitchū sensōshi* (History of the Sino-Japanese War).[21] He regretted that methodologically the writing of modern Japanese history had leaned too heavily on the "substructure," and that empirical research into the "superstructure"—such as political, diplomatic, and military leadership—had been neglected. Such an assertion had something in common with the editorial policy of *Taiheiyō sensō e no michi* to focus on the diplomatic and military activities of the top and middle-ranking officers and officials.

This series is composed of lengthy monographic essays written by fourteen scholars whose standpoints were not necessarily the same. There existed, however, a basic agreement among all the contributors to adhere strictly to the orthodox approach to diplomatic and military history. In the words of Tsunoda Jun, who was in charge of the entire project, they aimed to write "straightforward historical accounts solidly based on primary source materials—narratives of diplomatic history (leading to the war) in the classical sense."

The most important groundwork for that contribution made by the joint project was to unearth systematically and make available to scholars an enormous amount of previously inaccessible documents, especially those of the army and navy. The basic documents were published as a supplementary volume, *Shiryōhen* (Documents), of *Taiheiyō sensō e no michi* in 1963. These materials were extensively utilized by the individual contributors to *Taiheiyō sensō e no michi*, and as a result the level of scholarship was impressively heightened in such research fields as the Manchurian Incident, the Sino-Japanese War, the Tripartite Pact, Japan's southward advance, and the Japanese-American negotiations of 1941. (Brief assessments of each essay contained in each volume will be made in the following chapters.)

Although the *Taiheiyō sensō e no michi* series was widely praised for the quality of the primary sources it exploited and the thoroughness of the analysis of these documents, it was by no means immune from critical comments from the Marxist school of historians. They were dissatisfied with what they construed as the series' insufficient attention to the all-important China question. They made a valid point that the succession of Japanese aggressions following the Manchurian Incident are treated largely within the narrow framework of the origins of the Japanese-American war. In the eyes of these critics, the series gave undue emphasis to the "inevitable" confrontation between Japanese and American "imperialism," while neglecting the conflict between Chinese nationalism and the "imperialist powers." This slant, the leftist critics asserted, obscured the real causes of and responsibility for the Pacific War.[22] In short, they charged hyperbolically that the series represented an "imperialistic view of history."

To be sure, this work, when compared with the *Taiheiyō sensōshi* series edited by the left-wing Rekishigaku Kenkyūkai, seems to lack systematic and consistent discussion on how to evaluate and characterize the Pacific War as a whole. But, on the other hand, we may observe that this series revealed, as fully as documentation allowed, the complex realities of the 1930s, which could not be neatly explained in terms of the Marxists' schematic framework. The value of the *Taiheiyō sensō e no michi* series is apparent from the fact that since 1979 an English-language version of selected essays is being published under the general editorship of James W. Morley, and that a slightly revised version was published in 1987–1988.[23]

New Methodologies

The late 1960s and early 1970s saw the appearance of able monographic works on specific subjects following the standards set by this series. However, taken together, these new works have not yet superseded the series.

One recent trend is an effort to apply new theoretical insights to the writing of diplomatic history. Since the mid-1960s some Japanese diplomatic historians have shown increasing eagerness to exploit new analytical concepts and methodologies derived from political and behavioral sciences that have been developed, especially in the United States. This opened wide possibilities for new approaches in such diverse areas as foreign policy decision making, political leadership, the formation of attitudes toward other nations, and communication processes.

The application of these approaches widened the scope of study of diplomatic history in Japan. For example, Hosoya Chihiro became influenced by the theory of decision making during his research in the United States in the 1960s. One result is a paper titled "Twenty-Five Years After Pearl Harbor: A New Look at Japan's Decision for War" presented at the 1966 convention of the American Historical Association.[24]

This paper was followed by a series of essays analyzing the characteristics of the foreign policy decision-making process in prewar Japan.[25] In these works, Hosoya emphasized that prewar Japan's decision-making process cannot be adequately explained in terms of the "rational actor" model advanced by Richard C. Snyder and his colleagues. In his analysis Hosoya emphasized the crucial role played by the middle-echelon officers and officials in the Japanese military and the Foreign Ministry who had gained substantial power in the course of the 1930s.

The questions he raised in these and other works drew both Japanese and American scholars to comparative studies of the decision-making process in both countries.

Joint Project: Pearl Harbor as History

A conference of Japanese and American scholars, which met at Kawaguchiko in July 1969, was organized by Hosoya, who closely collaborated with Dorothy Borg and her American colleagues. The aim of the conference was to reassess, from binational perspectives, Japanese-American relations during the decade preceding Pearl Harbor. The participants (fourteen Japanese scholars, two of whom were of leftist persuasion, and eleven American historians) endeavored to investigate the process of the mounting antagonism and the spiral of mutual misperceptions and distrust. This objective was to be achieved through comparative analyses of policymaking mechanisms in Japan and the United States (government heads, administrative bureaucracies, the legislatures, the armed forces, and others), and the examination of the different political cultures of the two nations (communication processes, the mass media and intellectuals, mutual images, and the role of private organizations).

The papers presented by the participants, together with the summaries of the proceedings, were published in Japan as Hosoya Chihiro et al., eds., *Nichi-Bei kankeishi: Kaisen ni itaru 10-nen, 1931–1941* (A history of Japanese-American relations: The decade preceding the war, 1931–1941), in four volumes.[26] Its English version, *Pearl Harbor as History,* edited by Dorothy Borg and Shumpei Okamoto (Columbia University Press, 1973), does not contain the proceedings of the conference. As reported by one of the participants, Akira Iriye,[27] the conference was an unusual success for an international dialogue of this sort, and it is unfortunate that the proceedings were never published in English.

This is not the place to summarize the conference discussions that covered so many aspects of the subject. Suffice it here to stress that substantial differences in the ways in which decisions were made in the two countries clearly emerged at the conference. For example, as delineated by Asada Sadao in his essay on the Japanese navy, the structure of decision making in Japan was centrifugal; the authority and power of the senior leadership was gravely weakened, and actual power shifted downward to middle-echelon officers. This marked a sharp contrast to the American style of decision making in which power was centralized at the very top.

Lively discussions also took place on the political cultures of the two nations. On the agenda were such topics as communication gaps between the two countries as well as within each country, the self-righteousness often observed in the individual leaders' and the nations' self-images, the discrepancies in mutual perceptions, and the personalities of political leaders.

The Kawaguchiko conference was often preoccupied with such questions as whether or not there ever existed a chance to avert the Japanese-American war, and, if so, when the "point of no return" was reached. As a result, some participants felts that attention was too narrowly focused on bilateral relations, leaving many important questions unanswered. For instance, to what extent were Japanese-American relations in the 1930s actually influenced by the European situation, as the Japanese perceived it? Regarding the East Asian scene, would it have been more fruitful to discuss U.S.-Japanese relations within the context of at least quadrilateral interaction among the United States, Great Britain, Japan, and China?

What seemed to some of the participants the most important question was how to evaluate the role of China in relation to the "road to Pearl Harbor." In his paper on the Foreign Ministry, Usui Katsumi shrewdly analyzed the Asia-oriented group (made up of men like Arita Hachirō, Shigemitsu Mamoru, and Hirota Kōki) and the "renovation faction" or the "Axis faction" (led by Shiratori Toshio). Then Usui explained why the "pro–Anglo-American" Shidehara group failed to become the "mainstream" within the Foreign Ministry. He placed special emphasis on the basic differences over China policy that existed between Shidehara and the other two factions. Shidehara's position was predicated, Usui argued, on the premise that China was becoming a unified, modern nation, and he sought to pursue his China policy accordingly.

Usui's paper and comments provoked heated debates on the nature of Japanese-American confrontation, real or imagined, over the China question, and raised many interesting questions. Did the United States really have faith in China's ability to modernize and unify itself? Was America's goal in China less to encourage China's modernization than to maintain the status quo in East Asia and promote America's own economic interests? Did not the optimistic view about the unification and modernization of China, held by Japan's pro–Anglo-American faction (the Shidehara group), somewhat overlap with the American perception of China? (The reader is reminded that these discussions are recorded only in the Japanese version.)

After the conference was over, two major criticisms appeared from leftist historians. One charged that by belittling Japanese-American rivalry in China the conference failed to lay bare the "true" historical nature of the two countries' relations and dwelt too much on the question of whether there had been any prospect for a reconciliation. The other criticism was that the intense preoccupation with bureaucratic institutions and the decision-making process on the part of participants, ironically enough, tended to degenerate into a sort of fatalism or "determinism," more characteristic of a Marxist interpretation. These critics took exception to the acceptance of what had happened in the past as inevitable; this relinquished the historian's task to probe into the responsibility for bringing Japan into the Pacific War.

Joint Study: The British Angle

In the summer of 1979 twenty-two Japanese and British specialists in diplomatic and military history met together in the Imperial War Museum (London) for an Anglo-Japanese conference, which had been organized by Hosoya Chihiro and Donald C. Watt. The conference papers were published as Hosoya Chihiro, ed., *Nichi-Ei kankeishi, 1917–1949* (A history of Anglo-Japanese relations, 1917–1949),[28] and subsequently in English as Ian Nish, ed., *Anglo-Japanese Alienation, 1919–1952: Papers of the Anglo-Japanese Conference on the History of the Second World War* (Cambridge University Press, 1982). In a sense, this conference was the Anglo-Japanese version of the 1969 Kawagu-chiko conference. As had been pointed out at the earlier conference, any study of "the road to Pearl Harbor" required a multilateral approach; the Anglo-Japanese conference was a further step in this direction.

Immediately after the conference, Hosoya made a rather provocative presentation: "Was the Pacific War not an Anglo-Japanese war?"[29] He suggested that "the Pacific War essentially stemmed from the clash of interests between Japan and Britain, which escalated into war." Anglo-Japanese conflict in China, according to Hosoya, was largely over substantive interests, but there was room for mutual accommodation; in fact, both nations searched for the possibilities of a compromise solution in the mid-1930s. In this respect, Anglo-Japanese relations were different from the U.S.-Japanese conflict over China, which largely involved a clash between American "principles" and Japanese "programs," leaving little room for diplomatic adjustment. However, after the efforts at Anglo-Japanese accommodation failed, and as Japan's advance into Southeast Asia came to threaten Britain's vital interests, any possibility for compromise between the two nations disappeared.

Other important issues were raised by the participants. How did responses to the China question, which largely defined Anglo-Japanese relations in the interwar period, change over the years, leading to "estrangement" between the two nations? Papers by Hosoya, Usui Katsumi, and Ian Nish, tracing the shifting mutual perceptions of Britain and Japan, highlighted gaps in perception on the part of decision makers in both countries. They also examined the significance of nostalgia for the Anglo-Japanese Alliance and complications in Anglo-American relations which affected Anglo-Japanese relations thereafter. As had been the case with the Kawaguchiko conference, the question of how to treat Chinese nationalism still remained only partially answered.

The Question of Fascism

The characteristic feature of the Japanese debate since the 1950s was its view of Japanese fascism as obstacle to modernization. Therefore, the "feudal" and "absolutistic" nature of Japan came under attack.

The debate on fascism, which revived after the mid-1960s, began to take different directions. One group of historians increasingly tended to understand Japanese fascism in terms of the peculiar sociopolitical mechanisms for national integration that accompanied the process of modernization. In other words, the process of how Japan became fascist came to be studied not only in the realm of thought and political movements but also in connection with the emergence of political and social systems in response to concrete historical situations. Such a viewpoint is reflected in the works of Kisaka Jun'ichirō[30] and Imai Seiichi.[31] Kisaka focuses on the process through which Japan in the 1920s began to build a system to cope with total war and national mobilization. This effort resulted in the establishment of the Imperial Rule Assistance Association in 1940, which, Kisaka concludes, signaled the culmination of Japanese fascism. In a similar vein, Imai Seiichi has also published an essay discussing the emergence of Japanese fascism against the background of "the system of total mobilization."

The above-mentioned trends in interpretation are related to recent reexaminations of the period of so-called "Taishō democracy"—liberalism that prevailed during the latter half of the Taishō period (1912–26). The results of new research, led by Matsuo Takayoshi,[32] have done much to change, if not reverse, the traditional view that this liberal movement of the 1920s was crushed by the forces of fascism. On the contrary, the new works raise the question of whether or not the beginnings of Japanese fascism were already inherent in "Taishō democracy" itself. For example, party politics, which was a concrete political manifestation of "Taishō democracy," did not last long, and its demise prompted the policy of total national mobilization. Detailed studies from such a viewpoint would suggest continuities rather than discontinuities between the 1920s and the 1930s.

The second trend in research on fascism criticizes Maruyama Masao's hypothesis of "fascism from above." A representative example is *Nihon fashizumu* (Japanese fascism),[33] edited by Fujiwara Akira. According to this interpretation, it is argued that even after the failure of the February 26th (1936) Incident, there was a voluntary movement of "fascism from below" that acted in concert with Konoe Fumimaro's movement for a "New Order." (It aimed at a fascist polity under Konoe that concentrated all political power in the state and sought total national mobilization.)

As a third trend, there are an increasing number of studies that emphasize external factors as a stimulus to the emergence and growth of Japanese fascism. Works by Eguchi Keiichi and Suzuki Takashi, among others, stress the interaction between Japan's sense of crisis about developments abroad and colonial problems on the one hand, and domestic fascism and militarization on the other.[34] According to these authors, "Japanese imperialism" was forced to seek a solution for its internal "contradictions" by aggression in Asia, but the resulting war in turn aggravated Japan's domestic contradictions and prompted its road to fascism.

Such a variety of approaches to Japanese fascism made it impossible to analyze the 1930s in terms of "Emperor-system fascism" alone. For example, Rekishigaku Kenkyūkai's collaborative work, *Taiheiyō sensōshi* (A history of the Pacific War),[35] was intended to be a rewriting of the older series, but the new edition diluted the thesis on "Emperor-system fascism." The authors of the new edition were divided over the question of fascism, and as a result failed to provide a clear definition of "fascism" that could serve as a unifying theme in these volumes.

The validity of "Emperor-system fascism" as an analytical framework for historical study was further called into question by Marxist historians as research on the 1930s became more sophisticated. From the late 1970s to the early 1980s, the defects of this framework were unequivocally pointed out by Abe Hirozumi,[36] Fujimura Michio,[37] and Eguchi Keiichi.[38] Fujimura, for example, discards the theory of "Emperor-system fascism" entirely and maintains that the focal point of research on Japanese fascism must be on analyzing the process through which Japan built a new political system to cope with total war, the foremost task for the Japanese military.

On the other hand, Eguchi asserts that the analytical framework of "Emperor-system fascism," with its emphasis on the unitary nature of the "ruling class" and its consensual views, cannot explain conflicts within the governing forces, nor can it account for the radical fascist movement that revolted against monopoly capitalists and the elite military leadership. Instead, Eguchi proposes to explain the characteristics of Japanese fascism in the 1930s in terms of a conflict between two foreign policy guidelines: "cooperation with the Anglo-American powers" and "the Monroe Doctrine in Asia." In other words, he depicts this decade as a period when the forces opposed to the Washington system and dedicated to the establishment of the autarchical sphere gradually gathered strength and in the end prevailed over the forces supporting "cooperation with the Anglo-American powers."

Characteristic of Eguchi's viewpoint is its emphasis on external factors rather than domestic problems in explaining the emergence of Japanese fascism. This new stress on foreign policy issues can be also found, for example, in Fujiwara Akira and Nozawa Yutaka, eds., *Nihon no fashizumu to Higashi Ajia* (Japanese fascism and East Asia).[39] This work emphasizes interrelationships between the formation of Japanese fascism and the Sino-Japanese War. Recent years have also seen works that further develop the analysis of external factors affecting the emergence of fascism by comparting similarities and differences in the cases of Japan, Germany, Italy, and Spain. Underlying such a comparative approach is an effort to formulate a new conceptual framework for studying Japanese fascism. Works from such a comparative perspective attempt to extract common attributes of "fascist diplomacy" such as the concept of *Lebensraum* and dual diplomacy.[40]

During 1973–1978 the Shakai Kagaku Kenkyūjo (the Social Science

Research Institute) of the University of Tokyo conducted a joint project on the theme of "Fascism and Democracy." The results, which were published in eight volumes,[41] compare countries that adopted the "fascist system" with Britain, the United States, France, and others in such areas as the economy, society, and national movements, attempting to bring out the historical characteristics of "the age of fascism."

Ironically enough, as specialized studies accumulate, differences rather than similarities among various fascist movements have become obvious, and eventually the question was raised whether the concept of "fascism" was useful at all for understanding Japan in the 1930s. For instance, Itō Takashi[42] rejects the use of the term "fascism" in his analysis of the political system of prewar Japan. Instead, he provides a different framework for understanding the conflict between the two contending groups—the "renovationists" (representing destruction) versus the "gradualists" (representing the status quo). In Itō's analysis, the key to the understanding of the late 1920s and the 1930s is the rise of the "renovationists," which actually consisted of both rightist and leftist political groups bent on destroying the "ancien regime."

Itō's thesis, solidly grounded on numerous personal manuscripts of political and military leaders in the Shōwa period, would appear to be quite effective for reexamining Japan's political process from the 1920s to 1950s in terms of continuities. His study contributes significantly to the method of analyzing the power structures of various groups involved in foreign policy decisions. For this purpose he focuses on the dynamics of conflict and cooperation among these groups. That Itō's approach has had considerable influence is clear from the fact that a number of articles that examine power relationships within a political group or its interactions with other groups on the basis of personal manuscripts have been published in the annals of Kindai Nihon Kenkyūkai (the Research Group on Modern Japan),[43] of which Itō is a leader.

Itō's new thesis, together with the essay by Gordon M. Berger that refuses to call Japanese national experiences in the 1930s "fascism,"[44] again raised controversy among Japanese contemporary historians.[45] It must be admitted, however, that these new interpretations have not led to constructive scholarly debates; at the time of this writing, the state of confusion regarding the "fascism controversy" seems to have grown.

The Fifteen Years War

In the early 1980s we have witnessed what might be called a second "boom" in the history of the Shōwa period. Representative surveys include: Fujiwara Akira et al., eds., *Shōwa no rekishi* (Series on the history of the Shōwa period);[46] and Kinbara Samon and Takemae Eiji, *Shōwashi* (A history of the Shōwa period).[47] These works, based as they are on monographic literature and printed sources, basically retain the thesis of the "fifteen years war," and do not present fresh viewpoints of importance.

The term "fifteen years war," however, poses important questions on how to define the Sino-Japanese hostilities in the context of Japanese history. Should Japan's conflict, beginning with the Manchurian Incident and ending with its surrender in 1945, be considered one continuous war? Or should the Manchurian Incident and the Sino-Japanese War of 1937–1945 be treated separately?

The "fifteen years war" thesis has recently been recapitulated in Eguchi Keiichi et al., eds., *Taikei Nihon gendaishi* (Series on contemporary Japanese history),[48] which interprets a succession of military conflicts after the Manchurian Incident as a Japanese war of aggression against the neighboring Asian countries. Ienaga Saburō's *Taiheiyō senso* (The Pacific War, 1931–1945)[49] takes a similar position, but its main focus is on the Japanese populace on the home front which oscillated between obedience and resistance to the authorities. Its English translation by Franklin Baldwin was published under the title *The Pacific War: World War II and the Japanese, 1931–1945* (New York: Pantheon, 1978.)

On the other hand, a recent representative survey that rejects the "fifteen years war" thesis is Itō Takashi's book, which is paradoxically titled *15-nen senso* (A history of the fifteen years war).[50]

Usui Katsumi admits that the "fifteen years war" may be an appropriate term to capture the essence of the Pacific War, but that to be historically accurate, the Manchurian Incident ended with the Tangku truce of 1933.[51] These and related questions of periodization will be dealt with in the following chapters.

From a standpoint distinctly different from the "fifteen years war" thesis, Miyake Masaki et al. published, in 1983, a five-volume work, *Shōwashi no gunbu to seiji* (The Japanese military and politics in the history of the Shōwa period.)[52] This work is the result of a collaborative study that mobilized more than thirty scholars in order to "reexamine the entire history of the Shōwa period from the perspective of civil-military relations." In an introductory essay, Miyake summarizes the various recent theories in the West (especially the United States) on civil-militay relations and briefly examines the patterns of the Japanese military's political interference in order to search for comparability with foreign countries. It is an ambitious attempt to be free from the traditional controversy over the nature of Japanese fascism. Unfortunately, many of the contributions do not provide indepth analyses along the lines intended by Miyake.

In this essay I have attempted to describe the research trends and historical debates concerning the turbulent period of 1930–1945. It is not my intention, however, to give the impression that the traditional approach to diplomatic history, with its emphasis on archival research and narrative style, is in full retreat. Far from it. It must be emphasized that traditional studies still enjoy wide popularity among Japanese diplomatic historians.

Notes

1. Inoue Kiyoshi, Suzuki Masashi, and Okonogi Shinzaburō 井上清, 鈴木正四, 小此木真三郎, eds., *Gendai Nihon no rekishi* 現代日本の歴史 (A history of contemporary Japan), 2 vols. (Aoki Shoten, 1952).
2. Fujiwara Akira 藤原彰, *Kindai Nihonshi* 近代日本史 (A history of modern Japan) vol. 3 (Iwanami Shoten, 1977).
3. Rekishigaku Kenkyūkai 歴史学研究会, ed., *Taiheiyō sensōshi* 太平洋戦争史, 5 vols. (Tōyō Keizai Shinpōsha, 1953–54).
4. Ishida Takeshi 石田雄, *Kindai Nihon seiji kōzō no kenkyū* 近代日本政治構造の研究 (A study on political structure in modern Japan) (Miraisha, 1956).
5. Maruyama Masao 丸山真男, *Gendai seiji no shisō to kōdō* 現代政治の思想と行動 (Thought and behavior in modern Japanese politics), 2 vols. (Miraisha, 1956–57); enlarged edition, 1964.
6. Nihon Gaikō Gakkai 日本外交学会, ed., *Taiheiyō sensō gen'inron* 太平洋戦争原因論 (Shinbun Gekkansha, 1953).
7. Gaimushō 外務省, ed., *Shūsen shiroku* 終戦史録 (Shinbun Gekkansha, 1951).
8. Tōyama Shigeki, Imai Seiichi, and Fujiwara Akira 遠山茂樹, 今井清一, 藤原彰, *Shōwashi* 昭和史 (Iwanami Shoten, 1955).

9. Kamei Katsuichirō 亀井勝一郎, "Gendaishika e no gimon" 現代史家へ の疑問, *Bungei shunjū* (March 1956), pp.58–68.

10. Takeyama Michio 竹山道雄, *Shōwa no seishinshi* 昭和の精神史 (Shinchōsha, 1956).

11. Shinohara Hajime 篠原一, "Gendaishi no omosa to fukasa" 現代史の重 さと深さ (The weight and depth of contemporary history), *Sekai* (December 1956) pp. 143–58.; "Gendai seijishi no hōhō" 現代政治史の 方法 (A methodology of modern political history), *Shisō* (October 1959), pp. 1–22.

12. Maruyama Masao, "Sutārin hihan no hihan" スターリン批判の批判 (Criticism of de-Stalinization), *Sekai* (November 1956), pp. 146–61.

13. Tōyama Shigeki 遠山茂樹, "Gendaishi kenkyū no mondaiten" 現代史 研究の問題点 (Issues in the study of contemporary history), *Chūō kōron* (June 1956), pp. 52–61.

14. Marius B. Jansen and Hosoya Chihiro 細谷千博, eds., *Nihon ni okeru kindaika no mondai* 日本における近代化の問題 (Iwanami Shoten, 1968).

15. Edwin Reischauer, "Kindaishi o mitsumeru" 近代史を見つめる, *Asahi jānaru*, (June 10, 1962), pp. 39–44.

16. Ikei Masaru 池井優, "Amerika no tai-Nichi seisaku: Raishawā taishi no yakuwari o chūshin to shite" アメリカの対日政策―ライシャワー大 使の役割を中心として (American policy toward Japan: With particular reference to the role of Ambassador Reischauer), in Keiō Gijuku Daigaku Chiiki Kenkyū Gurūpu 慶応義塾大学地域研究グループ, ed., *Amerika no taigai seisaku* アメリカの対外政策 (American foreign policy), pp. 250–89 (Kajima Kenkyūjo Shuppankai, 1971).

17. Hayashi Fusao 林房雄, *Dai Tōa sensō kōteiron* 大東亜戦争肯定論 (Chūō Kōronsha, 1964); *Zoku Dai Tōa sensō kōteiron* 続大東亜戦争肯定論 (Chūō Kōronsha, 1965).

18. Takeuchi Yoshimi 竹内好 et al., "Zadankai: Dai Tōa kyōeiken no rinen to genjitsu" 座談会―大東亜共栄圏の理論と現実 (Discussion: The ideals and realities of the Greater East Asia Coprosperity Sphere), *Shisō no kagaku* (December 1964), pp. 2–19.

19. Ueyama Shunpei 上山春平, *Dai Tōa sensō no imi* 大東亜戦争の意味 (Chūō Kōronsha, 1964).

20. Nihon Kokusai Seiji Gakkai, Taiheiyō Sensō Gen'in Kenkyūbukai 日本国 際政治学会, 太平洋戦争原因研究部会, ed., *Taiheiyō sensō e no michi: Kaisen gaikōshi* 太平洋戦争への道―開戦外交史, 7 vols. (Asahi Shimbunsha, 1962–63).

21. Hata Ikuhiko 秦郁彦, *Nitchū sensōshi* 日中戦争史 (Kawade Shobō Shinsha, 1962).

22. See, for example, Imai Seiichi, Fiujiwara Akira, Arai Shin'ichi, and

Nozawa Yutaka 今井清一, 藤原彰, 荒井信一, 野沢豊, "*Taiheiyō sensō e no michi* hihan" 『太平洋戦争への道』批判 (A critique of *Taiheiyō sensō e no michi*), *Rekishigaku kenkyū* (June 1964), no. 289, pp. 1–13.

23. English versions published by Columbia University Press thus far are listed in f.n. 13 of Introduction. The capstone volume, *The Final confrontation: Japan's Negotiations with the United States, 1941,* is forthcoming.

24. This is included in Grant K. Goodman, comp., *Imperial Japan and Asia: A Reassessment* (Occasional Papers of the East Asian Institute, Columbia University, 1967), pp. 52–63. See also Hosoya, "Miscalculation in Deterrent Policy: Japanese-U.S. Relations, 1938–1941," *Journal of Peace Research* (1969) no. 2, pp. 97–115.

25. "Retrogression in Japan's Foreign Policy Decision-Making Process," in James W. Morley, ed., *Dilemmas of Growth in Prewar Japan* pp. 81–105 (Princeton University Press, 1971); "Characteristics of the Foreign Policy Decision-Making System in Japan," *World Politics* (1974), 26(3):353–69; "The Prewar Japanese Military in Political Decision-Making," in Harold Z. Schiffrin, ed., *Military and State in Modern Asia,* pp. 19–29 (Jerusalem Academic Press, 1976).

26. Hosoya Chihiro et al., eds., *Nichi-Bei kankeishi: Kaisen ni itaru 10-nen, 1931–1941* 日米関係史—開戦に至る10年(1931—1941年), 4 vols. (Tokyo Daigaku Shuppankai, 1971–72).

27. Akira Iriye, "Nichi-Bei gaikōshika no mita 1930-nendai" 日米外交史家のみた1930年代 (The 1930s as seen by Japanese and American diplomatic historians), *Kokusai mondai* (October 1969), no. 115, p. 25.

28. Hosoya, ed., *Nichi-Ei kankeishi, 1917–1949* 日英関係史, 1917—1949 (Tokyo Daigaku Shuppankai, 1982). Note that the Japanese-language version does not contain the reports by Hagiwara Nobutoshi and Donald C. Watt which are included in the English edition.

29. Hosoya, "Taiheiyō sensō towa Nichi-Ei sensō dewa nakatta no ka" 太平洋戦争とは日英戦争ではなかったのか *Gaikō shiryōkan kōen shiryō* 外交史料館講演資料 (November 1979), no. 10.

30. Kisaka Jun'ichirō 木坂順一郎, "Gunbu to demokurashī" 軍部とデモクラシー (The military and "Taishō democracy"), *Kokusai seiji* (1969), no. 38: *Sensō to heiwa no kenkyū,* pp. 1–41; "Taisei Yokusan Kai no seiritsu" 大政翼賛会の成立. In *Iwanami kōza: Nihon rekishi,* vol. 20: *Kindai [7]* 岩波講座：日本歴史20, 近代[7] (Iwanami series on Japanese history, vol. 20: The Modern period, 7), pp. 270–314 (Iwanami Shoten, 1976).

31. Imai Seiichi 今井清一, "Sōdōin taisei to gunbu" 総動員体制と軍部 (The system of general mobilization and the military), in Tokyo Daigaku Shakai Kagaku Kenkyūjo 東京大学社会科学研究所, ed., *Fashizumuki*

no kokka to shakai ファシズム期の国家と社会 (The state and society in the age of fascism), 6:143–94 (Tokyo Daigaku Shuppankai, 1979).

32. Matsuo Takayoshi 松尾尊兊, *Taishō demokurashī*, 大正デモクラシー, Iwanami Shoten, 1974).

33. Nihon Gendaishi Kenkyūkai 日本現代史研究会 (representative, Fujiwara Akira 藤原彰), ed., *Nihon fashizumu* 日本ファシズム, vols. 1 and 2 (Ōtsuki Shoten, 1981–82).

34. Eguchi Keiichi 江口圭一, "Nihon teikokushugi to Manshū mondai" 日本帝国主義と満州問題, in *Iwanami kōza: Sekai rekishi*, vol. 27: *Gendai [4]* 岩波講座：世界歴史27, 現代4 (Iwanami series: World history vol. 27: The contemporary period, 4), pp. 210–41 (Iwanami Shoten, 1971); Suzuki Takashi 鈴木隆史, "Senjika no Shokuminchi" 戦時下の植民地, in *Iwanami-kōza: Nihon rekishi*, 21: *Kindai, 8* 岩波講座：日本歴史21, 近代 8(Iwanami series: Japanese history, vol. 21: The modern period, 8), pp. 213–64. (Iwanami Shoten, 1977).

35. Rekishigaku Kenkyūkai 歴史学研究会, *Taiheiyō sensōshi* 太平洋戦争史, 6 vols. (Aoki Shoten, 1972–73).

36. Abe Hirozumi 安部博純, *Nihon fashizumu kenkyū josetsu* 日本ファシズム研究序説 (An introduction to the study of Japanese fascism) (Miraisha, 1975); "Kyūshin fashizumu undōron" 急進ファシズム運動論 (On radical fascist movements), in Eguchi Keiichi 江口圭一, ed., *Taikei Nihon gendaishi* 体系日本現代史 (Series on contemporary Japanese history), 1:125–66 (Ninon Hyōronsha, 1978).

37. Fujimura Michio 藤村道生, "Iwayuru Jūgatsu jiken no saikentō: Nihon fashizumuron oboegaku" いわゆる十月事件の再検討—日本ファシズム論覚書 (A reexamination of the so-called "October incident": A note on Japanese fascism), *Nihon Rekishi* (February 1981), no. 393, pp. 52–65; "Kokka sōryokusen taisei to kūdetā keikaku" 国家総力戦体制とクーデター計画 (The system for total war and plans for coup d'etat), in Miwa Kimitada 三輪公忠, ed., *Saikō: Taiheiyō sensō zen'ya* 再考—太平洋戦争前夜 (A reconsideration: The eve of the Pacific War), pp. 87–140 (Sōseiki, 1981).

38. Eguchi Keiichi 江口圭一, "Manshū jihen kenkyūshi no saikentō" 満州事変研究史の再検討 (A reexamination of the historiography of the Manchurian Incident), *Rekishi hyōron* (September 1981), no. 377, 2–11; "1930-nendai ron" 1930年代論 (On the 1930s), in Eguchi, ed., *Taikei Nihon gendaishi*, 1:1–37 (Nihon Hyōronsha, 1978).

39. Fujiwara Akira and Nozawa Yutaka 藤原彰, 野沢豊, eds., *Nihon no fashizumu to Higashi Ajia* 日本のファシズムと東アジア (Aoki Shoten, 1977).

40. Yamaguchi Yasushi 山口定, *Fasshizumu: Sono hikaku kenkyū no tameni*

ファシズム—その比較研究のために (Fascism: Toward a comparative study (Yūhikaku, 1979); Arai Shin'ichi 荒井信一, "Dainiji taisen to sangoku dōmei" 第二次大戦と三国同盟 (World War II and the Tripartite Pact) in Eguchi Keiichi, ed. *Taikei Nihon gendaishi,* 3:135–69; Abe Hirosumi, "Fashizumu gaikō no ronri to kokusai ninshiki" ファシズム外交の論理と国際認識 (The logic and world view of fascist diplomacy in Japan), *Kokusai seiji* (1974) no. 51, pp. 109–28.

41. Tokyo Daigaku Shakai Kagaku Kenkyūjo 東京大学社会科学研究所 ed., *Fashizumuki no kokka to shakai* ファシズム期の国家と社会 (The state and society in the age of fascism), 8 vols. (Tokyo Daigaku Shuppankai, 1978–79).

42. Itō Takashi 伊藤隆, *Shōwa shoki seijishi kenkyū: Rondon kaigun jōyaku o meguru sho seiji shūdan no taikō to teikei* 昭和初期政治史研究—ロンドン海軍条約をめぐる諸政治集団の対抗と提携 (A study in the political history of the early Shōwa period: Conflicts and alignments of political groups over the issue of the London Naval Treaty [1930]) (Tokyo Daigaku Shuppankai, 1969). See also Itō Takashi, "Shōwa seijishi kenkyū e no ichi shikaku" 昭和政治史研究への一視角 (A perspective on the study of political history of the Shōwa period), *Shisō* (June 1976), no. 624, pp. 949–62.

43. Kindai Nihon Kenkyūkai 近代日本研究会, eds., *Kindai Nihon kenkyū nenpō* 近代日本研究年報 (Journal of modern Japanese studies), vol. 1 (Yamakawa Shuppansha, 1979; 9 vols. published so far.)

44. Gordon M. Berger, "Shōwashi kenkyū josetsu: Atarashii hikakushiteki hōhō o motomete" 昭和史研究序説—新しい比較史的方法を求めて (Introduction to the study of Shōwa history: In search of a new method of comparative history), *Shisō* (June 1976), no. 624, pp. 198–214.

45. A representative criticism of Itō's work is Awaya Kentaō 粟屋憲太郎, "Shohyō: Itō Takashi, *Shōwaki no seiji*" 書評・伊藤隆『昭和期の政治』 (A review of Itō Takashi, *Shōwaki no seiji*), *Shigaku zasshi* (December 1985), 94(12):57–66.

46. Fujiwara Akira 藤原彰 et al., eds., *Shōwa no rekishi* 昭和の歴史, 11 vols. (Shōgakkan, 1982–83).

47. Kinbara Samon and Takemae Eiji 金原左門, 竹前栄治, *Shōwashi* (Yūhikaku, 1983).

48. Eguchi Keiichi et al., eds., *Taikei Nihon gendaishi* 大系日本現代史 (Series on contemporary Japanese history), 5 vols. (Nihon Hyōronsha, 1979).

49. Ienaga Saburō 家永三郎, *Taiheiyō sensō* 太平洋戦争 (Iwanami Shoten, 1968).

50. Itō Takashi 伊藤隆, *15-nen sensō* 十五年戦争, vol. 30 of *Nihon no rekishi* 日本の歴史 (Shōgakkan, 1976).
51. Usui Katsumi 臼井勝美, "Taiheiyō sensō nōto" 太平洋戦争ノート (A note on the Pacific War), in Usui, *Chūgoku o meguru kindai Nihon no gaikō* 中国をめぐる近代日本の外交 (Modern Japanese diplomacy toward China), pp. 3–22 (Chikuma Shobō, 1983).
52. Miyake Masaki 三宅正樹, ed., *Shōwashi no gunbu to seiji* 昭和史の軍部と政治, 5 vols. (Daiichi Hōki, 1983). See also Miyake, "Seigun kankei no shiten kara mita 1930-nendai no Nihon" 政軍関係の視点からみた1930年代の日本 (Japan in the 1930s as reexamined from the viewpoint of civil-military relations), in Miwa, ed., *Saikō: Taiheiyō sensō zen'ya,* pp. 44–86.

NOTES ON BASIC SOURCES

Hatano Sumio
Asada Sadao

Two important source materials deserve immediate notice: *Shōwashi no tennō* (The Emperor in the history of the Shōwa period), published in thirty volumes in 1967–76,[1] and *Gendaishi shiryō* (Documents on contemporary history).[2]

Shōwashi no Tennō

This project, undertaken by the staff of the *Yomiuri* newspaper, is journalistic in conception and style, but the series contains a vast body of detailed information of great value to the contemporary historian. The work is based on extensive interviews with approximately 10,000 individuals who were involved in important political and diplomatic events from 1935 to 1945. This is the product of the first systematic oral history project undertaken in Japan.

The series is not in chronological order and is not always easy to use. We shall, therefore, list the volumes that are specially relevant to the diplomatic historian.

Vol. 1: The peace maneuvers of the former prime ministers in 1945; the last of Japanese attempts at "peace maneuvers" with Chungking; the formation of the Suzuki cabinet in April 1945.

Vol. 2: Peace negotiations through the Soviet Union; the abortive plan to send Konoe on a special mission to Moscow; the secret peace efforts in Europe (contacts with Allen W. Dulles and peace maneuvers through Sweden (1945).

Vol. 3: The Potsdam Conference; the Potsdam Declaration and the Emperor system; Prime Minister Suzuki's attitude toward the declaration.

Vol. 4: The impact of the A-bombs.

Vol. 5: The Soviet entry into the Pacific War; the last days of the Kwantung Army; the disintegration of Manchukuo.

Vol. 6: The liquidation of the management of Manchukuo; the end of the war in Sakhalin (1945).

Vol. 7: The Emperor's decision to end the war; the Suzuki cabinet's attitude; the positions taken by the navy, the army, and the Foreign Ministry (1945).

Vols. 8–11 and 13–14: Japan's military administration in Southeast Asia and the fate of Japan's puppet regimes in Burma, India, the Philippines, and Nanking at the time of Japan's surrender.

Vol. 15: The Japanese military's invasion of China, culminating in the Marco Polo Bridge incident (1937).

Vol. 16: The Japanese army and the Sino-Japanese War; total national mobilization for the war.

Vol. 17: The Cabinet Research Bureau; the Cabinet Planning Board.

Vol. 18: Developments leading up to the Anti-Comintern Pact (1936).

Vol. 20: The conclusion of the Anti-Comintern Pact (1936).

Vol. 21: Efforts to strengthen the Anti-Comintern Pact; deliberations at the Five-Minister Conferences (over hypothetical enemies and the conditions under which Japan would be obliged to enter war) (1937–38).

Vol. 22: The army's initiative for a Tripartite Pact; the role of Ambassadors Ōshima and Shiratori; Prime Minister Hiranuma's reluctance to conclude a military alliance with Germany and Italy (1938–39).

Vol. 23: The question of Japan's obligation to enter the war under the proposed pact and the Emperor's misgivings (1939).

Vol. 24: Germany's compromise (Friedrich Gaus) plans in 1939; army-navy differences over the proposed Tripartite Pact.

Vol. 25: The navy's continued opposition to the army's plan for a Tripartite Pact; the Tientsin incident; the Nomonhan Incident (1939).

Vols. 26–29: The Nomonhan Incident.

Vol. 30: The conclusion of the Tripartite Pact (1940) and the Japan-USSR Neutrality Pact (1941); the Japanese-American negotiations in 1941.

The success of the *Shōwashi no Tennō* series proved to be a great impetus to oral history projects at various universities. (For the results of oral history projects conducted by academics, see chapter 1.)

Gendaishi Shiryō

The *Gendaishi shiryō* series, published by Misuzu Shobō, is a collection of basic source materials on the military, diplomatic, and political history of the Taishō and Shōwa periods. Each volume is accompanied by a detailed introductory essay and annotations, which give essential background information and helpful explanations of documents. Listed below are the volumes most relevant for our purposes.

Vol. 7: *Manshū jihen* (The Manchurian Incident).[3]
> Edited with an introduction by Kobayashi Tatsuo and Shimada Toshihiko. The London Naval Conference of 1930 and the Manchurian Incident. The latter subject is traced up to the conclusion of the Tangku truce. Especially valuable is "Manshū jihen kimitsu seiryaku nisshi" (A secret war diary of the Manchurian Incident) recorded by the General Staff of the Kwantung Army.[4]

Vol. 8: *Nitchū sensō, 1* (The Sino-Japanese War, 1).[5]
> Edited with an introduction by Shimada Toshihiko and Inaba Masao. Japan's China policy up to the Marco Polo Bridge incident; Japanese activities in Mongolia; the Sian Incident of 1936; the defense and economic development of Manchukuo; and Ishiwara Kanji's idea of preparing for the coming war.

Vol. 9: *Nitchū sensō, 2* (The Sino-Japanese War, 2).[6]
> Edited with an introduction by Usui Katsumi and Inaba Masao. Japan's military operations in and policy toward China following the Marco Polo Bridge incident, and Ishiwara Kanji's defense strategy against the Soviet Union.

Vol. 10: *Nitchū sensō, 3* (The Sino-Japanese War, 3).[7]
> Edited with an introduction by Tsunoda Jun. The Chankufeng incident of 1938; the Nomonhan Incident; Japan's advance into northern and southern French Indochina; and the question in 1938 of strengthening the Anti-Comintern Pact.

Vol. 11: *Zoku Manshū jihen* (Sequel volume on the Manchurian Incident).[8]
> Edited with an introduction by Kobayashi Tatsuo, Shimada Toshihiko, and Inaba Masao. The London Naval Conference of 1930 and the Manchurian Incident (the major portion of the materials pertaining to the creation of Manchukuo).

Vol. 12: *Nitchū sensō, 4* (The Sino-Japanese War, 4).[9]
   Edited with an introduction by Kobayashi Tatsuo, Inaba Masao, Shimada Toshihiko, and Usui Katsumi. The London Naval Conference of 1935; Japan's activities in Inner Mongolia; the Sian Incident; and developments following the Macro Polo Bridge Incident.
Vol. 13: *Nitchū sensō, 5* (The Sino-Japanese War, 5).[10]
   Edited with an introduction by Usui Katsumi. The Wang Ching-wei regime and the Japanese blockade of the British and French concessions in Tientsin (1939).
Vol. 38: *Taiheiyō sensō, 4* (The Pacific War, 4).[11]
   Edited with an introduction by Usui Katsumi. Military operations in China and the Supreme Command in the early phase of the Pacific War.

Next, we shall simply list volumes that are useful for studying interrelationships between foreign policy and domestic politics, the economy and public opinion.

Vols. 1–3: *Zoruge jiken,* 1–3 (The Sorge case, 1–3).[12]
   Edited with an introduction by Obi Toshito.
Vol. 42: *Zoruge jiken, 4* (The Sorge case, 4).[13]
   Edited with an introduction by Ishidō Kiyotomo.
Vols. 4–5: *Kokkashugi undō, 1, 2* (Nationalist movements).[14]
   Edited with an introduction by Imai Seiichi and Takahashi Masae.
Vol. 17: *Kokkashugi undō, 3* (Nationalist movements).
   Edited with an introduction by Takahashi Masae.
Vol. 41: *Masu media tōsei* (Control of the mass media).[15]
   Edited with an introduction by Uchikawa Yoshimi.
Vol. 43: *Kokka sōdōin. 1* [Seiji] (Total national mobilization [Politics], 1).[16]
   Edited with an introduction by Nakamura Takafusa and Hara Akira.
Vol. 44: *Kokka sōdōin, 2* [Keizai] (Total national mobilization [The economy], 2.[17] Edited with an introduction by Imai Seiichi and Itō Takashi.

Japan's colonial rule in Taiwan and Korea and the anti-Japanese movements for national independence during the 1920s and the early 1930s are treated in the following volumes:

Vols. 21–22: *Taiwan, 1, 2.*
   Edited with an introduction by Yamabe Kentarō.[18]
Vols. 25–30: *Chōsen, 1–4.*
   Edited with an introduction by Kan Dok-san (Kyo Toku-sō).[19]

Takahashi Masae, ed., *Bekkan: Sakuin* (Supplementary volume: Index)[20] contains the tables of contents of all forty-five volumes, a chronologically arranged catalogue of all the documents contained in the series, and an index of names.

Military Records

Most of the materials on the Manchurian Incident and Sino-Japanese War, contained in the above-listed volumes of the *Gendaishi shiryō* series, were printed from the army and navy records in the custody of the War History Department, the Defense Agency.[21]

For the crucial period from late 1940 on, the important collection is Sanbō Honbu (Army General Staff), ed., *Sugiyama memo* (The memoranda of General Sugiyama Hajime),[22] which emanates from the same sources. General Sugiyama Hajime, appointed chief of the Army General Staff in October 1940, personally took detailed minutes of deliberations at the Imperial Headquarters–Cabinet Liaison Conferences, the Imperial Conferences, and the Supreme War Council. *Sugiyama memo*, which prints his minutes together with documents on important national policies and decisions, is an essential collection that allows the historian to trace the decision-making process in the highest council of the state. Its first volume covers the period up to December 1941. The second volume, devoted to the conduct of war, ends in February 1944, when he resigned. The sequel to *Sugiyama memo* is Sanbō Honbu, ed., *Haisen no kiroku* (The record of defeat).[23] This volume, however, does not contain the record of policy deliberations (after Sugiyama's departure from office, the practice of keeping conference minutes disappeared). Together, the three-volume series constitute a basic collection of official documents on the nation's policy and strategy during the Konoe (1941), Tōjō (1941–44), Koiso-Yonai (1944), and Suzuki (1945) cabinets. The series contain detailed introductory essays by Inaba Masao.

The proceedings of the Liaison Conferences and Imperial Conferences have been selectively translated by Nobutake Ike as *Japan's Decision for War: Records of the 1941 Policy Conferences* (Stanford University Press, 1967). Ike's introductory essay and commentaries are useful.

In addition, there is Tanemura Suketaka's *Daihon'ei kimitsu nisshi* (The confidential war diary of the imperial headquarters).[24] This is by no means an official record but takes the form of a private diary. The author, attached to the Army General Staff since 1939, based his account on an official journal (1940–45) of the War Guidance Section (directly responsible to the vice-chief of the Army General Staff). Entitled the "Confidential War Diary," the documents vividly reveal the often acrimonious interservice deliberations with the navy representatives before the war and discussions of basic strategy during the war, often delving into political matters. The documents are of special interest because they show the role and thinking of middle-grade officers who often took the initiative in major policymaking. Never published in its entirety, the original diary is deposited at the War Histroy Department, the Defense Agency (see chapter 1).

A single-volume collection of major documents is: *Teiheiyō sensō e no michi: Bekkan—shiryōhen* (The road to the Pacific War: Supplementary volume—documents),[25] edited with an introduction by Inaba Masao, Kobayashi Tatsuo, Shimada Toshihiko, and Tsunoda Jun. This volume is a compilation of crucial military and diplomatic documents covering the years from 1930 through 1941. They were collected from the army and navy records at the War History Department, the defense Agency, as well as from various places such as the Ministry of Justice, Shiryō Chōsakai (Historical Materials Research Society), and Yōmei Bunko (the Konoe family papers in Kyoto).

We shall next mention some of the more important private diaries. The publication of the *Gendaishi shiryō* series has been renewed as *Zoku-Gendaishi shiryō* (Sequel: Documents on contemporary history), and its fourth volume is titled *Rikugun* (The army),[26] edited with an introduction by Itō Takashi and Terunuma Yasutaka. This volume consists of the detailed diary of General Hata Shunroku from 1929 to 1945. The most important portion for our purposes is the entries from late 1938 to late 1944, the period when Hara served as army minister, chief aide-de-camp to the Emperor, and commander in chief of the China Expeditionary Force.

At the time of this writing, General Mazaki Jinzaburō's personal papers and diaries are being printed in the new series *Kindai Nihon shiryō sensho* (Selected documents on modern Japanese history), published by Yamakawa Shuppansha. *Mazaki Jinzaburō nikki* (The dairy of Mazaki Jinzaburō), consists of six volumes,[27] which cover the years 1932–1947, and is edited with an introduction by Itō Takashi and Sasaki Takashi et al.

Another major diary published in the same series is Itō, et al., eds., *Honjō Shigeru nikki* (The diary of Honjō Shigeru), in five projected volumes spanning the years 1925–1945.[28] Two volumes (1925–33) have appeared to date. A portion of the diary, covering the period of the Manchurian crisis and the years of Honjō's service as the chief aide-de-camp to the Emperor (July 1931 to March 1936), had been previously published as *Honjō nikki* (The Honjō diary) by Hara Shobō in 1967. About one-third of the diary, covering the years 1933–36, has been expertly translated with an introduction by Mikiso Hane as *Emperor Hirohito and His Chief Aide-de-Camp: The Honjō Diary* (University of Tokyo Press, 1983). The three-volume *Ugaki Kazushige nikki* (the diary of Ugaki Kazushige),[29] published in 1968–1971, fully covers the period from 1902 to 1949 and replaces an earlier (1954) abridged edition *(Ugaki nikki)*.

Naval Sources

Published source materials on the Japanese navy are comparatively few in number. One large collection of official documents, deposited at Daitō Bunka Daigaku, is the record of the Navy Ministry's Research Section from 1934 to 1945—headed intermittently by Rear Admiral Takagi Sōkichi. They are being published as Doi Akira et al., eds., *Shōwa shakai keizai shiryō shūsei: Kaigunshō shiryō* (Collections of sources on the social and economic history of the Shōwa period: Documents of the Navy Ministry).[30] Of the scheduled twenty volumes, twelve have been published to date, covering up to April 1941. The important topics covered are: the development of the navy's plans for southward advance; Japan's perception of and response to the outbreak and development of World War II in Europe; and the navy's attitude toward the Tripartite Pact.

Another official record is the Navy Minister's Secretariat, ed., *Kaigun kankei giji sokkiroku* (The transcripts of Diet proceedings related to naval matters),[31] recently reprinted in ten volumes. These volumes, edited by the Navy Ministry, contain the deliberations on matters relating to the navy at the Imperial Diet (including subcommittees). However, they do not include the transcripts of secret meetings.

Turning to private sources, Okada Sadanori, ed., *Okada Keisuke kaikoroku: Fu Rondon gunshuku mondai nikki* (Memoirs of Okada Kisuke,

with his diary concerning the London Naval Treaty)[32] not only reprints the memoirs (originally published in 1950) but contains his
hitherto unpublished diary which covers the eventful years of the
London Naval Conference of 1930 and its aftermath. The volume is
accompanied by an excellent introductory essay by Ikeda Kiyoshi.

Takagi Sōkichi and Sanematsu Yuzuru, eds., *Kaigun taishō Yonai
Mitsumasa oboegaki* (The memoranda of Admiral Yonai Mitsumasa)[33]
highlights Navy Minister Yonai's attempt to gain an early surrender.
The role of Rear Admiral Takagi who secretly assisted Yonai is revealed in his *Takagi kaigun shōshō oboegaki* (The memoranda of Rear
Admiral Takagi Sōkichi),[34] a volume carefully annotated by Takagi
himself on the basis of his diary. Only a small portion of Takagi's
diary has been published,[35] and there is a plan to publish a main portion of Takagi's papers together with his complete diary (1936–45).

Also scheduled for publication in the *Zoku-Gendaishi shiryō* series in
the near future is *Katō Kanji kankei bunsho* (Papers relating to Admiral
Katō Kanji), under the editorship of Itō Takashi;[36] it should add much
new information on the moves of the so-called Fleet faction, which
was opposed to the treaties of naval limitation.

In addition, the previously mentioned series *Kindai Nihon shiryō
sensho* includes the diary of Rear Admiral Jō Eiichirō, who was a naval
aide-de-camp to the Emperor during 1940–44,[37] and *Kaigun Taishō
Kobayashi Seizō oboegaki* (The memoranda of Admiral Kobayashi
Seizō).[38] Scheduled for publication in the near future are: the diaries
of Admiral Sawamoto Yorio[39] and those of Rear Admiral Ishikawa
Shingo,[40] an ardent follower of Katō Kanji.

Other Sources

The compilation and publication of the diplomatic papers preserved at
the Diplomatic Record Office of the Foreign Ministry is progressing
slowly. It has finally reached the Shōwa period. Diplomatic documents relating to the Manchurian Incident and the Geneva and
London Naval Conferences have also been published. (For a detailed
treatment, see chapter 1.)

The most complete diary of a diplomat published to date is Amō
Daihei et al., ed., *Amō Eiji nikki, shiryōshū* (The diary of Amō Eiji and
related materials).[41] Five volumes are scheduled for publication to

cover the long time span from 1906 to 1948. To date, the first volume (1906–26) and the fourth volume (1941–45, when Amō was vice–foreign minister and the head of the cabinet's Information Bureau) have appeared.

The memoirs that Shigemitsu Mamoru wrote from 1938 to 1950 have been recently discovered. During these years he served as ambassador to Britain (1938–41) and China (1941–42), became foreign minister (1942–45), and was imprisoned at Sugamo as a war criminal (1945–50). Containing many memoranda and diary entries, *Shigemitsu Mamoru shuki*, published in 1987, is an important primary source.[42]

Finally, students of the political and diplomatic history of the Shōwa period cannot afford to ignore two famous diaries: One is Kido Nikki Kenkyūkai, ed., *Kido Kōichi nikki* (The diary of Kido Kōichi);[43] and the other is Harada Kumao, *Saionjikō to seikyoku* (Prince Saionji and politics).[44] The latter volumes are popularly known as "Harada nikki" (The Harada diary).

The Kido diary was written by Kido Kōichi, who was close to the Emperor and successively held various posts including Lord Keeper of the Privy Seal. From 1930 through 1945 he daily kept a diary. This diary had been partly diclosed and hastily translated into English for use by the International Military Tribunal for the Far East. In 1966 Kido's diary was published in its entirety in two well-edited volumes accompanied by a useful introductory essay by Oka Yoshitake. The first volume covers the years 1930–37, and the second volume contains entries until December 15, 1945. The sequel volume, subtitled *Tokyo saibanki* (The period of Tokyo war crimes trials),[45] was subsequently published in 1980; it contains his diary from December 15, 1945 (when he was imprisoned) to the end of 1948, with related materials—Kido's draft testimonies for the trials and record of his conversations (in the form of oral history) regarding the termination of the Pacific War and the Tokyo trials. In addition, the same study group that edited the Kido diary has also compiled *Kido Kōichi kankei bunsho* (Papers relating to Kido Kōichi).[46] It consists of three parts: Kido's own memoirs on his efforts to prevent the Pacific War and subsequently to terminate it; "documents," including official papers and written opinions sent to Kido; and letters, mostly incoming.

Perhaps even more valuable to the specialist in contemporary history is the "Harada diary," which was faithfully kept by Harada

Kumao, secretary to the last *'genrō,'* Prince Saionji Kinmochi. Serving as Saionji's political "antenna" with an almost uncanny ability to collect information, the ever-energetic Harada reported to Saionji what he had seen and heard in Japanese political circles—from prime ministers, various civilian ministers, and the army and the navy—during these years, dictating his reports in detail in the form of a diary. When compared with the Kido diary, the "Harada diary" is naturally richer in content, sometimes reproducing Harada-Saionji conversations verbatim, and it remains a veritable mine of information for historians. Only a small portion of the diary was translated, and that hurriedly, for the Tokyo trials. Recently, Thomas F. Mayer-Oakes has translated the parts relating to the London Naval Conference as *Fragile Victory: Prince Saionji and the 1930 Treaty Issue* (Detroit: Wayne State University Press, 1968).

Full as it is as a source material, the "Harada diary" perhaps requires some scrutiny by historians as to the veracity of the lengthy accounts it contains in the light of "primary" documents now available. Yet no Japanese scholar has made such an attempt. The best—and most absorbing—account of the intimate relations between Prince Saionji, Marquis Kido, Prince Konoe, and Baron Harada in the context of contemporary history is a nonfiction treatment by Harada's son-in-law, Shōda Tatsuo, *Jūshin tachi no Shōwashi* (A history of the Shōwa period as shaped by senior statesmen).[47]

Important materials that supplement the Kido diary and the Harada diary are, among others, the following personal accounts: *Ogawa Heikichi kankei bunsho* (Papers relating to Ogawa Heikichi);[48] *Ōkura Kinmochi nikki* (The diary of Ōkura Kinmochi);[49] *Yabe Teiji nikki* (The diary of Yabe Teiji);[50] and *Hosokawa nikki* (The diary of Hosokawa Morisada).[51]

IMTFE Documents

Thus far we have not mentioned the huge body of material that was accumulated by the International Military Tribunal for the Far East (IMTFE). From May 1946 to November 1948, when the Tokyo war crimes trials were held, both the prosecution and defense staffs gathered numerous exhibits and witnesses, presenting them as evidence. Materials that were admitted as evidence are contained in the transcript of the IMTFE proceedings. The official version of the transcript was in English, and its Japanese translation has been published by Gannandō as *Kyokutō kokusai gunji saiban sokkiroku* (Japanese Record of Proceedings of the International Military Tribunal for the Far East).[52]

The first to collect IMTFE materials, including documents that were not presented to the court or rejected, was Asahi Shimbunsha. Its intensive efforts during 1947–1950 resulted in the publication in 1953 of *Kyokutō kokusai gunji saiban kiroku, mokuroku oyobi sakuin* (The record of the International Military Tribunal for the Far East, with a catalogue and indices).[53]

The most complete and useful version is R. John Pritchard and Sonia M. Zaide, eds., *Tokyo War Crimes Trial* (New York and London: Garland Publishing, 1981; 22 vols. and a 5 volume index and guide). This English-language version is more helpful than the earlier Asahi Shimbun and Gannandō editions, for the Pritchard and Zaide edition (vols. 1–2 of the guide) contains detailed name and subject indices including roughly 30,000 cross-listed headings and subheadings.

Except during the early 1950s, specialists in contemporary Japanese history have not exploited this rich mine of information. The main reason may be that the prevailing view of the Tokyo war crimes trial as "victors' justice" made Japanese historians reluctant to rely on the IMTFE materials. (On Japanese feelings about the Tokyo trials, see chapter 8.) Second, the publication of such primary sources as the *Gendaishi shiryō* series and access to various archives and personal papers seemingly made the IMTFE materials insignificant.

Third, the Japanese government which possesses exhibits and testimonies that were not presented or rejected, has not yet made the materials fully available to researchers. For example, the Ministry of Justice, which holds these documents, has taken an illiberal policy in this regard, although it did compile *Kyokutō kokusai gunji saiban shiryō mokuroku* (A catalogue of materials relating to the International Military Tribunal for the Far East) in 1971.[54] The Supreme Court Library, which holds some materials not presented at the Tokyo war crimes trials, is exceptional in allowing the researcher to peruse them; this library has catalogues in Japanese as well as in English.

Exhibits and testimonies not presented to the court have also been kept by individual defense lawyers. One of them donated his set of materials to Shakai Kagaku Kenkyūjō (the Social Science Research Institute) of the University of Tokyo. With this as the core, the institute has built an extensive collection of evidence and defense materials that cannot be found elsewhere. They are open to researchers, and a catalogue of materials at the institute was prepared in 1971–72,[55] although it is not as detailed as that prepared by the Asahi Shimbunsha.

The IMTFE materials, we feel, have been slighted by Japanese scholars in recent years, and careful research into them with the use of new guides, such as Pritchard and Zaide, will fill in gaps in government documents.

War History Series

Frequent mention has been made to the *Senshi sōsho* (War History) series of the Defense Agency throughout this book. Although this series (102 vols.) cannot be regarded as source materials as such, it is replete with factual information not available elsewhere, liberally quoting from the army and navy records with a modicum of interpretation. Given the difficulty in gaining full access to the military archives at the War History Department (see chapter 1), the diplomatic historian must often use this series as the only available source material. Because of the nature of this series and the time span it covers, this chapter is a logical place to discuss the volumes that are specially relevant for our purposes.

The War History Office (the predecessor of the War History Department) devoted its first ten years (beginning in 1956) to collecting source materials, and it began publishing the results in 1965. The *Senshi sōsho* (War History) series is the "official" history of the Pacific War written by former army or navy officers (unlike the practice in the West, where academic historians are involved or consulted). Whether consciously or not, therefore, service viewpoints (especially those of staff officers) pervade these volumes. Footnotes (or, more accurately, endnotes) are often awkwardly arranged, and their citations of sources are too brief to be convenient for scholars.

The volumes were not published in chronological or any other meaningful order, so that it is not always easy for a researcher to find the specific volume he or she needs. Therefore, these volumes have been divided into several categories to give a clearer picture of the series as a whole and to indicate which volumes are important for our purposes. For this reason the convenient categories devised by Morimatsue Toshio in his contribution to *Revue Internationale d'Histoire Militaire*, (Tokyo: Commission Japan d'Histoire Militaire, 1978, No. 38, pp. 93–105) have been used. Numbers in parentheses before the titles indicate the general volume numbers, and those that follow are serial numbers for volumes within a group.

[I] The Road to War (Political Affairs) Series. *Daihon'ei rikugunbu: Dai Tōa sensō kaisen keii* (The Imperial Headquarters, army: Circumstances leading to the outbreak of the Greater East Asian War). 5 vols. Asagumo Shinbunsha, 1973–74.[56]

> This series treats Japan's political and military strategies from the outbreak of the European war in 1939 to Japan's commencement of hostilities in December 1941 from the viewpoint of the Army General Staff. The first volume is of special interest to diplomatic historians.
>
> (65) *Daihon'ei rikugunbu: Dai Toa sensō kaisen keii* (vol. 1) (The imperial headquarters, army: Circumstances leading to the outbreak of the Greater East Asian War). September 1933–August 1940. The foreign policy of the Yonai cabinet, especially its efforts to settle the Sino-Japanese War, and political maneuvers at the time of the formation of the second Konoe cabinet.
>
> (68) *Daihon'ei rikugunbu: Dai Tōa sensō kaisen keii* (vol. 2). July–September 1940. The Japanese army's advance into northern Indochina; the conclusion of the Tripartite Pact; and the Dutch-Japanese negotiations.
>
> (69) *Daihon'ei rikugunbu: Dai Tōa sensō kaisen keii* (vol. 3). June 1940–June 1941. Protracted battles in China; Japan's policies toward French Indochina and Thailand; the army's and navy's preparations for operations in Southeast Asia; the conclusion of the Neutrality Pact with the Soviet Union; and the opening of the Japanese-American negotiations.
>
> (70) *Daihon'ei rikugunbu: Dai Tōa sensō kaisen keii* (vol. 4). October 1940–September 1941. The collapse of the Dutch-Japanese negotiations; Japan's advance into southern Indochina; the determination for war with the United States, Britain, and the Netherlands.
>
> (76) *Daihon'ei rikugunbu: Dai Tōa sensō kaisen keii* (vol. 5). September 1941 to the outbreak of the Pacific War. The latter phase of the

Japanese-American negotiations; the Tōjō cabinet's reexamination of national policy; the acceleration of preparations and war planning; and the final decision to open hostilities.

(100) *Daihon'ei kaigunbu: Dai Tōa sensō kaisen keii* (vol. 1) (The imperial headquarters, navy: Circumstances leading to the outbreak of the Greater East Asian War). The first chapter is devoted to a discussion of the traditional naval "mentality" which the author compares with the army's. He goes back to the Manchurian Incident and stresses differences between the army and navy. Interservice clashing was also apparent in coping with the China war. This volume carries the story down to the end of 1939.

(101) *Daihon'ei kaigunbu: Dai Tōa sensō kaisen keii* (vol. 2). Starting with January 1940, the volume covers such topics as: the outbreak of the European war and the question of Japan's southward expansion; negotiations for the Tripartite Pact; advance into southern Indochina and its international impact; the failure of "Japanese-American negotiations"; and war preparation.[57]

These volumes describe Japan's political and naval strategies from the viewpoint of the Navy General Staff. The fact that the army *and* the navy versions were separately compiled is in itself revealing; prewar and wartime differences between the two services are reflected in their historical treatment of the road to war.

[II] The Imperial Headquarters, Army series. *Daihon'ei rikugunbu* (The imperial headquarters, army). 10 vols.[58]

This series describes the development of the army's policy for national defense and strategy; it presents, from the standpoint of the high command, overviews of major wars and "incidents" Japan fought; and explains its relationship with the army. We shall mention only the most relevant volumes.

(8) *Daihon'ei rikugunbu* 1: *Shōwa 15-nen 5-gatsu made* (up to May 1940). A condensed but well-documented survey beginning with the establishment of the Army Ministry (1872), this is a useful history of the army's policies of national defense, strategy, and the military system. Particularly valuable for compact treatments of the Russo-Japanese War and after, the Manchurian Incident, and—most importantly—the escalation of the Sino-Japanese War. Extremely useful to the diplomatic historian.

(20) *Daihon'ei rikugunbu 2: Shōwa 16-nen 12-gatsu made* (up to December 1941). Covering the period since September 1939 from the viewpoint of the army supreme command, this volume describes in detail the army's policy and strategy of advancing southward; efforts to settle the war in China; preparations and war planning against Britain, the Netherlands, and the United States; policy and strategy toward the Soviet Union; and decision to invade Southeast Asia; and the determination for war.

[III] The Imperial Headquarters, Navy Series. *Daihon'ei kaigunbu, Rengō kantai* (The imperial headquarters, navy: The Combined Fleet). 7 vols.[59]

This series describes the history of the Japanese navy from its establishment to Pearl Harbor and then gives detailed narratives of political and strategic guidelines of the Navy General Staff for the Combined Fleet during the Pacific War.

(91) *Daihon'ei kaigunbu, Rengō kantai* (1): *Kaisen made* (up to the outbreak of the war). This volume—authored by Nomura Minoru, a foremost naval historian—is by far the best single-volume history of the imperial Japanese navy from the establishment of the Navy Ministry in 1872 to Japan's opening of hostilities in December 1941. From the viewpoint of the naval supreme command, it traces the changes in the organization of the system; the policies of naval defense, strategies, and tactics, and the treaties of naval limitation and Japan's with--drawal from them in 1936. The latter half of the book is devoted to the navy's policy on such issues as the Sino-Japanese War, the Tripartite Pact and cooperation with the German navy, Japan's southward advance, and the crucial oil question. The author skillfully describes the Japanese navy's preparations and war planning in the context of the an aggravated international situation, and explains the process through which the Japanese navy reached its "determination" for war with the United States, Britain, and the Netherlands. Massively documented, Nomura's work is one of the best to appear in the War History series (see chapters 3 and 6).

(80) *Daihon'ei kaigunbu, Rengō kantai* (2): *Shōwa 17-nen 6-gatsu made* (up to June 1942). Covering from November 1941, this volume describes the Japanese Navy's determination for war and the opening of the hostilities; discusses army-navy differences over the question of the early termination of war; and deals with the conduct of the war from Pearl Harbor to Midway.

[IV] Armaments and War Preparation Series. 13 vols.

This series examines the policy of and progress in armaments, war preparations, and the maintenance and expansion of the war potential of the
army, navy, and air force.

(9) *Rikugun gunju dōin* (1): *Keikakuhen* (The army's mobilization of munitions, vol. 1: Program).[60] This volume describes the army's system,
plans, and preparations for munitions mobilized during the period
1917–1937 . Rather technical in treatment.

(33) *Rikugun gunju dōin* (2): *Jisshihen* (The army's munitional mobilization,
vol. 2: Implementation).[61] This volume describes year by year the
actual condition of mobilization of munitions since 1937 and traces
the decline in Japan's war potential and national power until 1945.

(99) *Rikugun gunsenbi* (The army's armaments and preparations for war).[62]
This volume compactly describes the development of the army's system of war preparations and traces armaments policy from the establishment of the Japanese army to the end of the Pacific War. It covers
all of the major wars Japan fought, with special emphasis on the
period after 1937.

(31) *Kaigun gunsenbi* (1): *Shōwa 16-nen 11-gatsu made* (Naval armaments
and preparations for war, vol. 1: Up to November 1941).[63] Authored
by the foremost expert Suekuni Masao, this authoritative volume
broadly traces the growth of the Japanese navy from 1905 to the eve
of Pearl Harbor. It describes the system of deciding the size of armaments and how it worked in practice; the history of strategic and
tactical ideas; developments in weaponry; budgetary considerations;
and the training of officers and men. The latter half of the book treats
in great detail the navy's efforts, after it withdrew from the naval
treaties, to accelerate preparations against the United States. This is
one of the most distinguished and useful volumes in the *Senshi* series.

(88) *Kaigun gunsenbi* (2): *Kaisen igo* (Naval armaments and preparations,
vol. 2: After the outbreak of the war).[64] This volume describes the
deteriorating condition of armaments—ships and aircraft—during
the war. It shows how the navy's armaments policy changed more
than once. The book also deals with such subjects as "special air
attacks" (*kamikaze* attacks), the training of officers, recruitment, and
the fuel problem.

[V] Advance operations Series. 9 vols.

The volumes in this series describe advance operations by the army, the
navy, and the air force in the initial period of the Pacific War (December
1941–June 1942). Below, we shall list only the most relevant volumes.

(10) *Hawai sakusen* (Naval attack against Hawaii).[65] This volume, perhaps the most interesting in the whole series, describes in detail the inception and development of the surprise attack idea; discusses how Admiral Yamamoto Isoroku forced the Navy General Staff to accept the bold plan; examines the careful planning and preparations; and ends with an estimate of the success of the "Hawaii operations."

(3) *Ran-In kōryaku sakusen* (Occupation of the Dutch East Indies).[66] Describes the guidance and conduct of operations of the 16th Army, which captured Borneo, southern Sumatra, and Java.

(5) *Biruma kōryaku sakusen* (Occupation of Burma).[67] Describes political and military strategies up to mid-1943, i.e., the capture of Burma, Sumatra, and the Andamans, and the Burmese independence movement.

[VI–XIII] Series that deal with strictly military and combat affairs of little interest to the diplomatic historian.

[XIV] Manchurian Theater Operations Series. 3 vols. The first two volumes of this series describe the Kwantung Army's preparations for war with the Soviet Union and involvements with the Soviets occasioned by border disputes.

(27) *Kantōgun* (1): *Tai-So senbi, Nomonhan jiken* (Kwantung Army, vol. 1: War preparations against USSR and the Nomonhan Incident).[68]

(73) *Kantōgun* (2): *Kan toku en, shūsenji no tai-So sen* (The Kwantung Army, vol. 2: Reinforcement of war preparations against USSR [in July 1941]; Operations against the Soviet forces immediately before the end of the war).[69]

[XV] China Theater Operations Series. 15 vols.
This series contains the following two-volume work, which is of great interest to the diplomatic historian. It describes battles between Japan's North China Army and the Chinese Communist Party forces. The first volume treats the period from 1937 to November 1941; the second volume covers up to 1945.

(18, 50) *Hokushi no chiansen* (Pacification of Communist subversion in North China). 2 vols.[70]

The following three volumes describe mainly the Army Supreme Headquarters' political and military strategies and its guidance of operations in the Sino-Japanese War.

(86) *Shina jihen rikugun sakusen, 1: Shōwa 13-nen 1-gatsu made* (Army operations in the China Incident, vol. 1: Up to January (1938).[71]

(89) *Shina jihen rikugun sakusen, 2: Shōwa 14-nen 9-gatsu made* (Army operations in the China Incident, vol. 2: Up to September 1939).[72]

(90) *Shina jihen rikugun sakusen, 3: Shōwa 16-nen 12-gatsu made* (Army operations in the China Incident, vol. 3: Up to December 1941).[73]

Essential for an effective use of the massive *Senshi sōsho* series is *Riku-kaigun nenpyō fu heigo, yōgo no kaisetsu* (A war chronology of the Japanese army and navy, and a dictionary of military terminology),[74] which was painstakingly edited by Suekuni Masao as the last volume in this series. This chronology, covering the years 1937 to 1945, provides a most convenient cross-reference that guides the reader to the proper volumes and pages of the series for the particular information he needs.

Documents

After the War History Department completed its 102-volume *Senshi sōsho*, it began editing and publishing materials from its archival holdings. Two document collections were published in 1986.

Senshi sōsho shiryōshū: Nanpō no gunsei (War History series: Collected documents—[Japan's] military administration of the Southern Areas).[75]

This volume collects documents relating to Japan's military administration of various areas in Southeast Asia, especially from the viewpoint of acquiring strategic resources. It also contains a comprehensive catalogue of all the documents in the custody of the War History Department relating to military administration in the south.

Senshi sōsho shiryōshū: Kaigun nendo sakusen keikaku (War History series: Collected documents—The navy's annual operational plans (1936–1941).[76]

This volume reproduces, in facsimile form, the top-secret documents, the annual operational plans of the navy against hypothetical enemies during the most crucial period. These documents, which accidentally survived at the end of war, are for the first time collected in their entirety and carefully annotated.

Notes

1. *Shōwashi no Tennō* 昭和史の天皇 (The Emperor in the history of the Shōwa period), 30 vols. (Yomiuri Shinbunsha, 1969–76).
2. *Gendaishi shiryō* 現代史資料 (Documents on contemporary [Japanese] history), 45 vols. (Misuzu Shobō, 1962–74). For detailed descriptions of the volumes on the Manchurian Incident and the Sino-Japanese War, see Akira Iriye's review article, "Japan's Foreign Policies between World Wars: Sources and Interpretations," *Journal of Asian Studies* (August 1967), 26(4):677–82.
3. Kobayashi Tatsuo and Shimada Toshihiko 小林龍夫, 島田俊彦, eds., *Manshū jihen* 満州事変, Misuzu Shobō (1964).
4. "Manshū jihen kimitsu seiryaku nisshi" 満州事変機密政略日誌.
5. Shimada Toshihiko and Inaba Masao 稲葉正夫, eds., *Nitchū sensō, 1* 日中戦争, 1 (1964).
6. Usui Katsumi 臼井勝美 and Inaba Masao, eds., *Nitchū sensō, 2* 日中戦争 2 (1964).
7. Tsunoda Jun 角田順, ed., *Nitchū sensō, 3* (1964).
8. Kobayashi Tatsuo, Shimada Toshihiko, and Inaba Masao eds., *Zoku Manshū jihen* 続満州事変 (Sequel volume on the Manchurian Incident) (1965).
9. Kobayashi Tatsuo, Inaba Masao, Shimada Toshihiko, and Usui Katsumi, eds., *Nitchū sensō, 4* (1965).
10. Usui Katsumi, ed., *Nitchū sensō, 5* (1966).
11. Usui Katsumi, ed., *Taiheiyō sensō, 4* (1972).
12. Obi Toshito 小尾俊人, ed., *Zoruge jiken, 1–3* (1962).
13. Ishidō Kiyotomo 石堂清倫, ed., *Zoruge jiken, 4* (1971).
14. Imai Seiichi and Takahashi Masae, 今井清一, 高橋正衛, eds., *Kokkashugi undō, 1, 2* 国家主義運動 (1963–64); Takahashi Masae, ed., *Kokkashugi undō, 3* (1974).
15. Uchikawa Yoshimi 内川芳美, ed., *Masu media tōsei* マス・メディア統制 (1973–75).
16. Nakamura Takafusa and Hara Akira 中村隆英, 原朗, eds., *Kokka sōdōin, 1* 国家総動員 (1970).
17. Imai Seiichi and Itō Takashi 伊藤隆, eds., *Kokka sōdōin, 2* (1974).
18. Yamabe Kentarō 山辺健太郎, ed., *Taiwan* 台湾 (1971).
19. Kan Dok-san 姜徳相, ed., *Chōsen* 朝鮮 (1965–76).
20. Takahashi Masae, ed., *Bekkan: Sakuin* 別巻・索引 (1980).
21. For the holdings of the War History Department, see chapter 2.
22. Sanbō Honbu 参謀本部, ed., *Sugiyama memo* 杉山メモ, 2 vols. (with an introductory essay by Inaba Masao 稲葉正夫) (Hara Shobō, 1967).

23. Sanbō Honbu ed., *Haisen no kiroku* 敗戦の記録 (with an introductory essay by Inaba Masao) (Hara Shobō, 1979).
24. Tanemura Suketaka 種村佐孝, *Daihon'ei kimitsu nisshi* 大本営機密日誌 (Daiyamondosha, 1952); reprinted by Fuyō Shobō, 1985.
25. Inaba Masao, Kobayashi Tatsuo, Shimada Toshihiko, and Tsunoda Jun 稲葉正夫, 小林龍夫, 島田俊彦, 角田順, eds., Nihon Kokusai Seiji Grakkai *Taiheiyō sensō e no michi: Bekkan—Shiryōhen* 太平洋戦争への道 ―別巻資料篇 (Asahi Shimbunsha, 1963).
26. *Rikugun* 陸軍 (The army), vol. 4 of *Zoku-Gendaishi shiryō* 続現代史資料 (Misuzu Shobō, 1983).
27. *Mazaki Jinzaburō nikki* 真崎甚三郎日記, edited with an introduction by Itō Takashi and Sasaki Takashi 伊藤隆, 佐々木隆 et al. 6 vols. (Yamakawa Shuppansha, 1982–87).
28. *Honjō Shigeru nikki* 本庄繁日記, edited by Itō Takashi et al. 2 vols. to date (Yamakawa Shuppansha, 1982–).
29. *Ugaki Kazushige nikki* 宇垣一成日記, edited by Tsunoda Jun, 3 vols. (Misuzu Shobō, 1968–71).
30. Doi Akira 土井章 et al., eds., *Shōwa shakai keizai shiryō shūsei: Kaigunshō shiryō* 昭和社会経済史料集成―海軍省資料, 12 vols. to date (Daitō Bunka Daigaku Tōyō Kenkyūjo, 1978–).
31. Kaibun daijin kanbō 海軍大臣官房, ed., *Kaigun kankei giji sokkiroku* 海軍関係議事速記録, 10 vols. (Hara Shobo, 1984).
32. Okada Sadanori 岡田貞寛, ed., *Okada Keisuke kaikoroku: Fu Rondon gunshuku mondai nikki* 岡田啓介回顧録・付ロンドン軍縮問題日記 (with an introductory essay by Ikeda Kiyoshi 池田清) (Mainichi Shinbunsha, 1972).
33. Takagi Sōkichi and Sanematsu Yuzuru 高木惣吉, 実松譲, eds., *Kaigun taishō Yonai Mitsumasa oboegaki* 海軍大将米内光政覚え書 (Kōjinsha, 1978).
34. Takagi Sōkichi, *Takagi kaigun shōshō oboegaki* 高木海軍少将覚え書 (Mainichi Shinbunsha, 1979).
35. Tagaki Sōkichi, *Takagi Sōkichi nikki* 高木惣吉日記 (Mainichi Shinbunsha, 1985).
36. Itō Takashi 伊藤隆, ed., *Katō Kanji kankei bunsho* 加藤寛治関係文書, (scheduled to be published by Misuzu Shobō).
37. Nomura Minoru 野村実, ed., *Jō Eiichirō nikki* 城英一郎日記 in the Kindai Nihon shiryō series (Yamakawa Shuppan, 1982).
38. Itō Takashi and Nomura Minoru, eds., *Kaigun Taishō Kobayashi Seizō oboegaki* 海軍大将小林躋造覚書 (Yamakawa Shuppan, 1981).
39. Sawamoto Yorio 沢本頼雄.
40. Ishikawa Shingo 石川信吾.

41. Amō Eiji Nikki, Shiryōshū Kankōkai 天羽英二日記, 資料集刊行会, ed., *Amō Eiji nikki, shiryōshu* 天羽英二日記, 資料, 2 vols. to date (Published by the editor, 1982).
42. Itō Takashi and Watanabe Yukio 伊藤隆, 渡辺行男 eds., *Shigemitsu Mamoru shuki* 重光葵手記 (Chūō Kōronsha, 1987).
43. Kido Kōichi Kenkyūkai 木戸幸一研究会, ed., *Kido Kōichi nikki* 木戸幸一日記, 2 vols. (Tokyo Daigaku Shuppankai, 1966). Aside from Oka's superb introductory essay, see a more intimate and informal account by Shōda Tatsuo 勝田龍夫 on "Kido Kōichi: A Hidden Witness," *Shokun* (June 1977), pp. 186–94.
44. Harada Kumao 原田熊雄, 西園寺公と政局 (Prince Saionji and politics), 8 vols. and 1 supp. (Iwanami Shoten, 1950–52, 1956); reprinted 1967.
45. Kido Kōichi Kenkyūkai, ed., *Kido Kōichi nikki: Tokyo saibanki* 木戸幸一日記—東京裁判期 (The diary of Kido Kōichi: The period of the Tokyo trials) (Tokyo Daigaku Shuppankai, 1980).
46. *Kido Kōichi kankei bunsho,* 木戸幸一関係文書 (Tokyo Daigaku Shuppankai, 1980).
47. Shōda Tatsuo 勝田龍夫, *Jūshin tachi no Shōwashi* 重臣たちの昭和史, 2 vols. (Bungei Shunjū, 1981).
48. Oka Yoshitake 岡義武 et al., ed., *Ogawa Heikichi kankei bunsho* 小川平吉関係文書, 2 vols. (Misuzu Shobō, 1973). (Ogawa was a politician belonging to the Seiyūkai.) These volumes contain his diary (1889–1941) in addition to his memoirs and letters.
49. Naiseishi Kenkyūkai 内政史研究会 and Nihon Kindai Shiryō Kenkyūkai 日本近代史料研究会, ed., *Ōkura Kinmochi nikki* 大蔵公望日記, 4 vols. (1973; not for general sale). (Ōkura was a politician who was known as a brain for Ugaki.) The diary covers the period 1932–1945.
50. Yabe Teiji Nikki Kankō Kai 矢部貞治日記刊行会, ed., *Yabe Teiji nikki* 矢部貞治日記, 4 vols. (Yomiuri Shinbunsha, 1974–75). Yabe, a professor of Tokyo Imperial University, was deeply involved in politics. The first volume (1937–45) is useful.
51. Hosokawa Morisada 細川護貞, *Jōhō Tennō ni tassezu: Hosokawa nikki* 情報天皇に達せず—細川日記 (Information that failed to reach the Emperor: Hosokawa diary), 2 vols. (Dōkōsha Isobe Shobō, 1953). Contains his diary during 1943–45 when he actively served as a brain for Prince Takamatsu.
52. *Kyōkutō kokusai gunji saiban sokkiroku* 極東国際軍事裁判速記録, 10 vols. (Gannandō, 1968).
53. Asahi Shimbun Chōsa Kenkyū Shitsu 朝日新聞調査研究室, ed., *Kyokutō kokusai gunji saiban kiroku, mokuroku oyobi sakuin* 極東国際軍事裁判記録, 目録及び索引 (Asahi Shimbunsha, privately printed in 1953).
54. Hōmu Daijin Kanbō Shihō Hōsei Chōsabu 法務大臣官房司法法制調

査部, ed., *Kyokutō kokusai gunji saiban shiryō mokuroku* 極東国際軍事裁判資料目録 (privately printed in 1971).

55. Tokyō Daigaku Shakai Kagaku Kenkyūjo 東京大学社会科学研究所, ed., *Kyokutō kokusai gunji saiban kiroku: Bengogawa shōko shorui* 極東国際軍事裁判記録—弁護側証拠書類 (The record of the International Military Tribunal for the Far East: A catalogue of the defendants' documentary evidence) (1971); *Kensatsugawa shōko shorui* 検察側証拠書類 (The prosecutors' documentary evidence) (1972); *Sōkihen* 総記篇 (General documents) (1973).

56. *Daihon'ei rikugunbu: Dai Tōa sensō kaisen keii* 大本営陸軍部・大東亜戦争開戦経緯 (1973-74).

57. *Daihon'ei kaigunbu: Dai Tōa sensō kaisen keii* 大本営海軍部・大東亜戦争開戦経緯 (1979).

58. *Daihon'ei rikugunbu* 大本営陸軍部 (1970-75).

59. *Daihon'ei kaigunbu, Rengō kantai* 大本営海軍部聯合艦隊 (1970-75).

60. *Rikugun gunju dōin, 1: Keikakuhen* 陸軍軍需動員, 1—計画編 (1967).

61. *Rikugun gunji dōin, 2: Jisshihen* 陸軍軍需動員, 2—実施編 (1970).

62. *Rikugun gunsenbi* 陸軍軍戦備 (1979).

63. *Kaigun gunsenbi, 1: Shōwa 16-nen 11-gatsu made* 海軍軍戦備, 1—昭和16年11月まで (1969).

64. *Kaigun gunsenbi, 2: Kaisen igo* 海軍軍戦備, Vol. 2—開戦以後, (1975).

65. *Hawai sakusen* ハワイ作戦 (1967).

66. *Ran-In kōryaku sakusen* 蘭印攻略作戦 (1967).

67. *Biruma kōryaku sakusen* ビルマ攻略作戦 (1967).

68. *Kantōgun, 1: Tai-So senbi, Nomonhan jiken* 関東軍, 1—対ソ戦備・ノモンハン事件 (1969).

69. *Kantōgen, 2: Kan toku en, shūsenji no tai-So sen* 関東軍, 2—関特演・終戦時の対ソ戦 (1974).

70. *Hokushi no chiansen* 北支の治安戦, 1 (1968).

71. *Shina jihen rikugun sakusen, 1: Shōwa 13-nen 1-gatsu made* 支那事変陸軍作戦, 1：昭和13年1月まで (1975).

72. *Shina jihen rikugun sakusen, vol. 2: Shōwa 14-nen 9-gatsu made* 支那事変陸軍作戦, Vol. 2：昭和14年9月まで (1976).

73. *Shina jihen rikugun sakusen, vol 3: Shōwa 16-nen 12-gatsu made* 支那事変陸軍作戦, Vol. 3—昭和16年12月まで (1975)

74. *Riku-kaigun nenpyō fu heigo, yōgo no kaisetsu* 陸海軍年表付兵語・用語の解説, edited by Suekuni Masao 末国正雄 (1980).

75. *Senshi sōsho shiryōshū: Nanpō no gunsei* 戦史叢書史料集—南方の軍政 (Asagumo Shinbunsha, 1985).

76. *Senshi sōsho shiryōshū: Kaigun nendo sakusen keikaku (Shōwa 11-nen-Shōwa 16-nen)* 戦史叢書史料集—海軍軍度作戦計画(昭和11年—昭和16年) (Asagumo Shinbunsha, 1986).

5

From the Manchurian Incident to the Sino-Japanese War

Hatano Sumio

THE MANCHURIAN INCIDENT

Basic Works

Scholarly efforts to delve into the Manchurian Incident had to wait until the military archives were opened. The first attempt to do so was made by Shimada Toshihiko, who contributed a full-length monographic essay on the development of the Manchurian Incident, 1931–1932, to Nihon Kokusai seiji gakkai, ed., *Taiheiyō sensō e no michi* (The road to the Pacific War), vol. 2. Shimada's comprehensive work traces a train of events which began with the outbreak of the Mukden Incident (September 1931), led to the creation of "Manchukuo" (March 1932), and ended with the Tangku truce agreement (May 1933). He examines the Kwantung army's invasion of Manchuria, the maneuvers within the Japanese military, and the shifting policies of the Tokyo government. Because of the thoroughness of his research, which is characteristic of this series, Shimada's work remains to this day the standard account of the subject.

Since its English translation is contained in James W. Morley, ed., *Japan Erupts: The London Naval Conference and the Manchurian Incident, 1928–1932* (Columbia University Press, 1984), it is only necessary here to note Shimada's particular contributions. This is an in-depth study on the escalation process of the September 18 incident, fully based on the unpublished sources of the Japanese army. Especially interesting is the author's account of the differences between the Kwantung Army (which originally had thought in terms of a military occupation of Manchuria) and the army's supreme command in Tokyo (which had less drastic plans).

Subsequently, Shimada wrote for general readers *Manshū jihen* (The Manchurian Incident), as well as a compact volume on *Kantōgun* (The Kwantung Army), succinctly describing the rise and fall of the Kwantung Army.

Another major monograph is Ogata Sadako, *Manshū jihen to seisaku no keisei katei* (The Manchurian Incident and the policymaking process), which also makes full use of army materials, the most significant among them being the secret war diary kept by Captain Katakura Tadashi, a staff officer of the Kwantung Army. The book is the author's own translation of the English version, *Defiance in Manchuria: The Making of Japanese Foreign Policy, 1931–1932* (Los Angeles: University of California Press, 1964). In this important work Ogata attempts to characterize the Manchurian Incident primarily as a change in power structure within the army, as dramatized by the Kwantung Army's challenge to and defiance of the top army leaders in Tokyo. From such a viewpoint the author succeeds in elucidating the process through which middle- and lower-grade army officers, intent on radically redirecting the course of the nation, took power into their own hands, thus making rational policymaking increasingly difficult.

Baba Akira is yet another diplomatic historian who has examined in detail the response of the Japanese government, especially the Foreign Ministry, to the Manchurian Incident. His solid and thoroughly documented monograph, *Manshū jihen* (The Manchurian Incident), is one of the best volumes in Kajima's series on Japanese diplomatic history, although its title page bears only the name of the "supervisors," Morishima Gorō and Yanai Hisao. Baba's work treats the three-month period from the outbreak of the Manchurian Incident to the collapse of the Wakatsuki Reijirō cabinet (December 1931). Although the author eschews a systematic evaluation of Shidehara diplomacy during this period, he gives a very favorable account of the Foreign Ministry and its legations abroad for their success in maintaining proper relationships with the Anglo-American powers and the League of Nations despite the Japanese army's military escalation in defiance of the powers.

Baba's essay [2] on the Manchurian Incident and the Inukai cabinet, also heavily based on the Foreign Ministry archives, is a careful study centering on Japan's response to the Shanghai incident. This essay is printed in his new book, *Nitchū kankei to gaisei kikō no kenkyū: Taishō-Shōwaki* (Studies on Sino-Japanese relations and Japan's foreign policy mechanisms: The Taishō and Shōwa periods.) Baba has also contributed a detailed commentary to the valuable manuscripts left by Hayashi Kyūjirō, who was consul general at the time of the Manchurian Incident.

Building on pioneering works by Shimada, Ogata, and others, Usui Katsumi has written *Manshū jihen: Sensō to gaikō to* (The Manchurian Incident: War and diplomacy), in which he advances a highly stimulating hypothesis. Usui argues that the Manchurian Incident of 1931 and the Shanghai incident of 1932 were essentially two different types of war: the former was a variation of recurrent warfare among warlords, whereas the latter was a "new type of war" which—at least on the local level—represented the Chinese people's "national resistance" against Japanese aggression. The basic theme of the book delineates the essential differences between military and foreign policies in Japan's decision-making process at the time of the Manchurian Incident.

The Demise of Shidehara Diplomacy

Fortified by many years of research on the history of Sino-Japanese relations, Usui has also published a number of distinguished articles dealing with the last phase of Shidehara diplomacy, on the basis of the Foreign Ministry archives. The more important among them examine the League of Nation's response to the Mukden incident [3] and the Japanese occupation of Chinchow and Shidehara diplomacy [4]. In these studies, Usui discusses the significance of the fact that the

Japanese government finally turned away from Chang Hsueh-liang to a pro-Japanese regime as the party with which to negotiate for a settlement. Usui has also published an essay [5] on the swan song of Shidehara diplomacy that desperately attempted to restore a cooperative relationship with the Anglo-American powers while under the strong pressure of, on the one hand, China's demand for the recovery of its "national rights," and, on the other, aggression by the Japanese military.

In the historical controversy over the nature of "Shidehara diplomacy" the central point at issue has been whether to regard the differences between Shidehara's cooperative policy and the military's "independent" policy as a basic conflict of principles or merely a difference in degree and tactics. This controversy, dormant during the past decade, was recently reopened by the Chinese scholar, Professor Yu Xin-qun of Nan Hai University (Tientsin), who visited Japan in 1982–83 to conduct research on Sino-Japanese relations. After his return to China, he contributed several articles to Japanese scholarly journals. In these studies, documented by the Japanese Foreign Ministry archives and the Chinese sources, he concludes that the so-called "dual diplomacy" since the Washington Conference revolved around differences merely in specific programs. In the process of coping with the Manchurian crisis, he contends, policy differences between the Foreign Ministry and the military gradually narrowed until finally the two came completely to agree on the creation of Manchukuo. Recently, Yu brought together his research results in a monograph, *Manshū jihenki no Chū-Nichi gaikōshi kenkyū* (A study of Sino-Japanese diplomatic history in the period of the Manchurian Incident). In it the author traces the course of Sino-Japanese relations from the spring of 1931 to Japan's withdrawal from the League of Nations in March 1933. To Yu's interpretation, no response from Japanese scholars has appeared to date.

Few studies are available on the short-lived cabinet of Inukai Tsuyoshi, who strove to settle the Manchurian Incident after the collapse of Shidehara diplomacy. One recent contribution is Tokitō Hideto's article [1]. It shows that Inukai, on the basis of his own long experience with Sino-Japanese relations, tried to contact the Chinese government through unofficial channels to make a beginning for a settlement of the Manchurian Incident, but that his efforts were obstructed by the military and bureaucrats who cooperated with the military.

Ishiwara Kanji

A Kwantung Army staff officer who engineered the Manchurian Incident, Ishiwara had developed a unique military philosophy that foresaw an armageddon between Japan and the United States. He elaborated such a view in his now famous treatise on the final global war as well as in many memoranda and lectures, which are collected in Tsunoda Jun, ed., *Ishiwara Kanji shiryō: Kokubō ronsaku* (Papers relating to Ishiwara Kanji: Treatises on national defense); and *Ishiwara Kanji shiryō: Sensō shiron* (Papers relating to Ishiwara Kanji: Treatises on war history). Ishiwara's published papers, essays, and writings are collected in *Ishiwara Kanji zenshū* (The complete work of Ishiwara Kanji). Because of his peculiar views on national defense as well as his powerful personality, Ishiwara has attracted keen attention from diplomatic historians.

As a commentary on *Kokubō ronshū,* Tsunoda Jun has written a useful introductory essay on Ishiwara's strategic thinking. Hata Ikuhiko's critical biographical essay [1] on Ishiwara incisively discusses the gaps that existed between Ishiwara's ideals as a policy planner and the existing political realities.

It was only in the 1970s, however, that full-scale research on Ishiwara Kanji's thought and behavior on the basis of primary sources began to be undertaken. Matsuzawa Tetsunari's essay [1] on Ishiwara's idea of the final global war goes back to his childhood to trace the formation of this notion. On the other hand, Kobayashi Hideo's essay on Ishiwara, contained in his *Shōwa fashisuto no gunzō* (A collective portrait of Shōwa fascists), describes Ishiwara as a "technocrat" devoting himself to the construction of an "advanced national defense state" fully prepared for a total war. Yet another viewpoint is provided by Kawahara Hiroshi in his *Kindai Nihon no Ajia ninshiki* (Modern Japan's perception of Asia), especially in a chapter dealing with Ishiwara and the East Asian League. Kawahara maintains that Ishiwara's ideology, because of his understanding of Chinese nationalism, was saved from falling into a dogmatic chauvinism that characterized other advocates of Pan-Asianism. One common feature of the above three essays is their emphasis on the interrelationship between the growth of Japanese fascism and Ishiwara's ideas and policies.

From a fresh perspective, Iokibe Makoto has written a series of original essays on the formation of Ishiwara's views on China [1], his idea of the East Asian League [4], and his plan to settle the Manchurian-Mongolian question [2]. These articles carefully examine the development of Ishiwara's strategic theories and his views of China, the development of his interest in and plan for the Manchurian question, and the way these problems were integrated in his thought on the East Asian League and philosophy of the final global war. However, as Iokibe himself admits, the most thorough monograph remains the work by an American historian, Mark R. Peattie, *Ishiwara Kanji and Japan's Confrontation with the West* (Princeton University Press, 1975), which is scheduled to appear in Japanese translation.

The Manchurian Incident and Fascism

Recently, there have been an increasing number of studies that have examined the Manchurian Incident in relation to the formation of Japanese fascism. A representative viewpoint is presented by Yoshimi Yoshiaki, who argues that during the period of the Manchurian Incident (1931−33) the "renovationist faction" and the status quo forces within the Japanese army reached a compromise to create a system for national unity. In this sense, Yoshimi concludes, the Manchurian Incident was the starting point of the Japanese type of fascism led by the military.

During 1981−83 a historical controversy recurred about whether or not the Manchurian Incident was, after all, caused by the Kwantung Army acting arbitrarily on its own responsibility. The controversy revolved around the question of how to evaluate the Manchurian Incident in the context of the army-led "fascist movement."

In his book and his 1981 articles [1] [2], Fujimura Michio maintained, on the basis of the documents of the General Staff, that the Manchurian Incident and the coup d'état plan that immediately followed (the October incident) were not caused by the Kwantung Army or middle-echelon officers in Tokyo; rather, he asserted, these were the actions of the Army General Staff who aimed at establishing military dictatorship. Rebuttals to this reinterpretation came from Morimatsu Toshio and Eguchi Keiichi [2]. Morimatsu, in particular, exposed Fujimura's "misreading" of the documents, reemphasizing that the initiative for staging the Manchurian Incident had throughout been taken by the Kwantung Army.

Although Fujimura's reinterpretation seemed to have been refuted, the real weight of his thesis was that the main thrust of research should be directed to the army-led planning for the exigencies of total war. It was in this context that Fujimura pointed to the importance of the "inner linkage" between the Manchurian Incident and domestic coup d'état plans such as the October and March (1931) incidents [2]. The backdrop of such a perspective is an accumulation of detailed studies on the moves of the military, the source of "renovationist" forces during the first half of the 1930s. Recent works on the subject include Karita Tōru's thorough analysis of the October incident and Yoshida Yutaka's essay that discusses the lineage between the rise of middle-grade officers, or "technocrats," and the "new bureaucrats." Tsutsui Kiyotada's new book analyzes the thought and behavior of the army's middle-echelon officers by applying sociological methodology. Sasaki Takashi's essay on the "renovationist faction" within the army is a detailed study of conflict and cooperation among various factions within the army. It is extensively based on the unpublished diary of General Minami Jirō (army minister and supreme military councilor, 1931–34).

The recent discovery of the diaries of General Minami and General Mazaki Jinzarubō—the twin central figures of the kōdōha (The "Imperial Way" faction)—enables the contemporary historian to go beyond the works on the army's factional struggles published in the 1960s, notably Hata Ikuhiko's Gun fashizumu undōshi (History of military fascism movements) and Tanaka Sōgorō's Nihon fashizumushi (History of Japanese fascism).

Fresh studies based on newly available sources have been published in: Kindai Nihon Kenkyūkai, ed., Nenpō kindai nihon kenkyū, no. 1: Shōwaki no gunbu (Journal of Modern Japanese Studies, no. 1: The Japanese military during the Shōwa period); and Miyake Masaki et al., eds., Shōwashi no gunbu to seiji (The military and politics in the history of the Shōwa period). These studies elucidate the political process through which the kōdōha (the "Imperial Way" faction) was replaced by the *tōseiha* (the "Control" faction) as the result of the February 26 (1936) mutiny. As researchers further delved into the subject, they raised new questions. Why did the Imperial Way faction so quickly disintegrate? What was the role of the Ugaki [Kazushige] faction and its successor, the Minami Jirō faction, which had constituted the "mainstream" within the army until the Manchurian Incident? Kitaoka Shin'ichi has attempted to answer these questions in the context of factional conflicts and compromises over defense and foreign policy issues.

There have also been recent studies on the navy's political activities during this period. Tanaka Hiromi, who discovered the diary of Vice-Admiral Ogasawara Naganari, has examined the political behavior of Ogasawara and Fleet Admiral Tōgō Heihachirō, who was close to him and his group, which in turn maintained close relations with the Imperial Way faction of the army and the Fleet faction of the navy. And the author shows how deeply the Ogasawara-Tōgō group was involved in the October (1931) incident as well as in the May 15 (1932) incident in which a group of young army and navy officers assassinated Prime Minister Inukai. The same group also played a role in the so-called "Ōsumi purge" (1933–34), in which Navy Minister Ōsumi forcefully retired moderate naval leaders who supported naval armament limitations.

The Manchurian Incident and Mass Media

In 1969 Etō Shinkichi analyzed in a stimulating essay the pattern of changing press coverage of the Sino-Japanese tension in the late 1920s by applying Charles E. Osgood's method of content analysis to the two major newspapers, the *Asahi* and the *Tokyo Nichi-Nichi*. Etō's conclusions are cautious: the editorial view of the *Asahi* was cool-headed and deliberate, whereas the *Nichi-Nichi* tended to appeal to the masses in emotional terms. Since then, no similar attempt has been made using such an approach.

The role of Japanese mass media in arousing chauvinistic public opinion at the time of the Manchurian Incident has attracted considerable scholarly attention. The essays by Ikei Masaru [2] and Eguchi Keiichi [1] trace the process through which newspapers and radio broadcasts led Japanese public opinion by presenting sensational reports that tended to justify the actions of the military. In another paper [4], contained in a joint study on *Tōyō Keizai Shinpō*, Eguchi examines how this liberal newspaper, which had initially opposed aggression in Manchuria, became isolated in a prevailing chauvinistic mood, and eventually reversed its position. Kakegawa Tomiko presents an original study on the government's control of the mass media in the fourth volume of *Nichi-Bei kankeishi* (also contained in Borg and Okamoto, eds., *Pearl Harbor as History*, pp. 533–549). In it she points to a sharp contrast between the English-language *Japan Chronicle* (published in Kobe), which consistently criticized Japanese foreign policy, and major Japanese newspapers, which vied with each other in ingratiating themselves to the government by spreading sensational news.

Withdrawal from the League

Japan's withdrawal from the League of Nations drove it into further international isolation. The ordeals of the Foreign Ministry and the Japanese delegation to Geneva are expertly examined in Uchiyama Masakuma's article. He emphasizes the responsibility of Japan's chief delegate Matsuoka Yōsuke, arguing that it was he who overrode the opposition of his colleagues to urge Tokyo to withdraw from the League. Uchiyama's interpretation is attacked in the official biography of Matsuoka (published in 1974), which attempts without success to defend him by asserting that a majority of the Japanese delegation were in agreement with Matsuoka.

Another astute study is Ogata Sadako's essay on Japanese public opinion and the withdrawal from the League of Nations. Focusing on the decision-making process leading to Japan's withdrawal, she examines the views of the League held by senior government figures, radical army leaders, intellectuals, and the general public. From this survey, Ogata concludes that Japan withdrew from the League without much domestic opposition, partly because the forces supporting the League had been weak from the very beginning.

In the domestic arena, the Manchurian Incident occasioned the rise of the so-called "new bureaucrats" *(kakushinha)*, an influential group within the Foreign Ministry that was critical of Shidehara diplomacy. The "new bureaucrats" (also known as the "Asian faction") were radical in their opposition to the so-called "Europe-America faction," and the leading members were Arita Hachirō, Shigemitsu Mamoru, Tani Masayuki, and Shiratori Toshio. After the Manchurian Incident Shiratori and junior officials who supported him came to spearhead the "new bureaucrats." This process is analyzed in Tobe Ryōichi's article on Shiratori and the Manchurian Incident. The increasing influence of the "new bureaucrats" is carefully treated in Usui Katsumi's contribution to the first volume of Hosoya et al., ed., *Nichi-Bei kankeishi* (also contained in Borg and Okamoto, eds., *Pearl Harbor as History*, pp. 127–148).

In this connection, Baba Akira has published an essay [1] on the Manchurian Incident and the question of a "Foreign Ministry general staff" (Gaimushō Kōsabu). In it he argues that the plan to establish a "diplomatic general staff," advocated by the "new bureaucrats" in the Foreign Ministry, had in reality been an attempt to resist the army's control of foreign policy. The plan never materialized, however.

The Creation of Manchukuo

The establishment of the puppet government of Manchukuo was led by the Kwantung Army and the members of the South Manchuria Railway Company who collaborated with the Kwantung Army. The participation of the Chinese residents was only nominal. The point at issue is how to interpret the rhetoric and realities of the Japanese administration of Manchuria and how to assess its impact on the Japanese settlers there.

For example, how did the creation of Manchukuo affect the thinking of Japanese settlers in Manchuria who were represented by the Manchurian Youth League (Manshū Seinen Renmei)? In return, how was the development of Manchukuo influenced by the ideas held by this league? These questions are examined in Hirano Ken'ichirō's essay on the movements and attitudes of Japanese residents in Manchuria. He throws light on the peculiar political functions of the Manchurian Youth League and analyzes its ideal of "interracial harmony" (harmony among the Japanese, Han, Manchu, Mongolian, and Korean peoples). This subject has also been studied by Matsuzawa Tetsunari: [1], [2]. (See chapter 3.)

There are dissenting views on the ideals for the founding of Manchukuo, such as the concept of the "Royal road" *(Ōdōshugi)* and "interracial harmony" in Manchuria. One interpretation asserts that an ideal such as "interracial harmony" was nothing more than an ideological facade for Japan's colonial rule. This view has been advanced by the work of Manshūshi Kenkyūkai (The Study Group on the History of Manchuria) on Manchuria under Japan's "imperialistic rule" and Suzuki Takashi's essay [2] on "Japanese imperialism" and the control of Manchukuo. Similarly, Okabe Makio regards the movement for "interracial harmony" in Manchuria as a form of "fascism from below" which failed to materialize within Japan.

On the other hand, there is an interpretation that emphasizes the idealistic vision, held by the Kwantung Army and Japanese residents in Manchuria, of building a model nation in Manchuria. Among those that positively evaluate this vision, one can cite, for example, the works of Hanzawa Hiroshi. He asserts that the concept of building a new nation as a multiracial state logically defied a parochial nationalism and contained an element of idealism that sought an international idea for Manchukuo.

A fresh study that challenges both positions is Hirano Ken'ichirō's essay [2] on Manshūkoku Kyōwakai and the political stabilization of Manchukuo. He points out that this officially guided political organization, aimed at promoting stability and unity in Manchuria, functioned as a peculiar mechanism for mobilizing the leaders of various "races" in Manchuria and integrating the newly established Manchukuo, thus bringing about a measure of political participation and stability in Manchuria.

With the creation of Manchukuo, there arose the question of how to unify Japan's administrative machineries in Manchukuo. This issue, which involved a sharp conflict of views and bureaucratic interests between the army and the Foreign Ministry, is carefully studied in Baba Akira's previously mentioned article [1]. The plan for a "diplomatic general staff" was a part of the efforts to create an organ to integrate the divisive administrative functions of the government since the May 15 (1932) coup d'état. On a broad background of changing administrative mechanism in Manchuria, Shimizu Hideko has written a seminal article [2].

On Japan's settlers in Manchuria, the pioneering study is Andō

Hikotarō's 1961 article on the prewar Japanese "administration" in Manchuria and Japanese immigration. Among studies on specific aspects of this question, the following are important: Asada Kyōji, *Nihon teikokushigi to kyū-shokuminchi jinushisei* (Japanese imperialism and landownership in her colonies); Okabe Makio's case study [2] on agricultural immigration to Manchuria; and Hasegawa Yūichi's essay on the Kwantung Army's plan for promoting immigration to Manchuria. An extremely useful book that gives an overall picture of Japanese economic activities in Manchuria, with a focus on agricultural immigrants, is Manshū Kaitakushi Kankōkai, ed., *Manshū kaitakushi* (A history of settlement in Manchuria). A comprehensive study of immigration to Manchuria is Manshū Iminshi Kenkyūkai, ed., *Nihon teikokushugika no Manshū imin* (Immigration to Manchuria under Japanese imperialism).

For a comprehensive bibliographical survey of studies on the Japanese administration of Manchukuo, the reader is referred to a useful article [1] by Suzuki Takashi; the sequel bibliography, ably covering works that appeared in the 1970s, has been published by Kaneko Fumio. A useful survey of the formation, development, and final collapse of Manchukuo is Okabe Makio's *Manshūkoku* (Manchukuo).

Documents on the Manchurian Incident

Heated historical controversies over the Manchurian Incident became a powerful stimulus for the Foreign Ministry to compile and publish special volumes on the Manchurian Incident, skipping the chronological order of the annually published diplomatic documents. Roughly half of the Foreign Ministry's *original* documents on the Manchurian Incident were destroyed by fire during the war, but through the painstaking efforts of Usui Katsumi and Kurihara Ken, these documents were substantially restored. In 1977 the seven-volume series of Gaimusho, ed., *Nihon gaikō bunsho: Manshū jihen* (Documents on Japanese foreign policy: The Manchurian Incident) began to be published; it was completed in 1981. The series covers from the outbreak of the Mukden Incident of September 18, 1931, to the Tangku truce agreement of May 1933. The contents can be roughly divided into the following three categories: the negotiations between the Japanese government and the Kuomintang government; anti-Japanese incidents in major Chinese cities; and Japan's withdrawal from the League of Nations and the Lytton Report. Shimizu Hideko, one of the editors of these volumes, has published a very useful essay [1] on the nature of the series.

The basic army documents relating to the Manchurian Incident that have survived had previously been published in the *Gendaishi shiryō* series. The seventh volume: *Manshū jihen* (The Manchurian Incident), edited by Kobayashi Tatsuo and Shimada Toshihiko, covers the period from the planning stage in 1927 to the Tangku truce agreement of 1933, and it is accompanied by a useful introductory essay and commentaries by Shimada Toshihiko. This useful collection was followed by the eleventh volume: *Zoku Manshū jihen* (Sequel volume on the Manchurian Incident), edited by Inaba Masao, Kobayashi Tatsuo, and Shimada Toshihiko (see chapter 4).

The most reliable account on the detailed military aspects of the Manchurian Incident is the Army General Staff, ed., *Manshū jihen sakusen keika no gaiyō* (A summary of the development of military operations during the Manchurian Incident). Mori Katsumi's *Manshū jihen no rimenshi* (The inside history of the Manchurian Incident) contains an abundance of interviews with and reminiscences of those directly involved in the Manchurian Incident. An extremely detailed record of the collaborations by the South Manchuria Railway Company is found in Minami Manshū Tetsudō Kabushiki Kaisha, ed., *Manshū jihen to Mantetsu* (The Manchurian Incident and the South Manchuria Railway Company).

FROM 1933 TO 1937

Sino-Japanese Relations, 1933–37

The pioneering work on the Sino-Japanese War is Hata Ikuhiko's monograph, *Nitchū sensōshi* (A history of the Sino-Japanese War), published in 1961. Covering the period 1933–39, this work represents the best product by the (then) younger generation of scholars who embarked on their study after World War II. It provides a detailed and well-documented account of military-political developments in Japanese-Chinese relations from the Tangku truce agreement of 1933 to the initial stages of the Sino-Japanese War. Hata's great contributions, among others, were: his reevaluation of the Sui-yuan incident of 1936, which prompted the various local regimes in north China to centralize and unite their power, thus giving the Chinese self-confidence vis-à-vis Japan; and his persuasive explanation of the reasons why the Marco Polo Bridge Incident could not be settled as a local affair, by reexaming the conflict between those who clamored for the extension of hostilities and those who opposed it. Until the publication of Hata's work there had been virtually no full-scale study on the crucial role the military played during this period. To this day, Hata's book remains the standard account of the subject. In 1963, Hata wrote a monographic essay [3] on the military developments of the Sino-Japanese War (1937−41) for the Nihon Kokusai Seiji Gakkai, ed., *Taiheiyō sensō e no michi* series (vol. 4). Its partial translation appeared in James W. Morley, ed., *The China Quagmire: Japan's Road to the Pacific War* (Columbia University Press, 1983).

The same English-language volume contains Shimada Toshihiko's detailed monographic essay on north China operations, 1933−37, which is solidly based on unpublished army records, especially those of the Kwantung Army. (The Japanese original was published in volume 3 of the *Taiheiyō sensō e no michi* series.) In his work, Shimada provides the essential prehistory of the Sino-Japanese War. His account of Sino-Japanese relations from the Tangku truce agreement to the opening of hostilities in 1937 revolves around Japan's covert operations to detach the northern provinces of China (Jehol, Hopei, Chahar, and Suiyan) conducted by the Kwantung Army and Tientsin Army. Shimada's detached narrative clearly shows that it was field officers, rather than the army authorities in Tokyo, who led Japanese policy at this critical juncture. Foreign Minister Hirota Kōki is treated in an unfavorable light: while announcing restoration of friendly relations with China, he failed to propose, much less advocate, a fundamental change in Japan's China policy.

In 1971 Kamimura Shin'ichi, a retired diplomat who was chief of the First Section of the East Asia Bureau of the Foreign Ministry in 1933−38, authored *Nikka jihen* (The Sino-Japanese War). A volume in the Kajima series on Japanese diplomatic history, it is a solid study extensively based on the Foreign Ministry archives and informed by his own first-hand experience. Especially valuable is his account on the developments leading to the establishment of the Wang Ching-wei regime in 1940.

Japan's China policy preceding the outbreak of the war in 1937 is discussed by Hoshino Akiyoshi and Furuya Tetsuo. Furuya asserts that Japan's basic policies were the establishment of pro-Japanese local regimes; the refusal to let third parties intervene in Sino-Japanese problems; and joint Sino-Japanese efforts to combat communism. All three policies came to a deadlock in 1935, according to Furuya.

Recently, with the progress of research on Sino-Japanese relations of this period, Japanese historians have come to see Foreign Minister Satō Naotake's diplomacy (March–June 1937) in a new light. Usui Katsumi's essay [6] on "Satō diplomacy" and Sino-Japanese relations in early 1937 points out that there was a strong move within the army to reconsider China policy since the Manchurian Incident and that this constituted the background of Satō's "new China policy," which called for an avoidance of war and the adjustment of relations with China on an equal footing.

Studies of currency reforms in China by Kobayashi Hideo and Hatano Sumio [2] assert that the Japanese military, faced with such new moves toward the unification of China as the successful currency reforms and the Sian incident (December 1936), began to modify their old images of China as a nation racked with rival warlords, and that this realization led to a "reexamination" of China policy. Such a reorientation of China policy, however, was never reflected in actual Sino-Japanese relations because "Satō diplomacy" was only too short-lived.

Abortive Rapprochement with Britain

After the Tangku truce agreement settled the Manchurian Incident for the moment, Japan once again searched for a policy of international cooperation in an effort to rescue itself from diplomatic isolation. The policy that surfaced in this process was intended rapprochement with Great Britain.

The subject is examined in detail in Hosoya Chihiro's essays on the proposal for an Anglo-Japanese nonaggression pact in the mid-1930s [3] and the diplomat Yoshida Shigeru's role in it [1]. Utilizing materials at the British Public Record Office as well as the Japanese Foreign Ministry, Hosoya analyzes the plan to conclude an Anglo-Japanese nonaggression pact in 1934 within the trilateral framework of Japan, Great Britain, and the United States. Hosoya believes that as far as Japan was concerned there was a possibility for concluding such a pact with Britain but it was aborted by the opposition from the British Foreign Office (especially its Far Eastern Department) and its fear of American response. These studies can be read most profitably within the broader context of Anglo-Japanese relations provided by Hosoya in his essay [2] on Japanese views of the Anglo-American powers in the interwar period, which is printed in Hosoya, ed., *Nichi-Ei kankeishi, 1917–1949*. The English version is Ian Nish, ed., *Anglo-Japanese Alienation, 1919–1952: Papers of the Anglo-Japanese Conference on the History of the Second World War* (Cambridge University Press).

Kibata Yōichi, a specialist in modern British history, has written a series of valuable articles on Britain's Far Eastern policy during the 1930s, all extensively based on British archival materials. One of them [1], on Anglo-Japanese relations in 1934, had examined the background of the proposed Anglo-Japanese nonaggression pact prior to Hosoya's study. Kibata's subsequent articles discuss the failure of Ambassador Yoshida's effort to bring about an Anglo-American rapprochement in 1936–37 [2] and the circumstances leading to Britain's dispatch of the Leith-Ross mission to China [3].

On the Leith-Ross mission of 1935–36, Hatano Sumio has published an essay [1] on its visit to the Far East and Japan's response, with particular reference to monetary reform in China. In this study Hatano analyzes the complicated relationship of cooperation and conflict between the Japanese military and the Foreign Ministry that surfaced over the Leith-Ross mission to China. In addition, Iyotani Toshio's article on the American plan for a cotton and wheat loan to China discusses Japan's reaction to the American loan proposal in 1933 within a multilateral framework of Japan, the United States, Great Britain, and China.

The most recent study on economic foreign policy during this period is a well-documented and closely argued essay by Mitani Taichirō. He examines how the new four-power China consortium (and especially, the American banker Thomas W. Lamont) reacted to a series of Sino-Japanese conflicts following the Manchurian Incident, and demonstrates that the changes the consortium underwent were none other than the transformation and then the final collapse of the "Washington system."

North China Operations

The insurmountable obstacle to Tokyo's search for a policy of international cooperation during the mid-1930s was the Japanese army's efforts to make north China a "second Manchukuo." Its operations to detach north China are treated in detail in Shimada Toshihiko's previously mentioned monographic essay [1]. Since the publication of this work, much progress has been made in this research area by the editing and publication of army and navy documents that were in Shimada's possession. The most important of them were printed in the above-mentioned volumes of the *Gendaishi shiryō* series (see chapter 4). The rest, in manuscript form, are preserved at the Social Science Research Institute, University of Tokyo. Their contents can be gleaned in Tokyo Daigaku Shakai Kagaku Kenkyūjo, ed., *Shimada bunsho mokuroku* (Catalogue of the papers of Shimada Toshihiko).

Fully utilizing these materials as well as the unpublished sources relating to the financial bureaucrats at the time, Nakamura Takafusa has presented a thorough study of the economic development of north China from 1933 to 1945 in his recent monograph, *Senji Nihon no Kahoku keizai shihai* (Japan's wartime economic control over north China). This book analyzes in dynamic details the process through which the plan for a "Japanese-Manchurian-Chinese economic bloc" went bankrupt in the end because of the conceptual gaps between Tokyo and Japanese authorities in north China, differences among various interest groups, the sectionalism of bureaucratic machineries within the army, and the premature planning and implementation of the plans by Japanese armed forces in north China. Imai Shun's essay on the smuggling trade into the East Hopei area discusses, on the basis of Chinese source materials, the political meaning of this smuggling and concludes that it was an integral part of the Japanese army's operations in north China.

Recently there has been a growing interest in Japanese economic expansion to north China and other Japanese-occupied areas in China.

The most comprehensive work is *Nihon teikokushugika no Chūgoku* (China under Japanese imperialism), the result of group research, headed by Asada Kyōji, on Japanese-occupied areas in China. Its central thesis is "the historical inevitability of Japanese imperialism to rule China." From this angle it analyzes the following problems: Japan's plundering of resources in its occupied areas in China; the manipulation of currency; the control of railways; and "economic warfare" in the areas occupied by Chinese Communist forces.

A useful collection of documents is Yoda Yoshiie, ed., *Nitchū sensōshi shiryō*, vol. 4: *Senryōchi shihai* (Historical materials on the Sino-Japanese War, vol. 4: Documents on Japan-occupied areas).

Economic Foreign Policy

What impact did the Great Depression have upon economic and trade relations between Japan and the countries in the Asia-Pacific basin? How did it influence the formation of Japan's economic bloc in this region? It was only in the 1970s that Japanese scholars began to pay serious attention to this question.

Recently Japanese trade with and investment in China during the first half of the 1930s have received considerable attention from Japanese scholars. Sakamoto Masako has published an article on a major Japanese trading company's expansion to the Manchurian and China markets; Matsumoto Toshirō has written on Sino-Japanese economic relations during the period of China's currency reforms. A research group (at Hitotsubashi University) that includes Sakamoto Masako and Matsumoto Toshirō undertook a joint project on Japan's export of capital to China. After eight years of collecting and analyzing source materials, the group has published Kokka Shihon Yushutsu Kenkyū-kai, ed., *Nihon no shihon yushutsu: Tai-Chūgoku shakkan no kenkyū* (Japanese export of capital: Studies on Japanese loans to China). This volume, the first work of this nature to be published after World War II, contains detailed statistical data on Japanese loans to China prior to 1945, and six articles that bring out the full picture of these loans.

To turn to another area of economic foreign policy, the economic friction between Japan and India occasioned by the intrusion of Japanese cotton products into the Indian market (1933–34) is studied by Yamamoto Mitsuru in the context of changes in the international economic structure after the Great Depression. Yanagisawa Asobu and Ishii Osamu have written articles on the first Japanese-Indian negotiations in 1933–34. Yanagisawa focuses on the Indian side, whereas Ishii solidly bases his study on British sources. Ishii has also authored *Cotton-Textile Diplomacy: Japan, Great Britain, and the United States, 1930–1936* (Arno Press, 1981). In this monograph Ishii shows that, contrary to the conventional argument that Japan's commercial expansion was ended by the Great Depression, the Japanese government adopted a new expansionary economic policy. The rapid expansion of Japanese exports of industrial products—mostly textiles—into new markets caused commercial disputes with Britain (and India) and the United States, leading them to take protectionist measures. On the basis of careful archival research, Ishii analyzes the interplay between the domestic conditions and foreign policies of the countries involved.

Alignment with Germany

The policy of rapprochement with Britain, which looked promising in 1934, came to naught on account of the army's north China operations. And in its place a policy of alignment with Germany emerged through the vigorous efforts of middle-echelon army officers who belonged to the "radical reformists" camp. The process through which these efforts resulted in the conclusion of the Anti-Comintern Pact of 1936 is fully examined in Ōhata Tokushirō's monographic essay on the Japanese-German Anti-Comintern Pact, contained in Nihon Kokusai Seiji Gakkai, ed., *Taiheiyō sensō e no michi*, vol. 5. The English version of this study appears in James W. Morley, ed., *Deterrent Diplomacy: Japan, Germany, and the USSR, 1935–1940* (Columbia University Press, 1976).

In this connection, Miyake Masaki has published an essay [1] on the Anti-Comintern Pact and the "Ribbentrop Bureau." Exploiting German sources, Miyake points out that there existed a form of "dual diplomacy" on the part of German leadership as well, namely the German Foreign Office and the "Büro Ribbentrop" ("Ribbentrop Bureau"). The Anti-Comintern Pact could be distinguished from ordinary international agreements on the following three scores: the pact was not signed by the German foreign minister; it was a highly ideological pact aimed at common defense against the Comintern; and

Germany was allowed to retain treaties with the Soviet Union, such as the Treaty of Rapallo. Miyake explains the reasons why Germany concluded such an anomalous pact with Japan by emphasizing differences between "Büro Ribbentrop," which desired friendly relations with the Soviets, and the German Foreign Office.

It is known that the Anti-Comintern Pact originated from unofficial negotiations between "Büro Ribbentrop" and Major General Ōshima Hiroshi, Japanese attaché to Berlin. It still remains uncertain which side took the initiative in proposing it. On the basis of Japanese sources, Nomura Minoru examines the role of Ōshima and concludes that Ōshima cannot be said to have initiated the matter. On the other hand, Miyake surmises that the lead was taken by Ōshima.

Relations with the Soviet Union

Japan's rapprochement with Nazi Germany can be said to have been prompted by the former's fear of the Soviet Union. On this subject, note should be taken of an essay [2] by Hirai Tomoyoshi, contained in the fourth volume of Nihon Kokusai Seiji Gakkai, ed., *Taiheiyō sensō e no michi*. This essay focuses on Soviet-Japanese relations following the Manchurian Incident (1933–39), and covers such issues as the problem of the sale of the Chinese Eastern Railway, border conflicts in northern Manchuria, Soviet reaction to the Anti-Comintern Pact, and the Soviet Union and the outbreak of the Sino-Japanese War. Kitaoka Shin'ichi's above-cited essay discusses the controversy in Japan over national defense against the Soviet Union in terms of factional strife within the Japanese army. Sakai Tetsuya, in his study on the shifting views of the Soviet Union held by Japanese leaders from the 1920s to the mid-1930s, suggests that Foreign Minister Hirota's diplomacy (1933–37) was aimed at preventing cooperation with the Anglo-American powers from collapsing on account of Japan's aggression in China; domestically, the author argues, Hirota attempted to placate the army by setting up a foreign policy goal of "anti-Comintern internationalism."

Details on Japan's defense policy and operational plannings in case of war with the Soviet Union are described in two volumes in the *Senshi sōsho* (War History) series of the Defense Agency: *Daihon'ei Rikugunbu* (The Imperial Headquarters: army), vol. 1, and *Kantōgun*

(The Kwantung Army), vol. 1. (For details on these volume, see above, chapter 4.)

The Crisis of 1935–36

While much has been written on the Japanese army in the mid-1930s, very few studies have been published on the navy centering on Japan's withdrawal from the Washington and London Naval Treaties. Kobayashi Tatsuo gives only a brief treatment of this crucial period in his contribution to Kokusai Seiji Gakkai, ed., *Taiheiyō sensō e no michi*. Shinmi Yukihiko's recent article on the collapse of the naval treaty system examines the parley between Japan, Britain, and the United States in the 1934 preliminary negotiations on the basis of the Foreign Ministry archives. The most detailed study on this subject remains Stephen E. Pelz's *Race to Pearl Harbor: The Failure of the Second London Naval Conference and the Onset of World War II* (Cambridge: Harvard University Press, 1974).

The factional struggle within the Japanese navy that revolved around the issue of naval limitation is succinctly treated by Hata Ikuhiko in his recent essay [2] on the "Fleet faction" versus the "Treaty faction." Asada Sadao's basic essay provides a broad historical context in which to understand this issue. Perhaps the most penetrating insights are to be found in *Kaigun to Nihon* (The navy and Japan), by Ikeda Kiyoshi, a former naval officer and a leading civilian authority on Japanese naval history. This compact volume contains, for example, critical reexamination of Japan's withdrawal from the naval treaties, the Japanese navy's misperception of China policy, and the political leadership of Navy Minister Yonai Mitsumasa.

Much of the surviving naval documents were published in the *Gendaishi shiryō* series: see especially vol. 11: *Nitchū Sensō, 4,* edited by Kobayashi Tatsuo, Inaba Masao, Shimada Toshihiko, and Usui Katsumi. For this volume Kobayashi has written a useful introductory essay focusing on the second London Naval Conference. Itō Takashi provides helpful commentaries on the letters and papers of Admiral Katō Kanji, the leader of the "Fleet faction," for the period 1933–34. The Foreign Ministry has published, as a supplement of its *Nihon gaikō bunsho* (Documents on Japanese foreign policy), *1935-nen Rondon kaigun* (The London Naval Conference of 1935). 1986.

Foreign Policy Leadership

Works on the makers of foreign policy are very few for this period, except those on Shidehara. On Prime Minister Inukai Tsuyoshi, Tokitō Hideto has published an essay [1] discussing how his images and perceptions of China since World War I were reflected in his China policy at the time of the Manchurian Incident. Foreign Minister Uchida Yasuya is the subject of Ikei Masaru's essay [3] which analyzes the background of his "scorched-earth" diplomacy. Ikei, together with Ōyama Azusa, have edited an official biography of Uchida, which appeared as Uchida Yasuya Denki Hensan Iinkai, ed., *Uchida Yasuya*.

Uchida's successor, and subsequently prime minister, Hirota Kōki, has been studied by Uno Shigeaki [2] and Usui Katsumi [2]. The former characterizes Hirota's policy toward Chiang Kai-shek as a diplomacy of watchful waiting. The latter is highly critical of Hirota for having opportunistically ingratiated himself with the military and fallen into line with them. Usui's stricture of "Hirota diplomacy" can also be found in his contribution [1] to Hosoya, et al., eds., *Nichi-Bei kankeishi* (also contained in *Pearl Harbor as History*). Usui takes sharp issue with the contention of Hirota's official biography that he chose to remain in office to perform the "difficult task" of opposing the military.

The official biography of Okada Keisuke gives a detailed account of his role in the controversy over the London Naval Treaty of 1930, but it is rather short and episodic in its coverage of the Second London Naval Conference and his prime ministership (1934–36).

Yoshida Shigeru's attempt at rapprochement with Britain has been treated in Hosoya Chihiro's previously mentioned essay [3]. A full-length biography is Inoki Masamichi, *Hyōden Yoshida Shigeru* (Yoshida Shigeru: A critical biography); its second volume covers the period discussed in this chapter.

In recent years Japanese historians have tended to rate Satō Naotake increasingly highly. Having played an active role as Japanese delegate to international conferences since the 1920s, he served briefly as foreign minister in 1937 and brought about a moderation of China policy. One example of work on Satō is a collection of essays on "Satō diplomacy" edited by Kurihara Ken. Especially relevant to this period is Unno Yoshirō's essay [2] on Satō's activities at the League of Nations and various conferences on arms limitation. Unno's monograph on Japan and the League of Nations also contains information on Satō as the head of the Japanese delegation in Geneva. Satō's memoirs are readable as well as instructive.

Prospects

The period under consideration in this chapter awaits further research and fresh interpretations; much has been written on the Manchurian Incident but relatively little attention has been paid by Japanese scholars to the important developments in the mid-1930s. With the exception of a few monographic essays in the *Taiheiyō sensō e no michi* series edited by Kokusai Seiji Gakkai, there has been no Japanese counterpart, for example, of Dorothy Borg's prize-winning monograph, *The United States and the Far Eastern Crisis of 1933–1938* (Cambridge: Harvard University Press, 1964) or Ann Trotter's *Britain and East Asia, 1933–1937* (Cambridge University Press, 1975). For that matter, there is no Japanese work comparable to James B. Crowley's somewhat dated revisionistic study, *Japan's Quest for Autonomy: National Security and Foreign Policy, 1930–1938* (Princeton University Press, 1966).

Bibliography

Andō Hikotarō 安藤彦太郎. "Senzen no Manshū keieiron to Nihon imin" 戦前の満州経営論と日本移民 (Prewar administration of Manchuria and Japanese immigration). *Waseda seiji keizaigaku zasshi* (October 1961), no. 171, pp. 1–20.

Asada Kyōji 浅田喬二. "Manshū ni okeru tochi shōsoken mondai" 満州における土地商租権問題 (The problem of the right to commercial land leases in Manchuria). In Manshūshi Kenkyūkai 満州史研究会, ed., *Nihon teikokushugi ka no Manshū*, pp. 317–97.

Asada Kyōji ed., *Nihon teikokushugika no Chūgoku: Chūgoku senryōchi keizai no kenkyū* 日本帝国主義下の中国―中国占領地経済の研究 (China under Japanese imperialism: Studies on the economy of Japan-occupied areas). Rakuyū Shobō, 1981.

―― *Nihon teikokushugi to kyū-shokuminchi jinushisei: Taiwan, Chōsen, Manshū ni okeru Nihonjin dai tochi shoyū no shiteki bunseki* 日本帝国主

義と旧植民地地主制—台湾，朝鮮，満州における日本人大土地所有の
史的分析 (Japanese imperialism and landlordism in former colonies: An
historical analysis of large landownership by the Japanese in Taiwan,
Korea, and Manchuria). Ochanomizu shobō, 1968.

Asada Sadao 麻田貞雄. "Nihon kaigun to tai-Bci scisaku oyobi senryaku"
(The Japanese navy and its policy and strategy toward the United States).
In Hosoya Chihiro et al., eds., *Nichi-Bei kankeishi: Kaisen ni itaru 10-nen*,
pp. 87–149. Also in Dorothy Borg and Shumpei Okamoto, eds., *Pearl
Harbor as History*, pp. 225–59.

Baba Akira 馬場明 (Morishima Gorō and Yanai Tsuneo 守島伍郎，柳井恒夫，
editorial supervisors). *Nihon gaikōshi, vol. 18: Manshū jihen* 日本外交史，
18—満州事変 (Japanese diplomatic history, 18: The Manchurian Incident). Kajima Kenkyūjo Shuppankai, 1973.

—— "Manshū jihen to Gaimushō kōsabu setchi mondai" 満州事変と外務
省考査部設置問題 (The Manchurian Incident and the question of a Foreign
Ministry general staff). *Kokusai seiji* (1968), no. 37: *Nihon gaikōshi no
shomondai, 3*, pp. 116–35. [1]

—— "Manshū jihen to Inukai naikaku" 満州事変と犬養内閣 (The Manchurian Incident and the Inukai cabinet). *Kokushigaku* (January 1974), no.
92, pp. 1–19. [2]

—— *Nitchū kankei to gaisei kikō no kenkyū: Taishō-Shōwaki* 日中関係と外政
機構の研究—大正・昭和期 (A study on Sino-Japanese relations and foreign policy machinery: Taishō and Shōwa periods). Hara Shobō, 1983.

Banno Junji 坂野潤治. "Gaikōkan no gokai to Manshū jihen no kakudai"
外交官の誤解と満州事変の拡大 (The misunderstanding of diplomats
and the escalation of the Manchurian Incident). *Shakai kagaku kenkyū*
(February 1984), 35(5):45–68.

Dorothy Borg and Shumpei Okamoto, eds., *Pearl Harbor as History: Japanese-
American Relations, 1931–1941*. New York: Columbia University Press,
1973. ·

Eguchi Keiichi 江口圭一. "Manshū jihen to daishinbun" 満州事変と大
新聞 (The Manchurian Incident and Japan's major newspapers). *Shisō*
(April 1973), no. 583, pp. 98–113. [1]

—— "Manshū jihen to gunbu: Fujimura shi no shosetsu ni tsuite" 満州事変
と軍部—藤村氏の所説について (The Manchurian Incident and the mili-
tary: Criticism of Mr. Fujimura's views). *Rekishigaku kenkyū* (October
1982), no. 509, pp. 16–23. [2]

—— "Rikugunshō no Manshū jihenkan" 陸軍省の満州事変観 (The Army
Ministry's view of the Manchurian Incident). In Fujiwara Akira and
Matsuo Takayoshi, eds., *Ronshū gendaishi*, pp. 305–35. Chikuma Shobō. [3]

—— "Santō shuppei, 'Manshū jihen' o megutte" 山東出兵,「満州事変」を

めぐって (On the Japanese expedition to Shantung and the Manchurian Incident). In Inoue Kiyoshi and Watanabe Tōru 井上清, 渡辺徹, eds., *Taishōki no kyūshinteki jiyūshugi: "Tōyō Keizai Shinpō" o chūshin to shite* 大正期の急進的自由主義―『東洋経済新報』を中心として (Radical liberalism of the Taishō period: Studies on the *Tōyō Keizai Shinpō*). Tōyō Keizai Shinpōsha, 1972, pp. 353–92. [4]

Etō Shin Kichi 衛藤瀋吉. "Keihōsen shadan mondai no gaikō katei" 京奉線遮断問題の外交過程 (The diplomatic negotiations concerning the suspension of traffic on the Peking-Mukden Railway). In Shinohara Hajime and Mitani Taichirō 篠原一, 三谷太一郎, eds., *Kindai Nihon no seiji shidō* 近代日本の政治指導 (Political leadership in modern Japan), pp. 375–425. Tokyo Daigaku Shuppankai, 1965.

Fujimura Michio 藤村道生. "Iwayuru 10-gatsu jiken no saikentō" いわゆる十月事件の再検討 (A reconsideration of the so-called October incident). *Nihon rekishi* (February 1981), no. 393, pp. 52–65. [1]

—— "Kokka sōryokusen taisei to kūdetā keikaku 国家総力戦体制とクーデター計画 (The total war system and coup d'état plots). In Miwa Kimitada 三輪公忠, ed., *Saikō: Taiheiyō sensō zenya* 再考―太平洋戦争前夜 (Reconsideration: The eve of the Pacific War), pp. 88–140. Sōseiki, 1981. [2]

—— "Kūdetā to shite no Manshū jihen" クーデターとしての満州事変 (The Manchurian Incident as a coup d'état). In Miyake Masaki et al., eds., *Shōwashi no gunbu to seiji*), 1983, 1:81–118. [3].

—— *Nihon gendaishi* 日本現代史 (Contemporary Japanese history). Yamakawa Shuppansha, 1981.

Fujiwara Akira 藤原彰, "Kokubō kokusaku o meguru riku-kaigun no tairitsu" 国防国策をめぐる陸海軍の対立 (The conflict between the army and the navy over national defense policy). In Fujiwara and Matsuo, eds., *Ronshū: Nihon gendaishi*, pp. 337–60.

Fujiwara Akira and Matsuo Takayoshi 松尾尊兊, eds., *Ronshū: Nihon Gendaishi* 論集―日本現代史 (A collection of essays on contemporary Japanese history). Chikuma Shobō, 1976.

Furuya Tetsuo 古屋哲夫. "Nitchū sensō ni itaru tai-Chūgoku seisaku no tenkai to sono kōzō" 日中戦争にいたる対中国政策の展開とその構造 (The development and structure of Japanese policy toward China prior to the Sino-Japanese War). In Furuya, ed., *Nitchū sensōshi kenkyū*, pp. 1–120.

Furuya Tetsuo, ed. *Nitchū sensōshi kenkyū* 日中戦争史研究 (Studies in the history of the Sino-Japanese War). Yoshikawa Kōbunkan, 1984.

Hanzawa Hiroshi 判沢弘. "'Manshūkoku' no isan wa nanika" 『満州国』の遺産はなにか (What is the legacy of "Manchukuo"?). *Chūō Kōron* (July 1964), 79(7):114–25.

Hasegawa Yūichi 長谷川雄一. "Manshū kaitakuron no kōzō" 満州開拓

論の構造 (The framework of the problem of settling in Manchuria). *Seiji keizai shigaku* (September 1978), no. 148, pp. 1–6 (November 1978), no. 150, pp. 113–22.

Hata Ikuhiko 秦郁彦. *Gun fashizumu undōshi* 軍ファシズム運動史 (A history of military fascist movements). Kawade Shobō Shinsha, 1972 (enlarged ed.).

—— "Hyōden Ishiwara Kanji" 評伝石原莞爾 (Ishiwara Kanji: A critical biography). In Hata, *Gun fashizumu undōshi*, pp. 215–65. [1]

—— "Kantaiha to jōyakuha: Kaigun no habatsu keifu" 艦隊派と条約派 —海軍の派閥系譜 (The Fleet Faction versus the Treaty Faction: The genealogy of naval factionalism). In Miyake et al., eds., *Shōwashi no gunbu to seiji*, 1:193–232. [2]

—— *Nitchū sensōshi* 日中戦争史 (A history of the Sino-Japanese War). Kawade Shobō Shinsha, 1962; revised, enlarged version, 1972.

—— "Nitchū sensō no gunjiteki tenkai, 1937–1941" 日中戦争の軍事的展開, 1937—1941 (The military developments of the Sino-Japanese War, 1937–1941). In Nihon Kokusai Seiji Gakkai, ed., *Taiheiyō sensō e no michi*, 4:3–110. [3]

Hatano Sumio 波多野澄雄. "Rīsu-Rosu no Kyokutō hōmon to Nihon: Chūgoku heisei kaikaku o megutte" リース・ロスの極東訪問と日本—中国幣制改革をめぐって (The Leith-Ross mission to the Far East, and the Japanese response: With particular reference to monetary reform in China). *Kokusai seiji* (1978), no. 58: *Nichi-Ei kankei no shiteki tenkai*, pp. 86–104. [1]

—— "Heisei kaikaku e no ugoki to Nihon no tai-Chū seisaku" 幣制改革への動きと日本の対中政策 (The making of currency reform in China [1935] and Japanese policy toward China). In Nozawa Yutaka 野沢豊, ed., *Chūgoku no heisei kaikaku to kokusai kankei*, pp. 265–98. [2]

Hayashi Kyūjirō 林久治郎 (introduction by Baba Akira 馬場明). *Manshū jihen to Hōten sōryōji: Hayashi Kyūjirō ikō* 満州事変と奉天総領事—林久治郎遺稿 (The Manchurian Incident and the Japanese consul general in Mukden: The posthumous manuscript of Hayashi Kyūjirō). Hara Shobō, 1978.

Hirai Tomoyoshi 平井友義. "Manshū jihen to Nisso kankei: Fushinryaku jōyaku mondai o chūshin ni" 満州事変と日ソ関係—不侵略条約問題を中心に (The Manchurian Incident and Japanese-Soviet relations: With particular reference to the problem of a nonaggression pact). *Kokusai seiji* (1966), no. 31: *Nichi-Ro Nisso kankei no tenkai*, pp. 99–113. [1]

—— "Soren no dōkō (1933–1939)" ソ連の動向 (1933–1939). (Soviet foreign policy, 1933–1939). In Nihon Kokusai Seiji Gakkai, ed., *Taiheiyō sensō e no michi*, 4:259–360. [2]

Hirano Ken'ichirō 平野健一郎. "Manshū jihen zen ni okeru zai-Man Nihon-

jin no dōkō: Manshūkoku seikaku keisei no ichi yōin" 満州事変前にお
ける在満日本人の動向―満州国性格形成の一要因　(The movements
and attitudes of Japanese residents in Manhuria, 1921–1931: Their idea
of "Interracial harmony"), *Kokusai seiji* (1978), no. 43: *Manshū jihen*,
pp. 51–76 [1]

—— "Manshūkoku Kyōwakai no seijiteki tenkai" 満州国協和会の政治
的展開 (The Kyōwakai and the political stabilization of Manchukuo).
Nenpō seijigaku, 1972, pp. 231–83. 1973. [2]

Hirota Kōki Denki Kankōkai 広田弘毅伝記刊行会, ed. *Hirota Kōki* 広田
弘毅. Published by the editor, 1966.

Hoshino Akiyoshi 星野昭吉. "'Rokōkyō jiken' made no Nihon no tai-Chū
seisaku no tenkai" 「蘆溝橋事件」までの日本の対中政策の展開 (The development of Japanese policy up to the outbreak of the "Marco Polo
Bridge Incident"). In Fujii Shōzō 藤井昇三, ed., *1930-nendai Chūgoku no
kenkyū* 1930年代中国の研究 (Studies on China in the 1930s), pp. 303–47.
Ajia Keizai Kenkyūjo, 1975.

Hosoya Chihiro 細谷千博. "Gaikōkan Yoshida Shigeru no yume to zasetsu:
Nichi-Ei teikei e no mosaku" 外交官吉田茂の夢と挫折―日英提携への
模索 (The dreams and frustrations of Yoshida Shigeru the diplomat: His
search for Anglo-Japanese cooperation). In Hosoya, *Nihon gaikō no zahyō*
日本外交の座標 (Thought and behavior in Japanese diplomacy), pp. 18–
52. Chūō Kōronsha, 1979. [1]

—— "Nihon no Ei-Beikan to senkanki no higashi Ajia" 日本の英米観と
戦間期の東アジア (Japanese views of the Anglo-American powers, and
East Asia in the interwar period). In Hosoya, ed., *Nichi-Ei kankeishi, 1917–
1949,* pp. 1–43. [2]

—— "1934-nen no Nichi-Ei fukashin kyōtei mondai" 1934年の日英不可侵
協定問題 (An attempt at a rapprochement with Britain in the mid-1930s:
The question of an Anglo-Japanese nonagression pact). *Kokusai seiji* (1978),
no. 58: *Nichi-Ei kankei no shiteki tenkai*, pp. 69–85. [3]

Hosoya Chihiro, Saitō Makoto, Imai Seiich, Royama Michio 斎藤真, 今井
清一, 蠟山道雄, eds. *Nichi-Bei kankeishi: Kaisen ni itaru 10-nen, 1931–
1941*日米関係史―開戦に至る十年, 1931—1941年 (A history of Japanese-
American relations: The decade preceding the war, 1931–1941). 4 vols.
Tokyo Dakigaku Shuppankai, 1971–72. Its English edition is Dorothy Borg
and Shumpei Okamoto, eds., *Pearl Harbor as History: Japanese-American
Relations, 1931–1941*. New York: Columbia University Press, 1973.

Hosoya Chihiro, ed., *Nichi-Ei kankeishi, 1917–1949* 日英関係史, 1917–1949
(History of Anglo-Japanese relations, 1917–1949). Tokyo Daigaku Shuppankai, 1982.

—— *Taiheiyō-Ajiaken no kokusai keizai funsōshi, 1922–1945* 太平洋・アジア

圏の国際経済紛争史, 1922—1945 (History of international economic conflicts in the Pacific and Asia, 1922–1945). Tokyo Daigaku Shuppankai, 1983. [4]

Ikeda Kiyoshi 池田清. *Kaigun to Nihon* 海軍と日本 (The navy and Japan). Chūō Kōronsha, 1981.

Ikei Masaru 池井優. "Manshū jihen o meguru Nichi-Bei sōgo imēgi" 満州事変をめぐる日米相互イメージ (Japanese and American images at the time of the Manchurian Incident). *Kokusai seiji* (1966), no. 34, pp. 58–74. [1]

—— "1930-nendai no masumedia: Manshū jihen e no taiō o chūshin to shite" 1930年代のマスメディア—満州事変への対応を中心として (The mass media during the 1930s: With particular reference to response to the Manchurian Incident). In Miwa Kimitada, ed., *Saikō: Taiheiyō sensō zenya* 再考—太平洋戦争前夜 (Reconsideration: The eve of the Pacific War), pp. 142–94. Sōseiki, 1981. [2]

—— "Uchida Yasuya: Shōdo gaikō e no kiseki" 内田康哉—焦土外交への軌跡 (Uchida Yasuya and the origins of his "scorched-land" diplomacy). *Kokusai seiji* (1976), no. 56: *1930-nendai no Nihon gaikō*, pp. 1–21. [3]

Imai Shun 今井駿. "Iwayuru 'Kitō mitsuyu' ni tsuite no ichi kōsatsu" いわゆる冀東密輸についての一考察 (A study on the so-called Chi-tung smuggling trade in the 1930s). *Rekishigaku kenkyū* (November 1976), no. 438, pp. 1–19, 37.

Inaba Masao, Kobayashi Tatsuo, and Shimada Toshihiko 稲葉正夫, 小林龍夫, 島田俊彦 eds. (with an introduction). *Zoku Manshū jihen* 続満州事変 (Sequel volume on the Manchurian Incident). Vol. 11 of *Gendaishi shiryō*.

Inoki Masamichi 猪木正道. *Hyōden Yoshida Shigeru* 評伝吉田茂 (Yoshida Shigeru: A critical biography), vol. 2. Yomiuri Shinbunsha, 1980.

Iokibe Makoto 五百旗頭真, "Ishiwara Kanji ni okeru Shinakan no keisei" 石原莞爾における支那観の形成 (The formation of Ishiwara Kanji's views of China). *Seikei ronsō* (Hiroshima Daigaku) (April 1972), 21(5–6): 377–415. [1]

—— "Manshū jihen no ichimen: Ishiwara Kanji no Manmō mondai kaiketsuan" 満州事変の一面—石原莞爾の満蒙問題解決案 (An aspect of the Manchurian Incident: Ishiwara Kanji's grand scheme for the solution of the Manchurian-Mongolian question). *Seikei ronsō* (December 1971), 21(3): 49–75. [2]

—— "Rikugun ni yoru seiji shihai: 2.26 jiken kara Nitchū sensō e" 陸軍による政治支配—2.26事件から日中戦争へ (The army's control of Japanese politics: From the February 26 incident to the Sino-Japanese War). In Miyake et al, eds., *Showashi no gunbu to seiji*, 2:3–56. [3]

—— "Tōa Renmeiron no kihonteki seikaku" 東亜連盟論の基本的性格

(Ishiwara Kanji's "East Asian League": Its fundamental features). *Ajia kenkyū* (April 1975), 22(1):22–58. [4]

Iriye, Akira and Aruga Tadashi 有賀貞, eds. *Senkanki no Nihon gaikō* 戦間期の日本外交 (Japanese diplomacy between the wars). Tokyo Daigaku Shuppankai, 1984.

Ishii Osamu 石井修. *Cotton-Textile Diplomacy: Japan, Great Britain, and the United States, 1930–36*. New York: Arno Press, 1981.

—— "Nichi-In kaishō, 1933–34" 日印会商, 1933—34 (Japanese-Indian negotiations, 1933–34). *Ajia keizai* (March 1980), 21(3):58–70.

Ishiwara Kanji Zenshū Kankōkai 石原莞爾全集刊行会, ed. *Ishiwara Kanji zenshū* 石原莞爾全集 (The complete writings of Ishiwara Kanji). 8 vols. Published by the editor, 1976–77.

Itō Takashi 伊藤隆. "Katō Kanji kankei bunsho: Shōwa 8–9 nen o chūshin ni" 加藤寛治関係文書—昭和8・9年を中心に (Papers relating to Katō Kanji, 1933–34). *Tokyo toritsu daigaku hōgakkai zasshi* (March 1970), 10(2): 165–234. [1]

Itō Takashi, Sasaki Takashi 佐々木隆 et al., eds. *Mazaki Jinzaburō nikki* 真崎甚三郎日記 (The diary of Mazaki Jinzaburō). 6 vols. Yamakawa Shuppansha, 1982–87.

Itō Takashi and Sasaki Takashi, eds. "Suzuki Teiichi nikki, Shōwa 8–9-nen" 鈴木貞一日記, 昭和8—9 -nen (Diary of Suzuki Teiichi 1933–34) *Shigaku zasshi*. (January 1978), 87(1):68–95; (April 1978), 87(4):57–82. [2]

Iyotani Toshio 伊豫谷登士翁. "Amerika no tai-Ka men baku shakkan kōshō to Nihon" アメリカの対華棉麦借款交渉と日本 (The American plan for a cotton and wheat loan to China, and the attitudes of Japan). In Onoi Kazui ichirō 小野一一郎 et al., eds., *Ryōtaisenkanki no Ajia to Nihon* 両大戦間期のアジアと日本 (Asia and Japan in the interwar period), pp. 97–122. Ōtsuki Shoten, 1979.

Japan, Bōeichō 防衛庁 (Defense Agency), Bōei Kenshūjo Senshi Shitsu 防衛研修所戦史室, ed. (The War History Office, National Defense College ed. *Senshi sōsho: Daihon'ei rikugunbu*, vol 1: *Shōwa 15-nen 5-gatsu made*. 戦史叢書, 大本営陸軍部, 1—昭和15年 5 月迄 (War History series: Imperial Headquarters, army, vol. 1—Up to May 1940). Asagumo Shinbunsha, 1967.

—— *Senshi sōsho: Kantōgun*, vol. 1: *Tai-So senbi, Nomonhan jiken* 戦史叢書, 関東軍, 1—対ソ戦備, ノモンハン事件. (War History series: The Kwantung Army, vol. 1: War preparations against the Soviet Union, the Nomonhan Incident). Asagumo Shinbunsha, 1969.

Japan, Gaimushō 外務省 (Foreign Ministry), ed. *Nihon gaikō bunsho: Manshū jihen* 日本外交文書—満州事変 (Documents on Japanese foreign policy: The Manchurian Incident). 7 vols. 1977–81.

—— *Nihon gaikō bunsho: 1935-nen Rondon kaigun kaigi* (Documents on Japanese foreign policy: The London Naval conference of 1935). 1986.

Japan, Sanbō Honbu 参謀本部 (Army General Staff), ed. *Manshū jihen sakusen keika no gaiyō* 満州事変作戦経過の概要 (A summary of the development of military operations during the Manchurian Incident). Gannandō Shoten, 1972.

Kakegawa Tomiko 掛川トミ子. "Masumedia no tōsei to tai-Bei ronchō" マスメディアの統制と対米論調 (The control of the press and its views of the United States). In Hosoya Chihiro et al., eds., *Nichi-Bei kankeishi: Kaisen ni itaru 10-nen*, 4:3–80; also in Borg and Okamoto, eds., *Pearl Harbor as History*, pp. 533–49.

Kamimura Shin'ichi 上村伸一. *Nikka Jihen* 日華事変 (The Sino-Japanese War). 2 vols. Vols. 19 and 20 of *Nihon gaikōshi* 日本外交史 (Japanese diplomatic History). Kajima Kenkyūjo Shuppankai, 1971.

Kaneko Fumio 金子文夫 "1970-nendai ni okeru 'Manshū' kenkyū no genjō (2): Manshū jihen kara 'Manshūkoku' no hōkai made" 1970年代における『満州』研究の現状(2)— 満州事変から『満州国』崩壊まで (The state of the art: "Manchurian" studies in the 1970s, 2: From the Manchurian Incident to the demise of "Manchukuo"). *Ajia keizai* (November 1979), 20(11):24–43.

Karita Tōru 刈田徹. *Showa shoki seiji, gaikōshi kenkyū: Jūgatsu jiken to seikyoku* 昭和初期政治, 外交史研究—十月事件と政局 (A study of political and diplomatic history of the early Shōwa period: The October [1931] incident and the political situation). Ningen no Kagakusha, 1981.

Kawahara Hiroshi 河原宏. *Kindai Nihon no Ajia ninshiki* 近代日本のアジア認識 (Modern Japan's perception of Asia). Daisan Bunmeisha, 1976.

Kibata Yōichi 木畑洋一. "Nitchū sensō zenshi ni okeru kokusai kankyō: Igirisu no tai-Nichi seisaku, 1934" 日中戦争前史における国際環境—イギリスの対日政策, 1934 (Anglo-Japanese relations in 1934: The international environment prior to the Sino-Japanese War). *Kyōyō gakka kiyō* (Tokyo Daigaku) (March 1976), no. 9, pp. 1–26. [1]

—— "Nitchū sensō zen'ya ni okeru Igirisu no tai-Nichi seisaku" 日中戦争前夜におけるイギリスの対日政策 (Britain's policy toward Japan on the eve of the Sino-Japanese War). *Tokyo gaikokugo daigaku ronshū* (March 1979), no. 29, pp. 175–91. [2]

—— "Rīsu-Rosu shisetsudan to kokusai kankei" リース・ロス使節団と英中関係 (The Leith-Ross mission and Anglo-Chinese relations). In Nozawa, ed., *Chūgoku no heisei kaikaku to kokusai kankei*, pp. 199–230. [3]

Kindai Nihon Kenkyūkai 近代日本研究会, ed. *Nenpō kindai Nihon kenkyū*, no. 1: *Shōwaki no gunbu* 年報近代日本研究, 1—昭和期の軍部 (Journal of modern Japanese studies, no. 1: The military in the Shōwa period). Yamakawa Shuppansha, 1979.

Kitaoka Shin'ichi 北岡伸一. "Rikugun habatsu tairitsu (1931–1935) no saikentō: Taigai kokubō seisaku o chūshin to shite" 陸軍派閥対立(1931–1935)の再検討—対外国防政策を中心として (A reexamination of the army's factional struggle, 1931–35: With particular reference to foreign and defense policy). *Nenpō kindai Nihon kenkyū* (1979), no. 1: *Shōwaki no gunbu*, pp. 44–95.

Kobayashi Hideo 小林英夫. "Heisei kaikaku o meguru Nihon to Chūgoku" 幣制改革をめぐる日本と中国 (Japan and China's currency reform). In Nozawa Yutaka, ed., *Chūgoku no heisei kaikaku to kokusai kankei,* pp. 233–36.

—— *Shōwa fashisuto no gunzō* 昭和ファシストの群像 (A collective portrait of Shōwa fascists). Aoki Shoten, 1984.

Kobayashi Tatsuo 小林龍夫. "Kaigun gunshuku jōyaku, 1921–1936" 海軍軍縮条約, 1921–1936 (Treaties of naval limitation, 1921–1936). In Nihon Kokusai Seiji Gakkai, ed., *Taiheiyō sensō e no michi,* vol. 1, pp. 33–160.

Kobayshi Tatsuo, Inaba Masao, Shimada Toshihiko, and Usui Katsumi 稲葉正夫, 島田俊彦, 臼井勝美, eds. *Gendaishi shiryō,* vol. 12: *Nitchū Sensō, 4* 現代史資料：日中戦争 (Documents on contemporary history, vol. 12: Sino-Japanese War, 4). Misuzu Shobō, 1964; edited with an introduction.

Kobayashi Tatsuo and Shimada Toshihiko, eds. *Gendaishi shiryō, Manshu jijen* 現代史資料：満州事変 (Documents on contemporary history, vol. 7: The Manchurian Incident). Misuzo Shobō, 1964.

Kokka Shihon Yushutsu Kenkyūkai 国家資本輸出研究会, ed. (Nakamura Masanori, 中村政則 representative). *Nihon no shihon yushutsu: Tai-Chūgoku shakkan no kenkyū* 日本の資本輸出—対中国借款の研究 (Japanese export of capital: Studies on Japanese loans to China). Taga Shuppan, 1986.

Kurihara Ken 栗原健, ed. *Satō Naotake no menboku* 佐藤尚武の面目 (The real achievements of Satō Naotake). Hara Shobō, 1981.

Manshū Iminshi Kenkyūkai 満州移民史研究会, ed. *Nihon teikokushugika no Manshū imin* 日本帝国主義下の満州移民 (Immigration to Manchuria under Japanese imperialism). Ryūkei Shosha, 1976.

Manshū Kaitakushi Kankōkai 満州開拓史刊行会, ed. *Manshū kaitakushi* 満州開拓史 (A history of settlement in Manchuria), published by the editor, 1966.

Manshūshi Kenkyūkai 満州史研究会, ed. *Nihon teikokushugika no Manshū* 日本帝国主義下の満州 (Manchuria under Japan's imperialistic rule). Ochanomizu Shobō, 1972.

Matsumoto Shigeharu 松本重治. *Shanhai jidai* 上海時代 (My years in Shanghai). 3 vols. Chūō Kōronsha, 1975.

Matsumoto Toshirō 松本俊郎. "Heisei kaikaku to Nitchū keizai kankei" 幣制改革と日中経済関係 (The Chinese currency reform and Sino-Japanese economic relations). In Nozawa, ed., *Chūgoku no heisei kaikaku to kokusai kankei*, pp. 299–333.

Matsuoka Yōsuke Denki Kankōkai 松岡洋右伝記刊行会. *Matsuoka Yōsuke: Sono hito to shōgai* 松岡洋右―その人と生涯 (Matsuoka Yōsuke: The man and his life). Kōdansha, 1974.

Matsuzawa Tetsunari 松沢哲成. "Ishiwara Kanji to sekai saishū sensōron: Manshū jihen zengo no Nihon fashizumu undō" 石原莞爾と世界最終戦争論―満州事変前後の日本ファシズム運動 (Ishiwara Kanji and his idea of the final global war: The Japanese fascist movement at the time of the Manchurian Incident), parts 1–2. *Shakai kagaku kenkyū* (January 1971), 22(3):95–162; (March 1971), 22(4):45–116. [1]

—— "Manshū jihen to 'Minzoku kyōwa undō'" 満州事変と「民族協和」運動 (The Manchurian Incident and the "interracial harmony" movement). *Kokusai seiji*, no. 43: *Manshū jihen*, 1970, pp. 77–99. [2]

Mikuriya Takashi 御厨貴. "Kokusaku tōgō kikan setchi mondai no shiteki tenkai" 国策統合機関設置問題の史的展開 (The historical development of the problem of establishing an organ to integrate national policies). *Nenpō kindai Nihon kenkyū*, no. 1: *Shōwaki no gunbu*, pp. 122–72.

Minami Manshū Tetsudō Kabushiki Kaisha 南満州鉄道株式会社 (South Manchuria Railway Company), ed. *Manshū jihen to Mantetsu* 満州事変と満鉄 (The Manchurian Incident and the South Manchuria Railway Company). 2 vols. Dairen: SMRC, 1934; reprinted by Hara Shobō, 1974.

Mitani Taichirō 三谷太一郎. "Kokusai kin'yū shihon to Ajia no sensō" 国際金融資本とアジアの戦争 (International finance and the war in Asia). *Nenpō kindai Nihon kenkyū*, no 2: *Kindai Nihon to higashi Ajia*, 1980, pp. 114–58.

Miwa Kimitada 三輪公忠. "Kokusai kankei no kōzō to tenkai: Higashi Ajia sekai kara no hitotsuno komentarī" 国際関係の構造と展開―東アジア世界からの一つのコメンタリー (The structure and development of international relations: A commentary from an East Asian perspective). In Mushakōji Kinhide and Rōyama Michio 武者小路公秀, 蠟山道雄, eds., *Kokusaigaku* 国際学 (International studies), pp. 100–8. Tokyo Daigaku Shuppankai. 1976.

Miyake Masaki 三宅正樹. "Nichi-Doku bōkyō kyōtei to 'Ribbentoroppu kikan'" 日独防共協定と「リッベントロップ機関」 (The Japanese-German Anti-Comintern Pact and the "Ribbentrop Bureau"). In Miyake, *Nichi-Doku-I sangoku dōmei no kenkyū*, pp. 35–36. [1]

Miyake Masaki. *Nichi-Doku-I sangoku dōmei no kenkyū* 日独伊三国同盟の研究 (A Study on the Tripartite Alliance: Berlin-Rome-Tokyo). Nansōsha, 1975.

—— "Nichi-Doku kankei no rekishiteki tenkai to Soren" 日独関係の歴史的展開とソ連 (The historical development of German-Japanese relations and the Soviet Union). In Miwa Kimitada, ed., *Sōgō kōza Nihon no shakai bunkashi*, vol. 7: *Sekai no nakano Nihon* 総合講座日本の社会文化史，7，世界の中の日本 (Series on Japanese social and cultural history, vol. 7: Japan in the world), pp. 362–431. Kōdansha, 1974. [2]

Miyake Masaki et al., eds. *Shōwashi no gunbu to seiji* 昭和史の軍部と政治 (The military and politics in the history of the Shōwa period), 5 vols. vols 1 and 2. Daiichi Hōki Shuppan, 1983.

Mori Katsumi 森克㊉. *Manshū jihen no rimenshi* 満州事変の裏面史 (The inside history of the Manchurian Incident). Kokusho Kankōkai, 1976.

Morimatsu Toshio 森松俊夫. "'Manshū jihen minaoshiron e no chūkoku'" 「満州事変見直し論」への忠告 (A suggestion on "reinterpretation of the Manchurian Incident"). *Gunji shigaku* (September 1983), 19(2):2–18.

Nakamura Takafusa 中村隆英. *Senji Nihon no Kahoku keizai shihai* 戦時日本の華北経済支配 (Japan's wartime economic control over north China). Yamakawa Shuppansha, 1983.

Nakanishi Osamu 中西治. "'Manshūkoku' o meguru Nisso kankei: Manshū jihen e no Soren no taiō to Tōshi Tetsudō baikyaku mondai" 『満州国』をめぐる日ソ関係—満州事変へのソ連の対応と東支鉄道売却問題 (Soviet-Japanese relations centering on "Manchuokuo": The Soviet response to the Manchurian Incident and the problem of the sale of the Chinese Eastern Railway). In Hosoya, ed., *Taiheiyō-Ajiaken no kokusai keizai funsōshi, 1922–1945*, pp. 265–86.

Nihon Kokusai Seiji Gakkai 日本国際政治学会 (Japan Association of International Relations), ed. *Kokusai seiji* (1970), no. 43: *Manshū Jihen.*

—— *Taiheiyō sensō e no michi*, vol. 2: *Manshū jihen* 太平洋戦争への道，2—満州事変 (The road to the Pacific War, vol. 2: The Manchurian Incident). Asahi Shimbunsha, 1962.

—— *Taiheiyō sensō e no michi*, vol. 3: *Nitchū sensō* 太平洋戦争への道，3—日中戦争(上) (The road to the Pacific War, vol. 3: The Sino-Japanese War), Asahi Shimbunsha, 1962.

Nihon Seiji Gakkai 日本政治学会 (Japanese Political Science Association), ed. *Nenpō seijigaku, 1972: "Konoe shin taisei" no kenkyū* 年報政治学 1972—「近衛新体制」の研究 *(The Annals of the Japanese Political Science Association, 1972: Studies on Prince Konoe's "New Order")*. Iwanami Shoten, 1973.

Nomura Minoru 野村実. "Bōkyō kyōtei kyōka kōshō to Doku-So fukashin jōyaku" 防共協定強化交渉と独ソ不可侵条約 (Negotiations to strengthen the Anti-Comintern Pact and the conclusion of the Nazi-Soviet Non-Aggression Pact). In *Nenpō kindai Nihon kenkyū*, no. 1: *Shōwaki no gunbu* (1979) no. 1: pp. 173–200.

—— *Taiheiyō sensō to Nihon no gunbu* 太平洋戦争と日本の軍部 (The Pacific War and the Japanese military). Yamakawa Shuppansha, 1983, pp. 31–63, 153–246.

Nozawa Yutaka 野沢豊, ed. *Chūgoku no heisei kaikaku to kokusai kankei* 中国の幣制改革と国際関係 (Currency reforms in China, and international relations). Tokyo Daigaku Shuppankai, 1981.

Ogata Sadako 緒方貞子. "Gaikō to yoron: Renmei dattai o meguru ichi kōsatsu" 外交と世論―連盟脱退をめぐる一考察 (Diplomacy and public opinion: A study on Japan's withdrawal from the League of Nations). *Kokusai seiji* (1970), no. 41: *Nihon gaikōshi kenkyū— Yoron to gaikō*, pp. 40–55.

—— *Manshū Jihen to seisaku no keisei katei* 満州事変と政策の形成過程 (The Manchurian Incident and the policymaking process). Hara Shobō, 1966.

Ōhata Tokushirō 大畑篤四郎. "Nichi-Doku bōkyō kyōtei, dō kyōka mondai (1935–1939)" 日独防共協定, 同強化問題, 1935—1939 (The problem of concluding and strengthening the Anti-Comintern Pact between Japan and Germany, 1935–1939). In Nihon Kokusai Seiji Gakkai, ed., *Taiheiyō sensō e no michi*, 5:3–155. [1]

—— "Tenkanki no keizai gaikō: 1925–35 nenki gaikō no ichi sokumen" 転換期の経済外交―1925—35年期外交の一側面 (Economic diplomacy in a transitional period: One aspect of foreign policy in 1925–35). *Seiji keizai shigaku* (November 1978), no. 150, pp. 103–12. [2]

Okabe Makio 岡部牧夫. *Manshūkoku* 満州国 (Manchukuo). Sanseidō, 1979. [1]

—— "Manshū nōgyō imin seisaku no tenkai" 満州農業移民政策の展開 (The development of [Japanese] agricultural immigration policy in Manchuria). In Fujwara Akira 藤原彰 et al., eds., *Nihon fashizumu to Higashi Ajia* 日本ファシズムと東アジア (Japanese fascism and East Asia), pp. 145–59. Aoki Shoten, 1977. [2]

—— "Shokuminchi fashizumu undō no seiritsu to tenkai" 植民地ファシズム運動の成立と展開 (The emergence and development of colonialist fascist movements). *Rekishigaku kenkyū* (March 1974), no. 406, pp. 1–16. [3]

Okada Taishō Kiroku Hensankai 岡田大将記録編纂会, ed. *Okada Keisuike*. 岡田啓介 Published by the editor, 1956.

Sakai Tetsuya 酒井哲哉 "Nihon gaikō ni okeru Sorenkan no hensen, 1923–

37″日本外交におけるソ連観の変遷, 1923—37 (Changing perceptions of the Soviet Union in Japanese diplomacy, 1923–37), *Kokka gakkai zasshi* (April 1984) 97(3–4):106–36.

Sakamoto Masako 坂本雅子. "Mitsui bussan to 'Manshū,' Chūgoku shijō" 三井物産と満州, 中国市場 (The Mitsui Bussan Company and the Manchurian and Chinese markets). In Fujiwara Akira and Nozawa Yutaka 藤原彰・野沢豊, eds., *Nihon fashizumu to Higashi Ajia* 日本ファシズムと東アジア (Japanese fascism and East Asia), pp. 106–44. Aoki Shoten, 1977.

Sasaki Takashi 佐々木隆. "Rikugun 'kakushinha' no tenkai" 陸軍「革新派」の展開 (The rise of the army's "renovationist" faction). *Nenpō kindai Nihon kenkyū*, vol. 1: *Shōwashi no gunbu*, pp. 1–43.

Satō Naotake 佐藤尚武. *Kaiko 80-nen* 回顧八十年 (My reminiscences of eighty years). Jiji Tsūshinsha, 1963.

Shidehara Heiwa Zaidan 幣原平和財団, ed. *Shidehara Kijūrō* 幣原喜重郎. Published by the editor, 1955.

Shimada Toshihiko 島田俊彦. "Kahoku kōsaku to kokkō chōsei (1933–1937)" 華北工作と国交調整(1933—1937年) (Operations in north China and readjustment in diplomatic relations, 1933–1937). In Nihon Kokusai Seiji Gakkai, ed., *Taiheiyō sensō e no michi*, 3:3–244. [1]

—— *Kantōgun* 関東軍 (The Kwantung Army). Chūō Kōronsha, 1965.

—— "Kawagoe-Chōgun kaidan no butaiura" 川越・張群会談の舞台裏 (Kawagoe–Chang Chun conversations), *Ajia kenkyū*, (April 1963), 10(1):49–68 (part 1); (October 1964), 10(3):23–49 (part 2). [2]

—— *Manshū jihen* 満州事変 (The Manchurian Incident). Vol. 7 of *Kindai no sensō* 近代の戦争 (Modern warfare series). Shin Jinbutsu Ōraisha, 1966.

—— "Manshū jihen no tenkai" 満州事変の展開, 1931–32 (The development of the Manchurian Incident, 1931–32). In Nihon Kokusai Seiji Gakkai, ed., *Taiheiyō sensō e no michi*, 2:3–188. [3]

—— "Umezu-Ka Ōkin kyōtei no seiritsu" 梅津・何応欽協定の成立 (The conclusion of the Umezu-Ho Ying-chin agreement). *Kokusai seiji: Nihon gaikōshi kenkyū—Shōwa jidai* (1960), no. 11, pp. 50–70. [4]

Shimada Toshihiko and Inaba Masao 稲葉正夫, (edited with an introduction). *Gendaishi shiryō, Vol. 8: Nitchū sensō, 1* 現代史資料, 8—日中戦争, 1 (Documents on contemporary history, Vol. 8: Sino-Japanese War 1). Misuzu Shobō 1964.

Shimizu Hideko 清水秀子, "Nihon gaikō bunsho 'Manshū jihen' ni tsuite" 日本外交文書『満州事変』について (On the *Documents on Japanese Foreign Policy: The Manchurian Incident*), *Gunji shigaku* (September 1982), 18(2):36–53. [1]

—— "Tai-Man kikō no hensen" 対満機構の変遷 (Changes in the Japanese administrative structure regarding Manchuria). *Kokusai seiji* (1968), no. 37, pp. 136–55. [2]

Shinmi Yukihiko 新見幸彦. "Jōyaku kaigun jidai no hōkai" 条約海軍時代の崩壊 (The collapse of the treaty period of naval limitation). *Kokugakuin daigaku hōken ronsō* (March 1983), no. 10, pp. 78–118.

Soejima Enshō 副島圓照 "'Manshūkoku' ni yoru Chūgoku kaikan sesshū" 「満州国」による中国海関接収 (The Manchukuo authorities' takeover of the Chinese maritime customs). *Jinbun gakuhō* (Kyoto Daigaku) (March 1979), no. 47, pp. 135–53.

Suzuki Takashi 鈴木隆史, "'Manshū kenkyū no genjō to kadai" 「満州」研究の現状と課題 (Manchurian studies: Its present state and future assignments). *Ajia keizai* (April 1971), 12(4):49–60. [1]

—— "Nihon teikokushugi to Manshū (Chūgoku tōhoku): 'Manshūkoku' no seiritsu oyobi sono tōchi ni tsuite" 日本帝国主義と満州(中国東北)—『満州国』の成立およびその統治について (Japanese imperialism and Manchuria: The creation and control of Manchukuo). *Tokushima daigaku kyōyōbu kiyō: Shakai kagakuhen* (March 1966), no. 1, pp. 47–63; (March 1967), no. 2, pp. 47–63. [2]

Tanaka Hiromi 田中宏巳. "Shōwa 7-nen zengo ni okeru Tōgō gurūpu no katsudō: Ogasawara Naganari nikki o tōshite" 昭和7年前後における東郷グループの活動—小笠原長生日記を通して (Activities of the Tōgō group about 1932: A study based on Ogasawara Naganari's diary). *Bōei daigakkō kiyō (Jinbun kagakuhen)* (September 1985), no. 51, pp. 7–37; (March 1986), no. 52, pp. 37–65.

Tanaka Sōgorō 田中惣五郎. *Nihon fashizumushi* 日本ファシズム史 (A history of Japanese fascism). Kawade Shobō Shinsha, 1960.

Tobe Ryōichi 戸部良一. "Shiratori Toshio to Manshū jihen" 白鳥敏夫と満州事変 (Shiratori Toshio and the Manchurian Incident). *Bōei daigakkō kiyō: Shakai kagakuhen* (September 1979), no. 39, pp. 77–130.

Tokitō Hideto 時任英人. "Inukai Tsuyoshi to Manshū jihen" 犬養毅と満州事変 (Inukai Tsuyoshi and the Manchurian Incident). *Seiji keizai shigaku* (December 1983), no. 209, pp. 45–66. [1]

—— "Manshūkoku shōnin to Saitō naikaku" 満州国承認と斎藤内閣 (The Saitō cabinet and the recognition of Manchukuo). *Kokusaigaku ronshū* (Jōchi Daigaku) (December 1982), 5(2):17–29. [2]

Tōkyō Daigaku Shakai Kagaku Kenkyūjo 東京大学社会科学研究所, ed. *Tōkyō Daigaku Shakai Kagaku Kenkyūjo shozō Shimada bunsho mokuroku* 東京大学社会科学研究所所蔵島田文書目録 (Catalogue of the papers of Shimada [Toshihiko] in the possession of the Social Science Research Institute, Tokyo University). 1978.

Tsunoda Jun 角田順, ed. *Ishiwara Kanji shiryō: Kokubō ronsaku* 石原莞爾

資料—国防論策 (Papers relating to Ishiwara Kanji: Treaties on national defense). Hara Shobō, 1967.

Tsunoda Jun, ed. *Ishiwara Kanji shiryō: Sensō shiron* 石原莞爾資料—戦争史論 (Papers relating to Ishiwara Kanji: Treaties on war history). Hara Shobō, 1968.

Tsutsui Kiyotada 筒井清忠. *Shōwaki Nihon no kōzō: Sono rekishi shakai-gakuteki kōsatsu* 昭和期日本の構造—その歴史社会学的考察 (The structure of Shōwa Japan: Its historical and sociological study). Yūhikaku, 1984.

Uchida Yasuya Denki Hensan Iinkai 内田康哉伝記編纂委員会, ed. *Uchida Yasuya* 内田康哉. Kajima Kenkyūjo Shuppandai, 1968.

Uchiyama Masakuma 内山正熊. "Manshūjihen to Kokusai Renmei dattai" 満州事変と国際連盟脱退 (The Manchurian Incident and [Japan's] withdrawal from the League of Nations). *Kokusai seiji* (1970), no. 43, pp. 155–81.

Unno Yoshirō 海野芳郎, "Dainiji Rondon gunshuku kaigi" 第2次ロンドン軍縮会議 (The second London Naval Conference). In Horinouchi Kensuke 堀内謙介, ed., *Nihon gaikōshi*, vol. 16: *Kaigun gunshuku kōshō, Fusen jōyaku* 日本外交史，16—海軍軍縮交渉，不戦条約 (Japanese diplomatic history, vol. 16: Negotiations for naval limitation and the Kellogg-Briand Pact), pp. 263–360. Kajima Kenkyūjo Shuppankai, 1973. [1]

—— "Kokusai Renmei oyobi gunshuku kaigi to Satō Naotake" 国際連盟および軍縮会議と佐藤尚武 (Satō Naotake and the League of Nations and conferences of arms limitation). In Kurihara, ed., *Satō Naotake no menboku*, pp. 25–84. [2]

Uno Shigeaki 宇野重昭. "Chūgoku no dōkō" 中国の動向 (Developments in China, 1933–1939). In Nihon Kokusai Seiji Gakkai, ed., *Taiheiyō sensō e no michi*, 3:247–363. [1]

—— "Hirota Kōki no tai-Ka seisaku to Shō Kai-seki: Jigotai gaikō no genkaisei" 広田弘毅の対華政策と蒋介石—自護体外交の限界性 (The limits of Hirota Kōki's diplomacy of watchful waiting toward Chiang Kai-shek). *Kokusai seiji* (1977), no. 56: *1930-nendai no Nihon gaikō—Yonin no gaisō o chūshin to shite*, pp. 22–45. [2]

Usui Katsumi 臼井勝美, "Gaimushō: Hito to kikō" 外務省—人と機構 (The Foreign Ministry: Its personnel and organization). In Hosoya Chihiro et al., eds., *Nichi-Bei kankeishi*, 1:113–40; also in Borg and Okamoto, eds., *Pearl Harbor as History*, pp. 127–48. [1]

—— "Hirota Kōkiron" 広田弘毅論 (On Hirota Kōki). *Kokusai seiji* (1966), no. 33, pp. 41–53. [2]

—— "Junēbu no hannō: 9.18 jiken chokugo" ジュネーブの反応—9.18事

件直後 (The reaction of Geneva: Immediately after the Mukden incident). *Nihon rekishi* (October 1972), no. 293, pp. 65–76. [3]

—— Kinshū senryō: Shidehara gaikō no ichi kōsatsu" 錦州占領—幣原外交 の一考察 (The occupation of Chinchow: A study of Shidehara diplomacy). *Shien* (March 1975), no. 112, pp. 1–17. [4]

—— *Manshū jihen: Sensō to gaikō to* 満州事変—戦争と外交と (The Manchurian Incident: War and diplomacy). Chūō Kōronsha, 1974.

—— "Manshū jihen to Shidehara gaikō" 満州事変と幣原外交 (The Manchurian Incident and Shidehara diplomacy). *Tsukuba hōsei* (March 1978), no. 1, pp. 53–74. [5]

—— "Satō gaikō to Nitchū kankei: 1937-nen sangatsu–gogatsu" 佐藤外交 と日中関係—1937年3月—5月 (Satō diplomacy and Sino-Japanese relations, March–May 1937). In Iriye and Aruga, eds., *Senkanki no Nihon gaikō*, pp. 241–66. [6]

Yamamoto Mitsuru 山本満. "Nichi-In (Nichi-Ei) mengyō funsō (1933–34)" 日印（日英）綿業紛争(1933—34) (Japanese-Indian [British] conflict over cotton industries). In Hosoya, ed., *Taiheiyō, Ajia-ken no kokusai keizai funsōshi, 1922–1945*, pp. 3–40.

Yanagisawa Asobu 柳沢遊 "Daiichiji Nichi-In kaishō (1933–34) o meguru Ei-In kankei" 第一次日印会商(1933—34)をめぐる英印関係 (Indian-British relations centering on the first Japanese-Indian conversations, 1933–34). *Bōeki to keizai* (1980), no. 129, pp. 30–48.

Yoda Yoshiie 依田憙家, ed. *Nitchū sensōshi shiryō*, vol. 4: *Senryōchi shihai, 1* 日中戦争史資料：占領地支配1. (Historical materials on the Sino-Japanese War: Documents on Japanese occupied areas.) Kawade Shobō Shinsha, 1975.

Yoshida Yutaka 吉田裕. "Manshū jihenka ni okeru gunbu" 満州事変下に おける軍部 (The military during the Manchurian Incident). *Nihonshi kenkyū* (June 1982), no. 238, pp. 39–74.

Yoshimi Yoshiaki 吉見義明. "Manshū jihenron" 満州事変論 (On the Manchurian Incident). In Eguchi Keiichi 江口圭一, ed., *Taikei Nihon gendaishi* 体系・日本現代史 (Series on contemporary Japanese history), 1:38–84. Nihon Hyōronsha, 1978.

Yu Xin-qun 兪辛焞, "Daiichiji Shanhai jihen to Gaimushō no yakuwari" 第一次上海事変と外務省の役割 (The first Shanghai incident and the role of the Japanese Foreign Ministry). *Hōkei ronshū: Hōritsuhen* (Aichi Daigaku) (August 1984), no. 105, pp. 55–87. [1]

—— "Kairai Manshūkoku no juritsu to Gaimushō" かいらい満州国の樹 立と外務省 (The creation of the puppet state Manchukuo, and the Foreign Ministry). *Shakai kagaku tōkyū* (February 1984), 29(2):87–128. [2]

Yu Xin-qun. *Manshū jihenki no Chū-Nichi gaikōshi kenkyū* 満州事変期の中日外交史研究 (A study of Sino-Japanese diplomatic history in the period of the Manchurian Incident). Tōhō Shoten, 1986.

—— "Manshū jihen to Shidehara gaikō" 満州事変と幣原外交 (The Manchurian Incident and Shidehara diplomacy). *Nihonshi kenkyū* (September 1983), no. 253, pp. 30–60. [3]

6

From the Sino-Japanese War to the Pacific War

Hatano Sumio
Asada Sadao

THE CHINA WAR AND JAPAN'S PEACE MANEUVERS

The Sino-Japanese War, which was waged from the Marco Polo Bridge Incident of 1937 to the end of the Pacific War in 1945, had so many facets that it is not always easy to draw a comprehensive picture of it.

Basic Works on the Sino-Japanese War

For some time after the war, memoirs written by those who participated in the China war were the only source materials. A breakthrough was made in 1961 by Hata Ikuhiko's work, *Nitchū sensōshi* (A history of the Sino-Japanese War), which elucidates the conflicting moves within Japan's field army in north China and the army leadership in Tokyo. Irreconcilable differences over the disposition of the Marco Polo Bridge Incident arose within the army between those who advocated expanding hostilities and those who insisted on scaling them down. In the end the former prevailed, making a local settlement impossible. Hata gives a detailed account of how by miscalculation a seemingly minor incident developed into full-scale, protracted warfare in China.

Subsequently Hata joined Kokusai Seijgakkai's research group for the *Taiheiyō senso̅ e no michi* series and wrote a monographic essay (in vol. 4) on military developments in the Sino-Japanese War, 1937–1941. For an English translation, see James Morley, ed., *The China Quagmire: Japan's Expansion on the Asian Continent, 1933–1941* (Columbia University Press, 1983). In comparison with his first book, Hata's contribution is a straightforward military and strategic account of events up to the Nomonhan Incident of 1939.

Usui Katsumi's contribution [2] to the same volume, translated also in *The China Quagmire*, parallels Hata's essay and carefully traces the political and diplomatic developments of the Sino-Japanese War (1937–41). In his usual way, Usui solidly based his account on Foreign Ministry archival materials and other new sources. He presents a detailed description of various episodes: German mediation efforts (involving German Ambassador Oskar Trautmann); Prime Minister Konoe Fumimaro's statement (January 1938) that the Japanese government would henceforth cease to deal with Chiang Kai-shek; the establishment of the Wang Ching-wei regime; and (contrary to Konoe's statement) Japan's secret peace maneuvers through direct negotiations with the Chungking government.

Subsequently Usui published a compact but valuable book, *Nitchū senso̅: Wahei ka sensen kakudai ka* (The Sino-Japanese War: Peace making or military escalation). In this book he depicts an overall picture of the Asian war up to 1945, succinctly bringing out its multifarious aspects: conflict of views within the Japanese military and the government, developments within China, and the involvement of the powers.

Usui's more recent essay [1] his contribution to Hosoya Chihiro, ed., *Nichi-Ei kankeishi, 1917–1949*) examines Japanese images of Britain that became increasingly hostile in the course of the Sino-Japanese War. He shows how Japan's policymakers took note of Britain's behind-the-scenes support of Chinese efforts to resist Japan and analyzes the process through which they came to define the Sino-

Japanese conflict as a part of the struggle between the status quo powers, represented by Britain, and the anti–status quo power, Japan. In this same study Usui notes the upsurge of anti-British movements instigated by the Japanese army that aimed at suppressing pro–Anglo-American forces at home. The anti-British movement, which reached a peak in 1939, is examined in great detail in Nagai Kazu's article [3].

The most recent survey of the Sino-Japanese War is Furuya Tetsuo's *Nitchū sensō* (The Sino-Japanese War), which appeared in 1985. This incisive book devotes much space to the prehistory of the war (the role of the Kwantung Army and Japan's "Manchurian-Mongolian interests," and the developments from the Manchurian Incident to the Marco Polo Bridge incident). He also analyzes the process through which the "China Incident" escalated into an all-out war. In particular, he traces Japan's changing war aims and inconsistent conduct of the war. He also offers a useful discussion on why Japan chose to keep it an "undeclared war."

Source Materials

During the 1960s important first-hand accounts of the Sino-Japanese War were published. Horiba Kazuo, a former staff officer of the China Expeditionary Army, published *Shina jihen sensō shidōshi* (A history of military strategy in the Sino-Japanese War). Imai Takeo, who was also a staff officer in the China Expeditionary Army, has published *Shina jihen no kaisō* (Recollections of the Sino-Japanese War). In addition, there are two useful books that throw light not only on the military but also on diplomatic aspects of the Sino-Japanese War. One is Imoto Kumao, *Sakusen nisshi de tsuzuru Shina jihen* (The China Incident as narrated through the war diary), based on the diary of Commander Imoto who served in the China Expeditionary Army and the Operations Section of the General Staff in 1939–1942. The other is Funaki Shigeru, *Shina hakengun sōshireikan Okamura Yasuji Taishō* (Biography of General Okamura Yasuji, the commander in chief of the China Expeditionary Army), which liberally quotes from his unpublished diary.

In addition, from the late 1960s onward a large quantity of basic army documents was edited and published as *Nitchū sensō* (The Sino-

Japanese War) in five volumes as part of the *Gendaishi shiryō* series. (For details, see chapter 4).

During the 1970s useful works with documentary value continued to appear. Kamimura Shin'ichi made the most of his own diplomatic experiences in writing his two-volume *Nikka jihen* (The Sino-Japanese War), which was published in the Kajima's series on Japanese diplomatic history. The work contains a detailed and reliable account of diplomatic developments leading to the establishment of the Wang Ching-wei government in 1940.

Materials on military affairs are fully provided in the "China Theater Operations Series" (15 vols.) of the official War History series edited by Bōeichō Senshishitsu. Of particular use are: Morimatsu Toshio et al., *Shina jihen rikugun sakusen* (Military operations in the Sino-Japanese War); and Morimatsu Toshio, *Hokushi no chiansen* (Operations to maintain public peace and order in north China). The latter contain a mine of information and material on economic and ideological warfare waged in north China between Japan's North China Expeditionary Forces and the Chinese Communists.

The Powers and Sino-Japanese Relations

In the 1970s research interest began to turn to the attitudes of the Western powers toward the Sino-Japanese War. For instance, Akira Iriye in his article [1] examines the process through which "invisible cooperation" between Great Britain and the United States in East Asia became increasingly apparent after 1938 and discusses the impact of this development on the Sino-Japanese War. In a recent essay [1] Watanabe Akio sharply analyzes the dilemma that the Japanese government faced in 1937–39: how to lessen the risk of economic sanctions by the United States and Britain, while at the same time pursuing a China policy that antagonized these powers.

A research topic that is recently attracting Japanese scholars is the question of British "appeasement" toward Japan over the China issue. Ikeda Kiyoshi's expert essays [1], [2] on the subject of Anglo-Japanese relations during 1937–41 and the Pacific War, examine Sir Robert Craigie's policy of appeasement toward Japan and attribute its failure to the hardening of Washington's attitude toward Japan. On the basis of British archival materials, Ikeda presents a dynamic picture of

British policy toward Japan in the broad context of increasingly close Anglo-American relations. Also utilizing the British sources, Satō Kyōzō has published an article [3] on the question of dispatching capital ships to Singapore against the background of Britain's Far Eastern strategy in 1939. He examines the circumstances that compelled the rejection of such an expedition as a case study in the declining importance of Far Eastern defense in Britain's global strategy. That decision, he concludes, was a strategic factor in Britain's "appeasement" of Japan.

Turning to the Japanese side, after Prime Minister Konoe Fumimaro's January 1938 statement (proclaiming that Japan would "stop dealing with the Kuomingtung government"), a plan took shape to adjust diplomatic relations with Britain in the hope of putting further pressure on the Chiang Kai-shek government and forcing a favorable settlement of the war. Hosoya Chihiro's essay [6] shows that, it was precisely in this context that the parley between Ambassador Craigie and Foreign Minister Ugaki Kazushige began, but that any possibility of Anglo-Japanese cooperation was shattered by the second Konoe statement (in November 1938) proclaiming the "New Order in East Asia."

On Anglo-Japanese relations and the Japanese military during this period, Nagai Kazu has also written some useful articles: [1], [2]. According to him, the Japanese army attempted to obtain concessions from Britain in return for guaranteeing its interests in central and south China; the army thus planned to bring pressure to bear on the Kuomingtung government by the combined diplomatic strategy of alliance with the Axis powers and improvement of relations with Britain. These efforts failed, however, because the United States began to aid China after the Arita-Craigie talks. Among recent works, there is Katō Yōko's article on Prime Minister Hiranuma Kiichirō's efforts to make peace with the Chunking government through Anglo-American mediation in 1939. She shows that the Hiranuma cabinet, while racked with controversies over the question of strengthening the Anti-Comintern Pact with Germany, made repeated approaches to the United States government asking its help for peace mediation with Chungking. When Hiranuma, utterly shaken by the conclusion of the Nazi-Soviet pact in 1939, made his parting statement that the European situation was "complex and inscrutable," the author contends that his real aim was to express his policy to abandon alignment with the Axis powers.

More detailed analyses of these Anglo-Japanese talks are found in the articles by Inoue Yūichi and Uchiyama Masakuma [2]. The former examines the attitude of Foreign Minister Arita Hachirō in his talks with Craigie. The latter discusses the blockading of the British concessions in Tientsin by Japanese forces, an incident that became the focal point of the Arita-Craigie talks. Also important are some of the essays contained in Furuya Tetsuo, ed., *Nitchū sensōshi kenkyū* (Studies on the history of the Sino-Japanese War).

Peace Maneuvers

In their research on a series of peace moves during the Sino-Japanese War, historians have been handicapped but by no means deterred by the scarcity of sources. The first overview of various peace efforts is Etō Shinkichi's essay on Japan's peace maneuvers toward China. Hata Ikuhiko has written a noteworthy essay [3] on Japan's peace maneuvers and its terms for peace. And Matsuzaki Shōichi—the chief compiler of the *Shōwashi no tennō* series (see chapter 4)—vividly portrays in a recent essay a comprehensive picture of peace manuevers from 1937 to 1945 on the basis of numerous interviews with surviving participants.

One mediation effort that seemed likely to succeed was the peace negotiations by the German ambassador to China in 1937–38, Oscar P. Trautmann. On this subject Miyake Masaki has analyzed the structure of "dual diplomacy" that existed on both the Japanese and German sides in his well-documented article [2]. A more recent study is Gerhard Krebs' article, which utilizes German documents to clarify the role of the Japanese Army General Staff in the Trautmann mediation. Also noteworthy is Unno Yoshirō's article on peace efforts by third parties during the early phase of the Sino-Japanese War.

As new army documents became available, more detailed studies on peace maneuvers began to appear. Shimada Toshihiko in his article [2] describes in detail: (a) the so-called "Sun Tzu-liang scheme," which the Japanese Army General Staff and the China Expeditionary Army attempted in 1940 to accomplish through Sun Tzu-liang who was influential with Chiang Kai-shek; and (b) the "Ch'ien Yung-ming scheme" of the same year, which was attempted by the leading figure of the Chekiang financial circle, under the initiative of Foreign Minister Matsuoka Yōsuke. In his article [1] on the "Funatsu Project", Shimada also provides documents relating to a maneuver that was engineered by Ishii Itarō, chief of the East Asia Bureau of the Foreign Ministry, and Funatsu Shin'ichirō, a former diplomat and a businessman who maintained ties with high officials in the Chinese Nationalist government. Tobe Ryōichi [3] discusses the activities of those "peace feelers" in relation to Japan's characteristic mode of decision making. Tobe contends that the simultaneous existence of so many peace maneuvers revealed a lack of leadership and coordination in policymaking.

On the other hand, Mitani Taichirō in his recent essay [1] explains the failure of peace efforts in terms of the shifts in Japan's international environment. He argues that anti-Communist ideology in Japan's China policy initially served to mobilize Japan against the Soviet Union but with the conclusion of the Nazi-Soviet pact in 1939 it was used as a means to turn attention to controlling the Chinese Communist Party, thus jeopardizing the chances of successful peace maneuver.

The peace conspiracy known as the "Wang Ching-wei scheme" underwent a peculiar process eventually leading to the creation of a "puppet regime" in China. The realities and historical characteristics of this peace effort have been examined in the previously cited works by Usui Katsumi [2], Etō Shinkichi, and Fujii Shōzō. Among recent works, the most noteworthy is Takahashi Hisashi's well-documented study [1] on the moves within the Japanese army up until Wang Ching-wei defected from the wartime capital of Chungking in December 1938, thus beginning his sixteen-month search for collaboration with Japan. Takahashi's extremely detailed analysis shows that there were differences and conflicts within Japan's army leadership concerning the "Wang scheme." However, Wang's true motives for defecting from Chungking and the nature of his pan-Asian idea remain obscure.

These peace maneuvers by Wang Ching-wei took place against a domestic political background that involved conflict between army and the Foreign Ministry's policies. The conflict that surfaced over the establishment of the Asia Development Board (Kōain) in 1938 is expertly treated in Baba Akira's works. Baba describes the struggle between the military, who attempted to take exclusive control over China issues and promote peace maneuvers through Wang Ching-wei by establishing the Asia Development Board on the one hand, and Foreign Minister Ugaki Kazushige, who endeavored to carry on negotiations with the Chungking government on the other. Although there are very few reliable materials on China's reaction to Japanese peace maneuvers in 1937–1941, Fujii Shōzō has made a valiant effort to examine this subject.

This would be an appropriate place to mention Japanese source materials on these peace maneuvers. Nishi Yoshiaki's *Higeki no shōnin* (A witness to tragedy) is valuable as a first-hand account of the history of Sino-Japanese peace talks. Nishi, a staff officer in the Army General Staff, was involved in the initial stages of the "Wang Ching-wei scheme" and the "Ch'ien Yung-ming scheme," and he had the support of Matsuoka Yōsuke and the South Manchuria Railway Company. Also important are the previously mentioned memoirs by Imai Takeo, who (as a member in the Army General Staff's China section and a staff officer of the China Expeditionary Army) was deeply involved in the Wang Ching-wei scheme and the "Sun Tzu-liang scheme." The third volume of Matsumoto Shigeharu's memoirs, *Shanhai jidai* (My Shanghai days), contains a personal account of his peace efforts including the Wang scheme. Matsumoto, then director of the Shanghai office of the Dōmei News Agency, maintained broad contacts with Chinese leaders. Lieutenant-Colonel Kagesa Sadaaki, the central army figure in the Wang Ching-wei scheme, wrote his memoir in 1944; it is included in *Gendaishi shiryō*, vol. 13: *Nitchū sensō*, vol. 5. Among the Foreign Ministry materials relating to this scheme, "Yano kiroku" (The records of Yano Seiki) is important. Yano, a middle-ranking diplomat, was involved in the Wang Ching-wei scheme along with Kagesa.

More recently, Itō Takashi and Toriumi Yasushi unearthed and printed the manuscripts of Matsumoto Kuraji relating to Kayano Naga-tomo's peace efforts in 1938–1941. (Kayano was a journalist and businessman long and deeply involved in Chinese affairs.) Also important are the papers and diary of Ogawa Heikichi, a member of Konoe's brain trust on Chinese affairs, who worked in collaboration with Kayano. These are published as Ogawa Heikichi Bunsho Kenkyūkai, ed., *Ogawa Heikichi kankei bunsho* (Papers relating to Ogawa Heikichi).

The "New Order in East Asia" as an Ideology

Concerning the concept of the "New Order in East Asia," which formed the ideological basis for the Wang Ching-wei peace scheme, Hashikawa Bunzō has thrown light on both its idealistic aspects and its dogmatic and exclusionist elements in a stimulating essay [2]. A more recent work is Miwa Kimitada's essay [1] surveying Pan-Asianism. Miwa analyzes the train of ideas on the unification of Asia (which culminated in the Konoe statement of January 1938), reinterpreting them as manifestations of the East Asian concept of international order peculiar to this region.

The idea of the "East Asia cooperative community" (Tōa kyōdōtairon) was advocated by the members of Shōwa Kenkyūkai (Shōwa Research Society)—the brain trust for Prime Minister Konoe—as the theoretical underpinning of the New Order in East Asia. The ideas of the East Asia cooperative community—and the "East Asian League" later—are as germane to an understanding of this period as is the concept of "racial harmony" in Manchukuo for an understanding of the previous period.

Miwa Kimitada [3] takes a positive view of the East Asia cooperative community idea as an attempt at forming a new international order on the basis of traditional values and outlooks in this area. In a similar vein, Takahashi Hisashi [3] analyzes the ideas held by intellectuals such as Rōyama Masamichi, Ozaki Hozumi, and Kada Tetsuji. Both Takahashi and Gomi Toshiki evaluate the East Asia cooperative community idea as an expression of the search by anguished intellectuals for a doctrine of Asian solidarity that would reject traditional Western colonialism and at the same time satisfy Chinese nationalism. Hashikawa Bunzō [2] also admits that this idea manifested the Japanese intellectuals' sympathy with Chinese nationalism. He points out, however, that for these intellectuals the idea of an East Asia cooperative community was in reality nothing more than a convenient way out of the dilemma of choosing between either the "invasion" or "liberation" of Asia. Going one step further, Imai Seiichi contends that the East Asia cooperative community idea was fundamentally a rationale to justify the Japanese invasion of China.

The East Asian League (Tōa Renmei)—another Pan-Asianist idea about solidarity between Japan, Manchukuo, and China—was advocated by the Ishiwara Kanji group and was adopted by the Wang Ching-wei regime. It took concrete institutional form when the East Asian League Association (Tōa Renmei Kyōkai) was founded in October 1939 as an ultranationalistic organization. Iokibe Makoto, in his basic essay, analyzes the idea of the East Asian League.

Because it called for a serious reexamination of Japan's previous continental policy, there are some intellectual historians, such as Hashikawa Bunzō, who have given the League credit for a positive role. The dissenting view is represented by Katsurahara Mitsumasa who argues that although the Ishiwara group at first accurately perceived the course of Chinese nationalism, it began gradually to lose this realistic viewpoint and tended toward a dogmatic view. The activities of the Tōa Renmei Kyōkai are treated in Terunuma Yasutaka's article.

Another study that discusses the intellectual aspects of Japanese policy toward China during this period is Uno Shigeaki's essay, which analyzes the affinity between the Japanese and Chinese perceptions of Asia in the context of their shared assertion of an Asian identity against modern Europe.

The Nanking Atrocities

The notorious Nanking atrocities (the "rape of Nanking") of December 1937 received sensational attention at the Tokyo war crimes trials. Since the restoration of Sino-Japanese diplomatic relations in 1972 the Nanking atrocities have once again became the subject of heated controversy among both academics and journalists. On the basis of many years of scholarly reseach, Hora Tomio wrote *Nankin jiken* (The Nanking incident) in 1972. In the following year he edited a two-volume collection of documents, *Nitchū sensōshi shiryō*, vols. 8 and 9: *Nankin jiken* (Documents concerning the Sino-Japanese War, vols. 8 and 9: The Nanking incident). Hora's studies resulted in confirming the number of the Chinese victims that the Tokyo trials presented— "more than 200,000 dead."

Meanwhile, this historical controversy became highly politicized when the Japanese Ministry of Education attempted, starting in 1981, to heavily censor high school history textbooks in order to tone down their descriptions of wartime Japanese atrocities, including the scaling down of the Nanking atrocities. Suzuki Akira, on the basis of his interviews with those involved in the incident, claimed that the "Nanking massacre" was "fictitious." To refute such an assertion, Hora published in 1983 *Ketteiban: Nankin dai gyakusatsu jiken* (The great Nanking massacre: The definitive story). Hora elaborated his points in a more polemical yet well-documented book, *Nankin dai gyakusatsu no shōmei* (The proof of the great Nanking massacre), published in 1986.

Recently, Hata Ikuhiko joined the controversy by publishing *Nankin jiken: "Gyakusatsu" no kōzō* (The Nanking incident: The making of a "massacre"). After pointing out the politicized nature of the controversy, Hata utilizes new sources to place the Nanking atrocities acurately in the context of military developments of the Sino-Japanese War. Hata's is the most balanced account. Another recent work that studies the incident against the broader background of the Sino-Japanese War is Yoshida Yutaka, *Tennō no guntai to Nankin jiken: Mō hitotsu no Nitchū sensōshi* (The Emperor's army and the Nanking atrocities: Another side of the Sino-Japanese War).

THE SOUTHWARD ADVANCE

Standard Account

The slogan "Greater East Asia Coprosperity Sphere," which publicly appeared for the first time in the summer of 1940, signaled that the agenda of Japanese expansionist policy had come to include control over resource-rich and strategically important European colonies in Southeast Asia. After the outbreak of the European war in 1939, and especially after sweeping German victories in the west in the summer of 1940, the Japanese were dazzled by the golden opportunity for aggressive thrusts southward.

How Japan took advantage of this opportunity to expand in the south is examined in great detail in volume 6 of Nihon Kokusai Seiji Gakkai, ed., *Taiheiyō sensō e no michi*. Nagaoka Shinjirō's contribution is a monographic essay, dealing with the diplomatic aspects of Japan's southern policy in 1937–1941. Though a useful work, it does not give an entirely satisfying analytical treatment of Japan's unsuccessful negotiations with the Dutch East Indies authorities (from September

1940 to June 1941) to purchase vital resources such as oil. No full-length work on these negotiations has appeared to date.

The second contributor, Hata Ikuhiko [1], focuses on the course of Japan's military advance into French Indochina in 1940–41. He closely analyzes the policymaking process (especially interservice deliberations and conflicts), emphasizing the ambivalent position taken by the navy. Initially the navy leaders were reluctant to force-fully advance to the south for fear of war with the United States. For this reason, in July 1940 the navy toned down the army-sponsored draft policy that called for southward thrust and preparations for war against the United States. Paradoxically, the army's pressure for a southward advance even at the risk of war provided the navy with a convenient pretext to demand priority in the allocation of strategic materials needed for war with the United States. Once the navy was granted this priority, the advocates of war (especially among the middle-echelon naval officers) became increasingly belligerent. Thus it was the navy that finally took the initiative in the decision to advance into southern Indochina in July 1941, and this became the immediate cause of the Pacific War. Hata's contribution, as sum-marized above, is perhaps the most stimulating of all of the essays in the *Taiheiyō sensō e no michi* series. Selected translations of Nagaoka's and Hata's essays are printed in James W. Morley, ed., *The Fateful Choice: Japan's Advance into Southeast Asia, 1939–1941* (Columbia University Press, 1980).

Subsequently Nagaoka has written an amplified version of the above-mentioned essay, with a focus on Indochina. Titled *Nanshin mondai* (The problems of the southward advance), and written under the editorial supervision of Matsumoto Shun'ichi and Andō Yoshirō, it was published as volume 22 of Kajima's Japanese diplomatic history series.

New Works

There are two recent studies that treat Japan's advance into northern Indochina. Tobe Ryōichi's essay [2] on the subject raises an important question: Was Japan's march there (September 1940) the first step toward an armed advance into southern Indochina, or was it carried out merely as a measure to force an early settlement of the Sino-

Japanese War? Tobe leans toward the former view. The most recent work on this subject is an article by Hatano Sumio which focuses on the Japanese army and the State policy paper "The Outline of the Main Principles for Coping with the Changing World Situation." In this essay Hatano points out that one of the key factors in the decision to move southward in the summer of 1940 was the rising expectation among the middle-grade army officers that the China war would be speedily settled with the success of the Sun Tzu-liang scheme.

Recently two monographs appeared on the subject of Japan's advance to northern and southern Indochina. Murakami Sachiko's posthumously published work, *Futsu-In shinchū, 1940–45* (Japan's thrust into French Indochina), is the translation of her Ph.D. dissertation for the City University of New York. Murakami also used French sources in order to examine her subject in the context of trilateral interactions between Tokyo, Vichy France, and Hanoi. She emphasizes that the actions of the Japanese army were neither reckless nor indiscreet but were rational and realistic, based on policies and strategies sanctioned by the government. According to the author, the fundamental reason why Japan chose a policy of southward expansion was the aggravation of Japanese-American relations after the outbreak of the China war.

Another new study is Yoshizawa Minami's work, *Sensō kakudai no kōzu: Nihongun no "Futsu-In shinchū"* (The scenario of the expansion of war: Japanese forces' "entry into French Indochina"), which emphasizes internal factors that contributed to military escalation. The author argues that the question of stationing forces in Indochina sharpened conflicts within policymaking groups, and, especially, that the parochial sectionalism within the army and navy created a structure of "decision making" that eschewed clear decisions and ended in a "parallel" pursuit of mutually incompatible aims. From such a perspective of bureaucratic politics, Yoshizawa criticizes interpretations that attribute to a small group of individuals or groups the responsibility for opening the hostilities.

The Oil Question

Regarding the petroleum question, in the context of Japan's southward advance, two early studies deserve mention. One is Itagaki

314 HATANO SUMIO AND ASADA SADAO

Yōichi's essay, which examines Japan's negotiations with European colonies in Southeast Asia centering on the petroleum issue. The other is Matsumoto Shigekazu's article [1] on the American military and the oil question, which analyzes Japan's oil negotiations with the Dutch East Indies and America's response.

Recent studies from the viewpoint of the Japanese Navy, contained in Nomura Minoru's collections of essays, emphasize how crucial the oil issue was as a factor in Japan's final decision for war. The most reliable account, solidly based on naval records, is contained in Suekuni Masao's *Kaigun gunsenbi*, vol. 1: *Shōwa 16-nen 11-gatsu made* (Naval armaments and preparations for war, vol. 1: Up to November 1941), a volume in the official *Senshi sōsho* (War History) series.

Basic source materials on Japan's southward advance, emanating mostly from the army, are printed in the following collections: Nihon Kokusai Seiji Gakkai (Inaba Masao et al.) eds., *Taiheiyō sensō e no michi: Bessatsu shiryōhen* (The road to the Pacific War: Supplementary volume of documents); and Tsunoda Jun, ed., *Gendaishi shiryō*, vol. 10: *Nitchū sensō, 3*.

The record of the Navy Ministry's Research Section from 1934 is being published as Doi Akira et al., eds., *Shōwa shakai keizai shiryō shūsei: Kaigunshō shiryō* (Collections of sources on social and economic history of the Shōwa period: Documents of the Navy Ministry). To date twelve volumes have appeared, covering up to April 1941. This series prints documents accumulated by the Research Section (Chōsaka) of the Navy Ministry from 1934 to 1945. Unfortunately, the editors of this collection did not carefully select relevant navy records; they included many documents that emanate from other ministries and do not directly relate to naval policy. But patient perusal will yield important naval documents (not available elsewhere) which show how the early program of "peaceful southern expansion" in search of oil resources gradually developed into plans and strategies for military expansion southward. Other important topics covered are: Japan's response to the outbreak and development of the European war and the navy's attitude toward the proposed Tripartite Pact. Especially valuable for our purposes are: vol. 8 (July–December 1939); vol. 9 (January–May 1940); vol. 10 (June–August 1940); vol. 11 (September–December 1940); vol. 12 (January–April 1941).

THE TRIPARTITE PACT AND JAPANESE-SOVIET RELATIONS

Basic Works

The first full-scale work is vol. 5 of Nihon Kokusai Seiji Gakkai's *Taiheiyo senso e no michi,* which is devoted to detailed studies on the Tripartite Pact and the Japanese-Soviet Neutrality Pact. The volume contains expert monographic essays by Ōhata Tokushirō on the Anti-Comintern Pact, 1935–39, and by Hosoya Chihiro [7] on the Tripartite Pact and the negotiations leading to the Japanese-Soviet Neutrality Treaty, 1939–41. These works present detailed accounts of the role played by the Japanese military in formulating policy toward Germany and the Soviet Union. Ōhata closely analyzes the Anti-Comintern Pact (1936) and traces the course of Japanese-German relations up to the signing of the German-Soviet Nonaggression Pact (1939).

Hosoya continues the account from there up to 1941 [8]. The author vividly depicts Japan's twisted road to the conclusion of the Tripartite Pact (September 1940) by highlighting interservice struggles, in which the navy opposed the pact with Germany for fear that it might involve Japan in war with the United States. Within the navy, too, middle-echelon officers who supported a military alliance with the Axis powers gained ascendancy. Hosoya [3] also presents an interesting account of Foreign Minister Matsuoka's policy of "brinkmanship": to take a "resolute stand" toward the United States in order to deter its entry into the European war and prevent its interference with Japan's southward advance. Matsuoka's "grand plan" was to include the Soviet Union and form a four-power pact. When he realized the infeasibility of his cherished plan during his tour in Europe, he dramatically concluded the Japanese-Soviet Neutrality Pact (April 1941).

This volume is one of the most outstanding works in the *Taiheiyō senso e no michi* series, and its selective translation was published as James R. Morley, ed., *Deterrent Diplomacy: Japan, Germany, and the USSR, 1935–1940* (Columbia University Press, 1976).

The Nature of the "Strange Alliance"

In 1975 Miyake Masaki published his massive work, *Nichi-Doku-I sangoku dōmei no kenkyū* (A study of the Tripartite Alliance: Berlin-

Rome-Tokyo), which brought together his previous studies on the subject. Based on a meticulous collation of the Japanese archives with German and other Western sources, this book attempts to throw new light on the realities of this alliance between Japan and Germany, both of whom attempted to use this pact for their own selfish and mutually incompatible purposes. The main emphasis of the book is on unraveling the German motives for concluding an alliance with Japan. Miyake closely examines the peculiar role of Foreign Minister Joachim von Ribbentrop, who was traditionally regarded as a faithful "watchdog" for Hitler, and comes up with the thesis that there was a form of "dual diplomacy" between the so-called "Ribbentrop Bureau" and the German Foreign Office.

Regarding Japanese motives, Miyake presents a close-knit analysis of the plan (September 1940) for a four-power pact, in which Germany is said to have promised to serve as an intermediary to persuade Russia to join the Tripartite Pact. There are many other stimulating points raised in Miyake's monograph, and some of them are presented in his subsequent essay [1] on the development of Japanese-German relations and the Soviet Union.

In 1977 Yoshii Hiroshi published his monograph, *Nichi-Doku-I sangoku dōmei to Nichi-Bei kankei: Taiheiyō senso zen kokusai kankei no kenkyū* (The Tripartite Pact and Japanese-American relations: A study in international relations prior to the outbreak of the Pacific War). In this book Yoshii traces the origins of the plan for a four-power pact among Japan, Germany, Italy, and the Soviet Union, and he discusses Japanese-Soviet talks looking toward such a pact. Especially interesting is Yoshii's close analysis of the reasons why the Japanese navy, hitherto opposed to the Tripartite Pact, changed its policy and decided to give its consent.

Nomura Minoru has published several articles on such topics as the negotiations leading to the Tripartite Pact and the German-Soviet Nonaggression Pact [1], a projected four-power pact including the Soviet Union [3], and the Japanese navy and the conclusion of the Tripartite Pact, with particular reference to Navy Minister Oikawa Koshirō and Admiral Yamamoto Isoroku [4]. These essays were subsequently collected in Normura's book, *Taiheiyō senso to Nihon gunbu* (The Pacific War and the Japanese military).

While these studies add much to our knowledge, there still remain questions about the behavior of the navy, which suddenly leaned toward the Tripartite Pact with the appointment of Admiral Oikawa as navy minister. In this regard, Asada Sadao [1] emphasizes the bureaucratic interests of the navy which utilized the Tripartite Pact as lever to demand a larger share of the budget and war materiel.

The Japanese-Soviet Neutrality Pact

Japanese-Soviet relations from the outbreak of the Sino-Japanese War to the conclusion of the neutrality pact present a dynamic picture in which large-scale border disputes—such as the Changkufeng incident (1938) and the Nomonhan Incident (1939)—were to be settled against the background of and in relation to the ongoing negotiations for the Tripartite Pact. What impacts did the Nomonhan Incident have on Japan's diplomatic policy? How did this incident affect Japanese plans for the Tripartite Pact and the neutrality treaty with the Soviet Union? These are interesting questions that await new research.

The only serious studies by Japanese scholars that have attracted our attention are Hirai Tomoyoshi's essay on Soviet-Japanese relations, 1933–39, and Hosoya Chihiro's work [8] on the developments leading to the Japanese-Soviet Neutrality Pact—monographic essays printed, respectively, in volumes 4 and 5 of the *Taiheiyō sensō e no michi* series. As for specific subjects, the Changkufeng incident is studied by Nakayama Takashi. Sasaki Chiyoko treats the Nomonhan Incident in her *Der Nomonhan Konflikt: Das fernostliche Vorspiel zum 2. Weltkrieg*. For military aspects of the Nomonhan Incident, the reader is referred to vol. 27 of the Senshi sōsho (War History) series, Nishihara Yukio (author), *Kantōgun*, vol. 1: *Tai-So senbi, Nomonhan jiken* (The Kwantung Army, vol. 1: War preparations against the Soviet Union, the Nomonhan Incident). A detailed record of the Kwantung Army relating to the Nomonhan Incident is contained in *Nitchū sensō, 3* (vol. 10 of the *Gendaishi shiryō* series), edited with an introduction by Tsunoda Jun. The *Shōwashi no tennō* series, edited by Yomiuri Shinbunsha, vols. 25–29, contains the record of interviews with numerous soldiers who participated in the Nomonhan Incident (see chapter 4.) By far the best work on the Nomonhan Incident, however, is by American scholar Alvin D. Coox. His recent study, based on thirty years of research, *Nomonhan: Japan Against Russia, 1939* (Stanford University Press, 1985; 2 vols.) is monumental. A specialist in military history, Coox thoroughly examined Japanese sources and interviewed more than four hundred individuals involved to depict in detail this crucial incident which turned Japan's strategy from "advance to the north" to "advance to the south." This important work, focusing on the operational activities of the Kwantung Army, also provides a useful history of the Kwantung Army and a detailed and comprehensive bibliography of Japanese source materials on this incident.

How Japan's policy toward the Soviet Union changed as the result of the Nomonhan Incident is elucidated in Momose Hiroshi's essay that analyzes, on the basis of the Foreign Ministry archives, the development of Japanese foreign policy toward Eastern Europe in the interwar period. According to Momose, an expert on Eastern Europe, the Japanese government until the Nomonhan Incident had made efforts to strengthen political ties with the Eastern European countries, but after Nomonhan Tokyo abandoned these efforts as it adopted the policy of not antagonizing the Soviet Union.

In addition to these works, there is Kameyama Ichiji et al. (Nishi Haruhiko, editorial supervisor), *Nisso kokkō mondai* (The problem of diplomatic relations between Japan and the Soviet Union, 1917–1945), vol. 15 of the Kajima series on Japanese diplomatic history. A detailed but prosaic account of bilateral relations from the Bolshevik Revolution to the end of the Pacific War in 1945, this volume is based heavily on "Nisso kōshōshi" (A history of Japanese-Soviet relations), which had been compiled by the Europe-Asia Bureau of the Japanese Foreign Ministry in 1942.

THE CAUSES OF THE PACIFIC WAR

By the late 1960s, both the accumulation of source materials and monographs as well as methodological sophistication made it possible for historians to take diverse approaches to the causes of the Pacific War. This was the background of the Kawaguchiko conference in 1969 (see "Overview" and chapter 4).

The Japanese Style of Decision Making

Hosoya Chihiro, the Japanese organizer of this binational conference, was one of the first scholars in Japan to apply the theories of decision-making to the study of diplomatic history. Among the many essays he has published, the most comprehensive are: "Retrogression in Japan's Foreign Policy Decision-Making Process" [7] and a succinct article [9] comparing the Japanese and American foreign policy decision-making processes. In the latter essay Hosoya characterizes the decision-making structure in prewar Japan as a "truncated pyramid system"— a system lacking strong leadership at the top to coordinate and unify diverse views within the government. In the course of the 1930s, Hosoya maintains, the government's integrative capacity further deteriorated, as its decision-making power became more and more diffuse and decentralized.

Applying this analytical framework, Hosoya has published a series of stimulating essays on the rupture of Japanese-American relations in 1941: [2], [4], [5]. In these works he demonstrated that America's economic sanctions, calculated to deter Japan from further military advances, failed to bring about the intended result; on the contrary, such a hard-line policy merely spurred the Japanese on to advance further southward, thus exacerbating the already strained relations between the two nations. Hosoya attributed this miscalculation on the part of American leaders to their lack of understanding of the highly "irrational" pattern of thought and behavior that characterized Japan's decision makers, who were dominated by middle-echelon officers.

This focus on the decision-making process was apparent at the Kawaguchiko meeting. In explaining the failure of Japan's leaders to prevent its drift toward war, Japanese participants tended to stress the organizational or bureaucratic imperatives. This approach was quite explicit in Asada Sadao's essay on the Japanese navy. Members of each section within Japan's policy machinery were preoccupied with their immediate and parochial bureaucratic interests. This tendency was particularly noticeable among staff officers who were often guided by narrowly strategic views in spasmodically making a chain of fateful decisions leading to war.

Such an approach, emphasizing institutional malfunctionings and deficiencies in Japan's policymaking process, has been attacked by Japanese critics who would rather stress the personalities and the roles of such political leaders as Matsuoka Yōsuke and Konoe Fumimaro.

Gaps in Mutual Images

One of the important points raised at the Kawaguchiko meeting was the gap in mutual perceptions. Mushakōji Kinhide addressed himself to this question in his concluding essay on the structure of Japanese-American relations in the 1930s. He theoretically analyzed the pattern and process of mounting distrust, explaining why distorted images could not be rectified.

Most specifically, two papers were presented by Japanese participants that dealt with Japanese perceptions of the United States and its Far Eastern policy. Mitani Taichirō's paper [2] examined the response of Japan's intellectuals to Japan's changing international position, while Kakegawa Tomiko's paper analyzed in detail the press and public opinion in Japan during the 1930s. The latter demonstrates that major Japanese newspapers, under the pretext of press control, in actuality promoted national jingoism by preempting hard-line policies to be followed by the government and the military. In regard to perceptions and images, Hosoya Chihiro has pointed out in the course of the conference, that "image studies" in Japan are marred by methodological inadequacies; often "images" are treated interchangeably with "perceptions," "public opinion," or even "ideas" and "attitudes." Nor have "image studies" been particularly successful in demonstrating how certain images affected the decision-making process. In this regard, the essays in *Nichi-Bei kankeishi* were not entirely immune from these difficulties.

Anglo-Japanese Antagonism

One major criticism of the Kawaguchiko meeting was that it did not entirely succeed in explaining the close interrelationship between Japanese-American relations and the radical changes in European international relations in the late 1930s.

Until recently Anglo-Japanese relations in the latter half of the

1930s (especially after the outbreak of the Sino-Japanese War) have received little attention in Japan. This was partly because the British archives for this period were inaccessible until 1967, but more importantly because Japanese historians have tended to see the international crises in East Asia and Southeast Asia primarily in the context of Japanese-American relations.

For Japanese historians, the first full-scale research on Anglo-Japanese relations during the 1930s may be said to have started with the binational conference on the history of Anglo-Japanese relations, held in 1979 in London. It resulted in Hosoya Chihiro, ed., *Nichi-Ei kankeishi, 1917–1949* (A history of Anglo-Japanese relations, 1917–1949). Its English version—Ian Nish, ed., *Anglo-Japanese Alienation, 1919–1952: Papers of the Anglo-Japanese Conference on the History of the Second World War* (Cambridge University Press, 1982)—contains two essays not printed in the Japanese edition: "Postscript: Anglo-Japanese attitudes, 1940–41," by Hagiwara Nobutoshi; and "Work Completed and Work as Yet Unborn," by Donald C. Watt.

In the course of the conference Hosoya presented a new viewpoint that comprehends the Pacific War as essentially an "Anglo-Japanese war." In comparison with the Japanese-American war, which resulted from a conflict between America's "principles" and Japan's "program," the Anglo-Japanese confrontation in the Far East was far more serious, Hosoya suggested, because it involved direct clashes of *interests* between the two nations. As long as Japanese aggression was confined to China, however, there still remained room for compromise. But when Japan advanced to the south, threatening British imperial interests in Southeast Asia, war with England became inevitable, concludes Hosoya.

The only thorough criticism of *Nichi-Ei kankeishi* is a review article [2] by Sato Kyozo. He argues that Britain simply could not "appease" Japan without incurring strong opposition from the United States, the one nation Britain could not afford to alienate. In other words, Sato questions any study of bilateral Anglo-Japanese relations that does not fully take into consideration the powerful presence of the United States.

Sato has published his own studies on Anglo-Japanese relations during the 1930s. In one article [1], on Great Britain and Japan's New Order in East Asia, he has argued that Britain abandoned even its feeble posture toward Japan with the onset of the European war in 1939, turning all its efforts to cementing its hitherto unsatisfactory relationship with the United States. Particularly after the proclamation of the Atlantic Charter in August 1941, he contends, Prime Minister Churchill left the handling of East Asian problems solely in the hands of the United States, so that Anglo–Japanese relations eventually came, in large part, to be subsumed under Japanese-American relations. These works point to the importance of examining the development of Anglo–Japanese-American relations as they affected the coming of the Pacific War.

Recently Satō published a monograph, *Japan and Britain at the Crossroads, 1939–1941: A Study in the Dilemmas of Japanese Diplomacy,* based heavily on the British Foreign Office Records as well as the Japanese archives. He examines Anglo–Japanese relations from the outbreak of war in Europe to Pearl Harbor. His criticism of conventional scholarship on the origins of the Pacific War is that it concentrates exclusively on "the final yet decisive bargaining between Japan and the United States." He claims, however, that until the end of the summer of 1941 "the British willy-nilly had to take the lead in the Far East" because of the indecisiveness of the United States.

THE JAPANESE-AMERICAN NEGOTIATIONS

Early Works

The first memoir to be published by a Japanese diplomat was Ambassador Nomura Kichisaburō's *Beikoku ni tsukai shite: Nichi-Bei kōshō no kaiko* (Ambassador the United States: Reminiscences of the Japanese-American negotiations), which appeared in 1946. It has retained its value since the diary kept by Nomura has not yet been located (except in an unsatisfactory translation submitted to the Tokyo war crimes trials). For example, the memoir contains Nomura's personal views of President Roosevelt and Secretary of State Cordell Hull, his impressions of American politics at a critical juncture, and the reasons why he accepted the ambassadorship to Washington when conflict seemed almost unavoidable. Kurusu Saburō, a special envoy sent to assist Nomura, published two memoirs: *Hōmatsu no 35-nen* (Thirty-five years of vain endeavor), in 1949, and *Nichi-Bei gaikō hiwa* (Secret stories of Japanese-American diplomacy), in 1953. Rather discursive, these volumes are less informative than Nomura's straightforward account.

In 1953 two full-length memoirs appeared. One was Tōgō Shigenori's *Jidai no ichimen* (An aspect of the Shōwa era). The latter half of the book was translated into English as *The Cause of Japan* (New York: Simon and Schuster, 1956), and it has a thoughtful preface that summarizes the deleted portions. The other is Shigemitsu Mamoru, *Shōwa no dōran* (Turbulence during the Shōwa period), translated as *Japan and Her Destiny* (New York: Dutton, 1958). Both Tōgō's and Shigemitsu's memoirs still remain useful sources.

On the basis of these materials as well as a plethora of documents released by the Tokyo war crime trials, Japanese historians early began to take an interest in the "Japanese-American negotiations," which were initiated toward the end of 1940 and lasted until December 1941.

It is of interest to note here that very few Japanese scholars have felt drawn to the American revisionism of a "back-door-to-war" variety (Charles C. Tansill) or a conspiracy theory (Charles A. Beard). Those who invoked American revisionist arguments did so to rationalize Japan's course and also to appeal to resurgent Japanese nationalism. A retired diplomat, Ōtaka Shōjirō, published *Dainiji sekai taisen sekininron* (On the responsibility for World War II) and *Kishū ka bōryaku ka: Shinjuwan no sekinin* (Surprise attack or plot: Responsibility for Pearl Harbor). A high-ranking army officer, Tanaka Shi'nichi, wrote *Taisen totsu'nyū no shinsō* (The truth about the plunge into the Pacific War). One of the very few Japanese diplomatic historians who have identified themselves with the Beard-Tansill school of revisionism is Uchiyama Masakuma [1].

The Navy's Responsibility

The capstone of the *Taiheiyō sensō e no michi* series was Tsunoda Jun's monographic work on the Japanese-American negotiations and their rupture, 1940–41. Since this volume is forthcoming in English translation (in the Columbia University Press series), suffice it here to note that Tsunoda, in contrast to the early works that emphasized the role of the army, throws fresh light on the navy's responsibility for commencing the hostilities with the United States. Tsunoda attaches special importance to the role played after 1940 by the newly established "First (policy) Committee" that was composed of middle-echelon naval officers. It was these pro-Axis, anti-American officers, he argues, who took the initiative in policymaking within the navy and even preempted the army in forcing the decision for war with the United States.

On the other hand, official naval historians, most prominently Nomura Minoru, writing in his history of the Combined Fleet (in the *Senshi sōsho* [War History] series) and elsewhere, deemphasize the role of the First Committee, regarding it merely as a niche for Captain Ishikawa Shingo's radical self-assertions. Thus, Nomura denies that this committee had any crucial influence on the navy's decision for war. In contrast, the personality and ideology of Captain Ishikawa are emphasized in Kudō Michihiro's *Nihon kaigun to Taiheiyō sensō* (The Japanese navy and the Pacific War), vol. 2.

Finally, regarding the navy's responsibility for Japan's plunge into war, there is an extraordinarily candid record of heated, sometimes acrimonious, post-morten discussions among the surviving admirals, which was recently published as Shinmyō Takeo, ed., *Kaigun sensō kentō kaigi kiroku: Taiheiyō sensō kaisen no keii* (the record of discussions about the navy and the Pacific War; Circumstances leading to the ourbreak of the Pacific War). Especially noteworthy are the testimonies of Admiral Inoue Shigeyoshi, a leading "liberal" in the navy; he was bitterly critical of the irresponsibility of the senior naval leaders who drifted into the decision for war. Inoue's views are shared by the leading naval historian Ikeda Kiyoshi in his concise *Kaigun to Nihon* (The navy and Japan). It contains a persuasive analysis of the reasons for the navy's failure to restrain the army on the road to the Pacific War.

The Failure of the Negotiations

In 1970 two books appeared that traced in detail Japanese-American negotiations from April to December 1941. These are: Kase Toshikazu, *Nichi-Bei kōshō* (Japanese-American negotiations), which was published as volume 23 of the Kajima series on Japanese diplomatic history, and Okumura Fusao, *Nichi-Bei kōshō to Taiheiyō sensō* (Japanese-American negotiations and the Pacific War).

Known abroad as the author of *Journey to the Missouri* (New Haven, Conn: Yale University Press, 1950), Kase served as secretary to Foreign Ministers Matsuoka Yōsuke, Toyoda Teijirō, and Tōgō Shigenori successively. In the new volume Kase asserts that the negotiations with the United States, begun without any sure prospect of success and in a highly irregular form, in the end resulted in war, and holds the Japanese government responsible for a series of miscalculations starting with the conclusion of the Tripartite Pact. At the same time he is also critical about the "self-righteous" policy of the United States, especially the rigid "principles" uncompromisingly insisted upon by Secretary of State Hull. However, the author does not fully sustain these themes in his cut-and-dried factual presentation. Okumura, more critical of the United States, argues that the unilateral and provocative demands of the United States, typified in the Hull note of November 26, 1941, "torpedoed" Japanese-American negotiations, and that the aim of American policy was just to play for time.

Next, we shall turn to more specialized studies. Tsunoda Jun's above-mentioned monographic study (in the final volume of Nihon Kokusai Seiji Gakkai, ed., *Taiheiyō sensō e no michi*), that appeared in 1963, presents massive details on Japan's decision-making process, utilizing a variety of archival and manuscript materials. As the concluding volume, however, this is a disappointing work in an otherwise excellent series; Tsunoda's presentation is often ambiguous, uneven in coverage, and scattered with questionable value judgments. It is expected that its English version *(The Final Confrontation: Japan's Negotiations with the United States, 1941)* by David Titus and the late Okamoto Shumpei, due for publication in 1990, will rectify some of the shortcomings.

Matsumoto Shigekazu has published an able article [3] on Foreign Minister Tōgō Shigenori's thought and behavior in the Japanese-American negotiations of 1941. This well-documented study was followed by an article [2] that examines the "agonies" of Terasaki Tarō, the head of the Foreign Ministry's America Bureau. According to this study, Terasaki, who favored withdrawal of Japanese forces from China, became isolated within the Foreign Ministry by the pressures from its "Axis faction" and the army; consequently, substantial decision-making leadership in the Foregn Ministry gradually came to be assumed by Yamamoto Kumaichi, head of the East Asia Bureau. Yamamoto, who regularly attended the Imperial Headquarters–Cabinet Liaison Conferences as assistant to the foreign minister, has written "Daitōa sensō hishi" (A hidden history of the Greater East Asian War), which was posthumously published in *Kokusai seiji*, no. 26. Drafted in April–October 1944, this brief memoir sketches the moves within the government leading to the decision for war.

The Tōjō cabinet's attitude toward Japanese-American negotiations is examined in detail in Sudō Shinji's recent article [6]. Sudō argues that there remained considerable differences between the final compromise plans of the two governments—between the Japanese proposal labeled "B" (a more moderate proposal) and the American plan for a *modus vivendi*—and that these differences basically stemmed from the problems created by Japan's southward advance during the second Konoe cabinet.

On the basis of a close analysis of the decision-making process in both countries, Hosoya Chihiro argues that there remained a modicum of possibility, until the last moment, of avoiding hostilities on the basis of a *modus vivendi:* [2], [4], [5], [9]. In an essay [1] that he contributed to Hosoya et al, eds., *Nichi-Bei kankeishi* (vol. 1), he emphasizes the gaps in communication between the Japanese Foreign Ministry and its embassy in Washington as well as differences in negotiating style between Japan and the United States as important factors that obstructed Japanese-American negotiations. A recent study by Shiozaki Hiroaki [5] discusses the factor of "bureaucratic politics" within the Japanese government as it affected the final phase of Japanese-American negotiations, on the basis of new source materials that add to our knowledge of the "new bureaucrats" (the anti-Shidehara, pro-Axis and nationalist faction) within the Foreign Ministry.

Shiozaki's articles, covering a wide range of subjects and based on research in unpublished American and British as well as Japanese sources, are brought together in his recent book, *Nich-Ei-Bei sensō no kiro: Taiheiyō no yūwa o meguru seisenryaku* (The crossroad of Japan's war with Britain and the United States: Political and military strategies of appeasement in the Pacific). The author presents multilateral perspectives and historiographical observations on "appeasement in the Pacific," attempting to explain why it failed. He discusses Japanese-American negotiations prior to the war in the context of the Anglo-American strategy of appeasement in the Pacific that includes Canada and Australia as well.

Yoshii Hiroshi's above-mentioned *Nichi-Doku-I sangoku dōmei to Nichi-Bei kankei* (The Tripartite Pact and Japanese-American relations) goes deeper into the subject than previous studies such as Paul W. Schroeder's *The Axis Alliance and Japanese-American Relations, 1941* (Ithaca, N.Y.: Cornell University Press, 1958) and focuses on problems neglected in earlier works. One of them is how to assess the impact of the outbreak of the German-Soviet war (June 1941) upon Japanese-American relations. Yoshii contends that this war, by making it no longer necessary for the United States to appease Japan and by inducing the United States to side with the Soviet Union, led to the hardening of the U.S. position toward Japan after July 1941. And the American response to the Japanese advance into southern Indochina, Yoshii concludes, made the Pacific War inevitable. Thus, he takes issue with Schroeder who regarded the problem of troop withdrawal from China as the crucil factor in the coming of the war; according to Yoshii, the China problem—like the Axis Alliance—was a mere pretext, rather than the determining factor, for American entry into war with Japan. Yoshii develops the same thesis in his "Influence of the German-Soviet War on the Japan-U.S. Negotiations: Particularly Centering on Studies on the Problem of Secession from the Axis Alliance."

Regarding the proposal for a Konoe-Roosevelt conference, Sudō Shinji [2] examines the opposition of the Far Eastern Division of the State Department. In particular, he focuses on the role of Stanley K. Hornbeck, the spearhead of the anti-Japanese forces, in torpedoing the proposed summit talk. The work is heavily documented by the Hornbeck papers.

John Doe Associates

It was on the basis of informal talks among private citizens of the two countries that Japanese-American negotiations began. Until the early 1970s most studies tended to lightly dispose of these informal talks merely as episodes or side stories. Japanese historians, therefore, took immediate interest in Robert J. C. Butow's *The John Doe Associates: Backdoor Diplomacy for Peace, 1941* (Stanford University Press, 1974), which traced in massive detail the activities of the "John Doe Associates"—Bishop James E. Walsh, Father James M. Drought, Colonel Iwakuro Hideo, and Ikawa Tadao—and discussed the way they interfered with or unintentionally obstructed the "official" negotiations.

Stimulated by Butow's work, Shiozaki Hiroaki has published two articles: one [2] on the origins and political background of "the John Doe Associates"; and the other [1] on "the John Doe Associates" and Japanese-American negotiations. Both of these studies utilize not only the bulky Drought papers and the Walker manuscripts but also papers of Ikawa Tadao. Ikawa's papers were recently published as Shiozake Hiroaki and Itō Takashi, eds., *Ikawa Tadao Nichi-Bei kōshō shiryō* (Historical materials relating to Ikawa Tadao's role in Japanese-American negotiations), with a detailed introductory essay. The volume consists mainly of Ikawa's bulky correspondence and telegrams, and his memoirs (apparently written shortly after the war began). Taken together, these materials reveal that Ikawa was acting in close touch with Prime Minister Konoe and army authorities such as Mutō Akira (the chief of the Military Affairs Bureau). While in Washington, Ikawa had the confidence of Ambassador Nomura.

On the basis of these materials Shiozaki attempts to reassess positively the role of the Japanese members of the John Doe Associates and sharply criticizes previous accounts of "Japanese-American negotiations" which regard the private talks as a mere aberration from the proper course of diplomatic negotiations. Shiozaki's previously mentioned monograph, *Nichi-Ei-Bei sensō no kiro* (The crossroad of Japan's war with Britain and the United States), represents his attempt to underscore the broader significance of the "John Doe Associates" in the context of "appeasement in the Pacific."

A more balanced treatment of the John Doe Associates is found in Sudō Shinji's article [4] on the limited role of private citizens in Japanese-American negotiations. Sudō [1] details the hitherto obscure behavior of Colonel Iwakuro Hideo during his informal mission to the United States. Building on these studies, Sudō has published a more general essay [5] on Japanese-American negotiations and the Japanese military.

Recently he brought together his works in one volume, *Nichi-Bei kaisen gaikō no kenkyū: Nichi-Bei kōshō no hottan kara Haru nōto made* (A study of Japanese-American diplomacy up to the outbreak of the war: From the beginning of Japanese-American negotiations to the Hull note). Eschewing the devil theory of war, he rejects the verdict of the Tokyo war trials, American "revisionist" views of the Beard-Tansill variety, and the Japanese leftlist position that explains the origins of the Pacific War in terms of imperialism and class struggle. Rather, Sudō stresses "communication and perception gaps "between the United States and Japan as a major factor that obstructed diplomatic adjustment, although both sides wanted to avoid war. He also emphasizes the roles and personalities of individuals—Roosevelt, Hull, Stanley K. Hornbeck, and Ambassador Joseph C. Grew on the one hand, and Konoe, Tōjō, Ambassador Nomura, Matsuoka, Kurusu Saburō, Ikawa, and Iwakuro, on the other. Sudō's treatment of "Japanese-American negotiations," which he claims never got even started on the official level, largely supercedes early works.

Official Histories and Documents

The army's attitude toward Japanese-American negotiations is detailed in Bōeichō Senshishitsu, ed., *Daihon'ei rikugunbu; Dai Tōa sensō kaisen keii* (The Imperial Headquarters, army: Circumstances leading to the outbreak of the Greater East Asian War, 5 vols.) in the *Senshi sōsho* (War History) series. Though abundantly based on military records, these volumes, authored by Hara Shirō, are rather diffuse in presentation, often lacking a clear focus on the cause of and processes leading to the war.

The first volume treats Japan's reaction to the European war, the peace maneuvers in China, and increasing cries to carry out a southward advance by taking advantage of the German successes in the west. The second volume deals with Japan's march to northern Indochina, the Dutch-Japanese negotiations in 1940, and the Tripartite Pact. The third volume narrates Japanese efforts to exploit the Thai-Indochina border dispute, and further developments in Japan's southern policy and strategy up to early 1941. The fourth volume treats Japan's advance into southern Indochina in the summer of 1941 and the process through which "the determination for war" was reached.

The final volumes carries the account up to Pearl Harbor (for more detail, see chapter 4).

The reader is reminded that these volumes, reflecting a service viewpoint, tend to be apologetic about the army's policies and actions, while they are often critical toward the navy, Prime Minister Konoe, and the Foreign Ministry.

The navy's response to the army volumes is Bōeichō Senshishitsu, ed., *Daihon'ei kaigunbu: Dai Tōa sensō kaisen keii* (The Imperial Headquarters, navy: Circumstances leading to the outbreak of the Greater East Asian War), authored by Uchida Kazuomi. These companion (or, more accurately, "rival") volumes in the *Senshi sōsho* (War History) series treat the role of the navy somewhat self-critically, yet a careful reader will detect interservice differences between the army and navy versions of the road to Pearl Harbor. And it needs to be reemphasized that these official volumes, written by former officers in uniform, are more useful for the documents they cite than for their historical interpretations.

The Foreign Ministry records for the period under consideration were published in 1978 as Gaimushō, ed., *Nichi-Bei kōshō shiryō: Shōwa 16-nen nigatsu—jūnigatsu* (Materials relating to Japanese-American negotiations: February to December 1941) with a brief introductory essay by Hosoya Chihiro. This volume is divided into two parts: diplomatic documents pertaining to Japanese-American negotiations in Washington; and detailed commentaries and background accounts prepared by senior Foreign Ministry officials involved in Japanese-American negotiations. The bulk of the diplomatic documents in part 1 is the Japanese counterpart of U.S. Department of state, *Papers Relating to the Foreign Relations of the United States, 1931–41*, vol. 2 (1943) and *Foreign Relations, of the United States 1941*, vol. 4 (1956), and these documents constitute the primary Japanese sources. Since some of them had already been published in Ambassador Nomura's memoirs and elsewhere, the more useful portion of the volume is part 2. Originally compiled in 1942, it was revised in 1946 by the Foreign Ministry principals who, penitent for their failure to stop the bellicose policy of the military, were determined to leave a candid record in the hope that Japan could make a fresh beginning as a peace-loving nation. Until recently this portion of the record (part 2) was presumed to have been destroyed at the time of Japan's surrender, hence this delay in publishing it. In terms of coverage, part 2 is far broader, treating such matters as the domestic situation that the Foreign Ministry had to face, the deliberations at the Imperial Headquarters—Cabinet Liaison Conferences, the reaction of and policies toward the Axis powers, and the activities of the John Doe Associates.

War Plans and Operational Matters

Ikeda Kiyoshi has published essays on Japan's plans for conducting the war [3] and Japanese strategy toward Britain in the Pacific War [4]. The former study emphasizes the lack of any concrete plan to conclude the war at the time when the Japanese government opened hostilities. The latter essay, presented to the Anglo-Japanese Conference of historians in 1979, emphasizes that from a naval viewpoint, the Pacific War was predominantly a war with the United States. Nomura Minoru has also written an article [2] on Japan's war plans at the outbreak of the Pacific War.

In this connection, attention should be called to the most recent publication of the War History Department of the Defense Agency: *Senshi sōshō shiryōshū: Kaigun nendo sakusen keikaku (Shōwa 11-nen— Shōwa 16-nen)* (Documents accompanying War History series: The navy's annual operational plans, 1936–1941), in facsimile form.

One of the most interesting and readable volumes in the entire War History series is Tsunoda Kyūshi, *Hawai sakusen* (Naval attack against Hawaii), which is vol. 10 of the series. It contains an absorbing description of the desperate strategy conceived by Admiral Yamamoto Isoroku to invade and conquer Hawaii with a view to forcing an early peace with the United States on the basis of a drastic compromise on Japan's part. Since Yamamoto kept his bold plan—and his true intentions—to himself and his few trusted subordinates in the Combined Fleet for fear of meeting opposition from the naval authorities in Tokyo, his strategy (which came to naught with Japan's defeat at the Battle of Midway) can be reconstructed only from fragmentary sources.

The whole subject is examined in a highly readable and well-researched study by an American scholar, John F. Stephen, in his *Hawaii Under the Rising Sun: Japan's Plans for Conquest after Pearl Harbor* (Honolulu: University of Hawaii Press, 1984). Not surprisingly, this monograph instantly appeared in Japanese translation.

LEADERS OF JAPANESE DIPLOMACY

Konoe and Matsuoka

Research interest in Japanese foreign policy leaders after the outbreak of the Sino-Japanese War seems to be focused on two figures: Konoe Fumimaro, who thrice served as prime minister; and Matsuoka Yōsuke, who masterminded the Tripartite Pact.

Konoe's memoirs, whose reliability as a historical source is open to question, were published as early as 1946 under the titles of *Ushinawareshi seiji* (Politics that failed) and *Heiwa e no doryoku* (My struggle for peace). Yabe Teiji, a member of Konoe's brain trust and a professor at the Imperial University of Tokyo, authored in 1952 a full-length biography (in two volumes) on the basis of Konoe's memoirs, the Konoe family papers preserved at Yōmei Bunko (in Kyoto), and the diaries and memoirs left by figures close to Konoe. This superb biography contains useful materials for the political and diplomatic history of this period. A distinguished recent study is Oka Yoshitake's succinct and well-balanced biography which analyzes Konoe's political career in the context of domestic politics. Its English version is Shumpei Okamoto, tr., *Konoe Fumimaro* (University of Tokyo Press, 1984).

The "new order movement" *(Shin taisei undō)* has attracted the attention of historians in relation to the domestic background. Konoe's attitude toward this movement is studied in a substantial essay by Kurihara Akira. He systematically applies the methods of psychohistory and social psychology to closely analyze Konoe's peculiar personality and political style, and the result is a highly sophisticated study of this complex man. The most recent study of the relationship between the Konoe group and the "new order movement" is Itō Takashi's *Konoe shin taisei: Taisei Yokusankai e no michi* (Konoe's new order: The road to the Imperial Rule Assistance Association).

No serious study on Matsuoka appeared until the 1960s. One reason is that for some time after the war Matsuoka continued to be regarded as responsible for concluding the Tripartite Pact, obstructing Japanese-American negotiations, and thus driving Japan to war with the United States. Such a simplistic interpretation began to be modified in the 1960s, when new studies brought to light his plan for a "four-power pact" aimed at strengthening Japan's negotiating position vis-à-vis the United States. Among these studies the following are important. Hosoya Chihiro gives a good treatment of Matsuoka diplomacy in his above-mentioned monographic essay [7], contained in volume 5 of Nihon Kokusai Seiji Gakkai, ed., *Taiheiyō sensō e no michi*. He has also published a readable essay [3] on Matsuoka's foreign policy, paying sufficient attention to his formative period, especially his youth in Oregon. In addition, Yoshii Hiroshi [2] has written an article on Matsuoka diplomacy. These works were followed by studies published in the 1970s: Miyake Masaki's previously mentioned monograph on the Tripartite Pact; and Sudō Shinji's essay [3] on Matsuoka diplomacy and Japanese-American negotiations, as well as his recent monograph.

In 1971 Miwa Kimitada published the first scholarly biography of Matsuoka. In this compact book Miwa argues that if Matsuoka had made a mistake in concluding the Tripartite Pact, he was compelled to do so by Japan's long-term historical predicament from which not even he could escape. Matsuoka's nationalistic, even jingoistic behavior, his hard-line policy toward the United States, and his demagogic political style aimed at winning mass support at home—all of these traits derived from the historical conditions of modern Japan. In this sense, Miwa concludes, Matsuoka was a "man who had to experience many times over the dialectic [in modern Japan] of the acceptance and rejection of Western civilization."

The official biography of Matsuoka was published in 1979 in a thick volume. Essentially a compilation of a large body of materials (most of them available elsewhere), it describes his life in great detail, but the end result goes little beyond an extended apologia.

Primary materials on Matsuoka's attitude and behavior during the negotiations leading to the Tripartite Pact are extremely scarce. They can be gleaned only from such sources as the reminiscences of Ōhashi

Chūichi, his vice–foreign minister, and the unpublished record left by Matsuoka's diplomatic advisor, Saitō Ryōei. The former was published as *Taiheiyō senso yuraiki: Matsuoka gaikō no shinsō* (The origins of the Pacific War: The true picture of Matsuoka diplomacy). The latter record is "Nichi-Doku-I sangoku jōyaku teiketsu yōroku" (A summary of negotiations leading to the Tripartite Pact between Japan, Germany, and Italy), which is printed in Miyake Masaki's previously mentioned monograph on the Tripartite Pact, with the author's careful commentary.

Other Personalities

On Tōgō Shigenori—who served twice as foreign minister, in 1941 to prevent the war and in 1945 to terminate the war—the basic source is his memoirs. They should be supplemented by Hagihara Nobutoshi's recent work on Tōgō which gives an expert multiarchival treatmet of his career before his foreign ministership—especially his years as ambassador in Berlin (1937–38) and in Moscow (1938–40). A most vidid account of Tōgō as foreign minister is contained in Kurihara Ken's *Tennō: Shōwashi oboegaki* (The Emperor: A note on the history of the Shōwa period) and *Shūsen shiroku* (Historical record of the termination of the Pacific War), compiled by him for Gaimushō (Foreign Ministry). In addition to Matsumoto Shigekazu's previously mentioned essay [3], there is Watanabe Akio's succinct essay [2] which critically compares Tōgō and Shigemitsu.

Arita Hachirō, who served as foreign minister four times during the brief period 1936–1940, has published two memoirs, in 1948 and 1959. Yet his foreign policy has been studied in only a few isolated articles: Gaylord Kubota on Arita and the conclusion of the Anti-Comintern Pact; and Inoue Yūichi on his negotiations with Ambassador Robert L. Craigie in 1939.

Shigemitsu Mamoru has been equally slightened by historians. He wrote two diplomatic memoirs in 1952 and 1953. The recently published *Shigemitsu Mamoru shuki* (Memoirs of Shigemitsu Mamoru) contains memoranda and diary accounts of important events during his ambassadorship in England (1938–1941) and in China (1941–1942), and his term as foreign minister (1943–1945). Usui Katsumi has written an essay (contained in vol. 1 of Hosoya et al., eds., *Nichi-Bei kankeishi*, vol. 1), incisively analyzing the ideas and policies of Shigemitsu and Arita in the context of the factional relationship and leadership within the Foreign Ministry.

On Shiratori Toshio, the leader of the "new bureaucrats" in the Foreign Ministry, Tobe Ryōichi has published a useful article [1] in which he discusses Shiratori's diplomatic views. Shiozaki Hiroaki [5] has traced the shifting views and positions of these "new bureaucrats" within the Foreign Ministry who came to form the "Shiratori group," utilizing the diary of Kawamura Shigehisa, a member of this group.

An ongoing publication of interest is the papers of Amō Eiji, vice–foreign minister from August to October 1941. His diaries contained in vol. 4) are especially valuable as one of the few journals left by high-ranking diplomats during this period.

Memoirs by other diplomats during this period include: the reminiscences of Nishi Haruhiko, vice-foreign minister when the war broke out; and the autobiography by Ishii Itarō, chief of the East Asia Bureau during 1937–38.

The diary of general Ugaki Kazushige, a typical "soldier statesman" who served as foreign minister in 1938 but never became prime minister despite repeated opportunities, has been published as *Ugaki Kazushige nikki*, edited by Tsunoda Jun. Ugaki is the sujbect of a concise biography by Inoue Kiyoshi. He places Ugaki in the context of the military's increasing control of political affairs, but the work is rather thin for the period after 1937. Itō Takashi has written a note [1] on new materials on Ugaki that also analyzes his political and diplomatic thought around 1940.

There are few studies on Tōjo Hideki, partly on account of the limited sources available and his unappealing personality. The prevailing view of Tōjō characterizes him not as a "dictator," but merely as a bureaucratic politician and administrative leader. Nor have there appeared full-scale biographies of Tōjō. The official biography, compiled by Jōhō Yoshio, brings together well-known sources and prints reminiscences by army survivors who were close to Tōjō, but the author's defense is not entirely successful. Frankly apologetic but useful for that purpose is a personal account by Tōjō's former subordinate, Lieutenant General Satō Kenryō, *Tōjō Hideki to Taiheiyō senso* (Tōjō Hideki and the Pacific War). For an understanding of

Tōjō's personality, the only work we can recommend is Hanzawa Hiroshi's critical biographical essay. The fullest biography remains Robert J. C. Butow's *Tojo and the Coming of the War* (Stanford University Press, 1961), which has been well received by the Japanese historical profession and has appeared in Japanese translation.

Bibliography

Amō Eiji Nikki, Shiryōshū Kankōkai 天羽英二日記, 資料集刊行会, ed. *Amō Eiji nikki, shiryōshū* 天羽英二日記, 資料集 (The diary and papers of Amō Eiji). Vol. 1 (1906–1926); vol. 4 (1941–1945). Amō Eiji Nikki Kankōkai, 1982.

Aoki Tokuzō 青木得三. *Taiheiyō sensō zenshi* 太平洋戦争前史 (The historical background of the Pacific War). 3 vols. Gakujutsu Bunken Fukyūkai, 1953.

Arita Hachirō 有田八郎. *Baka Hachi to hito wa iu: Gaikōkan no kaisō* 馬鹿八 と人は言う—外交官の回想 (People call me "Hachi" the fool: Memoirs of a diplomat). Kōwadō, 1959.

—— *Hito no me no chiri o miru: Gaikō mondai kaiko roku* 人の目の塵を見 る—外交問題回顧録 (Beholding the mote in other men's eyes: Memoirs of diplomatic problems). Dai Nihon Yūbenkai Kōdansha, 1948.

Asada Sadao 麻田貞雄. "Nihon kaigun to tai-Bei seisaku oyobi senryaku" 日本海軍の対米政策および戦略 (The Japanese navy and its policy and strategy toward the United States). In Hosoya Chihiro et al., eds., *Nichi-Bei Kankeishi: Kaisen ni itaru 10-nen* 日米関係史—開戦に至る10年 (1931–1941年)(A history of Japanese-American relations: The decade preceding the war, 1931–1941), 2:87–149. Tokyo Daigaku Shuppankai; also in Borg and Okamoto, eds., *Pearl Harbour as History*, pp. 225–59.

Baba Akira 馬場明. "Kōain setchi mondai" 興亜院設置問題 (The problem of establishing the Asia Development Board). *Gaimushō chōsa geppō* (July–August 1966), 7(7–8):46–83. [1]

—— "Kōain setchi mondai to Ugaki Kazushige" 興亜院設置問題と宇垣 一成 (Ugaki Kazushige and the problem of establishing the Asia Development Board). *Gunji shigaku* (June 1981), 17(1):2–16. [2]

Doi Akira 土井章 et al., eds. *Shōwa shakai keizai shiryō shūsei: Kaigunshō shiryō* 昭和社会経済史料集成—海軍省資料 (Collection of sources on social and economic history of the Shōwa period: Documents of the Navy Ministry). 12 vols. to date. Daitō Bunka Daigaku Tōyō Kenkyūjo, 1978–.

Etō Shinkichi 衛藤瀋吉. "Chūgoku ni taisuru sensō shūketsu kōsaku" 中国に対する戦争終結工作 (Japan's peace maneuvers toward China). In

Nihon Gaikō Gakkai 日本外交学会 (Association for the Study of Japanese Diplomacy), ed., *Taiheiyō sensō shūketsuron* 太平洋戦争終結論 (The termination of the Pacific War), pp. 383–423. Tokyo Daigaku Shuppankai, 1958.

Fujii Shōzō 藤井昇三. "Nitchū sensōchū no wahei kōsaku to Chūgoku no taiō" 日中戦争中の和平工作と中国の対応 (Japan's peace maneuvers during the Sino-Japanese War, and China's response). *Gaimushō chōsa geppō* (July 1968), 9(7): 17–49.

Funaki Shigeru 舩木繁. *Shina hakengun sōshireikan Okamura Yasuji Taishō* 支那派遣軍総司官岡村寧次大将 (The biography of General Okamura Yasuji, the Commander in Chief of the China Expeditionary Army). Kawade Shobō Shinsha, 1984.

Furuya Tetsuo 古屋哲夫. *Nitchū sensō* 日中戦争 (The Sino-Japanese War). Iwanami Shoten, 1985.

Furuya Tetsuo, ed. *Nitchū sensōshi kenkyū* 日中戦争史研究 (Studies in the history of the Sino-Japanese War). Yoshikawa Kōbunkan, 1984.

Gomi Toshiki 五味俊樹. "Kyokutō ni okeru Nichi-Bei kokusai chitsujokan no sōkoku" 極東における日米国際秩序観の相克 (The conflict between Japanese and American views of international order in the Far East). In Miwa, ed., *Nihon no 1930-nendai,* pp. 81–101.

Hagiwara Nobutoshi 萩原延寿. See under Tōgō Shigenori Kinenkai.

Hanzawa Hiroshi 判沢弘. "Tōjō Hideki" 東条英機 (Tōjō Hideki). In Kamishima Jirō 神島二郎, ed., *Gendai Nihon shisō taikei,* vol. 10. *Kenryoku no shisō* 現代日本思想体系, 10—権力の思想 (Series on contemporary Japanese political thought, vol. 10: The idea of power), pp. 327–50. Chikuma Shobō, 1965.

Hashikawa Bunzō 橋川文三. "Kokubō kokka no rinen" 国防国家の理念 (The idea of a national defense state). In Hashikawa and Matsumoto Sannosuke, eds., *Kindai Nihon seiji shisōshi,* 2: 232–51. [1]

—— "Tōa shin chitsujo no shinwa" 東亜新秩序の神話 (The myth of the New Order in East Asia). In Hashikawa and Matsumoto, eds., *Kindai Nihon seiji shisōshi* 2: 352–68. [2]

Hashikawa Bunzō and Matsumoto Sannosuke 松本三之介, eds., *Kindai Nihon seiji shisōshi* 近代日本政治思想史 (Essays on the history of modern Japanese political thought), vol. 2. Yūhikaku, 1970.

Hata Ikuhiko 秦郁彦. "Futsu-In shinchū to gun no nanshin seisaku, 1940–1941" 仏印進駐と軍の南進政策, 1940—1941 (The drive into Indochina and the military's policy of southern advance, 1940–1941). In Nihon Kokusai Seiji Gakki, ed., *Taiheiyō sensō e no michi,* 6: 143–274. [1]

—— *Nankin jiken: "Gyakusatsu" no kōzō* 南京事件—虐殺の構図 (The Nanking Incident: The making of a "massacre"). Chūō Kōronsha, 1986.

—— "Nikka jihen ni okeru 'Kakudaiha' to 'Fu-kakudaiha'"). 日華事変

における「拡大派」と「不拡大派」 (The "escalationists" versus. "anti-escalationists" in the Sino-Japanese War, 1, 2). *Kokusaihō gaikō zasshi* (December 1960), 59(4):58–101; (January 1961), 59(5):63–86. [2]

—— "Nikka jihen: Wahei kōsaku to wahei jōken o megutte" 日華事変—和平工作と和平条件をめぐって (The Sino-Japanese War: With special reference to peace maneuvers and their conditions). *Kokusai seiji* (1960), no. 11: *Nihon gaikōshi kenkyū—Shōwa jidai,* pp. 71–84. [3]

—— "Nitchū sensō no gunjiteki tenkai, 1937–1941" 日中戦争の軍事的展開, 1937—1941 (The military development of the Sino-Japanese War, 1937–1941). In Nihon Kokusai Seiji Gakkai, ed., *Taiheiyō sensō e no michi,* 4:3–108. [4]

—— *Nitchū sensōshi* 日中戦争史 (A history of the Sino-Japanese War). Kawade Shobō Shinsha, 1961 (revised enlarged version, 1972).

Hatano Sumio 波多野澄雄 "'Nanshin' e no senkai: 1940" 「南進」への旋回, 1940年 (The swing toward "southern advance," 1940). *Ajia keizai* (May 1985), 26(5):25–48.

Hirai Tomoyoshi 平井友義. "Soren no dōkō (1933–1939)" ソ連の動向 (1933—1939) (Soviet policy, 1933–1939). In Nihon Kokusai Seiji Gakkai, ed., *Taiheiyō sensō e no michi,* 4:259–360.

Hora Tomio 洞富雄. *Ketteiban: Nankin dai gyakusatsu jiken* 決定版南京大虐殺事件 (The great Nanking massacre: The definitive story). Gendaishi Shuppankai, 1983.

—— *Nankin dai gyakusatsu no shōmei* 南京大虐殺の証明 (The proof of the great Nanking massacre). Asahi Shimbunsha, 1986.

—— *Nankin jiken* 南京事件 (The Nanking Incident). Shin Jinbutsu Ōraisha, 1972.

Hora Tomio, ed. *Nitchū sensōshi shiryō,* vols. 8 and 9: *Nankin jiken* 日中戦争史資料, 8, 9—南京事件 (Documents concerning the Sino-Japanese War, vols. 8 and 9: The Nanking incident). Kawade Shobō Shinsha, 1973.

Horiba Kazuo 堀場一雄. *Shina jihen sensō shidō shi* 支那事変戦争指導史 (A history of military strategy in the Sino-Japanese War). 2 vols. Jiji Tsūshinsha, 1962.

Hosoya Chihiro 細谷千博. "Gaimushō to chū-Bei taishikan: 1940–41" 外務省と駐米大使館, 1940—1941 (The Foreign Ministry and the Japanese embassy in Washington, 1940–41). In Hosoya et al., eds., *Nichi-Bei kankeishi,* 1:201–30. [1]

—— "Japan's decision for war in 1941." *Peace Research in Japan* (The annual of the Japan Peace Research Group) (1967), pp. 41–51. [2]

—— "Matsuoka Yōsuke to hishōsuru gaikō" 松岡洋右と飛翔する外交 (Matsuoka Yōsuke and his soaring diplomacy). In Hosoya, *Nihon gaikō no zahyō,* pp. 53–87. [3]

—— "Miscalculation in Deterrent Policy: Japanese-U.S. relations, 1938–1941." *Journal of Peace Research* (1968), no. 2, pp. 97–115. [4]

—— "Nichi-Bei kankei no hakyoku, 1939–1941: Yokushi seisaku to sono gosan" 日米関係の破局, 1939—1941—抑止政策とその誤算 (The rupture of Japanese-American relations, 1939–1941: U.S. deterrent policy and its miscalculation). *Hitotsubashi ronsō* (July 1965), 54 (1): 55–79. [5]

Hosoya Chihiro, Saitō Makoto, Imai Seiichi, and Rōyama Michio 斎藤真, 今井清一, 蠟山道雄, eds. *Nichi-Bei kankeishi: Kaisen ni itaru 10-nen (1931–41)*. 4 vols. Tokyo Daigaku Shuppankai, 1971–72. Its English version is Dorothy Borg and Shumpei Okamoto, eds., *Pearl Harbor as History: Japanese-American Relations, 1931–1941*. Columbia University Press, 1973.

Hosoya Chihiro, ed. *Nichi-Ei kankeishi, 1917–1949* 日英関係史, 1917—1949 (A history of Anglo-Japanese Relations, 1917–1949). Tokyo Daigaku Shuppankai, 1982.

—— *Nihon gaikō no zahyō* 日本外交の座標 (The thought and behavior of Japanese diplomacy: Collected essays). Chūō Kōronsha, 1979.

—— "Nihon no Ei Bei kan to senkanki no Higashi Ajia" 日本の英米観と戦間期の東アジア (Japanese views of the Anglo-American powers and East Asia in the interwar period). In Hosoya, ed., *Nichi-Ei kankeishi, 1917–1949*, pp. 1–43. [6]

—— "Retrogression in Japan's Foreign Policy Decision-Making Process." in James W. Morley, ed., *Dilemmas of Growth in Prewar Japan* (Princeton University Press, 1971), pp. 81–105. [7]

—— "Sangoku dōmei to Nisso chūritsu jōyaku" 三国同盟と日ソ中立条約 (The Tripartite Pact and the Japanese-Soviet neutrality pact, 1939–1941). In Nihon Kokusai Seiji Gakkai, ed., *Taiheiyō sensō e no michi*, 5: 159–331. [8]

—— "Taigai seisaku kettei katei ni okeru Nichi-Bei no tokushitsu" 対外政策決定過程における日米の特質 (Characteristics of foreign policy decision-making processes in Japan and the United States). In Hosoya Chihiro and Watanuki Jōji 綿貫譲治, eds., *Taigai seisaku kettei katei no Nichi-Bei hikaku* 対外政策決定過程の日米比較 (Comparative study of the foreign policy decision-making process in Japan and the United States), pp. 1–20. Tokyo Daigaku Shuppankai, 1977. [9]

—— "Taiheiyō sensō wa sakerare nakkata no ka?" 太平洋戦争は避けられなかったのか (Was the Pacific War unavoidable?). *Rekishi to jinbutsu* (July 1973), pp. 30–47. [10]

Ichikawa Kenjirō 市川健二郎. "Nitchū sensō to Tōnan Ajia kakyō" 日中戦争と東南アジア華僑 (The Sino-Japanese War and the Chinese in the southeast). *Kokusai seiji* (1972), no. 47: *Nitchū sensō to kokusaiteki taiō*, pp. 75–87.

Ikeda Kiyoshi 池田清. *Kaigun to Nihon* 海軍と日本 (The navy and Japan). Chūō kōronsha, 1981.

—— "Nichi-Ei kankei to Taiheiyō sensō, 1937–1941, 1" 日英関係と太平洋戦争, 1937—1941, 1 (Anglo-Japanese relations and the Pacific War, 1). *Hōgaku* (Tōhoku Daigaku) February 1983, 46(6):1–40. [1]

—— "Nichi-Ei kara Nichi-Bei e: Tai-Nichi tōitsu sensen no keisei katei" 日英から日米へ—対日統一戦線の形成過程 (From Japanese-British to Japanese-American confrontation: The formation of the anti-Japanese united front). *Gunji shigaku* (December 1983), 19(3):2–14. [2]

—— "Nihon no sensō shidō keikaku" 日本の戦争指導計画 (Japan's plan for executing the war). *Hōgaku* (July 1979), 43 (2):1–34. [3]

—— "Nihon no tai-Ei senryaku to Taiheiyō sensō" 日本の対英戦略と太平洋戦争 (Japanese strategy toward Britain and the Pacific War). In Hosoya, ed., *Nichi-Ei kankeishi, 1917–1949*, pp. 81–104. [4]

Imai Seiichi 今井清一. "Nitchū sensō ron" 日中戦争論 (On the Sino-Japanese War). In Imai, ed., *Taikei Nihon gendaishi,* 体系日本現代史 (Series on contemporary Japanese history), 2:1–41. Nihon Hyōronsha, 1979.

Imai Takeo 今井武夫. *Shina jihen no kaisō* 支那事変の回想 (Recollections of the Sino-Japanese War). Misuzu Shobō, 1964.

Imoto Kumao 井本熊男. *Sakusen nisshi de tsuzuru Shina jihen* 作戦日誌で綴る支那事変 (The China Incident as narrated through the operational journal). Fuyō Shobō, 1978.

Inoki Masamichi 猪木正道. *Hyōden Yoshida Shigeru* 評伝吉田茂 (Yoshida Shigeru: A critical biography). 3 vols. Yomiuri Shinbunsha, 1978–1981.

Inoue Kiyoshi 井上清. *Ugaki Kazushige* 宇垣一成 Asahi Shimbunsha, 1975.

Inoue Yūichi 井上勇一. "Arita no 'kōiki keizaiken' kōsō to tai-Ei kōshō" 有田の「広域経済圏」構想と対英交渉 (Arita's proposal regarding an economic bloc for Japanese expansion and his conversations with Ambassador Craigie in July 1939). *Kokusai seiji* (1977), no. 56: *1930-nendai no Nihon gaikō,* pp. 65–84.

Iokibe Makoto 五百旗頭真. "Tōa renmeiron no kihonteki seikaku" 東亜連盟論の基本的性格 (The basic characteristics of the East Asian League). *Ajia kenkyū* (April 1975), 22(1):22–58.

Iriye, Akira 入江昭. *Nichi-Bei sensō* 日米戦争 (The Japanese-American War). Chūō Kōronsha, 1978.

—— "Nitchū kankei to Ei-Bei-kan no 'miezaru' kyōchō" 日中関係と英米間の「見えざる」協調 (Sino-Japanese relations and "invisible cooperation" between Britain and the United States). *Kokusai seiji* (1972), no. 47: *Nitchū sensō to kokusaiteki taiō,* pp. 17–32. [1]

—— "The failure of Military Expansionism." In James W. Morley, ed.,

Dilemmas of Growth in Prewar Japan, pp. 107–38. Princeton University Press, 1971. [2]

—— "The ideology of Japanese imperialism: Imperial Japan and China." In Grant K. Goodman, comp., *Imperial Japan and Asia: A Reassessement*, pp. 32–45. Occasional papers of the East Asian Institute, Columbia University, 1967. [3]

—— *The Origins of the Second World War in Asia and the Pacific*. London: Longman, 1987.

Iriye, Akira and Aruga Tadashi 有賀貞, eds. *Senkanki no Nihon gaikō* 戦間期の日本外交 (Japanese diplomacy in the interwar period). Tokyo Daigaku Shuppankai, 1984.

Ishii Itarō 石射猪太郎. *Gaikōkan no isshō* 外交官の一生 (The life of a diplomat). Yomiuri Shinbunsha, 1950; reprinted by Taihei Shuppan in 1972, with an introduction by Hashikawa Bunzō.

Itagaki Yoichi 板垣与一. "Taiheiyō sensō to sekiyu mondai" 太平洋戦争と石油問題 (The Pacific War and the oil question). In Nihon Gaikō Gakkai, ed., *Taiheiyō sensō gen'inron*, pp. 605–66. Shinbun Gekkansha, 1953.

Itō Takashi 伊藤隆. *Konoe shin taisei: Taisei Yokusankai e no michi* 近衛新体制―大政翼賛会への道 (Konoe's new order: The road to the Imperial Rule Assistance Association). Chūō Kōronsha, 1983.

—— "Ugaki Kaszushige no gaikō seisakuron: Showa 15-nen o chūshin ni" 守垣一成の外交政策論―昭和15年を中心に (Ugaki Kazushige's views on foreign policy: With focus on the year 1940). *Shigaku zasshi* (January 1985), 94(1):67–77. [1]

—— "Uyoku undō to tai-Bei kan" 右翼運動と対米観 (The right-wing organizations and their views of the United States). In Hosoya et al. eds., *Nichi-Bei kankeishi*, 3:257–306. [2]

Itō Takashi and Toriumi Yasushi 鳥海靖. "Nitchū wahei kōsaku ni kansuru ichi shiryō: Matsumoto Kuraji bunsho kara" 日中和平工作に関する一史料―松本蔵次文書から (A collection of documents relating to Sino-Japanese peace negotiations: The papers of Matsumoto Kuraji, 1, 2). *Rekishi to bunka* (March 1978), no. 12, pp. 227–92; (March 1980), no. 13, pp. 45–102.

Japan. Bōeichō 防衛庁 (Defense Agency). Bōei Kenshūjo Senshi Shitsu [The War History Office], ed. (Uchida Kazuomi 内田一臣), author. *Daihon'ei kaigunbu: Daitōa sensō kaisen keii* (The Imperial Headquarters, navy: Circumstances leading to the outbreak of the Greater East Asian War). 2 vols., Asagumo Shinbunsha, 1979. Details of this and the following volumes are provided in chapter 4, "Notes on Basic Sources."

—— (Nomura Minoru 野村実, author). *Daihon'ei kaigunbu, Rengō kantai,* vol. 1: *Kaisen made* (The Imperial Headquarters, navy: The Combined Fleet, vol. 1: Up to the outbreak of hostilities). Asagumo Shinbunsha, 1975.

—— (Shimanuki Takeharu, 島貫武治, author). *Daihon'ei rikugunbu,* vol. 1: *Shōwa-15 nen gogatsu made* (The Imperial Headquarters, army, vol. 1: Up to May 1940). Asagumo, Shinbunsha, 1967.

—— *Daihon'ei rikugunbu,* vol. 2: *Shōwa 16-nen jūnigatsu made* (The Imperial Headquarters, army, vol. 2: Up to December 1941). Asagumo Shinbunsha, 1968.

—— (Hara Shirō 原四郎, author). *Daihon'ei Rikugunbu, Daitōa sensō kaisen keii* (The Imperial Headquarters, army: Circumstances leading to the outbreak of the Greater East Asian war). 5 vols. Asagumo Shinbunsha, 1973–74.

—— (Tsunoda Kyūshi 角田求士, author). *Hawai sakusen* (Naval attack against Hawaii). Asagumo Shinbunsha, 1967.

—— (Morimatsu Toshio 森松俊夫, author). *Hokushi no chiansen* (Operations to maintain public peace and order in north China). 2 vols. Asagumo Shinbunsha, 1968–71.

—— (Suekuni Masao 末国正雄, author), *Kaigun gunsenbi,* vol. 1: *Shōwa 16-nen jūichigatsu made* 海軍軍戦備 1 —昭和16年11月まで (Naval armaments and preparations for war: Up to November 1941). Asagumo Shinbunsha, 1969.

—— (Nishihara Masao 西原征夫, author). *Kantōgun,* 1: *Tai-So senbi, Nomohan jiken* (The Kwantung Army, vol. 1: War preparations against the USSR and the Nomonhan Incident). Asagumo Shinbunsha, 1969.

—— (Nishihara) *Kantōgun,* vol. 2: *Kan Toku En, shūsenji no tai-So sen* (the Kwantung Army, vol 2: Reinforcement of war preparations against USSR [in July 1941]; Operations against the Soviet forces immediately before the end of the war). Asagumo Shinbunsha, 1974.

—— (Momimatsu Toshio 森松俊夫 et al., authors). *Shina jihen rikugun sakusen* (Army operations in the Chian Incident). 3 vols. Asagumo Shinbunsha, 1975–76.

Japan, Bōeichō Bōei Kenkyujo, Senshi-bu, ed. *Kaigun nendo sakusen keikaku* 海軍年度作戦計画 (The navy's annual operational plans). Asagumo Shinbunsha, 1986.

Japan, Gaimushō 外務省, ed. *Nichi-Bei kōshō shiryō: Shōwa 16-nen nigatsu— jūnigatsu* 日米交渉資料—昭和16年 2 月—12月 (Materials relating to Japanese-American negotiations: February–December 1941). Hara Shobō, 1978.

—— *Shūsen shiroku* 終戦史録 (Historical record of the termination of the Pacific War). 2 vols. Shinbun Gekkansha, 1951.

Jōhō Yoshio, ed., *Tōjō Hideki* 東条英機. Fuyō Shobō, 1974.

From Sino-Japanese War to Pacific War 343

Kagesa Sadaaki 影佐禎昭. "Sozorogaki" 曽走路我記 (My memoir of the path I once followed). In Usui Katsumi 臼井勝美, ed., *Gendaishi shiryō,* vol. 13: *Nitchū sensō,* 5, pp. 346–98. Misuzu Shobō, 1976.

Kakegawa Tomiko 掛川トミ子. "Masu media no tōsei to tai-Bei ronchō" マス・メディアの統制と対米論調 (The press and public opinion in Japan, 1931–1941). In Hosoya et al., eds., *Nichi-Bei kankeishi,* 4:3–80.

Kameyama Ichiji 亀山一二 et al. (Nishi Haruhiko 西春彦, editorial supervisor). *Nihon gaikōshi,* 15: *Nisso kokkō mondai, 1917–1945* 日本外交史, 15—日ソ国交問題 (Japanese diplomatic history, vol. 15: The problem of diplomatic relations between Japan and the Soviet Union, 1917–1945). Kajima Kenkyūjo Shuppankai, 1972.

Kamimura Shin'ichi 上村伸一. *Nihon gaikōshi,* vols. 19 and 20: *Nikka jihen* 日本外交史, 19—20—日華事変, 上, 下. (Japanese diplomatic history, vols. 19 and 20: The Sino-Japanese War). 2 vols. Kajima Kenkyūjo Shuppankai, 1971.

Kase Toshikazu 加瀬俊一. *Nihon gaikōshi,* 23: *Nichi-Bei kōshō* 日本外交史, 23—日米交渉 (Japanese diplomatic history, vol. 23: Japanese-American negotiations). Kajima Heiwa Kenkyūjo, 1970.

—— *Mizurī gō e no dōtei* ミズリー号への道程 (Journey to the U.S.S. *Missouri*). Bungei Shunjū Shinsha, 1951.

Katō Yōko 加藤陽子. "Shōwa 14-nen no tai-Bei kōsaku to Hiranuma Kiichirō" 昭和14年の対米工作と平沼騏一郎 (Prime Minister Hiranuma's approaches to the United States in 1939). *Shigaku zasshi* (November 1985), 95(11):43–75.

Katsurahara Mitsumasa 桂原光正. "Tōa renmei undōshi shōron" 東亜連盟運動史小論 (An essay on the history of the East Asian League movement). In Furuya Tetsuo, ed., *Nitchū sensōshi kenkyū,* pp. 363–439.

Kawahara Hiroshi 河川宏. *Ajia e no shisō* アジアへの思想 ([Japanese] ideas about Asia). Kawashima Shoten, 1968.

—— "Ishiwara Kanji to Tōa Renmei: "Kindai Nihon ni okeru Ajiakan" 石原莞爾と東亜連盟—近代日本におけるアジア観 (Ishiwara Kanji and the East Asian League: Perceptions of Asia in modern Japan). *Hōkei kenkyū* (Nihon Daigaku) (October 1965), 2(2):65–195.

Kōketsu Atsushi 纐纈厚. *Sōryokusen taisei kenkyū: Nihon rikugun no kokka sōdōin kōsō* 総力戦体制研究—日本陸軍の国家総動員構想 (A study of the total war system: The Japanese army's plan for total national mobilization). San'ichi Shobō, 1981.

Konoe Fumimaro 近衛文麿. *Heiwa e no doryoku* 平和への努力 (My struggle for peace). Nihon Denpō Tsūshinsha, 1946.

—— *Ushinawareshi seiji* 失はれし政治 (Politics that failed). Asahi Shimbunsha, 1946.

Krebs, Gerhard, "Sanbō honbu no wahei kōsaku, 1937–38" 参謀本部の和平工作, 1937—38 (The Army General Staff and peace meneuvers, 1937–38). *Nihon rekishi* (August 1980), 82(8): 36–51.

Kubota, Gaylord 窪田, ゲィロード. "Arita Hachirō: Nichi-Doku bōkyō kyōtei ni okeru usuzumi iro gaikō no tenkai" 有田八郎―日独防共協定における薄墨色外交の展開 (Arita Hachirō and the conclusion of the Anti-Comintern Pact: A case study in "thin ink" diplomacy). *Kokusai seiji* (1977), no. 56: *1930-nendai no Nihon gaikō*, pp. 46–64.

Kudō Michihiro 工藤美知尋. *Nihon kaigun to Taiheiyō sensō* 日本海軍と太平洋戦争 (The Japanese navy and the Pacific War). 2 vols. Nansōsha, 1982.

Kurihara Akira 栗原彬. "Konoe Fumimaro no pāsonaritī to shin-taisei" 近衛文麿のパーソナリティと新体制 (Konoe Fumimaro: Identity and the new order). *Nenpō seijigaku* 1972: *"Konoe shin taisei" no kenkyū* (The annals of the Japanese Political Science Association, 1972: Studies on Prince Konoe's New Order) (1973), pp. 181–230.

Kurihara Ken 栗原健. *Tennō: Shōwashi oboegaki* 天皇―昭和史覚書 (The emperor: A note on the history of the Shōwa period). Yūshindō, 1955.

Kurusu Saburō 来栖三郎. *Hōmatsu no 35-nen: Gaikō hishi* 泡末の35年 (Thirty-five years of vain endeavor: A secret history of my diplomacy). Bunka Shoin, 1949.

—— *Nichi-Bei gaikō hiwa: Waga gaikōshi* 日米外交祕話―わが外交史 (Secret stories of Japanese-American diplomacy: My diplomatic history). Sōgensha, 1952.

Masumi Junnosuke 升味準之輔. *Nihon seitōshi ron* 日本政党史論 (A history of Japanese party politics), vols. 6 and 7. Tokyo Daigaku Shuppankai, 1980.

Matsumoto Shigeharu 松本重治. *Shanhai jidei: Jānaristo no kaisō* (My Shanghai days), vol. 3. Chūō Kōronsha, 1975.

Matsumoto Shigekazu 松本繁一. "Amerika gunbu to sekiyu mondai" アメリカ軍部と石油問題 (The American military and the oil question). *Ajia kenkyū* (July 1962), 9(2): 47–66. [1]

—— "Nichi-Bei kōshō to Chūgoku mondai: Terasaki Amerika kyokuchō no shūhen" 日米交渉と中国問題―寺崎アメリカ局長の周辺 (U.S.-Japanese conversations and the China problem: Centering on Terasaki Tarō, the director of the American Bureau, Foreign Ministry). *Kokusai seiji* (1968), no. 37: *Nihon gaikōshi no shomondai, 3*, pp. 72–95. [2]

—— "Tōgō gaishō to Taiheiyō sensō" 東郷外相と太平洋戦争 (Foreign Minister Tōgō Shigenori and the Pacific War). *Kokusai seiji* (1967), no. 33: *Nihon gaikōshi kenkyū—Gaikō shidōsharon*, pp. 54–76. [3]

Matsuoka Yōsuke Denki Kankōkai 松岡洋右伝記刊行会, ed. *Matsuoka*

Yōsuke: Sono hito to shōgai 松岡洋右—その人と生涯 (Matsuoka Yōsuke: The man and his life). Kōdansha, 1974.

Matsuzaki Shōichi 松崎昭一. "Nitchū wahei kōsaku to gunbu" 日中和平工作と軍部 (The Japanese military and the peace maneuvers with China). In Miyake Masaki et al., eds., *Shōwashi no gunbu to seiji*, 2:201–242.

Mitani Taichirō 三谷太一郎. "Doku-So fukashin jōyakuka no Nitchū sensō gaikō: Ideorogī to kenryoku seiji" 独ソ不可侵条約下の日中戦争外交—イデオロギーと権力政治 (The Nazi-Soviet Non-Aggression Pact and the Sino-Japanese War and diplomacy). In Iriye and Argua eds., *Senkanki no Nihon gaikō*, pp. 299–328. [1]

—— "Kokusai kankyō no hendō to Nihon no chishikijin" 国際環境の変動と日本の知識人 (Changes in Japan's international position and the response of Japanese intellectuals). In Hosoya et al., eds., *Nichi-Bei kankeishi*, 4: 131–73. [2]

Miwa Kimitada 三輪公忠. "Ajiashugi no rekishiteki kōsatsu" アジア主義の歴史的考察 (A historical survey of pan-Asianism). In Hirano Ken'ichirō 平野健一郎, ed., *Sōgō kōza Nihon no shakai bunkashi, 4: Nihon bunka no hen'yō* 総合講座日本の社会文化史, 4—日本文化の変容 (Series on Japanese social and cultural history, vol. 4: Transformations of Japanese culture), pp. 386–462. Kodansha, 1973. [1]

—— *Matsuoka Yōsuke* 松岡洋右. Chūō Kōronsha, 1971.

—— *Nichi-Bei kankei no ishiki to kōzō* 日米関係の意識と構造 (The images and structure of Japanese-American relations). Nansōsha, 1974.

Miwa Kimitada, ed. *Nihon no 1930-nendai: Kuni no uchi to soto kara* 日本の1930年代—国の内と外から (The 1930s in Japan: Views from within and without the country). Sairyūsha, 1980.

—— *Saikō, Taiheiyō sensō zenya: Nihon no 1930-nendairon to shite* 再考, 太平洋戦争前夜—日本の1930年代論として (Reconsiderations: The eve of the Pacific War—Essays on Japan in the 1930s). Sōseiki, 1981.

—— "The Wang Ching-wei regime and Japanese efforts to terminate the China conflict." In Joseph Roggendof, ed., *Studies in Japanese Culture*, pp. 23–42. Tokyo: Sophia University, 1963. [2]

Miyake Masaki 三宅正樹. "Die Lage Japans beim Ausbruch des Zweiten Weltkrieges." In Wolfgang Benz and Herman Graml, eds., *Sommer 1939: Die Grossmächte und der Europäische Krieg*, pp. 195–222. Stuttgart: Deutsche Verlag, 1979.

—— *Nichi-Doku-I sangoku dōmei no kenkyū* 日独伊三国同盟の研究 (A study of the Tripartite Alliance: Berlin-Rome-Tokyo). Nansōsha, 1975.

—— "Nichi-Doku kankei no rekishiteki tenkai to Soren: Hitorā, Sutārin to Nichi-Doku-I dōmei" 日独関係の歴史的展開とソ連—ヒトラー, スターリンと日独伊同盟 (The historical development of Japanese-German relations and the Soviet Union: Hitler, Stalin and the Tripartite Alliance). In Miwa Kimitada 三輪公忠, ed., *Sōgō kōza: Nihon no shakai bunkashi*, 7: *Sekai no naka no Nihon* 総合講座—日本の社会文化史，7 —世界の中の 日本 (Comprehensive series: Social and cultural history of Japan, vol. 7: Japan in the world), pp. 361–431. Kōdansha, 1974. [2]

Miyake Masaki et al., eds. *Shōwashi no gunbu to seiji* 昭和史の軍部と政治 (The military and politics in the Shōwa period), vols. 2 and 3. Daiichi Hōki Shuppan, 1983.

—— "Torautoman kōsaku no seikaku to shiryō: Nitchū sensō to Doitsu gaikō" トラウトマン工作の性格と史料—日中戦争とドイツ外交 (The nature and record of Oskar Trautman's diplomacy during the Sino-Japanese War). *Kokusai seiji* (1972), no. 47: *Nitchū sensō to kokusaiteki taiō*, pp. 33–74. [3]

Momose Hiroshi 百瀬宏. "Senkanki Nihon no tai-Tōō gaikō ni kansuru oboegaki" 戦間期日本の対東欧外交に関する覚書 (A note on Japanese diplomacy toward Eastern Europe during the interwar period). *Kokusai kankeigaku kenkyū* (March 1982), no. 8, pp. 27–44.

Morimatsu Toshio 森松俊夫. "Shina jihen boppatsu tōsho ni okeru riku-kaigun no tai-Shi senryaku" 支那事変勃発当初における陸海軍の対支 戦略 (Japanese army and navy strategy toward China in 1937). *Seiji keizai shigaku* (May 1980), no. 168, pp. 19–32.

Murakami Sachiko 村上さち子. *Futsu-In shinchū, 1940–45* 仏印進駐, 1940—45 (Japan's thrust into French Indochina). Privately printed, 1984.

Mushakōji Kinhide 武者小路公秀. "30-nendai Nichi-Bei kankei no kōzō" 30年代日米関係の構造 (The structure of Japanese-American relations in the 1930s). In Hosoya Chihiro et al., eds., *Nichi-Bei kankeishi*, 4:263–82.

Nagai Kazu 永井和. "Nichi-Ei kankei to gunbu" 日英関係と軍部 (Anglo-Japanese relations and the military). In Miyake et al., eds., *Shōwashi no gunbu to seiji*, 2:159–199. [1]

—— "Nitchū sensō to Nichi-Ei tairitsu: Nihon no Kahoku senryōchi shihai to Tenshin Ei-Futsu sokai" 日中戦争と日英対立—日本の華北占領地支配 と天津英仏租界 (The Sino-Japanese War and Anglo-Japanese antago-nism: Japan's control of the occupied areas in North China and British and French settlements). In Furuya Tetsuo, ed., *Nitchū sensōshi kenkyū*, 日中 戦争史研究 (A study of the history of the Sino-Japanese War), pp. 237–362. [2]

—— "1939-nen no hai-Ei undō" 1939年の排英運動 (Anti-British move-ments in 1939). *Nenpō kindai Nihon kenkyū*, 5: *Shōwaki no shakai undō* pp. 191–258. [3]

Nagaoka Shinjirō 長岡新治郎. "Nanpō shisaku no gaikōteki tenkai (1937–

1941 nen)" 南方施策の外交的展開 (Diplomatic developments of measures toward the southern areas). In Nihon Kokusai Seiji Gakkai, ed., *Taiheiyō sensō e no michi,* 6:3–140.

—— *Nihon gaikōshi,* Vol. 22: *Nanshin monda* 日本外交史, 22—南進問題 (Japanese diplomatic history, Vol. 22: The problem of southern advance. o shiryō, 12: Nitchū sensō 4: (Documents on contemporary history). Kajima Kenkyūjo Shuppankai, 1973.

Nakanishi Osamu 中西治. "Kantōgun to Nisso taiketsu" 関東軍と日ソ対決 (The Kwantung Army and Japanese-Soviet confrontation). In Miyake et al., eds., *Shōwashi no gunbu to seiji,* 2:123–157.

Nakayama Takashi 中山隆志. "Chōkohō jiken no saikentō" 張鼓峯事件の再検討 (A reexamination of the Changkufeng incident). *Shin bōeironshū* (October 1983), 11(2):79–99.

Nihon Kokusai Seiji Gakkai 日本国際政治学会 (Japan Association of International Relations), ed. *Taiheiyō sensō e no michi* 太平洋戦争への道 (The road to the Pacific War), vols. 5–7. Asahi Shimbunsha, 1963.

—— (Inaba Masao 稲葉正夫 et al., eds. *Taiheiyō sensō e no michi: Bekkan shiryōhen* 太平洋戦争への道—別巻資料篇 (The road the Pacific War: Supplementary volume of documents). Asahi Shimbunsha, 1963.

Nishi Haruhiko 西春彦. *Kaisō no Nihon gaikō* 回想の日本外交 (My reminiscences of Japanese diplomacy). Iwanami Shoten, 1965.

Nishi Yoshiaki 西義顕. *Higeki no shōnin: Nitchū wahei kōsaku hishi* 悲劇の証人—日中和平工作秘史 (Witness to tragedy: A secret history of Sino-Japanese peace nagotiations). Bunkensha, 1962.

Nomura Kichisaburō 野村吉三郎. *Beikoku ni tsukai shite: Nichi-Bei kōshō no kaiko* 米国に使して—日米交渉の回顧 (My mission to the United States: Reminiscences of the Japanese-American negotiations). Iwanami Shoten, 1946.

Nomura Minoru 野村実. "Bōkyō kyōtei kyōka kōshō to Doku-So fukashin jōyaku" 防共協定強化交渉と独ソ不可侵条約 (Negotiations to strengthen the Anti-Comintern Pact and the German-Soviet Nonaggression Pact. *Nenpō kindai Nihon kenkyū,* no. 1: *Shōwaki no gunbu* (The military in the Shōwa period), pp. 173–200. 1979. [1]

—— "Japan's plans for World War II." *Revue Internationale d'Histoire Militaire* (1978), no. 38, pp. 199–217. [2]

—— "Nichi-Doku-I-So rengō shisō no hōga to hōkai" 日独伊ソ連合思想の萌芽と崩壊 (The inception and debacle of the scheme for a pact among Japan, Germany, Italy, and the Soviet Union). *Gunji shigaku* (March 1976), 11(4):2–14. [3]

—— "Nihon kaigun o chūshin to suru nenryo mondai no ichi tenbyō 日本海

軍を中心とする燃料問題の一点描 (A note on the fuel oil question centering on the Japanese navy). *Kaikankō hyōron* (November 1969), 7(6):6–17.

—— *Rekishi no naka no Nihon kaigun* 歴史の中の日本海軍 (The Japanese navy in historical perspectives). Hara Shobō, 1980.

—— "Sangoku dōmei teiketsu to kaigun: Oikawa Koshirō to Yamamoto Isoroku" 三国同盟締結と海軍—及川古志郎と山本五十六 (The Japanese navy and the conclusion of the Tripartite Pact: Navy Minister Oikawa Koshirō and Admiral Yamamoto Isoroku). *Nihon rekishi* (July 1978), no. 362, pp. 67–75. [4]

—— *Taiheiyō sensō to Nihon gunbu* 太平洋戦争と日本軍部 (The Pacific War and the Japanese military). Yamakawa Shuppansha, 1983.

—— "Taiheiyō sensō to Nihon no senryaku" 太平洋戦争と日本の戦略 (The Pacific War and Japanese strategy). In Hosoya, ed., *Nichi-Ei kankeishi*, pp. 105–13. [5].

Ogata Sadako 緒方貞子. "Gaikō to yoron: Renmei dattai o meguru ichi kōsatsu" 外交と世論—連盟脱退をめぐる一考察 (Public opinion and foreign policy: Opinion regarding Japan's withdrawal from the League of Nations). *Kokusai seiji (1969), no. 41: Nihon gaikōshi—Yoron to gaikō*, pp. 40–55.

Ogawa Heikichi Bunsho Kenkyūkai 小川平吉文書研究会, ed., *Ogawa Heikichi kankei bunsho* 小川平吉関係文書 (Papers relating to Ogawa Hei-kichi). 2 vols. Misuzu Shobō, 1973.

Ōhashi Chūichi 大橋忠一. *Taiheiyō sensō yuraiki: Matsuoka gaikō no shinsō* 太平洋戦争由来記—松岡外交の真相 (The origins of the Pacific War: The true picture of Matsuoka diplomacy). Takane Shobō, 1952.

Ōhata Tokushirō 大畑篤四郎. "Nichi-Doku bōkyō kyōtei, dō kyōka mondai, 1935–1939" 日独防共協定, 同強化問題 (The Japanese-German Anti-Comintern Pact and the problem of strengthening it). In Nihon Kokusai Seiji Gakkai, ed., *Taiheiyō sensō e no michi*, 5:3–155.

Oka Yoshitake 岡義武. *Konoye Fumimaro: "Unmei" no seijika* 近衛文磨—『運命』の政治家 (Konoye Fumimaro: A statesman of "fate"). Iwanami Shoten, 1972.

Okumura Fusao 奥村房夫. *Nichi-Bei kōshō to Taiheiyō sensō* 日米交渉と太平洋戦争 (The Japanese-American negotiations and the Pacific War). Maeno Shoten, 1970.

Ōtaka Shōjirō 大鷹正次郎. *Dainiji sekai taisen sekininron* 第二次世界大戦責任論 (On the responsibility for World War II). Jiji Tsūshinsha, 1959.

—— *Kishū ka bōryaku ka: Shinjuwan no sekinin* 奇襲か謀略か—真珠湾の責任 (Surprise attack or plot: Responsibility for Pearl Harbor). Jiji Tsūshinsha, 1954.

Saitō Yoshie 斎藤良衛. *Azamukareta rekishi: Matsuoka to Sangoku dōmei no rimen* 欺かれた歴史—松岡と三国同盟の裏面 (History deceived: The inside story of Matsuoka and the Tripartite Pact). Yomiuri Shinbunsha, 1955.

Sasaki Chiyoko 佐々木千代子. "Der Nomonhan Konflict: Das fernostliche Vorspiel zum 2, Weltkrieg." Bonn: Rheinishe Friedrich-Wilhelms-Universität, 1968.

Satō Kenryō 佐藤賢了. *Tōjō Hideki to Taiheiyō sensō* 東条英機と太平洋戦争 (Tōjō Hideki and the Pacific War). Bungei Shunjū Shinsha, 1960.

Satō Kyōzō 佐藤恭三. "Eikoku to Tōa shin chitsujo: Nichi-Ei Kyokutō seisaku no kairi" 英国と東亜新秩序 (Great Britain and Japan's "New Order in East Asia"). In Miwa, ed., *Nihon no 1930-nendai*, pp. 195–220. [1]

—— *Japan and Britain at the Crossroads, 1939–1941*. Tokyo: Senshū University Press, 1986. [1]

—— "Miotosareta mono to rekishi no zentaizō: Hosoya Chihiro hen *Nichi-Ei kankeishi, 1917–1945* hihan" 見落とされたものと歴史の全体像—細谷千博編『日英関係史, 1917—1945』批判 (The historical perspective and what is missing: A critique of Hosoya [ed.], *Nichi-Ei kankeishi, 1917–1945*). *Hōgaku kenkyūjo kiyō* (Senshū Daigaku) (April 1984), no. 19, pp. 63–87. [2]It appeared in English as "The Historical Perspective and What Is Missing. *Anglo-Japanese Alienation, 1919–1952*." *Modern Asian Studies* (April 1986) 20(2):375–87.

—— "1941-nen nigatsu no 'kiki': Eikoku no kyokutō seisaku to Matsuoka gaishō no taiō" 1941年2月の「危機」—英国の極東政策と松岡外相の対応 (The "crisis" of February 1941: Britain's Far Eastern policy and Foreign Minister Matsuoka's response). *Gunji shigaku* (June 1980), 16(1):2–17.

—— "Shingapōru kantai haken mondai to Igirisu no Kyokutō senryaku" シンガポール艦隊派遣問題とイギリスの極東戦略, 1939 (Relief of capital ships to Singapore and Britain's Far Eastern strategy, 1939). *Kokusai seiji* (1982), no. 72: *Dainiji taisen zenya*, pp. 120–34 [3]

Shigemitsu Mamoru 重光葵. *Gaikō kaisōroku* 外交回想録 (Diplomatic reminiscences). Mainichi Shinbunsha, 1953; reprinted in 1978.

—— *Shigemitsu Mamoru shuki* 重光葵手記 (The memoirs of Shigemitsu Mamoru). Itō Takashi and Watanaba Yukio, 伊藤隆, 渡辺行男 eds. Chūō Kōronsha, 1986.

—— *Shōwa no dōran* 昭和の動乱 (Turbulence during the Shōwa period). 2 vols. Chūō Kōronsha, 1952.

Shimada Toshihiko 島田俊彦. "'Funatsu kōsaku' nado" 「船津工作」など (The "Funatsu operations" during the Sino-Japanese War). *Kokusai seiji* (1972), no. 47: *Nitchū sensō to kokusaiteki taiō*, pp. 505–19. [1]

Shimada Toshihiko. "Nikka jihen ni okeru wahei kōsaku tokuni 'kiri kōsaku' oyobi 'Matsuoka-Sen Eimei kōsaku' ni tsuite" 日華事変における和平工作：とくに「桐工作」および「松岡・銭永銘工作」について (On peace maneuvers during the Sino-Japanese War: With special reference to the "Kiri operations" and the "Matsuoka-Ch'ien Yung-min operations." *Musashi daigaku jinbun gakkai zasshi* (June 1971), 3(1):1–75; (October 1971), 3(2):1–23. [2]

Shinmyō Takeo 新名丈夫, ed. *Kaigun sensō kentō kaigi kiroku: Taiheiyō sensō kaisen no keii* 海軍戦争検討会議記録—太平洋戦争開戦の経緯 (The record of the discussions about the navy and the Pacific War—Circumstances leading to the outbreak of the Pacific War). Mainichi Shinbunsha, 1976.

Shiozaki Hiroaki 塩崎弘明. "'John Doe Associates' to Nichi-Bei kōshō" "John Doe Associates" と日米交渉 (The "John Doe Associates" and Japanese-American negotiations). *Nihon rekishi* (September 1978), no. 364, pp. 58–75. [1]

—— "'Nichi-Bei kaidan' zenshi: 'John Doe Associates' no seiritsu to sono seijiteki haikei" 「日米会談」前史—"John Doe Associates" の成立とその政治的背景 (The origins and political background of the "John Doe Associates"). *Shigaku zasshi* (July 1976), 84(7):39–64. [2]

—— *Nichi-Ei-Bei sensō no kiro: Taiheiyō no yūwa o meguru seisenryaku* 日英米戦争の岐路—太平洋の宥和をめぐる政戦略 (The crossroad of Japan's war with Britain and the United States: Political and military strategies of the appeasement in the Pacific). Yamakawa Shuppan, 1984. [3]

—— "Ryōkaian kara Haru nōto made" 諒解案からハル・ノートまで (From the "draft understanding" to the "Hull note"). *Kokusai seiji* (1982) no. 71: *Nihon gaikō no shisō*, pp. 141–59. [4]

—— "Gaimushōnai kakushinha no genjō daha ninshiki to seisaku" 外務省内革新派の現状打破認識と政策 (The "new bureaucrats" within the Foreign Ministry: Their idea of challenge to the status quo), *Nenpō kindai Nihon kenkyū* (1985), no. 7: *Nihon gaikō no kiki ninshiki*, pp. 151–85.

Shiozaki Hiroaki and Itō Takashi 伊藤隆, eds. *Ikawa Tadao Nichi-Bei kōshō shiryō* 井川忠雄日米交渉史料 (Historical materials relating to Ikawa Tadao's role in the Japanese-American negotiations). Yamakawa Shuppansha, 1982.

Sudō Shinji 須藤真志. "Iwakuro Hideo to tai-Bei kōshō" 岩畔豪雄と対米交渉 (Colonel Iwakuro Hideo and the Japanese-American negotiations). *Kyoto sangyō daigaku ronshū* (January 1980). 9(1):1–40. [1]

—— "Konoe-Rūzuveruto kaidan no teishō to Kokumushō Kyokutōbu no hantai" 近衛・ローズベルト会談の提唱と国務省極東部の反対 (The proposal for a Konoe-Roosevelt conference and the opposition of the

Far Eastern Division, the State Department). *Kyoto sangyō daigaku ronshū* (September 1978), 8(1): 141–66. [2]

—— "Matsuoka gaikō to Nichi-Bei kōshō" 松岡外交と日米交渉 (Matsuoka diplomacy and the Japanese-American negotiations). *Kyōto sangyō daigaku ronshū* (January 1977), 6(1): 1–39. [3]

—— *Nichi-Bei kaisen gaikō no kenkyū: Nichi-Bei kōshō no hottan kara Haru nōto made* 日米開戦外交の研究—日米交渉の発端からハル・ノートまで (A study of Japanese-American diplomacy up to the outbreak of the war: From the beginning of Japanese-American negotiations to the Hull note). Keiō Tsūshin, 1986.

—— "Nichi-Bei kōshō ni miru minkanjin gaikō no genkai" 日米交渉にみる民間人外交の限界 (Private citizens as diplomats in the Japanese-American negotiations of 1941: The limitations of Hashimoto Tetsuma and Ikawa Tadao). *Kokusai seiji* (1983), no. 75: *Nihon gaikō no hiseishiki channeru*, pp. 49–63. [4]

—— "Nichi-Bei kōsho to gunbu" 日米交渉と軍部 (The Japanese-American negotiations and the Japanese military). In Miyake et al., eds. *Showashi no gunbu to seiji*, 3: 119–54. [5]

—— "Tōjō naikaku to Nichi-Bei kōshō" 東条内閣と日米交渉 (The Tōjō cabinet and the Japanese-American negotiations). *Kyōto sangyō daigaku ronshū* (October 1980), 10(1): 1–39. [6]

Suzuki Akira 鈴木明. *Nankin "dai gyakusatsu" no maboroshi* 南京「大虐殺」のまぼろし (The phantom of the "great Nanking massacre"). Bungei Shunjūsha, 1973.

Takahashi Hisashi 高橋久志. "Nikka jihen shoki ni okeru rikugun chūsūbu: Fukakudaiha no zasetsu kara Ō Chō Mei kōsaku e" 日華事変初期における陸軍中枢部—不拡大派の挫折から汪兆銘工作へ (The Japanese army during the early stage of the Sino-Japanese War: From the collapse of the antis to the "Wang Ching-wei scheme"). *Nenpō kindai Nihon kenkyū* (1985), 7: *Nihon gaikō no kiki ninshiki* pp. 187–220. [1]

—— "Ō Seiei ni okeru Ajiashugi no kinō" 汪精衛におけるアジア主義の機能 (The role of Pan-Asianism in Wang Ching-wei's thought and behavior). *Kokusaigaku ronshū* (January 1981), 4(1): 25–39. [2]

—— "Tōa kyōdōtairon"—Rōyama Masamichi, Ozaki Hotsumi, Kada Tetsuji no baai"「東亜協同体論」—蠟山政道, 尾崎秀実, 加田哲二の場合 ("East Asia cooperative community" idea: With particular reference to Rōyama Masamichi, Ozaki Hotsumi, and Kada Teiji). In Miwa, ed., *Nihon no 30-nendai*, pp. 81–101. [3]

Tanaka Shin'ichi 田中新一. *Taisen totsu'nyū no shinsō* 大戦突入の真相 (The truth about the plunge into the Pacific War). Gengensha, 1955.

Terunuma Yasutaka 照沼康隆. "Tōa Renmei Kyōkai" 東亜連盟協会 (A study on the East Asia League Association). *Nenpō kindai Nihon kenkyū* (1983), no. 5: *Shōwaki no shakai undō*. Yamakawa Shuppansha, pp. 297–328.

Tobe Ryōichi 戸部良一. "Gaikō ni okeru 'shisōteki rikyo' no tankyū: Shiratori Toshio no kōdō gaikōron" 外交における「思想的理拠」の探求—白鳥敏夫の皇道外交論 (Kōdō diplomacy in the thought of Shiratori Toshio). *Kokusai seiji*, (1982), no. 71: *Nihon gaikō no shisō*, pp. 124–40. [1]

—— "Hokubu Futsu-In shinchū: 'Nanshin' no ichi danmen to shiteno kōsatsu" 北部仏印進駐—『南進』の一断面としての考察 (Japan's advance into northern Indochina: An aspect of the southward avance). *Bōei Daigakkō kiyō: Shakai kagakuhen* (November 1978), no. 37, pp. 37–88. [2]

—— "Nikka jihen ni okeru pīsu fīrā" 日華事変におけるピースフィーラー (Peace feelers in the Sino-Japanese War). *Kokusai seiji* (1983), no. 75: *Nihon gaikō no hi-kōshiki channeru*, pp. 30–48. [3]

Tōgō Shigenori 東郷茂徳. *Jidai no ichimen: Taisen gaikō no shuki* 時代の一面—大戦外交の手記 (An aspect of the Shōwa era: Memoirs of wartime diplomacy). Kaizōsha, 1952. Reprinted as *Tōgō Shigenori gaikō shuki* (Diplomatic Memoirs of Tōgō Shigenori). Hara Shobō, 1967.

Tōgō Shigenori Kinenkai 東郷茂徳記念会, ed. *Gaisō Tōgō Shigenori* 外相東郷茂徳 (Foreign Minister Tōgō Shigenori). 2 vols. Hara Shobō, 1985. Vol. 1 reprints Tōgō's *Jidai no ichimen*, and vol. 2 is Hagiwara Nobutoshi 萩原延寿, *Tōgō Shigenori: Denki to kaisetsu* 東郷茂徳—伝記と解説 (Tōgō Shigenori: A biography and commentaries).

Tōjō Hideki Kankōkai (Jōhō Yoshio 上法快男), comp. *Tōjō Hideki* 東条英機. Fuyō Shobō, 1974.

Tsunoda Jun 角田順, ed. *Gendaishi shiryō*, vol. 10: *Nitchū sensō, 3* 現代史資料10：日中戦争 3 (Documents on contemporary history, vol. 10: The Sino-Japanese War, 3). Misuzu Shobō, 1964.

—— "Nihon no tai-Bei kaisen, 1940–41" 日本の対米開戦, 1940—41 (Japanese-American negotiations and their rupture, 1940–1941). In Nihon Kokusai Seiji Gakkai, ed., *Taiheiyō sensō e no michi*, 7:3–387.

Uchiyama Masakuma 内山正熊. "'Pāru Hābā' no sekinin mondai" パール・ハーバーの責任問題 (The problem of responsibility for "Pearl Harbor"). In Uchiyama, *Gaikō to kokusai seiji* 外交と国際政治 (Diplomacy and international relations), pp. 331–50. Keiō Tsūshin, 1960. [1]

—— "Tenshin Eikoku sokai fūsa no haikei" 天津英国租界封鎖の背景 (The background of the blockading of the British concessions in Tiensien). In Uchiyama Masakuma, *Gendai Nihon gaikōshi ron* 現代日本外交史論 (Essays on contemporary Japanese diplomatic history), pp. 213–69. Keiō Tsūshin, 1971. [2]

Ugaki Kazushige 宇垣一成. *Ugaki Kazushige nikki* 宇垣一成日記 (The diary of Ugaki Kazushige). 3 vols. Misuzu Shobō, 1968–71. These volumes supercede an earlier abridged edition published by Asahi Shimbunsha, 1954.

Unno Yoshirō 海野芳郎. "Nitchū sensō shoki no wahei doryoku: Tokuni daisangoku no ugoki" 日中戦争初期の和平努力—特に第三国の動き (Peace efforts during the early phase of the Sino-Japanese War: With special reference to the moves of neutral countries), *Gunji shigaku* (May 1967), 3(1):64–80.

Uno Shigeaki 宇野重昭. "1930-nendai ni okeru Nitchū no shinkinkan to sōkoku" 1930年代における日中の親近感と相剋 (Affinity and conflict in Sino-Japanese relations during the 1930s). In Miwa Kimitada, ed., *Saikō taiheiyō sensō zenya*, pp. 234–65.

Usui Katsumi 臼井勝美. "Gaimusho: Hito to Kikō" 外務省—人と機構 (The Foreign Ministry: Its personnel and organization). In Hosoya et al., eds., *Nichi-Bei kankeishi*, 1:113–40.

—— "Nihon no tai-Ei imēgi to Taiheiyō sensō" 日本の対英イメージと太平洋戦争 (Japan's images of Britain and the Pacific War). In Hosoya, ed., *Nichi-Ei kankeishi, 1917–1945*, pp. 134–56.

—— *Nitchū sensō: Wahei ka sensen kakudai ka* 日中戦争—和平か戦線拡大か (The Sino-Japanese War: Peacemaking or escalation). Chūō Kōronsha, 1967.

—— "Nitchū sensō no seijiteki tenkai, 1937–1941" 日中戦争の政治的展開 (1937—1941年) The political development of the Sino-Japanese War). In Nihon Kokusai Seiji Gakkai, ed., *Taiheiyō sensō e no michi*, 4:113–256. [3]

Watanabe Akio 渡辺昭夫. "Ei-Bei ni yoru keizai seisai no kiki to Nihon no taiō, 1937–39" 英米による経済制裁の危機と日本の対応 (Japan's response to [the risk of] economic sanction by the United States and Britain), *Nenpō kindai Nihon kenkyū*, no. 7: *Nihon gaikō no kiki ninshiki*, pp. 221–44. [1]

—— "Shigemitsu Mamoru to Tōgō Shigenori" 重光葵と東郷茂徳 (Shigemitsu Mamoru and Tōgō Shigenori). *Rekishi to jinbutsu* (August 1975), pp. 52–59. [2]

Yabe Teiji 矢部貞治. *Konoe Fumimaro* 近衛文麿. Kōbundō, 1952, 2 vols.; reprinted by Yomiuri Shinbunsha, 1976.

Yamamoto Kumaichi 山本熊一. "Yamamoto Kumaichi ikō: Daitōa sensō hishi" 山本熊一遺稿—大東亜戦争秘史 (The posthumous manuscript of Yamamoto Kumaichi: A hidden history of the Greater East Asia War). *Kokusai seiji* (1963), no. 26: *Nihon gaikōshi no shomondai, 1*, pp. 1–69.

Yano Seiki 矢野征記 "Yano kiroku" 矢野記録 (The records of Yano Seiki). Not printed, Foreign Ministry archives.

Yomiuri Shinbunsha 読売新聞社. *Shōwashi no Tennō* 昭和史の天皇 (The Emperor in the history of the Shōwa period), 30 vols., published by the editor, 1967–76. (For itemized details, see chapter 4.)

Yoshida Yutaka 吉田裕. *Tennō no guntai to Nankin jiken: Mō hitotsuno Nitchū Sensōshi* 天皇の軍隊と南京事件－もう一つの日中戦争史 (The Emperor's army and the Nanking atrocities: Another side of the Sino-Japanese War). Aoki Shoten, 1985.

Yoshii Hiroshi 義井博. "The influence of the German-Soviet War on the Japan-U.S. Negotiations: Particularly Centering on Studies on the Problem of Secession from the Axis Alliance." *Revue Internationale d'Histoire Militaire*, no. 38. Hara Shobō, 1978, pp. 183–98. [1]

—— "Matsuoka gaikō no tenkai to sono zasetsu" 松岡外交の展開とその挫折 (The development and failure of Matsuoka diplomacy). *Rekishi kyōiku* (February 1967), 15(2):64–72. [2]

—— "Nichi-Doku-I sangoku dōmei to gunbu" 日独伊三国同盟と軍部 (The Tripartite Pact and the Japanese military). In Miyake et al., eds., *Showashi no gunbu to seiji*, 3:3–39. [3]

—— *Nichi-Doku-I sangoku dōmei to Nichi-bei kankei: Taiheiyō sensōzen kokusai kankei no kenkyū* 日独伊三国同盟と日米関係－太平洋戦争前国際関係の研究 (The Tripartite Pact and Japanese-American relations: A study on international relations prior to the outbreak of the Pacific War). Nansōsha, 1977.

—— *Shōwa gaikōshi* 昭和外交史 (A diplomatic history of the Shōwa period). Nansōsha, 1971.

Yoshizawa Minami 吉沢南. *Sensō kakudai no kōzu: Nihongun no "Futsu-In shinchū"* 戦争拡大の構図－日本軍の「仏印進駐」 (The scenario of the expansion of the war: The Japanese forces' "entry into French Indo-china"). Aoki Shoten, 1986.

7

The Pacific War, 1941–1945

Hatano Sumio

WARTIME DIPLOMACY AND THE "GREATER EAST ASIA COPROSPERITY SPHERE"

War Histories

Although there is a vast literature on the Pacific War, reliable accounts of wartime diplomacy are relatively few in number. As early as 1947 ex-colonel Hattori Takushirō, former chief of the Operations Section of the Army General Staff, and his group began to conduct extensive research on the history of the Pacific War under the auspices of the Historical Section of General MacArthur's General Headquarters. Their research led not only to the gathering of scattered materials but also to the recording of a large number of interviews with surviving Japanese officers.

The large body of materials thus accumulated were translated into English and have been available as the U.S. Army Center of Military History, *Japanese Monographs* series (fourteen reels of microfilm). The major monographs in this series were published in fifteen volumes as Donald Witwiler and Charles Burdick, eds., *War in Asia and the Pacific, 1937–1945* (New York: Garland, 1980).

On the Japanese side, the same project resulted in Hattori Takushirō, *Dai Tōa sensō zenshi* (A complete history of the Greater East Asia War), which was published in 1953. Because of the "official" sponsorship of the project, Hattori's war history may seem like a condensed version of the *Senshi sōsho* (War History) series compiled by the War History Office of the Defense Agency. The English version of Hattori's work is contained in the above-cited *War in Asia and the Pacific*.

For the purpose of this chapter, it is not necessary to itemize the massive War History series (totaling 102 vols.). Volumes that are especially relevant to foreign policy matters or concerned with the military's role in the road to the Pacific War have been mentioned in previous chapters. Suffice it here to make some general observations.

As pointed out by Fujiwara Akira in his critical collective review of the *Senshi sōsho* (Military History) series, the volumes in this series were written mainly from the viewpoint of staff officers tracing the strategic planning and conduct of military operations. With the exception of the two volumes treating the invasion of Malaya (vol. 1) and the Dutch East Indies (vol. 3), little space is given to Japan's military administration of these areas. Army and navy operations are often treated in separate volumes, and their respective service viewpoints are sometimes at odds with each other. Peculiarly abbreviated footnotes (endnotes) make it difficult for researchers to trace the sources in the archives of the War History Department.

Despite these limitations, the factual information presented in this monumental series is basic to any study of the Pacific War. A concise annotated list of all the volumes, as well as an account of the origins of this ambitious publication, are contained in Hirata Toshiharu, ed., *Revue Internationale d'Histoire Militaire: Edition de la Commission Japon d'Histoire Militaire* (Hara Shobō, 1978), pp. 92–105.

An important survey history, written from the point of view of the Army General Staff, is ex-colonel Hayashi Saburō, *Taiheihō sensō rikusen gaishi* (A short history of land battles during the Pacific War). Its English version is Hayashi Saburō, in collaboration with Alvin D.

Coox, *Kōgun: The Japanese Army in the Pacific* (Marine Corps Association Press, 1959; reprinted by Westport, Conn.: Greenwood Press, 1978). On the navy side, a more personal and revealing account has been written by Rear Admiral Tomioka Sadatoshi, former chief of the Operations Division of the Navy General Staff: *Kaisen to shūsen: Hito to kikō to keikaku* (The making and losing of the war: Men, organization, and plans).

General Histories

The most comprehensive study from the viewpoint of "Emperor-system fascism" is Rekishigaku Kenkyūkai (Historical Science Society), ed., *Taiheiyō sensōshi* (History of the Pacific War), in five volumes. This is a joint product of historians who find one long continuous war of Japanese aggression starting with the Manchurian Incident and "inevitably" expanding into the Sino-Japanese War and the Pacific War. This interpretation is known as the "fifteen years war" thesis. The authors of the series agree that the Pacific War had three faces: a struggle among imperialist powers; a war between fascist and antifascist forces; and a war for the liberation of oppressed peoples in Asia (especially China) from Japanese as well as Western imperialism. They also sought to place the whole responsibility for the war on "Emperor-system fascism," monopoly capitalists, and parasitic landholders—in fact, the entire "ruling class" (see chapter 4, "Historiographical Survey").

Survey histories written from this perspective of the "fifteen years war" are: Ienaga Saburō's *Taiheiyō sensō* (The Pacific War) and Fujiwara Akira's *Taiheiyō sensō*. The former appeared in English as *The Pacific War: World War II and the Japanese, 1931–1945* (New York: Pantheon, 1978). Among recently published surveys, we note Kisaka Jun'ichirō's *Taiheiyō sensō*. In this book Kisaka shows that by 1942 "Emperor-system fascism" had been firmly established with the spread of bureaucratic control over almost every aspect of national life.

There are a number of historians who reject the viewpoint of "Emperor-system fascism" as sketched above, but no multivolume work by non-Marxists has yet appeared that matches Rekishigaku

Kenkyūkai, ed., *Taiheiyō sensōshi*. Examples of less overtly ideological treatments of the Pacific War are: Ōhata Tokushirō, *Taiheiyō sensō* (The Pacific War), 2 vols.; Hayashi Shigeru, *Taiheiyō sensō* (The Pacific War); and Arai Shin'ichi, *Dainiji sekai taisen: Sengo sekaishi no kiten* (World War II: The starting point for the history of the postwar world). Arai's compact book pays full attention to the linkage between the European war and the Asian theater. An original and strikingly revisionist interpretation—of neither the leftist nor rightist variety—is Akira Iriye's *Nichi-Bei sensō* (The Japanese-American war), which will be discussed below.

A convenient one-volume account of Japan's wartime diplomatic activities is Ōta Ichirō, editional supervisor, *Dai Tōa sensō: senji gaikō* (The Greater East Asian War: Wartime diplomacy), published as a volume in Kajima's series on Japanese diplomatic history. The book brings together Japan's policies toward neutral nations, relations with Asian nations, and policies toward the occupied areas in the south.

"The Greater East Asia Coprosperity Sphere"

The idea of the "Greater East Asia Coprosperity Sphere" was spelled out in the summer of 1940 at the time when the Japanese were eager to advance southward, and it was to become Japan's war aim. It was presented as an all-embracing doctrine to unify Japan, Manchukuo, and China together with Southeast Asia. However, its content was so dogmatic and at such variance with its actual implementation that until recently few Japanese scholars have been drawn to serious study on the subject.

Among published works, the following are noteworthy: Hashikawa Bunzō's essay on the ideal and realities of the Greater East Asia Coprosperity Sphere; Kawahara Hiroshi's *Shōwa seiji shisō kenkyū* (A study in the political thought of the Shōwa period); Miwa Kimitada's essay [2] on the differences between the "New Order in East Asia" and the "Greater East Asia Coprosperity Sphere"; and a few essays contained in Miwa Kimitada, ed., *Nihon no 1930-nendai: Kuni no uchi to soto kara* (The 1930s in Japan: Views from within and without the country). Kawahara's original study analyzes the ideological components of the "Greater East Asia Coprosperity Sphere" and the process through which they were translated into concrete policies, by focusing on the activities of technocrats who formed a brain trust for Prime Minister Konoe. Miwa's essay [2] attempts to contrast the two "grand policies": the idea of the "New Order in East Asia," according to the author, stemmed from the historical and moralistic ideal of Pan-Asianism, whereas the plan for the "Greater East Asia Coprosperity Sphere" was heavily influenced by the Western concept of "scientific" geopolitics and power-political "rationalism."

The question of why the German school of Geopolitik was so eagerly accepted by Japan in the late 1930s and early 1940s is studied in Hatano Sumio's essay [3]. Hatano finds the key to this question in a strong sense of crisis in Japan as a "have-not" nation facing international upheavals, and in the need of its intellectuals to find a "scientific and logical" rationale for the "Greater East Asia Coprosperity Sphere."

The economic aspects of the "Greater East Asia Coprosperity Sphere" have attracted the attention of Japanese scholars. Among them, I shall cite two representative examples: Kobayashi Hideo, *"Dai Tōa kyōeiken" no keisei to hōkai* (The formation and collapse of the "Greater East Asia Coprosperity Sphere"); and Hara Akira's essay on the economic realities of the Greater East Asia Coprosperity Sphere. Kobayashi's work elucidates the mechanism of Japan's economic control of all of the occupied areas in Southeast Asia as well as Manchuria, China, Taiwan, and Korea. Praised as "the crowning achievement of research in Japanese colonial history conducted during the 1970s," Kobayashi's book is aimed at refuting the "imperialistic interpretation" that attempts to favorably reevaluate the record of Japanese colonial rule. On the other hand, Hara's study presents an empirical analysis of the interrelationship between commercial and financial structures in the Japanese-occupied areas. Hara shows how Japan's "Coprosperity Sphere" as an "economic bloc" became completely paralyzed under its own weight.

The establishment of the Greater East Asia Ministry (Dai Tōashō) in 1942 came as a great blow to the Foreign Ministry, which was deprived of most of its diplomatic functions. The army forcefully prevailed over the Foreign Ministry to institute a new ministry under its control to integrate the administration of the Japanese-occupied areas in Asia. The intense struggle waged between the Foreign Ministry and the army is carefully studied in Baba Akira's article. [1]

Iriye's Japanese-American War

Almost all of the previous Japanese studies on the Pacific War dealt with military, diplomatic, and political policies only from Japanese viewpoints. Akira Iriye's *Nichi-Bei sensō* (The Japanese-American war), published in Japan in 1979, was all the more refreshing for its bifocal approach to the meaning of the Pacific War against a broad background of contemporary international history. (It received the prestigious Yoshida Shigeru prize in Japan.) Iriye's approach has been praised by Hata Ikuhiko as a model of "equidistant analysis" of international history, in which the historian takes his own stand at the midpoint ("equidistant") from the nations he treats. The English-language version of this work has subsequently appeared as *Power and Culture: The Japanese-American War, 1941–1945* (Cambridge: Harvard University Press, 1981); it is more explicit in its application of his framework of "power and culture."

In this work, Iriye underscores the essentially peaceful nature of the course of Japanese-American relations, arguing that the late 1930s and the Pacific War constituted aberrations. During the war, Iriye points out, there existed between the American and Japanese leaderships a broad spectrum of shared perceptions of the international system, and their proclaimed war aims had a great deal in common. For instance, he contends that the declaration of the Greater East Asia Conference of 1943 was strikingly similar to the Atlantic Charter of 1941, and that this fact in turn prepared the way for a quick Japanese-American rapprochement after the war. Iriye portrays the wartime American plan toward defeated Japan as that of "reintegrating" it into a peaceful and interdependent world order—an international system that Iriye calls "Wilsonian," and which he claims had defined Japanese-American relations during the 1920s.

Iriye's provocative thesis has encountered criticism in Japan from various directions. The most common one is that his book confuses the realities of Japanese wartime policy with its hollow rhetoric. Some have pointed out that the post-1945 period was far from a return to the Wilsonian world order, and that even in the 1920s Japan had not wholeheartedly adhered to Wilsonianism. Others have charged that Iriye minimizes differences between Japanese and American cultures as a factor in the Pacific War. The most thorough-going antithesis of Iriye's book is John W. Dower, *War without Mercy: Race and Power in the Pacific War* (New York, Pantheon, 1986) which stresses racial hatred that characterized both sides.

Hata, while generally favorable to Iriye's book in his review, questions Iriye's emphasis on the continuities of Japanese-American relations in the 1940s. Whereas Iriye argues that the American occupation policy toward Japan was merely an extension and implementation of wartime policy planning and was little affected by the emerging cold war, Hata contends that the cold war in Asia caused changes in occupation policies in 1948.

NATIONALIST MOVEMENTS IN JAPAN-OCCUPIED ASIA

Early Works

How did Japan's military administration of the occupied areas in Asia—especially in Southeast Asia—affect national independence movements in the regions? This question remained the focal point of Japanese works in the 1950s dealing with wartime Southeast Asia. Tanigawa Yoshihiko published pioneering works [1] [2] on the anti-Japanese nationalist movement in Indonesia, Vietnam, Burma, Malaya, and Indochina. As the result, research on Japan's military administration of Southeast Asia lagged far behind.

Japan's Military Administration

A path-breaking study of Japanese military administration is Nishijima Shigetada and Kishi Kōichi, eds., *Indoneshia ni okeru Nihon gunsei no kenkyū* (A study of Japanese military administration in Indonesia), published in 1959. In 1963 its English translation appeared, prepared by the Joint Publication Research Service (Washington, D.C.), titled *Japanese Military Administration in Indonesia*. Since this version lacked the scholarly apparatus, Harry J. Benda of Yale University took the initiative to publish an English translation of the documents (which constitute the latter half of the book) and supplemented them by important additional documents since collected in Japan and the Netherlands. The result is Benda et al., eds., *Japanese Military Administration in Indonesia: Selected Documents* (New Haven, Conn.: Southeast Asia Studies, Yale University, 1965.)

There is also the previously cited *Taiheiyō sensōshi* (A history of the Pacific War), vols. 4 and 5, edited by Rekishigaku Kenkyūkai. These volumes maintain that the postwar upsurge of national independence movements in Southeast Asia was not spurred by the Japanese military's slogan of "national liberation," but was caused by the Asian people's resistance to Japan's colonialistic oppression. On the other hand, Ōta Tsunezō's *Biruma ni okeru Nihon gunseishi no kenkyū* (A study of the history of Japanese military administration in Burma) is a substantial study written from the viewpoint of favorably assessing the impact of Japan's military administration on the Burmese national independence movement.

Impact on Nationalism

Since Ōta's work was published in 1967, scholarly interest in Southeast Asia has increased rapidly, and there has emerged a conspicuous tendency among Japanese scholars to reexamine the interrelation between the development of Japanese occupation policy and national liberation movements in Southeast Asia. As a result, a number of monographs have appeared that focus on particular aspects of Japan's military administration. Recent studies that cover Southeast Asia as a whole are: Tanaka Hiroshi, ed., *Nihon gunsei to Ajia no minzoku undō* (Japanese military administration and nationalist movements in Asia); and Iwatake Teruhiko, *Nanpō gunseika no keizai shisaku* (Economic policies in Southeast Asia under Japanese occupation). The former work, containing nine articles, is the product of a joint research project that addressed itself to the question: "How was Japan's military administration reflected in postwar relations between Japan and Southeast Asia?" A symposium contained in the volume presents interesting viewpoints concerning the impact that the Japanese military administration had on Asian nationalism. The latter work traces the development of the economic aspects of the Japanese military administration in Malaya, Sumatra, and Java. Its second volume contains a comprehensive list of primary sources relating to Japan's military administration in Southeast Asia, such as documents available at the War History Department of the Defense Agency, the Nishijima Shigetada collection at Shakai Kagaku Kenkyūjo (the Institute of Social Sciences) at Waseda University, and the Kishi Kōichi collection at Ajia Keizai Kenkyūjo (the Institute of Developing Economies).

Documents

Recently, the War History Department of the Defense Agency (Bōeichō) published *Nanpō no gunsei* (Military administration in the Southern region) as an addition to the War History series. This volume consists mainly of official documents that elucidate the process through which the Japanese army procured vital strategic resources from the various parts of Southeast Asia, but it also contains the personal recollections of those involved in this effort. The usefulness of this volume is enhanced by a full catalogue of all of the materials relating to Japan's military administration of Southeast Asia that are in the archives of the War History Department.

Indonesia

Of all of the Japanese-occupied areas, Indonesia, where the Japanese military administration is said to have left its strongest marks, has attracted particular attention from Japanese scholars. The military administration of Java—the touchstone of the Japanese occupaton of Indonesia—has been treated, among others, by Shiraishi Aiko's studies on the creation of the PETA army (Indonesian Pembela Tanah Air [National Defense Forces]) [3] and on the Ankatan Muda movement in Western Java [1]. The former discusses the role of the PETA Army, which was established under the guidance of the Japanese army; the latter examines the role of the Indonesian youth as subleaders. The views of Japan held by Achmed Sukarno and Mohammed Hatta, influential collaborators with the Japanese occupation authorities, are examined by Gotō Ken'ichi's study [4]. In a recent article [1], Gotō discusses Japanese military administration and the nature of the independence question on the basis of memoirs left by the Japanese military and civilians who were involved in the independence of Indonesia in 1945. Gotō presents a favorable evaluation of the psychological and spiritual impacts that Japan's military administration gave to the Indonesian independence movement.

The opposite position is taken by Shinbo Jun'ichirō. While admitting that the occupation of the Dutch East Indies by the Japanese forces had served as a leverage for the formation of the united anti-imperialistic people's front, Shinbō contends that "anti-Western education" imposed by Japan's military administration weakened the anti-imperialistic nature of Indonesian nationalism, thus hampering the Indonesian revolution.

A comprehensive survey from the viewpoint of the national liberation movement, including the period of Japanese occupation, is provided in Masuda Atau's account for the general reader, *Indoneshia gendaishi* (A history of contemporary Indonesia).

Regarding anti-Japanese movements and riots in Indonesia under Japanese rule, the following studies are of interest: Shiraishi Aiko's article [1] on Japanese occupation and social change with particular reference to peasant uprisings in Indramayu; Gotō Ken'ichi's essay on the "Pontianak incident" [3]; and Hara Fujio's study on the Japanese military administration and the "Api incident." The Pontianak incident was a large-scale uprising against the Japanese that took place in the city of Pontianak (western Borneo) in the fall of 1943, lasting until 1944. The Api incident was a similar uprising that occurred in October 1943 in north Borneo.

The Philippines

On Japan's occupation policy toward the Philippines, Ikehata Setsuho has published a distinguished study of the role played by Artemio Ricarte, one of the leading Philippine collaborators with the Japanese. The diary of Murata Shōzō, who as ambassador to the Philippines (1943–45) acted in close cooperation with President Jose P. Laurel, has been edited by Murata's colleague Fukushima Shintarō as *Murata Shōzō ikō: Hitō nikki* (The memoirs of Murata Shōzō: The Philippine diary).

Indochina

Indochina, where French colonial rule was preserved even after the stationing of Japanese forces, did not experience Japanese military administration until the collapse of the French Indochinese government in March 1945. The characteristics of Japanese rule over Indochina are examined by Shiraishi Masaya and Furuta Motoo in their joint pioneering essay. The Indochina question has also been treated in Akagi Kanji's well-documented article, which explains Japan's wartime policy toward Indochina in terms of conflict between the army and the Foreign Ministry over Japan's war aims. Akagi shows that there existed a sharp conflict between the Foreign Ministry and the army over the mode of administration in Indochina: the former, which stressed the war aim of national liberation, insisted on the independence and liberation of Indochina, whereas the army was reluctant, for military reasons. In the end, it was the impact of the Soviet-French alliance of December 1944 that forced the Japanese military to yield.

Burma

On the Japanese occupation policy toward Burma, we have, in addition to Ōta Tsunezō's above-cited monograph, articles by Ōno Tōru on the Burmese national army. In the process that led to the independence of Burma and subsequent Burmese-Japanese relations, the role of the "Minami kikan"—the Japanese intelligence bureau concerned with Burma (1941–42)—has received much attention, and Western scholars have tended to emphasize the close relationship between the leaders of Burmese independence and the "Minami kikan." In sharp contrast, Saitō Teruko maintains that in the final analysis the "Minami kikan" merely engaged in independent activities by exploiting confusions in the strategies of the Imperial Headquarters.

On the history of Japanese-Burmese relations, including the occupation of Burma by Japanese forces, there is a detailed and annotated bibliography prepared by a group located at the Tokyo University of Foreign Studies. See Biruma Kenkyū Gurūpu (Burma Research Group), ed., *Biruma kankei hōbun bunken no kaidai oyobi mokuroku* (Burmese studies in Japan, 1868–1985: A guide to literature and annotated bibliography).

Thailand

As for relations with Thailand, which managed to maintain nominal independence throughout the Pacific War, Ichikawa Kenjirō has published a noteworthy essay on Phibul's defection to Japan [2] and another essay on the Free Thai movement [1]. The former study focuses on Phibul Songkhram, the Thai prime minister who tried to pursue pro-Axis policies and eventually defected to Japan. The latter is a study of the Free Thai movement, which was promoted by Thai residents in the United States in close cooperaton with anti-Japanese elements within Thailand. On the Phibul regime during the Pacific War, Yoshikawa Toshiharu has published an excellent study.

Malaya

On the Japanese military administration of Malaya, Akashi Yōji has published several excellent articles: "Japanese Military Administration in Malaya: Its Formation and Evolution in Reference to Sultans, the Islamic Religion, and the Muslim Malays: 1941–45" [2]; and "Bureaucracy and the Japanese Military Administration, with Special Reference to Malaya" [1]. The latter essay is especially interesting, because it examines how the characteristics of the Japanese bureaucracy were reflected in Japan's military administration of the southern regions, Malaya in this instance. Useful as source materials are documents relating to Japanese military administration in Malaya, edited by Tonooka Akirō. Nagai Shin'ichi's Gendai Marēshia seiji kenkyū (A study of contemporary Malaysian politics) contains a good overall picture of the Malaysian nationalist movement during the Pacific War.

India

Japanese-Indian relations during the World War II period, with emphasis on the Indian National Army, has been the subject of a joint research, published as Nagasaki Nobuko, ed., Minami Ajia no minzoku undō to Nihon (Japan and nationalist movements in South Asia). This work includes, among others, the following studies: Nagasaki Nobuko on the formation of the Indian National Army; Oshikawa Fumiko on India's independence movement during World War II; and Kona Yasuyuki on the activities of the Indian Independence League in Southeast Asia in 1943. Ogata Kōhei, ed., Nihon to Indo (Japan and India) contains Arai Shin'ichi's essay on Japan's southward advance and India.

Finally, a mention must be made of Ōta Kōki's solid study [2] of the structure and functions of Japan's military administrative agencies for the southern areas. Ōta has also published a concise account [3] of the characteristics and development of Japan's military administration in the southern regions on the basis of his previous studies on the army's and navy's organizations for military administration as well as their local agencies.

THE DIPLOMACY OF TERMINATING THE WAR

Shūsen Shiroku

The Foreign Ministry, ed. (Kurihara Ken, comp.), *Shūsen shiroku* (Historical record of the termination of the war), published in 1951, contains not only the memoirs of Japan's main policymakers and records of the Tokyo war crimes trials but also a number of manuscripts and memoranda written specifically for this volume by those leaders who are known as the "peace party." As a basic collection of documentary sources, the volume has retained great value to researchers. (Robert J. C. Butow's classical account, *Japan's Decision to Surrender* [Stanford University Press, 1954], which has been translated into Japanese, makes full use of these materials.) For historiographical comments on *Shūsen shiroku*, see chapter 4, "Historiographical Survey."

Long out of print, *Shūsen shiroku* has recently been reprinted in a new format in six volumes. The fifth volume contains some important documents discovered since the publication of the original edition: notably a long message to Foreign Minister Tōgō from Ryū Shintarō, an *Asahi* newspaper correspondent in Europe; and telegraphic exchanges between Foreign Minister Shigemitsu and Ambassador Satō Naotake in Moscow which reveal fundamental differences of views between these two men on negotiations with the Soviet Union. A noteworthy new document contained in the sixth volume is the Foreign Ministry's report on "diplomatic processes leading to the termination of war" (declassified in 1976).

The sixth volume of the new edition also contains an extended historiographical essay by Hatano Sumio that places *Shūsen shiroku* in proper historical perspective. This analytical essay is followed by a bibliography listing more than 1,300 items, some of which are briefly annotated. The discursive and tendentious introductory essay for each volume by a right-wing literary critic Etō Jun is strangely out of place for such a documentary collection, and it can best be disregarded.

The supplementary volume to the new edition, *Bekkan: Shūsen o toinaosu* (Reexamining the termination of the war), consists of a symposium between diplomatic historians and political scientists. Some of the interesting controversies revolved around the issues raised by Iriye, for example the problem of how to assess the declaration of the Greater East Asia Conference of 1943.

In 1986 Kurihara Ken and Hatano Sumio thoroughly revised *Shūsen shiroku*, and the new edition was published as *Shūsen kōsaku no kiroku* (The record of maneuvers to terminate the war). It contains materials not found in *Shūsen shiroku*, such as Foreign Ministry materials that were recently released; the records (in Japanese) of interviews with Japan's political and military leaders, conducted by the Historical Section of General MacArthur's General Headquarters; Rear Admiral Takagi Sōkichi's materials relating to the navy's maneuvers to overthrow the Tōjō cabinet; the plan to dispatch Konoe to the Soviet Union for peace mediation; and hitherto unpublished materials of the army and the Army General Staff relating to war plans.

Earlier Studies

The first important research project on Japan's surrender was organized by Nihon Gaikō Gakkai (the Association for the Study of Japanese Diplomacy), headed by Ueda Toshio. In 1958, *Taiheiyō sensō shūketsuron* (Studies on the termination of the Pacific War) was published as the fruit of joint work involving some twenty specialists in diplomatic history, political science, economics, and international law. By clarifying, as far as documentary evidence then available permitted, the multifaceted aspects of Japan's surrender, this book provided the basis for further research. In a more popular vein is Hayashi Shigeru, ed., *Nihon shūsenshi* (A history of Japan's termination of the war).

Efforts for Peace Through Mediation

During the Pacific War, the Japanese-Soviet Neutrality Pact (1941–45) provided Japan with its sole official diplomatic channel with foreign nations other than the Axis powers. And the "peace party" in Japan pinned upon Soviet mediation their last hope to end the war (with acceptable conditions). The gap between this unrealistic expectation and the actualities of international politics is expertly discussed in Hosoya Chihiro's essay on Japanese wartime policy toward the Soviet Union, which he calls a "diplomacy of illusions." Hatano Sumio's recent article [1], focusing on the Soviet factor in Japan's war plans during 1942–45, assesses the significance of the Army General Staff's plan for mediating between Germany and the Soviet Union as it related to Japanese political and military strategy during the Pacific War.

Another useful study of the Japanese-Soviet negotiations of this period is Baba Akira's essay [2], which is based on unpublished exchanges between Foreign Minister Shigemitsu Mamoru and Ambassador to Russia Satō Naotake (August 1944–April 1945). Yubashi Shigeto, who acted in close concert with Ambassador Satō, has left a detailed account on the negotiations with the Soviet Union in his *Senji Nisso kōshōshi* (A history of Japanese-Soviet relations during the Pacific War). In addition, Morishima Gorō—who as minister plenipotentiary under Ambassador Satō, ably assisted him—left his memoirs, which contain much useful information. Unusually candid and revealing accounts are found in Satō's own diplomatic memoirs, *Kaiko 80-nen* (Reminiscences of my eighty years).

The details of wartime negotiations with the Soviet Union, such as those over the issue of the north Sakhalin oil, are carefully examined in Nishi Haruhiko, ed., *Nisso kokkō mondai* (Japanese-Soviet relations), vol. 15 of the Kajima series in Japanese diplomatic history. Somewhat prosaic, its accounts are based on Foreign Ministry materials. However, Ōta Ichirō, Matsumoto Shun'ichi, and Andō Yoshirō, eds., *Dai Tōa sensō, shūsen gaikō* (The Greater East Asian War and the termination of war), vol. 25 of the same series, contains little new information on Soviet-Japanese relations.

Concerning "peace feelers" emanating from such neutral countries as Switzerland and Sweden, as well as the Vatican, there are few works other than the essays by Kobayashi Tatsuo and Motohashi Tadashi, which were contained in the previously cited Nihon Gaikō Gakkai, ed., *Taiheiyō sensō shūketsuron*. Recently, both Kobayashi [1] and Motohashi [2] expanded on their essays by adding newly discovered materials. The only other noteworthy study in this area is Shiozaki Hiroaki's article, which surveys the Japanese efforts to end the war by Vatican mediation.

Regarding the Sino-Japanese peace maneuvers through Miao Pin, an influential figure in the Nanking regime, which became an occasion for the Koiso Kuniaki cabinet to collapse, few primary sources have survived, and historians must of necessity rely on such secondary sources as Tamura Shinsaku, *Myouhin kōsaku* (The Miao Pin maneuver) and Koiso's autobiography.

The Activities of the Peace Party

With regard to the activities of the "peace party," which came to the surface just when the Tōjō cabinet was beginning to collapse, Itō Takashi has thrown light on the interrelationship of various groups in his well-documented study [1] on the "Konoe-Mazaki group" in 1942–45 and the move to form a Kobayashi Seizō cabinet. According to Itō's study, the "Konoe-Mazaki group" (including Yoshida Shigeru, Iwabuchi Tatsuo, and army leaders of the "Kōdō faction"), feeling that for the sake of an early peace it was necessary to clean the army of the dominant "Control faction," was working for a cabinet to be headed by General Ugaki Kazushige or Admiral Kobayashi Seizō.

In addition to *Shūsen shiroku* and *Shūsen kōsaku no kiroku*, important source materials on the activities of the "peace party" are: Kyōdō Tsūshin Konoe Nikki Henshū Iinkai, ed., *Konoe nikki*, the dictated diary of Konoe Fumimaro, who as one of the foremost senior statesmen plotted for the downfall of the Tōjō cabinet; *Dai Tōa sensō shūshū no shinsō* (The real facts about the termination of the Greater East Asian War), by Matsutani Makoto, who was secretary to Prime Minister Suzuki Kantarō; and *Dai Tōa sensō hishi* (The secret history of the Greater East Asian War), by Vice-Admiral Hoshina Zenshirō, the last of the chiefs of the Naval Affairs Bureau. Concerning the activities of men close to Konoe, important works include the following: Tomita Kenji, *Haisen Nihon no uchigawa: Konoekō no omoide* (Inside defeated Japan: Recollections of Prince Konoe); Hosokawa Morisada's diary; and the detailed diary by Yabe Teiji, a member of Konoe's brain trust. A detailed analysis of the Yabe diary is contained in Itō Takashi's work, *Shōwa 10-nendaishi danshō* (Studies on the history of the decade 1935–45), which shows the delicate interrelationships between various peace activities.

There are very few primary sources that reveal the moves of cabinet members and ranking military leaders who were involved in the decision to surrender. One important exception is the rich diary of Kido Kōichi, Lord Keeper of the Privy Seal. There are numerous memoirs and biographies of the top leaders, but few contain reliable accounts. Recently, however, Prime Minister Suzuki Kantarō has been treated in a readable biography by Kobori Keiichirō.

The clandestine activities of the navy's "peace party" (headed by Navy Minister Yonai Mitsumasa) can be traced in Takagi Sōkichi and Sanematsu Yuzuru, eds., *Kaigun taishō Yonai Mitsumasa oboegaki* (The memoranda of Admiral Yonai Mitsumasa), which contains records dictated by Yonai himself and his memoranda. Also useful are the recently published memoranda of Rear Admiral Takagi Sōkichi who secretly served under Navy Minister Yonai to bring about a speedy end to the war. The hitherto unpublished manuscripts of Rear Admiral Takagi are partially printed and commented on by Kudō Michihiro in his recent article, which attempts to clarify the navy's role in the peace efforts. There are plans to publish the entire Takagi collection, including his valuable diary (see chapter 1).

The Politics of Surrender

The political process from the downfall of the Tōjō cabinet to the decision to surrender was expertly treated as early as 1955 by Kurihara Ken in his pioneering work, *Tennō: Shōwashi oboegaki* (The Emperor: A note on the history of the Shōwa period), which devotes more than half of the volume to the efforts to terminate the war.

It was followed by a series of noteworthy studies: in 1968, Ishida Takeshi, *Hakyoku to heiwa* (The catastrophe and peace); Fujiwara Akira's essay on Japan's defeat; Nomura Minoru's study [2] of the collapse of the Tōjō cabinet in the context of military developments; Fujimura Michio's essay on Japan's surrender and the collapse of the military; and Masumi Junnosuke, *Nihon seitō shiron* (A history of Japanese party politics), vol. 7. One theme common to the interpretations of the works of Ishida, Fujimura, and Masumi is the continuity of the "Emperor system" and of the governing functions of the Japanese state from the prewar to the postwar periods.

Fujiwara's essay points out that the military's political influence had been on the decline since the latter phase of the Koiso cabinet. Nomura examines the process through which Tōjō's "dictatorial" ruling system was undermined by the conflicting strategic views of the army and navy. Nomura suggests that Emperor Hirohito's opposition to the proposal to integrate the army and navy in April 1945 virtually amounted to his decision in favor of terminating the war.

In 1967 the official documents at the highest level of the Japanese military and government were collected and published as Sanbō Honbu, ed., *Haisen no kiroku* (The record of defeat). Essentially a sequel to *Sugiyama memo* (see chapter 4), this collection, also edited by the Army General Staff and published only in 1979, contains the official documents of the Imperial Headquarters–Cabinet Liaison Conferences, the Supreme War Council, and the Imperial Conferences during the crucial years 1944–1945. To supplement these documents, Inaba Masao provides in this volume a lengthy "commentary" that brings together a number of related documents emanating from other quarters, which are useful for a better understanding of Japan's decision to surrender. In this volume one can trace, on the highest policy level, such important developments as the collapse of the Tōjō cabinet; the disintegration of Japanese strategy and war efforts; the last desperate attempts at a mediated peace, abortive negotiations with the Soviet Union; the clandestine peace maneuvers under the Koiso-Yonai cabinets; and, most importantly, the final decision to surrender.

Appended to *Haisen no kiroku* is the confidential diary of the Military Affairs Section of the Army Ministry, the most staunch advocate of continued fighting. This diary gives detailed information on the plan for a coup d'état, prepared among the army's middle-echelon officers, to prevent Japan's surrender.

Few studies have yet appeared that compare the characteristics of Japan's surrender with that of Germany or Italy. Yoshida Teruo argues that Japan's surrender was a "domestic question" in the sense that the consent of the army leaders was the absolute prerequisite. For this reason, Yoshida concludes, the Japanese government simply could not make an active decision about the timing and method of surrender, as the Badoglio government did.

The A-Bomb Decision

One of the historical issues relating to Japan's surrender is whether the determining factor in its decision to accept "unconditional surrender" was the dropping of the A-bombs or the Soviet entry into the war. The prevailing view among Japanese scholars, as represented in Fujiwara's previously mentioned essay [2], holds that the shock of the Soviet entry was a more potent factor.

As to the American motives for dropping the atomic bombs, the majority of Japanese historians reject the "official" explanation of the U.S. government—the avoidance of further casualties by putting an early end to the war. Rather, they tend to accept the Cold War "revisionist" thesis that emphasizes the political aim of "containing" Soviet influence in East Asia and making the Russians more "manageable" in Eastern Europe. A typical example of such an interpretation is Nishijima Ariatsu, *Genbaku wa naze otosaretaka: Nihon kōfuku o meguru senryaku to gaikō* (Why the A-bombs were dropped: The strategy and diplomacy of Japan's surrender). This book, which appeared in 1971, essentially restates the thesis of P. M. S. Blackett, *Fear, War, and the Bomb* (New York: Whittlesey House, 1949) and Gar Alpevoritz, *Atomic Diplomacy: Hiroshima and Potsdam* (New York: Vintage, 1965) and connects the A-bomb decision with the American conduct of the Vietnam War, both having a racist overtone. A more recent monograph (1985) by Arai Shin'ichi, *Genbaku tōka e no michi* (The road to the dropping of the A-bombs), also follows the thesis advanced by the American "revisionists."

An original and useful work for our purposes is a joint study by Shōno Naomi et al., *Kaku to heiwa: Nihonjin no ishiki* (The nuclear weapon and peace: An investigation into Japanese consciousness), which is based on a public opinion survey and statistical data. Using his own data, Asada Sadao has analytically traced shifting Japanese attitudes about the atomic bomb in his essay, "Japanese Perceptions of the A-bomb Decision, 1945–1980." Originally presented at an international conference, held at the U.S. Air Force Academy (1980), Asada tries to explain the striking differences between Japanese and American perceptions of the A-bomb decision.

The Termination of War in Asia

Regarding the end of the war in the various parts of Asia and post-surrender financial transactions, several useful studies and collections of documents have been published by organizations and individuals that were involved in the task of massive demobilization and expatriation.

On Korea the authoritative monograph is *Chōsen shūsen no kiroku* (Korea at the end of the war: Collected documents) by Morita Yoshio, who was long engaged in the repatriation from Korea and is himself an expert on Korean-Japanese relations. Morita has also published an article on the termination of the Japanese rule of Korea. In addition, he has co-edited *Chōsen shūsen no kiroku: Shiryōhen* (Korea at the end of the war: Collected documents).

Basic documents regarding the cease-fire, the negotiations with the Chinese forces for a truce agreement, and expatriation from China are contained in Usui Katsumi, ed., *Gendaishi shiryō,* vol. 12: *Taiheiyō sensō, 4* (Source materials on contemporary history, vol. 12: The Pacific War, 4). This volume contains a detailed introductory essay by the editor.

On Taiwan, the standard works are: Mukōyama Hiroo, "Taiwan ni okeru Nihon tōchi to sengo naigai jōsei" (The Japanese administration of Taiwan and the domestic and external situations after the war); and Taiwan Sōtokufu (Government-General of Taiwan), *Taiwan tōchi shimatsu hōkokusho* (Report on the disposition of the administration of Taiwan). Both works are, however, not easily accessible.

The most detailed treatment of the battles between the Kwantung Army and the Soviet forces which invaded Manchuria, Korea, Sakhalin, and the Kurile Islands on August 15, 1945, as well as of the ensuing truce negotiations is: Bōeichō Senshishitsu (War History Office, Defense Agency), ed. (Nishihara Yukio, author), *Kantōgun* (The Kwantung Army), vol. 2 in the *Senshi sōsho* (War History) series.

On the subject of Japanese residents in Manchuria and their expatriation, the basic work is Manmō Dōhō Engokai, ed., *Manmō shūsenshi* (A history of the termination of the war in Manchuria and Mongolia). Regarding Sakhalin and the Kuriles, there is Karafuto Shūsenshi Kankōkai ed., *Karafuto shūsenshi* (Sakhalin at the end of the war).

On Java, Miyamoto Shizuo, who was an army officer there, has written a massive account, *Java shūsen shoriki* (An account of the end of the war in Java). This work provides particularly useful information on the realities of the last phase of Japan's military administration in Java.

Finally, I shall mention works touching on the leaders of Japan's "puppet" regimes—their behavior and attempt to take refuge in Japan. Interesting materials on the subject are contained in Yomiuri Shinbunsha, ed., *Shōwashi no tennō*, vols. 8–15; and Gaimushō (Foreign Ministry), ed. *Senryō shiroku* (Historical documents on the Allied occupation of Japan), vol. 2. The latter is a collection of relevant documents in the Foreign Ministry archives.

Bibliography

Akagi Kanji 赤木完爾. "Futsu-In buryoku shori o meguru gaikō to gunji: 'Jizon jiei' to 'Dai Tōa kaihō' no aida" 仏印武力処理をめぐる外交と軍事—「自存自衛」と「大東亜解放」の間 (Diplomacy and strategy of the armed settlement in French Indochina: Between "self-existence" and the "liberation of Greater East Asia"). *Hōgaku kenkyū* (Keiō gijuku Daigaku) (September 1984), 57(9):28–62.

Akashi Yōji 明石陽至. "Bureaucracy and the Japanese Military Administration in reference to Sultans, the Islamic Religion, and the Muslim Malays, *in Asia*, pp. 46–82. Singapore University Press, 1981. [1]

—— "Japanese Military Administration in Malaya: Its Formation and Evolution in reference to Sultans, the Islamic Religion, and the Muslim Malays, 1941–45." *Asian Studies* (April 1969), 7(1):81–110. [2]

—— "Japanese Policy Toward the Malayan Chinese, 1941–1845." *Journal of Southeast Asian Studies* (September 1970), 1(2):61–89.

—— "The Japanese Occupation of Malaya: Interruption or Transformation?" In Alfred W. McCoy, ed., *Southeast Asia Under Japanese Occupation*, pp. 54–74. Yale University, Southeast Asia Studies (Monograph series no. 22), 1980. [3]

Arai Shin'ichi 荒井信一. *Dainiji sekai taisen: Sengo sekaishi no kiten* 第二次世界大戦—戦後世界史の起点 (World War II: The starting point for the history of the postwar world). Tokyo Daigaku Shuppankai, 1973.

Arai Shin'ichi. *Genbaku tōka e no michi* 原爆投下への道 (The road to the dropping of the A-bombs). Tokyo Daigaku Shuppankai, 1985.

—— "Nihon no nanshin to Indo" 日本の南進とインド (Japan's southward advance and India). In Ōgata Kōhei, ed., *Nihon to Indo*, pp. 111–29.

Asada Sadao 麻田貞雄. "Japanese Perceptions of the A-Bomb Decision, 1945–1980." In Joe Dixon, ed., *The American Military and the Far East: Proceedings of the Ninth Military History Symposium, 1–3 October 1980*, pp. 199–217, 276–79. U.S. Air Force Academy and Office of Air Force History. Washington, D.C.: GPO, 1980.

Baba Akira 馬場明. "Dai Tōashō setchi mondai" 大東亜省設置問題 (The problem of establishing the Greater East Asia Ministry, 1, 2). *Gaimushō chōsa geppō* (October 1967), 8(10):55–84; (November 1967), 8(11):32–69. [1]

—— "Shigemitsu, Satō ōfuku denpō ni miru senji Nisso kōshō" 重光, 佐藤往復電報にみる戦時日ソ交渉 (Wartime Soviet-Japanese negotiations as seen in the Shigemitsu-Satō telegraphic exchanges). *Kokushigaku* (March 1980), nos. 110–11, pp. 113–33. [2]

Biruma Kenkyū Gurūpu ビルマ研究グループ, ed. *Biruma kankei hōgo bunken no kaidai oyobi mokuroku* ビルマ関係邦文文献の解題および目録 (Burmese studies in Japan, 1868–1985: A guide to literature and bibliography). Tokyo Gaikokugo Daigaku Biruma Kenkyūshitsu, 1985.

Etō Jun 江藤淳, ed., annotated by Hatano Sumio 波多野澄雄. *Senryō shiroku, 2: Teisen to gaikōken teishi* 占領秘録, 2：停戦と外交権停止 (Historical documents on the Allied occupation of Japan, vol. 2: The cease-fire and suspension of Japan's diplomatic rights). Kōdansha, 1982.

Fujimura Michio 藤村道生. "Nihon no kōfuku to gunbu no hōkai" 日本の降伏と軍部の崩壊 (Japan's surrender and the collapse of the Japanese military). In Miyake Masaki, ed., *Shōwashi no gunbu to seiji*, 4:227–65.

Fujiwara Akira 藤原彰. "Bōeichō Bōei Kenshūjo Senshi Shitsu: *Senshi Sōsho*" 防衛庁防衛研修所戦史室『戦史叢書』 ([Review of] Defense Agency, War History Office, ed., *Senshi sōsho*), *Rekishigaku kenkyū* (December 1979), no. 451, pp. 51–57. [1]

—— "Haisen" 敗戦 (Japan's defeat). In *Iwanami kōza: Nihon rekishi*, vol. 21: *Kindai*, 岩波講座日本歴史21, 近代[8] (Iwanami series: A history of Japan, vol. 21: The modern period, 8), pp. 322–70. Iwanami Shoten, 1977. [2]

—— *Taiheiyō sensō* 太平洋戦争 (The Pacific War). Bun'eidō, 1970.

—— *Taiheiyō sensōshiron* 太平洋戦争史論 (Historical essays on the Pacific War). Aoki Shoten, 1982.

Fukushima Shintarō 福島慎太郎. *Murata Shōzō ikō: Hitō nikki* 村田省蔵

遺稿—比島日記 (Memoirs of Murata Shōzō: The Philippine diary). Hara Shobō, 1969.

Gotō Ken'ichi 後藤乾一. "Nihon gunsei to Indoneshia dokuritsu mondai: Nihon gawa kankeisha no kaisōroku o tegakarini" 日本軍政とインドネシア独立問題—日本側関係者の回想録を手掛りに (Japanese military occupation and the problem of Indonesian independence: On the basis of Japanese principals' reminiscences). *Shakai kagaku tōkyū* (September 1984), 30(1): 99–134. [1]

—— "Nihon gunseiki ni okeru Indonesia no teikō undō" 日本軍政期におけるインドネシアの抵抗運動 (Resistance movement in Indonesia under Japanese military administration), *Shakai kagaku tōkyū* (June 1981), 26(2): 1–38. [2]

—— "Ponchianakku jiken no shiteki kōsatsu" ポンチアナック事件の史的考察 (A historical examination of the Pontianak incident). In Tanaka, ed., *Nihon gunsei to Ajia no minzoku undō*, pp. 21–40. [3]

—— "1930-nendai no Nihon-Indonesia kankeishiron josetsu" 1930年代の日本・インドネシア関係史論序説 (An introduction to history of Japanese-Indonesian relations in the 1930s). *Ajia kenkyū* (April 1979), 20(1): 1–29. [4]

—— "Shingaparuna jiken ni kansuru ichi kōsatsu: Nihon gunseiki ni okeru Indoneshia no teikō undō" シンガパルナ事件に関する一考察—日本軍政期におけるインドネシアの抵抗運動 (A historical analysis of the Singaparna uprising: Resistance movement in Indonesia during the Japanese occupation). *Shakai kagaku tōkyū* (June 1981), 26(2): 1–38. [5]

Hara Akira 原朗. "'Dai Tōa kyōeiken' no keizaiteki jittai" 『大東亜共栄圏』の経済的実態 (The economic realities of the "Greater East Asia Coprosperity Sphere"). *Tochi seido shigaku* (April 1976), no. 71, pp. 1–28.

Hara Fujio 原不二夫. "Nihon no kita Boruneo tōchi to Api jiken" 日本の北ボルネオ統治とアピ事件 (Japanese occupation of north Borneo and the "Api incident"). In Tanaka, ed., *Nihon no gunsei to Ajia no minzoku undō*, pp. 41–80.

Hashikawa Bunzō 橋川文三. "Dai Tōa kyōeiken no rinen to jittai" 大東亜共栄圏の理念と実態 (The Greater East Asia Coprosperity Sphere: Its ideal and realities). In *Iwanami kōza: Nihon rekishi*, vol. 21: *Kindai 8* 岩波講座日本歴史21, 近代 8 (Iwanami series: A history of Japan, vol. 21: The modern period, 8), pp. 265–320. Iwanami Shoten, 1977. [3]

Hata Ikuhiko 秦郁彦. Review of Akire Iriye, *Nichi-Bei sensō*, *Kokusai seiji* (1976), no. 6, pp. 171–74.

Hatano Sumio 波多野澄雄. "Nihon no sensō keikaku ni okeru Soren yōin, 1942–1945" 日本の戦争計画におけるソ連要因, 1942—1945 (The Soviet factor in Japan's war plans, 1942–1945). *Shin bōei ronshū* (October 1984), 12(2):49–69. [1]

—— "Shigemitsu Mamoru to Ajia gaikō" 重光葵とアジア外交 ([Foreign Minister] Shigemitsu Mamoru and his Asian policy, *Kokusaigaku ronshū* (January 1983), no. 10, pp. 16–29. [2]

—— "'Tōa shin chitsujo' to chiseigaku" 「東亜新秩序」と地政学 (The "New Order in East Asia" and geopolitics). In Miwa Kimitada, ed., *Nihon no 1930-nendai: Kuni no uchi to soto kara,* pp. 13–47. [3]

Hattori Takushirō 服部卓四郎. *Dai Tōa sensō zenshi* 大東亜戦争全史 (A complete history of the Greater East Asia War). 8 vols. Masu Shobō, 1953–56; reprinted by Hara Shobō, 1965.

Hayashi Saburō 林三郎. Taiheiyō sensō rikusen gaishi 太平洋戦争陸戦概史 (A short history of land battles during the Pacific War). Iwanami Shoten, 1951.

Hayashi Shigeru 林茂, ed. *Nihon shūsenshi* 日本終戦史 (A history of Japan's termination of the war). 3 vols. Yomiuri Shinbunsha, 1963.

—— *Taiheiyō sensō* 太平洋戦争 (The Pacific War). Chūō Kōronsha, 1967.

Hoshina Zenshirō 保科善四郎. *Dai Tōa sensō hishi: Ushinawareta wahei kōsaku* 大東亜戦争秘史—失われた和平工作 (A secret history of the Pacific War: Peace efforts that failed). Hara Shobō, 1975.

Hosokawa Morisada 細川護貞. *Jōhō Tennō ni tassezu* 情報天皇に達せず (Information that never reached the Emperor). 2 vols. Dōkōsha Isobe Shobō, 1953 (reprinted by Chūō Kōronsha in 1979 as *Hosokawa nikki;* 2 vols.)

Hosoya Chihiro 細谷千博. "Taiheiyō sensō to Nihon no tai-So gaikō: Gensō no gaikō" 太平洋戦争と日本の対ソ外交—幻想の外交 (The Pacific War and Japanese policy toward the Soviet Union: Diplomacy of illusions). In Hosoya Chihiro and Minakawa Takashi 皆川洸, eds., *Hen'yō suru kokusai shakai no hō to seiji,* 変容する国際社会の法と政治 (Law and politics in the changing international society), pp. 275–307. Yūshindō, 1971.

Ichikawa Kenjirō 市川健二郎. "Jiyū Tai undō" 自由タイ運動 (The Free Thai movement). In Yamamoto Hakase Kanreki Kinen Tōyōshi Ronsō Henshū Iinkai 山本博士還暦記念東洋史論叢編集委員会, ed., *Yamamoto Hakase kanreki kinen Tōyōshi ronshū* (Festschrift for Dr. Yamamoto), pp. 39–50. Yamamoto Shuppansha, 1972. [1]

—— "Pibun no Nihon bōmei to Nihon no Ajia fukki" ピブンの日本亡命と日本のアジア復帰 (Phibul's defection to Japan and Japan's return to Asia). *Tokyo suisan daigaku ronshū* (March 1975), no. 10, pp. 1–14. [2]

Ienaga Saburō 家永三郎. *Taiheiyō sensō* 太平洋戦争 (The Pacific War). Iwanami Shoten, 1968.

Ikehata Setsuho 池端雪輔. "Firipin ni okeru Nihon gunsei no ichi kōsatsu:

Rikarute shōgun no yakuwari o megutte" フィリピンにおける日本
軍政の一考察—リカルテ将軍の役割をめぐって (A study of Japan's
military administration in the Philippines: With special reference to the
role of Artemio Ricarte). *Ajia kenkyū* (July 1975) 22(2): 40–74.

Iriye, Akira 入江昭. *Nichi-Bei sensō* 日米戦争 (The Japanese-American
War). Chūō Kōronsha, 1978.

—— "Sengo Ajia e no senji Nihon no kōsō" 戦後アジアへの戦時日本
の構想 (Wartime Japan's plan for postwar Asia). In Hosoya Chihiro
細谷千博, ed., *Nichi-Ei kankeishi, 1917–1949* 日英関係史, 1917—1949
(Anglo-Japanese relations, 1917–1949), pp. 179–201. Tokyo Daigaku
Shuppankai, 1982.

Ishida Takeshi 石田雄. *Hakyoku to heiwa* 破局と平和 (The catastrophe and
peace). Tokyo Daigaku Shuppankai, 1968.

Itō Takashi 伊藤隆. "Shōwa 17–20 nen no Konoe-Mazaki gurūpu" 昭和
17—20年の近衛・真崎グループ (The Konoe-Mazaki group in 1942–
1945). *Kindai Nihon kenkyū*, vol. 1: *Shōwaki no gunbu*, pp. 221–52.

—— *Shōwa 10-nendaishi danshō* 昭和十年代史断章 (Studies on the decade
1935–1945). Tokyo Daigaku Shuppankai, 1981.

Iwatake Teruhiko 岩武照彦. *Nanpō gunseika no keizai shisaku: Marai,
Sumatora, Jawa no kiroku* 南方軍政下の経済施策—マライ, スマトラ,
ジャワの記録 (Economic policies in Southeast Asia under Japanese
occupation: Records in Malay, Sumatra, and Java). 2 vols. Kyūko Shoten,
1981.

Iwatake Teruhiko, ed. *Nanpō no gunsei* 南方の軍政 (Military administration
in the southern region). Asagumo Shinbunsha, 1985.

Japan, Bōeichō Senshishitsu 防衛庁戦史室 (War History Office, Defense
Agency), ed. (Nishihara Yukio 西原征夫, author). *Kantōgun* 関東軍 (The
Kwantung Army), vol. 2. Asagumo Shinbunsha, 1974.

Japan, Gaimushō 外務省 (Foreign Ministry). "Gaikō shiryo: Nisso gaikō
kōshō kiroku no bu: Chūritsu jōyaku teiketsu yori shūsen made" 外交
資料—日ソ外交交渉記録の部—中立条約締結より終戦まで (Diplomat-
ic documents; Record of Soviet-Japanese negotiations—From the conclusion of the Neutrality Treaty to Japan's defeat." Unpublished, 1946.

Japan, Gaimusho, ed., (Kurihara Ken 栗原健, comp.). *Shūsen shiroku* 終戦
史録 (Historical record of the termination of the war). Shinbun Gekkansha,
1952 (enlarged and reprinted in 6 vols. with introduction by Etō Jun
江藤淳 and annotations by Hatano Sumio 波多野澄雄, Hokuyōsha, 1977–
78).

Japan, Sanbō Honbu 参謀本部, ed. *Haisen no kiroku* 敗戦の記録 (The record
of defeat). Hara Shobō, 1979.

Japan, Taiwan Sōtokufu Zanmu Seiri Jimusho 台湾総督府残務整理事務所

(Offices for the disposal of remaining matters, Government-General of Taiwan). *Taiwan tōchi shimatsu hōkokusho* 台湾統治始末報告書 (Report on the disposal of the administration of Taiwan). Taiwan Sōtokufu, 1946.

Karafuto Shūsenshi Kankōkai 樺太終戦史刊行会, ed. *Karafuto shūsenshi* 樺太終戦史 (Sakhalin at the end of the war). Zenkoku Karafuto Renmei, 1973.

Kawahara Hiroshi 河原宏. *Shōwa seiji shisō kenkyū.* 昭和政治思想研究 (A study in the political thought of the Shōwa period). Waseda Daigaku Shuppanbu, 1979.

Kido Kōichi Nikki Kenkyūkai 木戸幸一日記研究会. *Kido Kōichi nikki* 木戸幸一日記 (The diary of Kido Kōichi). 2 vols. Tokyo Daigaku Shuppankai, 1967.

Kisaka Jun'ichirō 木坂順一郎. *Taiheiyō sensō* 太平洋戦争 (The Pacific War). Shōgakkan, 1982.

Kobayashi Hideo 小林英夫. *"Daitōa kyōeiken" no keisei to hōkai*「大東亜共栄圏」の形成と崩壊 (The formation and collapse of the "Greater East Asia Coprosperity Sphere"). Ochanomizu Shobō, 1973.

Kobayashi Tatsuo 小林龍夫. "Suēden o tsūjiru Taiheiyō sensō shūketsu kōsaku" スエーデン通じる太平洋戦争終結工作 (Maneuvers to end the Pacific War by way of Sweden). *Kokugakuin hōgaku* (February 1980), 18(4):91–136. [1]

—— "Tai-Suēden wahei kōsaku" 対スエーデン和平工作 (Peace maneuvers by way of Sweden). In Nihon Gaikō Gakkai, ed., *Taiheiyō sensō shūketsuron*, pp. 468–506. [2]

Kobori Keiichirō 小堀桂一郎. *Saishō Suzuki Kantarō* 宰相鈴木貫太郎 (Suzuki Kantarō as prime minister). Bungei Shunjū, 1982.

Koiso Kuniaki Jijoden Kankōkai 小磯国昭自叙伝刊行会, ed. *Katsuzan Kōsō* 葛山鴻爪 (Pen name of Koiso Kuniaki). Chūō Kōron Jigyō Shuppan, 1963.

Kona Yasuyuki 小名康之. "1943-nen no Tōnan Ajia ni okeru Indo dokuritsu renmei no katsudō" 1943年の東南アジアにおけるインド独立連盟の活動 (The activities of the Indian independence league in Southeast Asia in 1943). In Nagasaki Nobuko, ed., *Minami Ajia no minzoku undō to Nihon*, pp. 63–79.

Kudō Michihiro 工藤美知尋. "'Takagi Sōkichi shiryō' ni miru Nihon kaigun no shūsen kōsaku"『高木惣吉資料』にみる日本海軍の終戦工作 (The Japanese navy's efforts to end the war: As seen through the materials of Takagi Sōkichi). *Nihon hōgaku* (January 1983), 48(2):53–141.

Kurihara Ken 栗原健. *Tennō: Shōwashi oboegaki.* 天皇—昭和史覚書 (The Emperor: A note on the history of the Shōwa period). Yūshindō, 1955.

Kurihara Ken and Hatano Sumio 波多野澄雄, eds., *Shūsen kōsaku no kiroku*

終戦工作の記録 (The record of maneuvers to terminate the war). 2 vols. Kōdansha, 1986.

Kyōdō Tsūshinsha *Konoe Nikki* Henshū Iinkai 共同通信社『近衛日記』編集委員会, ed., *Konoe Fumimaro nikki* 近衛文磨日記 (The diary of Konoe Fumimaro). Kyōdō Tsūshinsha, 1968.

Manmō Dōhō Engokai 満蒙同胞援護会, ed. *Manmō shūsenshi* 満蒙終戦史 (A history of the termination of the war in Manchuria and Mongolia). Kawade Shobō, 1962.

Masuda Atau 増田与. *Indoneshia gendaishi* インドネシア現代史 (A history of contemporary Indoneshia). Chūō Kōronsha, 1971.

Masumi Junnosuke升味準之輔. *Nihon seitō shiron* 日本政党史論 (A history of Japanese political parties), vol. 7. Tokyo Daigaku Shuppankai, 1980.

Matsumoto Shun'ichi, Andō Yoshio 松本俊一, 安東義良 (supervisors). *Nihon gaikōshi*, vol. 25: *Dai Tōa sensō, Shūsen gaikō* 日本外交史, 25—大東亜戦争, 終戦外交 (Japanese diplomatic history, vol. 25: The Greater East Asia War and the termination of the war). Kajima Kenkyūjo Shuppankia, 1972.

Matsunari Makoto 松谷誠. *Daitōa sensō shūshū no shinsō* 大東亜戦争収拾の真相 (The real facts about the termination of the Greater East Asia War). Fuyō Shobō, 1980.

Miwa Kimitada 三輪公忠. "Nichi-Bei Higashi Ajia-kan no sōkoku" 日米東アジア観の相剋 (Conflict between Japanese and American views of East Asia). In Miyake Masaki, ed., *Shōwashi no gunbu to seiji*, 3:195–232. [1]

Miwa Kimitada, ed. *Nihon no 1930-nendai: Kuni no uchi to soto kara* 日本の1930年代—国の内と外から (The 1930s in Japan: Views from within and without the country). Sairyūsha, 1980.

—— "'Tōa shin chitsujo' sengen to 'Dai Tōa kyōeiken' kōsō no dansō" 『東亜新秩序』宣言と『大東亜共栄圏』構想の断層 (A gap between the declaration for the "New Order in East Asia" and the plan for the "Great East Asia Coprosperity Sphere"). In Miwa Kimitaka, ed., *Saikō taiheiyō sensō zenya* 再考太平洋戦争前夜 (Reconsiderations: The eve of the Pacific War). Sōseiki, 1981. [2]

Miyake Masaki 三宅正樹 et al., eds. *Shōwashi no gunbu to seiji* 昭和史の軍部と政治 (The military and politics in the Shōwa period), Vol. 4. Daiichi Hōki, 1983.

Miyamoto Shizuo 宮元静雄. *Jawa shūsen shoriki* ジャワ終戦処理記 (An account of the end of the war in Java). Jawa Shūsen Shoriki Kankōkai, 1973.

Morishima Gorō 守島伍郎. *Kunō suru chū-So taishikan: Nisso gaikō no omoide* 苦脳する駐ソ大使館—日ソ外交の思い出 (The anguished embassy in Moscow: My reminiscences of Soviet-Japanese diplomacy). Kōhoku Shuppan Gassakusha, 1952.

Morita Yoshio 森田芳夫. "Chōsen ni okeru Nihon tōchi no shūen" 朝鮮
における日本統治の終焉 (The end of Japanese rule in Korea). *Kokusai
seiji* (1962), no. 22, *Nikkan kankei no tenkai*, pp. 82–97.

—— *Chōsen shūsen no kiroku* 朝鮮終戦の記録 (Korea at the end of the war:
Collected documents). Gannandō, 1964.

—— and Osada Kanako 長田かな子 eds. *Chōsen shūsen no kiroku: Shiryōhen*
朝鮮終戦の記録—資料篇 (Korea at the end of the war: Collected documents). 3 vols. Gannandō, 1979–80.

Motohashi Tadashi 本橋正. "Daresu kikan o tsūzuru wahei kōsaku" ダレス
機関を通ずる和平工作 (Peace feelers through Allen W. Dulles). In Nihon
Gaikō Gakkai, ed., *Taiheiyō sensō shūketsuron*, pp. 507–71. [1]

—— "Sairon: Suisu ni okeru wahei kōsaku" 再論—スイスにおける和平
工作 (A reexamination of the peace feelers in Switzerland). *Kenkyū nenpō*
(Gakushūin Daigaku Hōgakubu) (1984), no. 9, pp. 407–75. [2]

Mukōyama Hiroo 向山寛夫. "Taiwan ni okeru Nihon tōchi to sengo naigai
jōsei" 台湾における日本統治と戦後内外情勢 (The Japanese administra-
tion of Taiwan and the domestic and external situations after the war).
Unpublished. 1963.

Nagai Shin'ichi 長井信一. *Gendai Marēshia seiji kenkyū* 現代マレーシア
政治研究 (A study on contemporary Malaysian politics). Ajia Keizai
Kenkyūjo, 1978.

—— "Taiheiyō sensōki no Marē minzokushugi undō" 太平洋戦争期の
マレー民族主義運動 (Nationalist movement in Malaya during the Pacific
War). *Ajia keizai* (October 1975), 16(10):40–50.

Nagasaki Nobuko 長崎暢子. "Indo kokumingun no keisei" インド国民軍
の形成 (The formation of the Indian national army). In Nagasaki, ed.,
Minami Ajia no minzoku undō to Nihon, pp. 1–62.

Nagasaki Nobuko, ed. *Minami Ajia no minzoku undō to Nihon* 南アジアの
民族運動と日本 (Japan and Nationalist movements in South Asia). Ajia
Keizai Kenkyūjo, 1980.

Nihon Gaikō Gakkai 日本外交学会 (Association for the Study of Japanese
Diplomacy), ed. (Ueda Toshio 植田捷雄, supervisory editor). *Taiheiyō
sensō shūketsuron* 太平洋戦争終結論 (Termination of the Pacific War).
Tokyo Daigaku Shuppankai, 1958.

Nishi Haruhiko 西春彦 (supervisor). *Nihon gaikōshi*, vol. 15: *Nisso kokkō
mondai, 1917–1945* 日本外交史,15：日ソ国交問題 (Japanese diplomatic
history, 15: The problem of diplomatic relations between Japan and the
Soviet Union, 1919–1945). Kajima Kenkyūjo Shuppankai, 1970.

Nishijima Ariatsu 西嶋有厚. *Genbaku wa naze otosaretaka: Nihon kōfuku
o meguru senryaku to gaikō* 原爆はなぜ投下されたか—日本降伏をめぐ

る戦略と外交 (Why the A-bombs were dropped: The strategy and diplomacy of Japan's surrender). Aoki Shoten, 1971.

Nishijima Shigetada and Kishi Kōichi 西嶋重忠, 岸幸一, eds. *Indoneshia ni okeru Nihon gunsei no kenkyū* インドネシアにおける日本軍政の研究 (A study of Japanese military administration in Indonesia). Completed under the auspices of Waseda Daigaku Ōkuma Kinen Shakai Kagaku Kenkyūjo. Kinokuniya Shoten, 1959.

Nomura Minoru 野村実. "Taiheiyō sensō no Nihon no sensō shidō" 太平洋戦争の日本の戦争指導 (Japanese strategy in the Pacific War). *Nenpō kindai Nihon kenkyū*, no. 4, pp. 29–50. [1]

—— "Taiheiyō sensōka no 'gunbu dokusai'" 太平洋戦争下の『軍部独裁』 ("Military dictatorship" during the Pacific War). In Miyake Masaki et al., eds., *Shōwashi no gunbu to seiji* 4:3–39. [2]

Ōgata Kōhei, 大形孝平. *Nihon to Indo* 日本とインド (Japan and India), Sanseidō, 1978.

Ōhata Tokushirō 大畑篤四郎. *Taiheiyō sensō* 太平洋戦争 (The Pacific War). 2 vols. Jinbutsu Ōraisha, 1966.

Ōno Tōru 大野徹. "Biruma kokugunshi" ビルマ国軍史 (A study of the history of the Burmese national army). *Tōnan Ajia kenkyū* (September 1970), 8(2):218–51; (December 1970), 8(3):345–76; (March 1971), 8(4):534–65.

Oshikawa Fumiko 押川文子. "Dainiji taisenki ni okeru Indo dokuritsu undō–Gandi, Nerū, Bōse o chūshin ni" 第二次大戦期におけるインド独立運動—ガンディー, ネルー, ボースを中心に (India's independence movement during World War II: With special reference to the roles of Mahatma Gandhi, Jawaharlal Nehru, and S. C. Bose), in Nagasaki Nobuko, ed., *Minami Ajia no minzoku undō to Nihon*, pp. 79–114.

Ōta Ichirō 太田一郎. *Nihon gaikōshi*, vol. 24: *Dai Tōa sensō, senji gaikō* 日本外交史, 16—大東亜戦争, 戦時外交 (The Greater East Asian War and wartime diplomacy). Kajima Kenkyūjo Shuppankai, 1972.

Ōta Kōki 太田弘毅. "Firipin ni okeru gunsei kikan to Hitō gyōseifu no kenkyū" フィリピンにおける軍政機関と比島行政府の研究 (A study of [Japan's] military administrative agencies in the Philippines and the Philippine executive). *Seiji keizai shigaku* (January 1977), no. 128, pp. 32–42; (February 1977), no. 129, pp. 20–32. [1]

—— "Nanpōgun gunsei sōkanbu no soshiki to ninmu" 南方軍政総監部の組織と任務 (The organization and function of the Military Administration General Headquarters for the southern areas). *Tōnan Ajia kenkyū* (June 1978), 16(1):103–18. [2]

—— "Nanpō gunsei no tenkai to tokushitsu" 南方軍政の展開と特質 (The

development and characteristics of Japanese military administration in the southern regions). In Miyake Masaki et al., eds., *Shōwashi no gunbu to seiji,* 4:41–76. [3]

Ōta Tsunezō 太田常蔵. *Biruma ni okeru Nihon gunseishi no kenkyū* ビルマにおける日本軍政史の研究 (A study of the history of Japanese military administration in Burma). Yoshikawa Kōbunkan, 1967.

Rekishigaku Kenkyūkai 歴史学研究会 (Historical Science Society), ed. *Taiheiyō sensōshi* 太平洋戦争史 (A history of the Pacific War). 5 vols. Toyō Keizai Shinpōsha, 1953–54 (revised edition, in 6 vols., published by Aoki Shoten, 1971–73).

Saitō Teruko 斎藤照子. "Kaisenki ni okeru Biruma kōsaku kikan" 開戦期におけるビルマ工作機関 (The Japanese intelligence bureau in Burma at the outbreak of the war). In Tanaka, ed., *Nihon gunsei to Ajia no minzoku undō,* pp. 99–112.

Satō Naotake 佐藤尚武. *Kaiko 80-nen* 回顧八十年 (Reminiscences of my eighty years). Jiji Tsūshinsha, 1963.

Shinbo Jun'ichirō 真保潤一郎. "Tōnan Ajia ni okeru minzoku undō" 東南アジアにおける民族運動 (Nationalist movements in Southeast Asia). In *Iwanami kōza Sekai rekishi, Gendai 6* 岩波講座世界歴史 29, 現代 6 (Iwanami series on world history, vol. 26: Contemporary history 6), pp. 104–38. Iwanami Shoten, 1971.

Shiozaki Hiroaki 塩崎弘明. "Taiheiyō sensō ni miru kaisen-shūsen gaikō: Tai-Bachikan gaikō o tōshite" 太平洋戦争にみる開戦終戦外交—対バチカン外交を通して (Japanese diplomacy at the time of the outbreak and termination of the Pacific War: With particular reference to diplomacy toward the Vatican). *Nihon rekishi* (October 1980), no. 389, pp. 55–73.

Shiraishi Aiko 白石愛子. "Ankatan muda undō no keisei to tenkai" アンカタン・ムダ運動の形成と展開 (The Ankatan Muda movement in Western Java: Its formation and development). *Ajia kenkyū* (April 1975), 22(1): 59–92. [1]

—— "Forced Delivery of Paddy and Peasant: Uprisings in Indramayu, Indonesia: Japanese Occupation and Social Change." *The Developing Economy* (March 1983), 21(1):52–97. [2]

—— "Jawa bōei giyūgun no setsuritsu" ジャワ防衛義勇軍の設立 (The creation of the PETA army). *Tōnan Ajia* (November 1974), no. 4, pp. 3–41. [3]

Shiraishi Masaya 白石昌也. "La Présence Japonaise en Indochine, 1940–1945." In Pierre Brocheux et al., *L'Indochine Francaise: 1940–1945,* pp. 215–41. Paris: Presses universitaires de France, 1982. [1]

—— "Chan Chon Kimu naikaku setsuritsu (1945-nen shigatsu) no haikei: Nihon tōkyoku no tai-Betonamu tōchi kōsō o chūshin to shite" チャン・

チョン・キム内閣設立（1945年4月）の背景―日本当局の対ベトナム統治構想を中心として (The background of forming the Tran Trong Kim cabinet: With particular reference to the Japanese authorities' plans to control Vietnam). In Tsuchiya Kenji and Shiraishi Takashi 土屋健治, 白石隆, eds., *Kokusai kankeiron no furontia* 国際関係論のフロンティア (The frontier of studies in international relations), 3: 33–69. Tokyo Daigaku Shuppankai, 1984. [2]

Shiraishi Masaya and Furuta Motoo 古田元夫. "Taiheiyō sensōki no Nihon no tai-Indoshina seisaku" 太平洋戦争期の日本の対インドシナ政策 (Japan's policy toward Indochina during the Pacific War). *Ajia kenkyū* (October 1976), 23(3): 1–37. [3]

Shōno Naomi 庄野直美, et al., *Kaku to heiwa: Nihonjin no ishiki* 核と平和―日本人の意識 (The nuclear weapon and peace: An investigation into Japanese consciousness). Kyoto: Hōritsu Bunkasha, 1978.

Takagi Sōkichi 高木惣吉. *Takagi kaigun shōshō oboegaki* 高木海軍少将覚え書 (The memoranda of Rear Admiral Takagi Sōkichi). Mainichi Shinbunsha, 1979.

Takagi Sōkichi and Sanematsu Yuzuru 実松譲, eds. *Kaigun taishō Yonai Mitsumasa oboegaki* 海軍大将米内光政覚書 (The memoranda of Admiral Yonai Mitsumasa). Kōjinsha, 1978.

Tamura Shinsaku 田村真作. *Myōhin kōsaku* 繆斌工作 (The Miao Pin maneuver). Sanei Shuppan, 1953.

Tanaka Hiroshi 田中宏, ed. *Nihon gunsei to Ajia no minzoku undō* 日本軍政とアジアの民族運動 (Japanese military administration and nationalist movements in Asia). Ajia Keizai Shuppankai, 1983.

Tanigawa Yoshihiko 谷川栄彦. "Taiheiyō sensōchū no Indoneshia minzoku undō: Jawa o chūshin to shite" 太平洋戦争中のインドネシア民族運動―ジャワを中心として (Nationalist movement in Indonesia during the Pacific War: With special reference to Java). *Hōsei kenkyū* (Kyūshū Daigaku) (October 1958), 21(1): 105–31. [1]

—— "Taiheiyō sensōchū no Tōnan Ajia kō-Nichi undō: Biruma, Vetonamu, Indoneshia, Maraya no kō-Nichi undō o chūshin to shine" 太平洋戦争中の東南アジア抗日運動―ビルマ，ベトナム，インドネシア，マラヤの抗日運動を中心として (Anti-Japanese movements in Southeast Asia during the Pacific War), *Ajia kenkyū* (September 1957), 4(1): 41–60. [2]

Tomioka Sadatoshi 富岡定俊. *Kaisen to shūsen: Hito to kikō to keikaku* 開戦と終戦―人と機構と計画 (The making and losing of the war: Men, organizations, and plans). Mainichi Shinbunsha, 1968.

Tomita Kenji 富田健治. *Haisen Nihon no uchigawa: Konoekō no omoide* 敗戦日本の内側―近衛公の思い出 (Inside defeated Japan: Recollections of Prince Konoe). Kokin Shoin, 1962.

Tonooka Akio 殿岡昭郎, ed. "Maraya ni okeru Nihon gunsei shiryō" マラヤにおける日本軍政史料 (Historical documents relating to Japanese military administration in Malaya). *Hōgaku ronshū* (Komazawa Daigaku) (December 1972), no. 9, pp. 324–49.

Usui Katsumi, Inaba Masao 臼井勝美, 稲葉正夫 eds., with an introduction. *Gendaishi shiryō,* vol. 38: *Taiheiyō sensō* 4 現代史料38—太平洋戦争4 (Documents on contemporary history, vol. 38: The Pacific War 4). Misuzu Shobō, 1972.

Yabe Teiji Nikki Kankōkai 矢部貞治日記刊行会, ed. *Yabe Teiji nikki* 矢部貞治日記. 4 vols. Yomiuri Shinbunsha, 1974–75.

Yomiuri Shinbunsha 読売新聞社, ed. *Shōwashi no tennō* 昭和史の天皇 (The Emperor in the history of the Shōwa period), vols. 8–15 (see chapter 4, "Notes on Basic Sources.")

Yoshida Teruo 吉田輝夫. "Fashizumu taisei no hōkai katei" ファシズム体制の崩壊 (The process of the collapse of the Fascist system), in *Iwanami kōza: Sekai rekishi, 29: Dainiji sekai taisen* 岩波講座：世界歴史29, 第二次世界大戦 (Iwanami series on world history, vol. 29: The Second World War), pp. 333–82. Iwanami Shoten, 1971.

Yoshikawa Toshiharu 吉川利治 "Taikoku Pibūn seiken to Taiheiyō sensō" タイ国ピブーン政権と太平洋戦争 (The Phibum regime in Thailand, and the Pacific War). *Tōnan Ajia kenkyū* (March 1982), 19(4):363–87.

Yuhashi Shigeto 油橋重遠. *Senji Nisso kōshōshi* 戦時日ソ交渉史 (A history of Japanese-Soviet relations during the Pacific War). Kasumigaseki Shuppan, 1974.

8

The Allied Occupation of Japan, 1945–1952

Iokibe Makoto

Asada Sadao

Hosoya Masahiro

OVERVIEW

Research on the Allied occupation of Japan has now reached maturity. It took a generation for occupation studies to become a field of serious academic research. A bibliographical guide edited by Nihon Gaku-jutsu Shinkōkai, *Nihon senryō bunken mokuroku* (A bibliography of the Allied occupation of Japan), published in 1972, is an eloquent testimony to the state of occupation studies twenty years after Japan regained its independence. This bibliographical volume—the companion volume to Robert E. Ward and Frank Joseph Shulman, eds., *The Allied Occupation of Japan, 1945–1952: An Annotated Bibliography* (1974)—is a compilation of approximately 2,500 books and articles on the Allied occupation, in Japanese, that had appeared up to June

1971. It covers not only major publications but also documents deposited in various Japanese archives. Although this bibliography has become somewhat outdated, it is still valuable as a basic guide and starting point for occupation studies.

The present essay claims to be neither comprehensive nor exhaustive in its coverage; rather it is intended to be an introductory guide to major works on the various aspects of the Allied occupation of Japan, focusing on recent works that have appeared since the publication of *Nihon senryō bunken mokuroku*.

For a selective treatment of Japanese works that appeared in the 1970s, the reader is referred to Asada Sadao's critical bibliographical essay, "Recent Works on the American Occupation of Japan." The most recent full-length historiographical essay on the literature both in Japanese and English is Carol Gluck's astute essay, "Entangling Illusions—Japanese and American Views of the Occupation," in Warren I. Cohen, ed., *New Frontiers in American–East Asian Relations* (Columbia University Press, 1983), pp. 169–236.

For a compact history of General MacArthur's headquarters, Takemae Eiji's *GHQ*, published in 1983, is invaluable. A pioneer of occupation studies in Japan, Takemae not only provides biographical information on MacArthur's staff but also evaluates various "democratization" programs that GHQ initiated. For somewhat more detailed surveys of the Allied occupation, Ōe Shinobu's *Sengo henkaku* (Postwar reforms) and Kanda Fuhito's *Senryō to minshushugi* (The occupation of Japan and democracy) are to be recommended. Realizing that previous studies on the Allied occupation did not cover Okinawa, Ōe set out to write about postwar Japan with particular emphasis on how Okinawa was treated in relation to American occupation policy. Kanda's book is focused on the occupation itself and gives a more detailed account of various "democratization" programs, drawing upon documents that have recently been made available. Since Kanda rarely refers to specific primary sources, however, his book may be more helpful to those who wish to gain an overall picture of the Allied occupation.

In 1980 Takemae published a general survey, *Senryō sengoshi* (The American occupation and postwar Japanese history). In this reflective book the author argues at length that during the occupation the Japanese people accepted, or were forced to accept, political, social, and economic *institutions* but failed to learn enough from "the democratic *spirit*" that underlay them.

Strictly speaking, Masamura Kimihiro's most recent publication, *Sengoshi* (Postwar Japanese history), is not a study on the occupation of Japan, but this economist's two-volume, thousand-page general survey, covering the thirty-year period from 1945 to 1975, argues that regardless of one's ideological bent one cannot deny that the basic framework laid during the occupation has defined and shaped the contours of postwar Japanese history. In this lengthy work, Masamura tries to evaluate the occupation reforms, including their merits and demerits, primarily on the basis of secondary sources. Masumi Junnosuke's *Sengo seiji, 1945–1955* (Postwar politics, 1945–1955) also deals with American-sponsored "democratization" programs, but his main focus is on party politics and political reorganization in postwar Japan.

There exists a whole series of books based on testimonies of eyewitnesses. In 1970, the staff of *Shūkan Shinchō* (a weekly journal) published *Makkāsā no Nihon* (MacArthur's Japan), which is based on numerous interviews with American occupation personnel. Somewhat journalistic in its presentation, the book succeeds in vividly re-creating various aspects of the occupation, thus demonstrating the usefulness of this type of approach. By the 1970s the time span since the end of the occupation was long enough to permit the selective declassification of the bulk of that period's documents, but not so long that all of the personalities involved had passed away.

In the field of oral history, Takemae himself had made an important contribution by publishing his extensive interviews with the successive chiefs of GHQ's Labor Division and their subordinates in his *Shōgen Nihon senryōshi: GHQ Rōdōka no gunzō* (Witnesses of the history of the occupation of Japan: A collective portrait of GHQ's Labor Division). While the value of oral history as significant evidence remains to be fully evaluated, Takemae makes conscious efforts to verify and substantiate his interviewees' statements with as many supporting documents as possible.

Basic printed documents for any scholarly study of the occupation period are conveniently collected in *Shiryō sengo 20-nenshi* (Basic documents: A twenty-year history of postwar Japan), compiled by Tsuji Kiyoaki et al. in 1966–67. This set consists of six volumes, dealing with politics, the economy, law, society, and labor, and providing a chronology and index. An even more comprehensive collection of original documents, specifically relating to the Allied occupation of Japan, is a four-volume *Senryō shiroku* (Historical documents on the Allied occupation of Japan), published in 1981–82. This set, compiled by Etō Jun et al., reproduces important documents held by the Japanese Foreign Ministry, with useful commentaries and brief annotations by Hatano Sumio.

A portion of the Foreign Ministry archives that has also appeared in print is *Shoki tai-Nichi senryō seisaku* (Early occupation policy toward Japan), which contains a series of reports that Asakai Kōichirō submitted to the Central Liaison Office (CLO), the Japanese government's official body for contacts with the Supreme Commander of the Allied Powers (SCAP). The "Asakai reports" record this diplomat's observations of SCAP officials and foreign diplomats from November 1945 to late 1948 when Asakai was chief of the General Affairs Section and later of the General Affairs Department of the CLO.

On the other hand, a Japanese Finance Ministry official, Watanabe Takeshi, has printed his diary as *Tai-senryōgun kōshō hiroku* (A secret account of negotiations with the occupation forces). In this valuable book the author meticulously chronicles his official dealings with SCAP officials on a wide variety of pressing issues, particularly economic and financial matters, from May 1946 to May 1951. This volume also reproduces his "official reports." Watanabe's previous publication, *Senryōka no Nihon zaisei oboegaki* (Notes on the financial history of occupied Japan), was also based on his diary, but *Tai-senryōgun kōshō hiroku* prints the original Watanabe diary itself. It is a truly indispensable source of information which vividly illuminates the inner formulation and implementation of SCAP's policy and Japanese responses.

As for the archives of the Foreign Ministry and other governmental agencies, the reader is referred to chapter 1 for practical information on their availability and restrictions.

Early Studies

Research on the Allied occupation of Japan was initiated by specialists in international law. As early as 1946 Yokota Kisaburō and his colleagues at the Faculty of Law, the University of Tokyo, commenced publication of *Nihon kanri hōrei kenkyū* (Studies on SCAP directives to Japan), 35 vols., which consisted of a comprehensive and detailed examination of the implementation of occupation policy toward Japan. In 1947 Yokota edited *Rengōkoku no Nihon kanri* (The Allied administration of Japan), which contained all of the major research that had been done in these early years.

At this time, Japanese scholars of international law were confronted by unprecedented issues. Japan's defeat in the Pacific War had, indeed, created a unique set of circumstances: The Allied powers sought not only to impose "unconditional surrender" on Japan but also to implement a long-term occupation that went well beyond solely military objectives. Faced with such a predicament, which did not accord with conventional practice or their understanding of international law, Japanese scholars had to examine its significance for postwar Japan by studying the details of SCAP directives.

Although the outline of occupation policies was readily apparent, Japanese scholars at the time were totally at a loss to discover how they had been formulated. Only toward the end of the occupation did there appear a considerable number of memoirs and autobiographies. These included accounts by American wartime leaders, and writings by occupation officials and journalists (most notably, Mark Gayn's *Japan Diary*, which quickly became a best-seller in its Japanese translation).

Even at this early stage of research, scholars of international law were working together with diplomatic historians such as Irie Keishirō. Their efforts resulted in Kokusai Hōgakkai, ed., *Heiwa jōyaku no sōgō kenkyū* (A comprehensive study of the peace treaty), which appeared in 1952. This work was followed by the publication of *Sengo Nihon no seiji katei* (Political processes in postwar Japan), the 1953 annual of the Nihon Seiji Gakkai (Japanese Political Science Association).

The academic and intellectual climate in the early postwar period was dominated by leftist-oriented "progressives" who called for the total condemnation of the militarism and ultra-nationalism of prewar Japan. Many intellectuals—adopting an anti-American, antigovernment stance—attacked changes in occupation policy as a "reverse course" and criticized the U.S.-Japan peace treaty, concluded at San

Francisco, as "one-sided." One history that reflects this tendency is
Shinobu Seizaburō's detailed four-volume work, *Sengo Nihon seijishi,
1945–1952* (A political history of postwar Japan, 1945–1952), which
was completed in the late 1960s. Characteristically, Shinobu treats the
occupation as a democratic revolution that basically failed. Another
example of a leftist survey history is a multivolume work, *Taiheiyō
sensōshi* (A history of the Pacific War), edited by Rekishigaku Kenkyūkai (Historical Science Society). The final volume of this series
deals with the Allied occupation in the broad context of international
developments.

The Occupation Reevaluated

In the 1960s, as Japan rebuilt itself and began to enjoy unprecedented economic growth, there appeared a new tendency among
Japanese scholars. This was to reevaluate the positive legacy of the
occupation in relation to postwar Japanese politics and diplomacy.
Indicative of this new trend was Kōsaka Masataka's *Saishō Yoshida
Shigeru* (Prime Minister Yoshida Shigeru). Kōsaka evaluates postwar
Japanese developments from the viewpoint that Yoshida skillfully
coped with occupation policies and sought to turn Japan into a
nonmilitary, commercial power within a broad framework of pro-
Americanism. Written in a similar vein is Kōsaka's survey history of
postwar Japan, *Ichioku no Nihonjin,* which was translated as *One Hundred Million Japanese: The Postwar Experience* (Kōdansha International,
1972). Kōsaka was one of the champions of the "realist" school which
emerged in the 1960s under the influence of the "political realism" of
Americans like George F. Kennan and Hans J. Morgenthau.

The works cited above were essential groundwork, but it was not
until the 1970s that full-fledged research on the occupation began.
What prompted this spectacular development was, first and foremost,
the declassification of archives by the United States government. Of
the State Department's series, *Foreign Relations of the United States,*
the first to deal with occupied Japan *(1945,* vol. 6: *The Far East)*
appeared in 1969, and subsequent volumes dealing with diplomatic
aspects of occupation policy continued to be published throughout
the 1970s. At approximately the same time, the United States National

Archives and related depositories throughout the United States also began opening vast amounts of basic source material for scholarly research. During the 1970s, serious works based on these materials appeared in rapid succession and made much previous research unsatisfactory.

The second factor aiding progress in the field was that a quarter of a century after the end of the Pacific War, the legacy of the occupation became increasingly apparent, so that it was possible to study the totality of the occupation period as history, with much greater detachment. Also, the existence of divergent viewpoints among Japanese scholars helped to stimulate occupation studies.

In 1976, Hata Ikuhiko published his major work, *Amerika no tai-Nichi senryō seisaku* (American occupation policy toward Japan), which appeared as vol. 3 of *Shōwa zaiseishi: Shūsen kara kōwa made* (Economic and financial history of the Shōwa period: From the end of the war to the peace), sponsored by the Japanese Finance Ministry. Hata, then head of the study group as a councilor in the Finance Ministry, energetically led the team of Japanese scholars and bureaucrats in preparing a twenty-volume official history of postwar Japanese public finance. For this purpose he and his colleagues collected a vast quantity of primary sources in the United States in the early 1970s. Hata himself wrote his massive book as the capstone of the series. This superbly documented 600-page volume is a comprehensive history of the occupation which covers the entire period—from U.S. presurrender preparations for postwar Japan to the conclusion of the San Francisco Peace Treaty.

On the basis of abundant American documents, Hata makes sophisticated analyses of the decision-making process. He shows that the same conflicts in political ideas, economic theories, and bureaucratic interests that had confused and encumbered wartime planning in Washington continued to plague the implementation of American occupation policy. He is particularly helpful in unraveling the maze of bureaucratic infighting in Washington as well as the internal power struggles within GHQ in Tokyo as they affected the occupation policy.

While Hata's book remains the standard work on the occupation, the very nature of the Finance Ministry project forced him to give

394 IOKIBE, ASADA, HOSOYA

weight to its economic and financial aspects. Considering the circumstances, it is to Hata's credit that he managed to include as much of the political, diplomatic, and strategic background as he did.

While Hata's work covers the entire occupation period, Morita Hideyuki's *Tai-Nichi senryō seisaku no keisei* (The formulation of American occupation policy toward Japan) specifically deals with policy preparation within the State Department for the period 1940–44. Focusing on the State Department's wartime planning for a defeated Japan, Morita traces major policymakers' thoughts on America's national defense which, he claims, underlay what came to be U.S. occupation policy toward Japan.

The most recent work on American presurrender planning for an occupied Japan is Iokibe Makoto's *Beikoku no Nihon senryō seisaku* (American occupation policy for Japan). This book will be discussed later in connection with Iokibe's other works.

DOMESTIC ENVIRONMENTS

The Tokyo Trials

The International Military Tribunal for the Far East, or the "Tokyo war crimes trials" as it is commonly called, was highly controversial in Japan from the very beginning. On the one hand, the Japanese people were shocked by the full exposure of what their military and political leaders had done on the Asian continent ever since the Manchurian Incident. On the other hand, the legitimacy and validity of the Tokyo trials were questioned by Kiyose Ichirō, chief of the Japanese defense counsel, at the outset of the trials. But "victors' justice" had its way, and later Japan's economic prosperity, stimulated by the Korean War, pushed aside the debate on the "international justice" of the Tokyo trials. The issue was rekindled during the war in Vietnam. (Overseas scholars will be interested to know that Richard H. Minear's polemical *Victors' Justice: The Tokyo War Crimes Trial* [Princeton University Press, 1971] was instantly translated into Japanese.) However, there is no denying that the memories of their "wartime experiences" failed to take permanent root among the Japanese people.

In 1982 a cinematic reproduction of the Tokyo trials, *Tokyo saiban*, based on the lengthy documentary films taken at the time, drew considerable attention from the Japanese people. A year later (May 1983) an international symposium was held on the Tokyo war crimes trials. Taken together, these events may be seen as attempts to reactivate the debate on the meanings of these trials. Hosoya Chihiro, Andō Nisuke (the translator of *Victors' Justice*), and Ōnuma Yasuaki edited the proceedings of the 1983 symposium as *Tokyo saiban o tou* (The Tokyo trials questioned), which contains papers presented by various specialists not only from Japan but also from the United States, the Soviet Union, Britain, China, Burma, West Germany, and Korea. It also includes a paper by the late B. V. A. Rolling of the Netherlands who had served as a judge at the Tokyo trials. The symposium consisted of four sessions dealing with international law, historical aspects, peace research, and the meaning of the trials for today.

War Responsibility

The May 1984 issue of the journal *Shisō* was devoted to the problem of the Tokyo trials. It contains Ōnuma Yasuaki's article on "war responsibility" and Ubukata Naokichi's essay on "crimes against humanity," while Sumitani Takeshi and others contribute a useful bibliography on the Tokyo trials, Class-B and Class-C war crimes, and "war responsibility." The twenty-eight-page bibliography covers major books and articles published as recently as December 1983.

In 1985 Ienaga Saburō published *Sensō sekinin* (War responsibility), which is a historian's attempt to probe into Japan's responsibility for initiating the "fifteen years war" that started in 1931. The author makes a sweeping denunciation of all Japanese leaders in the political, military, and other fields, and his indictment does not exempt the Emperor who, according to Ienaga, was involved—whether of his own volition or not—in the decision to initiate and expand the war in China. Ienaga maintains that in addition to intellectuals and journalists, the Japanese people as a whole must bear responsibility for the war. While the Japanese people may plead that they were victimized by their rulers, they are nonetheless responsible, at least in the moral sense, for the devastations inflicted upon the peoples of former Japanese colonies and Japanese-occupied territories. (While

Ienaga primarily places war responsibility on Japan, he does not condone American and Soviet culpabilities during the war; but that is another story.)

Ienaga concludes that since the Japanese people have not subjected themselves to serious soul searching, they must make sustained efforts to reexamine the whole question of Japan's war responsibility on the basis of empirical research, so that the "miseries of war" will never be repeated in the future.

In this connection, Ōnuma Yasuaki has approached the subject of war responsibility from a different angle. His *Tokyo saiban kara sengo sekinin no shisō e* (From the Tokyo trials to the idea of postwar responsibility) is a collection of articles he published in various journals and newspapers from 1978 to 1984. Admitting that "victors' justice" prevailed in the Tokyo trials, Ōnuma asserts that this does not exempt Japan and the Japanese people from responsibility for the "fifteen years war." He points out that since this war was defined as the Pacific War or, more narrowly, the Japanese-American War, by the Tokyo trials, Japan's war responsibility in Asia has not been sufficiently brought out. Ōnuma, who regards the war as a logical extension of the Japanese ideology of "throwing off Asia and joining the West" (a slogan that stemmed from the late nineteenth century), holds that the Japanese people, not just their leaders, must realize their war responsibility to their Asian victims. Some of them (like Koreans in Japan), he reminds the readers, still suffer to this date from the consequences of the war.

Having discussed the legacy of the war, let us next turn to various reforms made under the Allied occupation.

The New Constitution

As a result of research carried out on the framing of the new Japanese Constitution of 1947, legal scholars again came to contribute significantly to occupation studies. In 1964 Kenpō Chōsakai Jimukyoku (Commission for the investigation of the Constitution) produced an important report, *Kenpō seitei no keika ni kansuru shō-iinkai hōkokusho* (Report of the subcommittee on the process of the enactment of the Constitution) and *Kenpō chōsakai hōkokusho* (Report of the commission on the Constitution). The latter was edited and translated into English by John M. Maki as *Japan's Commission on the Constitution: The Final Report* (Seattle: University of Washington Press, 1980). The fruit of seven years of research, this report represented the advent of the new stage of documented study of the occupation period. Further progress in scholarly research on constitutional reform is indicated by the following works: the 1973 joint study under the editorship of Takayanagi Kenzō, Ōtomo Ichirō, and Tanaka Hideo, *Nihonkoku kenpō seitei no katei* (The process of framing the Japanese Constitution), which presented and analyzed Lieutenant Colonel Milo Rowell's important papers, in the first volume, and reproduced some of Rowell's basic memoranda in Japanese translations in the second volume; and Tanaka Hideo's *Kenpō seitei katei no oboegaki* (Notes on the process of the framing of the Constitution). One should not neglect an earlier but authoritative study by Satō Tatsuo, *Nihonkoku kenpō seiritsushi* (A history of the framing of the Japanese Constitution).

The most recent addition to the literature is Nishi Osamu's *Dokyumento Nihonkoku kenpō* (A documentary history of the Japanese Constitution). Mindful of the fact that more than 60 percent of the Japanese population were born after World War II, Nishi makes special efforts to present, in a concise and easy style, his account of the process through which the Japanese Constitution was framed and shaped. In particular, Nishi utilized pertinent portions of the Alfred Hussey papers at the University of Michigan as well as the English translation of the secret proceedings of the so-called "Ashida (Hitoshi) subcommittee," the Japanese originals of which still remain closed except to members of the Japanese Diet. As shown above, there exists a considerable body of scholarly work on the framing of the new Constitution.

As a by-product of his previously cited "official volume," *Amerika no tai-Nichi senryō seisaku,* Hata Ikuhiko has written a highly readable book, *Shiroku Nihon saigunbi* (A history of Japan's postwar rearmament). This focuses on the origins of Article Nine of the new Japanese Constitution that "renounces" war, and the issue of rearmament in the latter phase of the occupation. The question of Article Nine has been one of the most controversial issues in the field. A variety of interpretations and hypotheses have been put forth about its origins. Some argue that this article was first proposed by Prime Minister Shidehara Kijūrō; others contend that it was imposed upon Japan by General MacArthur and his staff. Others even claim that it was suggested by the Emperor himself. Hata dismisses the "idealistic" motivations for the proposal of this article, which previous studies tended to emphasize, asserting that there must have been more realistic considerations on the part of the American *shōgun* MacArthur and Japan's veteran diplomatist Shidehara. Hata's own interpretation (and he was the first to present it) is that Article Nine was a joint creation of Shidehara and MacArthur, and that it grew out of their bargaining over the issues of Japan's renunciation of war and the continuation of the Emperor system.

On this matter, Tanaka Hideo's previously cited work, *Kenpō seitei katei no oboegaki,* presents a two-stage theory, according to which Shidehara proposed to MacArthur that Japan be rebuilt as a non-military nation and the latter, in response, suggested that some such idea be incorporated in the new Constitution. Hata's and Tanaka's interpretations are not necessarily contradictory but can be understood as supplementing each other.

In passing, we may note that Owen Lattimore, a Far Eastern expert and the author of the radical work *Solution in Asia* (Boston: Little Brown, 1945), was one of those who unequivocally advocated the abolition of the Emperor system, and favored revolutionary changes in Japanese society—a position in sharp conflict with that of former Ambassador Joseph C. Grew and his "Japan crowd." Lattimore is the subject of Nagao Ryūichi's interesting biographical study, *Amerika chishikijin to Kyokutō: Ratimoa to sono jidai* (American intellectuals and the Far East: Owen Lattimore and his time).

Financial Reforms

The economic and financial policies of the American occupation are expertly studied in the massive series titled *Shōwa zaiseishi* (The economic and financial history of the Shōwa period), sponsored by the Ministry of Finance's Office of Financial History. Especially valuable among its twenty volumes is Nakamura Takafusa's work (in vol. 12: *Kin'yū* 1 [Money and banking 1]), which treats U.S. policy in great detail on the basis of the Finance Ministry archives and such basic American sources as the Joseph M. Dodge papers. Also important is

Uematsu Morio's excellent study of tax administration under the occupation (contained in vol. 8: *Sozei 2 Zeimu gyōsei* (Taxation 2: Tax administration)—one of the few existing treatments of this subject. Hara Akira's work (in vol. 1: *Sōsetsu: Baishō, shūsen shori* [General survey: Reparations, and postwar financial settlements]) is a most thorough study of Japan's postwar settlements, especially reparations.

The fullest account of antimonopoly policy is Miwa Ryōichi, *Dokusen kinshi* (Antimonopoly policy), which is volume 2 of the series. Miwa meticulously traces occupation policy to democratize the Japanese economic system, including the enactment of the Anti-Monopoly Law and the Deconcentration Law. Miwa's 600-page volume, with more than 100 pages of appended documents, will remain a definitive work for some time.

Volumes 17 and 18 of the *Shōwa zaiseishi* series are collections of Japanese documents on economic and financial affairs, mostly held by the Finance Ministry. Volume 20 is a collection of English-language documents which the Finance Ministry's research project team gathered at various major archives and depositories in the United States and Britain. This collection, which complements Hata Ikuhiko's history, is perhaps the best single collection available of documents on American economic policy toward Japan. Volume 19 is another important collection, devoted to various vital statistical information on economic and financial matters during the occupation. All in all, no student of the economic and financial aspects of the occupation can afford to neglect this twenty-volume series.

A recent collection of important essays is Nakamura Takafusa, ed., *Senryōki Nihon no keizai to seiji* (Japanese economy and politics during the occupation period), which draws on a variety of Japanese materials now available, though these are not as extensive as American source materials. This collection of well-documented essays examines various aspects of occupation policy, focusing on how they were affected by the "reverse course" or redirection of American policy influenced by the worsening cold war. Miwa Ryōichi's essay on the revision of the Anti-Monopoly Law in 1949 is an expert treatment of the subject. Takemae Eiji's contribution to this collective work is an excellent, well-researched study of the revision of the Labor Union Law and Labor Relations Adjustment Law in 1949. It examines GHQ's policymaking process, motives, and guidelines for changes in labor policy, with an emphasis on preparations up to September 1948.

Zaibatsu Dissolution

American policymakers in Washington regarded Japanese *zaibatsu* or "financial cliques" as excessive concentrations of economic power that stood in the way of a "democratic" Japan. Thus the *zaibatsu* had to be dissolved for Japan to be economically "democratized." Umezu Kazurō's *Zaibatsu kaitai* (Zaibatsu dissolution) provides a general account of the subject during the occupation period, but the author did not conduct archival research either in Japan or the United States.

Indispensable to any study of this aspect of economic democratization is: Mochikabu Kaisha Seiri Iinkai (Holding Company Liquidation Commission: HCLC), ed., *Nihon zaibatsu to sono kaitai* (The Japanese *zaibatsu* and their dissolution), which is an "official" collection of major documents held by the HCLC as well as HCLC's descriptions of their duties relating to the dissolution of the *zaibatsu*. Incidentally, this study, which covers the period up to March 1950, should be supplemented by its much briefer follow-up report, *Mochikabu kaisha seiri iinkai hakusho* (White paper of the Holding Company Liquidation Commission). Its English version is *Final Report on Zaibatsu Dissolution* (HCLC, July 10, 1951), which covers up to the day before the commission was dissolved.

Noda Iwajirō, who took over the chairmanship of the commission after Sasayama Tadao, describes in his memoirs, *Zaibatsu kaitai shiki* (Reminiscences on *zaibatsu* dissolution), the difficulties the commission had in dealing with the SCAP-sponsored economic democratization. He recalls how hard it was for the commission to deal with the SCAP, the Japanese government bureaucracy, and individual Japanese companies that were to be either reorganized or dissolved. His account also includes sketches of various SCAP officials including Eleanor Hadley and Edward Welsh.

Miwa Ryōichi's well-documented work on antimonopoly policy (volume 2 of the Finance Ministry's *Shōwa zaiseishi* series) has already been mentioned. In addition, Hosoya Masahiro has written "Economic Democratization and the 'Reverse Course' during the Allied

Occupation of Japan, 1945–1952" [2] and an essay [1] on SCAP prohibition of the use of *zaibatsu* trade names and trademarks. Hosoya attempts to elucidate the dynamics of mutual interaction among GHQ, the main *zaibatsu*, and Japanese bureaucrats, and shows how the leaders of Japanese *zaibatsu* succeeded in staging a "counteroffensive" to resist the implementation of the Deconcentration Law of 1947. He also traces the shift in American occupation policy from "democratization" to "economic recovery" and the way in which *zaibatsu* leaders responded to it.

Labor Reform

Takemae Eiji's well-documented monograph, *Amerika tai-Nichi rōdō seisaku no kenkyū* (A study of American labor policy toward Japan), published in 1970, was an epoch-making work demonstrating a new level of scholarship. This book does not limit itself to the specialized area of labor policy, but is a more comprehensive study than its title suggests. It places labor policy within the broad context of American occupation policy as a whole and against the international background of the emerging cold war. Takemae presents a rather sophisticated analysis of the multiple splits within the GHQ bureaucracy. Rectifying stereotyped dichotomies of the "New Dealers" versus "anti–New Dealers"; "progressive reformers" versus "right-wing conservatives"; or "the military" versus "the civilians," Takemae emphasizes that the basic conflict within GHQ revolved around the question of how to combine carrot and stick in introducing the "American way of life"—in this particular instance, what the American occupiers believed to be "sound" industrial relations.

After this pioneering work was published, a large quantity of documents became available in the United States, and Takemae's follow-up study drawing upon these new documents and interviews with former occupation staff resulted in his *Sengo rōdō kaikaku: GHQ rōdō seisakushi* (Postwar labor reform: A history of GHQ's labor policy). Takemae reinforces and revises with new archival evidence, his previous contentions. In particular, he analyzes the dynamics of Washington's policymaking process regarding labor policy; the negotiating process between GHQ and the Japanese concerning the Labor Standards Law and the National Public Service Law; GHQ's initiative in the "February 1947 General Strike Incident"; and the establishment of Sōhyō (General Council of Trade Unions of Japan). For the first time, he explains GHQ action in relation to the "labor purge" and the establishment of the Labor Ministry.

Agricultural Reform

One major policy that General MacArthur and his senior advisers handled with greater subtlety than other programs was land reform. The subject is ably treated in Ōwada Keiki's recent study, *Hishi Nihon no nōchi kaikaku: Ichi nōsei tantōsha no kaisō* (The secret history of Japan's land reform: Reminiscences of an agricultural administrator). The author, who as a young bureaucrat directly witnessed the entire course of the land reform, deftly combines his personal recollections with substantial research in the U.S. archives and interviews with surviving American principals. Ōwada demonstrates that in the case of the land reform the Japanese government took a "surprising" degree of initiative from the beginning, and that "internal factors" (the Japanese government's preparations, prompted by accumulated demands and historical forces) converged with "external factors" (the American demand to remove the rural roots of Japanese militarism) to bring about a successful land reform.

For a more detailed account of the land reform, the reader is referred to the Ministry of Agriculture and Forestry (editorial supervisors), *Nōchi kaikaku tenmatsu gaiyō* (Land reform: A general account), a voluminous work which records land reform in its totality—the legislative process and detailed administrative steps taken for the implementation of the reform. The work also attempts to place land reform in its historical and international perspective. While this volume was meant to be "general," the sixteen-volume *Nōchi kaikaku shiryō shūsei* (Collected documents on the land reform), compiled by Nōchi Kaikaku Shiryō Hensan Iinkai and published in 1974–82, is a comprehensive collection of source materials covering almost every aspect of the entire land reform program.

Social and Cultural Impacts and Reforms

Prominent examples of study of the social and cultural aspects of Japan under the occupation are: *Kyōdō kenkyū: Nihon senryō* (Joint research on the occupation of Japan); and its sequel, *Kyōdō kenkyū: Nihon senryōgun—Sono hikari to kage* (Joint research on the occupation forces in Japan: Their light and shadows), with a companion volume of reference, *Kyōdō kenkyū: Nihon senryō kenkyū jiten* (Encyclopedia of the Allied occupation of Japan), all edited by Shisō no Kagaku Kenkyūkai (The Research Group on the Science of Thought). These volumes cover practically every aspect of grass-roots life in Japan under the occupation and contain some penetrating essays written from the Japanese viewpoint. However, they often tend to be a mere collection of separate treatments of a wide range of topics, without any great attempt to fully integrate them.

As for more academic studies, Shakai Kagaku Kenkyūjo (The Social Science Research Institute) of the University of Tokyo has published an eight-volume series, *Sengo kaikaku* (Postwar reform), which resulted from a joint research project. Its eight volumes are: vol. 1, Problems and Perspectives; vol. 2, The International Environment; vol. 3, The Political Process; vol. 4, Legal Reform; vol. 5, Labor Reform; vol. 6, Land Reform; vol. 7, Economic and Financial Reforms; and vol. 8, The Japanese Economy Since Occupation Reforms. With the exception of able works based on U.S. archives—such as essays by Takemae Eiji on labor policy (in vol. 5) and Amakawa Akira [2] on reforms of local government (in vol. 3)—most of the papers are disappointing for our purposes. They focus primarily on the Japanese side, thus minimizing the impact of the occupation of Japan. The confused reader might get an impression that the postwar reforms took place somehow independently from and without the driving force of the occupation authorities.

Foreign scholars about to undertake occupation studies will find more stimulating and helpful *Nihon senryō hishi* (A secret history of the occupation of Japan), co-authored by Takemae and Amakawa (vol. 1) and Hata and Sodei (vol. 2). These books are written in a popular vein but informed by extensive archival research. Another well-documented work that appeared in the mid-1970s is Sodei Rinjirō, *Makkāsā no 2000-nichi* (MacArthur's two thousand days), which utilizes such materials as documents in the MacArthur Memorial in Norfolk, Virginia. This highly readable and popularly received book seeks to brush aside the veil of mystery surrounding the "blue-eyed Shogun" and presents a more realistic portrait.

Educational Reforms

The Allies' attempt to eradicate ultranationalistic and militaristic tendencies from the Japanese mind found its partial expression in their educational reforms. For a general history of this ideological reorientation, Ōta Takashi, ed., *Sengo Nihon kyōikushi* (A history of education in postwar Japan), is recommended. A collaborative work of five authors, the book does not specifically focus on occupation educational reforms as such but provides some keen insights into the significance of these reforms.

A recent monograph by Suzuki Eiichi, *Nihon senryō to kyōiku kaikaku* (Educational reforms in occupied Japan), is a well-documented study. Drawing on the vast amount of SCAP documents now available, Suzuki analyzes the educational policy of the United States during the occupation period. Suzuki emphasizes continuities in American educational policy, preparations for which began soon after the outbreak of the Pacific War; the author argues that the consistent policy of the United States remained that of rooting out militarism and ultranationalism through the reform and reeducation of the Japanese people by democratizing their entire educational system. The author concludes that educational reforms in postwar Japan were the product of the Allies' initiative and Japanese willingness to cooperate.

Kubo Yoshizō's carefully documented study, *Tai-Nichi senryō seisaku to sengo kyōiku kaikaku* (Allied occupation policy toward Japan and postwar educational reforms), reconstructs in detail specific aspects of educational reforms by liberally quoting from a number of documents deposited at the National Archives, the Washington National Records Center, and the Hoover Institution at Stanford (the Trainor papers). Kubo points out that American educational policy toward Japan had two aspects: one was a thorough democratization of Japanese education, and the other was dictated by the strategic considerations of the United States. While the former resulted in what we call "educational reforms" as such, the latter considerations envisaged the use of Japanese schools for the propaganda purposes of the occupation forces. This meant, the author argues, the establishment of Japan as a democracy on the model of Western capitalist nations, particularly the United States, which would serve as a barrier against Communist states such as the Soviet Union and, later, China. Kubo's interesting distinction between the two aspects of American educational policy toward Japan may serve as a helpful springboard for discussion on the "reverse course," reflecting the exigencies of the cold war.

INTERNATIONAL ENVIRONMENT

The Role of Britain and Other Allies

Admittedly, the United States played the dominant role in the Allied occupation of Japan, but Japanese scholars are gradually turning their attention to the policies of other Allied powers involved in the occupation.

Hosoya Chihiro has written an excellent article [1] on the role of the leading Japanologist in the British diplomatic corps, Sir George Sansom, which draws upon British sources. Its English version was printed in Ian Nish and Charles Dunn, eds., *European Studies on Japan* (Kent, England: Norbury, 1979), pp. 113–19. Hosoya argues that Great Britain exercised a subtle but important influence upon the mitigation of conditions to be imposed on defeated Japan, since the American draft of the Potsdam Declaration was revised in accordance with the British draft which was, in turn, based on Sansom's proposals.

Hosoya's most recent publication on the subject is a solid monograph, *San Furanshisuko kōwa e no michi* (The road to the San Franciso Peace Treaty). Hosoya treats British policy at length on the basis of newly available materials at the Public Record Office, and he also utilizes U.S. archival and manuscript sources as well as the recently opened archives of the Japanese Foreign Ministry. This monograph expertly unravels, among other problems, power-political complications between the United States and Britain over the issue of the peace settlement with Japan. While the two powers were united in their opposition to the Soviet Union, London did stage a strong resistance to the peace terms proposed by Washington, because they clashed with Britain's desire to retain whatever remained of its former glories and colonial interests which were the remnants of *Pax Britannica* in the Asia-Pacific region.

As to other Allies, Bamba Nobuya has examined the role played by the outstanding Canadian Japanologist and diplomat E. Herbert

Norman in his essay on Norman and the occupation of Japan. Wada Haruki has traced Soviet policy toward Japan during this period.

An intellectual historian, Takeda Kiyoko, has published *Tennōkan no sōkoku* (Conflict of views regarding the Emperor system), examining the ways in which the Emperor system was perceived by government leaders and intellectuals in the United States, Great Britain, Australia, and China, as well as solutions they prescribed for this problem. Because the Emperor system had always presented two faces, that of an absolute monarchy and "democratic" rule, Takeda asks how the images of these dual elements were reflected in the "mirrors" held in the Allied countries and how their leaders proposed to deal with or dispose of the Emperor. The process through which SCAP transformed the Emperor into a "symbolic existence" is explained as a sort of "compromise agreement" between the American zeal for democratization and the prevailing Japanese desire to retain the imperial institution.

The international environment of the Allied occupation of Japan is brilliantly examined in Nagai Yōnosuke's *Reisen no kigen: Sengo Ajia no kokusai kankyō* (The origins of the cold war: The international environment of post–World War II Asia). This work by a leading political scientist in Japan starts with the latter phase of World War II and ends with the Korean War, giving a broad, in-depth analysis of postwar international politics that affected Japan.

The Impact of the Cold War

Occupation studies have also reached the stage where Japanese scholars are systematically examining the evolution of American policy toward Japan during the occupation against the background of the global cold war. Igarashi Takeshi, one of the younger generation of historians, has published a series of articles on such themes as the cold war and redirection of occupation policy toward Japan [5], the role of George F. Kennan [1], and MacArthur's proposal for a Japanese peace treaty and his anti-Communist views [3], [4]. In these essays, Igarashi describes the process by which the framework of American anti-Communism during the cold war was built into the U.S. occupation policy toward Japan.

Igarashi addresses himself to the following questions: (a) how

MacArthur's proposal for an early peace in March 1947 became, ironically, the occasion for Washington to intervene in the management of affairs in Tokyo and to call for a redirection of occupation policy; (b) how George Kennan, chief of the Policy Planning Staff in the State Department, actively took steps to block the peace proposals initiated by the department's Office of Far Eastern Affairs; (c) how Kennan's report on his inspection tour of Japan came to be adopted by the U.S. government; and (d) how this led to a program for economic stabilization designed to prevent the spread of Communism in Japan. In examining these questions, Igarashi applies the "bureaucratic politics" approach to analyze the conflicts between the State and War departments.

In our view, however, Igarashi somewhat overemphasizes the role of Kennan and the cold war fixation. In his articles, Igarashi focused on the American side. However, his recent book, *Tai-Nichi kōwa to reisen: Sengo Nichi-Bei kankei no keisei* (The peace with Japan and the cold war: The formation of postwar Japanese-American relations), devotes considerable space to Prime Minister Yoshida Shigeru's response to the American initiatives, especially after the Korean War broke out. The author's main theme is the linkage between the "domestic cold war" and "international cold war."

In addition, other recent works indicate the degree to which occupation studies have grown in Japan. These studies include: Yamagiwa Akira's "reconsideration" of U.S. occupation policy toward Japan in the context of its East Asian policy; Shindō Eiichi's essay, which traces the formulation of American policy to separate Okinawa and the Kurile Islands from Japanese territory; and Miyasato Seigen's substantial monograph on the formulation and development of American policy toward Okinawa).

Continuities and Discontinuities

Since the mid-1970s Japanese historians and political scientists have increasingly come to examine the occupation policy in the context of America's global foreign policy and international politics. Akira Iriye actively participated in the above-mentioned joint research project on Japan's postwar international environment, and presented papers at two of the symposia sponsored by this project. In them Iriye powerfully presented his thesis that, although the United States government never defined a clear policy for the rest of East Asia, the State Department began to develop concrete plans for postwar policy toward Japan as early as 1943.

His "Continuities in U.S.-Japanese Relations, 1941–49" asserts that U.S. policy toward Japan was characterized by a high degree of continuity throughout this period. Challenging the view, widely held in Japan, that the onset of the cold war caused a major switch ("reverse course") in America's occupation policy, he maintains that American occupation policy was little affected by the cold war. His argument is based upon several considerations. First, he emphasizes the ameliorating effect that "moderate" Japan specialists within the State Department had upon policy formulation. Second, he stresses the influence of the doctrine of universalism within the American government, which called for the reintegration of the defeated enemies into the international community on American terms. Third, Iriye underscores the importance of the postwar framework of international politics, the "Yalta system," which assured that Japan would be placed under American control. From such a viewpoint, Iriye reiterates his thesis that, despite apparent fluctuations in occupation policy, the United States consistently sought to reintegrate Japan into the international order as a nonmilitary, capitalist nation friendly to the United States.

This view is further elaborated in his book, *Nichi-Bei sensō* (The Japanese-American War), English version of which was subsequently published as *Power and Culture: The Japanese-American War, 1941–1945* (Cambridge: Harvard University Press, 1981).

Some Japanese scholars have raised questions concerning Iriye's emphasis on the "continuities" in U.S.-Japanese relations. The most prominent among them is Hosoya Chihiro, who cautions [2] that the role of Japan experts within the State Department should not be overemphasized.

"Reverse Course"

In August 1980 an international symposium on the occupation of Japan was held at Amherst, Massachusetts, and selected papers presented were published as Ray Moore ed., *Tennō ga baiburu o yonda hi*

(The days when the Emperor read the Bible). The original English version of these and other papers will eventually be published, but until then this Japanese version may be of help to those who have no access to the original papers. An important section of the book is devoted to the problem of the so-called "reverse course." Igarashi Takeshi's paper emphasizes the role of George Kennan in redirecting American occupation policy. Howard Schonberger, in his "General William Draper, the 80th Congress, and the Origins of Japan's 'Reverse Course,'" attributes such "redirection" to domestic politics in the United States and claims that the central figure in this process was Undersecretary of the Army Draper. The most polemical paper, "Changing Gears: The Concept of the 'Reverse Course' in Studies of the Occupation of Japan," presented by Peter Frost, boldly asserts that there was no "reverse course" in American occupation policy toward Japan.

TO THE PEACE TREATY

The final phase of the occupation is discussed from the viewpoint of the Japanese government at that time in Nishimura Kumao, *San Furanshisuko heiwa jōyaku* (The San Francisco Peace Treaty), which is volume 27 of the Kajima series on Japanese diplomatic history. Nishimura was involved in the treaty negotiations as an assistant to Prime Minister Yoshida.

The most recent work on the last stage of the occupation is Hosoya Chihiro's previously mentioned *San Furanshisuko kōwa e no michi* (The road to the San Francisco peace treaty). Against the international background of the intensifying cold war and from the theoretical perspective of "bureaucratic politics," Hosoya examines in detail the differences between the State Department and the Pentagon in the relative weight they assigned to Japan as a military base against the Soviet Union, and shows that these differences were obstacles preventing the earlier conclusion of a peace treaty with Japan. Hosoya also emphasizes the importance of Anglo-American disagreement on the path to the Japanese Peace Treaty. (Portions of this book had previously appeared in an English-language article [2], "The Road to San Francisco: The Shaping of American Policy on the Japanese Peace Treaty."

Joint Study

A recent joint work on the peace treaty is Watanabe Akio and Miyasato Seigen, eds., *San Furanshisuko kōa* (The peace at San Francisco), which contains twelve essays that multilaterally study the roles played by the several countries involved in the peacemaking at San Francisco.

Watanabe Akio and Amakawa Akira [3] focus on the activities of the Japanese Foreign Ministry, drawing on its recently declassified archival materials. Sakeda Masatoshi treats the movement among a large segment of the Japanese people who demanded an "overall peace" including settlements with the Soviet Union and the People's Republic of China. He traces this movement from the autumn of 1949 to the outbreak of the Korean War. The author then examines the responses of the Yoshida cabinet and the United States government to this movement.

American policy and politics regarding the treaty issue are studied by Miyasato Seigen [1] and Umemoto Tetsuya. The former analyzes the decision-making process of the United States government, particularly the rivalry between the State Department and the Pentagon, and the latter examines the role played by Congress.

British policy toward Japan from the autumn of 1949 to the conclusion of the Japanese peace treaty is examined by Kibata Yōichi, who focuses on Britain's policy toward Japan's rearmament. Kibata concludes that, essentially, London and Washington agreed with each other on the issues of the U.S.-Japan security arrangement and Japan's rearmament; where their policies diverged was over the "China question"—whether the peace conference should be attended by the People's Republic of China or the Nationalist government. Taking up this "China question," Hosoya Chihiro [3] expertly examines Anglo-American differences on the basis of the U.S. and British archives and other sources.

The unique feature of this joint work is that in addition to the above-mentioned essays dealing with the parties directly involved, it discusses the positions of other nations in Asia and the Pacific. For example, Kikuchi Tsutomu examines Australia's changing roles in the question of the treaty issue, and P. N. Narasimha Murphy presents an Indian view. Roger Dingman highlights the roles of small countries in the negotiations, examining the cases of the Philippines and New Zealand. In order to analyze the process through which the Republic of China came to conclude the peace treaty with Japan, Ishii Akira delves into the archival materials of the Nationalist government. This volume contains no study on the response of the People's Republic of China, perhaps because the archives are not available. In addition, Kimura Hiroshi reviews the Soviet literature on Russian moves concerning the Japanese peace treaty issue in order to detect some pattern of behavior in Soviet foreign policy. All in all, this joint work is the first multinational attempt to study the Japanese peace treaty on the basis of multiarchival research.

FUTURE TASKS

A New Generation of Researchers

In the mid-1970s occupation studies were further activated by the emergence of a new generation of scholars. In 1974 Amakawa Akira published an original article [4], which focused on the process of formulating occupation policy at the administrative level in Washington. This study was followed by a series of works on the political process of the early occupation years in Tokyo, with special reference to occupation policy and the response of the Japanese bureaucracy [3]. His other works include essays on such subjects as reforms in self-government [2]; the Government Section of GHQ and the counteraction of the Ministry of Home Affairs [6]; and the structure of the self-government law [1].

Iokibe Makoto has also made extensive use of American sources in order to write detailed studies of the process of formulating American occupation policy toward Japan [2] and of the "Blueprint for Japan: Planning the Occupation" [3]. By setting this process within America's postwar planning as a whole, he attempts to develop a systematic interpretation. In his article [4] on the Cairo Declaration and Japan's postwar territories, he brings to light the serious divergence of views, and even lack of communication, between President Roosevelt and the State Department's Japan specialists in the decision-making process. Iokibe further argues that a compatible working relationship could hardly have existed between them. After all, the President had a vision of the postwar world characterized by a vertical international order in which the enemies would surrender unconditionally and the great powers would then cooperate in maintaining world peace. In contrast, the State Department invoked the universalistic principles embodied in the Atlantic Charter and sought moderate treatment for Japan.

In his article on unconditional surrender and the Potsdam Declaration [5], Iokibe contends that, reflecting the deterioration of U.S.-Soviet relations from the spring of 1945, the Committee of Three (the Secretary of State, the army, and the navy) sought to displace the concept of a vertical world order and called for a mitigation of American conditions to be imposed on Japan.

Regarding the problem of "unconditional surrender," Iokibe shows that the meaning of the term was broadly understood as "unconditional acceptance of the victor's conditions by the defeated party." In contrast to the case of Germany, the State Department's Japan specialists devised a policy of implying conditions for and encouraging an early surrender. This, Iokibe argues, was embodied in the Potsdam Declaration. The English translation of this article [1] was subsequently published as "American Policy Toward Japan's 'Unconditional Surrender.'"

Building on these articles, Iokibe has recently published a prize-winning monograph, Beikoku no Nihon senryō seisaku (American occupation policy for Japan) in two volumes, which aims at a systematic and comprehensive explanation of the making of postwar policy toward Japan. In addition to the themes already indicated, it encompasses wartime international relations and such domestic factors as the state of American public opinion, perceived "lessons of the past" as they related to postwar planning, and the role of private organizations like the Council on Foreign Relations. Iokibe's monograph is a meticulously researched and detailed study on American presurrender planning for the occupation of Japan, but the book does not cover the actual occupation period (in that sense, the title is perhaps misleading).

Assignment for the Future

Reviewing Japanese scholarship of the 1970s and early 1980s as a whole, we notice that a large number of works have tended to focus on wartime American preparations for the occupation of Japan and that outstanding studies have shown a marked trend to concentrate on the policymaking process within the United States government. The principal reason is, of course, the overwhelming superiority, in quantity and quality, of available American materials. In addition, Japanese scholars have been especially interested in investigating the factors and circumstances that decided Japan's national destiny at a place and time far removed from its control or even knowledge. Thus, not only experts in American diplomatic history but also specialists in contemporary Japanese history have come to delve into American sources. Indeed, given the need for bifocal perspectives for any balanced treatment of the occupation period, it is hardly surprising that some of the best Japanese studies on the subject are being produced by a handful of scholars trained in or familiar with both the American *and* Japanese fields: Hata, Takemae, Amakawa, Iokibe, Igarashi, and Hosoya Chihiro.

In a sense, occupation studies in Japan can be compared to a manufacturing company that imports raw materials from America and processes them for domestic consumption. With regard to the procurement of source materials, Japanese scholars have in no way lagged behind their American colleagues. Perhaps in no other field but occupation studies have Japanese and American scholars come closer to achieving parity in their use of primary sources. As proof of this, one might note the papers presented at a number of international conferences on the occupation, beginning with the biannual conference held under the auspices of the MacArthur Memorial.

The Legacy of the Occupation

Standpoints adopted by Japanese scholars, like those adopted by Americans, are quite diverse. Just as there are "orthodox" and "revisionist" schools of interpretation in the United States, so are there "conservative" and "leftist" historians in Japan. However, in comparison with the days of "the politics of polarization" which defined the 1960 crisis over the revision of the U.S.-Japan Mutual Security Pact, the distance between the right and left wing has narrowed, and relatively few Japanese would now deny the legacy of the occupation in toto or praise it uncritically in every aspect. On the contrary, most Japanese scholars are aiming at constructing middle-of-the-road interpretations by using primary materials to elucidate the international processes of the occupation.

Yet one cannot ignore the fact that Japanese historians, of whatever political persuasion, owe much to American scholarship in methodologies and analytical concepts. Leftist historians in Japan derive many of their ideas from the writings of revisionists such as Gabriel and Joyce Kolko. Other scholars have utilized the models or modes of analysis developed by Ernest R. May or Graham Allison, to cite a few examples.

If Japanese scholars succeed in incorporating these analytical insights and their own perspectives into their studies, they might find occupation studies one field in which they can hope to make a significant international contribution. Thus far, few studies have succeeded in fully marshalling U.S. and Japanese sources, and there is yet to appear a major work that analyzes the dynamic interrelationships of the occupier and the occupied. The prospect is improved by the selective declassification of Japanese Foreign Ministry archives (as of December 1987, partially open up to 1955).

Prospects

In November 1972, Takemae Eiji, Fukushima Jurō, and Amakawa Akira met in Tokyo to organize a study group on the Allied occupation of Japan. This group, Senryōshi Kenkyūkai, or the Japan Association for the Study of the History of the Occupation (JASHO), has grown in membership, which now counts more than one hundred not only in Japan but also in the United States and Britain. It embraces various disciplines. The Association issues the *JASHO Newsletter* every other month, and since 1981 has held a public symposium every year. This organization serves as a forum where members of various persuasions can exchange ideas and information.

As Takemae suggests in his book *GHQ* and elsewhere, the Allied occupation of Japan should be studied from a comparative perspective. It should be compared with other instances of occupation in history, for example, the Allies' occupation of Germany after World War II. It can also be profitably studied alongside Japanese rule in Korea and Taiwan or its occupation of the southeast Asian region during the Pacific War.

In this regard, the international symposium on the Allied occupation of Japan, hosted by Hōsei University in Tokyo in November–December 1983, indicates the likely direction of future research. The proceedings of this three-day international symposium were recently published as Sodei Rinjirō, ed., *Sekaishi no naka no Nihon senryō* (The Allied occupation of Japan in world history). The record of this symposium shows the rich possibilities of a comparative approach to the Allied occupation of Japan. Topics discussed include the Japanese occupation of the Philippines, Indonesia, and Malaya, and the American occupation of Micronesia, Okinawa and South Korea. In addition to the usual discussion of how to evaluate various occupation reforms and the two main figures of the occupation—General Douglas MacArthur and Prime Minister Yoshida Shigeru—the symposium devoted one session to highlighting conflicting interests among the Allies involved in the administration of occupied Japan: the United States, the Soviet Union, Great Britain, Australia, Canada, and China.

The predominant trend of occupation studies during the 1970s was to examine separate issues and problems at the micro level. In the latter half of the 1980s one can anticipate a revival of macro level studies, which will lead to a broad synthesis of monographic literature. In order to produce a masterly study that goes beyond the particular dramas enacted in the inner chambers of Washington or Tokyo and allows us to hear the very footsteps of contemporary history, we need historians who, in addition to familiarity with the political and diplomatic history of both Japan and the United States, are endowed with a broad insight into international history. Rather than anticipating a magnum opus by a single individual, one suspects, historians will move in the direction of collaborative research among scholars representing a broad spectrum of disciplines and nationalities (in particular, Japan, the United States, the United Kingdom, and—for comparative purposes—Germany).

Bibliography

Amakwa Akira 天川晃. "Chihō jichihō no kōzō" 地方自治法の構造 (The structure of the local self-government law). In Nakamura, ed., *Senryōki Nihon no keizai to seiji*, pp. 119–76. [1]
—— "Chihō jichi seido no kaikaku" 地方自治制度の改革 (Reforms in local

self-government). In Tokyo Daigaku Shakai Kagaku Kenkyūjo, ed., *Sengo kaikaku,* vol. 3: *Seiji katei,* pp. 231–86. Tokyo Daigaku Shuppankai, 1974. [2]

—— "Kōwa to kokunai tōchi taisei no saihen" 講和と国内統治体制の再編 (The peace treaty and the reorganization of the Japanese political system). In Watanabe and Miyasato, eds., *San Furanshisuko kōwa,* pp. 57–86. [3]

—— "Sengo seiji kaikaku no zentei: Amerika ni okeru tai-Nichi senryō no junbi katei" 戦後政治改革の前提—アメリカにおける対日占領の準備過程 (The premises of postwar political reform: The preparatory stages of American occupation policy toward Japan). In Taniuchi Yuzuru 溪内謙 et al., eds., *Gendai gyōsei to kanryōsei* 現代行政と官僚制 (Modern administration and the bureaucracy), 2:131–99. Tokyo Daigaku Shuppankai, 1974. [4]

—— "Senryō seisaku to kanryō no taiō" 占領政策と官僚の対応 (Occupation policy and the response of the Japanese bureaucracy). In Shisō no Kagaku Kenkyūkai, ed., *Kyōdō kenkyū: Nihon senryōgun: Sono hikari to kage,* pp. 215–26. [5]

—— "Senryō shoki no seiji jōkyō: Naimushō to Minseikyoku no taiō" 占領初期の政治状況—内務省と民政局の対応 (Political conditions during the early phase of the occupation: The response of the Ministry of Home Affairs and the Government Section of GHQ). *Shakai kagaku kenkyū* (Tokyo Daigaku) (January 1975), 26(2):1–59. [6]

Asada Sadao 麻田貞雄. "Recent Works on the American Occupation of Japan: The State of the Art." *The Japanese Journal of American Studies* (1981), no. 1, pp. 175–91.

Bamba Nobuya 馬場伸也. "Senryō to Nōman" 占領とノーマン (Norman and the occupation of Japan). *Shisō* (April 1977), no. 634, pp. 55–84.

Dingman, Roger. "Tai-Nichi kōwa to shōkoku no tachiba: Nyūjīrando to Firipin no baai" 対日講和と小国の立場—ニュージーランドとフィリピンの場合 (The Japanese peace settlement and the attitudes of small countries: The cases of New Zealand and the Philippines). In Watanabe and Miyasato, eds., *San Furanshisuko kōwa,* pp. 255–92.

Etō Jun 江藤淳 comp. (with annotations by Hatano Sumio 波多野澄雄). *Senryō shiroku* 占領史録 (Historical documents on the Allied occupation of Japan). 4 vols. Kōdansha, 1981–82.

Gayn, Mark. *Japan Diary.* New York: William Sloane Associates, 1948. Translated by Imoto Takeo 井本威夫 into Japanese in 1951; reprinted by Chikuma Shobō in 1963 as *Nippon nikki* ニッポン日記.

Hara Akira 原朗. *Shōwa zaiseishi,* vol. 1: *Sōsetsu: Baishō, shūsen shori* 昭和財政史1総説 賠償・終戦処理 (The economic and financial history of the Shōwa period, vol. 1: General survey: Reparations and postwar settlements). Tōyō Keizai Shinpōsha, 1984.

Hata Ikuhiko 秦郁彦. *Shiroku Nihon saigunbi* 史録日本再軍備 (A history of Japan's postwar rearmament). Bungei Shunjūsha, 1976.

—— *Shōwa zaiseishi*, vol. 3: *Amerika no tai-Nichi senryō seisaku* 昭和財政史 3 アメリカの対日占領政策 (The economic and financial history of shōwa period, vol. 3: American occupation policy toward Japan). Tōyō Keizai Shinpōsha, 1976.

Hata Ikuhiko and Sodei Rinjirō 袖井林二郎. *Nihon senryō hishi* 日本占領 秘史 (A secret history of the occupation of Japan), vol. 2. Asahi Shimbunsha, 1977.

Hosoya Chihiro 細谷千博. "Jōji Sansomu to haisen Nihon: Ichi chi-Nichiha gaikōkan no kiseki" ジョージ・サンソムと敗戦日本——"知日派"外交 官の軌跡 (Sir George Sansom and a defeated Japan: The footprint of a pro-Japanese diplomat). In Hosoya, *Nihon gaikō no zahyō* 日本外交の座標 (The thought and behavior of Japanese diplomacy), pp. 140–66. Chūō Kōronsha, 1979. [1]

—— *San Furanshisuko kōwa e no michi* サンフランシスコ講和への道 (The road to the San Francisco Peace Treaty). Chūō Kōronsha, 1984.

—— "The Road to San Francisco: The Shaping of American Policy on the Japanese Peace Treaty." *The Japanese Journal of American Studies* (1981), no. 1, pp. 87–117. [2]

—— "San Furanshisuko kōwa jōyaku to kokusai kankyō" サンフランシ スコ講和条約と国際環境 (The San Francisco Peace Treaty and the international environment). In Watanabe and Miyasato, eds., *San Furanshisuko kōwa*, pp. 1–16. [3]

Hosoya Chihiro, Andō Nisuke, and Ōnuma Yasuaki 安藤仁介, 大沼保昭, eds., *Kokusai shinpojiumu: Tokyo saiban o tou* 国際シンポジウム——東京 裁判を問う (The Tokyo war crimes trials questioned: The proceedings of an international symposium). Kōdansha, 1984.

Hosoya Masahiro 細谷正宏. "Amerika no tai-Nichi senryō seisaku no ichi sokumen: Zaibatsu shōgō-shōhyō no shiyō kinshi o megutte" アメリカ の対日占領政策の一側面——賊閥商号商標の使用禁止をめぐって (An aspect of American occupation policy toward Japan: The case of SCAP prohibition of the use of *zaibatsu* trade names and trademarks). *Doshisha Amerika kenkyū* (1984), no. 20, pp. 53–72. [1]

—— "Economic Democratization and the 'Reverse Course' during the Allied occupation of Japan, 1945–1952." *Kokusaigaku ronshū* (July 1983), no. 11, pp. 59–104. [2]

Ienaga Saburō 家永三郎. *Sensō sekinin* 戦争責任 (War responsibility). Iwanami Shoten, 1985.

Igarashi Takeshi 五十嵐武士. "Jōji Kenan to tai-Nichi senryō seisaku no tenkan: Kokka Anzen Hoshō Kaigi bunsho 13/2' no seiritsu ジョージ・ケナンと対日占領政策の転換 — 国家安全保障会議文書 13/2の成立 (George F. Kennan and the redirection of occupation policy: The formation of National Security Council Paper 13/2). In Nakamura, ed., *Senryōki Nihon no keizai to seiji*, pp. 59–85. [1]

—— "MacArthur's Proposal for an Early Peace with Japan and the Redirection of Occupation Policy Toward Japan." *Japanese Journal of American Studies* (1981), no. 1, pp. 55–86. Originally published as "Tai-Nichi kōwa no teishō to tai-Nichi senryō seisaku no tenkan" (see below). [2]

—— "Tai-Nichi kōwa no teishō to hankyōkan no isō" 対日講和の提唱と反共観の位相 (MacArthur's proposal of a Japanese peace treaty and his anti-Communist views). *Kokusai mondai* (July 1976), no. 196, pp. 41–59. [3]

—— "Tai-Nichi kōwa no teishō to tai-Nichi senryō seisaku no tenkan: Reisen no hazama ni okeru Amerika gaikō" 対日講和の提唱と対日占領政策の転換—冷戦の狭間におけるアメリカ外交 (MacArthur's proposal for peace with Japan and the transition of American occupation policy toward Japan: U.S. diplomacy in the cold war). *Shisō* (October 1976), no. 628, pp. 21–43. [4]

—— *Tai-Nichi kōwa to reisen: Sengo Nichi-Bei kankei no keisei* 対日講和と冷戦：戦後日米関係の形成 (The peace with Japan and the cold war: The formation of postwar Japanese-American relations). Tokyo Daigaku Shuppankai, 1986.

—— "Tai-Nichi senryō seisaku no tenkan to reisen: Tai-Nichi keizai fukkō seisaku no ritsuan o chūshin ni shite" 対日占領政策の転換と冷戦—対日経済復興政策の立案を中心にして (The cold war and the redirection of occupation policy: Shaping policy for the revival of the Japanese economy). In Nakamura, ed., *Senryōki Nihon no keizai to seiji*, pp. 25–57. [5]

Iokibe Makoto 五百旗頭真. "American policy toward Japan's 'unconditional surrender.'" *The Japanese Journal of American Studies* (1981), no. 1, pp. 19–53. [1]

—— "Beikoku ni okeru tai-Nichi senryō seisaku no keisei katei: Sono kikōteki sokumen to senryōgun kōsei no mondai" 米国における対日占領政策の形成過程—その機構的側面と占領軍構成の問題 (The formulation of U.S. policy concerning the occupation of Japan: Its structural mechanism and the problem of the composition of occupying forces). *Kokusaihō gaikō zasshi* (October 1975), 74(3); 1–62; (December 1975), 74(4): 35–65. [2]

—— *Beikoku no Nihon senryō seisaku: Sengo Nihon no sekkeizu* 米国の日本

占領政策—戦後日本の設計図 (American occupation policy for Japan: Blueprint for postwar Japan). 2 vols. Chūō Kōronsha, 1985.

—— "Blueprint for Japan: Planning the occupation." *Hiroshima hōgaku* (October 1980), 4(2):152–72. [3]

—— "Kairo sengen to Nihon no ryōdo" カイロ宣言と日本の領土 (The Cairo Declaration and Japan's postwar territory). *Hiroshima hōgaku* (March 1981), 4(3–4):59–127. [4]

—— "Mujōken kōfuku to Potsudamu sengen" 無条件降伏とポツダム宣言 (Unconditional surrender and the Potsdam Declaration). *Kokusaihō gaikō zasshi* (December 1980), 79(5):29–72. [5]

Irie Keishirō 入江啓四郎. *Nihon kōwa jōyaku no kenkyū* 日本講和条約の研究 (A study of the Japanese peace treaty). Itagaki Shoten, 1951.

Iriye, Akira 入江昭. "Continuities in U.S.-Japanese Relations, 1941–49." In Yōnosuke Nagai and Akira Iriye, eds., *The Origins of the Cold War in Asia,* pp. 378–407. University of Tokyo Press and Columbia University Press, 1977.

—— *Nichi-Bei sensō* 日米戦争 (The Japanese-American War). Chūō Kōronsha, 1978.

—— *Power and Culture: The Japanese-American War, 1941–1945.* Cambridge: Harvard University Press, 1981.

Ishii Akira 石井明. "Chūgoku to tai-Nichi kōwa: Chūka minkoku seifu no tachiba o chūshin to shite" 中国と対日講和—中華民国政府の立場を中心として (China and the Japanese peace settlement: With special reference to the position of the government of the Republic of China). In Watanabe and Miyasato, eds., *San Furanshisuko kōwa,* pp. 292–316.

Japan, Gaimushō 外務省 (Foreign Ministry), ed. *Shoki tai-Nichi senryō seisaku: Asakai Kōichirō hōkokusho* 初期対日占領政策—朝海浩一郎報告書 (Early occupation policy toward Japan). 2 vols. Mainichi Shinbunsha, 1979.

Japan, Gaimushō, ed. *Shūsen shiroku* 終戦史録 (Historical record of the termination of the Pacific War). 2 vols. Shinbun Gekkansha, 1951.

Japan, Nōrinshō 農林省 (Ministry of Agriculture and Forestry), supervisor; Nōchi Kaikaku Kiroku Iinkai 農地改革記録委員会 (Committee to record agricultural reforms), ed. *Nōchi kaikaku tenmatsu gaiyō* 農地改革顛末概要 (Land reform: A general account). Nōsei Chōsakai, 1951; reprinted by Ochanomizu Shobō in 1977.

Japan, Ōkurashō 大蔵省 (Finance Ministry), ed. *Tai-senryōgun kōshō hiroku: Watanabe Takeshi nikki* 対占領軍交渉秘録—渡辺武日記 (A secret account of negotiations with the occupation forces: The Watanabe Takeshi diary). Tōyō Keizai Shinpōsha, 1983.

—— Ōkurashō Zaiseishi Shitsu 大蔵省財政史室 (Finance Ministry, Office of

420 IOKIBE, ASADA, HOSOYA

Financial History), ed. *Shōwa zaiseishi: Shūsen kara kōwa made* 昭和財政史—終戦から講和まで (An economic and financial history of the Shōwa period: From the end of the war to the peace). 20 vols. Tōyō Keizai Shinpōsha, 1976–84.

Kanda Fuhito 神田文人. *Senryō to minshushugi* 占領と民主々義 (The occupation of Japan, and democracy). Shōgakkan, 1983.

Kenpō Chōsakai Jimukyoku 憲法調査会事務局 (Commission for the investigation of the Constitution). *Kenpō seitei no keika ni kansuru shō iinkai hōkokusho* 憲法制定の経過に関する小委員会報告書 (Report of the subcommittee on the process of the enactment of the Constitution). Kenpō Chōsakai, 1964.

—— *Kenpō Chōsakai hōkokusho* 憲法調査会報告書 (Report of the commission on the Constitution). Kenpō Chōsakai, 1964.

Kibata Yōichi 木畑洋一. "Tai-Nichi kōwa to Igirisu no Ajia seisaku" 対日講和とイギリスのアジア政策 (The Japanese peace settlement and British policy toward Asia). In Watanabe and Miyasato, eds., *San Furanshisuko kōwa*, pp. 165–92.

Kikuchi Totsumu 菊地努. "Ōsutoraria no tai-Nichi kōwa gaikō" オーストラリアの対日講和外交 (Australian diplomacy in the Japanese peace settlement). In Watanabe and Miyasato, eds., *San Furanshisuko kōwa*, pp. 193–224.

Kimura Hiroshi 木村汎. "Soren to tai-Nichi kōwa" ソ連と対日講和 (The Soviet Union and the Japanese peace settlement). In Watanabe and Miyasasto, eds., *San Furanshisuko kōwa*, pp. 317–46.

Kokusai Hōgakkai 国際法学会 ed., *Heiwa jōyaku no sōgō kenkyu* 平和条約の総合研究 (A comprehensive study of the peace treaty). 2 vols. Yūhikaku, 1952.

Kōsaka Masataka 高坂正堯. *Ichioku no Nihonjin* 一億の日本人 (One hundred million Japanese). Bungei Shunjū, 1969.

—— *Saishō Yoshida Shigeru* 宰相吉田茂 (Prime Minister Yoshida Shigeru). Chūō Kōronsha, 1968.

Koseki Shōichi 古関彰一. "Shōchō tennōsei no seiritsu katei," 象徴天皇制の成立過程 (The process of the emergence of the "symbolic" emperor system). *Hōritsu jihō* (July 1980), 52(7):92–99; (August 1980), 52(8):95–101; (October 1980), 52(10):78–83; (November 1980), 52(11):81–87.

Kubo Yoshizō 久保義三. *Tai-Nichi senryō seisaku to sengo kyōiku kaikaku* 対日占領政策と戦後教育改革 (The Allied occupation policy toward Japan and postwar educational reforms). Sanseidō, 1984.

Masamura Kimihiro 正村公宏. *Sengoshi* 戦後史 (Postwar Japanese history). 2 vols. Chikuma Shobō, 1985.

Masumi Junnosuke 升味準之輔. *Sengo seiji, 1945–55* 戦後政治, 1945—55 (Postwar politics, 1945–55). 2 vols. Tokyo Daigaku Shuppankai, 1983.

Miwa Ryōichi 三和良一. "1949-nen no dokusen kinshihō kaisei" 1949年の独占禁止法改正 (The revision of the Anti-Monopoly Law in 1949). In Nakamura, ed., *Senryōki Nihon no keizai to seiji*, pp. 223–66.

—— *Shōwa zaiseishi* vol. 2: *Dokusen kinshi* 昭和財政史[2]独占禁止 (The economic and financial history of the Shōwa period, vol. 2: Antimonopoly policy). Tōyō Keizai Shinpōsha, 1981.

Miyasato Seigen 宮里政玄. "Amerika Gasshūkoku seifu to tai-Nichi kōwa" アメリカ合衆国政府と対日講和 (The United States government and the Japanese peace settlement). In Watanabe and Miyasato, eds., *San Furanshisuko kōwa*, pp. 113–44. [1]

—— "Amerika no tai-Okinawa seisaku no keisei to tenkai" アメリカの対沖縄政策の形成と展開 (The formulation and development of American policy toward Okinawa). In Miyasato, ed., *Sengo Okinawa no seiji to hō*, pp. 3–116. [2]

Miyasato Seigen, ed. *Sengo Okinawa no seiji to hō, 1945–1972* 戦後沖縄の政治と法 (Politics and law in postwar Okinawa, 1945–1972). Tokyo Daigaku Shuppankai, 1975.

Mochikabu Kaisha Seiri Iinkai 持株会社整理委員会 (Holding Company Liquidation Commission), ed. *Mochikabu Kaisha Seiri Iinkai hakusho: Zaibatsu kaitai wa kaku okonawareta* 持株会社整理委員会白書—財閥解体は斯く行われた (White Paper of the Holding Company Liquidation Commission: This is how *zaibatsu* dissolution was carried out!). HCLC, 1951. Its English version is *Final Report on Zaibatsu Dissolution* (HCLC, July 10, 1951).

—— ed. *Nihon zaibatsu to sono kaitai* 日本財閥とその解体 (The Japanese *zaibatsu* and their dissolution). 2 vols. and a supp. HCLC, 1951; reprinted by Hara Shobō in 1973–74.

Moore, Ray, ed. *Tennō ga baiburu o yonda hi* 天皇がバイブルを続んだ日 (The days when the Emperor read the Bible). Kōdansha, 1982.

Morita Hideyuki 森田英之. *Tai-Nichi senryō seisaku no keisei: Amerika Kokumushō, 1940–44* 対日占領政策の形成—アメリカ国務省, 1940—44 (The formulation of American occupation policy toward Japan: The U.S. Department of State, 1940–44). Ashi Shobō, 1982.

Murphy, P. N. Narasimha. "Indo to tai-Nichi kōwa" インドと対日講和 (India and the Japanese peace settlement, in retrospect). In Watanabe and Miyasato, eds., *San Furanshisuko kōwa*, pp. 225–54.

Nagai Yōnosuke 永井陽之助. *Reisen no kigen: Sengo Ajia no kokusai kankyō* 冷戦の起源—戦後アジアの国際環境 (The origins of the cold war: The international environment of post–World War II Asia). Chūō Kōronsha, 1978.

Nagao Ryūichi 長尾龍一. *Amerika chishikijin to Kyokutō: Ratimoa to sono jidai* アメリカの知識人と極東—ラティモアとその時代 (American intellectuals and the Far East: Owen Lattimore and his time). Tokyo Daigaku Shuppankai, 1985.

Nakamura Takafusa 中村隆英, ed. *Senryōki Nihon no keizai to seiji* 占領期日本の経済と政治 (Japanese economy and politics during the occupation period). Tokyo Daigaku Shuppankai, 1979.

—— *Shōwa zaiseishi,* vol. 12: *Kin'yu* 昭和財政史12金融 (Economic and financial history of the Shōwa period, vol. 12: Money and banking, part 1). Tōyō Keizai Shinpōsha, 1976.

Nihon Gaikō Gakkai 日本外交学会 (Association for the Study of Japanese Diplomacy), ed. *Taiheiyō sensō shūketsuron* 太平洋戦争終結論 (Studies on the termination of the Pacific War). Tokyo Daigaku Shuppankai, 1958.

Nihon Gakujutsu Shinkōkai 日本学術振興会, ed. *Nihon senryō bunken mokuroku* 日本占領文献目録 (A bibliography of the Allied occupation of Japan). Nihon Gakujutsu Shinkōkai, 1972.

Nihon Kanri Hōrei Kenkyūkai 日本管理法令研究会, ed., *Nihon kanri hōrei kenkyū* 日本管理法令研究 (Studies on SCAP directives to Japan), nos. 1–35. Yūhikaku, 1946–53.

Nihon Seiji Gakkai 日本政治学会 (Japanese Political Science Association), ed. *Nenpō seijigaku 1953: Sengo Nihon no seiji katei* 年報政治学1953—戦後日本の政治過程 (The annual of the Japanese Political Science Association, 1953: Political processes in postwar Japan). Iwanami Shoten, 1953.

Nishi Osamu 西修. *Dokyumento Nihonkoku kenpō* ドキュメント日本国憲法 (A documentary history of the Japanese Constitution). Sanshūsha, 1986.

Nishimura Kumao 西村熊雄. *Nihon gaikōshi,* vol. 27: *San Furanshisuko heiwa jōyaku,* 日本外交史27—サンフランシスコ平和条約 (Japanese diplomatic history, vol. 27: The San Francisco Peace Treaty). Kajima Kenkyūjo Shuppankai, 1971.

Nōchi Kaikaku Shiryō Hensan Iinkai 農地改革資料編纂委員会 (Committee to compile documents on land reform), ed. *Nōchi kaikaku shiryō shūsei* 農地改革資料集成 (Collected documents on the land reform). 16 vols. Nōsei Chōsakai, Ochanomizu Shobō, 1974–82.

Nōchi Seido Shiryō Shūsei Hensan Iinkai 農地制度資料集成編纂委員会 (Editorial committee for collecting and editing documents on land reform), ed. *Nōchi seido shiryō shūsei* 農地制度資料集成 (Collected documents on the land system). 10 vols. and 2 supps. Ochanomizu Shobō, 1968–73.

Noda Iwajirō 野田岩次郎. *Zaibatsu kaitai shiki* 財閥解体私記 (Reminiscenses on *zaibatsu* dissolution). Nihon Keizai Shinpōsha, 1983.

Ōe Shinobu 大江志乃夫. *Sengo henkaku* 戦後変革 (Postwar reforms). Shōgakkan, 1976.

Ōnuma Yasuaki ·大沼保昭. *Tokyo saiban kara sengo sekinin no shisō e* 東京裁判から戦後責任の思想へ (From the Tokyo trials to the idea of postwar responsibility). Yūshindō, 1985.

—— "Tokyo saiban, sensō sekinin, sengo sekinin" 東京裁判, 戦争責任, 戦後責任 (The Tokyo trials, war responsibility, and postwar responsibility). *Shisō* (May 1984), no. 719, pp. 70–100.

Ōta Takashi 太田堯, ed. *Sengo Nihon kyōikushi* 戦後日本教育史 (A history of education in postwar Japan). Iwanami Shoten, 1978.

Ōwada Keiki 大和田啓氣. *Hishi Nihon no nōchi kaikaku: Ichi nōsei tantōsha no kaisō* 秘史日本の農地改革——一農政担当者の回想 (The secret history of Japan's land reform: Reminiscences of an agricultural administrator). Nihon Keizai Shinbunsha, 1981.

Rekishigaku Kenkyūkai 歴史学研究会 (Historical Science Society), ed. *Taiheiyō sensōshi,* 太平洋戦争史 (A history of the Pacific War). 5 vols. Tōyō Keizai Shinpōsha, 1953–54. (Revised edition in 6 vols. published by Aoki Shoten, 1971–73.)

Sakeda Masatoshi 酒田正敏. "Kōwa to kokunai seiji: Nitchū bōeki mondai to no kanren o chūshin ni" 講和と国内政治—日中貿易との関連を中心に (The peace treaty question and domestic politics: With special reference to Sino-Japanese trade issues). In Watanabe and Miyasato, eds., *San Furanshisuko kōwa,* pp. 87–114.

Satō Tatsuo 佐藤達夫. *Nihonkoku kenpō seiritsushi* 日本国憲法成立史 (A history of the framing of the Japanese Constitution). 2 vols. Yūhikaku, 1962.

Shindō Eiichi 進藤榮一. "Bunkatsu sareta ryōdo: Okinawa, Chishima, soshite Anpo" 分割された領土—沖縄, 千島, そして安保 (The divided territory: Okinawa, the Kuriles, and the U.S.-Japan Security Treaty). *Sekai* (April 1979), no. 401, pp. 31–51.

Shinobu Seizaburō 信夫清三郎. *Sengo Nihon seijishi, 1945–1952* 戦後日本政治史, 1945—52 (A political history of postwar Japan, 1945–1952). 4 vols. Keisō Shobō, 1965–1967.

Shisō no Kagaku Kenkyūkai 思想の科学研究会 (The Research Group on the Science of Thought), ed. *Kyōdō kenkyū: Nihon senryō* 共同研究—日本占領 (Joint research on the occupation of Japan). Tokuma Shoten, 1972.

—— *Kyōdō kenkyū: Nihon senryōgun—Sono hikari to kage* 共同研究—日本占領軍, その光と影 (Joint research on the occupation forces in Japan: Their light and shadows). 2 vols. Tokuma Shoten, 1978.

Shisō no Kagaku Kenkyūkai. *Kyōdō kenkyū: Nihon senryō kenkyū jiten* 共同研究—日本占領研究事典 (Encyclopedia of the Allied occupation of Japan). Tokuma Shoten, 1978.

Shūkan Shinchō 週刊新潮 (A weekly journal *Shinchō*), ed. *Makkāsā no Nihon* マッカーサーの日本 (MacArthur's Japan). Shinchōsha, 1970.

Sodei Rinjirō 袖井林二郎. *Makkāsā no 2000-nichi* マッカーサーの二千日 (MacArthur's two thousand days). Chūō Kōron-sha, 1974.

Sodei Rinjirō, ed. *Sekaishi no naka no Nihon senryō* 世界史のなかの日本占領 (The Allied occupation of Japan in world history). Nihon Hyōronsha, 1985.

Sumitani Takeshi 住谷雄幸, Utsumi Aiko 内海愛子, and Akazawa Shirō 赤沢史朗, eds. "Tokyo saiban, BC-kyū sensō hanzai, sensō sekinin kankei shuyō bunken mokuroku" 東京裁判, BC級戦争犯罪, 戦争責任関係主要文献目録 (A bibliography of major documents relating to the Tokyo trials, Class B and Class C war crimes and war responsibility) *Shisō* (May 1984), no. 719, pp. 1–28.

Suzuki Eiichi 鈴木英一. *Nihon senryō to kyōiku kaikaku* 日本占領と教育改革 (Educational reform in occupied Japan). Keisō Shobō, 1983.

Takayanagi Kenzō, Ōtomo Ichirō, and Tanaka Hideo 高柳賢三, 大友一郎, 田中英郎, eds., *Nihonkoku kenpō seitei no katei* 日本国憲法制定の過程 (The process of framing the Japanese Constitution). 2 vols. Yūhikaku, 1973.

Takeda Kiyoko 武田清子. *Tennōkan no sōkoku: 1945-nen zengo* 天皇観の相剋—1945年前後 (The conflict of views regarding the Emperor: Circa 1945). Iwanami, 1978.

Takemae Eiji 竹前栄治. *Amerika tai-Nichi rōdō seisaku no kenkyū* アメリカ対日労働政策の研究 (A study of American labor policy toward Japan). Nihon Hyōronsha, 1970.

—— *GHQ*. Iwanami Shoten, 1983.

—— *Sengo rōdōkaikaku: GHQ rōdō seisakushi* 戦後労働改革—GHQの労働政策史 (Postwar labor reform: A history of GHQ's labor policy). Tokyo Daigaku Shuppankai, 1982.

—— "1949-nen rōdōhō kaisei zenshi: Senryō seisaku o chūshin to shite" 1949年労働法改正前史—占領政策を中心として (Circumstances leading to the revision of the labor law in 1949: With particular reference to [American] occupation policy). In Nakamura, ed., *Senryōki Nihon no keizai to seiji*, pp. 301–38.

—— *Senryō sengoshi* 占領戦後史 (The American occupation and postwar Japanese history). Keisō Shobō, 1980.

—— *Shōgen Nihon senryōshi: GHQ Rōdōka no gunzō* 証言日本占領史—GHQ

労働課の群像 (Witnesses of the history of the occupation of Japan: A collective portrait of GHQ's Labor Division). Iwanami Shoten, 1983.

Takemae Eiji and Amakawa Akira 天川晃. *Nihon senryō hishi* 日本占領秘史 (A secret history of the occupation of Japan), vol. 1. Asahi Shimbunsha, 1977.

Tanaka Hideo 田中英夫. *Kenpō seitei katei no oboegaki* 憲法制定過程の 覚え書 (Notes on the process of framing the Constitution). Yūhikaku, 1979.

Tokyo Daigaku Shakai Kagaku Kenkyūjo 東京大学社会科学研究所 (Social Science Research Institute, University of Tokyo), ed. *Sengo kaikaku* 戦後 改革 (Postwar reform). 8 vols. Tokyo Daigaku Shuppankai, 1974–75.

Tsuji Kiyoaki 辻清明 et al. *Shiryō sengo 20-nenshi* 資料戦後二十年史 (Basic documents: A twenty-year history of postwar Japan). 6 vols. Nihon Hyōronsha, 1966–67.

Ubukata Naokichi 幼方直吉. ''Tokyo saiban o meguru shoronten: 'Jindō ni taisuru tsumi' to jikō'' 東京裁判をめぐる諸論点—「人道に対する罪」 と時効 (Issues concerning the Tokyo trials: 'Crimes against humanity' and legal prescription). *Shisō* (May 1984), no. 719, pp. 101–12.

Uematsu Morio and Ishi Hiromitsu 植松守雄, 石弘光. *Shōwa zaiseishi*, vol. 8: *Sozei 2 Zeimu gyōsei* 昭和財政史 8 租税, 税務行政 (The economic and financial history of the Shōwa period, vol. 8: Taxation [2], Tax administration). Tōyō Keizai Shinpōsha, 1977.

Umemoto Tetsuya 梅本哲也. ''Amerika Gasshūkoku gikai to tai-Nichi kōwa'' アメリカ合衆国議会と対日講和 (The United States Congress and the Japanese peace settlement). In Watanabe and Miyasato, eds., *San Furanshisuko kōwa*, pp. 145–64.

Umezu Kazurō 梅津和郎. *Zaibatsu kaitai* 財閥解体 (*Zaibatsu* dissolution). Kyōikusha, 1978.

Wada Haruki 和田春樹. ''Sobieto Renpō no tai-Nichi seisaku'' ソビエト 連邦の対日政策 (The USSR's policy toward Japan). In Tokyo Daigaku Shakai Kagaku Kenkyūjo, ed., *Sengo kaikaku*, vol. 2: *Kokusai kankyō* 戦後 改革, 2 —国際環境 (Postwar reform, vol. 2: The international environment). Tokyo Daigaku Shuppankai, 1974.

Ward, Robert E. and Frank Joseph Shulman, eds. *The Allied Occupation of Japan, 1945–52: An Annotated Bibliography of Western-Language Materials.* Chicago: American Library Association, 1974.

Watanabe Akio 渡辺昭夫. ''Kōwa mondai to Nihon no sentaku'' 講和問題 と日本の選択 (The peace treaty question and Japan's options). In Watanabe and Miyasato, eds., *San Furanshisuko kōwa*, pp. 17–54.

Watanabe Akio and Miyasato Seigen 宮里政玄, eds., *San Furanshisuko kōwa*

サンフランシスコ講和 (The peace at San Francisco). Tokyo Daigaku Shuppankai, 1986.

Watanabe Takeshi 渡辺武. *Senryōka no Nihon zaisei oboegaki* 占領下の日本財政覚え書 (Notes on the financial history of occupied Japan). Nihon Keizai Shinbunsha, 1966.

—— *Watanabe Takeshi nikki* (see entry under Japan, Ōkurashō, above.)

Yamagiwa Akira 山極晃. Amerika no sengo kōsō to Ajia: Tai-Nichi senryō seisaku o minaosu" アメリカの戦後構想とアジア—対日占領政策を見直す (America's postwar planning and East Asia: A reconsideration of U.S. Occupation policy toward Japan). *Sekai* (October 1976), no. 371, pp. 245–58.

Yokota Kisaburō 横田喜三郎, ed. *Rengōkoku no Nihon kanri: Sono kikō to seisaku* 連合国の日本管理—その機構と政策 (The Allied administration of Japan: Its organization and policy). Kyoto: Taigadō, 1947.

ADDENDUM

At the proof-reading stage of this book, two important publications came out; they are so valuable that they at least deserve mention here. One is Robert E. Ward and Sakamoto Yoshikazu, eds. *Democratizing Japan: The Allied Occupation*. It is a joint Japanese-American project and was published in both Japanese and English. We shall cite here the English edition.

Ward, Robert E. and Sakamoto Yoshikazu, eds. *Democratizing Japan: The Allied Occupation*. Honolulu: University of Hawaii Press, 1987.

Contents:

Kurt Steiner, "The Occupation and the Reform of the Japanese Civil Code," pp. 188–220.

Susan J. Pharr, "The Politics of Women's Rights," pp. 221–52.

Amakawa Akira, "The Making of the Postwar Local Government System," pp. 253–83.

Ōta Masahide, "The U.S. Occupation of Okinawa and Postwar Reforms in Japan Proper," pp. 284–305.

Uchida Kenzō, "Japan's Postwar Conservative Parties," pp. 306–38.

Takemae Eiji, "Early Postwar Reformist Parties," pp. 339–65.

Ōtake Hideo, "The *Zaikai* Under the Occupation: The Formation and Transformation of Managerial Councils," pp. 366–91.

Robert E. Ward, "Conclusion," pp. 392–433.

Another useful publication is *Kokusai seiji,* no. 85: *Nihon senryō no takakuteki kenkyū* 日本占領の多角的研究 (The occupation of Japan: Studies from various viewpoints) (May 1987).

Iokibe Makoto 五百旗頭真 "Josetsu senryō kenkyū no genkyō" 序説占領研究の現況 (Editor's introduction), pp. 1–6.

Hirai Tomoyoshi 平井友義 "Soren no shoki tai-Nichi senryō kōsō" ソ連の初期対日占領構想 (Soviet policy for Japanese occupation), pp. 7–24.

Ishii Akira 石井明 "Chūgoku no tai-Nichi senryō seisaku" 中国の対日占領政策 (The Republic of China's policy towards Japanese occupation), pp. 25–40.

Manabe Shunji 真鍋俊二 "Amerika no Doitsu senryō seisaku" アメリカのドイツ占領政策 (The Hoover Plan and U.S. occupation policy for Germany), pp. 41–54.

Shindō Eiichi 進藤榮一 "Ashida Hitoshi to sengo kaikaku" 芦田均と戦後改革 (Ashida Hitoshi and postwar reform: Between liberalism and conservatism), pp. 55–72.

Masuda Hiroshi 増田弘 "Kōshoku tsuihōrei (SCAPIN-550·548) no keisei-katei" 公職追放令 (SCAPIN-550·548) の形成過程 (The formulation of the purge directives, SCAPIN-550 & 548), pp. 73–96.

Kajiura Atsushi 梶浦篤 "Hoppō ryōdo o meguru Beikoku no seisaku" 北方領土をめぐる米国の政策 (The policy of the United States concerning the northern territories: The Dulles initiative in making peace with Japan), pp. 97–114.

Ishii Osamu 石井修 "Tai-Chū kin'yu to Nihon no keizai jiritsu" 対中禁輸と日本の経済自立 (China trade embargo and Japan's economic viability), pp. 115–32.

Miyasato Seigen 宮里政玄 "Gyōsei kyōtei no sakusei katei" 行政協定の作成過程 (Making of the administrative agreement between the United States and Japan), pp. 133–50.

Japanese-Language Periodicals

Ajia daigaku shogaku kiyō 亜細亜大学諸学紀要
Ajia keizai アジア経済
Ajia kenkyū アジア研究
Amerika kenkyū アメリカ研究
Asahi jānaru 朝日ジャーナル
Bessatsu chisei, 5: himerareta shōwashi 別冊知性, 5：秘められた昭和史
Bōei daigakkō kiyō : Jinbun kagaku-hen 防衛大学校紀要人文科学編
Bōei Daigakkō kiyō: Shakai kagaku-hen 防衛大学校紀要・社会科学編
Bōei ronshū 防衛論集
Bōei to keizai 防衛と経済
Bungei shunjū 文芸春秋
Bunka 文化
Bunka shigaku 文化史学
Chiba shōdai ronsō 千業商大論叢
Chōsen gakuhō 朝鮮学報
Chōsenshi kenkyūkai ronbunshū 朝鮮史研究会論文集
Chūkyō hōgaku 中京法学
Chūō daigaku bungakubu kiyō (Shigakuka) 中央大学文学部紀要（史学科）
Chūō kōron 中央公論
Chūō shigaku 中央史学
Doshisha Amerika kenkyū 同志社アメリカ研究

Furansugaku kenkyū 仏蘭西学研究

Gaikō jihō 外交時報

Gaimushō chōsa geppō 外務省調査月報

Gunji shigaku 軍事史学

Handai hōgaku 阪大法学

Hiroshima hōgaku 広島法学

Hisutoria ヒストリア

Hitotsubashi daigaku kenkyū nenpō: Hōgaku kenkyū 一橋大学研究年
報・法学研究

Hitotsubashi ronsō 一橋論叢

Hō to seiji 法と政治

Hōgaku (Kinki Daigaku) 法学(近畿大学) → *Kindai hōgaku*

Hōgaku (Tōhoku Daigaku) 法学(東北大学)

Hōgaku kenkyū (Keiō Gijuku Daigaku) 法学研究(慶応義塾大学)

Hōgaku kenkyūjo kiyō (Senshū Daigaku) 法学研究所紀要(専修大学)

Hōgaku ronshū (Komazawa Daigaku) 法学論集(駒沢大学)

Hōgaku ronsō (Kyoto Daigaku) 法学論叢(京都大学)

Hōgaku shinpō (Chūō Daigaku) 法学新報(中央大学)

Hōgaku shirin (Hōsei Daigaku) 法学志林(法政大学)

Hōgaku zasshi (Osaka Ichiritsu Daigaku) 法学雑誌(大阪市立大学)

Hōkei kenkyū (Nihon Daigaku) 法経研究(日本大学)

Hōkei ronshū: Hōritsu-hen (Aichi Daigaku) 法経論集・法律篇(愛
知大学)

Hoppō bunka kenkyū 北方文化研究

Hōritsu jihō 法律時報

Hōsei daigaku daigakuin kiyō 法政大学大学院紀要

Hōsei kenkyū (Kyūshū Daigaku) 法政研究(九州大学)

Hōsei shigaku 法政史学

Ibaragi daigaku kyōyōbu kiyō 茨城大学教養部紀要

Jinbun gakuhō (Kyoto Daigaku) 人文学報(京都大学)

Jinbun gakuhō (Tokyo Toritsu Daigaku) 人文学報(東京都立大学)

Jōchi shigaku 上智史学

Kaikankō hyōron 海幹校評論

Kakankai kaihō 霞関会会報

Kan (*The Han*) 韓

Keizai shirin 経済志林

Kenkyū nenpō (Gakushūin Daigaku Hōgakubu) 研究年報(学習院大学
法学部)

Kindai Chūgoku kenkyū 近代中国研究
Kindai hōgaku 近大法学
Kindai Nihon kenkyū 近代日本研究
Kōbe hōgaku zasshi 神戸法学雑誌
Kokka gakkai zasshi 国家学会雑誌
Kokugakuin daigaku hōken ronsō 国学院大学法研論叢
Kokugakuin daigaku kiyō 国学院大学紀要
Kokugakuin hōgaku 国学院法学
Kokugakuin zasshi 国学院雑誌
Kokuritsu kokkai toshokan geppō 国立国会図書館月報
Kokusai hōsei kenkyū 国際法政研究
Kokusai kankeigaku kenkyū (Tsuda Juku Daigaku) 国際関係学研究
　（津田塾大学）
Kokusai mondai 国際問題
Kokusai mondai kenkyū 国際問題研究
Kokusaigaku ronshū (Sophia University) 国際学論集
Kokusaihō gaikō zasshi 国際法外交雑誌
Kokushigaku 国史学
Kokushikan daigaku bungakubu jinbungakkai kiyō 国土館大学文学部人
　文学会紀要
Komazawa shigaku 駒沢史学
Kyoto sangyō daigaku ronshū 京都産業大学論集
Kyōyō gakka kiyō (Tokyo Daigaku) 教養学科紀要（東京大学）
Kyūshū kōgyō daigaku kenkyū hōkoku: Jinbun shakai kagaku 九州工業
　大学研究報告・人文社会科学
Meiji bunka kenkyū 明治文化研究
Musashi daigaku jinbun gakkai zasshi 武蔵大学人文学会雑誌
Nagoya daigaku bungakubu 10-shūnen kinen ronshū 名古屋大学文学部
　十周年記念論集
Nagoya daigaku bungakubu kenkyū ronshū: Shigaku 名古屋大学文学部
　研究論集・史学
Nanpō bunka 南方文化
Nenpō kindai Nihon kenkyū 年報近代日本研究
Nenpō seijigaku 年報政治学
Nihon hōgaku 日本法学
Nihon rekishi 日本歴史
Nihonshi kenkyū 日本史研究
Ochanomizu shigaku お茶の水史学

Ōita daigaku keizai ronshū 大分大学経済論集
Ōkuma kenkyū 大隈研究
Rekishi hyōron 歴史評論
Rekishi kyōiku 歴史教育
Rekishi to bunka (Tokyo Daigaku kyōyōgakubu) 歴史と文化(東京大学教養学部)
Rekishi to jinbutsu 歴史と人物
Rekishigaku kenkyū 歴史学研究
Roshiashi kenkyū ロシア史研究
Ryūdai hōgaku 琉大法学
Saitama daigaku kiyō: Shakai kagaku-hen 埼玉大学紀要・社会科学編
Saitama daigaku kyōyōbu kiyō 埼玉大学教養部紀要
Seiji keizai shigaku 政治経済史学
Seikei ronsō (Hiroshima Daigaku) 政経論叢(広島大学)
Seikei ronsō (Meiji Daigaku) 政経論叢(明治大学)
Seiyō shigaku 西洋史学
Sekai 世界
Sekai keizai 世界経済
Shakai kagaku jānaru 社会科学ジャーナル
Shakai kagaku kenkyū (Tokyo Daigaku) 社会科学研究(東京大学)
Shakai kagaku tōkyū (Waseda Daigaku) 社会科学討究(早稲田大学)
Shakai keizai shigaku 社会経済史学
Shakai undōshi 社会運動史
Shien 史淵
Shigaku zasshi 史学雑誌
Shin bōei ronshū 新防衛論集
Shingai kakumei kenkyū 辛亥革命研究
Shirin 史林
Shisō 思想
Shisō (Kyoto Joshi Daigaku) 思窓(京都女子大学)
Shisō no kagaku 思想の科学
Shokun 諸君
Sundai shigaku 駿台史学
Surabu kenkyū スラブ研究
Teikyō hōgaku 帝京法学
Tochi seido shigaku 土地制度史学
Tōhōgaku 東方学
Tōhoku daigaku bungakubu kenkyū nenpō 東北大学文学部研究年報

Tōkai daigaku kiyō (Bungakubu) 東海大学紀要（文学部）

Tokushima daigaku kyōyō gakubu kiyō (Jinbun shakai kagaku) 徳島大学教養学部紀要（人文社会科学）

Tokyo gaikokugo daigaku ronshū 東京外国語大学論集

Tokyo suisan daigaku ronshū 東京水産大学論集

Tokyo toritsu daigaku hōgakkai zasshi 東京都立大学法学会雑誌

Tōnan Ajia kenkyū 東南アジア研究

Tōnan Ajia: Rekishi to bunka 東南アジア・歴史と文化

Tōyō bunka kenkyūjo kiyō 東洋文化研究所紀要

Tōyō gakuhō 東洋学報

Tsuda juku daigaku kiyō 津田塾大学紀要

Tsukuba hōsei 筑波法政

Waseda hōgaku 早稲田法学

Waseda hōgakkaishi: Hōritsu-hen 早稲田法学会誌・法律編

Waseda jinbun shizen kagaku kenkyū 早稲田人文自然科学研究

Waseda seiji keizaigaku zasshi 早稲田政治経済学雑誌

Yamagata daigaku kiyō (Jinbun kagaku) 山形大学紀要（人文科学）

Yokohama kaikō shiryōkan kiyō 横浜開港資料館紀要

Yokohama shiritsu daigaku ronsō (Jinbun kagaku keiretsu) 横浜市立大学論叢（人文科学系列）

Notes on the Contributors

ASADA SADAO graduated from Carleton College (B. A., history) in 1958 and received his Ph. D. (American history and diplomatic history) from Yale University in 1963. Formerly Executive Secretary of the Center for American Studies, he is professor of international history in the Political Science Department, Doshisha University.

HATANO SUMIO was trained at Keiō University (B. A. 1972, and M. A., 1974). After having served as a researcher/archivist in the Foreign Ministry, the War History Department, and the National Institute for Defense Studies of the Defense Agency, he is associate professor of history at Tsukuba University.

HOSOYA CHIHIRO, professor of international relations at the International University of Japan, is a graduate of the Faculty of Law, Tokyo University (1945) and he received his Doctor of Law from Kyoto University in 1961. Professor emeritus of diplomatic history and international relations at Hitotsubashi University, he has served as President of the International Studies Association and JAIR.

HOSOYA MASAHIRO, associate professor at the Center for American Studies, Doshisha University, holds B. A. (history, 1968) and M. A. (political science, 1976) from Sophia University, and in 1982 he received his Ph. D. in history from Yale University.

IKEI MASARU, professor of diplomatic history in the Faculty of Law at Keiō University, graduated from that university in 1959. He has served as visiting professor at Columbia University.

INOUE YŪICHI, an archivist in the Foreign Ministry, was trained in the Faculty of Law at Keiō University, receiving his B. A. in 1974, M. A. in 1976, and Doctor of Law in 1983.

IOKIBE MAKOTO, professor of Japanese political and diplomatic history in the Faculty of Law, Kobe University, was trained at Kyoto University, where he received his B. A. in 1967 and M. A. in 1969.

ŌHATA TOKUSHIRŌ, professor of diplomatic history in the Faculty of Law, Waseda University, was graduated from that university's Faculty of Letters in 1951 with a major in history.

YASUOKA AKIO, professor of Japanese history in the Faculty of Letters, Hōsei University, was trained at that university, receiving his B. A. in 1953 and Litt. D. in 1971. He is director of the Hōsei Institute of Okinawan Studies.

Author Index

Subject Index

Abe Moritarō, 43

A-Bombs, in Pacific War (1941–45), 374–75

Advisory Council on Foreign Relations (1917–23), 152–53

Akiyama Saneyuki, 101

Alcock, Rutherford, 74

Allied occupation of Japan (1945–52): American presurrender policy toward Japan, 411–12; antimonopoly policy, 399; cold war and, 406–7; comparative studies of, 414–15; Constitution of 1947, 396–98; cultural impact, 402–3; documents (Finance Ministry), 30–31; documents (Foreign Ministry), 27, 390; documents (Gendai Seijishi Shiryō Shitsu), 30; educational reforms, 404–5; financial reforms, 398–400; generally, 387–92, 411–15; GHQ, 388; international environment, 405–9; labor reform, 399, 401–2; land reform, 402; New Constitution of 1947, 396–98; oral history, 389; peace treaty, 406, 409–11; reevaluation efforts, 392–94; "reverse course," 399, 408–9; role of Britain, 405; social impact, 402–3; Soviet policy toward, 406; State Department's wartime planning, 394, 411–12; Tokyo war crime trials, 394–96; war responsibility, 395–96; Zaibatsu dissolution, 400–1; see also International Military Tribunal of the Far East; MacArthur, Douglas; New Constitution of 1947

Amō Eiji, 247–48, 335

Amoy incident (1900), 93–94

An Chung gǔn, 144

Anglo-Japanese Alliance: abrogation of, 142; Canada's opposition to, 141–42; Chinese railroads and, 94; and Chinese Revolution of 1911, 143; conclusion of, 138; history of, 94–95; problem of renewing the third Alliance, 158

Anglo-Japanese relations: and Anglo-American relations in 1930s, 230, 277; Anglo-Japanese Conference on the History of the Second World War (1979), 321; antagonism in late 1930s, 320–21; and China question in interwar period, 230; commercial disputes in first half of 1930s, 280; during Allied occupation of Japan (1945–52), 405; Japan's attempted rapprochement with Britain, 276–77; Leith-Ross mission, 277; 1917 to 1949, 7, 229; 1933 to 1937, 276–78; in 1934, 277; 1937–41, 304–5; Pacific War and, 320–22; role of Yoshida Shigeru, 276–77; in Shōwa period, 229–30; in Sino-Japanese War (1937–41), 304–6

Anti-Comintern Pact (1936), 280–81, 305, 315

Aoki Shūzō, 90, 92, 99

Studies of the East Asian Institute

The Ladder of Success in Imperial China, by Ping-ti Ho. New York: Columbia University Press, 1962.

The Chinese Inflation, 1937–1949, by Shun-hsin Chou. New York: Columbia University Press, 1963.

Reformer in Modern China: Chang Chien, 1853–1926, by Samuel Chu. New York: Columbia University Press, 1965.

Research in Japanese Sources: A Guide, by Herschel Webb with the assistance by Marleigh Ryan. New York: Columbia University Press, 1965.

Society and Education in Japan, by Herbert Passin. New York: Teachers College Press, 1965.

Agricultural Production and Economic Developments in Japan, 1873–1922, by James I. Nakamura. Princeton: Princeton University Press, 1966.

Japan's First Modern Novel: Ukigumo of Futabatei Shimei, by Marleigh Ryan. New York: Columbia University Press,1967.

The Korean Communist Movement, 1918–1948, by Dae-Sook Suh. Princeton: Princeton University Press, 1967.

The First Vietnam Crisis, by Melvin Gurtov. New York: Columbia University Press, 1967.

Cadres, Bureaucracy, and Political Power in Communist China, by A. Doak Barnett. New York: Columbia University Press, 1968.

The Japanese Imperial Institution in the Tokugawa Period, by Herschel Webb. New York: Columbia University Press, 1968.

Higher Education and Business Recruitment in Japan, by Koya Azumi. New York: Teachers College Press, 1969.

The Communists and Peasant Rebellions: A Study in the Rewriting of Chinese History, by James P. Harrison, Jr. New York: Atheneum, 1969.

How The Conservatives Rule Japan, by Nathaniel B. Thayer. Princeton: Princeton University Press, 1969.

Aspects of Chinese Education, edited by C. T. Hu. New York: Teachers College Press, 1970.

Documents of Korean Communism, 1918–1948, by Dae-Sook Suh. Princeton: Princeton University Press, 1970.

Japanese Education: A Bibliography of Materials in the English Language, by Herbert Passin. New York: Teachers College Press, 1970.

Economic Development and the Labor Market in Japan, by Koji Taira. New York: Columbia University Press, 1970.

The Japanese Oligarchy and the Russo-Japanese War, by Shumpei Okamoto. New York: Columbia University Press, 1970.

Imperial Restoration in Medieval Japan, by H. Paul Varley. New York: Columbia University Press, 1971.

Japan's Postwar Defense Policy, 1947–1968, by Martin E. Weinstein. New York: Columbia University Press, 1971.

Election Campaigning Japanese Style, by Gerald L. Curtis. New York: Columbia University Press, 1971.

China and Russia: The "Great Game," by O. Edmund Clubb. New York: Columbia University Press, 1971.

Money and Monetary Policy in Communist China, by Katharine Huang Hsiao. New York: Columbia University Press, 1971.

The District Magistrate in Late Imperial China, by John R. Watt. New York: Columbia University Press, 1972.

Law and Policy in China's Foreign Relations: A Study of Attitude and Practice, by James C. Hsiung. New York: Columbia University Press, 1972.

Pearl Harbor as History: Japanese-American Relations, 1931–1941, edited by Dorothy Borg and Shumpei Okamoto, with the assistance of Dale K. A. Finlayson. New York: Columbia University Press, 1973.

Japanese Culture: A Short History, by H. Paul Varley. New York: Praeger, 1973.

Doctors in Politics: The Political Life of the Japan Medical Association, by William E. Steslicke. New York: Praeger, 1973.

The Japan Teachers Union: A Radical Interest Group in Japanese Politics, by Donald Ray Thurston. Princeton: Princeton University Press, 1973.

Japan's Foreign Policy, 1868–1941: A Research Guide, edited by James William Morley. New York: Columbia University Press, 1974.

Palace and Politics in Prewar Japan, by David Anson Titus. New York: Columbia University Press, 1974.

The Idea of China: Essays in Geographic Myth and Theory, by Andrew March. Devon, England: David and Charles, 1974.

Origins of the Cultural Revolution, by Roderick MacFarquhar. New York: Columbia University Press, 1974.

Shiba Kōkan: Artist, Innovator, and Pioneer in the Westernization of Japan, by Calvin L. French. Tokyo: Weatherhill, 1974.

Insei: Abdicated Sovereigns in the Politics of Late Heian Japan, by G. Cameron Hurst. New York: Columbia University Press, 1975.

Embassy at War, by Harold Joyce Noble. Edited with an introduction by Frank Baldwin, Jr. Seattle: University of Washington Press, 1975.

Rebels and Bureaucrats: China's December 9ers, by John Israel and Donald W. Klein. Berkeley: University of California Press, 1975.

Deterrent Diplomacy, edited by James William Morley. New York: Columbia University Press, 1976.

House United, House Divided: The Chinese Family in Taiwan, by Myron L. Cohen. New York: Columbia University Press, 1976.

Escape From Predicament: Neo-Confucianism and China's Evolving Political Culture, by Thomas A. Metzger. New York: Columbia University Press, 1976.

Cadres, Commanders, and Commissars: The Training of the Chinese Communist Leadership, 1920–45, by Jane L. Price. Boulder, Colo.: Westview Press, 1976.

Sun Yat-Sen: Frustrated Patriot, by C. Martin Wilbur. New York: Columbia University Press, 1977.

Japanese International Negotiating Style, by Michael Blaker. New York: Columbia University Press, 1977.

Contemporary Japanese Budget Politics, by John Creighton Campbell. Berkeley: University of California Press, 1977.

The Medieval Chinese Oligarchy, by David Johnson. Boulder, Colo.: Westview Press, 1977.

The Arms of Kiangnan: Modernization in the Chinese Ordnance Industry, 1860–1895, by Thomas L. Kennedy. Boulder, Colo.: Westview Press, 1978.

Patterns of Japanese Policymaking: Experiences from Higher Education, by T. J. Pempel. Boulder, Colo.: Westview Press, 1978.

The Chinese Connection: Roger S. Greene, Thomas W. Lamont, George E. Sokolsky, and American-East Asian Relations, by Warren I. Cohen. New York: Columbia University Press, 1978.

Mulitarism in Modern China: The Career of Wu P'ei-Fu, 1916–1939, by Odoric Y. K. Wou. Folkestone, England: Dawson, 1978.

A Chinese Pioneer Family; The Lins of Wu-Feng, by Johanna Meskill. Princeton: Princeton University Press, 1979.

Perspectives on a Changing China, edited by Joshua A. Fogel and William T. Rowe. Boulder, Colo.: Westview Press, 1979.

The Memoirs of Li Tsung-Jen, by T. K. Tong and Li Tsung-jen. Boulder, Colo.: Westview Press, 1979.

Unwelcome Muse: Chinese Literature in Shanghai and Peking, 1937–1945, by Edward Gunn. New York: Columbia University Press, 1979.

Yenan and the Great Powers: The Origins of Chinese Communist Foreign Policy, by James Reardon-Anderson. New York: Columbia University Press, 1980.

Uncertain Years: Chinese-American Relations, 1947–1950, edited by Dorothy Borg and Waldo Heinrichs. New York: Columbia University Press, 1980.

The Fateful Choice: Japan's Advance Into South-East Asia, edited by James William Morley. New York: Columbia University Press, 1980.

Tanaka Giichi and Japan's China Policy, by William F. Morton. Folkestone, England: Dawson, 1980; New York: St. Martin's Press, 1980.

The Origins of the Korean War: Liberation and the Emergence of Separate Regimes, 1945–1947, by Bruce Cumings. Princeton: Princeton University Press, 1981.

Class Conflict in Chinese Socialism, by Richard Curt Kraus. New York: Columbia University Press, 1981.

Education Under Mao: Class and Competition in Canton Schools, by Jonathan Unger. New York: Columbia University Press, 1982.

Private Academies of Tokugawa Japan, by Richard Rubinger. Princeton: Princeton University Press, 1982.

Japan and the San Francisco Peace Settlement, by Michael M. Yoshitsu. New York: Columbia University Press, 1982.

New Frontiers in Amercian-East Asian Relations: Essays Presented to Dorothy Borg, edited by Warren I. Cohen. New York: Columbia University Press, 1983.

The Origins of the Cultural Revolution: II, the Great Leap Forward, 1958–1960, by Roderick MacFarquhar. New York: Columbia University Press, 1983.

The China Quagmire: Japan's Expansion of the Asian Continent, 1933–1941, edited by James William Morley. New York: Columbia University Press, 1983.

Fragments of Rainbows: The Life and Poetry of Saito Mokichi, 1882–1953, by Amy Vladeck Heinrich. New York: Columbia University Press, 1983.

The U.S.-South Korean Alliance: Evolving Patterns of Security Relations, edited by Gerald L. Curtis and Sung-joo Han. Lexington, Mass.: Lexington Books, 1983.

Discovering History in China: American Historical Writing on the Recent Chinese Past, by Paul A. Cohen. New York: Columbia University Press, 1984.

The Foreign Policy of the Republic of Korea, edited by Youngnok Koo and Sungjoo Han. New York: Columbia University Press, 1984.

State and Diplomacy in Early Modern Japan, by Ronald Toby. Princeton: Princeton University Press, 1983.

Japan and the Asian Development Bank, by Dennis Yasutomo. New York: Praeger, 1983.

Japan Erupts: The London Naval Conference and the Manchurian Incident, edited by James W. Morley. New York: Columbia University Press, 1984.

Japanese Culture, third edition, revised, by Paul Varley. Honolulu: University of Hawaii Press, 1984.

Japan's Modern Myths: Ideology in the Late Meiji Period, by Carol Gluck. Princeton: Princeton University Press, 1985.

Shamans, Housewives, and Other Restless Spirits: Women in Korean Ritual Life, by Laurel Kendall. Honolulu: University of Hawaii Press, 1985.

Human Rights in Contemporary China, by R. Randle Edwards, Louis Henkin, and Andrew J. Nathan. New York: Columbia University Press, 1986.

The Pacific Basin: New Challenges for the United States, edited by James W. Morley. New York: Academy of Political Science, 1986.

The Manner of Giving: Strategic Aid and Japanese Foreign Policy, by Dennis T. Yasutomo. Lexington, Mass.: Lexington Books, 1986.

China's Political Economy: The Quest for Development Since 1949, by Carl Riskin. Oxford: Oxford University Press, 1987.

Anvil of Victory: The Communist Revolution in Manchuria, by Steven I. Levine. New York: Columbia University Press, 1987.

Single Sparks: China's Rural Revolutions, edited by Kathleen Hartford and Steven M. Goldstein. Armonk, N.Y.: M. E. Sharpe, 1987.

Urban Japanese Housewives: At Home and in the Community, by Anne E. Imamura. Honolulu: University of Hawaii Press, 1987.

China's Satellite Parties, by James D. Seymour. Armonk, N.Y.: M. E. Sharpe, 1987.

The Japanese Way of Politics, by Gerald L. Curtis. New York: Columbia University Press, 1988.

Kim Il Sung: The North Korean Leader, by Dae-Sook Suh. New York: Columbia University Press, 1988.